The American Spirit

Selected and Edited with
Introduction and Commentary by

Thomas A. Bailey
David M. Kennedy
Stanford University

The American Spirit

United States History
as Seen by Contemporaries

Ninth Edition

Volume 1: To 1877

Houghton Mifflin Company
Boston   New York

Senior Sponsoring Editor: Patricia A. Coryell
Assistant Editor: Keith Mahoney
Senior Project Editor: Rosemary R. Jaffe
Production/Design Coordinator: Jennifer Meyer Dare
Senior Manufacturing Coordinator: Florence Cadran
Permissions Editor: Craig Mertens
Editorial Assistant: Kevan Lee Rinehart

Cover Designer: Len Massiglia
Cover Image: *Harvesting*, by Olaf Krans. Bishop Hill State Historic Site/Illinois Historic Preservation Agency.

Printed in the United States of America.

Library of Congress Catalog Card Number: 97-72500

International Standard Book Number: 0-395-87100-X

6 7 8 9-DH-01 00

Contents

v

3 Settling the Northern Colonies, 1619–1700   **38**

4 American Life in the Seventeenth Century, 1607–1692   **61**

5 Colonial Society on the Eve of Revolution, 1700–1775 82

6 The Duel for North America, 1608–1763 100

16 *The Ferment of Reform and Culture, 1790–1860*   **309**

17 *The South and the Slavery Controversy, 1793–1860*   *347*

18 *Manifest Destiny and Its Legacy, 1841–1848*   *376*

19 *Renewing the Sectional Struggle, 1848–1854*   396

20 *Drifting Toward Disunion, 1854–1861*   413

21 Girding for War: The North and the South, 1861–1865   *433*

22   *The Furnace of Civil War, 1861–1865*   452

23 The Ordeal of Reconstruction, 1865–1877   485

Maps

Preface

The documents collected in *The American Spirit* are meant to recapture the spirit of the American past as expressed by the men and women who lived it. Movers and shakers who tried to sculpt the contours of history share these pages with the humble folk whose lives were grooved by a course of events they sometimes only dimly understood, and not infrequently resented. In all cases I have tried to present clear and pungent documents that combine intrinsic human interest with instructive historical perspectives. Students in American history courses will discover in these selections the satisfaction of working with primary documents—the raw human record from which meaningful historical accounts are assembled.

Taken together, the readings in the pages that follow convey a vivid sense of the wonder and the woe, the passion and the perplexity, with which Americans have confronted their lives and their times. *The American Spirit* seeks especially to stimulate reflection on the richness, variety, and complexity of American history, and an appreciation of both the problems and the prejudices of people in the past. Accordingly, it devotes much attention to the clash of opinion and judgment, including the unpopular or unsuccessful side of controversial issues. It gives special emphasis to problems of social justice, including the plight of religious, ethnic, and racial minorities; the evolving status of women; the problems of the poor; the responsibilities of world power; and the ongoing debate about the meaning of democracy itself.

I have revised the ninth edition of *The American Spirit* to make it fully compatible with its companion text, the eleventh edition of *The American Pageant*. Every chapter in the *Pageant* has a corresponding chapter of the same title in the *Spirit*. Instructors and students may use the two books together if they choose, but the chronological organization of the *Spirit* and its extensive explanatory materials make it usable with virtually any American history text. It may also be read on its own. Prologues for each chapter, headnotes for each document, explanatory inserts, and questions at the end of each headnote and at the end of every chapter will guide students in learning to appraise the documents thoughtfully and critically.

I have added a new feature to this edition. In many chapters, readers will find visual materials—cartoons, paintings, or posters, for example—that are treated as documents in their own right, fully equivalent in their evidentiary value and their historical interest to the more traditional verbal texts. This ninth edition of the *Spirit* presents these visual documents with the same kind of explanatory and other editorial apparatus that frames the conventional texts. It is my hope that students will thereby be encouraged to interrogate the past in new ways—not only by analyzing the written record, but by developing a critical attitude toward other kinds of historical evidence as well.

Like the eleventh edition of *The American Pageant,* this edition of the *Spirit* has been substantially revised to emphasize the interaction of social, economic, and cultural developments with political history. It contains many new documents on Native Americans, on Shays's rebellion, the Jacksonian era, slavery and the abolitionist crusade, the Ku Klux Klan during Reconstruction, the westward movement, women's history, segregation in the post–Civil War South, environmental controversies, the Great Depression, the 1960s, the rise of political conservatism, and the end of the Cold War. In response to suggestions from users, I have also undertaken to shorten some documents so that their essential significance might be more accessible and apparent to readers.

I wish to acknowledge the following instructors who read and commented on the eighth edition in preparation for this revision.

Donald S. Bodwell, East Lyme High School
Thomas Britten, Briar Cliff College
Catherine Clinton, Howard University
Wilfred Duchesneau, Coventry High School
L. T. Easley, Campbell University
Rose Ann Hardy, East Lyme High School
Gary Huey, Ferris State University
Diane Langley, Natick High School
Richard Parker, East Lyme High School

The result of these revisions, I hope, is a fresher and more provocative *Spirit* whose documents will enable students to savor the taste and to feel the texture of the American past, while engaging themselves in its frequently emotional and sometimes explosive controversies.

D. M. K.

The American Spirit

1

New World Beginnings, 33,000 B.C.–A.D. 1769

> . . . May it not then be lawful now to attempt the possession of such lands as are void of Christian inhabitants, for Christ's sake?
>
> William Strachey, c. 1620

Prologue: Each ignorant of the other's existence, Native Americans and Europeans lived in isolation on their separate continents for millennia before Columbus's revolutionary voyage in 1492. For the Europeans, the Native Americans were both a wonder and a mystery, unexplained in either the Bible or the classical writings of the ancients that were being revived in the dawning age of the Renaissance. Learned European scholars earnestly debated whether the "Indians" were "true men." For their part, the Native Americans were no less baffled by the arrival of the Europeans, and they looked to their own folklore and traditions in order to understand this new race of people who had suddenly appeared among them. The Europeans, especially the Portuguese and the Spanish, had begun to penetrate and exploit Africa even before they made contact with the New World of the Americas. A fateful triangle was established as Europe drew slave labor from Africa to unlock and develop the riches of the Americas. Spain soon spread its empire over a vast American domain, exciting the jealousy of the English, who began in the late 1500s to launch their own imperial adventure in the New World.

A. The Native Americans

1. Visualizing the New World (1505, 1509)

Early in the sixteenth century, the explorer Amerigo Vespucci wrote a letter detailing his experiences in the New World (a place to which he gave his name—America). The letter was translated and published throughout Europe, accompanied by illustrations that were often drawn by artists who themselves had never seen the newly discovered Western Hemisphere. How did the artists whose work is reproduced here imagine the Indians? What differences between the Indians and the Europeans did they think important? Did the various artists portray a consistent view of the Native Americans? From what sources in the history of European culture might these illustrators have drawn in their effort to understand Native Americans?

---

[1]The British Library, London.

Illustrations to Vespucci (top) 1509, (bottom) c. 1506–1510.

2. Juan Ginés de Sepúlveda Belittles the Indians (1547)

Juan Ginés Sepúlveda was an outstanding example of the "Renaissance man." A Spaniard who studied in the cradle of the Renaissance, Italy, he achieved fame as a theologian, philosopher, historian, and astronomer. When Emperor Charles V convened a debate in Valladolid, Spain, in 1550–1551 to determine the future of Spain's relationship with the American aborigines, he naturally turned to Sepúlveda as one of the most learned men in his realm. As a student of Aristotle, Sepúlveda relied heavily on the classical distinction between "civilized" Greeks and "barbarians." The selection that follows is not a transcript of the debate at Valladolid but an excerpt from Sepúlveda's book The Second Democrates, *published in 1547, in which he set forth his basic arguments. What differences does Sepúlveda emphasize between Europeans (especially Spaniards) and the Indians, and on what grounds does he assert the superiority of European culture?*

The Spanish have a perfect right to rule these barbarians of the New World and the adjacent islands, who in prudence, skill, virtues, and humanity are as inferior to the Spanish as children to adults, or women to men, for there exists between the two as great a difference as between savage and cruel races and the most merciful, between the most intemperate and the moderate and temperate and, I might even say, between apes and men.

You surely do not expect me to recall at length the prudence and talents of the Spanish. . . . And what can I say of the gentleness and humanity of our people, who, even in battle, after having gained the victory, put forth their greatest effort and care to save the greatest possible number of the conquered and to protect them from the cruelty of their allies?

Compare, then, these gifts of prudence, talent, magnanimity, temperance, humanity, and religion with those possessed by these half-men (*homunculi*), in whom you will barely find the vestiges of humanity, who not only do not possess any learning at all, but are not even literate or in possession of any monument to their history except for some obscure and vague reminiscences of several things put down in various paintings; nor do they have written laws, but barbarian institutions and customs. Well, then, if we are dealing with virtue, what temperance or mercy can you expect from men who are committed to all types of intemperance and base frivolity, and eat human flesh? And do not believe that before the arrival of the Christians they lived in that pacific kingdom of Saturn which the poets have invented; for, on the contrary, they waged continual and ferocious war upon one another with such fierceness that they did not consider a victory at all worthwhile unless they sated their monstrous hunger with the flesh of their enemies. . . . Furthermore these Indians were otherwise so cowardly and timid that they could barely endure the presence of our soldiers, and many times thousands upon thousands of them scattered in flight like women before Spaniards so few that they did not even number one hundred. . . . Although some of them show a certain ingenuity for various works of artisanship, this is no proof of human cleverness, for we can

---

²Juan Ginés de Sepúlveda, *The Second Democrates* (1547).

observe animals, birds, and spiders making certain structures which no human accomplishment can competently imitate. And as for the way of life of the inhabitants of New Spain and the province of Mexico, I have already said that these people are considered the most civilized of all, and they themselves take pride in their public institutions, because they have cities erected in a rational manner and kings who are not hereditary but elected by popular vote, and among themselves they carry on commercial activities in the manner of civilized peoples. But see how they deceive themselves, and how much I dissent from such an opinion, seeing, on the contrary, in these very institutions a proof of the crudity, the barbarity, and the natural slavery of these people; for having houses and some rational way of life and some sort of commerce is a thing which the necessities of nature itself induce, and only serves to prove that they are not bears or monkeys and are not totally lacking in reason. But on the other hand, they have established their nation in such a way that no one possesses anything individually, neither a house nor a field, which he can leave to his heirs in his will, for everything belongs to their masters whom, with improper nomenclature, they call kings, and by whose whims they live, more than by their own, ready to do the bidding and desire of these rulers and possessing no liberty. And the fulfillment of all this, not under the pressure of arms but in a voluntary and spontaneous way, is a definite sign of the servile and base soul of these barbarians. They have distributed the land in such a way that they themselves cultivate the royal and public holdings, one part belonging to the king, another to public feasts and sacrifices, with only a third reserved for their own advantage, and all this is done in such a way that they live as employees of the king, paying, thanks to him, exceedingly high taxes. . . . And if this type of servile and barbarous nation had not been to their liking and nature, it would have been easy for them, as it was not a hereditary monarchy, to take advantage of the death of a king in order to obtain a freer state and one more favorable to their interests; by not doing so, they have stated quite clearly that they have been born to slavery and not to civic and liberal life. Therefore, if you wish to reduce them, I do not say to our domination, but to a servitude a little less harsh, it will not be difficult for them to change their masters, and instead of the ones they had, who were barbarous and impious and inhuman, to accept the Christians, cultivators of human virtues and the true faith. . . .

3. Bartolomé de Las Casas Defends the Indians (1552)

The Dominican friar Bartolomé de Las Casas was Sepúlveda's great antagonist in the debates of 1550–1551 at Valladolid. As a young man, Las Casas had sailed with one of the first Spanish expeditions to the West Indies in 1502. A humane, sensitive priest, he was soon repelled by his countrymen's treatment of the native peoples of the New World. He eventually became bishop of Guatemala and devoted himself to reforming Spanish colonial policies—for which he was recognized as the "Protector of the Indians." His vivid and polemical account The Destruction of the Indies *did much to spread the "Black Legend" of Spain's brutal behavior in the New World—a*

---

[3]Bartolomé de Las Casas, *Thirty Very Judicial Propositions* (1552).

legend not without substance, and eagerly exploited by the rival English. How are his views of the Indians different from those of Sepúlveda? What ideas did the two debaters share?

Now if we shall have shown that among our Indians of the western and southern shores (granting that we call them barbarians and that they are barbarians) there are important kingdoms, large numbers of people who live settled lives in a society, great cities, kings, judges and laws, persons who engage in commerce, buying, selling, lending, and the other contracts of the law of nations, will it not stand proved that the Reverend Doctor Sepúlveda has spoken wrongly and viciously against peoples like these, either out of malice or ignorance of Aristotle's teaching, and, therefore, has falsely and perhaps irreparably slandered them before the entire world? From the fact that the Indians are barbarians it does not necessarily follow that they are incapable of government and have to be ruled by others, except to be taught about the Catholic faith and to be admitted to the holy sacraments. They are not ignorant, inhuman, or bestial. Rather, long before they had heard the word Spaniard they had properly organized states, wisely ordered by excellent laws, religion, and custom. They cultivated friendship and, bound together in common fellowship, lived in populous cities in which they wisely administered the affairs of both peace and war justly and equitably, truly governed by laws that at very many points surpass ours, and could have won the admiration of the sages of Athens. . . .

Now if they are to be subjugated by war because they are ignorant of polished literature, . . . I would like to hear Sepúlveda, in his cleverness, answer this question: Does he think that the war of the Romans against the Spanish was justified in order to free them from barbarism? And this question also: Did the Spanish wage an unjust war when they vigorously defended themselves against them?

Next, I call the Spaniards who plunder that unhappy people torturers. Do you think that the Romans, once they had subjugated the wild and barbaric peoples of Spain, could with secure right divide all of you among themselves, handing over so many head of both males and females as allotments to individuals? And do you then conclude that the Romans could have stripped your rulers of their authority and consigned all of you, after you had been deprived of your liberty, to wretched labors, especially in searching for gold and silver lodes and mining and refining the metals? . . . For God's sake and man's faith in him, is this the way to impose the yoke of Christ on Christian men? Is this the way to remove wild barbarism from the minds of barbarians? Is it not, rather, to act like thieves, cut-throats, and cruel plunderers and to drive the gentlest of people headlong into despair? The Indian race is not that barbaric, nor are they dull witted or stupid, but they are easy to teach and very talented in learning all the liberal arts, and very ready to accept, honor, and observe the Christian religion and correct their sins (as experience has taught) once priests have introduced them to the sacred mysteries and taught them the word of God. They have been endowed with excellent conduct, and before the coming of the Spaniards, as we have said, they had political states that were well founded on beneficial laws.

Furthermore, they are so skilled in every mechanical art that with every right they should be set ahead of all the nations of the known world on this score, so very beautiful in their skill and artistry are the things this people produces in the grace of its architecture, its painting, and its needlework. But Sepúlveda despises these mechanical arts, as if these things do not reflect inventiveness, ingenuity, industry, and right reason. For a mechanical art is an operative habit of the intellect that is usually defined as "the right way to make things, directing the acts of the reason, through which the artisan proceeds in orderly fashion, easily, and unerringly in the very act of reason." So these men are not stupid, Reverend Doctor. Their skillfully fashioned works of superior refinement awaken the admiration of all nations, because works proclaim a man's talent, for, as the poet says, the work commends the craftsman. Also, Prosper [of Aquitaine] says: "See, the maker is proclaimed by the wonderful signs of his works and the effects, too, sing of their author."

In the liberal arts that they have been taught up to now, such as grammar and logic, they are remarkably adept. With every kind of music they charm the ears of their audience with wonderful sweetness. They write skillfully and quite elegantly, so that most often we are at a loss to know whether the characters are handwritten or printed. . . .

The Indians are our brothers, and Christ has given his life for them. Why, then, do we persecute them with such inhuman savagery when they do not deserve such treatment? The past, because it cannot be undone, must be attributed to our weakness, provided that what has been taken unjustly is restored.

Finally, let all savagery and apparatus of war, which are better suited to Moslems than Christians, be done away with. Let upright heralds be sent to proclaim Jesus Christ in their way of life and to convey the attitudes of Peter and Paul. [The Indians] will embrace the teaching of the gospel, as I well know, for they are not stupid or barbarous but have a native sincerity and are simple, moderate, and meek, and, finally, such that I do not know whether there is any people readier to receive the gospel. Once they have embraced it, it is marvelous with what piety, eagerness, faith, and charity they obey Christ's precepts and venerate the sacraments. For they are docile and clever, and in their diligence and gifts of nature, they excel most peoples of the known world. . . .

B. The Spanish in America

1. Hernán Cortés Conquers Mexico (1519–1526)

In 1519 the Spanish conquistador Hernán Cortés landed in Mexico and quickly conquered the Aztecs, a powerful people who had long dominated their neighbors in the central Mexican highlands. In the passage below, Cortés, writing to his king in Spain, describes his first encounter with the Aztec ruler Muteczuma (Montezuma), as well as his efforts to suppress the religious practices of the Aztecs, especially those involving human sacrifice. What advantages did Cortés possess in his confrontation

[1]Hernán Cortés, *Five Letters, 1519–1526* (New York: Robert M. McBride, 1929), pp. 69–92.

with the Aztecs? How did his own cultural background influence his treatment of the native people?

The Second Letter

The Second Despatch of Hernán Cortés to the Emperor: sent from Segura de la Frontera on the 30th of October, 1520.

Most High Mighty and Catholic Prince, Invincible Emperor, and our Sovereign Liege:

. . . Muteczuma himself came out to meet us with some two hundred nobles, all barefoot and dressed in some kind of uniform also very rich, in fact more so than the others. They came forward in two long lines keeping close to the walls of the street, which is very broad and fine and so straight that one can see from one end of it to the other, though it is some two-thirds of a league in length and lined on both sides with very beautiful, large houses, both private dwellings and temples. . . . And while speaking to Muteczuma I took off a necklace of pearls and crystals which I was wearing and threw it round his neck; whereupon having proceeded some little way up the street a servant of his came back to me with two necklaces wrapped up in a napkin, made from the shells of sea snails, which are much prized by them; and from each necklace hung eight prawns fashioned very beautifully in gold some six inches in length. The messenger who brought them put them round my neck and we then continued up the street in the manner described until we came to a large and very handsome house which Muteczuma had prepared for our lodging. There he took me by the hand and led me to a large room opposite the patio by which we had entered, and seating me on a daïs very richly worked, for it was intended for royal use, he bade me await him there, and took his departure. After a short time, when all my company had found lodging, he returned with many various ornaments of gold, silver and featherwork, and some five or six thousand cotton clothes, richly dyed and embroidered in various ways, and having made me a present of them he seated himself on another low bench which was placed next to mine, and addressed me in this manner:

"Long time have we been informed by the writings of our ancestors that neither myself nor any of those who inhabit this land are natives of it, but rather strangers who have come to it from foreign parts. We likewise know that from those parts our nation was led by a certain lord (to whom all were subject), and who then went back to his native land, where he remained so long delaying his return that at his coming those whom he had left had married the women of the land and had many children by them and had built themselves cities in which they lived, so that they would in no wise return to their own land nor acknowledge him as lord; upon which he left them. And we have always believed that among his descendants one would surely come to subject this land and us as rightful vassals. Now seeing the regions from which you say you come, which is from where the sun rises, and the news you tell of this great king and ruler who sent you hither, we believe and hold it certain that he is our natural lord: especially in that you say he has long had knowledge of us. Wherefore be certain that we will obey you and hold you as lord in place of that great lord of whom you speak, in which service there shall be neither slackness nor deceit: and throughout all the land, that is to say all that I rule, you may command anything you desire, and it shall be obeyed and done, and all that we have is at your will and pleasure. And since you are in your own land and house, rejoice and take your leisure from the fatigues of your journey and the battles you have fought; for I am well informed of all those that you have been forced to engage in on your way here from Potonchan, as also that the natives of Cempoal and Tlascala have told you many evil things of me; but believe no more than what you see with your own eyes, and especially not words from the lips of those who are my enemies, who were formerly my vassals and on your coming rebelled against me and said these things in order to find favour with you: I am aware, moreover, that they have told you that the walls of my houses were of gold as was the matting on my floors and other household articles, even that I was a god and claimed to be so, and other like matters. As for the houses, you see that they are of wood, stones and earth." Upon this he lifted his clothes showing me his body, and said: "and you see that I am of flesh and blood like yourself and everyone else, mortal and tangible."

Grasping with his hands his arms and other parts of his body, he continued: "You see plainly how they have lied. True I have a few articles of gold which have remained to me from my forefathers, and all that I have is yours at any time that you may desire it. I am now going to my palace where I live. Here you will be provided with all things necessary for you and your men, and let nothing be done amiss seeing that you are in your own house and land.". . .

There are three large halls in the great mosque where the principal idols are to be found, all of immense size and height and richly decorated with sculptured figures both in wood and stone, and within these halls are other smaller temples branching off from them and entered by doors so small that no daylight ever reaches them. Certain of the priests but not all are permitted to enter, and within are the great heads and figures of idols, although as I have said there are also many outside. The greatest of these idols and those in which they placed most faith and trust I ordered to be dragged from their places and flung down the stairs, which done I had the temples which they occupy cleansed for they were full of the blood of human victims who had been sacrificed, and placed in them the image of Our Lady and other saints, all of which made no small impression upon Muteczuma and the inhabitants. They at first remonstrated with me, for should it be known, they said, by the people of the country they would rise against me, believing as they did that to these idols were due all temporal goods, and that should they allow them to be ill used they would be wroth against them and would give them nothing, denying them the fruits of the earth, and thus the people would die of starvation. I instructed them by my interpreters how mistaken they were in putting their trust in idols made by their own hands from unclean things, and that they must know that there was but one God, Lord of all, Who created the sky, the earth and all things, Who made both them and ourselves, Who was without beginning and immortal, Whom alone they had to adore and to believe in, and not in any created thing whatsoever: I told them moreover all things else that I knew of touching this matter in order to lead them from their idolatry and bring them to the knowledge of Our Lord: and all, especially Muteczuma, replied that they had already told me that they were not natives of this land but had come to it long time since, and that therefore they were well prepared to believe that they had erred somewhat from the true faith during the long time since they had left their native land, and I as more lately come would know more surely the things that it was right for them to hold and believe than they themselves: and that hence if I would instruct them they would do whatever I declared to be best. Upon this Muteczuma and many of the chief men of the city went with me to remove the idols, cleanse the chapels, and place images of the saints therein, and all with cheerful faces. I forbade them moreover to make human sacrifice to the idols as was their wont, because besides being an abomination in the sight of God it is prohibited by your Majesty's laws which declare that he who kills shall be killed. From this time henceforth they departed from it, and during the whole time that I was in the city not a single living soul was known to be killed and sacrificed.

The images of the idols in which these people believed are many times greater than the body of a large man. They are made from pulp of all the cereals and green-stuffs which they eat, mixed and pounded together. This mass they moisten with blood from the hearts of human beings which they tear from their breasts while still alive, and thus make sufficient quantity of the pulp to mould into their huge statues: and after the idols have been set up still they offer them more living hearts which they sacrifice in like manner and anoint their faces with the blood. Each department of human affairs has its particular idol after the manner of the ancients who thus honoured their gods: so that there is one idol from whom they beg success in war, another for crops, and so on for all their needs. . . .

2. Aztec Chroniclers Describe the Spanish Conquest of Mexico (1519)

The Spanish Franciscan friar Bernardino de Sahagún arrived in Mexico in 1529, swiftly mastered the indigenous language Nahuatl, and proceeded to gather from his Aztec informants a history of their civilization. In the selection that follows, one of Sahagún's witnesses describes the encounter between Montezuma and Cortés from the Aztec perspective. How does this account differ, either factually or interpretively, from Cortés's description?

. . . The Spaniards arrived in Xoloco, near the entrance to Tenochtitlan. That was the end of the march, for they had reached their goal.

Motecuhzoma now arrayed himself in his finery, preparing to go out to meet them. The other great princes also adorned their persons, as did the nobles and their chieftains and knights. They all went out together to meet the strangers.

They brought trays heaped with the finest flowers—the flower that resembles a shield; the flower shaped like a heart; in the center, the flower with the sweetest aroma; and the fragrant yellow flower, the most precious of all. They also brought

[2]From *The Broken Spears* by Miguel Leon-Portilla. © 1962, 1990 by Beacon Press. Expanded and Updated Edition © 1992 by Miguel Leon-Portilla. Reproduced by permission of Beacon Press, Boston.

garlands of flowers, and ornaments for the breast, and necklaces of gold, necklaces hung with rich stones, necklaces fashioned in the petatillo style.

Thus Motecuhzoma went out to meet them, there in Huitzillan. He presented many gifts to the Captain and his commanders, those who had come to make war. He showered gifts upon them and hung flowers around their necks; he gave them necklaces of flowers and bands of flowers to adorn their breasts; he set garlands of flowers upon their heads. Then he hung the gold necklaces around their necks and gave them presents of every sort as gifts of welcome.

When Motecuhzoma had given necklaces to each one, Cortes asked him: "Are you Motecuhzoma? Are you the king? Is it true that you are the king Motecuhzoma?"

And the king said: "Yes, I am Motecuhzoma." Then he stood up to welcome Cortes; he came forward, bowed his head low and addressed him in these words: "Our lord, you are weary. The journey has tired you, but now you have arrived on the earth. You have come to your city, Mexico. You have come here to sit on your throne, to sit under its canopy.

"The kings who have gone before, your representatives, guarded it and preserved it for your coming. The kings Itzcoatl, Motecuhzoma the Elder, Axayacatl, Tizoc and Ahuitzol ruled for you in the City of Mexico. The people were protected by their swords and sheltered by their shields.

"Do the kings know the destiny of those they left behind, their posterity? If only they are watching! If only they can see what I see!

"No, it is not a dream. I am not walking in my sleep. I am not seeing you in my dreams. . . . I have seen you at last! I have met you face to face! I was in agony for five days, for ten days, with my eyes fixed on the Region of the Mystery. And now you have come out of the clouds and mists to sit on your throne again.

"This was foretold by the kings who governed your city, and now it has taken place. You have come back to us; you have come down from the sky. Rest now, and take possession of your royal houses. Welcome to your land, my lords!"

When Motecuhzoma had finished, La Malinche translated his address into Spanish so that the Captain could understand it. Cortes replied in his strange and savage tongue, speaking first to La Malinche: "Tell Motecuhzoma that we are his friends. There is nothing to fear. We have wanted to see him for a long time, and now we have seen his face and heard his words. Tell him that we love him well and that our hearts are contented."

Then he said to Motecuhzoma: "We have come to your house in Mexico as friends. There is nothing to fear."

La Malinche translated this speech and the Spaniards grasped Motecuhzoma's hands and patted his back to show their affection for him. . . .

The Spaniards examined everything they saw. They dismounted from their horses, and mounted them again, and dismounted again, so as not to miss anything of interest. . . .

When the Spaniards entered the Royal House, they placed Motecuhzoma under guard and kept him under their vigilance. They also placed a guard over Itzcuauhtzin, but the other lords were permitted to depart.

Then the Spaniards fired one of their cannons, and this caused great confusion in the city. The people scattered in every direction; they fled without rhyme or reason; they ran off as if they were being pursued. It was as if they had eaten the mushrooms that confuse the mind, or had seen some dreadful apparition. They were all overcome by terror, as if their hearts had fainted. And when night fell, the panic spread through the city and their fears would not let them sleep.

In the morning the Spaniards told Motecuhzoma what they needed in the way of supplies: tortillas, fried chickens, hens' eggs, pure water, firewood and charcoal. Also: large, clean cooking pots, water jars, pitchers, dishes and other pottery. Motecuhzoma ordered that it be sent to them. The chiefs who received this order were angry with the king and no longer revered or respected him. But they furnished the Spaniards with all the provisions they needed—food, beverages and water, and fodder for the horses. . . .

The Aztecs begged permission of their king to hold the fiesta of Huitzilopochtli. The Spaniards wanted to see this fiesta to learn how it was celebrated. A delegation of the celebrants came to the palace where Motecuhzoma was a prisoner, and when their spokesman asked his permission, he granted it to them. . . .

On the evening before the fiesta of Toxcatl, the celebrants began to model a statue of Huitzilopochtli. They gave it such a human appearance that it seemed the body of a living man. Yet they made the statue with nothing but a paste made of the ground seeds of the chicalote, which they shaped over an armature of sticks.

When the statue was finished, they dressed it in rich feathers, and they painted crossbars over and under its eyes. They also clipped on its earrings of turquoise mosaic; these were in the shape of serpents, with gold rings hanging from them. Its nose plug, in the shape of an arrow, was made of gold and was inlaid with fine stones.

They placed the magic headdress of hummingbird feathers on its head. They also adorned it with an *anecuyotl,* which was a belt made of feathers, with a cone at the back. Then they hung around its neck an ornament of yellow parrot feathers, fringed like the locks of a young boy. Over this they put its nettle leaf cape, which was painted black and decorated with five clusters of eagle feathers.

Next they wrapped it in its cloak, which was painted with skulls and bones, and over this they fastened its vest. The vest was painted with dismembered human parts: skulls, ears, hearts, intestines, torsos, breasts, hands and feet. They also put on its *maxtlatl,* or loincloth, which was decorated with images of dissevered limbs and fringed with amate paper. This *maxtlatl* was painted with vertical stripes of bright blue.

They fastened a red paper flag at its shoulder and placed on its head what looked like a sacrificial flint knife. This too was made of red paper; it seemed to have been steeped in blood.

The statue carried a *tehuehuelli,* a bamboo shield decorated with four clusters of fine eagle feathers. The pendant of this shield was blood-red, like the knife and the shoulder flag. The statue also carried four arrows.

Finally, they put the wristbands on its arms. These bands, made of coyote skin, were fringed with paper cut into little strips.

Early the next morning, the statue's face was uncovered by those who had been chosen for that ceremony. They gathered in front of the idol in single file and offered it gifts of food, such as round seedcakes or perhaps human flesh. But they did not carry it up to its temple on top of the pyramid.

All the young warriors were eager for the fiesta to begin. They had sworn to dance and sing with all their hearts, so that the Spaniards would marvel at the beauty of the rituals.

The procession began, and the celebrants filed into the temple patio to dance the Dance of the Serpent. When they were all together in the patio, the songs and the dance began. Those who had fasted for twenty days and those who had fasted for a year were in command of the others; they kept the dancers in file with their pine wands. (If anyone wished to urinate, he did not stop dancing, but simply opened his clothing at the hips and separated his clusters of heron feathers.)

If anyone disobeyed the leaders or was not in his proper place they struck him on the hips and shoulders. Then they drove him out of the patio, beating him and shoving him from behind. They pushed him so hard that he sprawled to the ground, and they dragged him outside by the ears. No one dared to say a word about this punishment, for those who had fasted during the year were feared and venerated; they had earned the exclusive title "Brothers of Huitzilopochtli."

The great captains, the bravest warriors, danced at the head of the files to guide the others. The youths followed at a slight distance. Some of the youths wore their hair gathered into large locks, a sign that they had never taken any captives. Others carried their headdresses on their shoulders; they had taken captives, but only with help.

Then came the recruits, who were called "the young warriors." They had each captured an enemy or two. The others called to them: "Come, comrades, show us how brave you are! Dance with all your hearts!"

At this moment in the fiesta, when the dance was loveliest and when song was linked to song, the Spaniards were seized with an urge to kill the celebrants. They all ran forward, armed as if for battle. They closed the entrances and passageways, all the gates of the patio: the Eagle Gate in the lesser palace, the Gate of the Canestalk and the Gate of the Serpent of Mirrors. They posted guards so that no one could escape, and then rushed into the Sacred Patio to slaughter the celebrants. They came on foot, carrying their swords and their wooden or metal shields.

They ran in among the dancers, forcing their way to the place where the drums were played. They attacked the man who was drumming and cut off his arms. Then they cut off his head, and it rolled across the floor.

They attacked all the celebrants, stabbing them, spearing them, striking them with their swords. They attacked some of them from behind, and these fell instantly to the ground with their entrails hanging out. Others they beheaded: they cut off their heads, or split their heads to pieces.

They struck others in the shoulders, and their arms were torn from their bodies. They wounded some in the thigh and some in the calf. They slashed others in the abdomen, and their entrails all spilled to the ground. Some attempted to run away, but their intestines dragged as they ran; they seemed to tangle their feet in their own entrails. No matter how they tried to save themselves, they could find no escape.

Some attempted to force their way out, but the Spaniards murdered them at the gates. Others climbed the walls, but they could not save themselves. Those who ran into the communal houses were safe there for a while; so were those who lay down among the victims and pretended to be dead. But if they stood up again, the Spaniards saw them and killed them.

The blood of the warriors flowed like water and gathered into pools. The pools widened, and the stench of blood and entrails filled the air. The Spaniards ran into the communal houses to kill those who were hiding. They ran everywhere and searched everywhere; they invaded every room, hunting and killing. . . .

3. Francisco Coronado Explores the American Southwest (1541)

In 1540–1542 Francisco Coronado led a Spanish expedition from Mexico into the present-day territory of Arizona and New Mexico and as far east as Kansas. Seeking fabled cities of gold, he found instead the modest villages of the Pueblo Indians, who urged him to continue eastward to a region they called Quivira. As he struggled across the vast and forbidding American wilderness, the truth gradually dawned on Coronado that Quivira held no more gold than did the land of the Pueblos. How does Coronado describe the landscape? How does his cultural background influence what he sees and how he estimates its usefulness?

. . . While I was engaged in the conquest and pacification of the natives of this province, some Indians who were natives of other provinces beyond these had told me that in their country there were much larger villages and better houses than those of the natives of this country, and that they had lords who ruled them, who were served with dishes of gold, and other very magnificent things; and although, as I wrote Your Majesty, I did not believe it before I had set eyes on it, because it was the report of Indians and given for the most part by means of signs, yet as the report appeared to me to be very fine and that it was important that it should be investigated for Your Majesty's service, I determined to go and see it with the men I have here. I started from this province on the 23d of last April, for the place where the Indians wanted to guide me.

After nine days' march I reached some plains, so vast that I did not find their limit anywhere that I went, although I traveled over them for more than 300 leagues. And I found such a quantity of cows in these, of the kind that I wrote Your Majesty about, which they have in this country, that it is impossible to number them, for while I was journeying through these plains, until I returned to where I first found them, there was not a day that I lost sight of them. And after seventeen days' march I came to a settlement of Indians who are called Querechos, who travel around with these cows, who do not plant, and who eat the raw flesh and drink the blood of the cows they kill, and they tan the skins of the cows, with which all the people of this country dress themselves here. They have little field tents made of the hides of the

---

[3]George Parker Winship, trans. and ed., *The Journey of Coronado, 1540–1542* (New York: A. S. Barnes, 1904), pp. 213–220.

cows, tanned and greased, very well made, in which they live while they travel around near the cows, moving with these. They have dogs which they load, which carry their tents and poles and belongings. These people have the best figures of any that I have seen in the Indies. They could not give me any account of the country where the guides were taking me. I traveled five days more as the guides wished to lead me, until I reached some plains, with no more landmarks than as if we had been swallowed up in the sea, where they strayed about, because there was not a stone, nor a bit of rising ground, nor a tree, nor a shrub, nor anything to go by. . . .

It was the Lord's pleasure that, after having journeyed across these deserts seventy-seven days, I arrived at the province they call Quivira, to which the guides were conducting me, and where they had described to me houses of stone, with many stories; and not only are they not of stone, but of straw, but the people in them are as barbarous as all those whom I have seen and passed before this; . . .

The province of Quivira is 950 leagues from Mexico. Where I reached it, it is in the fortieth degree. The country itself is the best I have ever seen for producing all the products of Spain, for besides the land itself being very fat and black and being very well watered by the rivulets and springs and rivers, I found prunes like those of Spain [*or* I found everything they have in Spain] and nuts and very good sweet grapes and mulberries. I have treated the natives of this province, and all the others whom I found wherever I went, as well as was possible, agreeably to what Your Majesty had commanded, and they have received no harm in any way from me or from those who went in my company. I remained twenty-five days in this province of Quivira, so as to see and explore the country and also to find out whether there was anything beyond which could be of service to Your Majesty, because the guides who had brought me had given me an account of other provinces beyond this. And what I am sure of is that there is not any gold nor any other metal in all that country, and the other things of which they had told me are nothing but little villages, and in many of these they do not plant anything and do not have any houses except of skins and sticks, and they wander around with the cows; so that the account they gave me was false, because they wanted to persuade me to go there with the whole force, believing that as the way was through such uninhabited deserts, and from the lack of water, they would get us where we and our horses would die of hunger. And the guides confessed this, and said they had done it by the advice and orders of the natives of these provinces. . . .

4. Don Juan de Oñate Conquers New Mexico (1599)

Don Juan de Oñate, inspired by tales of Coronado's expedition some fifty years earlier, led a heavily armed expedition into present-day New Mexico in 1598 and proceeded to impose Spanish rule on the native Pueblo Indians. The Indians of the

---

[4]From *Don Juan de Oñate: Colonizer of New Mexico, 1595–1628,* by George P. Hammond and Agapito Rey, pp. 456–459. Copyright © 1953. Reprinted by permission of The University of New Mexico Press.

village of Acoma inflicted a humiliating defeat on Oñate's forces on December 4, 1599, prompting a swift and harsh reprisal from the Spanish. In the selection that follows, Oñate instructs his officers on how to deal with the Indians at Acoma (eventually they severed one foot of every adult male survivor). What motives prompted Oñate? In what ways did he try to promote the cause of Christianity among the Indians? How did he justify his action?

. . . Instructions to you, Vicente de Zaldívar, sargento mayor [sergeant-major] of the expedition to New Mexico, my lieutenant governor and captain general for the punishment of the pueblo of Acoma for having killed Don Juan de Zaldívar Oñate, my maese de campo [second-in-command], ten other captains and soldiers, and two servants, which resulted in disrupting the general peace of the land, which is now in serious danger of revolting if the offenders are not properly punished, as their vileness would be emulated by other savages whenever they wished; in this situation one can see the obvious danger of slavery or death for the innocent people entrusted to my protection and care by his majesty; these innocent ones are the ministers of the holy gospel, whom the Indians would not spare any more than they did others in the past, and they would also kill the many women and children in the expedition, who would suffer without cause once the natives overcame their fear of rebelling. The greatest force we possess at present to defend our friends and ourselves is the prestige of the Spanish nation, by fear of which the Indians have been kept in check. Should they lose this fear it would inevitably follow also that the teaching of the holy gospel would be hindered, which I am under obligation to prevent, as this is the main purpose for which I came. For the gospel is the complete remedy and guide for their abominable sins, some of them nefarious and against nature. For the following just cases, such as general peace in the land, protection of the innocent, punishment of those who transgress against their king and his ministers and against their obligations to him as ruler of these Indies, to whom they voluntarily swore obedience, and furthermore to obtain redress for such serious offenses as the killing of such worthy persons, disregarding the recovery of the goods they took from us, and finally to remove such pernicious obstacles and open the way for the spreading of the holy gospel, I have determined that in the discharge of your commission to the pueblo of Acoma, you should make more use of royal clemency than of the severity that the case demands, take into serious consideration the stupidity (*brutalidad*) and incapacity of the Indians, if that is what they showed in this case rather than malice, and observe the following instructions:

First: On receiving your commission and the instructions that follow, you will acknowledge receipt of them before the secretary. With these you will have sufficient authority for what you are to do and you must bind yourself to observe and obey exactly what you are ordered, as we expect from you.

Since the good success of the undertaking depends on the pleasure of God our Lord in directing you to appropriate and effective methods, it is right that you should seek to prevent public or private offenses to Him in the expedition. You must exercise particular care in this respect, admonishing and punishing in exemplary fashion those who cause them, so that one may readily see that you take special interest in this matter.

You will proceed over the shortest route to the pueblo of Acoma, with all the soldiers and war equipment. At the places and pueblos that you pass through on the way you will treat the natives well and not allow any harm to be done them, and to this end you may issue whatever proclamations that seem desirable or necessary.

When you come to the pueblo of Acoma, you must weigh very carefully and calmly the strength of the Indians, plant at once your artillery and musketry at the places that seem most practical, and assign the captains and soldiers to their posts in battle formation, without making any noise or firing an harquebus [heavy musket].

This done, you will, in the presence of Juan Velarde, my secretary, and with the help of Don Tomás and Don Cristóbal, Indian interpreters who are expert in the language, or with the aid of any other interpreters that you may deem suitable, summon the Indians of Acoma to accept peace, once, twice, and thrice, and urge them to abandon their resistance, lay down their arms, and submit to the authority of the king our lord, since they have already rendered obedience to him as his vassals.

You will ask the people of Acoma to surrender the leaders responsible for the uprising, and the murderers, assuring them that they will be justly dealt with.

The Acomas must abandon at once the fortified place in which they live and move down into the valley, where the ministers of the holy gospel who were sent to these kingdoms and provinces by his majesty for this purpose may be able to teach them more easily the matters of our holy Catholic faith.

The Indians must deliver up the bodies of those killed, their personal belongings and weapons, and the horseshoes and other iron that they had dug up three leagues from the pueblo. You must record their answers before my secretary in the presence of as many as can conveniently be brought together to hear them. If the Indians should do all that is prescribed above and come down and submit peacefully, you will establish them in the valley at a safe place where they will not run away and disappear. You will keep them under strict guard and bring them before me in order that we may hear their pleas and administer justice.

After the Indians have been removed from the pueblo and placed under custody, you will send back to the pueblo as many soldiers as you deem necessary, burn it to the ground, and leave no stone on stone, so that the Indians may never be able again to inhabit it as an impregnable fortress.

If the Indians are entrenched and should have assembled many people and you think there is danger of losing your army in trying to storm the pueblo, you will refrain from doing so, for there would be less harm in postponing the punishment for the time being than in risking the people with you and those left here for the protection of the church of God, its ministers, and me. In this matter you must exercise the utmost care and foresight.

If the people should have deserted the pueblo, you will burn it to the ground and destroy it. You will then consult with the council of war as to whether or not it is desirable to pursue the natives, since the council must consider the matter. This must be handled with much discretion.

If God should be so merciful as to grant us victory, you will arrest all of the people, young and old, without sparing anyone. Inasmuch as we have declared war on them without quarter, you will punish all those of fighting age as you deem best, as a warning to everyone in this kingdom. All of those you execute you will expose to public view at the places you think most suitable, as a salutary example. If you should want to show lenience after they have been arrested, you should seek all possible means to make the Indians believe that you are doing so at the request of the friar with your forces. In this manner they will recognize the friars as their benefactors and protectors and come to love and esteem them, and to fear us. To execute this punishment as you may see fit, I grant you the same powers I myself hold from his majesty.

And since all matters properly discussed and thought out lead to a happy and successful end, you already know that I have named as members of the council of war of this expedition, Alonso Sánchez, contador of the royal treasury, Diego de Zubía, captain of cavalry and purveyor general; Marcos Farfán de los Godos, captain of my guard; Captain Gaspar de Villagrán, procurator general; Pablo de Aguilar Inojosa, captain of cavalry; and Gerónimo Márquez, captain of artillery. All six of them are men of much experience and well informed in all that pertains to warfare. You will hold councils of war whenever it seems desirable to you, to them, or to the majority of them. Whatever is agreed upon by all or by the majority in council must be observed. The councils held are to be attended by my secretary who will record what may be determined. I have given these men the appropriate commissions as members of the council of war.

All of the aforesaid you will fulfill with proper diligence and care in order that God and his majesty may be served, and this offense punished.

Stamped with the seal of my office at the pueblo of San Juan Bautista on January 11, 1599. Don Juan de Oñate. By order of the governor, Juan Gutiérrez Bocanegra, secretary.

C. The African Slave Trade

1. Mungo Park Describes Slavers in the African Interior (c. 1790)

Mungo Park, a Scottish explorer, spent nearly two years in the 1790s in the interior of Africa—still terra incognita *to most Europeans. Although his description dates from nearly three centuries after the initial European development of the African slave trade, it provides a rare and probably reliable glimpse of the practices of the African slave traders with whom the Europeans made contact in the late fifteenth and sixteenth centuries. Does Park's account suggest any differences between the African and European slavers? What inferences might be drawn from Park's narrative about the influence of the Europeans on those interior tribes, far from the coast, that never came into direct contact with the whites?*

---

[1]Mungo Park, *Travels in the Interior of Africa* (Edinburgh: Adam and Charles Black, North Bridge, 1860), pp. 291–293.

. . . The slaves which Karfa [a slave trader] had brought with him were all of them prisoners of war; they had been taken by the Bambarran army in the kingdoms of Wassela and Kaarta, and carried to Sego, where some of them had remained three years in irons. From Sego they were sent, in company with a number of other captives, up the Niger in two large canoes, and offered for sale at Yamina, Bammakoo, and Kancaba, at which places the greater number of the captives were bartered for gold dust, and the remainder sent forward to Kankaree.

Eleven of them confessed to me that they had been slaves from their infancy; but the other two refused to give any account of their former condition. They were all very inquisitive; but they viewed me at first with looks of horror, and repeatedly asked if my countrymen were cannibals. They were very desirous to know what became of the slaves after they had crossed the salt water. I told them that they were employed in cultivating the land, but they would not believe me; and one of them, putting his hand upon the ground, said, with great simplicity, "Have you really got such ground as this to set your feet upon?" A deeply-rooted idea that the whites purchase Negroes for the purpose of devouring them, or of selling them to others, that they may be devoured hereafter, naturally makes the slaves contemplate a journey towards the coast with great terror, insomuch that the Slatees are forced to keep them constantly in irons, and watch them very closely to prevent their escape. They are commonly secured by putting the right leg of one, and the left of another into the same pair of fetters. By supporting the fetters with a string, they can walk, though very slowly. Every four slaves are likewise fastened together by the necks with a strong rope of twisted thongs; and in the night an additional pair of fetters is put on their hands, and sometimes a light iron chain passed round their necks.

Such of them as evince marks of discontent, are secured in a different manner. A thick billet of wood is cut about three feet long, and a smooth notch being made upon one side of it, the ankle of the slave is bolted to the smooth part by means of a strong iron staple, one prong of which passes on each side of the ankle. All these fetters and bolts are made from native iron; in the present case they were put on by the blacksmith as soon as the slaves arrived from Kancaba, and were not taken off until the morning on which the coffle [slave caravan] departed for Gambia.

In other respects, the treatment of the slaves during their stay at Kamalia was far from being harsh or cruel. They were led out in their fetters every morning to the shade of the tamarind tree, where they were encouraged to play at games of hazard, and sing diverting songs, to keep up their spirits; for though some of them sustained the hardships of their situation with amazing fortitude, the greater part were very much dejected, and would sit all day in a sort of sullen melancholy, with their eyes fixed upon the ground. In the evening their irons were examined and their hand fetters put on, after which they were conducted into two large huts, where they were guarded during the night by Karfa's domestic slaves. But notwithstanding all this, about a week after their arrival, one of the slaves had the address to procure a small knife, with which he opened the rings of his fetters, cut the rope, and made his escape; more of them would probably have got off had they assisted each other; but the slave no sooner found himself at liberty than he refused to stop and assist in breaking the chain which was fastened round the necks of his companions. . . .

2. A Slave Is Taken to Barbados (c. 1750)

Olauda Equiano was a remarkable African, born in 1745 in present-day Nigeria. After his capture as a boy by slave traders, he was taken to Barbados. He eventually bought his freedom and became a leading spokesperson for the cause of antislavery. His book The Interesting Narrative of the Life of Olaudah Equiano or Gustavus Vassa the African, *from which the selection below is taken, was a best-seller in both Europe and America in the late eighteenth and early nineteenth centuries. Although Equiano's narrative, like the preceding selection by Mungo Park, dates from nearly three centuries after the beginnings of large scale European slave trading in Africa, it affords a unique perspective on the experience of slavery through the eyes of an African slave. Equiano's account is probably faithful, at least psychologically, to the experiences of millions of Africans in the centuries before him. What differences does Equiano see between slavery as practiced in Africa and as practiced in Barbados? What is the most difficult part of his experience as a slave?*

. . . Our tillage is exercised in a large plain or common. . . . This common is often the theatre of war, and therefore when our people go out to till their land they not only go in a body but generally take their arms with them for fear of a surprise, and when they apprehend an invasion they guard the avenues to their dwellings by driving sticks into the ground, which are so sharp at one end as to pierce the foot and are generally dipped in poison. From what I can recollect of these battles, they appear to have been irruptions of one little state or district on the other to obtain prisoners or booty. Perhaps they were incited to this by those traders who brought the European goods . . . amongst us. Such a mode of obtaining slaves in Africa is common, and I believe more are procured this way and by kidnapping than any other. . . .

. . . I grew up till I was turned the age of 11, when an end was put to my happiness in the following manner. . . . One day, when all our people were gone out to their works as usual and only I and my dear sister were left to mind the house, two men and a woman got over our walls, and in a moment seized us both, and without giving us time to cry out or make resistance they stopped our mouths and ran off with us into the nearest wood. . . . The next day proved a day of greater sorrow than I had yet experienced, for my sister and I were then separated while we lay clasped in each other's arms. It was in vain that we besought them not to part us; she was torn from me and immediately carried away, while I was left in a state of distraction not to be described. I cried and grieved continually, and for several days I did not eat anything but what they forced into my mouth. At length, after many days' travelling, during which I had often changed masters, I got into the hands of a chieftain in a very pleasant country. This man had two wives and some children, and they all

---

[2]Olaudah Equiano, *Equiano's Travels: His Autobiography, The Interesting Narrative of the Life of Olaudah Equiano or Gustavus Vassa the African* (Oxford: Heinemann, 1967; first published 1789), pp. 8–32.

used me extremely well and did all they could to comfort me, particularly the first wife, who was something like my mother. Although I was a great many days' journey from my father's house, yet these people spoke exactly the same language with us. This first master of mine, as I may call him, was a smith, and my principal employment was working his bellows, which were the same kind as I had seen in my vicinity. . . .

Soon after this my master's only daughter and child by his first wife sickened and died, which affected him so much that for some time he was almost frantic, and really would have killed himself had he not been watched and prevented. However, in a small time afterwards he recovered and I was again sold. I was now carried to the left of the sun's rising, through many different countries and a number of large woods. . . .

From the time I left my own nation I always found somebody that understood me till I came to the sea coast. The languages of different nations did not totally differ, nor were they so copious as those of the Europeans, particularly the English. They were therefore easily learned, and while I was journeying thus through Africa I acquired two or three different tongues. . . .

All the nations and people I had hitherto passed through resembled our own in their manner, customs, and language: but I came at length to a country the inhabitants of which differed from us in all those particulars. I was very much struck with this difference, especially when I came among a people who did not circumcise and ate without washing their hands. They cooked also in iron pots and had European cutlasses and crossbows, which were unknown to us, and fought with their fists amongst themselves. Their women were not so modest as ours, for they ate and drank and slept with their men. But above all, I was amazed to see no sacrifices or offerings among them. In some of those places the people ornamented themselves with scars, and likewise filed their teeth very sharp. They wanted sometimes to ornament me in the same manner, but I would not suffer them, hoping that I might some time be among a people who did not thus disfigure themselves, as I thought they did. At last I came to the banks of a large river, which was covered with canoes in which the people appeared to live with their household utensils and provisions of all kinds. I was beyond measure astonished at this, as I had never before seen any water larger than a pond or a rivulet: and my surprise was mingled with no small fear when I was put into one of these canoes and we began to paddle and move along the river. . . . Thus I continued to travel, sometimes by land, sometimes by water, through different countries and various nations, till at the end of six or seven months after I had been kidnapped I arrived at the sea coast.

The first object which saluted my eyes when I arrived on the coast was the sea, and a slave ship which was then riding at anchor and waiting for its cargo. These filled me with astonishment, which was soon converted into terror when I was carried on board. I was immediately handled and tossed up to see if I were sound by some of the crew, and I was now persuaded that I had gotten into a world of bad spirits and that they were going to kill me. Their complexions too differing so much from ours, their long hair and the language they spoke (which was very different from any I had ever heard) united to confirm me in this belief. Indeed such were the horrors of my views and fears at the moment that, if ten thousand worlds had been my own, I would have freely parted with them all to have exchanged my condition with that of the meanest slave in my own country. When I looked round the ship too and saw a large furnace or copper boiling and a multitude of black people of every description chained together, every one of their countenances expressing dejection and sorrow, I no longer doubted of my fate; and quite overpowered with horror and anguish, I fell motionless on the deck and fainted. When I recovered a little I found some black people about me, who I believed were some of those who had brought me on board and had been receiving their pay; they talked to me in order to cheer me, but all in vain. I asked them if we were not to be eaten by those white men with horrible looks, red faces, and loose hair. They told me I was not, and one of the crew brought me a small portion of spirituous liquor in a wine glass, but being afraid of him I would not take it out of his hand. One of the blacks therefore took it from him and gave it to me, and I took a little down my palate, which instead of reviving me, as they thought it would, threw me into the greatest consternation at the strange feeling it produced, having never tasted such any liquor before. Soon after this the blacks who brought me on board went off, and left me abandoned to despair.

I now saw myself deprived of all chance of returning to my native country or even the least glimpse of hope of gaining the shore, which I now considered as friendly; and I even wished for my former slavery in preference to my present situation, which was filled with horrors of every kind, still heightened by my ignorance of what I was to undergo. I was not long suffered to indulge my grief; I was soon put down under the decks, and there I received such a salutation in my nostrils as I had never experienced in my life: so that with the loathsomeness of the stench and crying together, I became so sick and low that I was not able to eat, nor had I the least desire to taste anything. I now wished for the last friend, death, to relieve me; but soon, to my grief, two of the white men offered me eatables, and on my refusing to eat, one of them held me fast by the hands and laid me across I think the windlass, and tied my feet while the other flogged me severely. I had never experienced anything of this kind before, and although, not being used to the water, I naturally feared that element the first time I saw it, yet nevertheless could I have got over the nettings I would have jumped over the side, but I could not; and besides, the crew used to watch us very closely who were not chained down to the decks, lest we should leap into the water: and I have seen some of these poor African prisoners most severely cut for attempting to do so, and hourly whipped for not eating. This indeed was often the case with myself. In a little time after, amongst the poor chained men I found some of my own nation, which in a small degree gave ease to my mind. I inquired of these what was to be done with us; they gave me to understand we were to be carried to these white people's country to work for them. I then was a little revived, and thought if it were no worse than working, my situation was not so desperate: but still I feared I should be put to death, the white people looked and acted, as I thought, in so savage a manner; for I had never seen among my people such instances of brutal cruelty, and this not only shewn towards us blacks but also to some of the whites themselves. One white man in particular I saw, when we were permitted to be on deck, flogged so unmercifully with a large rope near the foremast that he died in consequence of it; and they tossed him over the side as they would have done a brute. This made me fear these people the more, and I expected nothing less than to be treated in the same manner. . . .

At last we came in sight of the island of Barbados, at which the whites on board gave a great shout and made many signs of joy to us. We did not know what to think of this, but as the vessel drew nearer we plainly saw the harbour and other ships of different kinds and sizes, and we soon anchored amongst them off Bridgetown. Many merchants and planters now came on board, though it was in the evening. They put us in separate parcels and examined us attentively. They also made us jump, and pointed to the land, signifying we were to go there. We thought by this we should be eaten by these ugly men, as they appeared to us; and when soon after we were all put down under the deck again, there was much dread and trembling among us, and nothing but bitter cries to be heard all the night from these apprehensions, insomuch that at last the white people got some old slaves from the land to pacify us. They told us we were not to be eaten but to work, and were soon to go on land where we should see many of our country people. This report eased us much; and sure enough soon after we were landed there came to us Africans of all languages. We were conducted immediately to the merchant's yard, where we were all pent up together like so many sheep in a fold without regard to sex or age. As every object was new to me everything I saw filled me with surprise. What struck me first was that the houses were built with storeys, and in every other respect different from those in Africa: but I was still more astonished on seeing people on horseback. I did not know what this could mean, and indeed I thought these people were full of nothing but magical arts. While I was in this astonishment one of my fellow prisoners spoke to a countryman of his about the horses, who said they were the same kind they had in their country. I understood them though they were from a distant part of Africa, and I thought it odd I had not seen any horses there; but afterwards when I came to converse with different Africans I found they had many horses amongst them, and much larger than those I then saw. We were not many days in the merchant's custody before we were sold after their usual manner, which is this: On a signal given, (as the beat of a drum) the buyers rush at once into the yard where the slaves are confined, and make choice of that parcel they like best. The noise and clamour with which this is attended and the eagerness visible in the countenances of the buyers serve not a little to increase the apprehensions of the terrified Africans, who may well be supposed to consider them as the ministers of that destruction to which they think themselves devoted. In this manner, without scruple, are relations and friends separated, most of them never to see each other again. I remember in the vessel in which I was brought over, in the men's apartment there were several brothers who, in the sale, were sold in different lots; and it was very moving on this occasion to see and hear their cries at parting. O, ye nominal Christians! might not an African ask you, Learned you this from your God who says unto you, Do unto all men as you would men should do unto you? Is it not enough that we are torn from our country and friends to toil for your luxury and lust of gain? Must every tender feeling be likewise sacrificed to your avarice? Are the dearest friends and relations, now rendered more dear by their separation from their kindred, still to be parted from each other and thus prevented from cheering the gloom of slavery with the small comfort of being together and mingling their sufferings and sorrows? Why are parents to lose their children, brothers their sisters, or husbands their wives? Surely this is a new refinement in cruelty which, while it has no advantage to atone for it, thus aggravates distress and adds fresh horrors even to the wretchedness of slavery.

D. New Worlds for the Taking

1. John Cabot Voyages for England (1497)

John Cabot was a Genoese (like Columbus) who became a naturalized Venetian and then took up residence at the port of Bristol, England. Inspired by the Columbian discovery and commissioned by Henry VII, he sailed into the stormy North Atlantic in 1497 with a single ship and eighteen men. Seeking the territory of the Grand Khan of China, he landed on or somewhere near Newfoundland, Labrador, or Cape Breton Island. A proud fellow Venetian dwelling in London wrote to his brothers in Venice describing the excitement. What does this account foreshadow about the future of English colonizing, especially the quality of the participants?

The Venetian, our countryman, who went with a ship from Bristol in quest of new islands, is returned, and says that 700 leagues hence he discovered land, the territory of the Grand Cham [Khan]. He coasted for 300 leagues and landed; saw no human beings, but he has brought hither to the King certain snares which had been set to catch game, and a needle for making nets. He also found some felled trees, wherefore he supposed there were inhabitants, and returned to his ship in alarm.

He was three months on the voyage, and on his return he saw two islands to starboard, but would not land, time being precious, as he was short of provisions. He says that the tides are slack and do not flow as they do here. The King of England is much pleased with this intelligence.

The King has promised that in the spring our countryman shall have ten ships, armed to his order, and at his request has conceded him all the prisoners, except such as are confined for high treason, to man his fleet. The King has also given him money wherewith to amuse himself till then, and he is now at Bristol with his wife, who is also Venetian, and with his sons. His name is Zuan Cabot, and he is styled the Great Admiral. Vast honor is paid him; he dresses in silk. And these English run after him like mad people, so that he can enlist as many of them as he pleases, and a number of our own rogues besides.

---

[1]Rawdon Brown, ed., *Calendar of State Papers . . . Venice . . .* (London, 1864), vol. 1, p. 262. Published by the authority of the Lords Commissioners of her majesty's treasury, under the direction of the master of the rools.

2. Richard Hakluyt Calls for an Empire (1582)

Richard Hakluyt, a remarkable clergyman-scholar-geographer who lies buried in Westminster Abbey, deserves high rank among the indirect founding fathers of the United States. His published collections of documents relating to early English explorations must be regarded as among the "great books" of American history for their stimulation of interest in New World colonization. (Hakluyt even gambled some of his own small fortune in the company that tried to colonize Virginia.) Passionately concerned about England's "sluggish security," he wrote the following in the dedicatory letter of his first published work (1582). It was addressed to Sir Philip Sidney— scholar, diplomat, author, poet, soldier, and knightly luminary of Queen Elizabeth's court. What were Hakluyt's various arguments for settling the Atlantic Coast north of Florida? Which ones probably appealed most strongly to Sidney's (a) patriotism and (b) religious faith?

I marvel not a little, right worshipful, that since the first discovery of America (which is now full four score and ten years), after so great conquests and plantings of the Spaniards and Portuguese there, that we of England could never have the grace to set fast footing in such fertile and temperate places as are left as yet unpossessed of them. But . . . I conceive great hope that the time approacheth and now is that we of England may share and part stakes [divide the prize] (if we will ourselve) both with the Spaniard and the Portuguese in part of America and other regions as yet undiscovered.

And surely if there were in us that desire to advance the honor of our country which ought to be in every good man, we would not all this while have forslown [neglected] the possessing of those lands which of equity and right appertain unto us, as by the discourses that follow shall appear most plainly.

Yea, if we would behold with the eye of pity how all our prisons are pestered and filled with able men to serve their country, which for small robberies are daily hanged up in great numbers, . . . we would hasten . . . the deducting [conveying] of some colonies of our superfluous people into those temperate and fertile parts of America, which, being within six weeks' sailing of England, are yet unpossessed by any Christians, and seem to offer themselves unto us, stretching nearer unto Her Majesty's dominions than to any other part of Europe. . . .

It chanced very lately that upon occasion I had great conference in matters of cosmography with an excellent learned man of Portugal, most privy to all the discoveries of his nation, who wondered that those blessed countries from the point of Florida northward were all this while unplanted by Christians, protesting with great affection and zeal that if he were now as young as I (for at this present he is three score years of age) he would sell all he had, being a man of no small wealth and honor, to furnish a convenient number of ships to sea for the inhabiting of those countries and reducing those gentile [heathen] people to Christianity. . . .

---

[2]Collected and published by Richard Hakluyt, *Divers Voyages Touching the Discovery of America and the Islands Adjacent,* . . . in the year 1582. Edited and with notes and an introduction by John Winter Jones (London: The Hakluyt Society, 1850), pp. 8–18.

If this man's desire might be executed, we might not only for the present time take possession of that good land, but also, in short space, by God's grace find out that short and easy passage by the Northwest which we have hitherto so long desired. . . .

Certes [certainly], if hitherto in our own discoveries we had not been led with a preposterous desire of seeking rather gain than God's glory, I assure myself that our labors had taken far better effect. But we forgot that godliness is great riches, and that if we first seek the kingdom of God, all other things will be given unto us. . . .

I trust that now, being taught by their manifold losses, our men will take a more godly course and use some part of their goods to his [God's] glory. If not, he will turn even their covetousness to serve him, as he hath done the pride and avarice of the Spaniards and Portuguese, who, pretending in glorious words that they made their discoveries chiefly to convert infidels to our most holy faith (as they say), in deed and truth sought not them, but their goods and riches. . . .

Here I cease, craving pardon for my overboldness, trusting also that Your Worship will continue and increase your accustomed favor toward these godly and honorable discoveries.

3. An English Landlord Describes a Troubled England (1623)

England's prosperity in the early sixteenth century had been built on the backs of bleating sheep, as exports of raw wool and finished woolen cloth boomed. Beginning about 1550, however, a severe depression descended upon the woolen districts. Thousands of sheepherders and weavers were pitched out of work and onto the roads of England. England suddenly seemed to be overflowing with paupers and vagabonds, as described in the following letter by a Lincolnshire landlord. What did he find most alarming?

Right honourable brother, the best news I can send you is that we are all in good health God be praised. I am now here with my son to settle some country affair, and my own private, which were never so burdensome unto me as now. For many insufficient tenants have given up their farms and sheepwalks, so as I am forced to take them into my own hands and borrow money upon use to stock them. It draweth me wholly from a contemplative life, which I most affected, and could be most willing to pass over my whole estate to the benefit of my children so as I were freed of the trouble. Our country was never in that want that now it is, and more of money than corn, for there are many thousands in these parts who have sold all they have even to their bed straw and cannot get work to earn any money. Dog's flesh is a dainty dish and found upon search in many houses, also such horse flesh as hath lain long in a deke for hounds. And the other day one stole a sheep who for mere hunger tore a leg out, and did eat it raw. All that is most certain true and yet

---

[3]*Lincolnshire Notes and Queries* (Horncastle, England: W. K. Morton, 1888), vol. 1, no. 1, pp. 15–16 (a quarterly journal devoted to the antiquities, parochial records, family history, folklore, quaint customs, etc., of the county).

the great time of scarcity not yet come. I shall rejoice to have a better subject to write of, and expect it with patience. In the mean time and ever

I will remain
Your honour's most loving brother to serve you
William Pelham

4. Hakluyt Sees England's Salvation in America (1584)

In one of his most widely read works, Discourse Concerning the Western Planting, *published in 1584, Richard Hakluyt further developed the argument that colonizing America might provide a remedy for England's festering economic and social problems. What did he identify as the most pressing problems to be solved? In what ways did he see America providing solutions to those problems? How prophetic was he about the role the American colonies were to play in England's commerce?*

It is well worth the observation to see and consider what the like voyages of discovery and planting in the East and West Indies have wrought in the kingdoms of Portugal and Spain; both which realms, being of themselves poor and barren and hardly able to sustain their inhabitants, by their discoveries have found such occasion of employment, that these many years we have not heard scarcely of any pirate of those two nations; whereas we and the French are most infamous for our outrageous, common, and daily piracies. . . . [W]e, for all the statutes that hitherto can be devised, and the sharp execution of the same in punishing idle and lazy persons, for want of sufficient occasion of honest employment, cannot deliver our commonwealth from multitudes of loiterers and idle vagabonds.

Truth it is that through our long peace and seldom sickness . . . we are grown more populous than ever heretofore; so that now there are of every art and science so many, that they can hardly live by one another, nay, rather, they are ready to eat up one another; yes, many thousands of idle persons are within this realm, which, having no way to be set on work, be either mutinous and seek alteration in the state, or at least very burdensome to the commonwealth, and often fall to pilfering and thieving and other lewdness, whereby all the prisons of the land are daily pestered and stuffed full of them, where either they pitifully pine away, or else at length are miserably hanged. . . .

Whereas if this voyage were put in execution, these petty thieves might be condemned for certain years to the western parts, especially in Newfoundland, in sawing and felling of timber for masts of ships; . . . in burning of the firs and pine trees to make pitch, tar, rosin, and soap ashes; in beating and working of hemp for cordage; and, in the more southern parts, in setting them to work in mines of gold, silver, copper, lead, and iron; in dragging for pearls and coral; in planting of sugar cane, as the Portuguese have done in Madera; in maintenance and increasing of silk worms for silk, and in dressing the same; in gathering of cotton whereof there is plenty; in tilling of the soil for grain; in dressing of vines whereof there is great abundance for wine; olives, whereof the soil is capable, for oil; trees for oranges,

⁴Richard Hakluyt, *Discourse Concerning the Western Planting* (1584), in Charles Deane, ed., *Documentary History of the State of Maine* (Cambridge: Press of John Wilson and Son, 1877), vol. 2, pp. 36–39.

lemons, almonds, figs, and other fruits, all which are found to grow there already; . . . in fishing, salting, and drying of ling, cod, salmon, herring; in making and gathering of honey, wax, turpentine. . . .

Besides this, such as by any kind of infirmity cannot pass the seas thither, and now are chargeable to the realm at home, by this voyage shall be made profitable members, by employing them in England in making of a thousand trifling things, which will be very good merchandise for those countries where we shall have most ample vente [sales] thereof.

And seeing the savages . . . are greatly delighted with any cap or garment made of coarse woolen cloth, their country being cold and sharp in winter, it is manifest we shall find great [demand for] our clothes . . . whereby all occupations belonging to clothing and knitting shall freshly be set on work, as cappers, knitters, clothiers, woolmen, carders, spinners, weavers, fullers, shearmen, dyers, drapers, hatters, and such like, whereby many decayed towns may be repaired.

Thought Provokers

1. How might we explain the attitudes of Renaissance era Europeans toward the newly discovered Indians? Was the concern for Christianizing the Native Americans sincere?
2. What motivated the Spanish to colonize the Americas in the sixteenth century? On balance, was the Spanish arrival good or bad for the New World? What advantages and disadvantages did the Spanish have as colonizers?
3. Why did Europeans look to Africa for labor with which to develop the riches of the New World? To what extent did Africans themselves help to promote the slave trade?
4. What were the most valid arguments used to promote English colonization in the sixteenth and seventeenth centuries? What relevance to the English did the example of Spain's colonizing venture in the New World have?

2

The Planting
of English America,
1500–1733

There is under our noses the great and ample country
of Virginia; the inland whereof is found of late to be
so sweet and wholesome a climate, so rich and
abundant in silver mines, a better and richer country
than Mexico itself.

Richard Hakluyt, 1599

Prologue: The spectacular success of the Spanish conquerors excited the cupidity
and rivalry of the English and partly inspired Sir Humphrey Gilbert's ill-fated colony
in Newfoundland in 1583 and Sir Walter Raleigh's luckless venture on Roanoke Island, off the North Carolina coast, in the 1580s. But England, though suffering from
blighting economic and social disruptions at home, was not prepared for ambitious
colonial ventures until the defeat of the Spanish Armada in 1588 and the perfection
of the joint-stock company—a device that enabled "adventurers" to pool their capital. Virginia, which got off to a shaky start in 1607, was finally saved by tobacco.
Launched in 1634 by Lord Baltimore as a Catholic haven, Maryland profited from Virginia's experience and assistance. In all the young colonies, people of diverse cultures—European, Indian, and African—commingled, and sometimes clashed.

A. Precarious Beginnings in Virginia

1. The Starving Time (1609)

*Captain John Smith—adventurer, colonizer, explorer, author, and mapmaker—also
ranks among America's first historians. Writing from England some fifteen years
later, about events that he did not personally witness, he tells a tale that had come
to him at second hand. What indications of modesty or lack of it are present? What
pulled the settlers through?*

[1]Edward Arber, ed., *Travels and Works of Captain John Smith* (A. G. Bradley, 1910), vol. 2, pp. 497–499.
(*The General History of Virginia by Captaine John Smith, sometymes Governour in those Countryes and
Admirall of New England.* [London: Printed by I. D. and I. H. for Michael Sparkes, 1674]).

The day before Captain Smith returned for England with the ships [October 4, 1609], Captain Davis arrived in a small pinnace [light sailing vessel], with some sixteen proper men more. . . . For the savages [Indians] no sooner understood Smith was gone but they all revolted, and did spoil and murder all they encountered. . . .

Now we all found the loss of Captain Smith; yea, his greatest maligners could now curse his loss. As for corn provision and contribution from the savages, we [now] had nothing but mortal wounds, with clubs and arrows. As for our hogs, hens, goats, sheep, horses, and what lived, our commanders, officers, and savages daily consumed them. Some small proportions sometimes we tasted, till all was devoured; then swords, arms, [fowling] pieces, or anything we traded with the savages, whose cruel fingers were so often imbrued in our blood that what by their cruelty, our Governor's indiscretion, and the loss of our ships, of five hundred [persons] within six months after Captain Smith's departure there remained not past sixty men, women, and children, most miserable and poor creatures. And those were preserved for the most part by roots, herbs, acorns, walnuts, berries, now and then a little fish. They that had starch [courage] in these extremities made no small use of it; yea, [they ate] even the very skins of our horses.

Nay, so great was our famine that a savage we slew and buried, the poorer sort took him up again and ate him; and so did divers one another boiled and stewed, with roots and herbs. And one amongst the rest did kill his wife, powdered [salted] her, and had eaten part of her before it was known, for which he was executed, as he well deserved. Now whether she was better roasted, boiled, or carbonadoed [broiled], I know not; but of such a dish as powdered wife I never heard of.

This was the time which still to this day [1624] we called the starving time. It were too vile to say, and scarce to be believed, what we endured. But the occasion was our own, for want of providence, industry, and government, and not the barrenness and defect of the country, as is generally supposed. For till then in three years . . . we had never from England provisions sufficient for six months, though it seemed by the bills of loading sufficient was sent us, such a glutton is the sea, and such good fellows the mariners. We as little tasted of the great proportion sent us, as they of our want and miseries. Yet notwithstanding they ever overswayed and ruled the business, though we endured all that is said, and chiefly lived on what this good country naturally afforded, yet had we been even in Paradise itself with these governors, it would not have been much better with us. Yet there were amongst us who, had they had the government as Captain Smith appointed but . . . could not maintain it, would surely have kept us from those extremities of miseries.

2. Governor William Berkeley Reports (1671)

Sir William Berkeley, a polished Oxford graduate, courtier, and playwright, was appointed governor of Virginia in 1642, when only thirty-six years of age. Conciliatory, energetic, and courageous, he served well in his early years, both as administrator and as military leader. He cultivated flax, cotton, rice, and silk on his own lands, and in one year sent a gift of three hundred pounds of silk to the king. In response to

---

[2]W. W. Hening, *The Statutes at Large . . . of Virginia . . .* (Richmond: Samuel Pleasants, 1823), vol. 2, pp. 514–517.

specific questions from London, he prepared the able report from which the following extract is taken. From what economic and social handicaps did Virginia suffer? Which one was the most burdensome? What is significantly revealed of Berkeley's character and outlook?

12. What commodities are there of the production, growth, and manufacture of your plantation [colony]; and particularly, what materials are there already growing, or may be produced for shipping in the same?

Answer. Commodities of the growth of our country we never had any but tobacco, which in this yet is considerable, that it yields His Majesty a great revenue. But of late we have begun to make silk, and so many mulberry trees are planted, and planting, that if we had skillful men from Naples or Sicily to teach us the art of making it perfectly, in less than half an age [generation] we should make as much silk in an year as England did yearly expend three score years since. But now we hear it is grown to a greater excess, and more common and vulgar usage. Now, for shipping, we have admirable masts and very good oaks; but for iron ore I dare not say there is sufficient to keep one iron mill going for seven years. . . .

15. What number of planters, servants, and slaves; and how many parishes are there in your plantation?

Answer. We suppose, and I am very sure we do not much miscount, that there is in Virginia above forty thousand persons, men, women, and children, and of which there are two thousand black slaves, six thousand Christian servants [indentured] for a short time. The rest are born in the country or have come in to settle and seat, in bettering their condition in a growing country

16. What number of English, Scots, or Irish have for these seven years last past come yearly to plant and inhabit within your government; as also what blacks or slaves have been brought in within the said time?

Answer. Yearly, we suppose there comes in, of servants, about fifteen hundred, of which most are English, few Scotch, and fewer Irish, and not above two or three ships of Negroes in seven years.

17. What number of people have yearly died, within your plantation and government, for these seven years last past, both whites and blacks?

Answer. All new plantations are, for an age or two, unhealthy, till they are thoroughly cleared of wood. But unless we had a particular register office for the denoting of all that died, I cannot give a particular answer to this query. Only this I can say, that there is not often unseasoned hands (as we term them) that die now, whereas heretofore not one of five escaped the first year. . . .

23. What course is taken about the instructing of the people, within your government, in the Christian religion; and what provision is there made for the paying of your ministry?

Answer. The same course that is taken in England out of towns: every man, according to his ability, instructing his children. We have forty-eight parishes, and our ministers are well paid, and by my consent should be better if they would pray oftener and preach less. But of all other commodities, so of this, the worst are sent us, and we had few that we could boast of, since the persecution in Cromwell's tyranny drove divers worthy men hither. But, I thank God, there are no free schools nor printing, and I hope we shall not have these hundred years. For learning has brought disobedience, and heresy, and sects into the world, and printing has divulged them, and libels against the best government. God keep us from both!

B. The Mix of Cultures in English America

1. The Great Indian Uprising (1622)

At the outset the Indians attacked the Virginia colonists with arrows, and relations between the two races remained uneasy for many years after 1607. As if deaths from famine, exposure, improper food, and malarial fever were not enough, the colonists lost perhaps a quarter of their number in the great attack of 1622. Among other grievances, the Indians resented the clearing of their forests and the seizure of their cornfields by the whites. Edward Waterhouse, a prominent Virginia official, sent home this firsthand report. What does it reveal about how the colony subsisted, how earnest the Christianizing efforts of the colonists were, and how the disaster could be used to the advantage of the Virginians?

And such was the conceit of firm peace and amity [with the Indians] as that there was seldom or never a sword worn and a [fowling] piece seldomer, except for a deer or fowl. By which assurance of security the plantations of particular adventurers and planters were placed scatteringly and stragglingly as a choice vein of rich ground invited them, and the farther from neighbors held the better. The houses generally sat open to the savages, who were always friendly entertained at the tables of the English, and commonly lodged in their bed-chambers . . . [thus] seeming to open a fair gate for their conversion to Christianity.

Yea, such was the treacherous dissimulation of that people who then had contrived our destruction, that even two days before the massacre, some of our men were guided through the woods by them in safety. . . . Yea, they borrowed our own boats to convey themselves across the river (on the banks of both sides whereof all our plantations were) to consult of the devilish murder that ensued, and of our utter extirpation, which God of his mercy (by the means of some of themselves converted to Christianity) prevented. . . .

On the Friday morning (the fatal day) the 22nd of March [1622], as also in the evening, as in other days before, they came unarmed into our houses, without bows or arrows, or other weapons, with deer, turkeys, fish, furs, and other provisions to sell and truck with us for glass, beads, and other trifles; yea, in some places, sat down at breakfast with our people at their tables, whom immediately with their own tools and weapons, either laid down, or standing in their houses, they basely and barbarously murdered, not sparing either age or sex, man, woman, or child; so sudden in their cruel execution that few or none discerned the weapon or blow that brought them to destruction. In which manner they also slew many of our people then at their several works and husbandries in the fields, and without [outside] their houses, some in planting corn and tobacco, some in gardening, some in making

---

[1]Susan M. Kingsbury, ed., *The Records of the Virginia Company of London* (Washington: Government Printing Office, 1933), vol. 3, pp. 550–551, 556–557.

, brick, building, sawing, and other kinds of husbandry—they well knowing in what places and quarters each of our men were, in regard of their daily familiarity and resort to us for trading and other negotiations, which the more willingly was by us continued and cherished for the desire we had of effecting that great masterpiece of works, their conversion.

And by this means, that fatal Friday morning, there fell under the bloody and barbarous hands of that perfidious and inhumane people, contrary to all laws of God and man, and nature and nations, 347 men, women, and children, most by their own weapons. And not being content with taking away life alone, they fell after again upon the dead, making, as well as they could, a fresh murder, defacing, dragging, and mangling the dead carcasses into many pieces, and carrying away some parts in derision, with base and brutish triumph. . . .

Our hands, which before were tied with gentleness and fair usage, are now set at liberty by the treacherous violence of the savages . . . so that we, who hitherto have had possession of no more ground than their waste and our purchase at a valuable consideration to their own contentment gained, may now by right of war, and law of nations, invade the country, and destroy them who sought to destroy us; whereby we shall enjoy their cultivated places. . . . Now their cleared grounds in all their villages (which are situate in the fruitfulest places of the land) shall be inhabited by us, whereas heretofore the grubbing of woods was the greatest labor.

2. A West Indian Planter Reflects on Slavery in Barbados (1673)

Richard Ligon, an English merchant, came to Barbados in 1647 to work on a sugarcane plantation. After suffering repeatedly from tropical diseases, he returned to England in 1650, only to be thrown in debtors' prison by his creditors. While incarcerated, he wrote the following account of his experiences in Barbados. What differences did he notice between the condition of indentured servants and the condition of slaves? What factors did he think prevented slave revolts? What role did Christianity play in the lives of slaves—and slave holders?

The Island is divided into three sorts of men, *viz.* Masters, Servants, and slaves. The slaves and their posterity, being subject to their Masters for ever, are kept and preserv'd with greater care then the servants, who are theirs but for five years, according to the law of the Island. So that for the time, the servants have the worser lives, for they are put to very hard labour, ill lodging, and their diet very sleight. . . .

It has been accounted a strange thing, that the *Negroes,* being more than double the numbers of the Christians that are there, and they accounted a bloody people, where they think they have power or advantages; and the more bloody, by how much they are more fearful than others: that these should not commit some horrid massacre upon the Christians, thereby to enfranchise themselves, and become Masters of the Island. But there are three reasons that take away this wonder; the one is, They are not suffered to touch or handle any weapons: The other, That they are held in such awe and slavery, as they are fearful to appear in any daring act; and

---

[2]Richard Ligon, *A True and Exact History of the Island of Barbadoes* (1673), pp. 51–59.

seeing the mustering of our men, and hearing their Gun-shot, (than which nothing is more terrible to them) their spirits are subjugated to so low a condition, as they dare not look up to any bold attempt. Besides these, there is a third reason, which stops all designs of that kind, and that is, They are fetch'd from several parts of *Africa,* who speake several languages, and by that means, one of them understands not another: For, some of them are fetch'd from *Guinny* and *Binny,* some from *Cutchew,* some from *Angola,* and some from the River of *Gambia.* And in some of these places where petty Kingdomes are, they sell their Subjects, and such as they take in Battle, whom they make slaves; and some mean men sell their Servants, their Children, and sometimes their Wives; and think all good traffick, for such commodities as our Merchants send them.

When they are brought to us, the Planters buy them out of the Ship, where they find them stark naked, and therefore cannot be deceived in any outward infirmity. They choose them as they do Horses in a Market; the strongest, youthfullest, and most beautiful, yield the greatest prices. Thirty pound sterling is a price for the best man Negroe; and twenty five, twenty six, or twenty seven pound for a Woman; the Children are at easier rates. And we buy them so, as the sexes may be equall; for, if they have more Men than Women, the men who are unmarried will come to their Masters, and complain, that they cannot live without Wives, and desire him, they may have Wives. . . .

Another, of another kind of speculation I found; but more ingenious then he: and this man with three or four more, were to attend me into the woods, to cut Church wayes, for I was imployed sometimes upon publick works; and those men were excellent Axe-men, and because there were many gullies in the way, which were impassable, and by that means I was compell'd to make traverses, up and down in the wood; and was by that in danger to miss of the point, to which I was to make my passage to the Church, and therefore was fain to take a Compasse with me, which was a Circumferenter, to make my traverses the more exact, and indeed without which, it could not be done, setting up the Circumferenter, and observing the Needle: This *Negre Sambo* comes to me, and seeing the needle wag, desired to know the reason of its stirring, and whether it were alive: I told him no, but it stood upon a point, and for a while it would stir, but by and by stand still which he observ'd and found it to be true.

The next question was, why it stood one way; and would not remove to any other point, I told him that it would stand no way but North and South, and upon that shew'd him the four Cardinal points of the compass, East, West, North, South, which he presently learnt by heart, and promis'd me never to forget it. His last question was, why it would stand North, I gave this reason, because of the huge Rocks of Loadstone that were in the North part of the world, which had a quality to draw Iron to it; and this Needle being of Iron, and touch'd with a Loadstone, it would alwayes stand that way.

This point of Philosophy as a little too hard for him, and so he stood in a strange muse; which to put him out of, I bad him reach his axe, and put it near to the Compass, and remove it about; and as he did so, the Needle turned with it, which put him in the greatest admiration that ever I saw a man, and so quite gave over his questions, and desired me, that he might be made a Christian; for, he thought to be a Christian, was to be endued with all those knowledges he wanted.

I promised to do my best endeavour; and when I came home, spoke to the Master of the Plantation, and told him, that poor *Sambo* desired much to be a Christian. But his answer was, That the people of that Island were governed by the Lawes of *England,* and by those Lawes, we could not make a Christian a Slave. I told him, my request was far different from that, for I desired him to make a Slave a Christian. His answer was, That it was true, there was a great difference in that: But, being once a Christian, he could no more account him a Slave, and so lose the hold they had of them as Slaves, by making them Christians; and by that means should open such a gap, as all the Planters in the Island would curse him. So I was struck mute, and poor *Sambo* kept out of the Church; as ingenious, as honest, and as good a natur'd poor soul, as ever wore black, or eat green.

3. A Missionary Denounces the Treatment of the Indians in South Carolina (1708)

Francis Le Jau served as an Anglican missionary in South Carolina from 1706 to 1717. In his regular reports to his superiors in London, he described Indian-white relations in the southern colony and was especially critical of the Indian slave trade. What did he see as the principal harm inflicted on the Indians by whites? In what ways did the whites' treatment of the native peoples complicate his efforts to spread Christianity among them?

. . . I perceive dayly more and more that our manner of giving Liberty to some very idle and dissolute Men to go and Trade in the Indian Settlements 600 or 800 Miles from us where they commit many Enormities & Injustices is a great Obstruction to our best designs. I have tryed to get some free Indians to live with me and wou'd Cloath them but they will not consent to it, nor part with their Children tho' they lead miserable poor lives. It is reported by some of our Inhabitants lately gone on Indian Trading that they excite them to make War amongst themselves to get Slaves which they give for our European Goods. I fear it is but too true and that the Slaves we have for necessary Service, (for our white Servants in a Months time prove good for nothing at all) are the price of great many Sins. . . .

. . . I gave you an account in my last of the desolate Condition of Renoque. it was in Octobr. or the latter End of September that the Tuscararo's Indians liveing near Cape fair Cutt off *137* of our people, most of them Palatines and some Switzers. I am not able to declare whether they were sett on by some of the partys that have been long at variance in that place or whether they were provoked by some great Injustice & taking their Land by force, it is so reported among us. our forces are Actualy marched to Suppress those Murderers. . . . Generall Called Barnewell and 16 White men, whome 6 or 700 Indians have Joined and they are to meet the Virginians. Many wise men in this Province doubt of the Success. It is evident that our Traders have promoted Bloody Warrs this last Year to get slaves and one of them brought lately *100* of those poor Souls. It do's not belong to me to say

---

[3]Frank J. Klingberg, ed., *The Carolina Chronicle of Dr. Francis Le Jau, 1706–1717* (Berkeley: University of California Press, 1956), pp. 41–116. Some of the punctuation in this document has been edited to conform to modern usage.

any more upon those Melancholy Affaires I submit as to the Justice of those Proceedings to Your Wisdom. When I am asked how we are to deal with those unfortunate slaves, I content my selfe to Exhort that they be used with Xtian Charity and yt. we render their Condition as tollerable as we can. . . .

The Indian traders have always discouraged me by raising a world of Difficultyes when I proposed any thing to them relating to the Conversion of the Indians. It appears they do not care to have Clergymen so near them who doubtless would never approve those perpetual warrs they promote amongst the Indians for the onely reason of making slaves to pay for their trading goods; and what slaves! poor women and children, for the men taken prisoners are burnt most barbarously. I am Informd It was done So this Last year & the women and children were brought among us to be sold.

C. Religious Strife in Maryland

1. The Intolerant Act of Toleration (1649)

Lord Baltimore, who had founded Maryland as a refuge for Catholics in 1634, pursued a policy of religious toleration from the outset. But the influx of hostile Protestants, combined with the success of the Puritans under Oliver Cromwell in the English Civil War, prompted him to protect his Catholic co-religionists. He appointed a Protestant governor, and urged the Maryland Assembly to pass "An Act Concerning Religion," which he had drafted back home in England. Protestants joined with Catholics in passing it. What specific protection for Catholics is mentioned? What would have happened to all Jews and atheists if the law had been strictly enforced?

Forasmuch as, in a well-governed and Christian commonwealth, matters concerning religion and the honor of God ought in the first place to be taken into serious consideration and endeavored to be settled, be it therefore ordered and enacted by the Right Honorable Cecilius Lord Baron of Baltimore, absolute Lord and Proprietary of this Province, with the advice and consent of this General Assembly:

That whatsoever person or persons within this Province . . . shall from henceforth blaspheme God, that is, curse him; or deny our Saviour Jesus Christ to be the son of God; or shall deny the Holy Trinity, the Father, Son, and Holy Ghost; or [shall deny] the Godhead of any of the said three Persons of the Trinity, or the unity of the Godhead; or shall use or utter any reproachful speeches, words, or language concerning the said Holy Trinity, or any of the said three Persons thereof, shall be punished with death and confiscation or forfeiture of all his or her lands and goods to the Lord Proprietary and his heirs.

And be it also enacted . . . that whatsoever person or persons shall from henceforth use or utter any reproachful words or speeches concerning the Blessed Virgin Mary, the Mother of our Saviour, or the Holy Apostles or Evangelists, or any of them, shall in such case for the first offense forfeit . . . the sum of five pounds ster-

[1]W. H. Browne, ed., *Archives of Maryland* (Baltimore: Maryland Historical Society, 1883), vol. 1, pp. 244–246.

ling. . . . But in case such offender or offenders shall not then have goods or chattels sufficient for the satisfying of such forfeiture . . . then such offender or offenders shall be publicly whipped and be imprisoned during the pleasure of the Lord Proprietary. . . .

[Harsher penalties are here prescribed for second and third offenses.]

And be it also further enacted . . . that whatsoever person or persons shall from henceforth . . . in a reproachful manner or way declare, call, or denominate any person or persons . . . an heretic, schismatic, idolater, Puritan, Independent, Presbyterian, popish priest, Jesuit, Jesuited papist, Lutheran, Calvinist, Anabaptist, Brownist, Antinomian, Barrowist, Roundhead, Separatist, or any other name or term in a reproachful manner relating to matter of religion, shall for every such offense forfeit and lose the sum of ten shillings . . . the one half thereof to be forfeited and paid unto the person and persons of whom such reproachful words are or shall be spoken or uttered. . . .

[Harsher penalties are here prescribed for those unable to pay the fine.]

Be it therefore also . . . enacted . . . that no person or persons whatsoever within this Province . . . professing to believe in Jesus Christ, shall from henceforth be in any ways troubled, molested, or discountenanced for . . . his or her religion nor in the free exercise thereof . . . nor any way compelled to the belief or exercise of any other religion against his or her consent, so as they be not unfaithful to the Lord Proprietary, or [do not] molest or conspire against the civil government established, or to be established, in this Province, under him or his heirs.

And that all and every person and persons that shall presume contrary to this act . . . to wrong, disturb, trouble, or molest any person whatsoever . . . professing to believe in Jesus Christ for or in respect of his or her religion or the free exercise thereof . . . shall be compelled to pay treble damages to the party so wronged or molested, and for every such offense shall also forfeit twenty shillings sterling in money or the value thereof, half thereof for the use of the Lord Proprietary and his heirs . . . and the other half for the use of the party so wronged or molested . . . or if the party so offending . . . shall refuse or be unable to recompense the party so wronged, or to satisfy such fine or forfeiture, then such offender shall be severely punished by public whipping and imprisonment during the pleasure of the Lord Proprietary. . . .

2. Persecutions of the Catholics (1656)

Lord Baltimore's beautiful dream soon turned into a nightmare. In 1654, after five years of so-called toleration, the aggressive Protestant majority in Maryland passed a law that specifically "restrained" Roman Catholics from worshiping according to their faith. Civil war broke out, with the Puritans, aided by Virginians, vanquishing the Catholics in a pitched battle in which some fifty men were killed or wounded. The subsequent persecutions of the Jesuit fathers, resembling anti-Catholic cruelties al-

---

[2]Peter Force, *Tracts* . . . (Washington: Peter Force, 1846), vol. 4, no. 12, pp. 43–44.

ready familiar in England, are graphically portrayed in the following report by a Jes-uit priest in 1656. What manifestations of the religious intolerance of the age are mentioned? What appropriate conclusions can you draw?

In Maryland, during the year last past, our [Catholic] people have escaped griev-ous dangers, and have had to contend with great difficulties and straits, and have suffered many unpleasant things, as well from enemies as [from] our own people.

The English who inhabit Virginia had made an attack on the colonists, them-selves Englishmen too; and safety being guaranteed on certain conditions, received indeed the governor of Maryland, with many others in surrender. But the conditions being treacherously violated, four of the captives, and three of them Catholics, were pierced with leaden balls. Rushing into our houses, they demanded for death the impostors, as they called them, intending inevitable slaughter to those who should be caught. But the Fathers, by the protection of God, unknown to them, were car-ried from before their faces [i.e., saved]; their books, furniture, and whatever was in the house, fell a prey to the robbers. With almost the entire loss of their property, private and domestic, together with great peril of life, they were secretly carried into Virginia; and in the greatest want of necessaries, scarcely, and with difficulty, do they sustain life. They live in a mean hut, low and depressed, not much unlike a cistern, or even a tomb, in which that great defender of the faith, St. Athanasius, lay con-cealed for many years.

To their other miseries this inconvenience was added, that whatever comfort or aid this year, under name of stipend, from pious men in England, was destined for them, had been lost, the ship being intercepted in which it was carried. But nothing affects them more than that there is not a supply of wine which is sufficient to per-form the sacred mysteries of the altar.

They have no servant, either for domestic use, or for directing their way through unknown and suspected places, or even to row and steer the boat, if at any time there is need. Often, over spacious and vast rivers, one of them, alone and unac-companied, passes and repasses long distances, with no other pilot directing his course than Divine Providence. By and by the enemy may be gone and they may return to Maryland; the things which they have already suffered from their people, and the disadvantages which still threaten, are not much more tolerable.

Thought Provokers

1. Why did the early Virginia colonists experience such punishing difficulties?
2. What were the relative advantages and disadvantages of Europeans, Africans, and Indi-ans as these three peoples commingled and clashed in seventeenth-century English America?
3. In what ways did English experiences in the West Indies provide a model for the colo-nization of mainland North America?
4. In what respects would the Maryland Act of Toleration be regarded as intoleration today?

3

Settling the Northern Colonies, 1619–1700

To Banbury [England] came I, O profane one!
Where I saw a Puritan once
Hanging of his cat on Monday,
For killing of a mouse on Sunday.

Richard Brathwaite, 1638

Prologue: The English authorities, angered by the efforts of Puritans further to de-Catholicize the established Church of England, launched persecutions that led to the founding of Plymouth in 1620 and the Massachusetts Bay Colony in 1630. The Bay Colony early fell under the leadership of Puritan (Congregational) clergymen. Although they had been victims of intolerance in old England, they understandably sought to enforce conformity in New England by persecuting Quakers and banishing dissenters like Anne Hutchinson and Roger Williams. Partly as a result of the uncongenial atmosphere in Massachusetts Bay, settlements in Connecticut and Rhode Island sprang into existence. These offshoot colonies, as well as the older ones, developed the pure-democracy town meeting and other significant institutions. All the colonies sometimes had troubled relationships with the Indians, especially in King Philip's War, 1675–1676. A more hospitable atmosphere in the Quaker colonies, notably William Penn's Pennsylvania, attracted heavy immigration, largely German. The Dutch in New Netherland, after a precarious existence from 1624 to 1664, were finally absorbed by the English, who renamed the colony New York.

A. The Planting of Plymouth

1. The Pilgrims Leave Holland (1620)

William Bradford, then a youth of nineteen, was one of the small group of Puritan Separatists who in 1609 fled from England to Holland in search of religious freedom.

---

[1]From *Of Plymouth Plantation* by William Bradford, edited by Samuel Eliot Morison. Copyright © 1952 by Samuel Eliot Morison and renewed 1980 by Emily M. Beck. Used by permission of Alfred A. Knopf, Inc.

But the new home proved to be unsatisfactory. The Pilgrims complained of theological controversy, unremitting toil, grinding poverty, and the unhealthy condition of their children, who were becoming "Dutchified" and developing "licentious habits." It seemed better to start anew in the New World, where they could all live and die as English subjects while advancing the "gospel of the Kingdom of Christ." Bradford became not only the leader of Plymouth but also its distinguished historian, as his classic History of Plymouth Plantation *attests. As the selection opens, Bradford has just reported that the Pilgrims first discussed the perils of the long sea voyage, the dangers of famine and nakedness, and the diseases that might come from the "change of air, diet, and drinking water." In his account of the decision to leave Holland, were the Pilgrims fully aware of their perils? What light does his analysis cast on their character?*

And also those which should escape or overcome these difficulties should yet be in continual danger of the savage people, who are cruel, barbarous, and most treacherous, being most furious in their rage, and merciless where they overcome; not being content only to kill and take away life, but delight to torment men in the most bloody manner that may be; flaying some alive with the shells of fishes, cutting off the members and joints of others by piecemeal and broiling on the coals, eat the collops [slices] of their flesh in their sight whilst they live, with other cruelties horrible to be related.

And surely it could not be thought but the very hearing of these things could not but move the very bowels of men to grate within them and make the weak to quake and tremble.

It was further objected that it would require greater sums of money to furnish such a voyage, and to fit them with necessaries, than their consumed estates would amount to; and yet they must as well look to be seconded with supplies as presently to be transported. Also many precedents of ill success and lamentable miseries befallen others in the like designs were easy to be found, and not forgotten to be alleged; besides their own experience, in their former troubles and hardships in their removal into Holland, and how hard a thing it was for them to live in that strange place, though it was a neighbor country and a civil and rich commonwealth.

It was answered that all great and honorable actions are accompanied with great difficulties, and must be both enterprised and overcome with answerable courages. It was granted the dangers were great, but not desperate. The difficulties were many, but not invincible. For though there were many of them likely, yet they were not certain. It might be sundry of the things feared might never befall; others by provident care and the use of good means might in a great measure be prevented. And all of them, through the help of God, . . . might either be borne or overcome.

True it was that such attempts were not to be made and undertaken without good ground and reason, not rashly or lightly, as many have done for curiosity or hope of gain, etc. But their condition was not ordinary, their ends were good and honorable, their calling lawful and urgent; and therefore they might expect the blessing of God in their proceeding. Yea, though they should lose their lives in this action, yet might they have comfort in the same and their endeavors would be honorable.

They lived here [in Holland] but as men in exile and in a poor condition, and as great miseries might possibly befall them in this place. For the twelve years of truce were now out,* and there was nothing but beating of drums and preparing for war, the events whereof are always uncertain. The Spaniard might prove as cruel as the savages of America, and the famine and pestilence as sore here as there, and their liberty less to look out for remedy.

After many other particular things answered and alleged on both sides, it was fully concluded by the major part to put this design in execution and to prosecute it by the best means they could.

2. Framing the Mayflower Compact (1620)

Leaving Plymouth (England) in the overburdened Mayflower, *the plucky band of Pilgrims crossed the Atlantic. After severe storms and much seasickness, they sighted the Cape Cod coast of Massachusetts, far to the north of the site to which they had been granted patent privileges by the Virginia Company. The absence of valid rights in the Plymouth area, so William Bradford recorded, caused "some of the strangers amongst them" to utter "discontented and mutinous speeches" to the effect that when they "came ashore they would use their own liberty; for none had the power to command them, the patent they had being for Virginia, and not for New England. . . ." In an effort to hold the tiny band together, the leaders persuaded forty-one male passengers to sign a solemn pledge known as the May-flower Compact. A constitution is "a document defining and limiting the func-tions of government." Was the Compact, as is often claimed, the first American constitution? In what ways did it foreshadow the development of democratic institutions?*

In the name of God, amen. We whose names are underwritten, the loyal sub-jects of our dread sovereign lord, King James, by the grace of God, of Great Britain, France, and Ireland King, Defender of the Faith, etc., having undertaken, for the glory of God, and advancement of the Christian faith, and honor of our King and country, a voyage to plant the first colony in the northern parts of Virginia, do by these presents solemnly and mutually, in the presence of God and one another, covenant and combine ourselves together into a civil body politic, for our better or-dering and preservation and furtherance of the ends aforesaid; and by virtue hereof to enact, constitute, and frame such just and equal laws, ordinances, acts, constitu-tions, and offices, from time to time, as shall be thought most meet and convenient for the general good of the colony, unto which we promise all due submission and obedience. In witness whereof we have hereunto subscribed our names at Cape Cod the eleventh of November, in the reign of our sovereign lord, King James, of England, France, and Ireland, the eighteenth, and of Scotland, the fifty-fourth. Anno Domini 1620.

---

*The twelve years' truce in Holland's bitter war of independence against Spain had been negotiated in 1609.

[2]B. P. Poore, ed., *The Federal and State Constitutions,* 2nd ed. (1878), part 1, p. 931.

3. Abandoning Communism at Plymouth (1623)

Some wag has said that the Pilgrims first fell on their knees, and then on the aborigines. The truth is that a plague—probably smallpox, possibly measles—had virtually exterminated the Indians near Plymouth, and the Pilgrims got along reasonably well with the few survivors. The Native Americans taught the whites how to grow maize (corn), which helped revitalize the ragged, starving, disease-decimated newcomers. The story of the first Thanksgiving (1621) is well known, but less well known is the fact that the abundant harvest of 1623 was made possible when the Pilgrims abandoned their early scheme of quasi-communism. For seven years there was to have been no private ownership of land, and everyone was to have been fed and clothed from the common stock. William Bradford, the historian and oft-elected governor of the colony, here tells what happened when each family was given its own parcel of land. Why did individual ownership succeed where communal enterprise had failed?

This had very good success, for it made all hands very industrious, so as much more corn was planted than otherwise would have been by any means the Governor or any other could use, and saved him a great deal of trouble, and gave far better content. The women now went willingly into the field and took their little ones with them to set corn, which before would allege weakness and inability, whom to have compelled would have been thought great tyranny and oppression.

The experience that was had in this common course and condition, tried sundry years and that amongst godly and sober men, may well evince the vanity of that conceit of Plato's and other ancients, applauded by some of later times, that the taking away of property and bringing in community [communism] into a commonwealth would make them happy and flourishing, as if they were wiser than God. For this community (so far as it was) was found to breed much confusion and discontent and retard much employment that would have been to their benefit and comfort. For the young men that were most able and fit for labor and service did repine that they should spend their time and strength to work for other men's wives and children, without any recompense. The strong, or man of parts, had no more in division of victuals and clothes than he that was weak and not able to do a quarter the other could; this was thought injustice. The aged and graver men to be ranked and equalized in labors and victuals, clothes, etc., with the meaner and younger sort, thought it some indignity and disrespect unto them. And for men's wives to be commanded to do service for other men, as dressing their meat, washing their clothes, etc., they deemed it a kind of slavery, neither could many husbands well brook it.

---

[3]From *Of Plymouth Plantation* by William Bradford, edited by Samuel Eliot Morison. Copyright 1952 by Samuel Eliot Morison and renewed 1980 by Emily M. Beck. Reprinted by permission of Alfred A. Knopf Inc.

B. Conformity in the Bay Colony

1. John Cotton Describes New England's "Theocracy" (1636)

Already a prominent Puritan minister in England, John Cotton arrived in Massachusetts Bay Colony in 1633 to become the principal preacher to the Boston Puritans. Something of a liberal in old England, he became an increasingly conservative defender of orthodoxy in the New World, as shown by his role in the banishment of Anne Hutchinson. Shortly after Cotton's arrival, he was asked by his fellow colonists to respond to inquiries (or "demands") from a group of English Puritan noblemen who desired to settle in Massachusetts, on the condition that the colony alter its form of government. Cotton's response constitutes a succinct statement of Puritan political theory. What social elements or interest did Cotton think government should represent? How did he define the relation of church and state? What did he think of "democracy"?

Demand 1. That the common-wealth should consist of two distinct ranks of men, whereof the one should be for them and their heirs, gentlemen of the country, the other for them and their heirs, freeholders.

Answer. Two distinct ranks we willingly acknowledge, from the light of nature and scripture; the one of them called Princes, or Nobles, or Elders (amongst whom gentlemen have their place), the other the people. Hereditary dignity or honours we willingly allow to the former, unless by the scandalous and base conversation of any of them, they become degenerate. Hereditary liberty, or estate of freemen, we willingly allow to the other, unless they also, by some unworthy and slavish carriage, do disfranchise themselves.

Demand 2. That in these gentlemen and freeholders, assembled together, the chief power of the common-wealth shall be placed, both for making and repealing laws.

Answer. So it is with us.

Demand 3. That each of these two ranks should, in all public assemblies, have a negative voice, so as without a mutual consent nothing should be established.

Answer. So it is agreed among us.

Demand 4. That the first rank, consisting of gentlemen, should have power, for them and their heirs, to come to the parliaments or public assemblies, and there to give their free votes personally; the second rank of freeholders should have the same power for them and their heirs of meeting and voting, but by their deputies.

Answer. Thus far this demand is practised among us. The freemen meet and vote by their deputies; the other rank give their votes personally, only with this difference, there be no more of the gentlemen that give their votes personally, but such as are chosen to places of office, either governors, deputy governors, councel-

---

[1]Thomas Hutchinson, *The History of the Colony of Massachusett's Bay,* 2nd ed. (London: M. Richardson, 1765), pp. 490–501.

lors, or assistants. All gentlemen in England have not that honour to meet and vote personally in Parliament, much less all their heirs. But of this more fully, in an answer to the ninth and tenth demand.

Demand 5. That for facilitating and dispatch of business, and other reasons, the gentlemen and freeholders should sit and hold their meetings in two distinct houses.

Answer. We willingly approve the motion, only as yet it is not so practised among us, but in time, the variety and discrepancy of sundry occurrences will put them upon a necessity of sitting apart.

Demand 6. That there shall be set times for these meetings, annually or half yearly, or as shall be thought fit by common consent, which meetings should have a set time for their continuance, but should be adjourned or broken off at the discretion of both houses.

Answer. Public meetings, in general courts, are by charter appointed to be quarterly, which, in this infancy of the colony, wherein many things frequently occur which need settling, hath been of good use, but when things are more fully settled in due order, it is likely that yearly or half yearly meetings will be sufficient. For the continuance or breaking up of these courts, nothing is done but with the joint consent of both branches.

Demand 7. That it shall be in the power of this parliament, thus constituted and assembled, to call the governor and all publick officers to account, to create new officers, and to determine them already set up: and, the better to stop the way to insolence and ambition, it may be ordered that all offices and fees of office shall, every parliament, determine, unless they be new confirmed the last day of every session.

Answer. This power to call governors and all officers to account, and to create new and determine the old, is settled already in the general court or parliament, only it is not put forth but once in the year, viz. at the great and general court in May, when the governor is chosen.

Demand 8. That the governor shall ever be chosen out of the rank of gentlemen.

Answer. We never practice otherwise, chusing [sic] the governor either out of the assistants, which is our ordinary course, or out of approved known gentlemen, as this year [1636] Mr. Vane.

Demand 9. That, for the present, the Right Honorable the Lord Viscount Say and Seale, the Lord Brooke, who have already been at great disbursements for the public works in New-England, and such other gentlemen of approved sincerity and worth, as they, before their personal remove, shall take into their number, should be admitted for them and their heirs, gentlemen of the country. But, for the future, none shall be admitted into this rank but by the consent of both houses.

Answer. The great disbursements of these noble personages and worthy gentlemen we thankfully acknowledge, because the safety and presence of our brethren at Connecticut is no small blessing and comfort to us. But, though that charge had never been disbursed, the worth of the honorable persons named is so well known to all, and our need of such supports and guides is so sensible to ourselves, that we do not doubt the country would thankfully accept it, as a singular favor from God and from them, if he should bow their hearts to come into this wilderness and help us. As for accepting them and their heirs into the number of gentlemen of the country, the custom of this country is, and readily would be, to receive and ac-knowledge, not only all such eminent persons as themselves and the gentlemen they speak of, but others of meaner estate, so be it is of some eminency, to be for them and their heirs, gentlemen of the country. Only, thus standeth our case. Though we receive them with honor and allow them pre-eminence and accommo-dations according to their condition, yet we do not, ordinarily, call them forth to the power of election, or administration of magistracy, until they be received as mem-bers into some of our churches, a privilege, which we doubt not religious gentlemen will willingly desire (as David did in Psal. xxvii. 4.) and christian churches will as readily impart to such desirable persons. . . .

Demand 10. That the rank of freeholders shall be made up of such, as shall have so much personal estate there, as shall be thought fit for men of that condition, and have contributed, some fit proportion, to the public charge of the country, either by their disbursements or labors.

Answer. We must confess our ordinary practice to be otherwise. For, excepting the old planters, i.e. Mr. Humphry, who himself was admitted an assistant at London, and all of them freemen, before the churches here were established, none are ad-mitted freemen of this commonwealth but such as are first admitted members of some church or other in this country, and, of such, none are excluded from the lib-erty of freemen. And out of such only, I mean the more eminent sort of such, it is that our magistrates are chosen. Both which points we should willingly persuade our people to change, if we could make it appear to them, that such a change might be made according to God; for, to give you a true account of the grounds of our proceedings herein, it seemeth to them, and also to us, to be a divine ordinance (and moral) that none should be appointed and chosen by the people of God, mag-istrates over them, but men fearing God. . . .

Now, if it be a divine truth, that none are to be trusted with public permanent authority but godly men, who are fit materials for church fellowship, then from the same grounds it will appear, that none are so fit to be trusted with the liberties of the commonwealth as church members. For, the liberties of the freemen of this commonwealth are such, as require men of faithful integrity to God and the state, to preserve the same. Their liberties, among others, are chiefly these. 1. To chuse all magistrates, and to call them to account at their general courts. 2. To chuse such burgesses, every general court, as with the magistrates shall make or repeal all laws. Now both these liberties are such, as carry along much power with them, either to establish or subvert the commonwealth, and therewith the church, which power, if it be committed to men not according to their godliness, which maketh them fit for church fellowship, but according to their wealth, which, as such, makes them no better than worldly men, then, in case wordly men should prove the major part, as soon they might do, they would as readily set over us magistrates like themselves, such as might hate us according to the curse . . . and turn the edge of all authority and laws against the church and the members thereof, the mainte-nance of whose peace is the chief end which God aimed at in the institution of Magistracy. . . .

It is better that the commonwealth be fashioned to the setting forth of God's house, which is his church: than to accommodate the church frame to the civill state.

Democracy. I do not conceyve that ever God did ordeyne as a fitt government eyther for church or commonwealth. If the people be governors, who shall be governed? As for monarchy, and aristocracy, they are both of them clearely approoved, and directed in scripture, yet so as referreth the soveraigntie to himselfe, and setteth up Theocracy in both, as the best forme of government in the commonwealth, as well as in the church.

2. Anne Hutchinson Is Banished (1637)

The powerful Massachusetts Bay Colony soon became a Bible commonwealth, centered at Boston, and the clergymen who dominated it could not permit heretics to undermine their authority. Mistress Anne Hutchinson, who bore her husband fourteen children, was a kindly woman of nimble wit and even more nimble tongue. Gathering a select group at her home, she would review and even reinterpret the ministers' sermons in the light of her own brand of Calvinism. Haled before the General Court, she was subjected to a rigid cross-examination. The case against her seemed to be breaking down when her voluble tongue revealed that she was in direct communication with God—a heresy that the religious leaders could not tolerate. What does this record of the court reveal about the Puritan way of thinking and the justice or injustice of these proceedings?

[*Anne Hutchinson.*] Therefore take heed what ye go about to do unto me. You have power over my body, but the Lord Jesus hath power over my body and soul; neither can you do me any harm, for I am in the hands of the eternal Jehovah, my Saviour. I am at his appointment, for the bounds of my habitation are cast in Heaven, and no further do I esteem of any mortal man than creatures in his hand. I fear none but the great Jehovah, which hath foretold me of these things, and I do verily believe that he will deliver me out of your hands. Therefore take heed how you proceed against me; for I know that for this you go about to do to me, God will ruin you and your posterity, and this whole state.

Mr. Nowell. How do you know that it was God that did reveal these things to you, and not Satan?

Mrs. Hutchinson. How did Abraham know that it was God that bid him offer [sacrifice] his son, being a breach of the sixth commandment?

Deputy-Governor Dudley. By an immediate voice.

Mrs. Hutchinson. So to me by an immediate revelation.

Deputy-Governor. How! an immediate revelation?

Mrs. Hutchinson. By the voice of his own spirit to my soul.

Governor Winthrop. Daniel was delivered by miracle; do you think to be delivered so too?

Mrs. Hutchinson. I do here speak it before the Court. I look that the Lord should deliver me by his providence. . . .

---

[2]C. F. Adams, *Three Episodes of Massachusetts History* (Boston and New York: Houghton Mifflin and Company, 1892), vol. 1, pp. 501–502, 507–508.

Governor Winthrop. The Court hath already declared themselves satisfied concerning the things you hear, and concerning the troublesomeness of her spirit, and the danger of her course amongst us, which is not to be suffered. Therefore, if it be the mind of the Court that Mrs. Hutchinson, for these things that appear before us, is unfit for our society, and if it be the mind of the Court that she shall be banished out of our liberties, and imprisoned till she be sent away, let them hold up their hands.

All but three held up their hands.

[Governor Winthrop.] Those that are contrary minded, hold up yours.

Mr. Coddington and Mr. Colburn only.

Mr. Jennison. I cannot hold up my hand one way or the other, and I shall give my reason if the Court require it.

Governor Winthrop. Mrs. Hutchinson, you hear the sentence of the Court. It is that you are banished from out our jurisdiction as being a woman not fit for our society. And you are to be imprisoned till the Court send you away.

Mrs. Hutchinson. I desire to know wherefore I am banished.

Governor Winthrop. Say no more. The Court knows wherefore, and is satisfied.

3. John Winthrop's Concept of Liberty (1645)

Governor John Winthrop, who pronounced Anne Hutchinson's banishment, was the most distinguished lay leader in the Massachusetts Bay Colony. Cambridge-educated and trained in the law, he was modest, tender, self-sacrificing, and deeply religious. After a furious quarrel had broken out at Hingham over the election of a militia leader, he caused certain of the agitators to be arrested. His foes brought impeachment charges against him, but they instead were fined. After his acquittal, Winthrop delivered this famous speech to the court. It illustrates the close connection between the aristocratic lay leaders of the Bay Colony and the leading clergymen. Would the kind of liberty that Winthrop describes be regarded as liberty today?

There is a twofold liberty: natural (I mean as our nature is now corrupt) and civil or federal. The first is common to man with beasts and other creatures. By this, man, as he stands in relation to man simply, hath liberty to do what he lists. It is a liberty to evil as well as to good. This liberty is incompatible and inconsistent with authority, and cannot endure the least restraint of the most just authority. The exercise and maintaining of this liberty makes men grow more evil, and in time to be worse than brute beasts. . . .

The other kind of liberty I call civil or federal. It may also be termed moral, in reference to the covenant between God and man in the moral law, and the politic covenants and constitutions amongst men themselves. . . . Whatsoever crosseth this, is not authority, but a distemper thereof. This liberty is maintained and exercised in

---

[3]John Winthrop, *The History of New England from 1630 to 1649* (Boston: Little, Brown and Company, 1853), vol. 2, pp. 281–282.

a way of subjection to authority. It is of the same kind of liberty wherewith Christ hath made us free.

The woman's own choice makes such a man her husband; yet being so chosen, he is her lord, and she is to be subject to him, yet in a way of liberty, not of bondage. And a true wife accounts her subjection her honor and freedom, and would not think her condition safe and free, but in her subjection to her husband's authority.

Such is the liberty of the church under the authority of Christ, her king and husband. His yoke is so easy and sweet to her as a bride's ornaments; and if through forwardness or wantonness, etc., she shake it off at any time, she is at no rest in her spirit until she take it up again. And whether her lord smiles upon her, and embraceth her in his arms, or whether he frowns, or rebukes, or smites her, she apprehends the sweetness of his love in all, and is refreshed, supported, and instructed by every such dispensation of his authority over her. On the other side, ye know who they are that complain of this yoke and say, let us break their bands, etc., we will not have this man to rule over us.

Even so, brethren, it will be between you and your magistrates. If you stand for your natural corrupt liberties, and will do what is good in your own eyes, you will not endure the least weight of authority, but will murmur, and oppose, and be always striving to shake off that yoke. But if you will be satisfied to enjoy such civil and lawful liberties, such as Christ allows you, then will you quietly and cheerfully submit unto that authority which is set over you, in all the administrations of it, for your good. Wherein if we [magistrates] fail at any time, we hope we shall be willing (by God's assistance) to hearken to good advice from any of you, or in any other way of God. So shall your liberties be preserved, in upholding the honor and power of authority amongst you.

4. Puritan Mistreatment of Quakers (1660)

The peace-loving Quakers, who opposed a paid clergy and a tax-supported church, likewise felt the restraining hand of Massachusetts authority. The Reverend Increase Mather wrote in 1684 that they were "under the strong delusion of Satan." Their stubborn devotion and courage under punishment were so exasperating as to provoke increasingly severe measures. Edward Burrough, one of their co-religionists in England, presented the following appeal on their behalf to the king, who thereupon sent orders to Massachusetts to end the persecutions. What were alleged to be the chief offenses of the Quakers? What were the most serious injustices, aside from physical abuse, that they suffered?

1. Two honest and innocent women stripped stark naked, and searched after such an inhumane manner, as modesty will not permit particularly to mention.

2. Twelve strangers in that country [Massachusetts], but free-born of this [English] nation, received twenty-three whippings, the most of them being with a whip

---

[4][Edward Burrough], *A Declaration of the Sad and Great Persecution and Martyrdom of the People of God, Called Quakers, in New England . . .* ([1660]), pp. 17–19.

of three cords, with knots at the ends, and laid on with as much strength as they could be by the arm of their executioner, the stripes amounting to three hundred and seventy. . . .

3. Eighteen inhabitants of the country, being free-born English, received twenty-three whippings, the stripes amounting to two hundred and fifty.

4. Sixty-four imprisonments of the Lord's people, for their obedience to his will, amounting to five hundred and nineteen weeks, much of it being very cold weather, and the inhabitants kept in prison in harvest time. . . .

5. Two beaten with pitched ropes, the blows amounting to an hundred thirty-nine. . . .

6. Also, an innocent man, an inhabitant of Boston, they banished from his wife and children, and put to seek a habitation in the winter. And in case he returned again, he was to be kept prisoner during his life; and for returning again, he was put in prison, and hath been now a prisoner above a year.

7. Twenty-five banishments, upon the penalties of being whipped, or having their ears cut; or branded in the hand, if they returned.

8. Fines laid upon the inhabitants for meeting together, and edifying one another, as the saints ever did; and for refusing to swear [take oaths], it being contrary to Christ's command, amounting to about a thousand pound. . . .

9. Five kept fifteen days (in all) without food, and fifty-eight days shut up close by the jailor. . . .

10. One laid neck and heels in irons for sixteen hours.

11. One very deeply burnt in the right hand with the letter H [for *heretic*], after he had been whipped with above thirty stripes.

12. One chained the most part of twenty days to a log of wood in an open prison in the winter-time.

13. Five appeals to England, denied at Boston.

14. Three had their right ears cut by the hangman in the prison, the door being barred, and not a friend suffered to be present while it was doing, though some much desired it. . . .

15. One of the inhabitants of Salem, who since is banished upon pain of death, had one half of his house and land seized on while he was in prison, a month before he knew of it.

16. At a General Court in Boston, they made an order, that those who had not wherewithal to answer the fines that were laid upon them (for their consciences) should be sold for bond-men and bond-women to Barbados, Virginia, or any of the English plantations. . . .

17. Eighteen of the people of God were at several times banished upon pain of death. . . .

18. Also three of the servants of the Lord they put to death [hanged], all of them for obedience to the truth, in the testimony of it against the wicked rulers and laws at Boston.

19. And since they have banished four more, upon pain of death. . . .

These things, O King, from time to time have we patiently suffered, and not for the transgression of any just or righteous law, either pertaining to the worship of God or the civil government of England, but simply and barely for our consciences to God. . . .

C. The Rule of Biblical Law

1. The Blue Laws of Connecticut (1672)

Blue laws—statutes governing personal behavior—were to be found both in Europe and the American colonies. They obviously could not be enforced with literal severity, and they generally fell into disuse after the Revolution. Connecticut's blue laws received unpleasant notoriety in the Reverend Samuel Peters's General History of Connecticut *(1781), which fabricated such decrees as, "No woman shall kiss her child on the Sabbath or fasting-day." But the valid laws of Connecticut, some of which are here reproduced with biblical chapter and verse, were harsh enough. How did the punishment fit the crime? Which offenses would still be regarded as criminal today?*

1. If any man or woman, after legal conviction, shall have or worship any other God but the Lord God, he shall be put to death. (Deuteronomy 13.6. Exodus 22.20.)

2. If any person within this colony shall blaspheme the name of God, the Father, Son, or Holy Ghost, with direct, express, presumptuous, or high-handed blasphemy, or shall curse in the like manner, he shall be put to death. (Leviticus 24.15, 16.)

3. If any man or woman be a witch, that is, has or consults with a familiar spirit, they shall be put to death. (Exodus 22.18. Leviticus 20.27. Deuteronomy 18.10, 11.)

4. If any person shall commit any willful murder, committed upon malice, hatred, or cruelty, not in a man's just and necessary defense, nor by casualty [accident] against his will, he shall be put to death. (Exodus 21.12, 13, 14. Numbers 35.30, 31.)

5. If any person shall slay another through guile, either by poisoning or other such devilish practices, he shall be put to death. (Exodus 21.14.) . . .

10. If any man steals a man or mankind and sells him, or if he be found in his hand, he shall be put to death. (Exodus 21.16.)

11. If any person rise up by false witness wittingly and of purpose to take away any man's life, he or she shall be put to death. (Deuteronomy 19.16, 18, 19.) . . .

14. If any child or children above sixteen years old, and of sufficient understanding, shall curse or smite their natural father or mother, he or they shall be put to death, unless it can be sufficiently testified that the parents have been very unchristianly negligent in the education of such children, or so provoked them by extreme and cruel correction that they have been forced thereunto to preserve themselves from death or maiming. (Exodus 21.17. Leviticus 20.9. Exodus 21.15.)

15. If any man have a stubborn or rebellious son, of sufficient understanding and years, viz. sixteen years of age, which will not obey the voice of his father, or the voice of his mother, and that when they have chastened him, he will not harken unto them; then may his father or mother, being his natural parents, lay hold on him, and bring him to the magistrates assembled in court, and testify unto them that their son is stubborn and rebellious, and will not obey their voice and chastisement, but lives in sundry notorious crimes, such a son shall be put to death. (Deuteronomy 21.20, 21.) . . .

---

[1]George Brinley, ed., *The Laws of Connecticut* (Hartford: printed for private distribution, 1865), pp. 9–10.

2. A Defense of Buying Indian Land (1722)

The Reverend Solomon Stoddard, for fifty-six years pastor of the Congregational church in Northampton, was easily the most influential figure of his day in western Massachusetts. Tall, dignified, and domineering, he was dubbed by his critics "the Pope." He advocated the frequent preaching of hellfire as a restraint against sin, and he bitterly opposed long hair and wigs for men, extravagance in dress, and intemperance in drink. The following is part of a tract that he published in 1722 entitled An Answer to Some Cases of Conscience Respecting the Country. *Which of his arguments is the most convincing? In what sense could the land be said to have "belonged" to the Indians in the first place?*

Question VIII. Did we any wrong to the Indians in buying their land at a small price?

Answer. 1. There was some part of the land that was not purchased, neither was there need that it should; it was *vacuum domicilium* [a vacant dwelling place]; and so might be possessed by virtue of God's grant to mankind, Genesis 1.28: "And God blessed them, and God said unto them, Be fruitful and multiply and replenish the earth, and subdue it; and have dominion over the fish of the sea, and over the fowl of the air, and over every living thing that moveth upon the earth." The Indians made no use of it but for hunting. By God's first grant men were to subdue the earth. When Abraham came into the land of Canaan, he made use of vacant land as he pleased; so did Isaac and Jacob.

2. The Indians were well contented that we should sit down by them. And it would have been for great advantage, both for this world and the other, if they had been wise enough to make use of their opportunities. It has been common with many people, in planning this world since the Flood, to admit neighbors, to sit down by them.

3. Though we gave but a small price for what we bought, we gave them their demands. We came to their market, and gave them their price. And, indeed, it was worth but little; and had it continued in their hands, it would have been of little value. It is our dwelling on it, and our improvements, that have made it to be of worth.

D. Indian-White Relations in Colonial New England: Three Views of King Philip's War

1. Mary Rowlandson Is Captured by Indians (1675)

Mary Rowlandson was taken prisoner in February 1675 by Indians who raided her home on the Massachusetts frontier some thirty miles west of Boston. Her account became one of the most popular "captivity narratives" that fascinated readers in Eng-

[2]Solomon Stoddard, *An Answer to Some Cases of Conscience Respecting the Country* (Boston: B. Green, 1722; reprinted Tarrytown, N.Y.: W. Abbott, 1917), pp. 14–15.

[1]From C. H. Lincoln, ed., *Original Narratives of Early American History: Narratives of Indian Wars, 1675–1699,* vol. 14 (New York: 1952).

land and America in the seventeenth and eighteenth centuries, providing a model for such later works as James Fenimore Cooper's The Last of the Mohicans. *What are the most harrowing aspects of Rowlandson's experience? What religious meaning did she find in the Indian attack and in her captivity?*

On the tenth of February 1675, came the Indians with great numbers upon Lancaster: their first coming was about sunrising; hearing the noise of some guns, we looked out; several houses were burning, and the smoke ascending to heaven. There were five persons taken in one house; the father, and the mother and a sucking child, they knocked on the head; the other two they took and carried away alive. There were two others, who being out of their garrison upon some occasion were set upon; one was knocked on the head, the other escaped; another there was who running along was shot and wounded, and fell down; he begged of them his life, promising them money (as they told me) but they would not hearken to him but knocked him in head, and stripped him naked, and split open his bowels. Another, seeing many of the Indians about his barn, ventured and went out, but was quickly shot down. There were three others belonging to the same garrison who were killed; the Indians getting up upon the roof of the barn, had advantage to shoot down upon them over their fortification. Thus these murderous wretches went on, burning, and destroying before them.

At length they came and beset our own house, and quickly it was the dolefulest day that ever mine eyes saw. The house stood upon the edge of a hill; some of the Indians got behind the hill, others into the barn, and others behind anything that could shelter them; from all which places they shot against the house, so that the bullets seemed to fly like hail; and quickly they wounded one man among us, then another, and then a third. About two hours (according to my observation, in that amazing time) they had been about the house before they prevailed to fire it (which they did with flax and hemp, which they brought out of the barn, and there being no defense about the house, only two flankers at two opposite corners and one of them not finished); they fired it once and one ventured out and quenched it, but they quickly fired it again, and that took. Now is the dreadful hour come, that I have often heard of (in time of war, as it was the case of others), but now mine eyes see it. Some in our house were fighting for their lives, others wallowing in their blood, the house on fire over our heads, and the bloody heathen ready to knock us on the head, if we stirred out. Now might we hear mothers and children crying out for themselves, and one another, "Lord, what shall we do?" Then I took my children (and one of my sisters', hers) to go forth and leave the house: but as soon as we came to the door and appeared, the Indians shot so thick that the bullets rattled against the house, as if one had taken an handful of stones and threw them, so that we were fain to give back. We had six stout dogs belonging to our garrison, but none of them would stir, though another time, if any Indian had come to the door, they were ready to fly upon him and tear him down. The Lord hereby would make us the more to acknowledge His hand, and to see that our help is always in Him. But out we must go, the fire increasing, and coming along behind us, roaring, and the Indians gaping before us with their guns, spears, and hatchets to devor us. No sooner were we out of the house, but my brother-in-law (being before wounded, in defending the house, in or near the throat) fell down dead, whereat the Indians scornfully shouted, and hallowed, and were presently upon him, stripping off his clothes, the bullets flying thick, one went through my side, and the same (as would seem) through the bowels and hand of my dear child in my arms. One of my elder sisters' children, named William, had then his leg broken, which the Indians perceiving, they knocked him on [his] head. Thus were we butchered by those merciless heathen, standing amazed, with the blood running down to our heels. My eldest sister being yet in the house, and seeing those woeful sights, the infidels hauling mothers one way, and children another, and some wallowing in their blood: and her elder son telling her that her son William was dead, and myself was wounded, she said, "And Lord, let me die with them," which was no sooner said, but she was struck with a bullet, and fell down dead over the threshold. I hope she is reaping the fruit of her good labors, being faithful to the service of God in her place. In her younger years she lay under much trouble upon spiritual accounts, till it pleased God to make that precious scripture take hold of her heart, "And he said unto me, my Grace is sufficient for thee" (2 Corinthians 12.9). More than twenty years after, I have heard her tell how sweet and comfortable that place was to her. But to return: the Indians laid hold of us, pulling me one way, and the children another, and said, "Come go along with us"; I told them they would kill me: they answered, if I were willing to go along with them, they would not hurt me.

Oh the doleful sight that now was to behold at this house! "Come, behold the works of the Lord, what desolations he has made in the Earth." Of thirty-seven persons who were in this one house, none escaped either present death, or a bitter captivity, save only one, who might say as he, "And I only am escaped alone to tell the News" [Job 1.15]. There were twelve killed, some shot, some stabbed with their spears, some knocked down with their hatchets. When we are in prosperity, Oh the little that we think of such dreadful sights, and to see our dear friends, and relations lie bleeding out their heart-blood upon the ground. There was one who was chopped into the head with a hatchet, and stripped naked, and yet was crawling up and down. It is a solemn sight to see so many Christians lying in their blood, some here, and some there, like a company of sheep torn by wolves, all of them stripped naked by a company of hell-hounds, roaring, singing, ranting, and insulting, as if they would have torn our very hearts out; yet the Lord by His almighty power preserved a number of us from death, for there were twenty-four of us taken alive and carried captive.

I had often before this said that if the Indians should come, I should choose rather to be killed by them than taken alive, but when it came to the trial my mind changed; their glittering weapons so daunted my spirit, that I chose rather to go along with those (as I may say) ravenous beasts, than that moment to end my days; and that I may the better declare what happened to me during that grievous captivity, I shall particularly speak of the several removes we had up and down the wilderness. . . .

But before I go any further, I would take leave to mention a few remarkable passages of providence, which I took special notice of in my afflicted time.

1. Of the fair opportunity lost in the long march, a little after the fort-fight, when our English army was so numerous, and in pursuit of the enemy, and so near as to take several and destroy them, and the enemy in such distress for food that our men might track them by their rooting in the earth for ground-nuts, whilest they were flying for their lives. I say, that then our army should want provision, and be forced to

leave their pursuit and return homeward; and the very next week the enemy came upon our town, like bears bereft of their whelps, or so many ravenous wolves, rending us and our lambs to death. But what shall I say? God seemed to leave his People to themselves, and order all things for his own holy ends. Shall there be evil in the City and the Lord hath not done it? They are not grieved for the affliction of Joseph, therefore shall they go captive, with the first that go captive. It is the Lord's doing, and it should be marvelous in our eyes.

2. I cannot but remember how the Indians derided the slowness, and dullness of the English army, in its setting out. For after the desolations at Lancaster and Medfield, as I went along with them, they asked me when I thought the English army would come after them? I told them I could not tell. "It may be they will come in May," said they. Thus did they scoff at us, as if the English would be a quarter of a year getting ready.

3. Which also I have hinted before, when the English army with new supplies were sent forth to pursue after the enemy, and they understanding it, fled before them till they came to Baquaug river, where they forthwith went over safely; that that river should be impassable to the English. I can but admire to see the wonderful providence of God in preserving the heathen for further affliction to our poor country. They could go in great numbers over, but the English must stop. God had an over-ruling hand in all those things.

4. It was thought, if their corn were cut down, they would starve and die with hunger, and all their corn that could be found, was destroyed, and they driven from that little they had in store, into the woods in the midst of winter; and yet how to admiration did the Lord preserve them for his holy ends, and the destruction of many still amongst the English! strangely did the Lord provide for them; that I did not see (all the time I was among them) one man, woman, or child, die with hunger.

Though many times they would eat that, that a hog or a dog would hardly touch; yet by that God strengthened them to be a scourge to his people.

The chief and commonest food was ground-nuts. They eat also nuts and acorns, artichokes, lilly roots, ground-beans, and several other weeds and roots, that I know not.

They would pick up old bones, and cut them to pieces at the joints, and if they were full of worms and maggots, they would scald them over the fire to make the vermine come out, and then boil them, and drink up the liquor, and then beat the great ends of them in a mortar, and so eat them. They would eat horse's guts, and ears, and all sorts of wild birds which they could catch; also bear, venison, beaver, tortoise, frogs, squirrels, dogs, skunks, rattlesnakes; yea, the very bark of trees; besides all sorts of creatures, and provision which they plundered from the English. I can but stand in admiration to see the wonderful power of God in providing for such a vast number of our enemies in the wilderness, where there was nothing to be seen, but from hand to mouth. Many times in a morning, the generality of them would eat up all they had, and yet have some further supply against they wanted. It is said, "Oh, that my People had hearkened to me, and Israel had walked in my ways, I should soon have subdued their Enemies, and turned my hand against their Adversaries" (Psalm 81.13–14). But now our perverse and evil carriages in the sight of the Lord, have so offended Him, that instead of turning His hand against them, the Lord feeds and nourishes them up to be a scourge to the whole land.

5. Another thing that I would observe is the strange providence of God, in turning things about when the Indians was at the highest, and the English at the lowest. I was with the enemy eleven weeks and five days, and not one week passed without the fury of the enemy, and some desolation by fire and sword upon one place or other. They mourned (with their black faces) for their own losses, yet triumphed and rejoiced in their inhumane, and many times devilish cruelty to the English. They would boast much of their victories; saying, that in two hours time they had destroyed such a captain and his company, at such a place; and such a captain and his company in such a place; and such a captain and his company in such a place; and boast how many towns they had destroyed, and then scoff, and say they had done them a good turn to send them to Heaven so soon. Again, they would say this summer that they would knock all the rogues in the head, or drive them into the sea, or make them fly the country; thinking surely, Agag-like, "The bitterness of Death is past." Now the heathen begins to think all is their own, and the poor Christian's hopes to fail (as to man) and now their eyes are more to God, and their hearts sigh heaven-ward; and to say in good earnest, "Help Lord, or we perish." When the Lord had brought his people to this, that they saw no help in anything but Himself; then He takes the quarrel into His own hand; and though they had made a pit, in their own imaginations, as deep as hell for the Christians that summer, yet the Lord hurled themselves into it. And the Lord had not so many ways before to preserve them, but now He hath as many to destroy them.

2. Plymouth Officials Justify the War (1675)

The officials of Plymouth Colony offered the following explanation for their actions in taking up arms against the Wampanoag chief Metacom (called King Philip by the English) in 1675. What do they see as the principal offenses by the Indians? Should Sassamon be regarded as "a faithful Indian" or as an English spy? Did the Puritan settlers go to war reluctantly or enthusiastically?

Anno Domini 1675

Not to look back further than the troubles that were between the Colony of New Plymouth and Philip, sachem [chieftain] of Mount Hope, in the year 1671, it may be remembered that . . . [he] was the peccant and offending party; and that Plymouth had just cause to take up arms against him; and it was then agreed that he should pay that colony a certain sum of money, in part of their damage and charge by him occasioned; and he then not only renewed his ancient covenant of friendship with them; but made himself and his people absolute subjects to our Sovereign Lord King Charles the Second. . . .

But sometime last winter the Governor of Plymouth was informed by Sassamon, a faithful Indian, that the said Philip was undoubtedly endeavoring to raise new troubles, and was endeavoring to engage all the sachems round about in a war against us; some of the English also that lived near the said sachem, communicated

---

[2]David Pulsifer, ed., "Acts of the Commissioners of the United Colonies of New England," in *Plymouth Colonial Records* (1675), vol. 10, pp. 362–364.

their fears and jealousies concurrent with what the Indian had informed. About a week after John Sassamon had given his information, he was barbarously murdered by some Indians for his faithfulness (as we have cause to believe) to the interest of God and of the English; some time after Sassamon's death Philip, having heard that the Governor of Plymouth had received some information against him and purposed to send for or to him to appear at their next Court that they might inquire into those reports, came down of his own accord to Plymouth a little before their Court, in the beginning of March last; at which time the Council of that colony upon a large debate with him, had great reason to believe, that the information against him might be in substance true, but not having full proof thereof and hoping that the discovery of it so far would cause him to desist they dismissed him friendly; giving him only to understand that if they hear further concerning that matter they might see reason to demand his arms to be delivered up for their security; which was according to former agreement between him and them; and he engaged [pledged] on their demand they should be surrendered unto them or their order.

At that Court we had many Indians in examination concerning the murder of John Sassamon but had not then testimony in the case but not long after, an Indian appearing to testify; we apprehended three by him charged to be the murderers of Sassamon; and secured them to a trial at our next Court (held in June) at which time, a little before the Court, Philip began to keep his men in arms about him and to gather strangers unto him and to march about in arms towards the upper end of the neck on which he lived and near to the English houses; who began thereby to be somewhat disquieted, but took as yet no further notice but only set a military watch in the next towns; as Swansea and Rehoboth some hints we had that Indians were in arms while our Court was sitting but we hoped it might arise from a guilty fear in Philip; that we would send for him and bring him to trial with the other murderers; and that if he saw the Court broken up and he not sent for, the cloud might blow over; and indeed our innocency made us very secure and confident it would not have broken out into a war.

But no sooner was our Court dissolved but we had intelligence from Lieut. John Brown of Swansea that Philip and his men continued constantly in arms, many strange Indians from several places flocked in to him & that they sent away their wives to Narragansett; and were giving our people frequent alarms by drums and guns in the night and invaded their passage towards Plymouth; and that their young Indians were earnest for a war; on the 7th of June Mr. Benjamin Church being on Rhode Island, Weetamoo and some of her chief men told him that Philip intended a war speedily with the English, some of them saying that they would help him; and that he had already given them leave to kill Englishmen's cattle and rob their houses; about the 14th and 15th of June Mr. James Brown went twice to Philip to persuade him to be quiet but at both times found his men in arms and Philip very high and not persuadable to peace; on the 14th June our Council wrote an amicable friendly letter to Philip therein showing our dislike of his practices; and advising him to dismiss his strange Indians and command his own men to fall quietly to their business that our people might also be quiet; and not to suffer himself to be abused by reports concerning us, who intended no wrong, nor hurt towards him; but Mr. Brown could not obtain an answer from him; on the 17th June Mr. Paine of Rehoboth and several others of the English going unarmed to Mount Hope to seek their horses at Philip's request, the Indians came and presented their guns at them and carried it very insolently though no way provoked by them; on the 18th or 19th Job Winslow his house was broken up and rifled by Philip's men; June the 20th being our Sabbath, the people at Swansea were alarmed by the Indians, two of our inhabitants burned out of their houses and their houses rifled; and the Indians were marching up as they judged to assault the town; and therefore entreated speedy help from us; we hereupon the 21 of June sent up some forces to relieve that town and dispatched more with speed; on Wednesday the 23 of June a dozen more of their houses at Swansea were rifled; on the 24th Thomas Layton was slain at the Fall River; on the 25th of June divers of the people at Swansea slain; and many houses burned until which time, and for several days, though we had a considerable force there both of our own and of the Massachusetts (to our grief and shame), they took no revenge on the enemy; thus slow were we and unwilling to engage ourselves and neighbors in a war; having many insolencies almost intolerable from them, of whose hands we had deserved better;

> *Josiah Winslow*
> *Thomas Hinckley*
> [Plymouth Commissioners to the United Colonies]

3. A Rhode Island Quaker Sympathizes with the Indians (1675)

John Easton, lieutenant governor of Rhode Island and a Quaker, took a different view of the war's causes than did the officials from Plymouth, as described in the preceding selection. In what ways does he disagree with them? What does he cite as the Indians' primary grievances against the English settlers?

. . . We said we knew the English said the Indians wronged them and the Indians said the English wronged them, but our desire was [that] the quarrel might rightly be decided in the best way, and not as dogs decide their quarrels. The Indians owned that fighting was the worst way, then they propounded how right might take place, we said by arbitration. They said all English agreed against them, and so by arbitration they had had much wrong, many miles square of land so taken from them, for English would have English arbitrators, and once they were persuaded to give in their arms, that thereby jealousy might be removed, [then] the English having their arms would not deliver them as they had promised, until they consented to pay 100 pounds, and now they had not so much land or money, that they were as good be killed as leave all their livelihood. We said they might choose an Indian king, and the English might choose the Governor of New York, that neither had cause to say either were parties in the difference. They said they had not heard of that way and said we honestly spoke, so we were persuaded if that way had been tendered they would have accepted. We did endeavor not to hear their complaints,

---

[3]John Easton, "A Relation of the Indian War," in Charles H. Lincoln, ed., *Narratives of the Indian Wars, 1675–1699* (New York: 1913), p. 11. Some of the punctuation in this document has been edited to conform to modern usage.

said it was not convenient for us now to consider of, but to endeavor to prevent war, said to them when in war against English, blood was spilt that engaged all Englishmen, for we were to be all under one king. We knew what their complaints would be, and in our colony [Rhode Island] had removed some of them in sending for [Narragansett] Indian rulers in so far as the crime concerned Indians' lives, which they very lovingly accepted and agreed with us to their execution and said so they were able to satisfy their subjects when they knew an Indian suffered duly, but said that was only between their Indians and not in townships that we had purchased, they would not have us prosecute and that they had a great fear lest any of their Indians should be called or forced to be Christian Indians. They said that such were in everything more mischievous, only dissemblers, and then the English made them not subject to their kings, and by their lying to wrong their kings.

We knew it to be true, and we promising them that however in government to Indians all should be alike and that we knew it was our King's will it should be so, that although we were weaker than other colonies, they having submitted to our King to protect them, others dared not otherwise to molest them, so they expressed they took that to be well, that we had little cause to doubt but that to us, under the King, they would have yielded to our determinations in what any should have complained to us against them, but Philip charged it to be dishonesty in us to put off the hearing [of] the complaints.

Therefore we consented to hear them. They said they had been the first in doing good to the English, and the English the first in doing wrong, said when the English first came their king's father [Massasoit] was as a great man and the English as a little child, he constrained other Indians from wronging the English and gave them corn and showed them how to plant and was free to do them any good and had let them have a 100 times more land than now the king had for his own people, but their king's brother when he was king came miserably to die by being forced to court, as they judged poisoned, and another grievance was if 20 of their own Indians testified that an Englishman had done them wrong, it was as nothing, and if but one of their worst Indians testified against any Indian or their king, when it pleased the English that was sufficient.

Another grievance was when their kings sold land, the English would say it was more than they agreed to and a writing must be proof against all them, and some of their kings had done wrong to sell so much. He left his people none, and some being given to drunkenness the English made them drunk and then cheated them in bargains, but now their kings were forewarned not to part with land for nothing in comparison to the value thereof. Now whom the English had owned for king or queen they [the English] would disinherit, and make another king that would give or sell them their land, that now they had no hopes left to keep any land. Another grievance the English cattle and horses still increased, that when they removed 30 miles from where English had anything to do, they could not keep their corn [there] from being spoiled, they never being used to fence, and thought when the English bought land of them that they [the English] would have kept their cattle upon their own land.

Another grievance, the English were so eager to sell the Indians liquor that most of the Indians spent all in drunkenness and then ravened upon the sober Indians and, they did believe, often did hurt the English cattle, and their kings could not prevent it. We knew before [that] these were their grand complaints, but then we only endeavored to persuade that all complaints might be righted without war, but could have no other answer but that they had not heard of that way for the Governor of York and an Indian king to have the hearing of it. We had cause to think if that had been tendered it would have been accepted. We endeavored that, however, they should lay down their arms, for the English were too strong for them. They said then the English should do to them as they did when they were too strong for the English. . . .

E. Founding the Middle Colonies

1. The Misrule of "Peter the Headstrong" (1650)

Henry Hudson's famous voyage in 1609 laid the foundations for the formal establishment of New Netherland (New York) in 1624. Hotheaded Peter Stuyvesant, who had lost a leg in the service of the Dutch West India Company, became governor in 1647, following several inept predecessors. Stuyvesant announced at the outset that he would be "as a father over his children." He proved to be covetous, dictatorial, and tyrannical. But he did attempt to curb drunkenness and knife-wielding in the streets, and ultimately instituted some overdue reforms. After three years of his misrule, eleven prominent members of the colony protested as follows over the head of the Dutch West India Company to the "High Mightinesses" of the Dutch government in Holland. What was the condition of "democracy" in the colony at this stage?

The fort under which we shelter ourselves, and from which as it seems all authority proceeds, lies like a mole-heap or a tottering wall, on which there is not one gun carriage or one piece of cannon in a suitable frame or on a good platform. . . .

His [Stuyvesant's] first arrival . . . was like a peacock, with great state and pomp. The declaration of His Honor that he wished to stay here only three years, with other haughty expressions, caused some to think that he would not be a father. The appellation of Lord General, and similar titles, were never before known here. Almost every day he caused proclamations of various import to be published, which were for the most part never observed, and have long since been a dead letter, except the wine excise, as that yielded a profit. . . .

At one time, after leaving the house of the minister, where the consistory had been sitting and had risen, it happened that Arnoldus Van Herdenbergh related the proceedings relative to the estate of Zeger Teunisz, and how he himself, as curator, had appealed from the sentence. Whereupon the Director [Stuyvesant], who had been sitting there with them as an elder, interrupted him and replied, "It may during my administration be contemplated to appeal, but if any one should do it, I will make him a foot shorter, and send the pieces to Holland, and let him appeal in that way.". . .

---

[1]*The Representation of New Netherland* (1650), in New-York Historical Society, *Collections,* Second Series (1849), vol. 2, pp. 298, 308, 309, 319.

In our opinion this country will never flourish under the government of the Honorable [West India] Company, but will pass away and come to an end of itself, unless the Honorable Company be reformed. And therefore it would be more profitable for them, and better for the country, that they should be rid thereof, and their effects transported hence.

To speak specifically. Care ought to be taken of the public property, as well ecclesiastical as civil, which, in beginnings, can be illy dispensed with. It is doubtful whether divine worship will have to cease altogether in consequence of the departure of the minister and the inability of the Company.

There should be a public school, provided with at least two good masters, so that first of all in so wild a country, where there are many loose people, the youth be well taught and brought up, not only in reading and writing, but also in the knowledge and fear of the Lord. As it is now, the school is kept very irregularly, one and another keeping it according to his pleasure and as long as he thinks proper. There ought also to be an almshouse, and an orphan asylum, and other similar institutions. The minister who now goes home can give a much fuller explanation thereof. The country must also be provided with godly, honorable, and intelligent rulers who are not very indigent, or, indeed, are not too covetous. . . .

[In 1664, fourteen years after this remonstrance, an English fleet, without firing a shot, forced a fuming Stuyvesant to surrender his flimsily fortified colony.]

2. Early Settlers in Pennsylvania (1682)

Richard Townsend, a Quaker who had come from England with William Penn in the ship Welcome, remembered through the haze of the years the founding of the colony. He set down his recollections about 1727, when he was eighty-three years old. What peculiar advantages did this colony have that the others had not enjoyed?

At our arrival [in Pennsylvania] we found it a wilderness. The chief inhabitants were Indians, and some Swedes, who received us in a friendly manner. And though there was a great number of us, the good hand of Providence was seen in a particular manner, in that provisions were found for us, by the Swedes and Indians, at very reasonable rates, as well as brought from divers other parts that were inhabited before.

Our first concern was to keep up and maintain our religious worship; and, in order thereunto, we had several meetings in the houses of the inhabitants; and one boarded meeting-house was set up, where the city was to be, near Delaware. And, as we had nothing but love and good will in our hearts, one to another, we had very comfortable meetings from time to time; and after our meeting was over, we assisted each other in building little houses, for our shelter.

After some time I set up a mill, on Chester creek, which I brought ready framed from London; which served for grinding of corn and sawing of boards, and was of great use to us. Besides, I with Joshua Tittery made a net and caught great quanti-

---

[2]Robert Proud, *The History of Pennsylvania* . . . (1797), vol. 1, pp. 229–231.

ties of fish, which supplied ourselves and many others; so that, notwithstanding it was thought near three thousand persons came in the first year, we were so providentially provided for that we could buy a deer for about two shillings, and a large turkey for about one shilling, and Indian corn for about two shillings and sixpence per bushel.

And, as our worthy Proprietor [Penn] treated the Indians with extraordinary humanity, they became very civil and loving to us, and brought in abundance of venison. As in other countries the Indians were exasperated by hard treatment, which hath been the foundation of much bloodshed, so the contrary treatment here hath produced their love and affection.

About a year after our arrival, there came in about twenty families from high and low Germany, of religious, good people; who settled about six miles from Philadelphia, and called the place Germantown. The country continually increasing, people began to spread themselves further back. . . .

About the time in which Germantown was laid out, I settled upon my tract of land, which I had purchased of the Proprietor in England, about a mile from thence; where I set up a house and a corn mill, which was very useful to the country for several miles round. But there not being plenty of horses, people generally brought their corn on their backs many miles. . . .

As people began to spread and improve their lands, the country became more fruitful; so that those who came after us were plentifully supplied; and with what we abounded we began a small trade abroad. And as Philadelphia increased, vessels were built, and many employed. Both country and trade have been wonderfully increasing to this day; so that, from a wilderness, the Lord, by his good hand of Providence, hath made it a fruitful field. . . .

Thought Provokers

1. In regard to the Plymouth Pilgrims, what support does one find for this statement: "The cowards never started; the weak died on the way"? An English writer claims that the brave ones were actually those who stayed at home and fought the authorities for religious freedom instead of fleeing from them. Comment.

2. How can one justify the so-called intolerance of the Puritans, especially since they were the victims of intolerance at home? What light does this statement of Pope Leo XIII in 1885 throw on the problem: "The equal toleration of all religions . . . is the same thing as atheism"?

3. It has been said that the Puritans were misguided in following biblical law, which did not fit conditions of the seventeenth century. Comment. The blacks of South Africa have this proverb: "At first we had the land and the white man had the Bible. Now we have the Bible and the white man has the land." Comment with reference to Indian-white relations in North America.

4. In which of the colonies from Pennsylvania to Massachusetts would you have preferred to be a settler? Explain fully why.

4

American Life in the Seventeenth Century, 1607–1692

Our fathers were Englishmen which came over this great ocean, and were ready to perish in this wilderness, but they cried unto the Lord, and he heard their voice, and looked on their adversity.

William Bradford, Of Plymouth Plantation

Prologue: The unhealthful environment of the Chesapeake region killed off the first would-be settlers in droves. Mostly single men, the earliest Virginia and Maryland colonists struggled to put their raw colonies on a sound economic footing by cultivating tobacco. At first, indentured servants provided much of the labor supply for tobacco culture, but after discontented former servants erupted in Bacon's Rebellion in 1676, the dominant merchant-planters shifted to importing African slaves. By the end of the seventeenth century, both white and black populations in the Chesapeake were growing through natural reproduction as well as through continued immigration. New England, in contrast, was settled from the start by colonists in family units, who thrived almost from the outset. As their numbers grew, they built a prosperous, diversified economy, founded schools and tidy towns, and established a tradition of self-government. The Puritan faith pervaded all aspects of New England life, encouraging, in one extreme instance, the persecution of a number of women for witchcraft at Salem in 1692.

A. Indentured Servants in the Chesapeake Region

1. A Londoner Agrees to Provide a Servant (1654)

The earliest Virginia settlers hungered for more workers so that they could plant more land in tobacco, the colony's richly profitable cash crop. Agents in England served as "brokers" who found laborers, arranged for their transportation to the New World,

---

[1]From *The Old Dominion in the Seventeenth Century: A Documentary History of Virginia, 1606–1686,* edited by Warren M. Billings, pp. 134–135, 144, 146–147. Published for the Institute of Early American History and Culture, Williamsburg, Virginia. Copyright © 1975 by The University of North Carolina Press. Used by permission of the publisher.

and drew up contracts specifying the terms of labor and the duration of the period of service. In the following contract, what sort of worker does Thomas Workman of Virginia want? What might be the implications of the contract's conspicuous failure to mention the terms of the servant's termination of service in four years' time?

Recorded this 20th Day of June 1654

Be it known unto all men by these presents that I Richard Garford of London Inhoulder doe Confess and acknowledge my selfe to owe and stand indebted unto Thomas Workman of the Little Creeke in the County of Lower Norffolk in Virginia, planter, his Executors Administrators or assignes the full and Just some of Tenn pounds of good and lawfull money of England to be paid uppon demand of the abovesaid Thomas Workman or his true and lawfull Atterny or Attornyes at the now dwelling house of Mr. Willyam Garford Innkeeper at the Red Lyon in fleet streete without either Equevocation fraud or delay, and to the true performance of the same well and truly to bee made and done I bind my selfe my Executors Administrators and Assignes, firmly by these presents in witnesse heereof I have hereunto sett my hand and seale this 4th day of Aprill 1653

Richard Garfford

The Condition of this obligation is such that the within bounden Richard Garford or his Assignes shall well and truly deliver or cause to be delivered unto the above mentioned Thomas Workman, his Executors Administrators or assignes here in Virginia a sound and able man servant betweene Eighteene and 25 yeres of age that shall have fower yeres to serve at the least, and that in the first second or third shipp that shall arrive in the Port of James River in Virginia from London, that then the bond above to be voyd and of noe effect or else to stand in full force and vertue

Richard Garfford

Sealed and delivered in the presence of
Thomas Ward

2. A Servant Describes His Fate (c. 1680)

Mostly impoverished and unemployed in England, the great mass of indentured servants possessed neither the learning nor the leisure to reflect in writing on their experience in Virginia. A notable exception was James Revel, a criminal with some education who was "transported" to Virginia as punishment for his offenses. He eventually returned to England and wrote the following remarkable poem. What did

---

[2]James Revel, "The Poor Unhappy Transported Felon's Sorrowful Account of His Fourteen Years Transportation at Virginia in America," ed. John Melville Jennings, *Virginia Magazine of History and Biography 56* (1948): 189–194. Reprinted by permission.

he find most difficult about life in Virginia? What was his attitude toward the blacks he encountered?

Part I

My loving Countrymen pray lend an Ear,
    To this Relation which I bring you here,
My sufferings at large I will unfold,
Which tho' 'tis strange, 'tis true as e'er was told,
    Of honest parents I did come (tho' poor,)
Who besides me had never Children more;
Near Temple Bar was born their darling son,
And for some years in virtue's path did run.

    My parents in me took great delight,
And brought me up-at School to read and write,
And cast accompts likewise, as it appears,
Until that I was aged thirteen years.

    Then to a Tin-man I was Prentice bound,
My master and mistress good I found,
They lik'd me well, my business I did mind,
From me my parents comfort hop'd to find.

    My master near unto Moorfields did dwell,
Where into wicked company I fell;
To wickedness I quickly was inclin'd
Thus soon is tainted any youthful mind.

    I from my master then did run away,
And rov'd about the streets both night and day:
Did with a gang of rogues a thieving go,
Which filled my parents heart with grief and woe.

    At length my master got me home again,
And used me well, in hopes I might reclaim, . . .
I promis'd fair, but yet could not refrain,

    But to my vile companions went again: . . .
One night was taken up one of our gang,
Who five impeach'd and three of these were hang'd.

    I was one of the five was try'd and cast,
Yet transportation I did get at last; . . .

    In vain I griev'd, in vain my parents weep,
For I was quickly sent on board the Ship:
With melting kisses and a heavy heart,
I from my dearest parents then did part.

Part II

In a few Days we left the river quite,
    And in short time of land we lost the sight,
The Captain and the sailors us'd us well,
But kept us under lest we should rebel.

    We were in number much about threescore,

A wicked lowsey crew as e'er went o'er;
Oaths and Tobacco with us plenty were,
For most did smoak, and all did curse and swear.

    Five of our number in our passage died,
Which were thrown into the Ocean wide:
And after sailing seven Weeks and more,
We at Virginia all were put on shore.

    Where, to refresh us, we were wash'd and cleaned
That to our buyers we might the better seem;
Our things were gave to each they did belong,
And they that had clean linnen put it on.

    Our faces shav'd, comb'd out our wigs and hair,
That we in decent order might appear,
Against the planters did come down to view,
How well they lik'd this fresh transported crew.
The Women s[e]parated from us stand,
As well as we, by them for to be view'd;
And in short time some men up to us came,
Some ask'd our trades, and others ask'd our names.

    Some view'd our limbs, and other's turn'd us round
Examening like Horses, if we're sound,
What trade are you, my Lad, says one to me,
A Tin-man, Sir, that will not do, says he[.]

    Some felt our hands and view'd our legs and feet,
And made us walk, to see we were compleat;
Some view'd our teeth, to see if they were good,
Or fit to chew our hard and homely Food.

    If any like our look, our limbs, our trade,
The Captain then a good advantage made:
For they a difference made it did appear.
'Twixt those for seven and for fourteen year.

    Another difference there is alow'd,
They who have money have most favour show'd;
For if no cloaths nor money they have got,
Hard is their fate, and hard will be their lot.

    At length a grim old Man unto me came,
He ask'd my trade, and likewise ask'd my Name:
I told him I a Tin-man was by trade,
And not quite eighteen years of age I said.

    Likewise the cause I told that brought me there,
That I for fourteen years transported were,
And when he this from me did understand,
He bought me of the Captain out of hand,

Part III

Down to the harbour I was took again,
    On board of a sloop, and loaded with a chain;

Which I was forc'd to wear both night and day,
For fear I from the Sloop should get away.
     My master was a man but of ill fame,
Who first of all a Transport thither came,
In Reppahannock county we did dwell,
Up Reppahannock river known full well,
     And when the Sloop with loading home was sent
An hundred mile we up the river went
The weather cold and very hard my fare,
My lodging on the deck both hard and bare,
     At last to my new master's house I came,
At the town of Wicocc[o]moco call'd by name,
Where my Europian clothes were took from me,
Which never after I again could see.
     A canvas shirt and trowsers then they gave,
With a hop-sack frock in which I was to slave:
No shoes nor stockings had I for to wear,
Nor hat, nor cap, both head and feet were bare.
     Thus dress'd into the Field I nex[t] must go,
Amongst tobacco plants all day to hoe,
At day break in the morn our work began,
And so held to the setting of the Sun.
     My fellow slaves were just five Transports more,
With eighteen Negroes, which is twenty four:
Besides four transport women in the house,
To wait upon his daughter and his Spouse,
     We and the Negroes both alike did fare,
Of work and food we had an equal share;
But in a piece of ground we call our own,
The food we eat first by ourselves were sown,
     No other time to us they would allow,
But on a Sunday we the same must do:
Six days we slave for our master's good,
The seventh day is to produce our food.
     Sometimes when that a hard days work we've done,
Away unto the mill we must be gone;
Till twelve or one o'clock a grinding corn,
And must be up by daylight in the morn.
     And if you run in debt with any one,
It must be paid before from thence you come;
For in publick places they'll put up your name,
That every one their just demands may claim,
     And if we offer for to run away,
For every hour we must serve a day;
For every day a Week, They're so severe,
For every week a month, for every month a year
But if they murder, rob or steal when there,

Then straightway hang'd, the Laws are so severe;
For by the Rigour of that very law
They're much kept under and to stand in awe.

Part IV

At length, it pleased God I sick did fall
But I no favour could receive at all,
For I was Forced to work while I could stand,
Or hold the hoe within my feeble hands.

Much hardships then in deed I did endure,
No dog was ever nursed so I'm sure,
More pity the poor Negroe slaves bestowed
Than my inhuman brutal master showed.

Oft on my knees the Lord I did implore,
To let me see my native land once more;
For through God's grace my life I would amend
And be a comfort to my dearest friends.

Helpless and sick and being left alone,
I by myself did use to make my moan;
And think upon my former wicked ways,
How they had brought me to this wretched case.

The Lord above who saw my Grief and smart,
Heard my complaint and knew my contrite heart,
His gracious Mercy did to me afford,
My health again was unto me restor'd.

It pleas'd the Lord to grant me so much Grace,
That tho' I was in such a barbarous place,
I serv'd the Lord with fervency and zeal,
By which I did much inward comfort feel.

Thus twelve long tedious years did pass away,
And but two more by law I had to stay:
When Death did for my cruel Master call,
But that was no relief to us at all.

The Widow would not the Plantation hold,
So we and that were both for to be sold,
A lawyer rich who at James-Town did dwell,
Came down to view it and lik'd it very well.

He bought the Negroes who for life were slaves,
But no transported Fellons would he have,
So we were put like Sheep into a fold,
There unto the best bidder to be sold.

Part V

A Gentleman who seemed something grave,
Unto me said, how long are you to slave;
Not two years quite, I unto him reply'd,
That is but very short indeed he cry'd.

He ask'd my Name, my trade, and whence I came
And what vile Fate had brought me to that shame?
I told him all at which he shook his head,
I hope you have seen your folly now, he said.
 I told him yes and truly did repent,
But that which made me most of all relent
That I should to my parents prove so vile,
I being their darling and their only child.
 He said no more but from me short did turn,
While from my Eyes the tears did trinkling run,
To see him to my overseer go,
But what he said to him I do not know.
 He straightway came to me again,
And said no longer here you must remain,
For I have bought you of that Man said he,
Therefore prepare yourself to come with me.
 I with him went with heart oppressed with woe,
Not knowing him, or where I was to go;
But was surprised very much to find
He used me so tenderly and kind.
 He said he would not use me as a slave,
But as a servant if I well behav'd;
And if I pleased him when my time expir'd,
He'd send me home again if I required.
 My kind new master did at James Town dwell;
By trade a Cooper, and liv'd very well:
I was his servant on him to attend.
Thus God, unlook'd for raised me up a friend.

Part VI

Thus did I live in plenty and at ease,
 Having none but my master for to please,
And if at any time he did ride out,
I with him rode the country round about
 And in my heart I often cry'd to see,
So many transport fellons there to be;
Some who in England had lived fine and brave,
Were like old Horses forced to drudge and slave.
 At length my fourteen years expired quite,
Which fill'd my very soul with fine delight;
To think I shoud no longer there remain,
But to old England once return again.
 My master for me did express much love,
And as good as his promise to me prov'd:
He got me ship'd and I came home again
With joy and comfort tho' I went asham'd,
 My Father and my Mother wel I found,

Who to see me, with Joy did much abound:
My Mother over me did weep for Joy,
My Father cry'd once more to see my Boy;
    Whom I thought dead, but does alive remain,
And is returned to me once again;
I hope God has so wrought upon your mind,
No more wickedness you'll be inclined,
    I told them all the dangers I went thro'
Likewise my sickness and my hardships too;
    Which fill'd their tender hearts with sad surprise,
While tears ran trinkling from their aged eyes.
    I begg'd them from all grief to refrain,
Since God had brought me to them home again,
The Lord unto me so much grace will give,
For to work for you both While I live,
    My country men take warning e'er too late,
Lest you should share my hard unhappy fate;
Altho' but little crimes you here have done,
Consider seven or fourteen years to come,
    Forc'd from your friends and country for to go,
Among the Negroes to work at the hoe;
In distant countries void of all relief,
Sold for a slave because you prov'd a thief.
    Now young men with speed your lives amend,
Take my advice as one that is your friend:
For tho' so slight you make of it while here,
Hard is your lot when once the[y] get you there.

3. A Servant Girl Pays the Wages of Sin (1656)

Single, lonely, and hard-used, indentured servants enjoyed few liberties. Those who did go astray could be severely punished. In the following record from Charles City County Court, Virginia, what are the consequences of the servant girl's having borne an illegitimate child?

Whereas Ann Parke servant to Elizabeth Hatcher widdow is Complained of and proved to have Comitted Fornication and borne a Child in the time of her service: It is therefore ordered that the said Ann shall double the time of service due to be performed by her to her mistress or her assigns, from the time of her departure, according to act in that Case made and provided.

---

[3]From *The Old Dominion in the Seventeenth Century: A Documentary History of Virginia, 1606–1609,* edited by Warren M. Billings. Published for the Institute of Early American History and Culture, Williamsburg, Virginia. Copyright © by The University of North Carolina Press. Used by permission of the publisher.

4. An Unruly Servant Is Punished (1679)

The planter-employers and masters struggled constantly to keep their hard-drinking, fractious servants in line. Sometimes matters got seriously out of hand, as in the following account from Virginia's Accomack County Court records in 1679. What were the terms of the offender's punishment? Were they justified?

The Examination of Elizabeth Bowen Widdow—
saith—That on Sunday evening being the eighteenth day of May 1679 Thomas Jones her servant did come into her Roome and with a naked Rapier in his hand did tell her he would kill her and said shee had sent Will Waight to her Mothers and that shee had got a master for them, but hee would bee her Master and allso said that he would not kill her if shee would let him lye with her all night and bade her goe to bed and she answered she would not and Runn in with his Rapier and bent it, then he said he woald cutt her throat but she getting [to] the dore did run out of dores and he after her and ketched [her] in the yard and as she was standing did endeavor to cutt her throat with a knife but could not and then he threw her down and did there allso indeavour to cutt her throat but she prevented it by defending her throat with her hands and bending the knife hee took her [petti]coats and threw [them] over her head and gave her two or three blows in the face with his fist and bade her get her gun and did in this act with the Knife scurrify her throat and brest and cut her right hand with six or seven cutts very much and that she with bending the Rapier and knife cut her hands and fingers very much

Elizabeth Bowen

Whereas Elizabeth Bowin Widdow did by her examination upon oath in open Court declare that Thomas Jones her servant in a most barbarous and villanous nature sett upon and most desparately attempted to murder the said Bowin with a naked Rapier and Knife to cut her throat which had been perpatrated and committed had it not bee[n] Providentially and strongly prevented by the said Bowins resistance recieving severall wounds in her endeavours to prevent the sam[e] which was allso confessed by the said Jones: The Court takeing the same into their serious Considerations do order as a just reward for his said horrid offense and crime that the sherriff Forthwith take him into Custody and that he forthwith receive thirty nine lashes on the bare back well laid on: and to have his haire cutt off and an Iron Coller forthwith put about his neck dureing the Courts pleasure and after the time for which he was to serve his said mistriss is expired to serve his said mistriss or assignes one whole yeare according to Act for laying violent hands on his said mistriss and allso two yeares for his wounding her as aforesaid and after due punishment inflicted accordingly The Court do further order that the sherriff deliver the said Jones to the

[4]From *The Old Dominion in the Seventeenth Century: A Documentary History of Virginia, 1606–1609,* edited by Warren M. Billings. Published for the Institute of Early American History and Culture, Williamsburg, Virginia. Copyright © by The University of North Carolina Press. Used by permission of the publisher.

said Elizabeth Bowin or order (it being by her request) and the said Bownig [sic] to Pay Court Charges the said Jones making satisfaction for the same after his time of service is expired—

B. Bacon's Rebellion and Its Aftermath

1. The Baconite Grievances (1677)

Angry former servants, impoverished and resentful, crowded into the untamed Virginia backcountry as the seventeenth century wore on. Governor William Berkeley's unwillingness to protect the hardscrabble planters on the frontier against Indian butcheries gave rise to ugly rumors of graft, and helped spark a rebellion led by his wife's kinsman, the well-born Nathaniel Bacon. After the uprising had collapsed, a royal commission sent out from England prepared the following report, which was not friendly to Berkeley. What were the governor's alleged shortcomings? Did they justify Bacon's defiance of his authority?

The unsatisfied people, finding themselves still liable to the Indian cruelties, and the cries of their wives and children growing grievous and intolerable to them, gave out in speeches that they were resolved to plant tobacco rather than pay the tax for maintaining of forts; and that the erecting of them was a great grievance, juggle, and cheat, and of no more use or service to them than another plantation with men at it; and that it was merely a design of the [tidewater] grandees to engross [monopolize] all their tobacco into their own hands.

Thus the sense of this oppression and the dread of a common approaching calamity made the giddy-headed multitude mad, and precipitated them upon that rash overture of running out upon the Indians themselves, at their own voluntary charge and hazard of their lives and fortunes. Only they first by petition humbly craved leave or commission to be led by any commander or commanders as the Governor should please to appoint over them to be their chieftain or general. But instead of granting this petition, the Governor by proclamation, under great penalty, forbade the like petitioning for the future.*

This made the people jealous that the Governor for the lucre of the beaver and otter trade, etc., with the Indians, rather sought to protect the Indians than them, since after public proclamation prohibiting all trade with the Indians (they complain), he privately gave commission to some of his friends to truck with them, and that those persons furnished the Indians with powder, shot, etc., so that they were better provided than His Majesty's subjects.

The peoples of Charles City County (near Merchants Hope) being devised [denied] a commission by the Governor, although he was truly informed . . . of several formidable bodies of Indians coming down on the heads of James River within fifty or sixty miles of the English plantations. . . , they begin to beat up drums for volunteers to go out against the Indians, and so continued sundry days drawing into arms,

---

[1]*The Virginia Magazine of History and Biography 4* (1896): 121–122.

*The governor feared that the settlers would attack, as they did, both friendly and unfriendly tribes.

the magistrates being either so remiss or of the same faction that they suffered this disaster without contradiction or endeavoring to prevent so dangerous a beginning and going on.

The rout [mob] being got together now wanted nor waited for nothing but one to head and lead them out on their design. It so happened that one Nathaniel Bacon, Jr., a person whose lost and desperate fortunes had thrown him into that part of the world about fourteen months before. . . , framed him fit for such a purpose. . . .

2. The Governor Upholds the Law (1676)

The youthful Bacon, putting himself at the head of about a thousand men, chastised both the Indians and Berkeley's forces. He died mysteriously at the moment of victory, and his rebellion ended. The ferocity with which Berkeley executed Bacon's followers (more than twenty all told) shocked Charles II, who allegedly remarked, "That old fool has killed more people in that naked country than I have done for the murder of my father." Before the rebellion collapsed, Berkeley pleaded his own case with the people of Virginia as follows. What is the strongest argument in defense of his position? Comment critically on it.

But for all this, perhaps I have erred in things I know not of. If I have, I am so conscious of human frailty and my own defects that I will not only acknowledge them, but repent of and amend them, and not, like the rebel Bacon, persist in an error only because I have committed it. . . .

And now I will state the question betwixt me as a governor and Mr. Bacon, and say that if any enemies should invade England, any counselor, justice of peace, or other inferior officer might raise what forces they could to protect His Majesty's subjects. But I say again, if, after the King's knowledge of this invasion, any the greatest peer of England should raise forces against the King's prohibition, this would be now, and ever was in all ages and nations, accounted treason. . . .

Now, my friends, I have lived thirty-four years amongst you, as uncorrupt and diligent as ever governor was. Bacon is a man of two years among you; his person and qualities unknown to most of you, and to all men else, by any virtuous action that ever I heard of. And that very action [against the Indians] which he boasts of was sickly and foolishly and, as I am informed, treacherously carried to the dishonor of the English nation. Yet in it he lost more men than I did in three years' war; and by the grace of God will put myself to the same dangers and troubles again when I have brought Bacon to acknowledge the laws are above him, and I doubt not but by God's assistance to have better success than Bacon hath had. The reasons of my hopes are, that I will take counsel of wiser men than myself; but Mr. Bacon hath none about him but the lowest of the people.

Yet I must further enlarge that I cannot, without your help, do anything in this but die in defense of my King, his laws and subjects, which I will cheerfully do, though alone I do it. And considering my poor fortunes, I cannot leave my poor

²Massachusetts Historical Society, *Collections,* Fourth Series (1871), vol. 9, pp. 179–181.

wife and friends a better legacy than by dying for my King and you: for his sacred Majesty will easily distinguish between Mr. Bacon's actions and mine; and kings have long arms, either to reward or punish.

Now after all this, if Mr. Bacon can show one precedent or example where such acting in any nation whatever was approved of, I will mediate with the King and you for a pardon and excuse for him. But I can show him an hundred examples where brave and great men have been put to death for gaining victories against the command of their superiors.

Lastly, my most assured friends, I would have preserved those Indians that I knew were hourly at our mercy to have been our spies and intelligence, to find out our bloody enemies. But as soon as I had the least intelligence that they also were treacherous enemies, I gave out commissions to destroy them all, as the commissions themselves will speak it.

To conclude, I have done what was possible both to friend and enemy; have granted Mr. Bacon three pardons, which he hath scornfully rejected, supposing himself stronger to subvert than I and you to maintain the laws, by which only, and God's assisting grace and mercy, all men must hope for peace and safety.

3. Slavery Is Justified (1757)

Following Bacon's ill-starred rebellion, tobacco culture continued to flourish. The Virginians had early learned that the path to wealth and leisure involved the use of African slaves. Even ministers of the gospel parroted the arguments in behalf of slavery, as is evident in this brutally frank letter by the Reverend Peter Fontaine, of Westover, Virginia, to his brother Moses. Is the attempt to shift the blame onto the British convincing? Was there a valid economic basis for slavery?

As to your second query, if enslaving our fellow creatures be a practice agreeable to Christianity, it is answered in a great measure in many treatises at home, to which I refer you. I shall only mention something of our present state here.

Like Adam, we are all apt to shift off the blame from ourselves and lay it upon others, how justly in our case you may judge. The Negroes are enslaved [in Africa] by the Negroes themselves before they are purchased by the masters of the ships who bring them here. It is, to be sure, at our choice whether we buy them or not; so this then is our crime, folly, or whatever you will please to call it. But our Assembly, foreseeing the ill consequences of importing such numbers amongst us, hath often attempted to lay a duty upon them which would amount to a prohibition, such as ten or twenty pounds a head. But no governor dare pass a law, having instructions to the contrary from the Board of Trade at home. By this means they are forced upon us, whether we will or will not. This plainly shows the African Company has the advantage of the colonies, and may do as it pleases with the [London] ministry.

Indeed, since we have been exhausted of our little stock of cash by the [French and Indian] war, the importation has stopped; our poverty then is our best security. There is no more picking for their [slave traders'] ravenous jaws upon bare bones, but should we begin to thrive, they will be at the same again. . . .

---

[3]Ann Maury, ed., *Memoirs of a Huguenot Family* (1853), pp. 351–352.

This is our part of the grievance, but to live in Virginia without slaves is morally impossible. Before our troubles, you could not hire a servant or slave for love or money, so that unless robust enough to cut wood, to go to mill, to work at the hoe, etc., you must starve, or board in some family where they both fleece and half starve you. There is no set price upon corn, wheat, and provisions, so they take advantage of the necessities of strangers, who are thus obliged to purchase some slaves and land. This, of course, draws us all into the original sin and the curse of the country of purchasing slaves, and this is the reason we have no merchants, traders, or artificers of any sort but what become planters in a short time.

A common laborer, white or black, if you can be so much favored as to hire one, is a shilling sterling or fifteen pence currency per day; a bungling carpenter two shillings or two shillings and sixpence per day; besides diet and lodging. That is, for a lazy fellow to get wood and water, £19.16.3 current per annum; add to this seven or eight pounds more and you have a slave for life.

C. Slavery in the Colonial Era

1. The Conscience of a Slave Trader (1694)

In September 1693 the thirty-six-gun ship Hannibal, *commanded by Thomas Phillips, set sail from England for West Africa, where Phillips bought slaves for sale on the West Indian sugar island of Barbados. What does Phillips's account reveal about the involvement of the Africans themselves in the slave trade? What was Phillips's own attitude toward the Africans? How could he reconcile such sentiments with the brutal business in which he was engaged?*

We mark'd the slaves we had bought in the breast, or shoulder, with a hot iron, having the letter of the ship's name on it, the place being before anointed with a little palm oil, which caus'd but little pain, the mark being usually well in four or five days, appearing very plain and white after.

When we had purchas'd to the number of 50 or 60 we would send them aboard, there being a cappasheir, intitled the captain of the slaves, whose care it was to secure them to the water-side, and see them all off; and if in carrying to the marine any were lost, he was bound to make them good, to us, the captain of the trunk being oblig'd to do the like, if any ran away while under his care, for after we buy them we give him charge of them till the captain of the slaves comes to carry them away: These are two officers appointed by the king for this purpose, to each of which every ship pays the value of a slave in what goods they like best for their trouble, when they have done trading; and indeed they discharg'd their duty to us very faithfully, we not having lost one slave thro' their neglect in 1300 we bought here.

---

[1]Elizabeth Donnan, *Documents Illustrative of the History of the Slave Trade to America* (Washington, D.C.: The Carnegie Institution, 1930), vol. 1, pp. 402–403. Reprinted by permission of the Carnegie Institution of Washington.

There is likewise a captain of the sand, who is appointed to take care of the merchandize we have come ashore to trade with, that the negroes do not plunder them, we being often forced to leave goods a whole night on the sea shore, for want of porters to bring them up; but notwithstanding his care and authority, we often came by the loss, and could have no redress.

When our slaves were come to the seaside, our canoes were ready to carry them off to the longboat, if the sea permitted, and she convey'd them aboard ship, where the men were all put in irons, two and two shackled together, to prevent their mutiny, or swimming ashore.

The negroes are so wilful and loth to leave their own country, that they have often leap'd out of the canoes, boat and ship, into the sea, and kept under water till they were drowned, to avoid being taken up and saved by our boats, which pursued them; they having a more dreadful apprehension of Barbadoes than we can have of hell, tho' in reality they live much better there than in their own country; but home is home, etc: we have likewise seen divers of them eaten by the sharks, of which a prodigious number kept about the ships in this place, and I have been told will follow her hence to Barbadoes, for the dead negroes that are thrown overboard in the passage. I am certain in our voyage there we did not want the sight of some every day, but that they were the same I can't affirm.

We had about 12 negroes did wilfully drown themselves, and others starv'd themselves to death; for 'tis their belief that when they die they return home to their own country and friends again.

I have been inform'd that some commanders have cut off the legs and arms of the most wilful, to terrify the rest, for they believe if they lose a member, they cannot return home again: I was advis'd by some of my officers to do the same, but I could not be perswaded to entertain the least thought of it, much less put in practice such barbarity and cruelty to poor creatures, who, excepting their want of christianity and true religion (their misfortune more than fault) are as much the works of God's hands, and no doubt as dear to him as ourselves; nor can I imagine why they should be despis'd for their colour, being what they cannot help, and the effect of the climate it has pleas'd God to appoint them. I can't think there is any intrinsick value in one colour more than another, nor that white is better than black, only we think so because we are so, and are prone to judge favourably in our own case, as well as the blacks, who in odium of the colour, say, the devil is white, and so paint him. . . .

The present king often, when ships are in a great strait for slaves, and cannot be supply'd otherwise, will sell 3 or 400 of his wives to compleat their number, but we always pay dearer for his slaves than those bought of the cappasheirs. . . .

2. The Stono River Rebellion in South Carolina (1739)

Black slaves made up a majority of the population in early eighteenth-century South Carolina. Naturally, they dreamed of freedom, and the refuge of nearby Spanish Florida held out the promise of turning their dream into reality. In 1739 a number of South Carolina slaves rose up in arms and struck out for Florida and freedom.

[2]Allen D. Candler, compiler, *The Colonial Records of the State of Georgia* (1913), vol. 22, part 2, pp. 232–236. Courtesy of Public Record Office (London)—CO 5/640ff.

What did their behavior suggest about the character of colonial slavery? In the following account by a white contemporary, what appear to be the greatest fears of the white slaveowning minority?

Sometime since there was a Proclamation published at Augustine, in which the King of Spain (then at Peace with Great Britain) promised Protection and Freedom to all Negroes [sic] Slaves that would resort thither. Certain Negroes belonging to Captain Davis escaped to Augustine, and were received there. They were demanded by General Oglethorpe who sent Lieutenant Demere to Augustine, and the Governor assured the General of his sincere Friendship, but at the same time showed his Orders from the Court of Spain, by which he was to receive all Run away Negroes. Of this other Negroes having notice, as it is believed, from the Spanish Emissaries, four or five who were Cattel-Hunters, and knew the Woods, some of whom belonged to Captain Macpherson, ran away with His Horses, wounded his Son and killed another Man. These marched f [sic] for Georgia, and were pursued, but the Rangers being then newly reduced [sic] the Countrey people could not overtake them, though they were discovered by the Saltzburghers, as they passed by Ebenezer. They reached Augustine, one only being killed and another wounded by the Indians in their flight. They were received there with great honours, one of them had a Commission given to him, and a Coat faced with Velvet. Amongst the Negroe Slaves there are a people brought from the Kingdom of Angola in Africa, many of these speak Portugueze [which Language is as near Spanish as Scotch is to English,] by reason that the Portugueze have considerable Settlement, and the Jesuits have a Mission and School in that Kingdom and many Thousands of the Negroes there profess the Roman Catholic Religion. Several Spaniards upon diverse Pretences have for some time past been strolling about Carolina, two of them, who will give no account of themselves have been taken up and committed to Jayl in Georgia. The good reception of the Negroes at Augustine was spread about, Several attempted to escape to the Spaniards, & were taken, one of them was hanged at Charles Town. In the latter end of July last Don Pedr, Colonel of the Spanish Horse, went in a Launch to Charles Town under pretence of a message to General Oglethorpe and the Lieutenant Governour.

On the 9th day of September last being Sunday which is the day the Planters allow them to work for themselves, Some Angola Negroes assembled, to the number of Twenty; and one who was called Jemmy was their Captain, they suprized a Warehouse belonging to Mr. Hutchenson at a place called Stonehow [Stono]; they there killed Mr. Robert Bathurst, and Mr. Gibbs, plundered the House and took a pretty many small Arms and Powder, which were there for Sale. Next they plundered and burnt Mr. Godfrey's house, and killed him, his Daughter and Son. They then turned back and marched Southward along Pons Pons, which is the Road through Georgia to Augustine, they passed Mr. Wallace's Tavern towards day break, and said they would not hurt him, for he was a good Man and kind to his Slaves, but they broke open and plundered Mr. Lemy's House, and killed him, his wife and Child. They marched on towards Mr. Rose's resolving to kill him; but he was saved by a Negroe, who having hid him went out and pacified the others. Several Negroes joyned them, they calling out Liberty, marched on with Colours displayed and two Drums beating, pursuing all the white people they met with, and killing Man Woman and Child when they could come up to them. Collonel Bull, Lieutenant

Governour of South Carolina, who was then riding along the Road, discovered them, was pursued, and with much difficulty escaped & raised the Countrey. They burnt Colonel Hext's house and killed his Overseer and his Wife. They then burnt Mr. Sprye's house, then Mr. Sacheverell's, and then Mr. Nash's house, all lying upon the Pons Pons Road, and killed all the white People they found in them. Mr. Bullock got off, but they burnt his House, by this time many of them were drunk with the Rum they had taken in the Houses. They increased every minute by new Negroes coming to them, so that they were above Sixty, some say a hundred, on which they halted in a field, and set to dancing, Singing and beating Drums, to draw more Negroes to them, thinking they were now victorious over the whole Province, having marched ten miles & burnt all before them without Opposition, but the Militia being raised, the Planters with great briskness pursued them and when they came up, dismounting; charged them on foot. The Negroes were soon routed, though they behaved boldly, several being killed on the Spot, many ran back to their Plantations thinking they had not been missed, but they were there taken and Shot. Such as were taken in the field also, were, after being examined, shot on the Spot. And this is to be said to the honour of the Carolina Planters, that notwithstanding the Provocation they had received from so many Murders, they did not torture one Negroe, but only put them to an easy death. All that proved to be forced & were not concerned in the Murders & Burnings were pardoned, And this sudden Courage in the field, & the Humanity afterwards hath had so good an Effect that there hath been no farther Attempt, and the very Spirit of Revolt seems over. About 30 escaped from the fight, of which ten marched about 30 miles Southward, and being overtaken by the Planters on horseback, fought stoutly for some time and were all killed on the Spot. The rest are yet untaken. In the whole action about 40 Negroes and 20 whites were killed. The Lieutenant Governour sent an account of this to General Oglethorpe, who met the advices on his return from the Indian Nation. He immediately ordered a Troop of Rangers to be ranged, to patrole through Georgia, placed some Men in the Garrison at Palichocolas, which was before abandoned, and near which the Negroes formerly passed, being the only place where Horses can come to swim over the River Savannah for near 100 miles, ordered out the Indians in pursuit, and a Detachment of the Garrison at Port Royal to assist the Planters on any Occasion, and published a Proclamation ordering all the Constables &ca. of Georgia to pursue and seize all Negroes, with a Reward for any that should be taken. It is hoped these measures will prevent any Negroes from getting down to the Spaniads.

D. Life Among New England's Puritans

1. Cotton Mather on the Education of His Children (1706)

Cotton Mather (1663–1728), grandson of John Cotton, was among the most famous of New England's Puritan preachers. Entering Harvard at age twelve, he went on to

---

[1]Worthington Chauncy Ford, ed., *Diary of Cotton Mather, 1681–1724,* Collections of the Massachusetts Historical Society, Seventh Series (Boston, 1911–1912), vol. 1, pp. 534–537.

a long and prolific career as a minister, political activist, and scientist. A pillar of orthodoxy, he lectured and wrote frequently on the application of Puritan doctrine to everyday life, including child-rearing. In the following selection, what does Mather see as the main responsibilities of parents? What was the role of religion in his ideal Puritan family? Did he assume that children are naturally good or evil? How do his child-rearing precepts differ from those popular today?

Some Special Points, relating to the Education of my Children

I. I pour out continual Prayers and Cries to the God of all Grace for them, that He will be a Father to my Children, and bestow His Christ and His Grace upon them, and guide them with His Councils, and bring them to His Glory.

And in this Action, I mention them distinctly, every one by Name unto the Lord.

II. I begin betimes to entertain them with delightful Stories, especially scriptural ones. And still conclude with some Lesson of Piety; bidding them to learn that Lesson from the Story.

And thus, every Day at the Table, I have used myself to tell a Story before I rise; and make the Story useful to the Olive Plants about the Table.

III. When the Children at any time accidentally come in my way, it is my custome to lett fall some Sentence or other, that may be monitory and profitable to them.

This Matter proves to me, a Matter of some Study, and Labour, and Contrivance. But who can tell, what may be the Effect of a continual Dropping?

IV. I essay betimes, to engage the Children, in Exercises of Piety; and especially secret [silent] Prayer, for which I give them very plain and brief Directions, and suggest unto them the Petitions, which I would have them to make before the Lord, and which I therefore explain to their Apprehension and Capacity. And I often call upon them; *Child, Don't you forgett every Day, to go alone, and pray as I have directed you!*

V. Betimes I try to form in the Children a Temper of Benignity. I put them upon doing of Services and Kindnesses for one another, and for other Children. I applaud them, when I see them Delight in it. I upbraid all Aversion to it. I caution them exquisitely against all Revenges of Injuries. I instruct them, to return good Offices for evil Ones. I show them, how they will by this Goodness become like to the Good GOD, and His Glorious CHRIST. I lett them discern, that I am not satisfied, except when they have a Sweetness of Temper shining in them.

VI. As soon as tis possible, I make the Children learn to write. And when they can write, I employ them in Writing out the most agreeable and profitable Things, that I can invent for them. In this way, I propose to fraight their minds with excellent Things, and have a deep Impression made upon their Minds by such Things.

VII. I mightily endeavour it, that the Children may betimes, be acted by Principles of Reason and Honour.

I first begett in them an high Opinion of their Father's Love to them, and of his being best able to judge, what shall be good for them.

Then I make them sensible, tis a Folly for them to pretend unto any Witt and Will of their own; they must resign all to me, who will be sure to do what is best; my word must be their Law.

I cause them to understand, that it is an hurtful and a shameful thing to do amiss. I aggravate this, on all Occasions; and lett them see how amiable they will render themselves by well doing.

The first Chastisement, which I inflict for an ordinary Fault, is, to lett the Child see and hear me in an Astonishment, and hardly able to beleeve that the Child could do so base a Thing, but beleeving that they will never do it again.

I would never come, to give a child a Blow; except in Case of Obstinacy; or some gross Enormity.

To be chased for a while out of my Presence, I would make to be look'd upon, as the sorest Punishment in the Family.

I would by all possible Insinuations gain this Point upon them, that for them to learn all the brave Things in the world, is the bravest Thing in the world. I am not fond of proposing Play to them, as a Reward of any diligent application to learn what is good; lest they should think Diversion to be a better and a nobler Thing than Diligence.

I would have them come to propound and expect, at this rate, *I have done well, and now I will go to my Father; He will teach me some curious Thing for it.* I must have them count it a Priviledge, to be taught; and I sometimes manage the Matter so, that my Refusing to teach them Something, is their Punishment.

The slavish way of Education, carried on with raving and kicking and scourging (in Schools as well as Families,) tis abominable; and a dreadful Judgment of God upon the World.

VIII. Tho' I find it a marvellous Advantage to have the Children strongly biased by Principles of Reason and Honour, (which, I find, Children will feel sooner than is commonly thought for:) yett I would neglect no Endeavours, to have higher Principles infused into them.

I therefore betimes awe them with the Eye of God upon them.

I show them, how they must love JESUS CHRIST; and show it, by doing what their Parents require of them.

I often tell them of the good Angels, who love them, and help them, and guard them; and who take Notice of them: and therefore must not be disobliged.

Heaven and Hell, I sett before them, as the Consequences of their Behaviour here.

IX. When the Children are capable of it, I take them alone, one by one; and after my Charges unto them, to fear God, and serve Christ, and shun Sin, I pray with them in my Study and make them the Witnesses of the Agonies, with which I address the Throne of Grace on their behalf.

X. I find much Benefit, by a particular Method, as of Catechising the Children, so of carrying the Repetition of the public Sermons unto them.

The Answers of the Catechism I still explain with abundance of brief Quaestions, which make them to take in the Meaning of it, and I see, that they do so.

And when the Sermons are to be Repeated, I chuse to putt every Trust, into a Quaestion, to be answered still, with Yes, or, No. In this way I awaken their Attention, as well as enlighten their Understanding. And in this way I have an Opportunity, to ask, *Do you desire such, or such a Grace of God?* and the like. Yea, I have an Opportunity to demand, and perhaps, to obtain their Consent unto the glorious Articles of the New Covenant. The Spirit of Grace may fall upon them in this Action; and they may be seiz'd by Him, and Held as His Temples, thro' eternal Ages.

2. A Dutchman Visits Harvard College (1680)

Jasper Danckaerts was an emissary from the Dutch Reformed church who in 1679–1680 visited a colony of his co-religionists who flourished briefly in Maryland and Delaware. On his way home, he spent nearly a month in the Boston area and, while there, called at Harvard College. Founded in 1636, Harvard was then nearly half a century old and already the proud citadel of New England learning. Danck-aerts, however, was unimpressed. What did he find lacking? How might Harvard's alleged deficiencies be explained?

9th, Tuesday. We started out to go to Cambridge, lying to the northeast of Boston, in order to see their college and printing office. We left about six o'clock in the morning, and were set across the river at Charlestown. We followed a road which we supposed was the right one, but went full half an hour out of the way, and would have gone still further, had not a negro who met us, and of whom we inquired, disabused us of our mistake. We went back to the right road, which is a very pleasant one. We reached Cambridge about eight o'clock. It is not a large village, and the houses stand very much apart. The college building is the most conspicuous among them. We went to it, expecting to see something unusual, as it is the only college, or would-be academy of the Protestants in all America, but we found ourselves mistaken. In approaching the house we neither heard nor saw anything mentionable; but, going to the other side of the building, we heard noise enough in an upper room to lead my comrade to say, "I believe they are engaged in disputation." We entered and went up stairs, when a person met us, and requested us to walk in, which we did. We found there eight or ten young fellows, sitting around, smoking tobacco, with the smoke of which the room was so full, that you could hardly see; and the whole house smelt so strong of it that when I was going up stairs I said, "It certainly must be also a tavern." We excused ourselves, that we could speak English only a little, but understood Dutch or French well, which they did not. However, we spoke as well as we could. We inquired how many professors there were, and they replied not one, that there was not enough money to support one. We asked how many students there were. They said at first, thirty, and then came down to twenty; I afterwards understood there are probably not ten. They knew hardly a word of Latin, not one of them, so that my comrade could not converse with them. They took us to the library where there was nothing particular. We looked over it a little. They presented us with a glass of wine. This is all we ascertained there. The minister of the place goes there morning and evening to make prayer, and has charge over them; besides him, the students are under tutors or masters. Our visit was soon

---

[2]Excerpted from Bartlett Burleigh James and J. Franklin Jameson, eds., *Original Narratives in Early American History—Journal of Jasper Danckaerts, 1679–1680,* pp. 266–268. Copyright 1913 Charles Scribner's Sons.

over, and we left them to go and look at the land about there. We found the place beautifully situated on a large plain, more than eight miles square, with a fine stream in the middle of it, capable of bearing heavily laden vessels. As regards the fertility of the soil, we consider the poorest in New York superior to the best here. As we were tired, we took a mouthful to eat, and left. We passed by the printing office, but there was nobody in it; the paper sash however being broken, we looked in, and saw two presses with six or eight cases of type. There is not much work done there. Our printing office is well worth two of it, and even more.

3. The Salem Witchcraft Hysteria (1692)

Thousands of suspected witches were hanged or burned in Europe in the sixteenth and seventeenth centuries, and belief in witches was common in the American colonies. In fact, the Bible decreed, "Thou shalt not suffer a witch to live" (Exodus 22:18). Hysteria swept Salem Village, Massachusetts, in 1692 after some children, mostly girls, brought witchcraft charges against certain persons, mostly women, whom they disliked. Before the special court had adjourned, nineteen persons and two dogs had been hanged, one man had been pressed to death in an attempt to wring from him an answer to the indictment, and 150 victims were in prison awaiting trial. Which aspects of the following testimony seem least credible? Would such testimony be allowed in courts today?

Martha Carrier was indicted for the bewitching of certain persons, according to the form usual in such cases pleading not guilty to her indictment. There were first brought in a considerable number of the bewitched persons, who not only made the court sensible to an horrid witchcraft committed upon them, but also deposed that it was Martha Carrier, or her shape, that grievously tormented them by biting, pricking, pinching, and choking of them. It was further deposed that while this Carrier was on her examination before the magistrates, the poor people were so tortured that every one expected their death upon the very spot, but that upon the binding [arrest] of Carrier they were eased. . . .

Before the trial of this prisoner, several of her own children had frankly and fully confessed, not only that they were witches themselves, but that this, their mother, had made them so. This confession they made with great shows of repentance, and with much demonstration of truth. They related place, time, occasion; they gave an account of journeys, meetings, and mischiefs by them performed, and were very credible in what they said. . . .

Benjamin Abbott gave in his testimony that. . . this Carrier was very angry with him upon laying out some land near her husband's. Her expressions in this anger were that she "would stick as close to Abbot as the bark stuck to the tree; and that he should repent of it afore seven years came to an end, so as Doctor Prescot should never cure him.". . . Presently after this he was taken with a swelling in his foot, and then with a pain in his side, and exceedingly tormented. It bred into a sore, which was lanced by Doctor Prescot, and several gallons of corruption [pus]

[3]G. L. Burr, ed., *Narratives of the Witchcraft Cases, 1648–1706* (1914), pp. 241–242, 244. Permission granted by Barnes & Noble Books, Totowa, New Jersey.

ran out of it. For six weeks it continued very bad, and then another sore bred in his groin, which was also lanced by Doctor Prescot. Another sore then bred in his groin, which was likewise cut, and put him to very great misery. He was brought unto death's door, and so remained until Carrier was taken and carried away by the constable, from which very day he began to mend and so grew better every day, and is well ever since.

Sarah Abbot also, his wife, testified that her husband was not only all this while afflicted in his body, but also that strange, extraordinary, and unaccountable calamities befell his cattle, their death being such as they could guess at no natural reason for. . . .

One Foster, who confessed her own share in the witchcraft for which the prisoner stood indicted, affirmed that she had seen the prisoner at some of their witch meetings, and that it was this Carrier who persuaded her to be a witch. She confessed that the devil carried them on a pole to a witch meeting; but the pole broke, and she hanging about Carrier's neck, they both fell down, and she then received an hurt by the fall whereof she was not at this very time recovered.

Thought Provokers

1. What sorts of people became indentured servants? How did the life of the servant compare with that of the slave?
2. What caused Bacon's Rebellion? Were the Baconites justified in revolting? In what ways did their rebellion foreshadow the American Revolutionary War?
3. How did slavery affect the spirit of the enslaved? of the enslavers? Would you rather have been a slave or an indentured servant in colonial Virginia?
4. How did seventeenth-century New England differ from the seventeenth-century Chesapeake region? In what ways did such differences between the two regions persist into later periods of American history?
5. What caused the Salem witchcraft hysteria, and why did the Puritan rulers respond as they did? Was their reaction justified?

5

Colonial Society on the Eve of Revolution, 1700–1775

Driven from every other corner of the earth, freedom
of thought and the right of private judgment in
matters of conscience direct their course to this happy
country as their last asylum.

Samuel Adams, 1776

Prologue: The population of the English colonies increased amazingly, owing largely to the fertility of a pioneer people. Slaves arrived from Africa in growing numbers in the eighteenth century, and they, too—like the whites—were soon increasing their ranks through their own natural fertility. Immigrants were pouring in from the British Isles and Europe, and although the English language remained predominant, the now-famed melting pot was beginning to bubble. As the population spread, the austerity of the old-time worship weakened, although it was given a temporary revival by the Great Awakening of the 1730s. The rational thought inspired by the European Enlightenment found a ready disciple in Benjamin Franklin, whose sly pokes at religion no doubt helped undermine the dominance of the clergy. Americans began dealing in international trade, straining against the commercial limitations imposed by British imperial rule. A ruling class of sorts existed in all the colonies, although the governing clique in New York received a sharp jolt in the famed Zenger libel case. The ease with which the individual colonial could rise from one social rung to another, quite in contrast with Old World rigidity, foreshadowed the emergence of a mobile, pluralistic society.

A. The Colonial Melting Pot

1. Benjamin Franklin Analyzes the Population (1751)

The baby boom in the English colonies was an object of wonderment. The itinerant Swedish scientist, Peter Kalm, recorded that Mrs. Maria Hazard, who died in her

[1]Jared Sparks, ed., *The Works of Benjamin Franklin* (1840), vol. 2, pp. 313–315.

hundredth year, left a total of five hundred children, grandchildren, great-grandchildren, and great-great-grandchildren. Benjamin Franklin, the incredibly versatile printer, businessman, philosopher, scientist, and diplomat, made the following observations in 1751. In his opinion, why were families so large, white labor so expensive, and slave labor so uneconomical?

Land being thus plenty in America, and so cheap as that a laboring man that understands husbandry can, in a short time, save money enough to purchase a piece of new land sufficient for a plantation, whereon he may subsist a family, such are not afraid to marry. For, if they even look far enough forward to consider how their children, when grown up, are to be provided for, they see that more land is to be had at rates equally easy, all circumstances considered.

Hence marriages in America are more general, and more generally early, than in Europe. And if it is reckoned there that there is but one marriage per annum among one hundred persons, perhaps we may here reckon two; and if in Europe they have but four births to a marriage (many of their marriages being late), we may here reckon eight, of which, if one half grow up, and our marriages are made, reckoning one with another, at twenty years of age, our people must at least be doubled every twenty years.

But notwithstanding this increase, so vast is the territory of North America that it will require many ages to settle it fully. And till it is fully settled, labor will never be cheap here, where no man continues long a laborer for others, but gets a plantation of his own; no man continues long a journeyman to a trade, but goes among those new settlers, and sets up for himself, etc. Hence labor is no cheaper now in Pennsylvania than it was thirty years ago, though so many thousand laboring people have been imported.

The danger therefore of these colonies interfering with their mother country in trades that depend on labor, manufactures, etc., is too remote to require the attention of Great Britain. . . .

It is an ill-grounded opinion that, by the labor of slaves, America may possibly vie in cheapness of manufactures with Britain. The labor of slaves can never be so cheap here as the labor of workingmen is in Britain. Any one may compute it. Interest of money is in the colonies from 6 to 10 percent. Slaves, one with another, cost thirty pounds sterling per head. Reckon then the interest of the first purchase of a slave, the insurance or risk on his life, his clothing and diet, expenses in his sickness and loss of time, loss by his neglect of business (neglect is natural to the man who is not to be benefited by his own care or diligence), expense of a driver to keep him at work, and his pilfering from time to time, almost every slave being by nature a thief, and compare the whole amount with the wages of a manufacturer of iron or wool in England, you will see that labor is much cheaper there than it ever can be by Negroes here.

Why then will Americans purchase slaves? Because slaves may be kept as long as a man pleases, or has occasion for their labor; while hired men are continually leaving their masters (often in the midst of his business) and setting up for themselves.

2. Gottlieb Mittelberger Voyages to Pennsylvania (c. 1750)

In the eighteenth century tens of thousands of Germans, largely from the war-ravaged Rhineland, came to Pennsylvania for economic and social betterment. Often they were lured to the dock by the glib misrepresentations of "soul-traffickers," who received a commission for each victim enticed. Floating down the Rhine past thirty-six customshouses, the immigrants were fleeced at every turn by greedy officials and delayed by as much as six weeks. Then came delays of up to six weeks more in Holland and another six weeks in England, while scanty savings melted away. Many immigrants were exhausted before the beginning of the real ordeal—the seven- to twelve-week voyage. It is here described by a German pastor, Gottlieb Mittelberger, who crossed the Atlantic about 1750 to investigate conditions and to alert the people back home to their peril. His description of "the sale of human beings" at the end of the voyage, though overdrawn (like his description of the voyage itself), is basically sound. Yet he failed to observe that this system, which forced many immigrants into indentured servitude to pay for their passage, also enabled tens of thousands of hard-working immigrants to get a start in America. Why were sickness and death on the voyage so common? In what respects was white indentured servitude similar to black slavery, and in what important respect was it dissimilar?

During the voyage there is on board these ships terrible misery, stench, fumes, horror, vomiting, many kinds of sea-sickness, fever, dysentery, headache, heat, constipation, boils, scurvy, cancer, mouth-rot, and the like, all of which come from old and sharply salted food and meat, also from very bad and foul water, so that many die miserably.

Add to this, want of provisions, hunger, thirst, frost, heat, dampness, anxiety, want, afflictions, and lamentations, together with other trouble, as for example, the lice abound so frightfully, especially on sick people, that they can be scraped off the body. The misery reaches the climax when a gale rages for two or three nights and days, so that every one believes that the ship will go to the bottom with all human beings on board. In such a visitation the people cry and pray most piteously. . . .

Among the healthy, impatience sometimes grows so great and cruel that one curses the other, or himself and the day of his birth, and sometimes come near killing each other. Misery and malice join each other, so that they cheat and rob one another. One always reproaches the other with having persuaded him to undertake the journey. Frequently children cry out against their parents, husbands against their wives and wives against their husbands, brothers and sisters, friends and acquaintances against each other. But most against the soul-traffickers.

Many sigh and cry: "Oh, that I were at home again, and if I had to lie in my pigsty!" Or they say: "O God, if I only had a piece of good bread, or a good fresh drop of water!" Many people whimper, sigh, and cry piteously for their homes; most of them get homesick. Many hundred people necessarily die and perish in such misery, and must be cast into the sea, which drives their relatives, or those who per-

---

[2]Gottlieb Mittelberger, *Journey to Pennsylvania in the Year 1750* . . . (1898), pp. 20–29.

suaded them to undertake the journey, to such despair that it is almost impossible to pacify and console them. . . .

No one can have an idea of the sufferings which women in confinement have to bear with their innocent children on board these ships. Few of this class escape with their lives; many a mother is cast into the water with her child as soon as she is dead. One day, just as we had a heavy gale, a woman in our ship, who was to give birth and could not give birth under the circumstances, was pushed through a loophole [porthole] in the ship and dropped into the sea, because she was far in the rear of the ship and could not be brought forward.

Children from 1 to 7 years rarely survive the voyage; and many a time parents are compelled to see their children miserably suffer and die from hunger, thirst, and sickness, and then to see them cast into the water. I witnessed such misery in no less than thirty-two children in our ship, all of whom were thrown into the sea. The parents grieve all the more since their children find no resting-place in the earth, but are devoured by the monsters of the sea. It is a notable fact that children who have not yet had the measles or smallpox generally get them on board the ship, and mostly die of them.

Often a father is separated by death from his wife and children, or mothers from their little children, or even both parents from their children; and sometimes whole families die in quick succession; so that often many dead persons lie in the berths beside the living ones, especially when contagious diseases have broken out on board the ship. . . .

[Pastor Mittelberger, after describing accidental falls that resulted in cripples or people lost overboard, turns to less serious inconveniences.]

That most of the people get sick is not surprising, because, in addition to all other trials and hardships, warm food is served only three times a week, the rations being very poor and very little. Such meals can hardly be eaten, on account of being so unclean. The water which is served out on the ship is often very black, thick, and full of worms, so that one cannot drink it without loathing, even with the greatest thirst. O surely, one would often give much money at sea for a piece of good bread, or a drink of good water, not to say a drink of good wine, if it were only to be had. I myself experienced that difficulty, I am sorry to say. Towards the end we were compelled to eat the ship's biscuit which had been spoiled long ago, though in a whole biscuit there was scarcely a piece the size of a dollar that had not been full of red worms and spiders' nests. Great hunger and thirst force us to eat and drink everything; but many a one does so at the risk of his life. . . .

At length, when, after a long and tedious voyage, the ships come in sight of land, so that the promontories can be seen, which the people were so eager and anxious to see, all creep from below on deck to see the land from afar, and they weep for joy, and pray and sing, thanking and praising God. The sight of the land makes the people on board the ship, especially the sick and the half dead, alive again, so that their hearts leap within them. They shout and rejoice, and are content to bear their misery in patience, in the hope that they may soon reach the land in safety.

But alas! When the ships have landed at Philadelphia after their long voyage, no one is permitted to leave them, except those who pay for their passage or can give good security. The others, who cannot pay, must remain on board the ships till they are purchased, and are released from the ships by their purchasers. The sick always fare the worst, for the healthy are naturally preferred and purchased first. And so the sick and wretched must often remain on board in front of the city for two or three weeks, and frequently die; whereas many a one, if he could pay his debt and were permitted to leave the ship immediately, might recover and remain alive. . . .

The sale of human beings in the market on board the ship is carried on thus: every day Englishmen, Dutchmen, and High-German people come from the city of Philadelphia and other places, in part from a great distance, say 20, 30, or 40 hours away, and go on board the newly arrived ship that has brought and offers for sale passengers from Europe, and select among the healthy persons such as they deem suitable for their business, and bargain with them how long they will serve for their passage-money, which most of them are still in debt for. When they have come to an agreement, it happens that adult persons bind themselves in writing to serve 3, 4, 5, or 6 years for the amount due by them, according to their age and strength. But very young people, from 10 to 15 years, must serve till they are 21 years old.

Many parents must sell and trade away their children like so many head of cattle; for if their children take the debt upon themselves, the parents can leave the ship free and unrestrained. But as the parents often do not know where and to what people their children are going, it often happens that such parents and children, after leaving the ship, do not see each other again for many years, perhaps no more in all their lives.

When people arrive who cannot make themselves free, but have children under 5 years, the parents cannot free themselves by them; for such children must be given to somebody without compensation to be brought up, and they must serve for their bringing up till they are 21 years old. Children from 5 to 10 years, who pay half price for their passage, viz. 30 florins, must likewise serve for it till they are 21 years of age. They cannot, therefore, redeem their parents by taking the debt of the latter upon themselves. But children above 10 years can take part of their parents' debt upon themselves.

A woman must stand for her husband if he arrives sick, and in like manner a man for his sick wife, and take the debt upon herself or himself, and thus serve 5 to 6 years, not alone for his or her own debt, but also for that of the sick husband or wife. But if both are sick, such persons are sent from the ship to the sick-house, but not until it appears probable that they will find no purchasers. As soon as they are well again they must serve for their passage, or pay if they have means.

It often happens that whole families—husband, wife, and children—are separated by being sold to different purchasers, especially when they have not paid any part of their passage-money.

When a husband or wife has died at sea when the ship has made more than half of her trip, the survivor must pay or serve not only for himself or herself, but also for the deceased. . . .

If some one in this country runs away from his master, who has treated him harshly, he cannot get far. Good provision has been made for such cases, so that a runaway is soon recovered. He who detains or returns a deserter receives a good reward.

If such a runaway has been away from his master one day, he must serve for it as a punishment a week, for a week a month, and for a month half a year. But if the master will not keep the runaway after he has got him back, he may sell him for so many years as he would have to serve him yet.

3. Michel-Guillaume Jean de Crèvecoeur Discovers a New Man (c. 1770)

Michel-Guillaume Jean de Crèvecoeur, a young Frenchman of noble family, served with the French army in Canada from 1758 to 1759. Upon reaching the English colonies in 1759, he traveled widely, married an American woman, and settled down to an idyllic existence on his New York estate, "Pine Hill." A born farmer, he introduced into America a number of plants, including alfalfa. Probably during the decade before 1775, he wrote in English the classic series of essays known as Letters from an American Farmer *(published in 1782). This glowing account was blamed for luring some five hundred French families to the wilds of the Ohio Country, where they perished. What does Crèvecoeur reveal regarding the racial composition of the colonies? What did he regard as the most important factors creating the new American man?*

. . . Whence came all these people?

They are a mixture of English, Scotch, Irish, French, Dutch, Germans, and Swedes. From this promiscuous breed, that race now called Americans have arisen. The Eastern [New England] provinces must indeed be excepted, as being the unmixed descendants of Englishmen. I have heard many wish that they had been more intermixed also. For my part, I am no wisher, and think it much better as it has happened. They exhibit a most conspicuous figure in this great and variegated picture; they too enter for a great share in the pleasing perspective displayed in these thirteen provinces. I know it is fashionable to reflect on them, but I respect them for what they have done; for the accuracy and wisdom with which they have settled their territory; for the decency of their manners; for their early love of letters; their ancient college, the first in this hemisphere;* for their industry, which to me, who am but a farmer, is the criterion of everything. There never was a people, situated as they are, who with so ungrateful a soil have done more in so short a time. . . .

In this great American asylum, the poor of Europe have by some means met together, and in consequence of various causes; to what purpose should they ask one another what countrymen they are? Alas, two-thirds of them had no country. Can a wretch who wanders about, who works and starves, whose life is a continual scene of sore affliction or pinching penury—can that man call England or any other kingdom his country? A country that had no bread for him, whose fields procured him no harvest, who met with nothing but the frowns of the rich, the severity of the laws, with jails and punishments; who owned not a single foot of the extensive surface of this planet? No! urged by a variety of motives, here they came. Everything has tended to regenerate them: new laws, a new mode of living, a new social system. Here they are become men. In Europe they were as so many useless plants, wanting vegetative

---

[3]M. G. J. de Crèvecoeur, *Letters from an American Farmer* (New York: Fox, Duffield & Company, 1904; reprint), pp. 51–56.

*In fact, the Spanish universities in Mexico City and Lima, Peru, antedated Harvard by eighty-five years.

mould, and refreshing showers; they withered, and were mowed down by want, hunger, and war. But now by the power of transplantation, like all other plants, they have taken root and flourished! Formerly they were not numbered in any civil lists of their country, except in those of the poor. Here they rank as citizens.

By what invisible power has this surprising metamorphosis been performed? By that of the laws and that of their industry. The laws, the indulgent laws, protect them as they arrive, stamping on them the symbol of adoption. They receive ample rewards for their labors; these accumulated rewards procure them lands; those lands confer on them the title of freemen, and to that title every benefit is affixed which men can possibly require. . . .

What then is the American, this new man? He is either an European, or the descendant of an European; hence that strange mixture of blood, which you will find in no other country. I could point out to you a family whose grandfather was an Englishman, whose wife was Dutch, whose son married a French woman, and whose present four sons have now four wives of different nations.

He is an American who, leaving behind him all his ancient prejudices and manners, receives new ones from the new mode of life he has embraced, the new government he obeys, and the new rank he holds. He becomes an American by being received in the broad lap of our great *alma mater.* Here individuals of all nations are melted into a new race of men whose labors and posterity will one day cause great changes in the world. Americans are the western pilgrims, who are carrying along with them the great mass of arts, sciences, vigor, and industry which began long since in the East. They will finish the great circle.

The American ought therefore to love this country much better than that wherein either he or his forefathers were born. Here the rewards of his industry follow with equal steps the progress of his labor; his labor is founded on the basis of nature, *self-interest;* can it want a stronger allurement? Wives and children, who before in vain demanded of him a morsel of bread, now, fat and frolicsome, gladly help their father to clear those fields whence exuberant crops are to arise to feed and to clothe them all; without any part being claimed, either by a despotic prince, a rich abbot, or a mighty lord. Here religion demands but little of him: a small voluntary salary to the minister, and gratitude to God. Can he refuse these?

The American is a new man, who acts upon new principles; he must therefore entertain new ideas, and form new opinions. From involuntary idleness, servile dependence, penury, and useless labor, he has passed to toils of a very different nature, rewarded by ample subsistence.

This is an American.

4. The Growth of the Colonial Population (1740–1780)

This table shows the growth and shifting composition of the colonial population in the several decades before independence. What are the principal trends in the

---

[4]Reprinted by permission of The Peters Fraser and Dunlop Group Limited on behalf of R. C. Simmons from *The American Colonies from Settlement to Independence.* Copyright © 1976 by R. C. Simmons.

changing population? How might one account for regional differences in the numbers and makeup of the American people in the colonial era? Why did some areas grow faster than others? To what extent can the subsequent history of the United States be predicted from these figures?

The Thirteen Colonies
Estimated Percentages of Blacks and Whites, 1740–1780

A = Total Population   B = % of Blacks   C = % of Whites

	1740			1760			1780		
	A	B	C	A	B	C	A	B	C
Maine*	—	—	—	—	—	—	49,133	0.93	99.07
New Hampshire	23,256	2.15	97.85	39,093	1.53	98.47	87,802	0.62	99.38
Massachusetts	151,613	2.00	98.00	222,600	2.18	97.82	268,627	1.79	98.21
Rhode Island	25,255	9.53	90.47	45,471	7.63	92.37	52,946	5.04	94.96
Connecticut	89,580	2.90	97.10	142,470	2.65	97.35	206,701	2.85	97.15
New York	63,665	14.13	85.87	117,138	13.94	86.06	210,541	10.00	90.00
New Jersey	51,373	8.50	91.50	93,813	7.00	93.00	139,627	7.49	92.51
Pennsylvania	85,637	2.40	97.60	183,703	2.40	97.60	327,305	2.40	97.60
Delaware	19,870	5.21	94.79	33,250	5.21	94.79	45,385	6.60	93.40
Maryland	116,093	20.70	79.30	162,267	30.20	69.80	245,474	32.80	67.20
Virginia	180,440	33.25	66.75	339,726	41.38	58.62	538,004	41.00	59.00
North Carolina	51,760	21.25	78.75	110,422	30.38	69.62	270,133	33.69	66.31
South Carolina	45,000	66.67	33.33	94,074	60.94	39.06	180,000	53.89	46.11
Georgia	2,021		100.00	9,578	37.36	62.64	56,071	37.15	62.85

*Massachusetts, of which Maine was a part until admitted to the Union as a state in 1820, did not establish a separate administrative district for Maine until the 1770s.

B. The Great Awakening

1. George Whitefield Fascinates Franklin (1739)

The frenzied religious revival that swept the colonies in the 1730s, known as the Great Awakening, featured George Whitefield as one of the Awakeners. Although he was only twenty-five years old when Benjamin Franklin heard him in Philadelphia during the second of Whitefield's seven trips to America, he had already preached with such emotional power in England that crowds would assemble at his church door before daybreak. When orthodox clergymen denied him their pulpits, he

[1]John Bigelow, ed., *Autobiography of Benjamin Franklin* (Philadelphia: J. B. Lippincott & Co., 1868), pp. 251–255.

would speak in the open air, at times to crowds of twenty thousand persons. Franklin, then thirty-six years old and a hardheaded Philadelphia businessman, was skeptical. What does this passage from his famed autobiography, written many years later, reveal about Franklin's character and about the atmosphere of toleration in Philadelphia?

In 1739 arrived among us from Ireland the Reverend Mr. Whitefield, who had made himself remarkable there as an itinerant preacher. He was at first permitted to preach in some of our churches; but the clergy, taking a dislike to him, soon refused him their pulpits, and he was obliged to preach in the fields. The multitudes of all sects and denominations that attended his sermons were enormous, and it was matter of speculation to me, who was one of the number, to observe the extraordinary influence of his oratory on his hearers, and how much they admired and respected him, notwithstanding his common abuse of them, by assuring them they were naturally *half beasts and half devils*. It was wonderful to see the change soon made in the manners of our inhabitants. From being thoughtless or indifferent about religion, it seemed as if all the world were growing religious, so that one could not walk through the town in an evening without hearing psalms sung in different families of every street.

And it being found inconvenient to assemble in the open air, subject to its inclemencies, the building of a house to meet in was no sooner proposed, and persons appointed to receive contributions, but sufficient sums were soon received to procure the ground and erect the building, which was one hundred feet long and seventy broad, about the size of Westminster Hall; and the work was carried on with such spirit as to be finished in a much shorter time than could have been expected. Both house and ground were vested in trustees, expressly for the use of any preacher of any religious persuasion who might desire to say something to the people at Philadelphia; the design in building not being to accommodate any particular sect, but the inhabitants in general; so that even if the Mufti of Constantinople were to send a missionary to preach Mohammedanism to us, he would find a pulpit at his service.

Mr. Whitefield, in leaving us, went preaching all the way through the colonies to Georgia. The settlement of that province had lately been begun, but, instead of being made with hardy, industrious husbandmen, accustomed to labor, the only people fit for such an enterprise, it was with families of broken shopkeepers and other insolvent debtors, many of indolent and idle habits, taken out of the jails, who, being set down in the woods, unqualified for clearing land, and unable to endure the hardships of a new settlement, perished in numbers, leaving many helpless children unprovided for. The sight of their miserable situation inspired the benevolent heart of Mr. Whitefield with the idea of building an Orphan House there, in which they might be supported and educated. Returning northward, he preached up this charity, and made large collections, for his eloquence had a wonderful power over the hearts and purses of his hearers, of which I myself was an instance.

I did not disapprove of the design, but, as Georgia was then destitute of materials and workmen, and it was proposed to send them from Philadelphia at a great expense, I thought it would have been better to have built the house there, and brought the children to it. This I advised, but he was resolute in his first project, rejected my counsel, and I therefore refused to contribute.

I happened soon after to attend one of his sermons, in the course of which I perceived he intended to finish with a collection, and I silently resolved he should get nothing from me. I had in my pocket a handful of copper money, three or four silver dollars, and five pistoles in gold. As he proceeded I began to soften, and concluded to give the coppers. Another stroke of his oratory made me ashamed of that, and determined me to give the silver; and he finished so admirably that I emptied my pocket wholly into the collector's dish, gold and all.

At this sermon there was also one of our club who, being of my sentiments respecting the building in Georgia, and suspecting a collection might be intended, had, by precaution, emptied his pockets before he came from home. Towards the conclusion of the discourse, however, he felt a strong desire to give, and applied to a [Quaker] neighbor, who stood near him, to borrow some money for the purpose. The application was unfortunately to perhaps the only man in the company who had the firmness not to be affected by the preacher. His answer was, "At any other time, Friend Hopkinson, I would lend to thee freely; but not now, for thee seems to be out of thy right senses."

2. Jonathan Edwards Paints the Horrors of Hell (1741)

Jonathan Edwards, a New England Congregational minister, was, like George Whitefield, a Great Awakener. Tall, slender, and delicate, Edwards had a weak voice but a powerful mind. He still ranks as the greatest Protestant theologian ever produced in America. His command of the English language was exceptional, and his vision of hell, peopled with pre-damned infants and others, was horrifying. As he preached hellfire to his Enfield, Connecticut, congregation, there was a great moaning and crying: "What shall I do to be saved? Oh, I am going to hell!" Men and women groveled on the floor or lay inert on the benches. Would Edwards's famous sermon, "Sinners in the Hands of an Angry God," be equally effective today?

The God that holds you over the pit of hell, much as one holds a spider or some loathsome insect over the fire, abhors you, and is dreadfully provoked. His wrath towards you burns like fire; he looks upon you as worthy of nothing else but to be cast into the fire. He is of purer eyes than to bear you in his sight; you are ten thousand times as abominable in his eyes as the most hateful, venomous serpent is in ours.

You have offended him infinitely more than ever a stubborn rebel did his prince, and yet it is nothing but his hand that holds you from falling into the fire every moment. It is to be ascribed to nothing else that you did not go to hell the last night; that you were suffered to awake again in this world, after you closed your

---

[2]Jonathan Edwards, *Works* (Andover, Mass.: Allen, Morrill & Wardwell, 1842), vol. 2, pp. 10–11.

eyes to sleep. And there is no other reason to be given why you have not dropped into hell since you arose in the morning, but that God's hand has held you up. There is no other reason to be given why you have not gone to hell since you have sat here in the house of God provoking his pure eye by your sinful, wicked manner of attending his solemn worship. Yea, there is nothing else that is to be given as a reason why you do not this very moment drop down into hell.

O sinner! consider the fearful danger you are in! It is a great furnace of wrath, a wide and bottomless pit, full of the fire of wrath that you are held over in the hand of that God whose wrath is provoked and incensed as much against you as against many of the damned in hell. You hang by a slender thread, with the flames of Divine wrath flashing about it, and ready every moment to singe it and burn it asunder. . . .

It would be dreadful to suffer this fierceness and wrath of Almighty God one moment; but you must suffer it to all eternity. There will be no end to this exquisite, horrible misery. When you look forward, you shall see along forever a boundless duration before you, which will swallow up your thoughts, and amaze your soul. And you will absolutely despair of ever having any deliverance, any end, any mitigation, any rest at all. You will know certainly that you must wear out long ages, millions of millions of ages in wrestling and conflicting with this Almighty, merciless vengeance. And then when you have so done, when so many ages have actually been spent by you in this manner, you will know that all is but a point [dot] to what remains. So that your punishment will indeed be infinite.

Oh! who can express what the state of a soul in such circumstances is! All that we can possibly say about it gives but a very feeble, faint representation of it. It is inexpressible and inconceivable: for "who knows the power of God's anger"!

How dreadful is the state of those that are daily and hourly in danger of this great wrath and infinite misery! But this is the dismal case of every soul in this congregation that has not been born again, however moral and strict, sober and religious, they may otherwise be. Oh! that you would consider it, whether you be young or old!

There is reason to think that there are many in this congregation, now hearing this discourse, that will actually be the subjects of this very misery to all eternity. We know not who they are, or in what seats they sit, or what thoughts they now have. It may be they are now at ease, and hear all these things without much disturbance, and are now flattering themselves that they are not the persons, promising themselves that they shall escape.

If we knew that there was one person, and but one, in the whole congregation, that was to be the subject of this misery, what an awful thing it would be to think of! If we knew who it was, what an awful sight would it be to see such a person! How might all the rest of the congregation lift up a lamentable and bitter cry over him!

But, alas! instead of one, how many is it likely will remember this discourse in hell! And it would be a wonder, if some that are now present should not be in hell in a very short time, before this year is out. And it would be no wonder if some persons that now sit here in some seats of this meeting-house, in health, and quiet and secure, should be there before tomorrow morning!

C. The Colonial Economy

1. The West Indian Connection (1766)

Serving as a colonial agent in England in 1766, many-sided Benjamin Franklin was summoned to testify about American commerce before a parliamentary committee. What does the following excerpt from his testimony reveal about the economic relationship between the colonies and the mother country, and about the importance of the West Indian trade?

Q. What may be the amount of one year's imports into Pennsylvania from Britain?

A. I have been informed that our merchants compute the imports from Britain to be above 500,000 Pounds.

Q. What may be the amount of the produce of your province exported to Britain?

A. It must be small, as we produce little that is wanted in Britain. I suppose it cannot exceed 40,000 Pounds.

Q. How then do you pay the ballance?

A. The Ballance is paid by our produce carried to the West-Indies, and sold in our own islands, or to the French, Spaniards, Danes and Dutch; by the same carried to other colonies in North-America, as to New-England, Nova-Scotia, Newfoundland, Carolina and Georgia; by the same carried to different parts of Europe, as Spain, Portugal and Italy. In all which places we receive either money, bills of exchange, or commodities that suit for remittance to Britain; which, together with all the profits on the industry of our merchants and mariners, arising in those circuitous voyages, and the freights made by their ships, center finally in Britain, to discharge the ballance, and pay for British manufactures continually used in the province, or sold to foreigners by our traders.

Q. Have you heard of any difficulties lately laid on the Spanish trade?

A. Yes, I have heard that it has been greatly obstructed by some new regulations, and by the English men of war and cutters stationed all along the coast in America.

2. The Pattern of Colonial Commerce (1766)

Gottfried Achenwall was a distinguished German scholar whom Benjamin Franklin visited at Göttingen, Germany, in July 1766. At that time few Germans had any reliable knowledge about America, so Achenwall seized the opportunity to interview the immensely knowledgeable Franklin. What does Achenwall's analysis, as inspired by Franklin, suggest about the colonists' situation in the British imperial system?

---

[1]From *The Papers of Benjamin Franklin,* ed. Leonard W. Labaree (Yale University Press, 1969), vol. 13, p. 133.

[2]From *The Papers of Benjamin Franklin,* ed. Leonard W. Labaree (Yale University Press, 1969), vol. 13, pp. 368–371.

Certainly it will in time be necessary to establish some manufacturers in the colonies. For with the growth of the North American colonies lasting for centuries, Great Britain and Ireland, as islands of limited resources (e.g., their wool production cannot be increased proportionately or without limit) will in the future find it beyond their power to supply from their output, the quantity of goods required by the colonies.

The three largest cities, centers of trade and seaports, in British America, are Boston in New England, New York in the province of that name, and Philadelphia in Pennsylvania. About 1720, Boston was as large as the other two cities together, but since that time New York and Pennsylvania have grown far more than Boston. For in New England there are many seaports, but the other two are the only ports in their respective provinces, as these have only a small coastal area. So both these cities are the common markets for their whole province and grow more in proportion to the province and have the hope in consequence of becoming the largest cities in America. Philadelphia has more than 3,000 houses and more than 20,000 inhabitants. The city is regularly laid out, the streets are all at right angles; they are extended every year and new houses are always being built beyond the first boundary. The houses are almost all of brick, like most of those in London.

All the American colonies have their cities and villages; but Virginia has the fewest villages and only one small city, Williamsburg, where the governor resides and the provincial Assembly and the courts meet. In this province the colonists are scattered and distant from each other, each on its own tobacco plantation. This is because of the nature of the country. Chesapeake Bay runs deep into the land, and many navigable streams flow into it. By these streams the colonists send down their tobacco in barges to the Bay, where the seagoing vessels load it. This transport is the easiest and cheapest, especially for a product taking up as much room as tobacco. Virginia is cut up by as many naturally navigable streams, as Holland by artificial canals.

New York has excellent advantage for the trade with the savages. It ships its goods up the Hudson River, to the city of Albany. Hence they are sent by other streams, and because of waterfalls, here and there partly by land several English miles, on to Oswego on Lake Ontario. Here the fairs for Indian trade are held. Lake Ontario is connected by water through the greater lakes lying inland with the *Obersee* (Lake Superior). The savages easily bring their skins and hides from the interior in their boats to Oswego. In this trade Pennsylvania has no share, as New York would not allow it. On the other hand, the trade of Pennsylvania profits by the commerce of New Jersey, as this by the convenience of the Delaware River is mostly directed to Philadelphia.

The English colonies lack salt and rarely make it for themselves. They import it from Spanish South America. There it is produced naturally, as in the Cape Verde Islands and Senegal. When the tide is high, it flows over the sand banks in certain valleys, and the heat of the sun makes salt. The colonies import it in 50 or 60 ships a year.

The colonies are generally restricted in all their foreign trade, and even more in their shipping in all sorts of ways. Nevertheless the continental colonies particularly maintain a considerable shipping trade of their own. Many products, particularly those for ship building and raw materials suitable for manufactures: mast trees, ship timber, iron, copper ore, hemp, flax, cotton, indigo, tobacco, ginger, tar, pitch, rosin, potash, skins and furs, they may not export. These are reserved for the British realm, must be bought by British merchants, and carried by British ships and sailors. In areas where an English company has the exclusive trade, they may not trade, for example, the East Indies. In 1765, trade also was prohibited with the West Indies colonies of the French and Spanish. But this prohibition had bad results, and has been lifted. To the Portuguese Sugar Islands they may carry all sorts of food stuffs, such as grain, flour, butter, meat, and cattle for butchering, wood and timber for house building and farm use, and in return bring back chiefly molasses, from which rum is made. Trade with the Spanish in America is a mere contraband trade; the Spanish government requires the confiscation of the goods and enforces the law by its coastguard ships. But the colonist risks it because he can bring back specie, which is so rare in the colonies.

Great Britain has now, 1766, established two free ports in the West Indies, one in Jamaica and one in Dominica. Other nations had formerly done so, the French a port in St. Domingo, the Dutch in St. Eustatius, an unproductive island, the Danes in the island of St. Thomas. Great Britain has done so to enjoy the same advantages, and particularly to reduce the contraband trade with the Spanish. Yet there are restrictions on this new arrangement: all foreigners can buy all goods there duty free, but for cash, not in exchange for goods.

That the shipping trade of their own which the colonies carry on, is so important rises partly from the trade referred to with the Spanish and French West Indies, partly from the intercolonial trade by exchange of their marketable over-production, especially between the continental colonies and the English Sugar Islands, partly from their great off-shore fisheries.

After the West Indies, the chief trade of the colonies goes to the regions lying south of Cape Finisterre. They traffic directly (in their own products and in their own ships) to Africa, the Canaries, and other islands in the ocean; as also in their own wares but in British ships to Portugal, Cadiz, Malaga, Marseilles, Leghorn, and Naples. They can in this way even trade to Turkey, but up to now have not. Hither they export their surplus, especially fish, grain, and flour, timber, also sugar and rice, and bring back their price partly in hard cash. The trade with Portugal has special restrictions. They can export their products there, but cannot bring back Portuguese wine for that must be carried by way of England. So they usually in return bring back salt as ballast. Sugar is the only product which the colonist can export as his own property, though in British ships, to all Europe and sell directly.

The greatest part of American goods are taken by the English, as they ship their manufactures to America. In general, no foreign nation is permitted to go to the colonies to buy their products and carry them away, much less to send their own goods over; both export and import remain a privilege for British subjects or especially for inhabitants of England. The import of English goods into the colonies increases as they grow. England sells annually to the colonies in North America and the West Indies more than three million pounds sterling of its own products, chiefly manufactures, and including Scotland and Ireland over five million pounds sterling. . . .

D. The Shoots of Democracy

1. The Epochal Zenger Trial (1735)

William Cosby, a hotheadedly incompetent New York governor, peremptorily re-moved the chief justice of the colony and substituted a stooge, young James Delancey. New Yorkers of the "popular party" decided to strike back by supporting the New-York Weekly Journal, *edited by John Peter Zenger, a struggling printer who had ear-lier come from Germany as an indentured servant. Zenger's attacks on Governor Cosby brought on a famous trial for seditious libel. The outlook seemed dark after Zenger's two attorneys were summarily disbarred. But at the crucial moment An-drew Hamilton, an aging but eminent Philadelphia lawyer, put in a surprise ap-pearance as defense counsel. At the outset he seemingly gave away his case when he admitted that Zenger had published the alleged libels, but he contended that since they were true, they were not libelous. The accepted law was that a libel was a libel, regardless of its truth. In the account excerpted here, Zenger describes his defense by Hamilton and the outcome of the trial. How did Hamilton's defense contribute to the development of American democracy?*[1]

Mr. Attorney. . . . The case before the court is whether Mr. Zenger is guilty of libel-ing His Excellency the Governor of New York, and indeed the whole adminis-tration of the government. Mr. Hamilton has confessed the printing and publishing, and I think nothing is plainer than that the words in the information [indictment] are scandalous, and tend to sedition, and to disquiet the minds of the people of this province. And if such papers are not libels, I think it may be said there can be no such thing as a libel.

Mr. Hamilton. May it please Your Honor, I cannot agree with Mr. Attorney. For though I freely acknowledge that there are such things as libels, yet I must in-sist, at the same time, that what my client is charged with is not a libel. And I ob-served just now that Mr. Attorney, in defining a libel, made use of the words "scandalous, seditious, and tend to disquiet the people." But (whether with de-sign or not I will not say) he omitted the word "false."

Mr. Attorney. I think I did not omit the word "false." But it has been said already that it may be a libel, notwithstanding it may be true.

Mr. Hamilton. In this I must still differ with Mr. Attorney; for I depend upon it, we are to be tried upon this information now before the court and jury, and to which we have pleaded not guilty, and by it we are charged with printing and publishing a certain false, malicious, seditious, and scandalous libel. This word "false" must have some meaning, or else how came it there? . . .

Mr. Chief Justice [Delancey]. You cannot be admitted, Mr. Hamilton, to give the truth of a libel in evidence. A libel is not to be justified; for it is nevertheless a libel that it is true [i.e., the fact that it is true makes it nonetheless a libel].

Mr. Hamilton. I am sorry the court has so soon resolved upon that piece of law; I expected first to have been heard to the point. I have not in all my reading met

---

[1] J. P. Zenger, *Zenger's Own Story* (1736; reprint Columbia, Mo.: Press of the Crippled Turtle, 1954), pp. 20–41, passim.

with an authority that says we cannot be admitted to give the truth in evidence, upon an information for a libel.

Mr. Chief Justice. The law is clear, that you cannot justify a libel. . . .

Mr. Hamilton. I thank Your Honor. Then, gentlemen of the jury, it is to you we must now appeal, for witnesses, to the truth of the facts we have offered, and are denied the liberty to prove. And let it not seem strange that I apply myself to you in this manner. I am warranted so to do both by law and reason.

The law supposes you to be summoned out of the neighborhood where the fact [crime] is alleged to be committed; and the reason of your being taken out of the neighborhood is because you are supposed to have the best knowledge of the fact that is to be tried. And were you to find a verdict against my client, you must take upon you to say the papers referred to in the information, and which we acknowledge we printed and published, are false, scandalous, and seditious. But of this I can have no apprehension. You are citizens of New York; you are really what the law supposes you to be, honest and lawful men. And, according to my brief, the facts which we offer to prove were not committed in a corner; they are notoriously known to be true; and therefore in your justice lies our safety. And as we are denied the liberty of giving evidence to prove the truth of what we have published, I will beg leave to lay it down, as a standing rule in such cases, that the suppressing of evidence ought always to be taken for the strongest evidence; and I hope it will have that weight with you. . . .

I hope to be pardoned, sir, for my zeal upon this occasion. It is an old and wise caution that when our neighbor's house is on fire, we ought to take care of our own. For though, blessed be God, I live in a government [Pennsylvania] where liberty is well understood, and freely enjoyed, yet experience has shown us all (I'm sure it has to me) that a bad precedent in one government is soon set up for an authority in another. And therefore I cannot but think it mine, and every honest man's duty, that (while we pay all due obedience to men in authority) we ought at the same time to be upon our guard against power, wherever we apprehend that it may affect ourselves or our fellow subjects.

I am truly very unequal to such an undertaking on many accounts. And you see I labor under the weight of many years, and am borne down with great infirmities of body. Yet old and weak as I am, I should think it my duty, if required, to go to the utmost part of the land, where my service could be of any use, in assisting to quench the flame of prosecutions upon informations, set on foot by the government, to deprive a people of the right of remonstrating (and complaining too) of the arbitrary attempts of men in power. Men who injure and oppress the people under their administration provoke them to cry out and complain; and then make that very complaint the foundation for new oppressions and prosecutions. I wish I could say there were no instances of this kind.

But to conclude. The question before the court and you, gentlemen of the jury, is not of small nor private concern. It is not the cause of a poor printer, nor of New York alone, which you are now trying. No! It may, in its consequence, affect every freeman that lives under a British government on the main[land] of America. It is the best cause. It is the cause of liberty. And I make no doubt but your upright conduct, this day, will not only entitle you to the love and esteem of your fellow citizens; but every man who prefers freedom to a life of slavery will bless and honor you, as men who have baffled the attempt of tyranny, and, by an impartial and uncorrupt verdict, have laid a noble foundation for securing to ourselves, our posterity, and our neighbors, that to which nature and the laws of our country have given us a right—the liberty both of exposing and opposing arbitrary power (in these parts of the world, at least) by speaking and writing truth. . . .

The jury withdrew, and in a small time returned, and being asked by the clerk whether they were agreed of their verdict, and whether John Peter Zenger was guilty of printing and publishing the libels in the information mentioned, they answered by Thomas Hunt, their foreman, "Not guilty." Upon which there were three huzzas in the hall, which was crowded with people, and the next day I was discharged from my imprisonment.

[The jurors, who might have suffered fines and imprisonment, were guilty of "bad law," for at that time they had no legal alternative to finding Zenger guilty. But the trial, which was widely publicized at home and abroad, provided a setback for judicial tyranny, a partial triumph for freedom of the press, a gain for the privilege of criticizing public officials, and a boost to the ideal of liberty generally. Andrew Hamilton, in truth, was contending for the law as it should be—and as it ultimately became. Not for many years, however, did the two principles for which he argued become accepted practice in England and America: (1) the admissibility of evidence as to the truth of an alleged libel, and (2) the right of the jury to judge the libelous nature of the alleged libel.]

2. Crèvecoeur Finds a Perfect Society (c. 1770)

Crèvecoeur, the happy Frenchman dwelling on a New York farm before the Revolution (see earlier, p. 87), wrote in glowing terms of the almost classless society developing in the colonies. Can you reconcile his statements with the existence of slavery and indentured servitude, a planter aristocracy, and a tax-supported church?

He [the English traveler to America] is arrived on a new continent; a modern society offers itself to his contemplation, different from what he had hitherto seen. It is not composed, as in Europe, of great lords who possess everything, and of a herd of people who have nothing. Here are no aristocratical families, no courts, no kings, no bishops, no ecclesiastical dominion, no invisible power giving to a few a very visible one; no great manufacturers employing thousands, no great refinements of luxury. The rich and the poor are not so far removed from each other as they are in Europe.

Some few towns excepted, we are all tillers of the earth, from Nova Scotia to West Florida. We are a people of cultivators, scattered over an immense territory, communicating with each other by means of good roads and navigable rivers, united by the silken bands of mild government, all respecting the laws, without

---

[2]M. G. J. de Crèvecoeur, *Letters from an American Farmer* (New York: Fox, Duffield & Company, 1904; reprint), pp. 49–50.

dreading their power, because they are equitable. We are all animated with the spirit of an industry which is unfettered and unrestrained, because each person works for himself.

If he [the English visitor] travels through our rural districts, he views not the hostile castle and the haughty mansion, contrasted with the clay-built hut and miserable cabin, where cattle and men help to keep each other warm, and dwell in meanness, smoke, and indigence. A pleasing uniformity of decent competence appears throughout our habitations. The meanest of our log-houses is a dry and comfortable habitation. Lawyer or merchant are the fairest titles our towns afford; that of a farmer is the only appellation of the rural inhabitants of our country. It must take some time ere he can reconcile himself to our dictionary, which is but short in words of dignity and names of honor.

There, on a Sunday, he sees a congregation of respectable farmers and their wives, all clad in neat homespun, well mounted, or riding in their own humble wagons. There is not among them an esquire, saving the unlettered magistrate. There he sees a parson as simple as his flock, a farmer who does not riot on the labor of others. We have no princes, for whom we toil, starve, and bleed: we are the most perfect society now existing in the world. Here man is free as he ought to be; nor is this pleasing equality so transitory as many others are.

Thought Provokers

1. Compare and contrast social conditions in the New World with those in the Old, and explain why the New World had certain advantages. In what ways did the composition of colonial society foreshadow the social structure of the modern United States?
2. Compare and contrast religion in colonial times with religion today. Did the threat of hell-fire promote better morals? Reconcile the wrathful Old Testament God of Jonathan Edwards with the New Testament concept "God is love."
3. In what ways did British imperial regulations work to the advantage of the American colonials? to their disadvantage?
4. How can one reconcile the case of Zenger with the classless society described by Crèvecoeur? Can the truth be libel today?

6

The Duel
for North America,
1608–1763

The most momentous and far-reaching question ever
brought to issue on this continent was: Shall France
remain here or shall she not?

Francis Parkman, 1884

Prologue: French exploration of North America penetrated deeply into Canada
and the Mississippi Valley. At first there was elbow room for both the French and
the English, but wars that were ignited in Europe spread to the New World and involved the colonials of both nations in a series of bloody clashes: King William's
War (1689–1697), Queen Anne's War (1702–1713), King George's War (1744–1748),
and the French and Indian War (1754–1763). Continuing rivalry between the English
colonists and the French traders gradually became intense, and the showdown came
in 1754 in the wilds of the Ohio Valley, where young George Washington's tiny
army of Virginians was forced to surrender. The French and Indian War (called the
Seven Years' War in Europe) thus began inauspiciously for the British, and continued disastrously for them. In 1755 General Edward Braddock's army was almost
wiped out near what is now Pittsburgh. At length a new prime minister, William Pitt,
infused life into the flagging cause. In 1759 Quebec fell to the heroic Wolfe, and the
next year Montreal capitulated. By the Treaty of 1763 France was completely and
permanently ejected from the mainland of North America.

A. The Development of New France

1. Father Isaac Jogues Endures Tortures (1642)

*The Catholic (Jesuit) missionaries in French Canada, among other activities, estab-
lished a mission among the two thousand or so disease-ridden Huron Indians of the
Lake Huron area. Father Isaac Jogues, returning from Quebec to this spiritual vine-
yard with two French associates and a small band of Huron Indians, was captured*

---

[1]New-York Historical Society, *Collections,* Second Series (1857), vol. 3, part 1, pp. 177–204, passim.

in 1642 by a hostile Mohawk (Iroquois) raiding party. He here relates his harrowing experiences to his superiors. As this part of the narrative begins, Father Jogues has just been captured, and one of his French associates (Couture) is being tortured. What is Father Jogues's attitude toward his captors? toward his fellow captives?

When I beheld him [Couture] thus bound and naked, I could not contain myself, but, leaving my keepers, rushed through the midst of the savages who had brought him; embraced him most tenderly; exhorted him to offer all this to God for himself, and those at whose hands he suffered. They at first looked on in wonder at my proceeding; then, as if recollecting themselves, and gathering all their rage, they fell upon me, and with their fists, thongs, and clubs beat me till I fell senseless. Two of them then dragged me back to where I had been before; and scarcely had I begun to breathe when some others, attacking me, tore out, by biting, almost all my nails, and crunched my two forefingers with their teeth, giving me intense pain. The same was done to René Goupil. . . .

We were twenty-two; three had been killed. By the favor of God our sufferings on that march, which lasted thirteen days, were indeed great: hunger and heat and menaces, the savage fury of the Indians, the intense pain of our untended and now putrefying wounds, which actually swarmed with worms. No trial, however, came harder upon me than to see them [the Iroquois] five or six days after approach us, jaded with the march, and, in cold blood, with minds in no wise excited by passion, pluck out our hair and beard and drive their [finger]nails, which are always very sharp, deep into parts most tender and sensitive to the slightest impression.

But this was outward; my internal sufferings affected me still more when I beheld that funeral procession of doomed [Indian] Christians pass before my eyes, among them five old converts, the main pillars of the infant Huron Church. Indeed I ingenuously admit that I was again and again unable to withhold my tears, mourning over their lot and that of my other companions, and full of anxious solicitude for the future. For I beheld the way to the Christian faith closed by these Iroquois on the Hurons and countless other nations, unless they were checked by some seasonable dispensation of Divine Providence. . . .

At last, on the eve of the Assumption of the Blessed Virgin, we reached the first village of the Iroquois. I thank our Lord Jesus Christ that on the day when the whole Christian world exults in the glory of his Mother's Assumption into heaven, he called us to some small share and fellowship of his sufferings and cross. Indeed we had, during the journey, always foreseen that it would be a sad and bitter day for us. It would have been easy for René and me to escape that day and the flames, for, being often unbound and at a distance from our guards, we might, in the darkness of night, have struck off from the road, and even though we should never reach our countrymen, we would at least meet a less cruel death in the woods. He constantly refused to do this, and I was resolved to suffer all that could befall me, rather than forsake in death Frenchmen and Christian Hurons, depriving them of the consolation which a priest can afford. . . .

[Father Jogues endured further tortures, including the cutting off of one thumb, but even so he managed quietly to baptize several Indian children, "two with raindrops gathered from the leaves of a stalk of Indian corn given us to chew. . . ." He

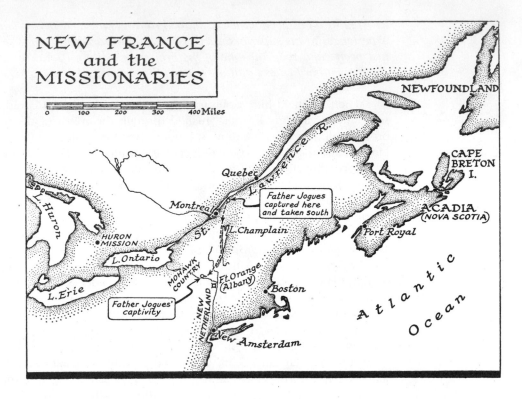

witnessed the brutal tomahawking of his French colleague René Goupil, and was made a slave by his captors.]

Mindful of the character imposed upon me by God, I began with modesty to discourse with them [Iroquois] of the adoration of one only God; of the observance of his commandments; of heaven, hell, and the other mysteries of our faith, as fully as I was able. At first, indeed, they listened; but when they saw me constantly recur to these things, and especially when the chase did not meet with the desired success, then they declared that I was a demon who caused them to take so little game. . . .

How often on the stately trees of the forest did I carve the most sacred name of Jesus, that, seeing it, the demons might fly, who tremble when they hear it! How often, too, did I not strip off the bark, to form the most holy cross of the Lord, that the foe might fly before it. . . .

Although I could in all probability escape either through the Europeans or the Indian nations around us did I wish to fly, yet on this cross to which our Lord has nailed me, beside himself, am I resolved by his grace to live and die. For who in my absence would console the French captives? who absolve the penitent? who remind the christened Huron of his duty? who instruct the prisoners constantly brought in? who baptize them dying, encourage them in their torments? who cleanse the infants in the saving waters? who provide for the salvation of the dying adult, the instruction of those in health? . . .

[After a year of slavery in central New York, Father Jogues escaped to the Dutch in New Netherland, and then sailed to France, where he was greeted as one raised

from the dead. The queen summoned him to an audience, and the Pope, as a special dispensation, granted him permission to celebrate mass with mutilated hands. Jogues, however, eager to continue his work of conversion among the unregenerate Mohawks, returned in 1646. He was promptly tortured, then tomahawked. In 1930 Pope Pius XI canonized him.]

2. A Swede Depicts the Indian Trade (1749)

Peter Kalm, a noted Swedish botanist then in his early thirties, was sent on a scientific expedition to America in 1748–1751. His primary purpose was to discover seeds and plants that could profitably be adapted to the rigorous climate of Sweden. Alert, open-minded, and energetic, he recorded in his journal a gold mine of information, ranging in subject from the vocal cords of bullfrogs to the shortness of women's skirts in Canada. He found in Benjamin Franklin a kindred scientific spirit, and while in New Jersey he not only occupied the pulpit of a deceased Swedish pastor but married his widow as well. In Kalm's account of the fur trade in Canada, what are the most surprising aspects of the Native Americans' sense of values, and the most significant impact of whites on Indian culture?

Indian Trade. The French in Canada carry on a great trade with the Indians; and though it was formerly the only trade of this extensive country, its inhabitants were considerably enriched by it. At present they have, besides the Indian goods, several other articles which are exported. The Indians in this neighborhood [Montreal], who go hunting in winter like the other Indian nations, commonly bring their furs and skins to sell in the neighboring French towns; however, this is not sufficient. The red men who live at a greater distance never come to Canada at all; and lest they should bring their goods to the English, or the English go to them, the French are obliged to undertake journeys and purchase the Indian goods in the country of the natives. This trade is carried on chiefly at Montreal, and a great number of young and old men every year undertake long and troublesome voyages for that purpose, carrying with them such goods as they know the Indians like and want. It is not necessary to take money on such a journey, as the Indians do not value it; and indeed I think the French who go on these journeys scarcely ever take a sol or penny with them.

Goods Sold to the Natives. I will now enumerate the chief goods which the French carry with them for this trade, and which have a good sale among the Indians:

1. *Muskets, powder, shot, and balls.* The Europeans have taught the Indians in their neighborhood the use of firearms, and so they have laid aside their bows and arrows, which were formerly their only arms, and use muskets. If the Europeans should now refuse to supply the natives with muskets, they would starve to death, as almost all their food consists of the flesh of the animals which they hunt; or they would be irritated to such a degree as to attack the colonists. The savages have hitherto never tried to make muskets or similar firearms, and their great indolence does

---

[2]A. B. Benson, ed., *The America of 1750: Peter Kalm's Travels in North America* (New York: Wilson-Erickson, Inc., 1937), vol. 2, pp. 518–522.

not even allow them to mend those muskets which they have. They leave this entirely to the settlers.

When the Europeans came into North America, they were very careful not to give the Indians any firearms. But in the wars between the French and English, each party gave their Indian allies firearms in order to weaken the force of the enemy. The French lay the blame upon the Dutch settlers in Albany, saying that the latter began in 1642 to give their Indians firearms, and taught the use of them in order to weaken the French. The inhabitants of Albany, on the contrary, assert that the French first introduced this custom, as they would have been too weak to resist the combined force of the Dutch and English in the colonies. Be this as it may, it is certain that the Indians buy muskets from the white men, and know at present better how to make use of them than some of their teachers. It is likewise certain that the colonists gain considerably by their trade in muskets and ammunition.

2. a. *Pieces of white cloth,* or of a coarse uncut material. The Indians constantly wear such cloth, wrapping it round their bodies. Sometimes they hang it over their shoulders; in warm weather they fasten the pieces round the middle; and in cold weather they put them over the head. Both their men and women wear these pieces of cloth, which have commonly several blue or red stripes on the edge.

b. *Blue or red cloth.* Of this the Indian women make their skirts, which reach only to their knees. They generally choose the blue color.

c. *Shirts and shifts of linen.* As soon as an Indian, either man or woman, has put on a shirt, he (or she) never washes it or strips it off till it is entirely worn out.

d. *Pieces of cloth,* which they wrap round their legs instead of stockings, like the Russians.

3. *Hatchets, knives, scissors, needles, and flint.* These articles are now common among the Indians. They all get these tools from the Europeans, and consider the hatchets and knives much better than those which they formerly made of stone and bone. The stone hatchets of the ancient Indians are very rare in Canada.

4. *Kettles of copper or brass,* sometimes tinned on the inside. In these the Indians now boil all their meat, and they produce a very large demand for this ware. They formerly made use of earthen or wooden pots, into which they poured water, or whatever else they wanted to boil, and threw in red hot stones to make it boil. They do not want iron boilers because they cannot be easily carried on their continual journeys, and would not bear such falls and knocks as their kettles are subject to.

5. *Earrings* of different sizes, commonly of brass, and sometimes of tin. They are worn by both men and women, though the use of them is not general.

6. *Cinnabar.* With this they paint their face, shirt, and several parts of the body. They formerly made use of a reddish earth, which is to be found in the country; but, as the Europeans brought them vermilion, they thought nothing was comparable to it in color. Many persons told me that they had heard their fathers mention that the first Frenchmen who came over here got a heap of furs for three times as much cinnabar as would lie on the tip of a knife.

7. *Verdigris,* to paint their faces green. For the black color they make use of the soot off the bottom of their kettles, and daub the whole face with it.

8. *Looking glasses.* The Indians like these very much and use them chiefly when they wish to paint themselves. The men constantly carry their looking glasses

with them on all their journeys; but the women do not. The men, upon the whole, are more fond of dressing than the women.

9. *Burning glasses.* These are excellent utensils in the opinion of the Indians because they serve to light the pipe without any trouble, which pleases an indolent Indian very much.

10. *Tobacco* is bought by the northern Indians, in whose country it will not grow. The southern Indians always plant as much of it as they want for their own consumption. Tobacco has a great sale among the northern Indians, and it has been observed that the further they live to the northward, the more tobacco they smoke.

11. *Wampum,* or as it is here called, *porcelain.* It is made of a particular kind of shell and turned into little short cylindrical beads, and serves the Indians for money and ornament.

12. *Glass beads,* of a small size, white or other colors. The Indian women know how to fasten them in their ribbons, bags, and clothes.

13. *Brass and steel wire,* for several kinds of work.

14. *Brandy,* which the Indians value above all other goods that can be brought them; nor have they anything, though ever so dear to them, which they would not give away for this liquor. But on account of the many irregularities which are caused by the use of brandy, the sale of it has been prohibited under severe penalties; however, they do not always pay implicit obedience to this order.

These are the chief goods which the French carry to the Indians and they do a good business among them. . . .

It is inconceivable what hardships the people in Canada must undergo on their hunting journeys. Sometimes they must carry their goods a great way by land. Frequently they are abused by the Indians, and sometimes they are killed by them. They often suffer hunger, thirst, heat, and cold, and are bitten by gnats, and exposed to the bites of poisonous snakes and other dangerous animals and insects. These destroy a great part of the youth in Canada, and prevent the people from growing old. By this means, however, they become such brave soldiers, and so inured to fatigue, that none of them fears danger or hardships. Many of them settle among the Indians far from Canada, marry Indian women, and never come back again.

B. The French and Indian War

1. Benjamin Franklin Characterizes General Edward Braddock (1755)

Once the French and Indian War had begun, the British aimed their main thrust of 1755 at Fort Duquesne, on the present site of Pittsburgh. Their commander was General Edward Braddock, a sixty-two-year-old veteran of European battlefields. Transportation over uncut roads from Virginia was but one of the many difficulties facing the invaders, and Benjamin Franklin won laurels by rounding up 150 wagons.

[1]John Bigelow, ed., *Autobiography of Benjamin Franklin* (Philadelphia: J. B. Lippincott & Co., 1868), pp. 309–313.

*Within about ten miles of Fort Duquesne, Braddock's vanguard of some 1,200 offi-
cers and men encountered an advancing force of about 250 French and 600 Indians. Both sides were surprised, but the French, at first driven back, rallied and
attacked the flanks of the crowded redcoats from nearby ravines. In Franklin's account, written some sixteen years after the event, who or what is alleged to have been
responsible for the disaster?*

This general [Braddock] was, I think, a brave man, and might probably have
made a figure as a good officer in some European war. But he had too much self-
confidence, too high an opinion of the validity of regular troops, and too mean a
one of both Americans and Indians. George Croghan, our Indian interpreter, joined
him on his march with one hundred of those people, who might have been of great
use to his army as guides, scouts, etc., if he had treated them kindly. But he slighted
and neglected them, and they gradually left them.

In conversation with him one day, he was giving me some account of his intended progress. "After taking Fort Duquesne," says he, "I am to proceed to [Fort]
Niagara; and, having taken that, to [Fort] Frontenac, if the season will allow time; and
I suppose it will, for Duquesne can hardly detain me above three or four days; and
then I see nothing that can obstruct my march to Niagara."

Having before revolved in my mind the long line his army must make in their
march by a very narrow road, to be cut for them through the woods and bushes,
and also what I had read of a former defeat of 1,500 French who invaded the Iroquois country, I had conceived some doubts and some fears for the event of the
campaign. But I ventured only to say, "To be sure, sir, if you arrive well before
Duquesne, with these fine troops, so well provided with artillery, that place, not yet
completely fortified, and as we hear with no very strong garrison, can probably
make but a short resistance. The only danger I apprehend of obstruction to your
march is from ambuscades of Indians, who, by constant practice, are dexterous in
laying and executing them; and the slender line, near four miles long, which your
army must make, may expose it to be attacked by surprise in its flanks, and to be cut
like a thread into several pieces, which, from their distance, cannot come up in time
to support each other."

He smiled at my ignorance, and replied, "These savages may, indeed, be a formidable enemy to your raw American militia, but upon the King's regular and disciplined troops, sir, it is impossible they should make any impression." I was
conscious of an impropriety in my disputing with a military man in matters of his
profession, and said no more.

The enemy, however, did not take the advantage of his army which I apprehended its long line of march exposed it to, but let it advance without interruption
till within nine miles of the place; and then, when more in a body (for it had just
passed a river, where the front had halted till all were come over), and in a more
open part of the woods than any it had passed, attacked its advanced guard by a
heavy fire from behind trees and bushes, which was the first intelligence the General had of an enemy's being near him. This guard being disordered, the General
hurried the troops up to their assistance, which was done in great confusion,
through wagons, baggage, and cattle; and presently the fire came upon their flank.
The officers, being on horseback, were more easily distinguished, picked out as

marks, and fell very fast; and the soldiers were crowded together in a huddle, having or hearing no orders, and standing to be shot at till two-thirds of them were killed; and then, being seized with a panic, the whole fled with precipitation.

The wagoners took each a horse out of his team and scampered. Their example was immediately followed by others; so that all the wagons, provisions, artillery, and stores were left to the enemy. The General, being wounded, was brought off with difficulty; his secretary, Mr. Shirley, was killed by his side; and out of 86 officers, 63 were killed or wounded, and 714 men killed out of 1,100. . . .

Captain Orme, who was one of the General's aides-de-camp, and, being grievously wounded, was brought off with him and continued with him to his death, which happened in a few days, told me that he was totally silent all the first day, and at night only said, "Who would have thought it?" That he was silent again the following day, saying only at last, "We shall better know how to deal with them another time"; and died in a few minutes after.

2. A Frenchman Reports Braddock's Defeat (1755)

An anonymous Frenchman, presumably stationed at Fort Duquesne, sent the following report of the battle home to Paris. In what important respects does it differ from Franklin's account just given? Where the two versions conflict, which is to be accorded the more credence? Why? What light does this report cast on the legend that Braddock was ambushed?

M. de Contrecoeur, captain of infantry, Commandant of Fort Duquesne, on the Ohio, having been informed that the English were taking up arms in Virginia for the purpose of coming to attack him, was advised, shortly afterwards, that they were on the march. He dispatched scouts, who reported to him faithfully their progress. On the 7th instant he was advised that their army, consisting of 3,000 regulars from Old England, were within six leagues [eighteen miles] of this fort.

That officer employed the next day in making his arrangements; and on the 9th detached M. de Beaujeu, seconded by Messrs. Dumas and de Lignery, all three captains, together with 4 lieutenants, 6 ensigns, 20 cadets, 100 soldiers, 100 Canadians, and 600 Indians, with orders to lie in ambush at a favorable spot, which he had reconnoitred the previous evening. The detachment, before it could reach its place of destination, found itself in presence of the enemy within three leagues of that fort.

M. de Beaujeu, finding his ambush had failed, decided on an attack. This he made with so much vigor as to astonish the enemy, who were waiting for us in the best possible order; but their artillery, loaded with grape[shot]. . . , having opened its fire, our men gave way in turn. The Indians, also frightened by the report of the cannon, rather than by any damage it could inflict, began to yield, when M. de Beaujeu was killed.

M. Dumas began to encourage his detachment. He ordered the officers in command of the Indians to spread themselves along the wings so as to take the enemy

²E. B. O'Callaghan, ed., *Documents Relative to the Colonial History of the State of New York* (Albany, N.Y.: Weed, Parsons, Printers, 1858), vol. 10, pp. 303–304.

in flank, whilst he, M. de Lignery, and the other officers who led the French, were attacking them in front. This order was executed so promptly that the enemy, who were already shouting their "Long live the King," thought now only of defending themselves.

The fight was obstinate on both sides and success long doubtful; but the enemy at last gave way. Efforts were made, in vain, to introduce some sort of order in their retreat. The whoop of the Indians, which echoed through the forest, struck terror into the hearts of the entire enemy. The rout was complete. We remained in possession of the field with six brass twelves and sixes [cannon], four howitz-carriages of fifty, eleven small royal grenade mortars, all their ammunition, and, generally, their entire baggage.

Some deserters, who have come in since, have told us that we had been engaged with only 2000 men, the remainder of the army being four leagues further off. These same deserters have informed us that the enemy were retreating to Virginia, and some scouts, sent as far as the height of land, have confirmed this by reporting that the thousand men who were not engaged had been equally panic-striken, and abandoned both provisions and ammunition on the way. On this intelligence, a detachment was dispatched after them, which destroyed and burnt everything that could be found.

The enemy have left more than 1000 men on the field of battle. They have lost a great portion of the artillery and ammunition, provisions, as also their general, whose name was Mr. Braddock, and almost all their officers. We have had 3 officers killed; 2 officers and 2 cadets wounded. Such a victory, so entirely unexpected, seeing the inequality of the forces, is the fruit of M. Dumas' experience, and of the activity and valor of the officers under his command.

3. Francis Parkman Analyzes the Conflict (1884)

Francis Parkman (1823–1893), the partially blind and nervously afflicted Boston historian, produced the classic multivolume epic of the struggle between England and France for supremacy in North America. Determined to absorb local color, he ranged widely by canoe and on foot over the region about which he wrote. Although he is best known for his descriptive powers, his analytical talents are brilliantly revealed in these observations following his account of the surrender of Montreal, the last French stronghold, in 1760. Why did the French hold out as long as they did? Why did the English seem inept?

Half the continent had changed hands at the scratch of a pen. Governor Bernard, of Massachusetts, proclaimed a day of thanksgiving for the great event, and the Boston newspapers recount how the occasion was celebrated with a parade of the cadets and other volunteer corps, a grand dinner in Faneuil Hall, music, bonfires, illuminations, firing of cannon, and, above all, by sermons in every church of the province; for the heart of early New England always found voice through her pulpits. . . .

---

[3]Francis Parkman, *Montcalm and Wolfe* (Boston: Little, Brown and Company, 1884; 1899 reprint), vol. 2, pp. 391–396, passim.

On the American continent the war was ended, and the British colonists breathed for a space, as they drifted unwittingly towards a deadlier strife. They had learned hard and useful lessons. Their mutual jealousies and disputes, the quarrels of their governors and assemblies, the want of any general military organization, and the absence, in most of them, of military habits, joined to narrow views of their own interest, had unfitted them to the last degree for carrying on offensive war. Nor were the British troops sent for their support remarkable in the beginning for good discipline or efficient command.

When hostilities broke out, the army of Great Britain was so small as to be hardly worth the name. A new one had to be created; and thus the inexperienced [Governor] Shirley [of Massachusetts] and the incompetent [Earl of] Loudon, with the futile [Prime Minister] Newscastle behind them, had, besides their own incapacity, the disadvantage of raw troops and half-formed officers; while against them stood an enemy who, though weak in numbers, was strong in a centralized military organization, skillful leaders armed with untrammeled and absolute authority, practiced soldiers, and a population not only brave, but in good part inured to war.

The nature of the country was another cause that helped to protract the contest. "Geography," says Von Moltke, "is three-fourths of military science"; and never was the truth of his words more fully exemplified. Canada was fortified with vast outworks of defense in the savage forests, marshes, and mountains that encompassed her, where the thoroughfares were streams choked with fallen trees and obstructed by cataracts. Never was the problem of moving troops, encumbered with baggage and artillery, a more difficult one. The question was less how to fight the enemy than how to get at him. If a few practicable roads had crossed this broad tract of wilderness, the war would have been shortened and its character changed.

From these and other reasons, the numerical superiority of the English was to some extent made unavailing. This superiority, though exaggerated by French writers, was nevertheless immense, if estimated by the number of men called to arms. But only a part of these could be employed in offensive operations. The rest garrisoned forts and blockhouses and guarded the far reach of frontier from Nova Scotia to South Carolina, where a wily enemy, silent and secret as fate, choosing their own time and place of attack, and striking unawares at every unguarded spot, compelled thousands of men, scattered at countless points of defense, to keep unceasing watch against a few hundred savage marauders. Full half the levies of the colonies, and many of the regulars, were used in service of this kind.

In actual encounters the advantage of numbers was often with the French, through the comparative ease with which they could concentrate their forces at a given point. Of the ten considerable sieges or battles of the war, five, besides the great bush-fight in which the Indians defeated Braddock, were victories for France; and in four of these—Oswego, Fort William Henry, Montmorenci, and Ste.-Foy—the odds were greatly on her side.

Yet in this most picturesque and dramatic of American wars, there is nothing more noteworthy than the skill with which the French and Canadian leaders used their advantages; the indomitable spirit with which, slighted and abandoned as they were, they grappled with prodigious difficulties; and the courage with which they were seconded by regulars and militia alike. In spite of occasional lapses, the defense of Canada deserves a tribute of admiration.

C. A New Restlessness

1. Andrew Burnaby Scoffs at Colonial Unity (1760)

Andrew Burnaby, the broad-minded Church of England clergyman who traveled extensively in the colonies during the closing months of the French and Indian War, recorded many penetrating observations. But he scoffed at the idea that the Americans would one day form a mighty nation or even come together in a voluntary union. Which of his arguments were borne out when the colonies did attempt to form one nation?

An idea, strange as it is visionary, has entered into the minds of the generality of mankind, that empire is traveling westward; and everyone is looking forward with eager and impatient expectation to that destined moment when America is to give law to the rest of the world. But if ever an idea was illusory and fallacious, I will venture to predict that this will be so.

America is formed for happiness, but not for empire. In a course of 1,200 miles I did not see a single object that solicited charity. But I saw insuperable causes of weakness, which will necessarily prevent its being a potent state. . . .

The Southern colonies have so many inherent causes of weakness that they never can possess any real strength. The climate operates very powerfully upon them, and renders them indolent, inactive, and unenterprising; this is visible in every line of their character. I myself have been a spectator—and it is not an uncommon sight—of a man in the vigor of life, lying upon a couch, and a female slave standing over him, wafting off the flies, and fanning him, while he took his repose. . . .

The mode of cultivation by slavery is another insurmountable cause of weakness. The number of Negroes in the Southern colonies is upon the whole nearly equal, if not superior, to that of the white men; and they propagate and increase even faster. Their condition is truly pitiable: their labor excessively hard, their diet poor and scanty, their treatment cruel and oppressive; they cannot therefore but be a subject of terror to those who so unhumanly tyrannize over them.

The Indians near the frontiers are a still farther formidable cause of subjection. The southern Indians are numerous, and are governed by a sounder policy than formerly; experience has taught them wisdom. They never make war with the colonists without carrying terror and devastation along with them. They sometimes break up entire counties together. Such is the state of the Southern colonies.

The Northern colonies are of stronger stamina, but they have other difficulties and disadvantages to struggle with, not less arduous, or more easy to be surmounted, than what have been already mentioned. . . . They are composed of people of different nations, different manners, different religions, and different languages. They have a mutual jealousy of each other, fomented by considerations of interest, power, and ascendancy. Religious zeal, too, like a smothered fire, is secretly burning in the hearts of the different sectaries that inhabit them, and were it not restrained by laws and superior authority, would soon burst out into a flame of uni-

---

[1]Andrew Burnaby, *Travels through the Middle Settlements in North-America in the Years 1759 and 1760* (London: J. Payne, 1775; reprinted Ithaca, N.Y.: Great Seal Books, 1960), pp. 110–114.

versal persecution. Even the peaceable Quakers struggle hard for pre-eminence, and evince in a very striking manner that the passions of mankind are much stronger than any principles of religion. . . .

Indeed, it appears to me a very doubtful point, even supposing all the colonies of America to be united under one head, whether it would be possible to keep in due order and government so wide and extended an empire, the difficulties of communication, of intercourse, of correspondence, and all other circumstances considered.

A voluntary association or coalition, at least a permanent one, is almost as difficult to be supposed: for fire and water are not more heterogeneous than the different colonies in North America. Nothing can exceed the jealousy and emulation which they possess in regard to each other. The inhabitants of Pennsylvania and New York have an inexhaustible source of animosity in their jealousy for the trade of the Jerseys. Massachusetts Bay and Rhode Island are not less interested in that of Connecticut. The West Indies are a common subject of emulation to them all. Even the limits and boundaries of each colony are a constant source of litigation.

In short, such is the difference of character, of manners, of religion, of interest, of the different colonies, that I think, if I am not wholly ignorant of the human mind, were they left to themselves there would soon be a civil war from one end of the continent to the other, while the Indians and Negroes would, with better reason, impatiently watch the opportunity of exterminating them all together.

2. A Lawyer Denounces Search Warrants (1761)

During the French and Indian War, the American merchant-smugglers kept up a lucrative illicit trade with the French and Spanish West Indies. They argued that they could not pay wartime taxes if they could not make profits out of their friends, the enemy. Angered by such disloyalty, the royal authorities in Massachusetts undertook to revive the hated writs of assistance. Ordinary search warrants describe the specific premises to be searched; writs of assistance were general search warrants that authorized indiscriminate search of ships and dwellings for illicit goods. Colonial participation in the recent war against the French had inspired a spirit of resistance, and John Adams, later president of the United States, remembered in his old age the following dramatic episode. Why were the colonials so alarmed? Were their fears exaggerated?

When the British ministry received from General Amherst his despatches announcing his conquest of Montreal, and the consequent annihilation of the French government in America, in 1759 [actually 1760], they immediately conceived the design and took the resolution of conquering the English colonies, and subjecting them to the unlimited authority of Parliament. With this view and intention, they sent orders and instructions to the collector of the customs in Boston, Mr. Charles Paxton, to apply to the civil authority for writs of assistance, to enable the customhouse officers, tidewaiters, landwaiters, and all, to command all sheriffs and constables, etc., to attend and aid them in breaking open houses, stores, shops, cellars,

---

[2]C. F. Adams, ed., *The Works of John Adams* (1856), vol. 10, pp. 246–248.

ships, bales, trunks, chests, casks, packages of all sorts, to search for goods, wares, and merchandises which had been imported against the prohibitions or without paying the taxes imposed by certain acts of Parliament, called "The Acts of Trade.". . .

An alarm was spread far and wide. Merchants of Salem and Boston applied to [lawyers] Mr. Pratt, who refused, and to Mr. Otis and Mr. Thacher, who accepted, to defend them against this terrible menacing monster, the writ of assistance. Great fees were offered, but Otis, and I believe Thacher, would accept of none. "In such a cause," said Otis, "I despise all fees."

I have given you a sketch of the stage and the scenery, and the brief of the cause; or, if you like the phrase better, the tragedy, comedy, or farce.

Now for the actors and performers. Mr. Gridley argued [for the government] with his characteristic learning, ingenuity, and dignity, and said everything that could be said in favor of Cockle's [deputy collector at Salem] petition, all depending, however, on the "If the Parliament of Great Britain is the sovereign legislature of all the British empire."

Mr. Thacher followed him on the other side, and argued with the softness of manners, the ingenuity, and the cool reasoning which were remarkable in his amiable character.

But Otis was a flame of fire! With a promptitude of classical allusions, a depth of research, a rapid summary of historical events and dates, a profusion of legal authorities, a prophetic glance of his eye into futurity, and a torrent of impetuous eloquence he hurried away everything before him. American independence was then and there born; the seeds of patriots and heroes were then and there sown. . . .

Every man of a crowded audience appeared to me to go away, as I did, ready to take arms against writs of assistance. Then and there was the first scene of the first act of opposition to the arbitrary claims of Great Britain. Then and there the child Independence was born. In fifteen years, namely in 1776, he grew up to manhood and declared himself free. . . .

Mr. Otis' popularity was without bounds. In May, 1761, he was elected into the House of Representatives by an almost unanimous vote. On the week of his election, I happened to be at Worcester attending a Court of Common Pleas, of which Brigadier Ruggles was Chief Justice, when the News arrived from Boston of Mr. Otis' election. You can have no idea of the consternation among the government people. Chief Justice Ruggles, at dinner at Colonel Chandler's on that day, said, "Out of this election will arise a d——d faction, which will shake this province to its foundation."

Thought Provokers

1. It has been said that the true martyr does not feel pain, as other humans do, but actually takes pleasure in suffering for a noble cause. Comment in the light of the Jesuit experience in Canada. Explain why there was prolonged conflict in New France between the missionaries and the fur traders. Did the whites "rob" the Indians when they exchanged a string of beads for valuable furs?

2. Did the British err in depriving France of Canada in 1763? How would the history of the English colonies have been changed in the eighteenth and nineteenth centuries if the French had been allowed to remain?

3. Compare and contrast the advantages and disadvantages of the French and the English in their intercolonial wars in America. Assess the effects of these wars on colonial attitudes.

4. The seeds of American nationalism were sown during the colonial period. In parallel columns list those forces and factors that made for a spirit of unity or nationality and those that militated against it. Then form conclusions as to which forces predominated and what they foreshadowed.

7

The Road to Revolution, 1763–1775

We cannot be happy without being free; we cannot be
free without being secure in our property; we cannot
be secure in our property if, without our consent,
others may, as by right, take it away; taxes imposed
on us by Parliament do thus take it away.

John Dickinson, 1767

Prologue: The British Empire was erected on the then-popular theory of mercantilism, which held that colonies existed for the benefit of the mother country.
British regulations imposed burdens and conferred benefits, but on balance the advantages to the colonials probably outweighed the disadvantages. After the Seven
Years' War had saddled Britain with a staggering debt, the British government
decided to tax the colonies for a portion of their defense upkeep. The result was
the Stamp Act of 1765, which stirred up such a furor that Parliament was forced
to repeal it the next year. A renewed attempt at taxation in 1773 goaded the colonials into destroying a number of tea cargoes, notably at Boston. Parliament retaliated by passing legislation directed at Massachusetts, which, among other
restrictions, closed the port of Boston. The other colonies rallied to the defense of
Massachusetts; tensions increased; and the first overt fighting erupted at Lexington
in 1775.

A. The Burden of Mercantilism

1. Virginia Resents Restrictions (1671)

*The foundation stones of British mercantilism in America were the Navigation Acts
of 1651 and 1660. They decreed that all commerce with the colonies had to be carried on in English-built and English-owned ships (a blow at Dutch competitors), and*

---

[1]W. W. Hening, *The Statutes at Large . . . of Virginia . . .* (Richmond: Samuel Pleasants, 1823), vol. 2, pp.
515–516.

that certain "enumerated articles," including sugar, tobacco, and indigo, could be exported only to England. To the English mainland colonies, tobacco was by far the most important enumerated product, and Virginia was especially hard hit. The Virginians, to be sure, were guaranteed a monopoly of the English market, but they were denied the profits of direct sales to Spanish and other European customers. As early as 1671 the testy Governor Berkeley of Virginia (see p. 29) lodged the following bitter protest with the London officials in response to specific questions from them. How did mercantilist restrictions hamper the development of Virginia?

What obstructions do you find to the improvement of the trade and navigation of the plantations within your government?

Answer. Mighty and destructive, by that severe act of Parliament which excludes us the having any commerce with any nation in Europe but our own, so that we cannot add to our plantation any commodity that grows out of it, as olive trees, cotton, or vines. Besides this, we cannot procure any skillful men for one now hopeful commodity, silk; for it is not lawful for us to carry a pipe stave, or a barrel of corn, to any place in Europe out of the King's dominions. If this were for His Majesty's service or the good of his subjects, we should not repine, whatever our sufferings are for it; but on my soul, it is the contrary for both. And this is the cause why no small or great vessels are built here; for we are most obedient to all laws, whilst the New England men break through, and men trade to any place that their interest lead them.

What advantages or improvement do you observe that may be gained to your trade or navigation?

Answer. None, unless we had liberty to transport our pipe staves, timber, and corn to other places besides the King's dominions.

2. Adam Smith's Balance Sheet (1776)

The Navigation Laws, as perfected in the eighteenth century, bore most harshly on the southern colonies, with their staple enumerated products. To strengthen the Royal Navy, the London government paid bounties for the production of pitch, tar, rosin, turpentine, hemp, masts, yards, and bowsprits, but the northern colonies came off with a lion's share of the bounty payments. The whole system was reviewed in 1776, the year the colonies declared independence, by the Scottish philosopher-economist Adam Smith in his monumental Wealth of Nations. *As a declaration of independence from current mercantilist restrictions, it ranks as one of the great books of all time. Smith, who has been dubbed the father of modern economics, was a liberal-minded exponent of the greatest good to the greatest number. In the passage here reproduced from his* Wealth of Nations, *what*

---

[2]Adam Smith, *An Inquiry into the Nature and Causes of the Wealth of Nations* (New York: G. P. Putnam's Sons, 1904), vol. 2, pp. 82–84.

British restrictions are viewed as most galling? Why were they tolerated as long as they were?

The most perfect freedom of trade is permitted between the British colonies of America and the West Indies, both in the enumerated and in the non-enumerated commodities. Those colonies are now become so populous and thriving that each of them finds in some of the others a great and extensive market for every part of its produce. All of them taken together, they make a great internal market for the produce of one another.

The liberality of England, however, towards the trade of her colonies has been confined chiefly to what concerns the market for their produce, either in its rude state or in what may be called the very first stage of manufacture. The more advanced or more refined manufactures, even of the colony produce, the merchants and manufacturers of Great Britain choose to reserve to themselves, and have prevailed upon the legislature [Parliament] to prevent their establishment in the colonies, sometimes by high duties, and sometimes by absolute prohibitions. . . .

While Great Britain encourages in America the manufactures of pig and bar iron, by exempting them from duties to which the like commodities are subject when imported from any other country, she imposes an absolute prohibition upon the erection of steel furnaces and slit-mills in any of her American plantations. She will not suffer her colonists to work in those more refined manufactures, even for their own consumption; but insists upon their purchasing of her merchants and manufacturers all goods of this kind which they have occasion for.

She prohibits the exportation from one province to another by water, and even the carriage by land upon horseback or in a cart, of hats, of wools and woolen goods, of the produce of America—a regulation which effectually prevents the establishment of any manufacture of such commodities for distant sale, and confines the industry of her colonists in this way to such coarse and household manufactures as a private family commonly makes for its own use, or for that of some of its neighbors in the same province.

To prohibit a great people, however, from making all that they can of every part of their own produce, or from employing their stock and industry in the way that they judge most advantageous to themselves, is a manifest violation of the most sacred rights of mankind.

Unjust, however, as such prohibitions may be, they have not hitherto been very hurtful to the colonies. Land is still so cheap and, consequently, labor so dear among them that they can import from the Mother Country almost all the more refined or more advanced manufactures cheaper than they could make them for themselves. Though [even if] they had not, therefore, been prohibited from establishing such manufactures, yet in their present state of improvement a regard to their own interest would probably have prevented them from doing so. In their present state of improvement these prohibitions, perhaps, without cramping their industry, or restraining it from any employment to which it would have gone of its own accord, are only impertinent badges of slavery imposed upon them, without any sufficient reason, by the groundless jealousy of the merchants and manufacturers of the Mother Country. In a more advanced state they might be really oppressive and insupportable.

B. The Tempest over Taxation

1. Benjamin Franklin Testifies Against the Stamp Act (1766)

In 1765 the British Parliament undertook to levy a direct (internal) stamp tax on the American colonies to defray one-third of the expenses of keeping a military force there. The colonials had long paid taxes voted by their own assemblies, as well as customs duties (external taxes) passed by Parliament primarily to regulate trade. But they objected heatedly to paying direct or internal taxes voted by a Parliament in which they were not specifically represented. Benjamin Franklin, then in London as a prominent colonial agent, testified as follows before a committee of the House of Commons. He made a brilliant showing with his incisive answers, especially since he had "planted" a number of questions in advance among his friends on the committee. Were the Americans financially able to bear additional taxes? What defenses did they have available against the odious stamp tax?

Q. What is your name, and place of abode?

A. Franklin, of Philadelphia.

Q. Do the Americans pay any considerable taxes among themselves?

A. Certainly many, and very heavy taxes.

Q. What are the present taxes in Pennsylvania, laid by the laws of the colony?

A. There are taxes on all estates, real and personal; a poll tax; a tax on all offices, professions, trades, and businesses, according to their profits; an excise on all wine, rum, and other spirit; and a duty of ten pounds per head on all Negroes imported, with some other duties.

Q. For what purposes are those taxes laid?

A. For the support of the civil and military establishments of the country, and to discharge the heavy debt contracted in the last [Seven Years'] war. . . .

Q. Are not all the people very able to pay those taxes?

A. No. The frontier counties, all along the continent, having been frequently ravaged by the enemy and greatly impoverished, are able to pay very little tax. . . .

Q. Are not the colonies, from their circumstances, very able to pay the stamp duty?

A. In my opinion there is not gold and silver enough in the colonies to pay the stamp duty for one year.

Q. Don't you know that the money arising from the stamps was all to be laid out in America?

A. I know it is appropriated by the act to the American service; but it will be spent in the conquered colonies, where the soldiers are, not in the colonies that pay it. . . .

Q. Do you think it right that America should be protected by this country and pay no part of the expense?

---

[1] *The Parliamentary History of England* . . . (1813), vol. 16, pp. 138–159, passim.

A. That is not the case. The colonies raised, clothed, and paid, during the last war, near 25,000 men, and spent many millions.

Q. Were you not reimbursed by Parliament?

A. We were only reimbursed what, in your opinion, we had advanced beyond our proposition, or beyond what might reasonably be expected from us; and it was a very small part of what we spent. Pennsylvania, in particular, disbursed about 500,000 pounds, and the reimbursements, in the whole, did not exceed 60,000 pounds. . . .

Q. Do not you think the people of America would submit to pay the stamp duty, if it was moderated?

A. No, never, unless compelled by force of arms. . . .

Q. What was the temper of America towards Great Britain before the year 1763?

A. The best in the world. They submitted willingly to the government of the Crown, and paid, in all their courts, obedience to acts of Parliament. . . .

Q. What is your opinion of a future tax, imposed on the same principle with that of the Stamp Act? How would the Americans receive it?

A. Just as they do this. They would not pay it.

Q. Have not you heard of the resolutions of this House, and of the House of Lords, asserting the right of Parliament relating to America, including a power to tax the people there?

A. Yes, I have heard of such resolutions.

Q. What will be the opinion of the Americans on those resolutions?

A. They will think them unconstitutional and unjust.

Q. Was it an opinion in America before 1763 that the Parliament had no right to lay taxes and duties there?

A. I never heard any objection to the right of laying duties to regulate commerce; but a right to lay internal taxes was never supposed to be in Parliament, as we are not represented there. . . .

Q. Did the Americans ever dispute the controlling power of Parliament to regulate the commerce?

A. No.

Q. Can anything less than a military force carry the Stamp Act into execution?

A. I do not see how a military force can be applied to that purpose.

Q. Why may it not?

A. Suppose a military force sent into America; they will find nobody in arms; what are they then to do? They cannot force a man to take stamps who chooses to do without them. They will not find a rebellion; they may indeed make one.

Q. If the act is not repealed, what do you think will be the consequences?

A. A total loss of the respect and affection the people of America bear to this country, and of all the commerce that depends on that respect and affection.

Q. How can the commerce be affected?

A. You will find that, if the act is not repealed, they will take very little of your manufactures in a short time.

Q. Is it in their power to do without them?

A. I think they may very well do without them.

Q. Is it their interest not to take them?

A. The goods they take from Britain are either necessaries, mere conveniences, or superfluities. The first, as cloth, etc., with a little industry they can make at home;

the second they can do without till they are able to provide them among themselves; and the last, which are much the greatest part, they will strike off immediately. They are mere articles of fashion, purchased and consumed because the fashion in a respected country; but will now be detested and rejected. The people have already struck off, by general agreement, the use of all goods fashionable in mournings. . . .

Q. If the Stamp Act should be repealed, would it induce the assemblies of America to acknowledge the right of Parliament to tax them, and would they erase their resolutions [against the Stamp Act]?

A. No, never.

Q. Is there no means of obliging them to erase those resolutions?

A. None that I know of; they will never do it, unless compelled by force of arms.

Q. Is there a power on earth that can force them to erase them?

A. No power, how great soever, can force men to change their opinions. . . .

Q. What used to be the pride of the Americans?

A. To indulge in the fashions and manufactures of Great Britain.

Q. What is now their pride?

A. To wear their old clothes over again, till they can make new ones.

2. Philadelphia Threatens Tea Men (1773)

Parliament, faced with rebellion and a crippling commercial boycott, repealed the Stamp Act in 1766. The next year the ministry devised a light indirect tax on tea, which, being external, presumably met the colonial objections to a direct tax. Opposition to the new levy was fading when, in 1773, the London officials granted a monopoly of the tea business in America to the powerful and hated British East India Company. These arrangements would make the tea, even with the three-penny tax included, cheaper than ever. The colonials, resenting this transparent attempt to trick them into paying the tax, staged several famous tea parties. Those at Boston and New York involved throwing the tea overboard; the affair at Annapolis resulted in the burning of both vessel and cargo. At Portsmouth and Philadelphia the tea ships were turned away. Of the reasons here given by the Philadelphians for action, which was the strongest? Was it strong enough to warrant the measures threatened?

TO CAPT. AYRES
Of the Ship *Polly,* on a Voyage
from London to Philadelphia

Sir: We are informed that you have imprudently taken charge of a quantity of tea which has been sent out by the [East] India Company, under the auspices of the Ministry, as a trial of American virtue and resolution.

Now, as your cargo, on your arrival here, will most assuredly bring you into hot water, and as you are perhaps a stranger to these parts, we have concluded to advise you of the present situation of affairs in Philadelphia, that, taking time by the forelock, you may stop short in your dangerous errand, secure your ship against the

---

[2]*Pennsylvania Magazine of History and Biography 15* (Philadelphia: Pennsylvania Historical Society, 1891): 391.

rafts of combustible matter which may be set on fire and turned loose against her; and more than all this, that you may preserve your own person from the pitch and feathers that are prepared for you.

In the first place, we must tell you that the Pennsylvanians are, to a man, passionately fond of freedom, the birthright of Americans, and at all events are determined to enjoy it.

That they sincerely believe no power on the face of the earth has a right to tax them without their consent.

That, in their opinion, the tea in your custody is designed by the Ministry to enforce such a tax, which they will undoubtedly oppose, and in so doing, give you every possible obstruction.

We are nominated to a very disagreeable, but necessary, service: to our care are committed all offenders against the rights of America; and hapless is he whose evil destiny has doomed him to suffer at our hands.

You are sent out on a diabolical service; and if you are so foolish and obstinate as to complete your voyage by bringing your ship to anchor in this port, you may run such a gauntlet as will induce you in your last moments most heartily to curse those who have made you the dupe of their avarice and ambition.

What think you, Captain, of a halter around your neck—ten gallons of liquid tar decanted on your pate—with the feathers of a dozen wild geese laid over that to enliven your appearance?

Only think seriously of this—and fly to the place from whence you came—fly without hesitation—without the formality of a protest—and above all, Captain Ayres, let us advise you to fly without the wild geese feathers.

Your friends to serve,
THE COMMITTEE OF TARRING AND FEATHERING

3. Connecticut Decries the Boston Port Act (1774)

The Boston Tea Party, which involved the destruction of three cargoes of tea by colonials thinly disguised as Indians, provoked an angry response in Parliament. Even as good a friend of America as Colonel Barré so far forgot his grammar as to burst out, "Boston ought to be punished; she is your eldest son!" Parliament speedily passed a series of punitive measures ("Intolerable Acts"), notably the act closing the port of Boston until the tea was paid for. The other colonies, deeply resentful, responded with assurances of support. Virginia raised food and money; Philadelphia contributed one thousand barrels of flour. Various groups, including the citizens of Farmington, Connecticut, passed resolutions of protest. To what extent did their resolution reflect a desire for independence?

Early in the morning was found the following handbill, posted up in various parts of the town, viz.:

---

[3]Peter Force, ed., *American Archives,* Fourth Series (Washington, D.C.: prepared and published under authority of an act of Congress, 1837), vol. 1, p. 336.

To pass through the fire at six o'clock this evening, in honor to the immortal goddess of Liberty, the late infamous Act of the British Parliament for farther distressing the American Colonies. The place of execution will be the public parade, where all Sons of Liberty are desired to attend.

Accordingly, a very numerous and respectable body were assembled of near one thousand people, when a huge pole, just forty-five feet high, was erected, and consecrated to the shrine of liberty; after which the Act of Parliament for blocking up the Boston harbor was read aloud, sentenced to the flames, and executed by the hands of the common hangman. Then the following resolves were passed, *nem. con.* [unanimously]:

1st. That it is the greatest dignity, interest, and happiness of every American to be united with our parent state while our liberties are duly secured, maintained, and supported by our rightful sovereign, whose person we greatly revere; whose government, while duly administered, we are ready with our lives and properties to support.

2nd. That the present Ministry, being instigated by the Devil, and led on by their wicked and corrupt hearts, have a design to take away our liberties and properties, and to enslave us forever.

3rd. That the late Act, which their malice hath caused to be passed in Parliament, for blocking up the port of Boston, is unjust, illegal, and oppressive; and that we, and every American, are sharers in the insults offered to the town of Boston.

4th. That those pimps and parasites who dared to advise their master [George III] to such detestable measures be held in utter abhorrence by us and every American, and their names loaded with the curses of all succeeding generations.

5th. That we scorn the chains of slavery; we despise every attempt to rivet them upon us; we are the sons of freedom, and resolved that, till time shall be no more, that godlike virtue shall blazon our hemisphere.

C. Britain at the Crossroads

1. Dean Josiah Tucker Advises a Divorce (1774)

Josiah Tucker, a British clergyman-economist, was a born controversialist who for fifty years penned numerous pamphlets on varied subjects. A man of prodigious energy, he had, as a student at Oxford, regularly walked the 150 miles between the university and his native Wales. Regarding England as underpopulated, he doubted the utility of colonies and criticized many aspects of mercantilism. After a crisis over taxation again developed with America in 1774, he examined, in a pamphlet, four possible courses: (1) let affairs drift; (2) persuade the colonies to accept representation in Parliament; (3) crush the colonies with arms; (4) separate peacefully from the colonies, with an offer of protection against foreign foes. In the following passage he develops the theme that the British Empire would actually be strengthened by the expulsion of its most valuable part. In the light of subsequent history, was he more right than wrong?

---

[1]From *Josiah Tucker* by R. L. Schuyler, pp. 259–266, passim. Copyright © 1931 Columbia University Press, New York. Reprinted with the permission of the publisher.

The first and capital supposed [dis]advantage is that if we separate from the colonies, we shall lose their trade. But why so? And how does this appear? The colonies, we know by experience, will trade with any people, even with their bitterest enemies, during the hottest of a war, and a war [French and Indian War] undertaken at their own earnest request, and for their own sakes—the colonies, I say, will trade even with them, provided they shall find it their interest so to do. Why then should any man suppose that the same self-interest will not induce them to trade with us? . . .

The second objection against giving up the colonies is that such a measure would greatly decrease our shipping and navigation, and consequently diminish the breed of sailors. But this objection has been fully obviated already. For if we shall not lose our trade, at least in any important degree, even with the northern colonies (and most probably we shall increase it with other countries), then it follows that neither the quantity of shipping nor the breed of sailors can suffer any considerable diminution; so that this supposition is merely a panic, and has no foundation. Not to mention that in proportion as the Americans shall be obliged to exert themselves to defend their own coasts in case of war, in the same proportion shall Great Britain be exonerated from that burden, and shall have more ships and men at command to protect her own channel trade, and for other services.

The third objection is that if we were to give up these colonies, the French would take immediate possession of them. Now this objection is entirely built on . . . very wild, very extravagant, and absurd suppositions. . . .

The manifold advantages attendant on such a scheme:

And first, a disjunction from the northern colonies would effectually put a stop to our present emigrations. . . .

Secondly. Another great advantage to be derived from a separation is that we shall then save between £300,000 and £400,000 a year, by being discharged from the payment of any civil or military establishment belonging to the colonies; for which generous benefaction we receive at present no other return than invectives and reproaches.

Thirdly. The ceasing of the payment of bounties on certain colony productions will be another great saving, perhaps not less than £200,000 a year. And it is very remarkable that the goods imported from the colonies, in consequence of these bounties, could not have been imported into any other part of Europe, were there a liberty to do it, because the freight and first cost would have amounted to more than they could be sold for. So that, in fact, we give premiums to the colonies for selling goods to us which would not have been sold at all anywhere else. . . .

Fourthly. When we are no longer connected with the colonies by the imaginary tie of an identity of government, then our merchant-exporters and manufacturers will have a better chance of having their debts paid than they have at present. For as matters now stand, the colonists choose to carry their ready cash to other nations, while they are contracting debts with their mother country, with whom they think they can take greater liberties. . . .

Fifthly. After a separation from the colonies, our influence over them will be much greater than ever it was since they began to feel their own weight and importance. For at present we are looked upon in no better a light than that of robbers and usurpers; whereas we shall then be considered as their protectors, mediators, benefactors. The moment a separation takes effect, intestine quarrels will begin. For it is well known that the seeds of discord and dissension between province and province are now ready to shoot forth; and they are only kept down by the present combination of all the colonies against us, whom they unhappily fancy to be their common enemy. When, therefore, this object of their hatred shall be removed by a declaration on our parts that, so far from usurping all authority, we, from henceforward, will assume none at all against their own consent, the weaker provinces will entreat our protection against the stronger, and the less cautious against the more crafty and designing. So that, in short, in proportion as their factious, republican spirit shall intrigue and cabal, shall split into parties, divide, and subdivide—in the same proportion shall we be called in to become their general umpires and referees.

2. Adam Smith Criticizes Empire (1776)

Like Dean Tucker and British officialdom, Adam Smith was concerned about the expense of mercantilism. When serious friction developed with America, he advocated colonial membership in Parliament, with representation based on taxes paid. If the American tax revenues should ultimately exceed those of England, as was not unlikely, the capital of the empire might be moved from London to the New World. Such views were not popular in the mother country. Smith here examines the alternatives in the concluding passage of his Wealth of Nations. *Did he regard the colonies as a burden or an asset?*

The expense of the peace establishment of the colonies . . . , though very great, is insignificant in comparison with what the defense of the colonies has cost us in time of war. The last war [Seven Years' War], which was undertaken altogether on account of the colonies, cost Great Britain, it has already been observed, upwards of ninety millions [of pounds]. The Spanish war of 1739 [War of Jenkins' Ear] was principally undertaken on their account; in which, and in the French war [King George's] that was the consequence of it, Great Britain spent upwards of forty millions, a great part of which ought justly to be charged to the colonies.

In those two wars the colonies cost Great Britain much more than double the sum which the national debt amounted to before the commencement of the first of them. Had it not been for those wars, that debt might, and probably would, by this time, have been completely paid. And had it not been for the colonies, the former of those wars might not, and the latter certainly would not, have been undertaken. It was because the colonies were supposed to be provinces of the British empire that this expense was laid out upon them.

But the countries which contribute neither revenue nor military force towards the support of the empire cannot be considered as provinces. They may perhaps

²Adam Smith, *An Inquiry into the Nature and Causes of the Wealth of Nations* (New York: G. P. Putnam's Sons, 1904), vol. 2, 432.

be considered as appendages, as a sort of splendid and showy equipage of the empire. But if the empire can no longer support the expense of keeping up this equipage, it ought certainly to lay it down. And if it cannot raise its revenue in proportion to its expense, it ought, at least, to accommodate its expense to its revenue. If the colonies, notwithstanding their refusal to submit to British taxes, are still to be considered as provinces of the British empire, their defense in some future war may cost Great Britain as great an expense as it ever has done in any former war.

The rulers of Great Britain have, for more than a century past, amused the people with the imagination that they possessed a great empire on the west side of the Atlantic. This empire, however, has hitherto existed in imagination only. It has hitherto been, not an empire, but the project of an empire; not a gold mine, but the project of a gold mine—a project which has cost, which continues to cost, and which, if pursued in the same way as it has been hitherto, is likely to cost, immense expense, without being likely to bring any profit. For the effects of the monopoly of the colony trade, it has been shown, are, to the great body of the people, mere loss instead of profit.

It is surely now time that our rulers should realize this golden dream, in which they have been indulging themselves, perhaps, as well as the people; or that they should awake from it themselves, and endeavor to awaken the people. If the project cannot be completed, it ought to be given up. If any of the provinces of the British empire cannot be made to contribute toward the support of the whole empire, it is surely time that Great Britain should free herself from the expense of defending those provinces in time of war, and of supporting any part of their civil or military establishments in time of peace, and endeavor to accommodate her future views and designs to the real mediocrity [moderateness] of her circumstances.

3. Samuel Johnson Urges the Iron Fist (1775)

The conservative Samuel Johnson, famed for his English dictionary, was no friend of Americans, who, he wrote, "multiplied with the fecundity of their own rattlesnakes." In 1762 he accepted a pension of £300 annually from the crown; in 1775 he repaid his royal master by publishing a pamphlet, Taxation No Tyranny, *in which he proved himself to be a political babe in the woods. He privately admitted that his manuscript was revised and shortened by the royal officials. Which of his proposals would be most likely to arouse the American frontier? which the South? Which would be most likely to stir up renewed rebellion generally? Which proposals have real merit, and which are the most fantastic?*

The Dean of Gloucester has proposed, and seems to propose it seriously, that we should, at once, release our claims, declare them [the Americans] masters of themselves, and whistle them down the wind. His opinion is that our gain from

---

[3] *The Works of Samuel Johnson* (Oxford, Eng.: Talboys and Wheeler, 1825), vol. 6, pp. 259–262.

them will be the same, and our expense less. What they can have most cheaply from Britain, they will still buy; what they can sell to us at the highest price, they will still sell.

It is, however, a little hard that, having so lately fought and conquered for their safety, we should govern them no longer. By letting them loose before the [Seven Years'] war, how many millions might have been saved? One wild proposal is best answered by another. Let us restore to the French what we have taken from them. We shall see our colonists at our feet, when they have an enemy so near them [Canada]. Let us give the Indians arms, and teach them discipline, and encourage them, now and then, to plunder a plantation. Security and leisure are the parents of sedition.

While these different opinions are agitated, it seems to be determined by the legislature that force shall be tried. Men of the pen have seldom any great skill in conquering kingdoms, but they have strong inclination to give advice. I cannot forbear to wish that this commotion may end without bloodshed, and that the rebels may be subdued by terror rather than by violence; and, therefore, recommend such a force as may take away not only the power but the hope of resistance, and, by conquering without a battle, save many from the sword.

If their obstinacy continues, without actual hostilities, it may, perhaps, be mollified by turning out the soldiers to free quarters, forbidding any personal cruelty or hurt. It has been proposed that the slaves should be set free, an act which, surely, the [American] lovers of liberty cannot but commend. If they are furnished with firearms for defense, and utensils for husbandry, and settled in some simple form of government within the country, they may be more grateful and honest than their masters. . . .

Since the Americans have made it necessary to subdue them, may they be subdued with the least injury possible to their persons and their possessions! When they are reduced to obedience, may that obedience be secured by stricter laws and stronger obligations!

Nothing can be more noxious to society than that erroneous clemency which, when a rebellion is suppressed, exacts no forfeiture and establishes no securities, but leaves the rebels in their former state. Who would not try the experiment which promises advantage without expense? If rebels once obtain a victory, their wishes are accomplished. If they are defeated, they suffer little, perhaps less than their conquerors. However often they play the game, the chance is always in their favor. In the meantime they are growing rich by victualing the troops we have sent against them, and, perhaps, gain more by the residence of the army than they lose by the obstruction of their post [Boston].

Their charters, being now, I suppose, legally forfeited, may be modeled as shall appear most commodious to the Mother Country. Thus the privileges [of self-government] which are found, by experience, liable to misuse will be taken away, and those who now bellow as patriots, bluster as soldiers, and domineer as legislators will sink into sober merchants and silent planters, peaceably diligent and securely rich. . . .

We are told that the subjection of Americans may tend to the diminution of our own liberties—an event which none but very perspicacious politicians are able to foresee. If slavery be thus fatally contagious, how is it that we hear the loudest yelps for liberty among the [American] drivers of Negroes?

4. Two Views of the British Empire (1767, 1775)

Benjamin Franklin played many roles in colonial America. In 1767, he commissioned the cartoon shown below, "Britannia: Her Colonies," to illustrate the importance of the North American colonies to the British Empire. Was his purpose to encourage independence or reconciliation? To whom is his cartoon principally addressed? The second cartoon "The Wise Men of Gotham and Their Goose," is from a London magazine in 1775, after the Revolutionary War had broken out. To what audience is it addressed? What are the cartoonist's sympathies in the conflict between Britain and its American colonies? To what extent does the British cartoon of 1775 express sentiments similar to Franklin's image of 1767?

---

[4] *(above)* John Carter Brown Library, Brown University; *(p. 127)* 1776 London Mezzotint from Stephen Hess and Milton Kaplan, *The Ungentlemanly Art,* 1968, MacMillan; courtesy Harvard College Library.

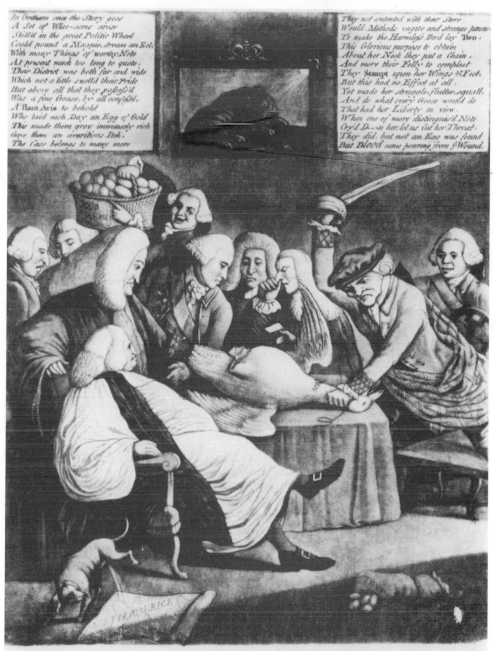

THE WISE MEN of GOTHAM and their GOOSE-

D. Loyalists Versus Patriots _____

1. Daniel Leonard Deplores Rebellion (1775)

Daniel Leonard, of an aristocratic Massachusetts family, was the cleverest Tory pamphleteer in America. His writings, declared his pen adversary John Adams, "shone like the moon among the lesser stars." Forced to flee from Boston when the British troops withdrew in 1776, he subsequently became chief justice of Bermuda and dean of the English bar. He is best known in America for a series of seventeen newspaper articles, published in 1774–1775 over the signature "Massachusettensis." He warned his readers that rebellion was "the most atrocious offense" and that it would open the doors to anarchy. Legal punishment for the rebel was that he be dragged to the gallows; "that he be hanged by the neck, and then cut down alive; that his entrails be taken out and burned while he is yet alive; that his head be cut off; that his body be divided into four parts; that his head and quarters be at the king's disposal." As the clash neared between the American Patriots (Whigs) and the British troops in Massachusetts, Leonard issued this final appeal to his countrymen two weeks before the bloodshed at Lexington. What were his most convincing and least convincing arguments in support of the view that the colonials could not win?

Do you expect to conquer in war? War is no longer a simple, but an intricate science, not to be learned from books or two or three campaigns, but from long experience. You need not be told that His Majesty's generals, Gage and Haldimand, are possessed of every talent requisite to great commanders, matured by long experience in many parts of the world, and stand high in military fame; that many of the officers have been bred to arms from their infancy, and a large proportion of the army now here have already reaped immortal honors in the iron harvest of the field.

Alas! My friends, you have nothing to oppose to this force but a militia unused to service, impatient of command, and destitute of resources. Can your officers depend upon the privates, or the privates upon the officers? Your war can be but little more than mere tumultuary rage. And besides, there is an awful disparity between troops that fight the battles of their sovereign and those that follow the standard of rebellion.

These reflections may arrest you in an hour that you think not of, and come too late to serve you. Nothing short of a miracle could gain you one battle; but could you destroy all the British troops that are now here, and burn the men-of-war that command our coast, it would be but the beginning of sorrow. And yet without a decisive battle, one campaign would ruin you. This province [Massachusetts] does not produce its necessary provision when the husbandman can pursue his calling without molestation. What then must be your condition when the demand shall be increased and the resource in a manner cut off? Figure to yourselves what must be your distress should your wives and children be driven from such places as the

_____

[1]Daniel Leonard, *Massachusettensis* (London: J. Mathews, 1776; reprinted Boston, 1810), pp. 187–188.

King's troops shall occupy, into the interior parts of the province, and they, as well as you, be destitute of support.

I take no pleasure in painting these scenes of distress. The Whigs [rebels] affect to divert you from them by ridicule; but should war commence, you can expect nothing but its severities. Might I hazard an opinion, but few of your leaders ever intended to engage in hostilities, but they may have rendered inevitable what they intended for intimidation. Those that unsheathe the sword of rebellion may throw away the scabbard; they cannot be treated with while in arms; and if they lay them down, they are in no other predicament than conquered rebels. The conquered in other wars do not forfeit the rights of men, nor all the rights of citizens. Even their bravery is rewarded by a generous victor. Far different is the case of a routed rebel host.

My dear countrymen, you have before you, at your election, peace or war, happiness or misery. May the God of our forefathers direct you in the way that leads to peace and happiness, before your feet stumble on the dark mountains, before the evil days come, wherein you shall say, we have no pleasure in them.

2. Patrick Henry Demands Boldness (1775)

Daniel Leonard's well-justified lack of confidence in the ill-trained colonial militia was more than shared by the earl of Sandwich. In the House of Lords he scorned the colonials as "raw, undisciplined, cowardly men," and hoped that they would assemble 200,000 "brave fellows" rather than 50,000, for they would thus starve themselves out and then run at the first "sound of cannon." But the great William Pitt (now Lord Chatham), also speaking in Parliament, warned against "an impious war with a people contending in the great cause of public liberty." "All attempts to enforce servitude upon such men must be vain, must be futile." A few weeks later Patrick Henry, the flaming young lawyer-orator, urging warlike preparations before the Virginia Assembly, spelled out the reasons for action in his famous speech ending with the immortal words, "Give me liberty or give me death!" Which of his several arguments is the strongest?

They tell us, sir, that we are weak; unable to cope with so formidable an adversary. But when shall we be stronger? Will it be the next week, or the next year? Will it be when we are totally disarmed, and when a British guard shall be stationed in every house? Shall we gather strength by irresolution and inaction? Shall we acquire the means of effectual resistance by lying supinely on our backs and hugging the delusive phantom of hope, until our enemies shall have bound us hand and foot?

Sir, we are not weak if we make a proper use of those means which the God of nature hath placed in our power. Three millions of people armed in the holy cause of liberty, and in such a country as that which we possess, are invincible by any force which our enemy can send against us. Besides, sir, we shall not fight our battles alone. There is a just God who presides over the destinies of nations and who

---

[2]C. M. Depew, ed., *The Library of Oratory* (New York: The Globe Publishing Company, 1902), vol. 3, pp. 30–31.

will raise up friends to fight our battles for us. The battle, sir, is not to the strong alone; it is to the vigilant, the active, the brave.

Besides, sir, we have no election. If we were base enough to desire it, it is now too late to retire from the contest. There is no retreat but in submission and slavery! Our chains are forged! Their clanking may be heard on the plains of Boston! The war is inevitable—and let it come! I repeat, sir, let it come!

It is vain, sir, to extenuate the matter. The gentlemen may cry, Peace, peace! but there is no peace. The war has actually begun! The next gale that sweeps from the north will bring to our ears the clash of resounding arms! Our brethren are already in the field! Why stand we here idle? What is it that the gentlemen wish? What would they have? Is life so dear or peace so sweet as to be purchased at the price of chains and slavery? Forbid it, almighty God. I know not what course others may take, but as for me, give me liberty or give me death!

3. New Yorkers Abuse Tories (1775)

In 1773 James Rivington, a former London bookseller who had emigrated to New York after losing his fortune in racetrack gambling, launched one of the best colonial newspapers, Rivington's New York Gazetteer. *Its columns at first were open to both sides in the increasingly bitter war of words between Loyalists (Tories) and Patriots (Whigs). But American Patriots (Sons of Liberty), resenting additional criticisms about to be published, wrecked Rivington's plant in November 1775. The pro-Loyalist publisher then fled to England. What did the ill will between Loyalists and Patriots portend for the course of the Revolutionary War?*

This afternoon, at New York, as William Cunningham and John Hill were coming from the North River, they stopped near the liberty pole to see a boxing match, but had not stood long when Cunningham was struck at by Smith Richards, James Vandyke, and several others; called Tory; and used in a most cruel manner by a mob of above two hundred men. Mr. Hill, coming up to his assistance, was beaten and abused most barbarously, though neither of them gave the least offense, except being on the King's side of the question at the meeting this morning.

The leaders of this mob brought Cunningham under the liberty pole, and told him to go down on his knees and damn his Popish King George, and they would then set him free. But, on the contrary, he exclaimed, "God bless King George!" They then dragged him through the green, tore the clothes off his back, and robbed him of his watch. They also insisted on Hill's damning the King, but he, refusing, was used in the same manner, and were it not for some of the peace officers, viz., Captain Welsh, John Taylor, William Dey, and Joseph Wilson, together with———— Goldstream, who rescued them from the violence of this banditti and brought them to the jail for the security of their persons from further injuries, they would inevitably have been murdered.

---

[3]*Rivington's New York Gazetteer,* March 9, 1775, in Frank Moore, *Diary of the American Revolution* (New York: C. Scribner; London: S. Low, Son & Company, 1860), vol. 1, pp. 36–37. For a variant Whig account of the episode, see ibid., vol. 1, pp. 45–48.

E. The Clash of Arms

1. Conflicting Versions of the Outbreak (1775)

British troops from Boston, seeking secret military stores and presumably rebel leaders, clashed with the colonials at Lexington and then at Concord, on April 19, 1775, in the first bloodshed of the American Revolution. Among the numerous conflicting accounts that exist, these two excerpts, representing an American version and an official British version, are noteworthy. To this day scholars have not proved who fired the first shot. What undisputed and what probable facts emerge from these accounts? How can historians extract truth from conflicting contemporary testimony?

American Version

At Lexington . . . a company of militia . . . mustered near the meeting house. The [British] troops came in sight of them just before sunrise; and running within a few rods of them, the Commanding Officer [Pitcairn] accosted the militia in words to this effect: "Disperse, you rebels—damn you, throw down your arms and disperse"; upon which the troops huzzaed, and immediately one or two officers discharged their pistols, which were instantaneously followed by the firing of four or five of the soldiers, and then there seemed to be a general discharge from the whole body. Eight of our men were killed and nine wounded. . . .

In Lexington [the British] . . . also set fire to several other houses. . . . They pillaged almost every house they passed. . . . But the savage barbarity exercised upon the bodies of our unfortunate brethren who fell is almost incredible. Not contented with shooting down the unarmed, aged, and infirm, they disregarded the cries of the wounded, killing them without mercy, and mangling their bodies in the most shocking manner.

British Version

. . . Six companies of [British] light infantry . . . at Lexington found a body of the country people under arms, on a green close to the road. And upon the King's troops marching up to them, in order to inquire the reason of their being so assembled, they went off in great confusion. And several guns were fired upon the King's troops from behind a stone wall, and also from the meetinghouse and other houses, by which one man was wounded, and Major Pitcairn's horse shot in two places. In consequence of this attack by the rebels, the troops returned the fire and killed several of them. . . .

On the return of the troops from Concord, they [the rebels] . . . began to fire upon them from behind stone walls and houses, and kept up in that manner a scattering fire during the whole of their march of fifteen miles, by which means several were killed and wounded. And such was the cruelty and barbarity of the rebels that they scalped and cut off the ears of some of the wounded men who fell into their hands.

---

[1]The American version is from the Salem (Massachusetts) *Gazette* of April 25, 1775, the British, from the London *Gazette* of June 10, 1775. Reprinted in Peter Force, ed., *American Archives,* Fourth Series (1839), vol. 2, pp. 391–392, 945–946. For numerous other versions, see A. C. McLaughlin et al., *Source Problems in United States History* (1918), pp. 3–53.

2. Franklin Embittered by Bloodshed (1775)

News of Lexington and Concord, embellished by atrocity stories that were either ex-aggerated or wholly fabricated, elicited the following reaction from the well-balanced and benign Franklin, who had recently returned to Philadelphia from England. He wrote, but apparently did not send, the following letter.

Mr. Strahan, You are a member of Parliament, and one of that majority which has doomed my country to destruction. You have begun to burn our towns and murder our people. Look upon your hands! They are stained with the blood of your relations! You and I were long friends; you are now my enemy, and I am

Yours,
B. Franklin

3. Why an Old Soldier Fought (1898)

Many years after the bloodshed at Lexington, Mellen Chamberlain, a prominent Massachusetts lawyer-politican-historian-librarian, published the following account of an interview with a veteran participant, Levi Preston. Why did Preston fight? What did his reasons have to do with traditional historical accounts?

When the action at Lexington, on the morning of the 19th [of April], was known at Danvers, the minute men there, under the lead of Captain Gideon Foster, made that memorable march—or run, rather—of sixteen miles in four hours, and struck Percy's flying column at West Cambridge. Brave but incautious in flanking the Redcoats, they were flanked themselves and badly pinched, leaving seven dead, two wounded, and one missing. Among those who escaped was Levi Preston, afterwards known as Captain Levi Preston.

When I was about twenty-one and Captain Preston about ninety-one, I "interviewed" him as to what he did and thought sixty-seven years before, on April 19, 1775. And now, fifty-two years later, I make my report—a little belated perhaps, but not too late, I trust, for the morning papers!

At that time, of course, I knew all about the American Revolution—far more than I do now! And if I now know anything truly, it is chiefly owing to what I have since forgotten of the histories of that event then popular.

With an assurance passing even that of the modern interviewer—if that were possible—I began: "Captain Preston, why did you go to the Concord fight, the 19th of April, 1775?"

The old man, bowed beneath the weight of years, raised himself upright, and turning to me said: "Why did I go?"

---

[2]To William Strahan, July 5, 1775, in A. E. Smyth, ed., *The Writings of Benjamin Franklin* (New York: The Macmillan Company, 1906), vol. 6, p. 407.

[3]Mellen Chamberlain, *John Adams, the Statesman of the American Revolution* (Boston and New York: Houghton, Mifflin and Company, 1898), pp. 248–249.

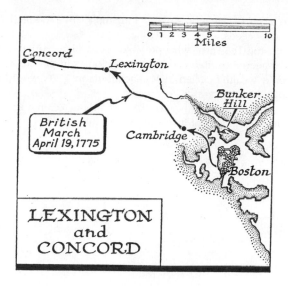

LEXINGTON and CONCORD

"Yes," I replied; "my histories tell me that you men of the Revolution took up arms against 'intolerable oppressions.' What were they?"

"Oppressions? I didn't feel them."

"What, were you not oppressed by the Stamp Act?"

"I never saw one of those stamps, and always understood that Governor Bernard [of Massachusetts] put them all in Castle William [Boston]. I am certain I never paid a penny for one of them."

"Well, what then about the tea-tax?"

"Tea-tax! I never drank a drop of the stuff; the boys threw it all overboard."

"Then I suppose you had been reading Harrington or Sidney and Locke about the eternal principles of liberty."

"Never heard of 'em. We read only the Bible, the Catechism, Watts' Psalms and Hymns, and the Almanack."

"Well, then, what was the matter? and what did you mean in going to the fight?"

"Young man, what we meant in going for those Redcoats was this: we always had governed ourselves, and we always meant to. They didn't mean we should."

Thought Provokers

1. It has been said that the American colonists attempted to reverse the maxim and have it read, "Mother countries exist for the benefit of their colonies." Comment on the reasonableness of such a position. Has mercantilism disappeared as an economic philosophy?

2. Is it justifiable for the people to take mob action against lawful measures that they deem harmful or illegal? Comment critically on the following propositions in the light of the

American Revolution: (a) He who strikes a king must strike to kill. (b) Rebellion is a great crime—unless it succeeds.

3. Following the Boston Tea Party, what possible courses were open to England, and which one would have been most likely to keep the colonies in the empire?

4. If you had been a wealthy citizen in Massachusetts in 1776, would you have remained loyal to the king? Explain.

5. Why did each side blame the other for the first shot at Lexington? Are the people who fight in a war the best judges of its causes and significance?

8

America Secedes from the Empire, 1775–1783

And if ever there was a just war since the world
began, it is this in which America is now engaged. . . .
We fight not to enslave, but to set a country free, and
to make room upon the earth for honest men to
live in.

Thomas Paine, The Crisis, *1776*

Prologue: Following the bloodshed at Lexington, the colonials raised a nonde-
script army and put George Washington in command. The undisciplined and unreli-
able amateur soldiers exasperated their leader, and not until later in the war was a
nucleus of several thousand trained veterans whipped into line. Meanwhile the
colonials, goaded by harsh British acts, finally declared their independence in 1776.
They kept their flickering cause alive with secret French aid until 1778, when France
formed an alliance with them following the decisive American victory over General
John Burgoyne at Saratoga in 1777. Spain and Holland ultimately entered the general conflict against the British. With much of the rest of Europe unfriendly, Britain
found that the war had become too big to handle. Following a crushing defeat by a
joint Franco-American force at Yorktown in 1781, the British decided to cut their
losses and come to terms with their rebellious subjects. The final treaty was signed
in 1783.

A. General Washington in Command

1. Washington Scorns Independence (1775)

*Jonathan Boucher, a prominent Virginia clergyman who had married a wealthy
woman, was so outspoken a Loyalist and an Anglican that he was ultimately burned
in effigy by Patriots. He had tutored George Washington's stepson and was on terms
of dinner-table friendship with the future general. At the time of which he writes, the*

---

[1]From *Reminiscences of an American Loyalist,* p. 109, edited by Edmund S. Bouchier. Copyright 1925 by
Houghton Mifflin Company.

*colonials were fighting near Boston for a redress of grievances, not for indepen-
dence, and the newly appointed George Washington was about to join them as their
commander. What does Boucher's account of the following incident reveal about
Washington's character and the aims of the Patriots?*

I happened to be going across the Potomac to Alexandria [Virginia] with my
wife and some other of our friends, exactly at the time that General Washington was
crossing it on his way to the northward, whither he was going to take command of
the Continental Army. There had been a great meeting of people, and great doings
in Alexandria on the occasion; and everybody seemed to be on fire, either with rum,
or patriotism, or both.

Some patriots in our boat huzzaed, and gave three cheers to the General as he
passed us; whilst Mr. Addison and myself contented ourselves with pulling off our
hats. The General (then only Colonel) Washington beckoned us to stop, as we did,
just, as he said, to shake us by the hand. His behavior to me was now, as it had always been, polite and respectful, and I shall forever remember what passed in the
few disturbed moments of conversation we then had.

From his going on the errand he was, I foresaw and apprised him of much that
has since happened; in particular that there would certainly then be a civil war, and
that the Americans would soon declare for independency. With more earnestness
than was usual with his great reserve, he scouted my apprehensions, adding (and I
believe with perfect sincerity) that if ever I heard of his joining in any such measures, I had his leave to set him down for everything wicked.

2. Washington's Deep Discouragements
(1775–1776)

*General Washington's homespun army of plowmen and artisans, gathered around
Boston, was an ill-disciplined force. It may not have frightened the British, but it certainly worried its commander. Washington's complaints, recorded in letters and repeated endlessly, are most revealing. Who and what were responsible for his chief
difficulties?*

[September 21, 1775, to the President of Congress] It gives me great pain to
be obliged to solicit the attention of the honorable Congress to the state of this
army. . . . But my situation is inexpressibly distressing, to see the winter fast approaching upon a naked army, the time of their service within a few weeks of expiring, and no provision yet made for such important events. Added to this, the
military chest is totally exhausted; the paymaster has not a single dollar in hand; the
commissary-general assures me he has strained his credit to the utmost for the subsistence of the army. The quartermaster-general is precisely in the same situation;
and the greater part of the army are in a state not far from mutiny, upon the deduc-
tion from their stated allowance. I know not to whom I am to impute this failure; but

---

[2]J. C. Fitzpatrick, ed., *The Writings of George Washington* (Washington, D.C.: U.S. Government Printing Office, 1931), vol. 3, p. 512; vol. 4, pp. 124–125, 243.

I am of opinion, if the evil is not immediately remedied, and more punctually observed in future, the army must absolutely break up.

[November 28, 1775, to Joseph Reed] What an astonishing thing it is that those who are employed to sign the Continental bills should not be able, or inclined, to do it as fast as they are wanted. They will prove the destruction of the army, if they are not more attentive and diligent. Such a dearth of public spirit and want of virtue, such stock-jobbing and fertility in all the low arts to obtain advantages of one kind or another, in this great change of military arrangement, I never saw before, and pray God I may never be witness to again. What will be the ultimate end of these manoeuvres is beyond my scan. I tremble at the prospect.

We have been till this time enlisting about three thousand five hundred men. To engage these I have been obliged to allow furloughs as far as fifty men a regiment, and the officers, I am persuaded, indulge as many more. The Connecticut troops will not be prevailed upon to stay longer than their term (saving those who have enlisted for the next campaign, and mostly on furlough), and such a dirty, mercenary spirit pervades the whole that I should not be at all surprised at any disaster that may happen.

In short, after the last of this month our lines will be so weakened that the minute men and militia must be called in for their defense. These, being under no kind of government themselves, will destroy the little subordination I have been laboring to establish, and run me into one evil whilst I am endeavoring to avoid another. But the lesser must be chosen. Could I have foreseen what I have, and am likely to experience, no consideration upon earth should have induced me to accept this command. . . .

[January 14, 1776, to Joseph Reed] . . . I have often thought how much happier I should have been if, instead of accepting of a command under such circumstances, I had taken my musket on my shoulder and entered the ranks; or, if I could have justified the measure to posterity and my own conscience, had retired to the back country, and lived in a wigwam. If I shall be able to rise superior to these and many other difficulties which might be enumerated, I shall most religiously believe that the finger of Providence is in it, to blind the eyes of our enemies. For surely, if we get well through this month, it must be for want of their knowing the disadvantages we labor under.

3. The Unreliable Militia (1776)

Washington's makeshift army, after finally forcing the British out of Boston in March 1776, was badly defeated later in the year while defending New York City. On one occasion Washington tried to beat the fleeing militia into line with the flat of his sword. From the discouraging letter that he wrote several weeks later to the president of Congress, determine why he regarded the militiamen as poor fighters, poor soldiers, and prone to desertion.

To place any dependence upon militia is assuredly resting upon a broken staff. Men just dragged from the tender scenes of domestic life, unaccustomed to the din

---

[3]J. C. Fitzpatrick, ed., *The Writings of George Washington* (1931), vol. 6, pp. 110–112 (September 24, 1776).

of arms, totally unacquainted with every kind of military skill, which (being followed by want of confidence in themselves when opposed to troops regularly trained, disciplined, and appointed, superior in knowledge and superior in arms) makes them timid and ready to fly from their own shadows.

Besides, the sudden change in their manner of living (particularly in the lodging) brings on sickness in many, impatience in all, and such an unconquerable desire of returning to their respective homes that it not only produces shameful and scandalous desertions among themselves, but infuses the like spirit in others.

Again, men accustomed to unbounded freedom and no control cannot brook the restraint which is indispensably necessary to the good order and government of an army, without which licentiousness and every kind of disorder triumphantly reign. . . .

The jealousies [suspicions] of a standing army, and the evils to be apprehended from one, are remote, and, in my judgment, situated and circumstanced as we are, not at all to be dreaded. But the consequence of wanting [lacking] one, according to my ideas formed from the present view of things, is certain and inevitable ruin. For, if I was called upon to declare upon oath whether the militia have been most serviceable or hurtful upon the whole, I should subscribe to the latter.

B. The Formal Break with Britain

1. Thomas Paine Talks Common Sense (1776)

Despite the shooting at Lexington, Concord, and Bunker Hill; despite the British burning of Falmouth (Maine) and Norfolk (Virginia); despite the king's hiring of German (Hessian) mercenaries, the American colonials professed to be fighting merely for reconciliation. But killing redcoats with one hand and waving the olive branch with the other seemed ridiculous to Thomas Paine, a thirty-nine-year-old agitator from England who had arrived in Philadelphia about a year earlier. Of humble birth, impoverished, largely self-educated, and early apprenticed to a corset maker, he was a born rebel who had failed at various undertakings. But he rocketed to fame with a forty-seven-page pamphlet published in January 1776 under the title Common Sense. *Selling the incredible total of 120,000 copies in three months, it sharply accelerated the drift toward independence. Paine urged an immediate break, not only to secure foreign assistance but also to fulfill America's moral mandate from the world. Were his views on mercantilism, isolationism, and reconciliation reasonable? Did his arguments appeal more to passion or to logic?*

In the following pages I offer nothing more than simple facts, plain arguments, and common sense: . . .

I have heard it asserted by some that, as America has flourished under her former connection with Great Britain, the same connection is necessary towards her fu-

---

[1]Thomas Paine, *Common Sense* (New York: G. P. Putnam's Sons, 1894), pp. 84–101, passim.

ture happiness, and will always have the same effect. Nothing can be more fallacious than this kind of argument. We may as well assert that, because a child has thrived upon milk, it is never to have meat, or that the first twenty years of our lives is to become a precedent for the next twenty. But even this is admitting more than is true. For I answer roundly that America would have flourished as much, and probably much more, had no European power taken any notice of her. The commerce by which she hath enriched herself are the necessaries of life, and will always have a market while eating is the custom of Europe.

But she [England] has protected us, say some. That she hath engrossed [monopolized] us is true, and defended the continent at our expense, as well as her own, is admitted; and she would have defended Turkey from the same motive, viz. for the sake of trade and dominion. . . .

But Britain is the parent country, say some. Then the more shame upon her conduct. Even brutes do not devour their young, nor savages make war upon their families; wherefore the assertion, if true, turns to her reproach. But it happens not to be true, or only partly so. . . . Europe, and not England, is the parent country of America. This new world hath been the asylum for the persecuted lovers of civil and religious liberty from every part of Europe. Hither have they fled, not from the tender embraces of the mother, but from the cruelty of the monster; and it is so far true of England that the same tyranny which drove the first emigrants from home pursues their descendants still. . . .

. . . Any submission to, or dependence on, Great Britain tends directly to involve this continent in European wars and quarrels, and set us at variance with nations who would otherwise seek our friendship, and against whom we have neither anger nor complaint. As Europe is our market for trade, we ought to form no partial [preferential] connection with any part of it. It is the true interest of America to steer clear of European contentions, which she never can do while, by her dependence on Britain, she is made the makeweight in the scale of British politics. . . .

Everything that is right or reasonable pleads for separation. The blood of the slain, the weeping voice of nature, cries, 'tis time to part. Even the distance at which the Almighty hath placed England and America is a strong and natural proof that the authority of the one over the other was never the design of Heaven. . . .

But if you say, you can still pass the violations over, then I ask, Hath your house been burnt? Hath your property been destroyed before your face? Are your wife and children destitute of a bed to lie on, or bread to live on? Have you lost a parent or a child by their hands, and yourself the ruined and wretched survivor? If you have not, then are you not a judge of those who have. But if you have, and can still shake hands with the murderers, then are you unworthy the name of husband, father, friend, or lover; and whatever may be your rank or title in life, you have the heart of a coward, and the spirit of a sycophant. . . .

Every quiet method for peace hath been ineffectual. Our prayers have been rejected with disdain. . . . Wherefore, since nothing but blows will do, for God's sake let us come to a final separation. . . .

Small islands, not capable of protecting themselves, are the proper objects for government to take under their care. But there is something absurd in supposing a continent to be perpetually governed by an island. In no instance hath nature made the satellite larger than its primary planet; and as England and America, with respect to each other, reverse the common order of nature, it is evident that they belong to different systems. England to Europe: America to itself. . . .

No man was a warmer wisher for a reconciliation than myself before the fatal nineteenth of April, 1775 [Lexington]. But the moment the event of that day was made known, I rejected the hardened, sullen-tempered Pharaoh of England [George III] for ever; and disdain the wretch that, with the pretended title of Father of his People, can unfeelingly hear of their slaughter, and composedly sleep with their blood upon his soul. . . .

And in order to show that reconciliation now is a dangerous doctrine, I affirm that it would be policy in the King at this time to repeal the acts, for the sake of re-instating himself in the government of the provinces; in order that *he may accom-plish by craft and subtlety in the long run what he cannot do by force and violence in the short one.* Reconciliation and ruin are nearly related. . . .

You that tell us of harmony and reconciliation, can you restore to us the time that is past? Can you give to prostitution its former innocence? Neither can you rec-oncile Britain and America. . . . There are injuries which nature cannot forgive; she would cease to be nature if she did. As well can the lover forgive the ravisher of his mistress as the continent forgive the murders of Britain. The Almighty hath im-planted in us these unextinguishable feelings for good and wise purposes . . . They distinguish us from the herd of common animals. . . .

O! you that love mankind! You that dare oppose not only the tyranny but the tyrant, stand forth! Every spot of the old world is overrun with oppression. Freedom hath been hunted round the globe. Asia and Africa have long expelled her. Europe regards her like a stranger, and England hath given her warning to depart. O! receive the fugitive, and prepare in time an asylum for mankind.

2. Richard Henry Lee's Resolution of Independence (1776)

Richard Henry Lee of Virginia, one of the earliest advocates of a complete break, pro-posed the following three resolutions in the Continental Congress at Philadelphia on June 7, 1776. After a spirited debate, the first one was approved on July 2 by the rep-resentatives of twelve states. This was in fact the original "declaration" of indepen-dence; and John Adams wrote his wife that the day would thereafter be observed by future generations as the great anniversary festival, with fireworks and other mani-festations of joy. But he miscalculated by two days. Why was this resolution for inde-pendence less memorable than Jefferson's historic document, which follows?

Resolved, That these United Colonies are, and of right ought to be, free and in-dependent States; that they are absolved from all allegiance to the British Crown; and that all political connection between them and the State of Great Britain is, and ought to be, totally dissolved.

That it is expedient forthwith to take the most effectual measures for forming foreign alliances.

---

[2]W. C. Ford, ed., *Journals of the Continental Congress* (1906), vol. 5, p. 425.

That a plan of confederation be prepared and transmitted to the respective Colonies for their consideration and approbation.

3. Thomas Jefferson's Declaration of Independence (1776)

Lee's immortal resolution of independence, passed on July 2, formally cut all ties with Britain. But so momentous a step could not be taken without a convincing explanation, partly in the hope of eliciting foreign sympathy and military aid. The Continental Congress had appointed a committee to prepare such an appeal, and the tall, sandy-haired Thomas Jefferson, then only thirty-three years old, was named chief draftsman. The Declaration (Explanation) of Independence, formally adopted on July 4, 1776, contained little new. It embodied the doctrine of natural rights and John Locke's ancient "compact theory" of government, as well as a formidable and partisan list of grievances, as though from a prosecuting attorney. But the language of the Declaration was so incisive and eloquent that this subversive document—designed primarily to subvert British rule—was magnificently successful. What persons or groups of persons are blamed, and which one is blamed the most? Does Jefferson offer any hint that the colonials themselves were partly at fault?

[I]

When, in the course of human events, it becomes necessary for one people to dissolve the political bands which have connected them with another, and to assume, among the powers of the earth, the separate and equal station to which the laws of nature and of nature's God entitle them, a decent respect to the opinions of mankind requires that they should declare the causes which impel them to the separation.

We hold these truths to be self-evident: that all men are created equal; that they are endowed by their Creator with certain unalienable rights; that among these are life, liberty, and the pursuit of happiness. That to secure these rights, governments are instituted among men, deriving their just powers from the consent of the governed. That, whenever any form of government becomes destructive of these ends, it is the right of the people to alter or to abolish it, and to institute new government, laying its foundation on such principles, and organizing its powers in such form, as to them shall seem most likely to effect their safety and happiness.

Prudence, indeed, will dictate that governments long established should not be changed for light and transient causes; and accordingly all experience hath shown that mankind are more disposed to suffer, while evils are sufferable, than to right themselves by abolishing the forms to which they are accustomed. But when a long train of abuses and usurpations, pursuing invariably the same object, evinces a design to reduce them under absolute despotism, it is their right, it is their duty, to throw off such government, and to provide new guards for their future security. Such has been the patient sufferance of these colonies; and such is now the necessity which constrains them to alter their former systems of government.

---

[3]W. C. Ford, ed., *Journals of the Continental Congress* (1906), vol. 5, pp. 510–515.

[II]

The history of the present King of Great Britain is a history of repeated injuries and usurpations, all having in direct object the establishment of an absolute tyranny over these states. To prove this, let facts be submitted to a candid world.

He has refused his assent to laws the most wholesome and necessary for the public good.

He has forbidden his governors to pass laws of immediate and pressing importance, unless suspended in their operation till his assent should be obtained, and when so suspended, he has utterly neglected to attend to them.

He has refused to pass other laws for the accommodation of large districts of people, unless those people would relinquish the right of representation in the legislature, a right inestimable to them and formidable to tyrants only.

He has called together legislative bodies at places unusual, uncomfortable, and distant from the depository of their public records, for the sole purpose of fatiguing them into compliance with his measures.

He has dissolved representative houses repeatedly for opposing, with manly firmness, his invasions on the rights of the people.

He has refused for a long time, after such dissolutions, to cause others to be elected; whereby the legislative powers, incapable of annihilation, have returned to the people at large for their exercise; the state remaining in the mean time, exposed to all the dangers of invasion from without and convulsions within.

He has endeavored to prevent the population [populating] of these states; for that purpose obstructing the laws for naturalization of foreigners, refusing to pass others to encourage their migration hither, and raising the conditions of new appropriations of lands.

He has obstructed the administration of justice by refusing his assent to laws for establishing judiciary powers.

He has made judges dependent on his will alone for the tenure of their offices and the amount and payment of their salaries.

He has erected a multitude of new offices, and sent hither swarms of officers to harass our people and eat out their substance.

He has kept among us, in time of peace, standing armies without the consent of our legislatures.

He has affected to render the military independent of and superior to the civil power.

[III]

He has combined with others to subject us to a jurisdiction [by Parliament] foreign to our constitution, and unacknowledged by our laws; giving his assent to their acts of pretended legislation:

For quartering large bodies of armed troops among us;

For protecting them, by a mock trial, from punishment for any murders which they should commit on the inhabitants of these states;

For cutting off our trade with all parts of the world;

For imposing taxes on us without our consent;

For depriving us, in many cases, of the benefits of trial by jury;

For transporting us beyond seas to be tried for pretended offenses;

For abolishing the free system of English laws in a neighboring province [Quebec], establishing therein an arbitrary government, and enlarging its boundaries so as to render it at once an example and fit instrument for introducing the same absolute rule into these colonies [a reference to the Quebec Act of 1774];

For taking away our charters, abolishing our most valuable laws, and altering fundamentally the forms of our governments;

For suspending our own legislatures and declaring themselves invested with power to legislate for us in all cases whatsoever.

[IV]

He has abdicated government here by declaring us out of his protection and waging war against us.

He has plundered our seas, ravaged our coasts, burnt our towns, and destroyed the lives of our people.

He is at this time transporting large armies of foreign mercenaries to complete the works of death, desolation, and tyranny already begun with circumstances of cruelty and perfidy scarcely paralleled in the most barbarous ages, and totally unworthy the head of a civilized nation.

He has constrained our fellow citizens, taken captive on the high seas, to bear arms against their country, to become the executioners of their friends and brethren, or to fall themselves by their hands.

He has excited domestic insurrections amongst us, and has endeavored to bring on the inhabitants of our frontiers the merciless Indian savages, whose known rule of warfare is an undistinguished destruction of all ages, sexes, and conditions.

In every stage of these oppressions we have petitioned for redress in the most humble terms; our repeated petitions have been answered only by repeated injury. A prince whose character is thus marked by every act which may define a tyrant is unfit to be the ruler of a free people.

[V]

Nor have we been wanting in attention to our British brethren. We have warned them from time to time of attempts by their legislature to extend an unwarrantable jurisdiction over us. We have reminded them of the circumstances of our emigration and settlement here. We have appealed to their native justice and magnanimity, and we have conjured them, by the ties of our common kindred, to disavow these usurpations, which would inevitably interrupt our connections and correspondence. They too have been deaf to the voice of justice and consanguinity. We must, therefore, acquiesce in the necessity which denounces [announces] our separation, and hold them, as we hold the rest of mankind, enemies in war, in peace friends.

[VI]

We, therefore, the representatives of the United States of America, in General Congress assembled, appealing to the Supreme Judge of the world for the rectitude of our intentions, do in the name and by the authority of the good people of these colonies, solemnly publish and declare, That these United Colonies are, and of right ought to be, *free and independent states;* that they are absolved from all allegiance to the British Crown, and that all political connection between them and the state of

Great Britain is, and ought to be, totally dissolved; and that as free and independent states they have full power to levy war, conclude peace, contract alliances, establish commerce, and to do all other acts and things which independent states may of right do. And for the support of this Declaration, with a firm reliance on the protection of Divine Providence, we mutually pledge to each other our lives, our fortunes, and our sacred honor.

4. The Abortive Slave Trade Indictment (1776)

Farsighted colonials had repeatedly attempted in their local assemblies to restrict or stop the odious African slave trade. But the London government, responding to the anguished cries of British (and New England) slave traders, had killed all such laws with the royal veto—five times in the case of Virginia alone. Jefferson added this grievance to the original indictment, but Congress threw it out, largely because of opposition from those parts of the South heavily dependent on the slave trade. Would this clause have added to the effectiveness of the Declaration of Independence? How, if at all, might its inclusion have changed the subsequent course of human history?

He [George III] has waged cruel war against human nature itself, violating its most sacred rights of life and liberty in the persons of a distant people who never offended him, captivating and carrying them into slavery in another hemisphere, or to incur miserable death in their transportation thither. This piratical warfare, the opprobrium of infidel powers, is the warfare of the Christian King of Great Britain. Determined to keep open a market where *men* should be bought and sold, he has prostituted his negative [royal veto] for suppressing every legislative attempt to prohibit or to restrain this execrable commerce. And that this assemblage of horrors might want no fact of distinguished dye [might lack no flagrant crime], he is now exciting those very people to rise in arms among us, and to purchase that liberty of which he has deprived them by murdering the people upon whom he also obtruded them: thus paying off former crimes committed against the liberties of one people with crimes which he urges them to commit against the lives of another.

C. Voices of Dissent

1. Lord Chatham Assails the War (1777)

Partisan clamor in England between the ruling Tories and the out-of-office Whigs aided the Patriot cause in America. Many English Whigs, partly to embarrass the Tory government, proclaimed that the Americans were merely fighting for English liberties. After the bloodshed at Lexington and Concord, some English Whigs wore mourning out of respect for the colonials who had died. William Pitt, the great

[4]J. H. Hazelton, *The Declaration of Independence* (New York: Dodd, Mead and Company, 1906), p. 144.
[1]D. J. Brewer, ed., *World's Best Orations* (St. Louis and Chicago: F. P. Kaiser, 1899), vol. 3, 1069–1073.

organizer of victory in the Seven Years' War, had become a peer (Lord Chatham) in 1766. Suffering acutely from gout and other afflictions, he pulled himself together for the following superlative oratorical effort six months before his death at the age of sixty-nine. The shocking news of General Burgoyne's surrender at Saratoga had not yet reached England. Was Pitt's speech treasonable? Did he favor independence? Was he justified in criticizing Britain's military policies?

My lords, this ruinous and ignominious situation, where we cannot act with success, nor suffer with honor, calls upon us to remonstrate in the strongest and loudest language of truth, to rescue the ear of majesty from the delusions which surround it.

The desperate state of our arms abroad is in part known: no man thinks more highly of them than I do. I love and honor the English troops. I know their virtues and their valor. I know they can achieve anything except impossibilities; and I know that the conquest of English America is an impossibility.

You cannot, I venture to say it, you cannot conquer America. Your armies in the last [Seven Years'] war effected everything that could be effected; and what was it? It cost a numerous army, under the command of a most able general [Amherst], now a noble lord in this house, a long and laborious campaign, to expel five thousand Frenchmen from French America. My lords, you cannot conquer America. What is your present situation there? We do not know the worst; but we know that in three campaigns we have done nothing and suffered much. . . .

As to conquest, therefore, my lords, I repeat, it is impossible. You may swell every expense and every effort still more extravagantly; pile and accumulate every assistance you can buy or borrow; traffic and barter with every little pitiful German prince that sells and sends his subjects to the shambles of a foreign prince. Your efforts are forever vain and impotent; doubly so from this mercenary aid on which you rely. For it irritates, to an incurable resentment, the minds of your enemies—to overrun them with the mercenary sons of rapine and plunder; devoting them and their possessions to the rapacity of hireling cruelty! If I were an American, as I am an Englishman, while a foreign troop was landed in my country, I never would lay down my arms—never—never—never!

Your own army is infected with the contagion of these illiberal allies. The spirit of plunder and of rapine is gone forth among them. . . . I know from authentic information, and the most experienced officers, that our discipline is deeply wounded. Whilst this is notoriously our sinking situation, America grows and flourishes; whilst our strength and discipline are lowered, hers are rising and improving.

But, my lords, who is the man that, in addition to these disgraces and mischiefs of our army, has dared to authorize and associate to our arms the tomahawk and scalping knife of the savage? To call into civilized alliance the wild and inhuman savage of the woods; to delegate to the merciless Indian the defense of disputed rights; and to wage the horrors of his barbarous war against our brethren? My lords, these enormities cry aloud for redress and punishment. Unless thoroughly done away, it will be a stain on the national character. It is a violation of the constitution. I believe it is against law. It is not the least of our national misfortunes that the strength and character of our army are thus impaired. Infected with the mercenary spirit of robbery and rapine, familiarized to the horrid scenes of savage cruelty, it can no longer boast of the noble and generous principles which dignify a soldier. . . .

My lords, no man wishes for the due dependence of America on this country more than I do. To preserve it, and not confirm that state of independence into which your measures hitherto have driven them, is the object which we ought to unite in attaining. The Americans, contending for their rights against arbitrary exactions, I love and admire. It is the struggle of free and virtuous patriots. But contending for independency and total disconnection from England, as an Englishman, I cannot wish them success. For, in a due constitutional dependency, including the ancient supremacy of this country in regulating their commerce and navigation, consists the mutual happiness and prosperity both of England and America. She derived assistance and protection from us; and we reaped from her the most important advantages. She was, indeed, the fountain of our wealth, the nerve of our strength, the nursery and basis of our naval power.

It is our duty, therefore, my lords, if we wish to save our country, most seriously to endeavor the recovery of these most beneficial subjects. And in this perilous crisis, perhaps the present moment may be the only one in which we can hope for success. For in their negotiations with France they have, or think they have, reason to complain: though it be notorious that they have received from that power important supplies and assistance of various kinds, yet it is certain they expected it in a more decisive and immediate degree. America is in ill humor with France on some points that have not entirely answered her expectations. Let us wisely take advantage of every possible moment of reconciliation. . . .

You cannot conciliate America by your present measures. You cannot subdue her by your present, or by any, measures. What, then, can you do? You cannot conquer; you cannot gain; but you can address. . . . In a just and necessary war, to maintain the rights or honor of my country, I would strip the shirt from my back to support it. But in such a war as this, unjust in its principle, impracticable in its means, and ruinous in its consequences, would not contribute a single effort, nor a single shilling.

2. Tories Fear French Catholics (1779)

The French, thirsting for revenge after the Seven Years' War, were eager to break up Britain's empire. After the hope-inspiring American victory at Saratoga, they concluded a treaty of alliance with the rebels in 1778. But France had been the traditional enemy of the colonials in four bitter wars, and was a Catholic monarchy besides. American Loyalists attempted to weaken the alliance by arousing anti-Catholic fears, notably in this fictitious diary prophesying horrible events ten years distant. It appeared in Rivington's New York Royal Gazette *(sometimes referred to as "Rivington's Lying Gazette"). Rivington (see p. 130) had fled New York in 1776 but had returned in 1777 to publish his new Loyalist journal under the protection of British bayonets. In the following satire, what are the most fundamental of the liberties allegedly lost, and what items would be most alarming to Protestant Patriots?*

---

[2]*Rivington's New York Royal Gazette,* March 17, 1779, quoted in Frank Moore, *Diary of the American Revolution* (New York: C. Scribner; London: S. Low, Son & Company, 1859), vol. 2, pp. 148–150.

Boston, November 10, 1789.—His Excellency Count Tyran has this day published, by authority from His [French] Majesty, a proclamation for the suppression of heresy and establishment of the Inquisition in this town, which has already begun its functions in many other places of the continent under His Majesty's dominion.

The use of the Bible in the vulgar tongue [English vernacular] is strictly prohibited, on pain of being punished by discretion of the Inquisition.

November 11.—The Catholic religion is not only outwardly professed, but has made the utmost progress among all ranks of people here, owing in a great measure to the unwearied labors of the Dominican and Franciscan friars, who omit no opportunity of scattering the seeds of religion, and converting the wives and daughters of heretics. We hear that the building formerly called the Old South Meeting is fitted up for a cathedral, and that several other old meeting-houses are soon to be repaired for convents. . . .

Philadelphia, November 16.—On Tuesday last arrived here the *St. Esprit,* from Bordeaux, with a most valuable cargo of rosaries, mass books, and indulgences, which have been long expected. . . .

. . . Father Le Cruel, president of the Inquisition in this city, out of a tender regard for the salvation of mankind, has thought proper that an example should be made of an old fellow of the age of ninety, convicted of Quakerism, and of reading the Bible, a copy of which, in the English language, was found in his possession. He was hardened and obstinate beyond measure, and could not be prevailed on to retract his errors. . . .

November 21.—Obadiah Standfast, the Quaker, was this day burnt, pursuant to his sentence. . . .

November 23.—His Majesty has directed his viceroy to send five hundred sons of the principal inhabitants of America to be educated in France, where the utmost care will be taken to imbue them with a just regard for the Catholic faith and a due sense of subordination to government. . . .

Such is the glorious specimen of happiness to be enjoyed by America, in case the interposition of France shall enable her to shake off her dependence on Great Britain.

D. A Civil War Within a Civil War

1. Pistols on the Pulpit (1775)

Jonathan Boucher, the slaveowning Anglican clergyman who knew Washington (see pp. 135–136), was so disdainfully Loyalist that he provoked violence. Once he felled with one punch a blacksmith armed with a stick and gun. Boucher was finally forced to abandon his valuable plantation property in Maryland and sail for England in September 1775, nine months before independence was declared. How does his account display Christian values?

---

[1]From *Reminiscences of an American Loyalist,* p. 113, edited by Edmund S. Bouchier. Copyright 1925 by Houghton Mifflin Company.

. . . In the usual and regular course of preaching, I happened one Sunday to recommend peaceableness; on which a Mr. Lee and sundry others, supposing my sermon to be what they called a stroke at the times, rose up and left the church. This was a signal to the people to consider every sermon of mine as hostile to the views and interests of America; and accordingly I never after went into a pulpit without something very disagreeable happening. I received sundry messages and letters threatening me with the most fatal consequences if I did not (not desist from preaching at all, but) preach what should be agreeable to the friends of America.

All the answer I gave to these threats was in my sermons, in which I uniformly and resolutely declared that I never could suffer any merely human authority to intimidate me from performing what in my conscience I believed and knew to be my duty to God and his Church. And for more than six months I preached, when I did preach, with a pair of loaded pistols lying on the cushion; having given notice that if any man, or body of men, could possibly be so lost to all sense of decency and propriety as to attempt really to do what had been long threatened, that is, to drag me out of my own pulpit, I should think myself justified before God and man in repelling violence by violence.

2. Vengeance on the Tories (1779)

The Loyalists, remaining true to their king, fought back against their Patriot neighbors with all the weapons at their command, including well-armed Indian allies. This was a civil war, and civil wars are inevitably bitter. Even the judicious Washington called the Loyalists "pests of society," many of whom, he thought, ought to commit suicide or be hanged. All told, about eighty thousand of these unfortunates were expelled; some of them later received partial compensation for their losses from the London government. The following outcry by "A Whig" summarizes the chief Patriot grievances, many of which were soundly based. What were the chief economic complaints? What practices would most hinder reconciliation between the Patriots and Loyalists after the war?

Among the many errors America has been guilty of during her contest with Great Britain, few have been greater, or attended with more fatal consequences to these States, than her lenity to the Tories. . . . We are all crying out against the depreciation of our money, and entering into measures to restore it to its value; while the Tories, who are one principal cause of the depreciation, are taken no notice of, but suffered to live quietly among us.

We can no longer be silent on this subject, and see the independence of the country, after standing every shock from without, endangered by internal enemies. Rouse, America! your danger is great—great from a quarter where you least expect it. The Tories, the Tories will yet be the ruin of you! 'Tis high time they were separated from among you. They are now busy engaged in undermining your liberties. They have a thousand ways of doing it, and they make use of them all.

---

[2]*Pennsylvania Packet,* August 5, 1779, in Frank Moore, *Diary of the American Revolution* (1859), vol. 2, pp. 166–168.

Who were the occasion of this war? The Tories! Who persuaded the tyrant of Britain to prosecute it in a manner before unknown to civilized nations, and shocking even to barbarians? The Tories! Who prevailed on the savages of the wilderness to join the standard of the enemy? The Tories! Who have assisted the Indians in taking the scalp from the aged matron, the blooming fair one, the helpless infant, and the dying hero? The Tories! Who advised and who assisted in burning your towns, ravaging your country, and violating the chastity of your women? The Tories! Who are the occasion that thousands of you now mourn the loss of your dearest connections? The Tories! Who have always counteracted the endeavors of Congress to secure the liberties of this country? The Tories!

Who refused their money when as good as specie, though stamped with the image of his most sacred Majesty? The Tories! Who continue to refuse it? The Tories! Who do all in their power to depreciate it? The Tories! Who propagate lies among us to discourage the Whigs? The Tories! Who corrupt the minds of the good people of these States by every species of insidious counsel? The Tories! Who hold a traitorous correspondence with the enemy? The Tories! Who daily send them intelligence? The Tories! Who take the oaths of allegiance to the States one day, and break them the next? The Tories! Who prevent your battalions from being filled? The Tories! Who dissuade men from entering the army? The Tories! Who persuade those who have enlisted to desert? The Tories! Who harbor those who do desert? The Tories! In short, who wish to see us conquered, to see us slaves, to see us hewers of wood and drawers of water? The Tories! . . .

Awake, Americans, to a sense of your danger. No time to be lost. Instantly banish every Tory from among you. Let America be sacred alone to freemen.

Drive far from you every baneful wretch who wishes to see you fettered with the chains of tyranny. Send them where they may enjoy their beloved slavery to perfection—send them to the island of Britain; there let them drink the cup of slavery and eat the bread of bitterness all the days of their existence—there let them drag out a painful life, despised and accursed by those very men whose cause they have had the wickedness to espouse. Never let them return to this happy land—never let them taste the sweets of that independence which they strove to prevent. Banishment, perpetual banishment, should be their lot.

3. The Hanging of a Loyalist (c. 1778)

The untroubled existence of the French émigré Crèvecoeur (see pages 87 and 98) ended with the Revolution. His aristocratic breeding caused him to recoil from the excesses of the Patriots, who forced him off his New York farm to the British sanctuary of New York City. Impoverished, he finally fled to France in 1780. Returning after the war, he learned that his home was in ashes, his wife was dead, and his two children had disappeared during an Indian raid. He ultimately found his offspring, and served for a number of years as French consul in New York City. In the following sketch he describes an incident that presumably occurred following a Tory-Indian raid on the Pennsylvania frontier. A Loyalist by the name of Joseph Wilson, accused of having sheltered three of the Tory attackers, is being hung by his toes and

---

[3]M. G. J. de Crèvecoeur, *Sketches of Eighteenth Century America* (1925 reprint), pp. 183–185.

thumbs to extort a confession. What light does this episode cast on the nature of fron-tier warfare and on the difficulties of remaining mildly Loyalist or even neutral? Could this man Wilson be regarded as a genuine Loyalist?

Whilst in this painful suspension he [Wilson] attested his innocence with all the energy he was master of. By this time his wife, who had been informed of the trag-ical scene, came from her house, with tears gushing in streams, and with a counte-nance of terror. In the most supplicating posture she implored their mercy, but they rejected her request. They accused her of having participated also in her husband's abominable crime. She repeated her entreaties, and at last prevailed on them to re-lieve her husband. They took him down after a suspension of six minutes, which will appear a long interval to whoever considers it anatomically.

The bitter cries of the poor woman, the solemn asseverations of her husband, seemed for a few moments to lull the violence of their rage, as in a violent gale of wind nature admits of some kind intermission which enables the seaman to bring his vessel to. But all of a sudden one of the company arose, more vindictive than the rest. He painted to them their conflagrated houses and barns, the murder of their re-lations and friends. The sudden recollection of these dreadful images wrought them up to a pitch of fury fiercer than before. Conscious as they were that he was the per-son who had harbored the destroyers of their country, they resolved finally to hang him by the neck.

Hard was this poor man's fate. He had been already suspended in a most ex-cruciating situation for not having confessed what was required of him. Had he con-fessed the crime laid to his charge, he must have been hung according to the principle of self-preservation which filled the breasts of these people. What was he then to do? Behold here innocence pregnant with as much danger as guilt itself, a situation which is very common and is characteristic of these times. You may be punished tomorrow for thoughts and sentiments for which you were highly com-mended the preceding day and alternately.

On hearing of his doom, he flung himself at the feet of the first man. He solemnly appealed to God, the searcher of hearts, for the truth of his assertions. He frankly owned that he was attached to the King's cause from ancient respect and by the force of custom; that he had no idea of any other government, but that at the same time he had never forcibly opposed the measures of the country; that his opin-ions had never gone beyond his house; that in peace and silence he had submitted to the will of heaven without ever intending to take part with either side; that he de-tested from the bottom of his heart this mode of war which desolated and ruined so many harmless and passive inhabitants who had committed no other crime than that of living on the frontiers. He earnestly begged and entreated them that they would give him an opportunity of proving his innocence: "Will none of you hear me with patience? I am no stranger, no unknown person; you well know that I am a home-staying man, laborious and peaceable. Would you destroy me on a hearsay? For the sake of that God which knows and sees and judges all men, permit me to have a judicial hearing."

The passive character of this man, though otherwise perfectly inoffensive, had long before been the cause of his having been suspected. Their hearts were hard-ened and their minds prepossessed; they refused his request and justified the sentence of death they had passed. They, however, promised him his life if he would confess who were those traitors that came to his house, and who guided them through the woods to————. With a louder voice than usual, the poor culprit denied his having the least knowledge whatever of these persons, but, seeing that it was all in vain, he peaceably submitted to his fate, and gave himself up to those who were preparing the fatal cord. It was soon tied round the limb of a tree to which they hanged him.

[Some of the executioners, Crèvecoeur relates, experienced a change of heart and cut Wilson down in time to revive him with water. He was subsequently given an impartial trial and acquitted.]

Thought Provokers

1. Why were many Patriot soldiers who had volunteered to defend their liberties so untrustworthy and even cowardly?
2. Paine's *Common Sense* and the Declaration of Independence have both been referred to as the most potent propaganda documents in American history. Comment. Prepare a British rejoinder to the Declaration of Independence. The Declaration was designed primarily to achieve American independence, but it was much more than that. Assess its worldwide, long-range significance.
3. It has been said that the Whigs in England and the Tories (Loyalists) in America were both traitors to a cause. Explain. Seneca wrote, "Loyalty is the holiest good in the human breast." If this is true, why were the American Loyalists regarded as despicable creatures?
4. The War of Independence has been called a civil war within a civil war. Comment. Were the Patriots justified in abusing the Loyalists and expelling them? Argue both sides, and then come to a conclusion.

9

The Confederation and the Constitution, 1776–1790

Should the states reject this excellent Constitution, the probability is that an opportunity will never again offer to make another in peace—the next will be drawn in blood.

George Washington, on signing the Constitution, 1787

Prologue: The nation's first written constitution—the Articles of Confederation (in force 1781–1789)—provided a toothless central government. Disorders inevitably erupted, notably in Massachusetts, though they were exaggerated by those who hoped to substitute a potent federal government. Such pressures eventually bore fruit in the new Constitution framed in Philadelphia during the humid summer of 1787. A century and a quarter later, Charles A. Beard advanced the sensational thesis that propertied men had foisted the Constitution upon the less privileged classes. He underscored the fact that many of the fifty-five framers owned depreciated government securities that would rise in value with the establishment of a powerful central regime. But recent scholarship has indicated Beard overemphasized economic motivation. The crucial struggle was between the big states, which had reluctantly accepted an equal vote in the Senate, and the small states, which rather promptly approved the Constitution. Several of the stronger and more self-sufficient commonwealths, notably Virginia and New York, were among the last to ratify.

A. The Shock of Shays's Rebellion

1. Daniel Gray Explains the Shaysites' Grievances (1786)

When debt-ridden farmers in Massachusetts failed in 1786 to persuade the state legislature to issue cheap paper money and take measures to halt farm foreclosures, violence erupted. One of the Shaysites, Daniel Gray, issued the following statement of

---

[1]George Richards Minot, ed., *History of the Insurrection in Massachusetts in 1786 and of the Rebellion Consequent Thereon* (Worcester, MA: Isaiah Thomas, 1788), as reprinted by Da Capo Press, 1971, pp. 83–84.

the farmers' grievances. What was their principal complaint? Were they justified in taking up arms?

An Address *to the People of the several towns in the county of* Hampshire, *now at arms.*

GENTLEMEN,

We have thought proper to inform you of some of the principal causes of the late risings of the people, and also of their present movement, viz.

1st. The present expensive mode of collecting debts, which, by reason of the great scarcity of cash, will of necessity fill our goals with unhappy debtors, and thereby a reputable body of people rendered incapable of being serviceable either to themselves or the community.

2d. The monies raised by impost and excise being appropriated to discharge the interest of governmental securities, and not the foreign debt, when these securities are not subject to taxation.

3d. A suspension of the writ of *Habeas corpus,* by which those persons who have stepped forth to assert and maintain the rights of the people, are liable to be taken and conveyed even to the most distant part of the Commonwealth, and thereby subjected to an unjust punishment.

4th. The unlimited power granted to Justices of the Peace and Sheriffs, Deputy Sheriffs, and Constables, by the Riot Act, indemnifying them to the prosecution thereof; when perhaps, wholly actuated from a principle of revenge, hatred and envy.

Furthermore, Be assured, that this body, now at arms, despise the idea of being instigated by British emissaries, which is so strenuously propagated by the enemies of our liberties: And also wish the most proper and speedy measures may be taken, to discharge both our foreign and domestic debt.

> Per Order,
> Daniel Gray, *Chairman of the Committee, for the above purpose.*

2. George Washington Expresses Alarm (1786)

The retired war hero Washington, struggling to repair his damaged fortunes at Mount Vernon, was alarmed by the inability of the Congress under the Articles of Confederation to collect taxes and regulate interstate commerce. The states, racked by the depression of 1784–1788, seemed to be going their thirteen separate ways. The worthy farmers of western Massachusetts were especially hard hit, burdened as they were with inequitable and delinquent taxes, mortgage foreclosures, and the prospect of imprisonment for debt. Hundreds of them, under the Revolutionary Captain Daniel Shays, formed armed mobs in an effort to close the courts and to force the issuance of paper money. "Good God!" burst out Washington on hearing of these disorders; "who, besides a Tory, could have foreseen, or a Briton have predicted them?"

---

[2]J. C. Fitzpatrick, ed., *Writings of George Washington* (Washington, D.C.: U.S. Government Printing Office, 1938), vol. 28, pp. 502–503 (August 1, 1786).

He wrote despairingly as follows to John Jay, the prominent New York statesman and diplomat. What single fear seems to disturb Washington most, and why?

Your sentiments, that our affairs are drawing rapidly to a crisis, accord with my own. What the event will be is also beyond the reach of my foresight. We have errors to correct; we have probably had too good an opinion of human nature in forming our Confederation. Experience has taught us that men will not adopt, and carry into execution, measures the best calculated for their own good, without the intervention of coercive power. I do not conceive we can exist long as a nation without lodging, somewhere, a power which will pervade the whole Union in as energetic a manner as the authority of the state governments extends over the several states.

To be fearful of investing Congress, constituted as that body is, with ample authorities for national purposes, appears to me the very climax of popular absurdity and madness. Could Congress exert them for the detriment of the people without injuring themselves in an equal or greater proportion? Are not their interests inseparably connected with those of their constituents? By the rotation of appointments [annual elections], must they not mingle frequently with the mass of citizens? . . .

What then is to be done? Things cannot go on in the same train forever. It is much to be feared, as you observe, that the better kind of people, being disgusted with these circumstances, will have their minds prepared for any revolution whatever. We are apt to run from one extreme to another. To anticipate and prevent disastrous contingencies would be the part of wisdom and patriotism.

What astonishing changes a few years are capable of producing! I am told that even respectable characters speak of a monarchical form of government without horror. From thinking proceeds speaking; thence to acting is often but a single step. But how irrevocable and tremendous! What a triumph for our enemies to verify their predictions! What a triumph for the advocates of despotism to find that we are incapable of governing ourselves, and that systems founded on the basis of equal liberty are merely ideal and fallacious. Would to God that wise measures may be taken in time to avert the consequences we have but too much reason to apprehend.

3. Thomas Jefferson Favors Rebellion (1787)

Thomas Jefferson was the successor to Dr. Benjamin Franklin as American minister to France, 1785 to 1789. ("I do not replace him, sir; I am only his successor," he remarked with both wit and modesty.) As an ultraliberal and a specialist in revolution, this author of the Declaration of Independence wrote as follows about Shays's Rebellion to his Virginia neighbor, James Madison. The complete crushing of the uprising had not yet occurred. What did Jefferson regard as the most important cause of the disturbance, and what was most extreme about his judgment?

. . . I am impatient to learn your sentiments on the late troubles in the Eastern [New England] states. So far as I have yet seen, they do not appear to threaten seri-

---

[3]P. L. Ford, ed., *Writings of Thomas Jefferson* (New York: G. P. Putnam's Sons, 1894), vol. 4, pp. 361–363.

ous consequences. Those states have suffered by the stoppage of the channels of their commerce, which have not yet found other issues. This must render money scarce, and make the people uneasy. This uneasiness has produced acts absolutely unjustifiable; but I hope they will provoke no severities from their governments. A consciousness of those in power that their administration of the public affairs has been honest may perhaps produce too great a degree of indignation; and those characters wherein fear predominates over hope may apprehend too much from these instances of irregularity. They may conclude too hastily that nature has formed man insusceptible of any other government but that of force, a conclusion not founded in truth, nor experience. . . .

Even this evil is productive of good. It prevents the degeneracy of government, and nourishes a general attention to the public affairs. I hold it that a little rebellion now and then is a good thing, and as necessary in the political world as storms in the physical. Unsuccessful rebellions indeed generally establish the encroachments on the rights of the people which have produced them. An observation of this truth should render honest republican governors so mild in their punishment of rebellions as not to discourage them too much. It is a medicine necessary for the sound health of government.

B. Clashes in the Philadelphia Convention

1. The Debate on Representation in Congress (1787)

After Shays's Rebellion collapsed, pressures for a stronger central government mounted. Finally, in the summer of 1787, delegates from twelve states met in Philadelphia to strengthen the Articles of Confederation—actually to frame a new constitution. The most complete record of the debates was kept by James Madison of Virginia, the youthful "Father of the Constitution." A portion of his notes follows. The reader must be warned that two of the speakers, Elbridge Gerry of Massachusetts and George Mason of Virginia, not only refused to sign the Constitution but fought against its adoption. Do these debates show the Framing Fathers to be truly democratic? What were the most impressive arguments for and against popular election of representatives? Which side was right?

Resolution 4, first clause: "that the members of the first branch [House of Representatives] of the national legislature ought to be elected by the people of the several states" (being taken up),

Mr. Sherman [of Connecticut] opposed the election by the people, insisting that it ought to be by the state legislatures. The people, he said, immediately should have as little to do as may be about the government. They want [lack] information and are constantly liable to be misled.

Mr. Gerry [of Massachusetts]. The evils we experience flow from the excess of democracy. The people do not want virtue, but are the dupes of pretended patriots.

---

[1]Max Farrand, ed., *The Records of the Federal Convention of 1787* (New Haven: Yale University Press, 1911), vol. 1, pp. 48–50 (May 31, 1787).

In Massachusetts, it has been fully confirmed by experience that they are daily misled into the most baneful measures and opinions by the false reports circulated by designing men, and which no one on the spot can refute. . . . He had, he said, been too republican heretofore: he was still, however, republican, but had been taught by experience the danger of the leveling spirit.

Mr. Mason [of Virginia] argued strongly for an election of the larger branch by the people. It was to be the grand depository of the democratic principle of the government. It was, so to speak, to be our House of Commons. It ought to know and sympathize with every part of the community, and ought therefore to be taken not only from different parts of the whole republic, but also from different districts of the larger members of it, which had in several instances, particularly in Virginia, different interests and views arising from difference of produce, of habits, etc., etc.

He admitted that we had been too democratic but was afraid we should incautiously run into the opposite extreme. We ought to attend to the rights of every class of the people. . . .

Mr. Wilson [of Pennsylvania] contended strenuously for drawing the most numerous branch of the legislature immediately from the people. He was for raising the federal pyramid to a considerable altitude, and for that reason wished to give it as broad a basis as possible. No government could long subsist without the confidence of the people. In a republican government this confidence was peculiarly essential. He also thought it wrong to increase the weight of the state legislatures by making them the electors of the national legislature. All interference between the general and local governments should be obviated as much as possible. On examination it would be found that the opposition of states to federal measures had proceeded much more from the officers of the states than from the people at large.

Mr. Madison [of Virginia] considered the popular election of one branch of the national legislature as essential to every plan of free government. . . . He thought, too, that the great fabric to be raised would be more stable and durable if it should rest on the solid foundation of the people themselves than if it should stand merely on the pillars of the legislatures. . . .

On the question for an election of the first branch of the national legislature by the people: Massachusetts, aye; Connecticut, divided; New York, aye; New Jersey, no; Pennsylvania, aye; Delaware, divided; Virginia, aye; North Carolina, aye; South Carolina, no; Georgia, aye. (Ayes—6; noes—2; divided—2.)

2. The Argument over Slave Importations (1787)

The issue of slavery provoked spirited debate at Philadelphia. Should the black slave count as a whole person or as no person at all in apportioning representation in Congress? The compromise: a slave would count as three-fifths of a person. Should the further importation of slaves be shut off or allowed to continue forever? The compromise: Congress could not touch slave importation for twenty years (a concession to the South), but Congress by a simple majority rather than by a two-thirds vote could pass laws to control shipping (a concession to the commercial North). As this

---

[2]Max Farrand, ed., *The Records of the Federal Convention of 1787* (New Haven: Yale University Press, 1911), vol. 2, pp. 364–365, 369–372.

portion of the debate opens, according to James Madison, delegate Luther Martin of Maryland, a man of well-known liberal tendencies, is endeavoring to amend a draft article stipulating that slave importation was not to be prohibited or taxed. What were the arguments for nonimportation and those for continued importation? What might have happened if the convention had voted to stop all slave importations at once?

[August 21.] *Mr. L. Martin* [of Maryland] proposed to vary article 7, sect. 4 so as to allow a prohibition or tax on the importation of slaves. First, as five slaves are to be counted as three freemen in the apportionment of representatives, such a clause would leave an encouragement to this traffic. Second, slaves [through danger of insurrection] weakened one part of the Union, which the other parts were bound to protect; the privilege of importing them was therefore unreasonable. Third, it was inconsistent with the principles of the Revolution, and dishonorable to the American character, to have such a feature in the Constitution.

Mr. Rutledge [of South Carolina] did not see how the importation of slaves could be encouraged by this section [as now phrased]. He was not apprehensive of insurrections, and would readily exempt the other states from the obligation to protect the Southern against them. Religion and humanity had nothing to do with this question. Interest alone is the governing principle with nations. The true question at present is whether the Southern states shall or shall not be parties to the Union. If the Northern states consult their interest, they will not oppose the increase of slaves, which will increase the commodities of which they will become the carriers.

Mr. Ellsworth [of Connecticut] was for leaving the clause as it stands. Let every state import what it pleases. The morality or wisdom of slavery are considerations belonging to the states themselves. What enriches a part enriches the whole, and the states are the best judges of their particular interest. The old Confederation had not meddled with this point; and he did not see any greater necessity for bringing it within the policy of the new one.

Mr. [Charles] Pinckney [of South Carolina]. South Carolina can never receive the plan if it prohibits the slave trade. In every proposed extension of the powers of Congress, that state has expressly and watchfully excepted that of meddling with the importation of Negroes. If the states be all left at liberty on this subject, South Carolina may perhaps, by degrees, do of herself what is wished, as Virginia and Maryland already have done. . . .

Mr. Sherman [of Connecticut] was for leaving the clause as it stands. He disapproved of the slave trade; yet, as the states were now possessed of the right to import slaves, as the public good did not require it to be taken from them, and as it was expedient to have as few objections as possible to the proposed scheme of government, he thought it best to leave the matter as we find it. He observed that the abolition of slavery seemed to be going on in the United States, and that the good sense of the several states would probably by degrees complete it. . . .

Col. Mason [of Virginia]. This infernal traffic originated in the avarice of British merchants. The British government constantly checked the attempts of Virginia to put a stop to it. The present question concerns not the importing states alone, but the whole Union. . . . Maryland and Virginia, he said, had already prohibited the importation of slaves expressly. North Carolina had done the same in substance. All this would be in vain if South Carolina and Georgia be at liberty to import. The Western people are already calling out for slaves for their new lands, and will fill that country with slaves, if they can be got through South Carolina and Georgia. Slavery discourages arts and manufactures. The poor despise labor when performed by slaves. They prevent the immigration of whites, who really enrich and strengthen a country. They produce the most pernicious effect on manners. Every master of slaves is born a petty tyrant. They bring the judgment of Heaven on a country. As nations cannot be rewarded or punished in the next world, they must be in this. By an inevitable chain of causes and effects, Providence punishes national sins by national calamities. He lamented that some of our Eastern [New England] brethren had, from a lust of gain, embarked in this nefarious traffic. . . . He held it essential, in every point of view, that the general government should have power to prevent the increase of slavery.

Mr. Ellsworth [of Connecticut], as he had never owned a slave, could not judge of the effects of slavery on character. He said, however, that if it was to be considered in a moral light, we ought to go further, and free those already in the country. As slaves also multiply so fast in Virginia and Maryland that it is cheaper to raise than import them, whilst in the sickly rice swamps foreign supplies are necessary, if we go no further than is urged, we shall be unjust towards South Carolina and Georgia. Let us not intermeddle. As population increases, poor laborers will be so plenty as to render slaves useless. Slavery, in time, will not be a speck in our country. . . .

Gen. [Charles C.] Pinckney [of South Carolina] declared it to be his firm opinion that if himself and all his colleagues were to sign the Constitution, and use their personal influence, it would be of no avail towards obtaining the assent of their constituents [to a slave trade prohibition]. South Carolina and Georgia cannot do without slaves. As to Virginia, she will gain by stopping the importations. Her slaves will rise in value, and she has more than she wants. It would be unequal to require South Carolina and Georgia to confederate on such unequal terms. . . . He contended that the importation of slaves would be for the interest of the whole Union. The more slaves, the more produce to employ the carrying trade; the more consumption also; and the more of this, the more of revenue for the common treasury. He admitted it to be reasonable that slaves should be duted like other imports; but should consider a rejection of the clause as an exclusion of South Carolina from the Union.

[The final compromise, as written into the Constitution, permitted Congress to levy a maximum duty of ten dollars a head on each slave imported. In 1808, the earliest date permitted by the framers, Congress ended all legal importation of slaves.]

3. Singing for the Constitution (1787)

When the results of the Philadelphia Convention were promulgated, popular passions for and against the new Constitution were aroused. In the pro-Constitution song below, what seems most to have shaped opinion favorable to the Constitution?

---

[3]*Publications of the Colonial Society of Massachusetts.* Vol. 8, *Transactions, 1902–1904* (Boston: Colonial Society of Massachusetts, 1906), pp. 273–275.

The Grand Constitution: A New Federal Song

To the Tune of—*"Our Freedom we've won, &c."*

From scenes of affliction—Columbia opprest—
Of credit expiring—and commerce distrest,
Of nothing to do—and of nothing to pay—
From such dismal scenes let us hasten away.

Our Freedom we've won and the Prize let's maintain,
  Our Hearts are all right,
  Unite, Boys, Unite,
And our EMPIRE *in glory shall ever remain.*

The *Muses* no longer the cypress shall wear.
For we turn our glad eyes to a prospect more fair:
The *Soldier* return'd to his small cultur'd farm,
Enjoys the reward of his conquering arm,
        Our Freedom, &c.

Our trade and our commerce shall reach far and wide,
And riches and honour flow in with each tide,
Kamschatka and *China* with wonder shall stare,
That the *Federal stripes* shou'd wave gracefully there.
        Our Freedom, &c.

With gratitude let us acknowledge the worth,
Of what the *Convention* has call'd into birth,
And the Continent wisely confirm what is done
By *Franklin* the Sage, and by brave *Washington.*
        Our Freedom, &c.

The wise *Constitution* let's truly revere,
It points out the course for our *Empire* to steer,
For Oceans of bliss, do they hoist the broad sail,
And *Peace* is the current, and *Plenty* the gale.
        Our Freedom, &c.

With gratitude fill'd—let the great *Commonweal*
Pass round the full glass to *Republican* zeal—
From ruin—their judgment and wisdom well aim'd,
Our *Liberties, Laws,* and our *Credit* reclaim'd.
        Our Freedom, &c.

Here *Plenty* and *Order,* and *Freedom* shall dwell,
And your *Shayses** and *Dayses*[†] won't dare to rebel—
Independence and culture shall graciously smile,
And the *Husbandman* reap the full fruit of his toil.
        Our Freedom, &c.

That these are the blessings *Columbia* knows—
The blessings the *Fed'ral Convention* bestows;

---

*Daniel Shays, the leader of Shays's Rebellion, 1786–1787.
[†]Luke Day, a leader of the insurgents in Shays's Rebellion.

O! then let the *People* confirm what is done
By *Franklin* the Sage, and by brave *Washington.*

Our Freedom we've won, and the prize let's maintain,
By Jove we'll Unite,
Approve and Unite—
And huzza for Convention *again and again.*

C. First Reactions to the Constitution

1. A Philadelphia Editor Is Expectant (1787)

A curious public had little inkling of what was going on in the Philadelphia convention. The delegates, who were sworn to secrecy, deliberated behind closed doors guarded by soldiers. But the general expectation was that a stronger government would emerge, designed to subdue disorders and bring the headstrong states to heel. The following Philadelphia editorial fairly glows with optimism. Which one of the anticipated arguments against the Constitution seems most formidable? Why could the Shaysites be compared to the Tories?

The year 1776 is celebrated (says a correspondent) for a revolution in favor of Liberty. The year 1787, it is expected, will be celebrated with equal joy for a revolution in favor of Government. The impatience with which all classes of people (a few officers of government only excepted) wait to receive the new federal constitution can only be equaled by their zealous determination to support it.

Every state (adds our correspondent) has its Shays, who either with their pens—or tongues—or offices—are endeavoring to effect what Shays attempted in vain with his sword. In one of the states, this demagogue tries to persuade the people that it is dangerous to increase the powers of Congress. In another, he denies the authority of the Convention to redress our national grievances. In a third, he whispers distrust, saying the states will not adopt the new frame of government. In a fourth, he says the state constitutions, and the officers who act under them, are of divine right, and can be altered by no human power—and of course considers all attempts to restore order and government in the United States as a "laughable" thing. In the fifth, he opposes a general confederacy, and urges the division of the states into three smaller confederacies, that he may the more easily place himself at the head of one of them.

The spirit and wickedness of Shays is in each of these principles and measures. Let Americans be wise. Toryism and Shayism are nearly allied. They both lead to slavery, poverty, and misery.

We hear that the Convention propose to adjourn next week, after laying America under such obligations to them for their long, painful, and disinterested labors to establish her liberty upon a permanent basis as no time will ever cancel.

---

[1]*Pennsylvania Gazette,* September 5, 1787.

2. Alexander Hamilton Scans the Future (1787)

Alexander Hamilton of New York, though only thirty-two, was probably the most brilliant and eloquent member of the Philadelphia assemblage. But his great contribution was in engineering the call for the convention and in campaigning for the Constitution. At Philadelphia, he was outvoted by his two antifederalist colleagues from New York, and his own federalist and centralist views were too extreme for the other delegates. His superlative five-hour oratorical effort championed a plan that, among other things, would have had the president and the senators holding office during good behavior, and the state governors appointed by the federal government. The scheme received one vote—his own. Hamilton evidently prepared the following memorandum shortly after the Constitution was drafted. Why would the rich be favorable to the new instrument? Why would the poor and the states' righters be unfavorable?

The new Constitution has in favor of its success these circumstances: A very great weight of influence of the persons who framed it, particularly in the universal popularity of General Washington. The good will of the commercial interest throughout the states, which will give all its efforts to the establishment of a government capable of regulating, protecting, and extending the commerce of the Union. The good will of most men of property in the several states, who wish a government of the Union able to protect them against domestic violence and the depredations which the democratic spirit is apt to make on property, and who are besides anxious for the respectability of the nation. The hopes of the creditors of the United States, that a general government, possessing the means of doing it, will pay the debt of the Union. A strong belief in the people at large of the insufficiency of the present Confederation to preserve the existence of the Union, and of the necessity of the Union to their safety and prosperity. Of course, a strong desire of a change, and a predisposition to receive well the propositions of the convention.

Against its success is to be put: The dissent of two or three important men in the convention, who will think their characters pledged to defeat the plan. The influence of many *inconsiderable* men in possession of considerable offices under the state governments, who will fear a diminution of their consequence, power, and emolument by the establishment of the general government, and who can hope for nothing there. The influence of some *considerable* men in office, possessed of talents and popularity, who, partly from the same motives, and partly from a desire of *playing a part* in a convulsion for their own aggrandizement, will oppose the quiet adoption of the new government. (Some considerable men out of office, from motives of ambition, may be disposed to act the same part.)

Add to these causes: The disinclination of the people to taxes, and of course to a strong government. The opposition of all men much in debt, who will not wish to see a government established, one object of which is to restrain the means of cheating creditors. The democratical jealousy of the people, which may be alarmed

---

[2]H. C. Lodge, ed., *The Works of Alexander Hamilton* (Boston and New York: Houghton, Mifflin and Company, 1904), vol. 1, pp. 420–423.

at the appearance of institutions that may seem calculated to place the power of the community in few hands, and to raise a few individuals to stations of great pre-eminence. And the influence of some foreign powers, who, from different motives, will not wish to see an energetic government established throughout the states.

In this view of the subject, it is difficult to form any judgment whether the plan will be adopted or rejected. It must be essentially matter of conjecture. The present appearances and all other circumstances considered, the probability seems to be on the side of its adoption. But the causes operating against its adoption are powerful, and there will be nothing astonishing in the contrary.

If it do not finally obtain, it is probable the discussion of the question will beget such struggles, animosities, and heats in the community that this circumstance, conspiring with the real necessity of an essential change in our present situation, will produce civil war. . . .

A reunion with Great Britain, from universal disgust at a state of commotion, is not impossible, though not much to be feared. The most plausible shape of such a business would be the establishment of a son of the present monarch [George III] in the supreme government of this country, with a family compact.

If the government be adopted, it is probable General Washington will be the President of the United States. This will ensure a wise choice of men to administer the government, and a good administration. A good administration will conciliate the confidence and affection of the people, and perhaps enable the government to acquire more consistency than the proposed Constitution seems to promise for so great a country. . . .

3. George Mason Is Critical (1787)

George Mason, a wealthy Virginia planter who owned five thousand acres, had played a leading role in the Revolutionary movement. A self-taught constitutional lawyer of high repute, a dedicated advocate of states' rights, and an undying foe of slavery, he was one of the five most frequent speakers at the Philadelphia convention. Shocked by the whittling down of states' rights, he finally refused to sign the Constitution and fought it bitterly in Virginia. His chief grievance was the compromise by which the South conceded a simple majority vote in Congress on navigation laws in return for twenty more years of African slave trade, of which he disapproved anyhow. He set forth his objections in the following influential pamphlet. Which of his criticisms relate to states' rights? which to the rights of the South? Which seem overdrawn in the light of subsequent events?

There is no Declaration [Bill] of Rights, and the laws of the general government being paramount to the laws and constitution of the several states, the declarations of rights in the separate states are no security. . . .

---

[3]Kate M. Rowland, *The Life of George Mason* (New York and London: G. P. Putnam's Sons, 1892), vol. 2, pp. 387–390.

The Judiciary of the United States is so constructed and extended as to absorb and destroy the judiciaries of the several states; thereby rendering law as tedious, intricate, and expensive, and justice as unattainable, by a great part of the community, as in England, and enabling the rich to oppress and ruin the poor.

The President of the United States has no Constitutional Council, a thing unknown in any safe and regular government. He will therefore be unsupported by proper information and advice, and will generally be directed by minions and favorites; or he will become a tool to the Senate—or a council of state will grow out of the principal officers of the great departments; the worst and most dangerous of all ingredients for such a council in a free country. From this fatal defect has arisen the improper power of the Senate in the appointment of public officers, and the alarming dependence and connection between that branch of the legislature and the Supreme Executive.

Hence also sprung that unnecessary officer, the Vice-President, who, for want of other employment, is made president of the Senate, thereby dangerously blending the executive and legislative powers, besides always giving to some one of the states an unnecessary and unjust pre-eminence over the others. . . .

By declaring all treaties supreme laws of the land, the Executive and the Senate have, in many cases, an exclusive power of legislation; which might have been avoided by proper distinctions with respect to treaties, and requiring the assent of the House of Representatives, where it could be done with safety.

By requiring only a majority [of Congress] to make all commercial and navigation laws, the five Southern states, whose produce and circumstances are totally different from that of the eight Northern and Eastern states, may be ruined. For such rigid and premature regulations may be made as will enable the merchants of the Northern and Eastern states not only to demand an exorbitant freight, but to monopolize the purchase of the commodities at their own price, for many years, to the great injury of the landed interest and impoverishment of the people. And the danger is the greater as the gain on one side will be in proportion to the loss on the other. Whereas requiring two-thirds of the members present in both Houses would have produced mutual moderation, promoted the general interest, and removed an insuperable objection to the adoption of this government.

Under their own construction of the general clause [Article I, Section VIII, para. 18], at the end of the enumerated powers, the Congress may grant monopolies in trade and commerce, constitute new crimes, inflict unusual and severe punishments, and extend their powers as far as they shall think proper; so that the state legislatures have no security for the powers now presumed to remain to them, or the people for their rights.

There is no declaration of any kind for preserving the liberty of the press, or the trial by jury in civil causes [cases]; nor against the danger of standing armies in time of peace. . . .

This government will set out a moderate aristocracy; it is at present impossible to foresee whether it will, in its operation, produce a monarchy or a corrupt, tyrannical aristocracy. It will most probably vibrate some years between the two, and then terminate in the one or the other.

4. Jefferson Is Unenthusiastic (1787)

Thomas Jefferson, the American minister in Paris, learned of the Philadelphia convention with some misgivings. While recognizing the need for a stronger central government, especially in foreign affairs, he regarded the Confederation as a "wonderfully perfect instrument," considering the times. A comparison of the United States government with the governments of continental Europe, he declared, "is like a comparison of heaven and hell. England, like the earth, may be allowed to take the intermediate station." He evidently believed that some judicious patchwork would provide the needed bolstering. Upon receiving a copy of the new Constitution, he was troubled by some of its features, particularly by the absence of a Bill of Rights. Why, in the following letter to the prominent New York jurist William Smith, did he belittle reports of anarchy? Why did he condone periodic rebellions?

I do not know whether it is to yourself or Mr. [John] Adams I am to give my thanks for the copy of the new Constitution. . . . There are very good articles in it; and very bad. I do not know which preponderate. What we have lately read in the history of Holland . . . would have sufficed to set me against a chief magistrate eligible for a long duration, if I had ever been disposed towards one. And what we have always read of the elections of Polish kings should have forever excluded the idea of one continuable for life.

Wonderful is the effect of impudent and persevering lying. The British ministry have so long hired their gazetteers to repeat, and model into every form, lies about our being in anarchy, that the world has at length believed them, the English nation has believed them, the ministers themselves have come to believe them, and what is more wonderful, we have believed them ourselves.

Yet where does this anarchy exist? Where did it ever exist, except in the single instance of [Shays's Rebellion in] Massachusetts? And can history produce an instance of rebellion so honorably conducted? I say nothing of its motives. They were founded in ignorance, not wickedness.

God forbid we should ever be twenty years without such a rebellion. The people cannot be all, and always, well informed. The part which is wrong will be discontented, in proportion to the importance of the facts they misconceive. If they remain quiet under such misconceptions, it is a lethargy, the forerunner of death to the public liberty.

We have had thirteen states independent for eleven years. There has been one rebellion. That comes to one rebellion in a century and a half for each state. What country before ever existed a century and a half without a rebellion? And what country can preserve its liberties if its rulers are not warned from time to time that their people preserve the spirit of resistance? Let them take arms. The remedy is to set them right as to facts, pardon, and pacify them.

What signify a few lives lost in a century or two? The tree of liberty must be refreshed from time to time with the blood of patriots and tyrants. It is its natural manure. Our convention has been too much impressed by the insurrection of Massa-

---

[4]P. L. Ford, ed., *The Writings of Thomas Jefferson* (New York: G. P. Putnam's Sons, 1894), vol. 4, pp. 466–467 (November 13, 1787).

chusetts; and on the spur of the moment they are setting up a kite [hawk] to keep the henyard in order.

I hope in God this article [perpetual reeligibility of the president] will be rectified before the Constitution is accepted.

D. The Ratification Debate in Massachusetts

1. A Delegate Fears for the Little People (1788)

When the crucial Massachusetts ratifying convention met, it first mustered a majority against the Constitution. As Hamilton had predicted, the propertied and commercial elements favored it; the debtors (including many Shaysites), small farmers, and states' rights people generally fought it. The following outburst by Amos Singletary, one of the small-fry group, who had never attended school, is typical of much of the debate in the state conventions. Did he fear taxation without representation or merely taxation in itself? To what extent did he anticipate the thesis of Charles A. Beard regarding the self-seeking economic motives of the propertied Founding Fathers?

We contended with Great Britain—some said for a three-penny duty on tea; but it was not that. It was because they claimed a right to tax us and bind us in all cases whatever. And does not this Constitution do the same? Does it not take away all we have—all our property? Does it not lay *all* taxes, duties, imposts, and excises? And what more have we to give?

They tell us Congress won't lay dry [direct] taxes upon us, but collect all the money they want by impost [import duties]. I say, there has always been a difficulty about impost. . . . They won't be able to raise money enough by impost, and then they will lay it on the land and take all we have got.

These lawyers, and men of learning, and moneyed men, that talk so finely and gloss over matters so smoothly, to make us poor illiterate people swallow down the pill, expect to get into Congress themselves. They expect to be the managers of this Constitution, and get all the power and all the money into their own hands. And then they will swallow up all of us little folks, like the great Leviathan, Mr. President; yes, just as the whale swallowed up Jonah. This is what I am afraid of. . . .

2. A Storekeeper Blasts Standing Armies (1788)

Samuel Nasson, a saddler and later a storekeeper, expressed a common fear in the Massachusetts ratifying convention. Why was this unmoneyed Massachusetts man so deeply concerned about an army?

---

[1]Jonathan Elliot, *The Debates on the Federal Constitution* (Philadelphia: J. B. Lippincott, 1836), vol. 2, pp. 101–102.

[2]Jonathan Elliot, *The Debates on the Federal Constitution* (1836), vol. 2, pp. 136–137.

The eighth section, Mr. President, provides that Congress shall have power to lay and collect taxes, duties, imposts, excise, etc. We may, sir, be poor; we may not be able to pay these taxes, etc. We must have a little meal, and a little meat, whereon to live, and save a little for a rainy day. But what follows? Let us see. To raise and support armies. Here, sir, comes the key to unlock this cabinet; here is the means by which you will be made to pay taxes! But will ye, my countrymen, submit to this?

Suffer me, sir, to say a few words on the fatal effects of standing armies, that bane of republican governments. A standing army! Was it not with this that Caesar passed the Rubicon and laid prostrate the liberties of his country? By this have seven eighths of the once free nations of the globe been brought into bondage! Time would fail me, were I to attempt to recapitulate the havoc made in the world by standing armies. . . .

Sir, had I a voice like Jove, I would proclaim it throughout the world; and had I an arm like Jove, I would hurl from the globe those villains that would dare attempt to establish in our country a standing army. I wish, sir, that the gentlemen of Boston would bring to their minds the fatal evening of the 5th of March, 1770, when by standing troops they lost five of their fellow townsmen [in the Boston Massacre]. I will ask them, What price can atone for their lives? What money can make satisfaction for the loss? . . .

What occasion have we for standing armies? We fear no foe. If one should come upon us, we have a militia, which is our bulwark. . . . Therefore, sir, I am utterly opposed to a standing army in time of peace. . . .

3. A Farmer Favors the Constitution (1788)

The Massachusetts convention finally ratified the Constitution by the narrow margin of 187 to 168 votes. But the majority did not fall into line until Samuel Adams, an experienced subverter of strong governments, reluctantly threw his weight behind the document, and not until the members agreed to recommend nine fear-quieting amendments (the Bill of Rights). Not all farmers opposed ratification, as this earthy convention speech of Jonathan Smith attests. How convincingly did he make his points that mob rule is tyranny, that anarchy begets despotism, and that the moneyed class was not thinking solely of its narrowly selfish interests?

Mr. President, I am a plain man, and get my living by the plough. I am not used to speak in public, but I beg your leave to say a few words to my brother plough-joggers in this house.

I have lived in a part of the country where I have known the worth of good government by the want of it. There was a black cloud [Shays's Rebellion] that rose in the east last winter, and spread over the west. . . . It brought on a state of anarchy and that led to tyranny. I say, it brought anarchy. People that used to live peaceably, and were before good neighbors, got distracted, and took up arms against government. . . . People, I say, took up arms, and then, if you went to speak to them, you had the musket of death presented to your breast. They would rob you of your property, threaten to burn your houses; oblige you to be on your guard night and

³Jonathan Elliot, *The Debates on the Federal Constitution* (1836), vol. 2, pp. 102–104.

day. Alarms spread from town to town; families were broken up; the tender mother would cry, O my son is among them! . . .

Our distress was so great that we should have been glad to snatch at anything that looked like a government. Had any person that was able to protect us come and set up his standard, we should all have flocked to it, even if it had been a monarch, and that monarch might have proved a tyrant. So that you see that anarchy leads to tyranny; and better have one tyrant than so many at once.

Now, Mr. President, when I saw this Constitution, I found that it was a cure for these disorders. It was just such a thing as we wanted. I got a copy of it and read it over and over. I had been a member of the convention to form our own state constitution, and had learnt something of the checks and balances of power; and I found them all here. I did not go to any lawyer, to ask his opinion—we have no lawyer in our town, and do well enough without. I formed my own opinion, and was pleased with this Constitution. . . .

But I don't think the worse of the Constitution because lawyers, and men of learning, and moneyed men are fond of it. I don't suspect that they want to get into Congress and abuse their power. I am not of such a jealous make. They that are honest men themselves are not apt to suspect other people. . . .

Brother farmers, let us suppose a case, now. Suppose you had a farm of 50 acres, and your title was disputed, and there was a farm of 5,000 acres joined to you that belonged to a man of learning, and his title was involved in the same difficulty. Would you not be glad to have him for your friend, rather than to stand alone in the dispute?

Well, the case is the same—these lawyers, these moneyed men, these men of learning, are all embarked in the same cause with us, and we must all swim or sink together. And shall we throw the Constitution overboard because it does not please us alike? Suppose two or three of you had been at the pains to break up a piece of rough land, and sow it with wheat—would you let it lie waste because you could not agree what sort of a fence to make? Would it not be better to put up a fence that did not please everyone's fancy, rather than not fence it at all, or keep disputing about it until the wild beasts came in and devoured it?

Some gentlemen say, don't be in a hurry; take time to consider; and don't take a leap in the dark. I say, take things in time—gather fruit when it is ripe. There is a time to sow, and a time to reap. We sowed our seed when we sent men to the federal convention. Now is the harvest; now is the time to reap the fruit of our labor. And if we won't do it now, I am afraid we never shall have another opportunity.

E. The Ratification Debate in New York

1. An Anti-Federalist Demands Deliberation (1787)

Last-ditch opposition to the Constitution formed in New York under the states' rights banner of George Clinton, the first governor and so-called Father of New York State. The strategic location of New York City, he saw clearly, promised commercial ascen-

[1]New York *Journal and Weekly Register,* November 8, 1787.

dancy, and he did not welcome the restraints of a powerful federal government. His views were evidently shared by this anonymous contributor to a New York newspaper. What were the strongest arguments against a hasty and uncritical acceptance of the Constitution? Could some of this reasoning be applied to present-day political affairs? What was the basis of this writer's optimism?

I have read with a degree of attention several publications which have lately appeared in favor of the new Constitution; and as far as I am able to discern, the arguments (if they can be so termed) of most weight which are urged in its favor may be reduced to the two following:

1st. That the men who formed it were wise and experienced; that they were an illustrious band of patriots and had the happiness of their country at heart; that they were four months deliberating on the subject; and therefore it must be a perfect system.

2nd. That if the system be not received, this country will be without any government, and, of consequence, will be reduced to a state of anarchy and confusion, and involved in bloodshed and carnage; and in the end a government will be imposed upon us, not the result of reason and reflection, but of force and usurpation. . . .

With respect to the first, it will be readily perceived that it precludes all investigation of the merits of the proposed Constitution, and leads to an adoption of the plan without enquiring whether it be good or bad. For if we are to infer the perfection of this system from the characters and abilities of the men who formed it, we may as well determine to accept it without any enquiry as with. A number of persons in this as well as the other states have upon this principle determined to submit to it without even reading or knowing its contents. . . .

In answer to the second argument, I deny that we are in immediate danger of anarchy and commotions. Nothing but the passions of wicked and ambitious men will put us in the least danger on this head. Those who are anxious to precipitate a measure will always tell us that the present is the critical moment; now is the time, the crisis is arrived, and the present minute must be seized. Tyrants have always made use of this plea; and nothing in our circumstances can justify it.

The country is in profound peace, and we are not threatened by invasion from any quarter. The governments of the respective states are in the full exercise of their powers; and the lives, the liberty, and property of individuals are protected. All present exigencies are answered by them.

It is true, the regulation of trade and a competent provision for the payment of the interest of the public debt is wanting; but no immediate commotion will rise from these. Time may be taken for calm discussion and deliberate conclusions.

Individuals are just recovering from the losses and embarrassments sustained by the late war. Industry and frugality are taking their station and banishing from the community idleness and prodigality. Individuals are lessening their private debts, and several millions of the public debt is discharged by the sale of Western territory.

There is no reason, therefore, why we should precipitately and rashly adopt a system which is imperfect or insecure. We may securely deliberate and propose amendments and alterations. I know it is said we cannot change for the worse; but if we act the part of wise men, we shall take care that we change for the better. It will be labor lost if, after all our pains, we are in no better circumstances than we were before.

If any tumults arise, they will be justly chargeable on those artful and ambitious men who are determined to cram this government down the throats of the people before they have time deliberately to examine it.

2. James Madison Defends the New Constitution (1787)

To promote ratification of the new Constitution in New York, Alexander Hamilton, James Madison, and John Jay teamed up to write a series of newspaper articles under the name "Publius." These articles, eighty-five in all, are known together as The Federalist Papers *and have become justly famous not only as high-class propaganda but as probably the most brilliant commentary ever written on the principles underlying the Constitution. Possibly the single most famous paper was Number Ten, written by James Madison. Madison ingeniously refuted the prevailing wisdom of the day that democracy was possible only in a small state. In the following excerpt from Federalist No. Ten, how does Madison justify the new central government envisioned in the Constitution? In particular, how does he handle the problem of "factions"?*

Among the numerous advantages promised by a well-constructed Union, none deserves to be more accurately developed than its tendency to break and control the violence of faction. Complaints are everywhere heard from our most considerate and virtuous citizens, equally the friends of public and private faith and of public and personal liberty, that our governments are too unstable, that the public good is disregarded in the conflicts of rival parties, and that measures are too often decided, not according to the rules of justice and the rights of the minor party, but by the superior force of an interested and overbearing majority. . . .

By a faction I understand a number of citizens, whether amounting to a majority or minority of the whole, who are united and actuated by some common impulse of passion, or of interest, adverse to the rights of other citizens, or to the permanent and aggregate interests of the community.

There are two methods of curing the mischiefs of faction: the one, by removing its causes; the other, by controlling its effects.

There are again two methods of removing the causes of faction: the one, by destroying the liberty which is essential to its existence; the other, by giving to every citizen the same opinions, the same passions, and the same interests.

It could never be more truly said than of the first remedy that it was worse than the disease. Liberty is to faction what air is to fire, an ailment without which it instantly expires. But it could not be a less folly to abolish liberty, which is essential to political life, because it nourishes faction than it would be to wish the annihilation

---

[2]H. C. Lodge, ed., *The Federalist* (New York: G. P. Putnam's Sons, 1895), pp. 61–66.

of air, which is essential to animal life, because it imparts to fire its destructive agency.

The second expedient is as impracticable as the first would be unwise. As long as the reason of man continues fallible, and he is at liberty to exercise it, different opinions will be formed. . . . The latent causes of faction are thus sown in the nature of man. . . .

The inference to which we are brought is that the *causes* of faction cannot be removed and that relief is only to be sought in the means of controlling its *effects*.

If a faction consists of less than a majority, relief is supplied by the republican principle, which enables the majority to defeat its sinister views by regular vote. It may clog the administration, it may convulse the society; but it will be unable to execute and mask its violence under the forms of the Constitution. When a majority is included in a faction, the form of popular government, on the other hand, enables it to sacrifice to its ruling passion or interest both the public good and the rights of other citizens. To secure the public good and private rights against the danger of such a faction, and at the same time to preserve the spirit and the form of popular government, is then the great object to which our inquiries are directed. . . .

From this view of the subject it may be concluded that a pure democracy, by which I mean a society consisting of a small number of citizens, who assemble and administer the government in person, can admit of no cure for the mischiefs of faction. A common passion or interest will, in almost every case, be felt by a majority of the whole; a communication and concert results from the form of government itself; and there is nothing to check the inducements to sacrifice the weaker party or an obnoxious individual. Hence it is that such democracies have ever been spectacles of turbulence and contention; have ever been found incompatible with personal security or the rights of property; and have in general been as short in their lives as they have been violent in their deaths. Theoretic politicians, who have patronized this species of government, have erroneously supposed that by reducing mankind to a perfect equality in their political rights, they would at the same time be perfectly equalized and assimilated in their possessions, their opinions, and their passions.

A republic, by which I mean a government in which the scheme of representation takes place, opens a different prospect and promises the cure for which we are seeking. Let us examine the points in which it varies from pure democracy, and we shall comprehend both the nature of the cure and the efficacy which it must derive from the Union.

The two great points of difference between a democracy and a republic are: first, the delegation of the government, in the latter, to a small number of citizens elected by the rest; secondly, the greater number of citizens and greater sphere of country over which the latter may be extended.

The effect of the first difference is, on the one hand, to refine and enlarge the public views by passing them through the medium of a chosen body of citizens, whose wisdom may best discern the true interest of their country and whose patriotism and love of justice will be least likely to sacrifice it to temporary or partial considerations. Under such a regulation it may well happen that the public voice, pronounced by the representatives of the people, will be more consonant to the public good than if pronounced by the people themselves, convened for the purpose. . . .

The other point of difference is the greater number of citizens and extent of territory which may be brought within the compass of republican than of democratic government; and it is this circumstance principally which renders factious combinations less to be dreaded in the former than in the latter. The smaller the society, the fewer probably will be the distinct parties and interests composing it; the fewer the distinct parties and interests, the more frequently will a majority be found of the same party; and the smaller the number of individuals composing a majority, and the smaller the compass within which they are placed, the more easily will they concert and execute their plans of oppression. Extend the sphere and you take in a greater variety of parties and interests; you make it less probable that a majority of the whole will have a common motive to invade the rights of other citizens; or if such a common motive exists, it will be more difficult for all who feel it to discover their own strength and to act in unison with each other. Besides other impediments, it may be remarked that, where there is a consciousness of unjust or dishonorable purposes, communication is always checked by distrust in proportion to the number whose concurrence is necessary.

Hence, it clearly appears that the same advantage which a republic has over a democracy in controlling the effects of faction is enjoyed by a large over a small republic—is enjoyed by the Union over the States composing it. Does this advantage consist in the substitution of representatives whose enlightened views and virtuous sentiments render them superior to local prejudices and to schemes of injustice? It will not be denied that the representation of the Union will be most likely to possess these requisite endowments. Does it consist in the greater security afforded by a greater variety of parties, against the event of any one party being able to outnumber and oppress the rest? In an equal degree does the increased variety of parties comprised within the Union increase this security? Does it, in fine, consist in the greater obstacles opposed to the concert and accomplishment of the secret wishes of an unjust and interested majority? Here again the extent of the Union gives it the most palpable advantage.

The influence of factious leaders may kindle a flame within their particular States but will be unable to spread a general conflagration through the other States. A religious sect may degenerate into a political faction in a part of the Confederacy; but the variety of sects dispersed over the entire face of it must secure the national councils against any danger from that source. A rage for paper money, for an abolition of debts, for an equal division of property, or for any other improper or wicked project, will be less apt to pervade the whole body of the Union than a particular member of it, in the same proportion as such a malady is more likely to taint a particular county or district than an entire State.

In the extent and proper structure of the Union, therefore, we behold a republican remedy for the diseases most incident to republican government. And according to the degree of pleasure and pride we feel in being republicans ought to be our zeal in cherishing the spirit and supporting the character of federalists.

Publius

Thought Provokers

1. Considering the conflicting testimony regarding conditions of anarchy under the Articles of Confederation, what conclusions may be safely drawn about the true state of affairs? To what extent may Daniel Shays be regarded as one of the indirect Founding Fathers? Was his "rebellion" justified? Would Jefferson today be permitted to express publicly his views on rebellion?

2. In what sense was the Constitution a democratic document, and in what sense a conservative one? What did democracy mean to the Founding Fathers?

3. What groups seem to have been the strongest supporters of the Constitution? the strongest foes? Why? What probably would have happened in the short run and in the long run if the Constitution had failed of ratification?

4. What is meant by "enlightened self-interest" in public affairs? Were the Founding Fathers motivated by it rather than by "pocketbook patriotism"?

5. Were *The Federalist Papers* really propaganda in the same sense as the Declaration of Independence and Paine's *Common Sense?*

10

Launching the New Ship of State, 1789–1800

Hamilton was honest as a man, but, as a politician, believed in the necessity of either force or corruption to govern men.

Thomas Jefferson, 1811

[Jefferson is] a man of profound ambition and violent passions.

Alexander Hamilton, 1792

Prologue: When Washington took the presidential oath at New York, the temporary capital, he was determined to get the ship of state off on an even keel. He therefore "packed" the new offices with federalists, as the supporters of the Constitution were called. The one conspicuous exception was the secretary of state, Thomas Jefferson. As a vigilant champion of states' rights, he was an antifederalist, or a foe of a powerful central government. One result was an inevitable clash between him and Secretary of the Treasury Alexander Hamilton, a staunch federalist, over foreign affairs and fiscal policy. From these heated differences there emerged, about 1793, two political parties: the Hamiltonian Federalists and the Jeffersonian Republicans. Jefferson naturally opposed the Hamiltonian plans for assuming the state debts, establishing the Bank of the United States, and levying an excise tax on whiskey. In his eyes, all these schemes would increase the power of the federal octopus, encroach on states' rights, promote corruption, and enrich the ruling class at the expense of the common folk.

A. Conflict in the Infant Republic

1. The Senate Snubs George Washington (1789)

The new Constitution empowered the president to "make treaties" with "the advice and consent of the Senate." Early in his administration Washington, accompanied

---

[1]E. S. Maclay, ed., *Journal of William Maclay* (New York: D. Appleton and Company, 1890), pp. 131–132.

by Secretary of War Henry Knox, appeared before the then-tiny group of senators to explain an Indian treaty. The deliberations proceeded so haltingly in the president's awesome presence that Senator William Maclay finally supported a motion to refer the papers to a committee. Washington was visibly annoyed. Tradition has him saying, as he left the chamber, that he would "be damned" if he ever came back again, but he did return—once. No president since has attempted to discuss treaties personally with the entire Senate. In reading the following extract from Senator Maclay's diary, one should bear in mind that the author was an ardent republican who resented Washington's aristocratic airs and who privately wished that the general "were in heaven" and not "brought forward as the constant cover to every unconstitutional and irrepublican act." As this diary entry begins, Maclay has just spoken for deferment. Why did this type of personal conferring with the senators fail?

As I sat down, the President of the United States started up in a violent fret. "This defeats every purpose of my coming here" were the first words that he said. He then went on that he had brought his Secretary of War with him to give every necessary information; that the Secretary knew all about the business; and yet he [Washington] was delayed and could not go on with the matter. He cooled, however, by degrees. Said he had no objection to putting off this matter until Monday, but declared he did not understand the matter of commitment [referral]. He might be delayed; he could not tell how long.

He rose a second time, and said he had no objection to postponement until Monday at ten o'clock. By the looks of the Senate this seemed agreed to. A pause for some time ensued. We waited for him to withdraw. He did so with a discontented air. Had it been any other man than the man whom I wish to regard as the first character in the world, I would have said, with sullen dignity.

I cannot now be mistaken. The President wishes to tread on the necks of the Senate. Commitment will bring the matter to discussion, at least in the committee, where he is not present. He wishes us to see with the eyes and hear with the ears of his Secretary [of War] only. The Secretary to advance the premises, the President to draw the conclusions, and to bear down our deliberations with his personal authority and presence. Form only will be left to us. This will not do with Americans. But let the matter work; it will soon cure itself.

August 24th, Monday.—The Senate met. The President of the United States soon took his seat, and the business began. The President wore a different aspect from what he did Saturday. He was placid and serene, and manifested a spirit of accommodation; declared his consent that his questions should be amended.

2. Alexander Hamilton Versus Thomas Jefferson on Popular Rule (1780s–1820s)

President Washington's aristocratic and monarchical appearance may have offended Senator Maclay, who became a follower of Thomas Jefferson, but it did not

---

[2]Excerpts found for the most part in S. K. Padover, ed., *The Mind of Alexander Hamilton* (New York: Harper & Row, 1958); R. B. Morris, ed., *The Basic Ideas of Alexander Hamilton* (1957); S. K. Padover, ed., *Thomas Jefferson on Democracy* (New York and London: D. Appleton-Century Company, 1939).

disturb Secretary of the Treasury Hamilton. The youthful financier, though born in humble circumstances, had developed a profound distrust of common people. In contrast, Jefferson, a Virginia planter-aristocrat, championed the common folk. Faith in the informed masses became the cornerstone of Jefferson's Democratic-Republican party; distrust of the masses and the cultivation of special interests became the cornerstone of Hamilton's Federalist party. Following are the conflicting opinions of the two great leaders over a period of years. The initial quotations from Hamilton formed a part of his five-hour speech before the Constitutional Convention in Philadelphia (see p. 161). To what extent were Hamilton and Jefferson both right in the light of subsequent history? Who, on balance, was the more sound? Note that Jefferson, particularly, was prone to exaggerate, and that some of these observations were written privately and in the heat of bitter partisan struggles.

Hamilton

All communities divide themselves into the few and the many. The first are the rich and well born; the other, the mass of the people. The voice of the people has been said to be the voice of God; and however generally this maxim has been quoted and believed, it is not true in fact. The people are turbulent and changing; they seldom judge or determine right. Give therefore to the first class a distinct, permanent share in the government. They will check the unsteadiness of the second; and as they cannot receive any advantage by a change, they therefore will ever maintain good government.

Can a democratic assembly, who annually [through annual elections] revolve in the mass of the people, be supposed steadily to pursue the public good? Nothing but a permanent body can check the imprudence of democracy. Their turbulent and uncontrolling disposition requires checks. (1787)

Take mankind in general, they are vicious—their passions may be operated upon. . . . Take mankind as they are, and what are they governed by? Their passions. There may be in every government a few choice spirits, who may act from more worthy motives.

Jefferson

Those who labor in the earth are the chosen people of God, if ever he had a chosen people, whose breasts he has made his peculiar deposit for substantial and genuine virtue. (1784)

Men . . . are naturally divided into two parties. Those who fear and distrust the people. . . . Those who identify themselves with the people, have confidence in them, cherish and consider them as the most honest and safe . . . depository of the public interest. (1824)

The mass of mankind has not been born with saddles on their backs, nor a favored few booted and spurred, ready to ride them legitimately, by the grace of God. (1826)

Every government degenerates when trusted to the rulers . . . alone. The people themselves are its only safe depositories. (1787)

I have such reliance on the good sense of the body of the people and the honesty of their leaders that I am not afraid of their letting things go wrong to any length in any cause. (1788)

Hamilton	Jefferson
One great error is that we suppose mankind more honest than they are. Our prevailing passions are ambition and interest; and it will be the duty of a wise government to avail itself of those passions, in order to make them subservient to the public good. (1787)	Whenever the people are well-informed, they can be trusted with their own government; whenever things get so far wrong as to attract their notice, they may be relied on to set them to rights. (1789)
Your people, sir, is a great beast. (According to legend, *c.* 1792)	I am not among those who fear the people. They, and not the rich, are our dependence for continued freedom. (1816)
I have an indifferent [low] opinion of the honesty of this country, and ill forebodings as to its future system. (1783)	I have great confidence in the common sense of mankind in general. (1800)
I said that I was affectionately attached to the republican theory. . . . I add that I have strong hopes of the success of that theory; but, in candor, I ought also to add that I am far from being without doubts. I consider its success as yet a problem. (1792)	My most earnest wish is to see the republican element of popular control pushed to the maximum of its practicable exercise. I shall then believe that our government may be pure and perpetual. (1816)

3. The Clash over States' Rights (1780s–1820s)

Hamilton, distrusting and fearing the states, strove to build up a powerful central government at their expense. Jefferson, distrusting and fearing a potent central government, strove to safeguard states' rights at its expense. Which of the two men was closer to the truth in the light of subsequent history, particularly in the matter of grass-roots supervision of government?

Hamilton	Jefferson
A firm Union will be of the utmost moment to the peace and liberty of the states, as a barrier against domestic faction and insurrection. (1787)	I am not a friend to a very energetic government. It is always oppressive. It places the governors indeed more at their ease, at the expense of the people. (1787)
A state government will ever be the rival power of the general government. (1787)	If ever this vast country is brought under a single government, it will be one of the most extensive corruption. (1822)

---

[3]See the works of Padover and Morris previously cited.

Hamilton

As to the destruction of state governments, the great and real anxiety is to be able to preserve the national [government] from the too potent and counteracting influence of those governments. . . . As to the state governments, the prevailing bias of my judgment is that if they can be circumscribed within bounds consistent with the preservation of the national government, they will prove useful and salutary.

If the states were all of the size of Connecticut, Maryland, or New Jersey, I should decidedly regard the local governments as both safe and useful. As the thing now is, however, I acknowledge the most serious apprehensions that the government of the United States will not be able to maintain itself against their influence. I see that influence already penetrating into the national councils and preventing their direction.

Hence, a disposition on my part towards a liberal construction of the powers of the national government, and to erect every fence to guard it from depredations which is, in my opinion, consistent with constitutional propriety. As to any combination to prostrate the state governments, I disavow and deny it. (1792)

Jefferson

Our country is too large to have all its affairs directed by a single government. Public servants, at such a distance and from under the eye of their constituents, must, from the circumstance of distance, be unable to administer and overlook all the details necessary for the good government of the citizens; and the same circumstance, by rendering detection impossible to their constituents, will invite the public agents to corruption, plunder, and waste. . . .

What an augmentation of the field for jobbing, speculating, plundering, office-building, and office-hunting would be produced by an assumption of all the state powers into the hands of the general government. The true theory of our Constitution [strict construction] is surely the wisest and best—that the states are independent as to everything within themselves, and united as to everything respecting foreign nations. Let the general government be reduced to foreign concerns only, and let our affairs be disentangled from those of all other nations, except as to commerce, which the merchants will manage the better, the more they are left free to manage themselves. And our general government may be reduced to a very simple organization and a very unexpensive one: a few plain duties to be performed by a few servants. (1800)

4. The Spectrum of Disagreement (1780s–1820s)

At the rear entrance of Jefferson's imposing Virginia home, Monticello, busts of Hamilton and Jefferson stood opposite each other. The guide used to tell tourists that Jefferson placed them there because the two men had opposed each other in life, and they might as well stand opposite each other in death. In the following quotations, what do they agree on, what are their most fundamental disagreements, and how fair are they in assessing each other?

---

[4]See the works of Padover and Morris previously cited.

Hamilton

A national debt, if it is not excessive, will be to us a national blessing. (1781)

If all the public creditors receive their dues from one source . . . their interest will be the same. And having the same interests, they will unite in support of the fiscal arrangements of the government. (*c.* 1791)

Real liberty is neither found in despotism or the extremes of democracy, but in moderate governments. (1787)

Beware, my dear sir, of magnifying a riot into an insurrection, by employing in the first instance an inadequate force. 'Tis better far to err on the other side. Whenever the government appears in arms, it ought to appear like a Hercules, and inspire respect by the display of strength. (1799)

I believe the British government forms the best model the world ever produced, and such has been its progress in the minds of the many that this truth gradually gains ground. (1787)

It must be by this time evident to all men of reflection . . . that it [Articles of Confederation] is a system so radically vicious and unsound as to admit not of amendment but by an entire change in its leading features and characters. (1787)

Let me observe that an Executive is less dangerous to the liberties of the people when in office during life than for seven years. (1787)

Jefferson

. . . No man is more ardently intent to see the public debt soon and sacredly paid off than I am. This exactly marks the difference between Colonel Hamilton's views and mine, that I would wish the debt paid tomorrow; he wishes it never to be paid, but always to be a thing wherewith to corrupt and manage the legislature [Congress]. (1792)

. . . Were it left to me to decide whether we should have a government without newspapers, or newspapers without a government, I should not hesitate a moment to prefer the latter. (1787)

. . . A little rebellion now and then is a good thing, and as necessary in the political world as storms in the physical. . . . It is a medicine necessary for the sound health of government. (1787)

. . . It is her [England's] government which is so corrupt, and which has destroyed the nation—it was certainly the most corrupt and unprincipled government on earth. (1810)

But with all the imperfections of our present government [Articles of Confederation], it is without comparison the best existing or that ever did exist. . . . Indeed, I think all the good of this new Constitution might have been couched in three or four new articles, to be added to the good, old, and venerable fabric. . . . (1787)

I disapproved, also, the perpetual re-eligibility of the President. (1789)

Hamilton	Jefferson
Standing armies are dangerous to liberty. (1787)	A naval force can never endanger our liberties, nor occasion bloodshed; a land force would do both. (1786)
[Jefferson is] an atheist in religion and a fanatic in politics. (1800)	I am a Christian, in the only sense in which he [Jesus] wished anyone to be: sincerely attached to his doctrines, in preference to all others. (1803)
It was not long before I discovered he [Washington] was neither remarkable for delicacy nor good temper. . . . The General [Washington] is a very honest man. His competitors have slender abilities, and less integrity. His popularity has often been essential to the safety of America. . . . These considerations have influenced my past conduct respecting him and will influence my future. (1781)	His [Washington's] integrity was most pure, his justice the most inflexible I have ever known. . . . He was, indeed, in every sense of the words, a wise, a good, and a great man. His temper was naturally irritable and high toned; but reflection and resolution had obtained a firm and habitual ascendancy over it. If ever, however, it broke its bonds, he was most tremendous in his wrath. (1814)
That gentleman [Jefferson] whom I once *very much esteemed,* but who does not permit me to retain that sentiment for him, is certainly a man of sublimated and paradoxical imagination, entertaining and propagating opinions inconsistent with dignified and orderly government. (1792)	Hamilton was indeed a singular character. Of acute understanding, disinterested, honest, and honorable in all private transactions, amiable in society, and duly valuing virtue in private life, yet so bewitched and perverted by the British example as to be under thorough conviction that corruption was essential to the government of a nation. (1818)

B. State Debts and the National Bank

1. Jefferson Duped (?) by Hamilton (1790)

The brilliant young Secretary Hamilton, in his First Report on the Public Credit, proposed to couple the national debt with an assumption of state debts amounting to $21.5 million. His argument was that the states had incurred these burdens while fighting for independence, and hence the obligation was shared by all. One of his main purposes was to weaken states' rights and strengthen the federal government by tying the states financially to the federal chariot. Those states staggering under large unpaid debts, chiefly in New England, applauded the scheme; those in better fi-

---

[1]A. A. Lipscomb, ed., *The Writings of Thomas Jefferson* (Washington, D.C.: Thomas Jefferson Memorial Association, 1904), vol. 1, pp. 273–276.

nancial shape, chiefly in the South, condemned it. The resulting stalemate was broken by a compromise allegedly engineered by Hamilton and Jefferson together. Jefferson, who had recently come to New York after a five-year sojourn in France as minister, here recounts the story from contemporary notes and the vantage point of 1818. Was he fair in his analysis of Hamilton's motives? What was the significance of the early talk of secession? Why should southern congressmen have been parties to this logrolling operation?

This [funding] game was over, and another was on the carpet at the moment of my arrival; and to this I was most ignorantly and innocently made to hold the candle. This fiscal manoeuvre is well known by the name of the Assumption.

Independently of the debts of Congress, the states had during the war contracted separate and heavy debts; . . . and the more debt Hamilton could rake up, the more plunder for his mercenaries. This money, whether wisely or foolishly spent, was pretended to have been spent for general purposes, and ought, therefore, to be paid from the general purse.

But it was objected that nobody knew what these debts were, what their amount, or what their proofs. No matter; we will guess them to be twenty millions. But of these twenty millions, we do not know how much should be reimbursed to one state, or how much to another. No matter; we will guess. And so another scramble was set on foot among the several states, and some got much, some little, some nothing. But the main object was obtained: the phalanx of the Treasury was reinforced by additional recruits [bureaucrats].

This measure produced the most bitter and angry contest ever known in Congress, before or since the Union of the states. I arrived [in New York] in the midst of it. But a stranger to the ground, a stranger to the actors on it, so long absent as to have lost all familiarity with the subject, and as yet unaware of its object, I took no concern in it.

The great and trying question [of assumption], however, was lost in the House of Representatives [31 to 29]. So high were the feuds excited by this subject that on its rejection business was suspended. Congress met and adjourned from day to day without doing anything, the parties being too much out of temper to do business together. The Eastern [New England] members particularly, who, with Smith from South Carolina, were the principal gamblers in these scenes, threatened a secession and dissolution.

Hamilton was in despair. As I was going to the President's one day, I met him in the street. He walked me backwards and forwards before the President's door for half an hour. He painted pathetically the temper into which the legislature had been wrought; the disgust of those who were called the creditor states; the danger of the secession of their members, and the separation of the states. He observed that the members of the Administration ought to act in concert; that though this question was not of my [State] Department, yet a common duty should make it a common concern; that the President was the center on which all administrative questions ultimately rested; and that all of us should rally around him, and support, with joint efforts, measures approved by him; and that the question having been lost by a small majority only, it was probable that an appeal from me to the judgment and discretion of some of my friends might effect a change in the vote, and the machine of government, now suspended, might be again set into motion.

I told him that I was really a stranger to the whole subject; that not having yet informed myself of the system of finances adopted, I knew not how far this was a necessary sequence; that undoubtedly, if its rejection endangered a dissolution of our Union at this incipient stage, I should deem that the most unfortunate of all consequences, to avert which all partial and temporary evils should be yielded. I proposed to him, however, to dine with me the next day, and I would invite another friend or two, bring them into conference together, and I thought it impossible that reasonable men, consulting together coolly, could fail, by some mutual sacrifices of opinion, to form a compromise which was to save the Union.

The discussion took place. I could take no part in it but an exhortatory one, because I was a stranger to the circumstances which should govern it. But it was finally agreed that, whatever importance had been attached to the rejection of this proposition, the preservation of the Union and of concord among the states was more important, and that therefore it would be better that the vote of rejection should be rescinded, to effect which some members should change their votes. But it was observed that this pill would be peculiarly bitter to the Southern states, and that some concomitant measure should be adopted, to sweeten it a little to them.

There had before been propositions to fix the [permanent] seat of government either at Philadelphia, or at Georgetown on the Potomac; and it was thought that by giving it to Philadelphia for ten years, and to Georgetown permanently afterwards, this might, as an anodyne, calm in some degree the ferment which might be excited by the other measure alone. So two of the Potomac members (White and Lee, but White with a revulsion of stomach almost convulsive) agreed to change their votes, and Hamilton undertook to carry the other point. In doing this, the influence he had established over the Eastern members, with the agency of Robert Morris with those of the Middle states, effected his side of the engagement.

And so the Assumption was passed, and twenty millions of stock divided among favored states, and thrown in as a pabulum to the stock-jobbing herd. This added to the number of votaries to the Treasury, and made its chief the master of every vote in the legislature which might give to the government the direction suited to his political views.

I know well . . . that nothing like a majority in Congress had yielded to this corruption. Far from it. But a division . . . had already taken place . . . between the parties styled republican and federal.

2. Hamilton Defends Assumption (1792)

The scheme for assuming the state debts, proposed formally by Hamilton early in 1790, was not passed by Congress until nearly seven months later—again with the votes of certain members who stood to gain personally. During this delay a brisk

[2]H. C. Lodge, ed., *The Works of Alexander Hamilton* (Boston and New York: Houghton, Mifflin and Company, 1904), vol. 2, pp. 468–470 (August 18, 1792).

speculation in the depreciated state securities occurred, largely among northern financiers. Hamilton, in this private memorandum for Washington, denies that there was anything sinister in such purchases. What was his strongest argument? Who took advantage of whom?

. . . Is a government to bend the general maxims of policy and to mold its measures according to the accidental course of private speculations? Is it to do this, or omit that, in cases of great national importance, because one set of individuals may gain, another lose, from unequal opportunities of information, from unequal degrees of resource, craft, confidence, or enterprise?

Moreover, there is much exaggeration in stating the manner of the alienation of the debt. The principal speculations in state debts, whatever may be pretended, certainly began after the promulgation of the plan for assuming by the report of the Secretary of the Treasury to the House of Representatives. The resources of individuals in this country are too limited to have admitted of much progress in purchases before the knowledge of that plan was diffused throughout the country. After that, purchasers and sellers were upon equal ground. If the purchasers speculated upon the sellers, in many instances the sellers speculated upon the purchasers. Each made his calculation of chances, and founded upon it an exchange of money for certificates. It has turned out generally that the buyer had the best of the bargain, but the seller got the value of his commodity according to his estimate of it, and probably in a great number of instances more. This shall be explained.

It happened that Mr. Madison, and some other distinguished characters of the South, started in opposition to the assumption. The high opinion entertained of them made it be taken for granted in that quarter that the opposition would be successful. The securities quickly rose, by means of purchases, beyond their former prices. It was imagined that they would soon return to their old station by a rejection of the proposition for assuming. And the certificate holders were eager to part with them at their current prices, calculating on a loss to the purchasers from their future fall. This representation is not conjectural; it is founded on information from respectable and intelligent Southern characters, and may be ascertained by inquiry.

Hence it happened that the inhabitants of the Southern states sustained a considerable loss by the opposition to the assumption from Southern gentlemen, and their too great confidence in the efficacy of that opposition.

Further, a great part of the debt which has been purchased by the Northern and Southern citizens has been at higher prices—in numerous instances beyond the true value. In the late delirium of speculation large sums were purchased at 25 percent above par and upward.

The Southern people, upon the whole, have not parted with their property for nothing. They parted with it voluntarily, in most cases, upon fair terms, without surprise or deception—in many cases for more than its value. 'Tis their own fault if the purchase money has not been beneficial to them; and, the presumption is, it has been so in a material degree.

3. Jefferson Versus Hamilton on the Bank (1791)

There were only three banks in the entire country when Hamilton, in 1790, proposed the Bank of the United States as the keystone of his financial edifice. Modeled on the Bank of England and located in Philadelphia, it would be capitalized at $10 million, one-fifth of which might be held by the federal government. As a private concern under strict government supervision, it would be useful to the Treasury in issuing notes, in safeguarding surplus tax money, and in facilitating numerous public financial transactions. Before signing such a bank bill, Washington solicited the views of his cabinet members. The opinions of Jefferson, given below, elicited a rebuttal from Hamilton, also given below. Note that Jefferson, the strict constructionist of the Constitution, based his case on the Tenth Amendment in the Bill of Rights, about to be ratified. Hamilton, the loose constructionist of the Constitution, based his views on the implied powers in Article I, Section VIII, paragraph 18, which stipulates that Congress is empowered "to make all laws which shall be necessary and proper for carrying into execution the foregoing powers." Which of the two men seems to be on sounder ground in interpreting "necessary"?

Jefferson
February 15, 1791

I consider the foundation of the Constitution as laid on this ground—that *all powers not delegated to the United States by the Constitution, nor prohibited by it to the states, are reserved to the states, or to the people* (12th [10th] amend.). To take a single step beyond the boundaries thus specifically drawn around the powers of Congress is to take possession of a boundless field of power, no longer susceptible of any definition.

The incorporation of a bank, and the powers assumed by this bill, have not, in my opinion, been delegated to the United States by the Constitution.

The second general phrase is "to make all laws *necessary* and proper for carrying into execution the enumerated powers." But they can all be carried into execution without a bank. A bank therefore is not *necessary,* and

Hamilton
February 23, 1791

If the *end* be clearly comprehended within any of the specified powers, and if the measure have an obvious relation to that *end,* and is not forbidden by any particular provision of the Constitution, it may safely be deemed to come within the compass of the national authority.

There is also this further criterion, which may materially assist the decision: Does the proposed measure abridge a pre-existing right of any state or of any individual? If it does not, there is a strong presumption in favor of its constitutionality. . . .

. . . "Necessary" often means no more than needful, requisite, incidental, useful, or conducive to. . . . [A] restrictive interpretation of the word "necessary" is also contrary to this sound maxim of construction: namely,

[3]H. C. Lodge, ed., *The Works of Alexander Hamilton* (1904), vol. 3, pp. 458, 452, 455, 485–486; P. L. Ford, ed., *The Writings of Thomas Jefferson* (New York: G. P. Putnam's Sons, 1895), vol. 5, pp. 285, 287.

Jefferson	Hamilton
consequently not authorized by this phrase.	that the powers contained in a constitution . . . ought to be construed liberally in advancement of the public good.
It has been much urged that a bank will give great facility or convenience in the collection of taxes. Suppose this were true; yet the Constitution allows only the means which are "necessary," not those which are merely "convenient," for effecting the enumerated powers. If such a latitude of construction be allowed to this phrase as to give any non-enumerated power, it [the latitude] will go to every one; for there is not one [power] which ingenuity may not torture into a convenience, in some instance or other, to some one of so long a list of enumerated powers. It would swallow up all the delegated powers [of the states], and reduce the whole to one power. . . .	A hope is entertained that it has, by this time, been made to appear to the satisfaction of the President, that a bank has a natural relation to the power of collecting taxes—to that of regulating trade—to that of providing for the common defense—and that, as the bill under consideration contemplates the government in the light of a joint proprietor of the stock of the bank, it brings the case within the provision of the clause of the Constitution which immediately respects [relates to] the property of the United States. [Evidently Art. IV, Sec. III, para. 2: "The Congress shall have power to . . . make all needful rules and regulations respecting the territory or other property belonging to the United States. . . ."]

C. Overawing the Whiskey Boys

1. Hamilton Upholds Law Enforcement (1794)

Secretary Hamilton's excise tax on whiskey hit the impoverished Pennsylvania frontiersmen especially hard. Their roads were so poor that they could profitably transport their corn and rye to market only in liquid concentrate form. If sued by the government, they were forced to incur the heavy expense of traveling three hundred miles and undergoing trial before strange judges and jurors. Numerous other grievances caused the Whiskey Boys to form armed mobs that intimidated would-be taxpayers or roughly handled the federal tax collectors. Some agents were tarred, feathered, and beaten; the home of one was burned. An outraged Hamilton, prejudiced against those who "babble republicanism," set forth these views in the press over the pen name "Tully." What are the strengths and weaknesses of his argument?

Let us see then what is this question. It is plainly this: Shall the majority govern or be governed? Shall the nation rule or be ruled? Shall the general will prevail, or the will of a faction? Shall there be government or no government? It is impossible

---

[1]H. C. Lodge, ed., *The Works of Alexander Hamilton* (1904), vol. 6, pp. 414–416 (August 26, 1794).

to deny that this is the true and the whole question. No art, no sophistry can involve it in the least obscurity.

The Constitution *you* have ordained for yourselves and your posterity contains this express clause: "The Congress shall have power to lay and collect taxes, duties, imposts, and excises, to pay the debts, and provide for the common defense and general welfare of the United States." You have, then, by a solemn and deliberate act, the most important and sacred that a nation can perform, pronounced and decreed that your representatives in Congress shall have power to lay excises. You have done nothing since to reverse or impair that decree.

Your representatives in Congress, pursuant to the commission derived from you, and with a full knowledge of the public exigencies, have laid an excise. At three succeeding sessions they have revised that act, and have as often, with a degree of unanimity not common, and after the best opportunities of knowing your sense, renewed their sanction to it. You have acquiesced in it; it has gone into general operation; and *you* have actually paid more than a million of dollars on account of it.

But the four western counties of Pennsylvania undertake to rejudge and reverse your decrees. You have said, "The Congress shall have power to lay excises." They say, "The Congress shall not have this power," or—what is equivalent—"they shall not exercise it": for a power that may not be exercised is a nullity. Your representatives have said, and four times repeated it, "An excise on distilled spirits shall be collected." They say, "It shall not be collected. We will punish, expel, and banish the officers who shall attempt the collection. We will do the same by every other person who shall dare to comply with your decree expressed in the constitutional charter, and with that of your representatives expressed in the laws. The sovereignty shall not reside with you, but with us. If you presume to dispute the point by force, we are ready to measure swords with you, and if unequal ourselves to the contest, we will call in the aid of a foreign nation [Britain]. We will league ourselves with a foreign power."

2. Jefferson Deplores Undue Force (1794)

Hamilton was accused of deliberately aggravating the Whiskey Rebellion so that he might strengthen the prestige of the new government with an overpowering show of might. At all events, he marched out to the disaffected region with an army of some thirteen thousand militiamen. Resistance evaporated before such a force. Jefferson was appalled that these extravagant measures should have been taken against "occasional riots," and charged that Hamilton was merely pursuing his "favorite purpose of strengthening government and increasing public debt," all under "the sanction of a name [Washington] which has done too much good not to be sufficient to cover harm also." From his luxurious home, Monticello, Jefferson wrote indignantly as follows to James Madison, his friend and neighbor. Six years later these same backcountry rebels, who had incurred Hamilton's upper-class scorn, helped elect Jefferson president. Hamilton's show of sledgehammer force no doubt helped the prestige of the national government, but in the light of Jefferson's letter, how did the government probably hurt itself?

---

[2]P. L. Ford, *The Writings of Thomas Jefferson* (New York: G. P. Putnam's Sons, 1895), vol. 6, pp. 518–519 (December 28, 1794).

The excise law is an infernal one. The first error was to admit it by the Constitution; the second, to act on that admission; the third and last will be to make it the instrument of dismembering the Union, and setting us all afloat to choose which part of it we will adhere to.

The information of our militia, returned from the westward, is uniform, that though the people there let them pass quietly, they were objects of their laughter, not of their fear; that a thousand men could have cut off their whole force in a thousand places of the Allegheny; that their detestation of the excise law is universal, and has now associated to it a detestation of the government; and that separation, which perhaps was a very distant and problematical event, is now near, and certain, and determined in the mind of every man.

I expected to have seen justification of arming one part of the society against another; of declaring a civil war the moment before the meeting of that body [Congress] which has the sole right of declaring war; of being so patient of the kicks and scoffs of our [British] enemies,* and rising at a feather against our friends; of adding a million to the public debts and deriding us with recommendations to pay it if we can, etc., etc.

D. The Birth of a Neutrality Policy

1. The French Revolution: Conflicting Views (1790s)

Hamilton and Jefferson, disagreeing as they did on many issues, naturally took opposite sides on the French Revolution. The philosophical Virginian, ever dedicated to liberty, rejoiced over the liberation of oppressed humanity. The practical-minded New Yorker, concerned about property, was profoundly shocked by the bloody excesses. Why did Hamilton reject the parallel to the American Revolution? Why was Jefferson so deeply concerned?

Hamilton	Jefferson
In France, he [Jefferson] saw government only on the side of its abuses. He drank freely of the French philosophy, in religion, in science, in politics. He came from France in the moment of a fermentation which he had a share in exciting, and in the passions and feelings of which he shared, both from temperament and situation. . . . He	But it is a fact, in spite of the mildness of their governors, the [French] people are ground to powder by the vices of the form of government. Of twenty millions of people supposed to be in France, I am of opinion there are nineteen millions more wretched, more accursed in every circumstance of human existence than the most con-

---

*A reference to British seizures of American ships prior to Jay's Treaty.

[1]Convenient compilations of quotations are found in S. K. Padover, ed., *The Mind of Alexander Hamilton* (New York: Harper & Row, 1958) and *Thomas Jefferson on Democracy* (New York and London: D. Appleton-Century Company, 1939).

Hamilton

came electrified with attachment to France, and with the project of knitting together the two countries in the closest political bands. (1792)

... The cause of France is compared with that of America during its late revolution. Would to heaven that the comparison were just. Would to heaven we could discern in the mirror of French affairs the same humanity, the same decorum, the same gravity, the same order, the same dignity, the same solemnity, which distinguished the cause of the American Revolution. Clouds and darkness would not then rest upon the issue as they now do. I own I do not like the comparison. (1793?)

... There was a time when all men in this country entertained the same favorable view of the French Revolution. At the present time, they all still unite in the wish that the troubles of France may terminate in the establishment of a free and good government; and dispassionate, well-informed men must equally unite in the doubt whether this be likely to take place under the auspices of those who now govern ... that country. But agreeing in these two points, there is a great and serious diversity of opinion as to the real merits and probable issue of the French Revolution. (1794)

None can deny that the cause of France has been stained by excesses and extravagances for which it is not easy, if possible, to find a parallel in the history of human affairs, and from which reason and humanity recoil. . . . (1794)

Jefferson

spicuously wretched individual of the whole United States. (1785)

You will have heard, before this reaches you, of the peril into which the French Revolution is brought by the flight of their King. Such are the fruits of that form of government which heaps importance on idiots, and of which the Tories of the present day are trying to preach into our favor. I still hope the French Revolution will issue happily. I feel that the permanence of our own leans in some degree on that; and that a failure there would be a powerful argument to prove there must be a failure here. (1791)

In the struggle which was necessary, many guilty persons fell without the forms of trial, and with them some innocent. These I deplore as much as anybody, and shall deplore some of them to the day of my death. But I deplore them as I should have done had they fallen in battle. . . . But time and truth will rescue and embalm their very liberty for which they would never have hesitated to offer up their lives. The liberty of the whole earth was depending on the issue of the contest, and was ever such a prize won with so little innocent blood? (1793)

My own affections have been deeply wounded by some of the martyrs to this cause, but rather than it should have failed I would have seen half the earth desolated; were there but an Adam and an Eve left in every country, and left free, it would be better than it now is. (1793)

2. A Jeffersonian Condemns Neutrality (1793)

The treaty of alliance with France in 1778 bound the United States "forever" to help defend the French West Indies. Britain's entrance into the War of the French Revolution in 1793 consequently threatened to involve the American people. Both Hamilton and Jefferson agreed (for once) on the wisdom of a neutrality proclamation. President Washington thereupon issued a stern admonition reminding Americans of their "duty" to be "friendly and impartial" toward both Britain and France. But many Jeffersonians, including the anonymous author of the following open letter to Washington, emitted pained outcries. What was the author's most serious grievance against the president, and the reason for it? Did moral considerations compel a policy of favoritism to France?

In countries where the people have little or no share in the government (as in Great Britain, for instance), it is not uncommon for the executive to act in direct opposition to the will of the nation. It is to be hoped that the practice of aping the absurd and tyrannical systems of Britain, though already carried to an alarming extent in this country, will never proceed so far as to induce our executive to try the vain experiment of officially opposing the national will. . . .

Had you, sir, before you ventured to issue a proclamation which appears to have given much uneasiness, consulted the general sentiments of your fellow citizens, you would have found them, from one extremity of the Union to the other, firmly attached to the cause of France. You would not have found them disposed to consider it as a "duty" to forget their debt of gratitude to the French nation; or to view with unconcern the magnanimous efforts of a faithful ally to baffle the infernal projects of those despots who have confederated for the purpose of crushing her infant liberty. Neither would you have found them so far divested of the feelings of men as to treat with "impartiality," and equal "friendship," those tigers who so lately deluged our country with the blood of thousands, and the men who generously flew to her rescue and became her deliverers.

No, sir—had even no written treaty existed between France and the United States, still would the strongest ties of amity have united the people of both nations; still would the republican citizens of America have regarded Frenchmen, contending for liberty, as their brethren; still would they have sympathized with them in their misfortunes, and have exulted in their success. . . .

It ought never to be forgotten by our magistrates that popular opinion is the basis of our government; and that when any public measure is not well understood, it would be by no means degrading to the authors of that measure, however exalted their station, to explain. Let me entreat you, sir, to deal candidly with the people; and, without loss of time, to remove their anxiety by informing them whether it is intended that the treaties with France are to be observed or not.

I am aware, sir, that some court satellites may have deceived you with respect to the sentiments of your fellow citizens. The first magistrate of a country, whether he be called a king or a president, seldom knows the real state of the nation, particularly if he be so much buoyed up by official importance as to think it beneath his

---

[2]*National Gazette* (Philadelphia), June 5, 1793.

dignity to mix occasionally with the people. Let me caution you, sir, to beware that you do not view the state of the public mind, at this critical moment, through a fallacious medium. Let not the little buzz of the aristocratic few and their contemptible minions, of speculators, Tories, and British emissaries, be mistaken for the exalted and general voice of the American people. The spirit of 1776 is again roused; and soon shall the mushroom-lordlings of the day, the enemies of American as well as French liberty, be taught that American Whigs of 1776 will not suffer French patriots of 1792 to be vilified with impunity by the common enemies of both.

E. The Controversial Jay Treaty

1. Virginians Oppose John Jay's Appointment (1794)

After British cruisers suddenly seized scores of American food ships bound for the French West Indies, a crisis developed. President Washington, desperately seeking to avoid hostilities, decided to send to London a pro-British Federalist, John Jay, in a last-gasp effort to preserve peace. Pro-French Jeffersonians reacted angrily, notably in this "Address to the People of the United States" from the Democratic Society in Wythe County, Virginia. Were these Jeffersonians pro-French, pro-British, or merely partisan?

While with anxious expectation we contemplate the affairs of Europe, it will be criminal to forget our own country. A session of Congress having just passed, the first in which the people were equally represented, it is a fit time to take a retrospective view of the proceedings of government. We have watched each motion of those in power, but are sorry we cannot exclaim, "Well done, thou good and faithful servant." We have seen the nation insulted, our rights violated, our commerce ruined—and what has been the conduct of government? Under the corrupt influence of the [Hamiltonian] paper system, it has uniformly crouched to Britain; while on the contrary our allies, the French, to whom we owe our political existence, have been treated unfriendly; denied any advantages from their treaties with us; their minister abused; and those individuals among us who desired to aid their arms, prosecuted as traitors—blush, Americans, for the conduct of your government.

Citizens! Shall we Americans who have kindled the spark of liberty stand aloof and see it extinguished when burning a bright flame in France, which hath caught it from us? Do you not see, if despots prevail, you must have a despot like the rest of the nations? If all tyrants unite against free people, should not all free people unite against tyrants? Yes! Let us unite with France and stand or fall together.

We lament that a man who hath so long possessed the public confidence as the head of the Executive Department [Washington] hath possessed it, should put it to so severe a trial as he hath by a late appointment [of Jay]. The Constitution hath been trampled on, and your rights have no security. . . .

---

[1]*Independent Chronicle* (Boston), August 11, 1794.

Fellow citizens!

We hope the misconduct of the Executive may have proceeded from bad advice; but we can only look to the immediate cause of the mischief. To us it seems a radical change of measures is necessary. How shall this be effected? Citizens! It is to be effected by a change of men. Deny the continuance of your confidence to such members of the legislative body as have an interest distinct from that of the people.

2. Hamilton Attacks Jay's Attackers (1795)

The Federalist diplomat John Jay, who held few high cards, finally signed a treaty in London in 1794 that was keenly disappointing. Although the British belatedly agreed to evacuate the half-dozen frontier trading posts on American soil and grant certain trade concessions, they gave no satisfaction regarding the impressment of American seamen, the future seizure of ships, and the alleged inciting of the Indians of the Northwest. But to a financially shaky America, a humiliating treaty was still better than a devastating war, and Federalists defended the pact with vigor. After he was bloodily stoned from a New York platform, Alexander Hamilton contributed a series of articles to the press, from which the following excerpt is taken. How did the democratic process operate then, as compared with now?

Before the treaty was known, attempts were made to prepossess the public mind against it. It was absurdly asserted that it was not expected by the people that Mr. Jay was to make any treaty; as if he had been sent, not to accommodate differences by negotiation and agreement, but to dictate to Great Britain the terms of an unconditional submission.

Before it was published at large, a sketch, calculated to produce false impressions, was handed out to the public, through a medium noted for hostility to the administration of the government. Emissaries flew through the country, spreading alarm and discontent; the leaders of [Jeffersonian] clubs were everywhere active to seize the passions of the people, and preoccupy their judgments against the treaty.

At Boston it was published one day, and the next a town-meeting was convened to condemn it; without ever being read, without any serious discussion, sentence was pronounced against it.

Will any man seriously believe that in so short a time an instrument of this nature could have been tolerably understood by the greater part of those who were thus induced to a condemnation of it? Can the result be considered as anything more than a sudden ebullition of popular passion, excited by the artifices of a party which had adroitly seized a favorable moment to furorize the public opinion? This spirit of precipitation, and the intemperance which accompanied it, prevented the body of the merchants and the greater part of the most considerate citizens from attending the meeting, and left those who met, wholly under the guidance of a set of men who, with two or three exceptions, have been the uniform opposers of the government.

---

[2]H. C. Lodge, ed., *The Works of Alexander Hamilton* (1904), vol. 5, pp. 195–197.

The intelligence of this event had no sooner reached New York than the leaders of the clubs were seen haranguing in every corner of the city, to stir up our citizens into an imitation of the example of the meeting at Boston. An invitation to meet at the city hall quickly followed, not to consider or discuss the merits of the treaty, but to unite with the meeting at Boston to address the President against its ratification.

This was immediately succeeded by a hand-bill, full of invectives against the treaty, as absurd as they were inflammatory, and manifestly designed to induce the citizens to surrender their reason to the empire of their passions.

In vain did a respectable meeting of the merchants endeavor, by their advice, to moderate the violence of these views, and to promote a spirit favorable to a fair discussion of the treaty; in vain did a respectable majority of the citizens of every description attend for that purpose. The leaders of the clubs resisted all discussion, and their followers, by their clamors and vociferations, rendered it impracticable, notwithstanding the wish of a manifest majority of the citizens convened upon the occasion.

Can we believe that the leaders were really sincere in the objections they made to a discussion, or that the great and mixed mass of citizens then assembled had so thoroughly mastered the merits of the treaty as that they might not have been enlightened by such a discussion?

It cannot be doubted that the real motive to the opposition was the fear of a discussion; the desire of excluding light; the adherence to a plan of surprise and deception. Nor need we desire any fuller proof of the spirit of party which has stimulated the opposition to the treaty than is to be found in the circumstances of that opposition.

F. The Retirement of Washington

1. A President Bids Farewell (1796)

Weary of body and outraged by political abuse, Washington announced his decision to retire in his Farewell Address, which he simply gave as a gratuitous "scoop" to a Philadelphia newspaper. At first a nonpartisan but now a Federalist, he had leaned heavily on Hamilton's collaboration in its composition. The bulk of the address deals with domestic difficulties, but the part relating to foreign affairs is best known. The document was clearly partisan. It served as the opening gun in the forthcoming presidential campaign of 1796 by indirectly defending Jay's Treaty and by directly alerting the public to flagrant French intrigue in the nation's capital. Many Jeffersonian Republicans, recognizing the attack on them, condemned the document. Why was it to the advantage of America to remain aloof? Did Washington reject all alliances in all circumstances?

[1]J. D. Richardson, ed., *Messages and Papers of the Presidents* (1896), vol. 1, pp. 221–223.

Observe good faith and justice toward all nations. Cultivate peace and harmony with all. Religion and morality enjoin this conduct. And can it be that good policy does not equally enjoin it? It will be worthy of a free, enlightened, and, at no distant period, a great nation to give to mankind the magnanimous and too novel example of a people always guided by an exalted justice and benevolence. . . .

In the execution of such a plan nothing is more essential than that permanent, inveterate antipathies against particular nations and passionate attachments for others should be excluded, and that, in place of them, just and amicable feelings toward all should be cultivated. The nation which indulges toward another an habitual hatred or an habitual fondness is in some degree a slave. It is a slave to its animosity or to its affection, either of which is sufficient to lead it astray from its duty and its interest. . . .

The nation prompted by ill will and resentment sometimes impels to war the government, contrary to the best calculations of policy. The government sometimes participates in the national propensity, and adopts through passion what reason would reject. . . .

So, likewise, a passionate attachment of one nation for another produces a variety of evils. Sympathy for the favorite nation, facilitating the illusion of an imaginary common interest in cases where no real common interest exists, and infusing into one the enmities of the other, betrays the former into a participation in the quarrels and wars of the latter without adequate inducement or justification. . . .

As avenues to foreign influence in innumerable ways, such attachments are particularly alarming to the truly enlightened and independent patriot. How many opportunities do they afford to tamper with domestic factions, to practice the arts of seduction, to mislead public opinion, to influence or awe the public councils! Such an attachment of a small or weak toward a great and powerful nation dooms the former to be the satellite of the latter.

Against the insidious wiles of foreign influence (I conjure you to believe me, fellow citizens) the jealousy of a free people ought to be *constantly* awake, since history and experience prove that foreign influence is one of the most baneful foes of republican government. . . .

The great rule of conduct for us in regard to foreign nations is, in extending our commercial relations, to have with them as little *political* connection as possible. So far as we have already formed engagements [French treaty], let them be fulfilled with perfect good faith. Here let us stop.

Europe has a set of primary interests which to us have none, or a very remote, relation. Hence she must be engaged in frequent controversies, the causes of which are essentially foreign to our concerns. Hence, therefore, it must be unwise in us to implicate ourselves by artificial ties in the ordinary vicissitudes of her politics, or the ordinary combinations and collisions of her friendships or enmities.

Our detached and distant situation invites and enables us to pursue a different course. If we remain one people, under an efficient government, the period is not far off when we may defy material injury from external annoyance; when we may take such an attitude as will cause the neutrality we may at any time resolve upon to be scrupulously respected; when belligerent nations, under the impossibility of making acquisitions upon us, will not lightly hazard the giving us provocation; when we may choose peace or war, as our interest, guided by justice, shall counsel.

Why forgo the advantages of so peculiar a situation? Why quit our own to stand upon foreign ground? Why, by interweaving our destiny with that of any part of Europe, entangle our peace and prosperity in the toils of European ambition, rivalship, interest, humor, or caprice?

It is our true policy to steer clear of permanent alliances with any portion of the foreign world, so far, I mean, as we are now at liberty to do it. For let me not be understood as capable of patronizing infidelity to existing engagements. I hold the maxim no less applicable to public than to private affairs that honesty is always the best policy. I repeat, therefore, let those engagements be observed in their genuine sense. But in my opinion it is unnecessary and would be unwise to extend them.

Taking care always to keep ourselves by suitable establishments on a respectable defensive posture, we may safely trust to temporary alliances for extraordinary emergencies.

Harmony, liberal intercourse with all nations, are recommended by policy, humanity, and interest. But even our commercial policy should hold an equal and impartial hand, neither seeking nor granting exclusive favors or preference; . . . constantly keeping in view that it is folly in one nation to look for disinterested favors from another; that it must pay with a portion of its independence for whatever it may accept under that character; that by such acceptance it may place itself in the condition of having given equivalents for nominal favors, and yet of being reproached with ingratitude for not giving more. There can be no greater error than to expect or calculate upon real favors from nation to nation. It is an illusion which experience must cure, which a just pride ought to discard.

2. Editor Benjamin Franklin Bache Berates Washington (1797)

Benjamin Franklin Bache, grandson of "Old Ben," was a newspaper editor notorious for his malicious attacks on the Federalists in general and on Washington in particular.* He published the following tirade when the president retired, but fortunately his sentiments were not shared by the vast majority of Washington's appreciative countrymen. In retaliation, Federalist rowdies wrecked the office of the Philadelphia Aurora and manhandled editor Bache. How much of this incendiary editorial is anti-Federalist partisanship and how much is pure libel?

"Lord, now lettest thou thy servant depart in peace, for mine eyes have seen thy salvation," was the pious ejaculation of a man who beheld a flood of happiness rushing upon mankind [Simeon, who had just seen Jesus]. If ever there was a time that would license the reiteration of the exclamation, that time is now arrived. For the man who is the source of all the misfortunes of our country is this day reduced to a level with his fellow citizens, and is no longer possessed of power to multiply evils upon the United States.

---

[2]Philadelphia *Aurora,* March 6, 1797, in Allan Nevins, ed., *American Press Opinion* (Boston and New York: D. C. Heath and Company, 1928), pp. 21–22.

*Benjamin Franklin Bache was nicknamed "Lightning Rod, Junior," an obvious reference to his inventive grandfather and to his own high-voltage journalism.

If ever there was a period for rejoicing, this is the moment. Every heart in unison with the freedom and happiness of the people ought to beat high with exultation that the name of Washington, from this day, ceases to give a currency to political iniquity and to legalize corruption. A new era is opening upon us—a new era which promises much to the people. For public measures must now stand upon their own merits, and nefarious projects can no longer be supported by a name.

When a retrospect is taken of the Washington administration for eight years, it is a subject of the greatest astonishment that a single individual should have canceled the principles of republicanism in an enlightened people, and should have carried his designs against the public liberty so far as to have put in jeopardy its very existence. Such, however, are the facts, and with these staring us in the face, this day ought to be a jubilee in the United States.

3. Editor William Cobbett Blasts Bache (1797)

Newspaper editor William Cobbett, a violent pro-Federalist, was the Federalist answer to Benjamin Franklin Bache. An English émigré who was so pro-British that he insolently displayed portraits of George III in his bookshop window, he was threatened with tar and feathers by the Philadelphia mob. Here he pays his editorial disrespects to his rival Bache. Note his explanation of Bache's hostility to Washington. What aspects of this type of journalism may no longer be found, and why?

This atrocious wretch (worthy descendant of old Ben) knows that all men of any understanding set him down as an abandoned liar, as a tool, and a hireling; and he is content that they should do so. He does not want to be thought anything else. . . . As this *Gazette* is honored with many readers in foreign countries, it may not be improper to give them some little account of this miscreant.

If they have read the old hypocrite Franklin's will, they must have observed that part of his library, with some other things, are left to a certain grandson; this is the very identical Market Street scoundrel. He spent several years in hunting offices under the federal government, and being constantly rejected, he at last became its most bitter foe. Hence his abuse of General Washington, whom, at the time he was soliciting a place, he panegyrized up to the third heaven.

He was born for a hireling, and therefore when he found he could not obtain employ in one quarter, he sought it in another. The first effect of his paw being greased appeared soon after [the French envoy] Genet's arrival, and he has from that time to this been as faithful to the cutthroats of Paris as ever dog was to his master.

He is an ill-looking devil. His eyes never get above your knees. He is of a sallow complexion, hollow-cheeked, dead-eyed, and has a *tout ensemble* [general effect] just like that of a fellow who has been about a week or ten days on a gibbet.

---

[3]*Porcupine's Gazette* (Philadelphia), November 15, 1797, in William Cobbett, *Porcupine's Works* . . . (1801), vol. 7, pp. 294–295.

G. The Alien and Sedition Hysteria

1. Timothy Pickering Upholds the Repressive Laws (1798)

Angered by Jay's pro-British treaty, the French seized scores of American ships, thereby paving the way for the undeclared naval war of 1798–1800, during the presidency of John Adams. The pro-British Federalists, riding the wave of anti-French hysteria, undertook to curb and gag the pro-French Jeffersonians by passing the Alien and Sedition Acts of 1798. The Alien Act empowered the president to deport undesirable aliens (largely Irish and French refugees); the Sedition Act prescribed fines and imprisonment for false maligning of federal officials. Timothy Pickering, secretary of state under President Adams, offered the following spirited defense of the Alien and Sedition Acts. What were his views regarding (a) inferior rights of aliens and (b) the similarity between abusing free speech and committing murder?

The Alien Law has been bitterly inveighed against as a direct attack upon our liberties, when in fact it affects only foreigners who are conspiring against us, and has no relation whatever to an American citizen. It gives authority to the First Magistrate [President] of the Union to order all such aliens as he shall judge dangerous to the peace and safety of the United States, or shall have reasonable grounds to suspect are concerned in any treasonable or secret machinations against the government thereof, to depart out of our territory.

It is only necessary to ask whether, without such a power vested in some department, any government ever did, or ever can, long protect itself. The objects of this act are strangers merely, persons not adopted and naturalized—a description of men who have no lot nor interest with us, and who even manifest a disposition the most hostile to this country, while it affords them an asylum and protection. It is absurd to say that, in providing by law for their removal, the Constitution is violated. For he must be ignorant indeed who does not know that the Constitution was established for the protection and security of American citizens, and not of intriguing foreigners.

The Sedition Act has likewise been shamefully misrepresented as an attack upon the freedom of speech and of the press. But we find, on the contrary, that it prescribes a punishment only for those pests of society and disturbers of order and tranquillity "who write, print, utter, or publish any false, scandalous, and malicious writings against the government of the United States, or either house of the Congress of the United States, or the President, with intent to defame, or bring them into contempt or disrepute, or to excite against them the hatred of the good people of the United States; or to stir up sedition, or to abet the hostile designs of any foreign nation."

What honest man can justly be alarmed at such a law, or can wish unlimited permission to be given for the publication of malicious falsehoods, and with intentions the most base? They who complain of legal provisions for punishing intentional defamation and lies as bridling the liberty of speech and of the press, may, with equal propriety, complain against laws made for punishing assault and murder,

---

[1]C. W. Upham, *Life of Timothy Pickering* (1873), vol. 3, pp. 475–476.

as restraints upon the freedom of men's actions. Because we have the right to speak and publish our opinions, it does not necessarily follow that we may exercise it in uttering false and malicious slanders against our neighbor or our government, any more than we may under cover of freedom of action knock down the first man we meet, and exempt ourselves from punishment by pleading that we are free agents. We may indeed use our tongues, employ our pens, and carry our cudgels or our muskets whenever we please. But, at the same time, we must be accountable and punishable for making such "improper use of either as to injure others in their characters, their persons, or their property."

2. The Virginia Legislature Protests (1798)

The Federalist Sedition Act was plainly a violation of the free-speech and free-press guarantees of the Constitution (First Amendment, Bill of Rights). But the Federalist Supreme Court was not yet declaring acts of Congress unconstitutional. When Jeffersonians branded the Sedition Act the "gag law," one Federalist editor replied: "Nothing can so completely gag a Jeffersonian Democrat as to restrain him from lying. If you forbid his lying, you forbid his speaking." A score or so of Jeffersonian editors were arrested, including the unbridled Benjamin Franklin Bache, who died before his trial. Vice President Jefferson and James Madison (who was then in private life) both feared that the Sedition Act would terrorize the Jeffersonian Republican party into silence and destroy it. Madison, working secretly with Jefferson, drafted the following resolutions, which were approved by the Virginia legislature. Note especially the views on the "compact theory," the First Amendment, and the proposed method of voiding the Alien and Sedition laws. Do they seem unreasonable?

[*Resolved,*] That this Assembly most solemnly declares a warm attachment to the union of the states, to maintain which it pledges its powers; and that, for this end, it is their duty to watch over and oppose every infraction of those principles which constitute the only basis of that union, because a faithful observance of them can alone secure its existence and the public happiness.

That this Assembly does explicitly and peremptorily declare that it views the powers of the federal government as resulting from the compact to which the states are parties, as limited by the plain sense and intention of the instrument [Constitution] constituting that compact, as no further valid than they are authorized by the grants enumerated in that compact; and that, in case of a deliberate, palpable, and dangerous exercise of other powers not granted by the said compact, the states who are parties thereto have the right, and are in duty bound, to interpose for arresting the progress of the evil, and for maintaining, within their respective limits, the authorities, rights, and liberties appertaining to them. . . .

That the General Assembly does also express its deep regret that a spirit has, in sundry instances, been manifested by the federal government to enlarge its powers by forced constructions of the constitutional charter which defines them, . . . so as to consolidate the states, by degrees, into one sovereignty, the obvious tendency and

---

[2]Jonathan Elliot, *The Debates . . . on the Adoption of the Federal Constitution* (Philadelphia: J. B. Lippincott, 1836), vol. 4, pp. 528–529.

inevitable result of which would be to transform the present republican system of the United States into an absolute, or, at best, a mixed monarchy.

That the General Assembly does particularly protest against the palpable and alarming infractions of the Constitution in the two late cases of the "Alien and Sedition Acts," passed at the last session of Congress; the first of which exercises a power nowhere delegated to the federal government, and which, by uniting legislative and judicial powers to those of executive, subverts the general principles of free government, as well as the particular organization and positive provisions of the federal Constitution; and the other of which acts exercises, in like manner, a power not delegated by the Constitution, but, on the contrary, expressly and positively forbidden by one of the amendments thereto—a power which, more than any other, ought to produce universal alarm, because it is leveled against the right of freely examining public characters and measures, and of free communication among the people thereon, which has ever been justly deemed the only effectual guardian of every other right.

That this state having, by its convention [of 1788] which ratified the federal Constitution, expressly declared that, among other essential rights, "the liberty of conscience and the press cannot be canceled, abridged, restrained, or modified by any authority of the United States," and, from its extreme anxiety to guard these rights from every possible attack of sophistry and ambition, having, with other states, recommended an amendment for that purpose, which amendment [the First] was, in due time, annexed to the Constitution, it would mark a reproachful inconsistency and criminal degeneracy if an indifference were now shown to the most palpable violation of one of the rights thus declared and secured, and to the establishment of a precedent which may be fatal to the other.

That the good people of the commonwealth having ever felt, and continuing to feel, the most sincere affection for their brethren of the other states, the truest anxiety for establishing and perpetuating the union of all, and the most scrupulous fidelity to that Constitution, which is the pledge of mutual friendship, and the instrument of mutual happiness, the General Assembly does solemnly appeal to the like dispositions in the other states, in confidence that they will concur with this commonwealth in declaring, as it does hereby declare, that the acts aforesaid are unconstitutional, and that the necessary and proper measures will be taken by each for cooperating with this state in maintaining unimpaired the authorities, rights, and liberties reserved to the states respectively, or to the people.

3. Rhode Island Rebuffs Virginia's Plea (1799)

The appeal of Virginia to her sister states for support fell on barren ground. A half-dozen or so northern state legislatures, with varying degrees of heat, registered dissent, particularly in the Federalist centers. Do the following Rhode Island resolutions propose a sounder solution of the constitutional problem than those of Virginia?

1. *Resolved,* That, in the opinion of this legislature, the second section of the third article of the Constitution of the United States, in these words, to wit, "The ju-

---

[3]Jonathan Elliot, *The Debates . . . on the Adoption of the Federal Constitution* (1836), vol. 4, p. 533.

dicial power shall extend to all cases arising under the laws of the United States," vests in the federal courts exclusively, and in the Supreme Court of the United States ultimately, the authority of deciding on the constitutionality of any act or law of the Congress of the United States.

2. *Resolved,* That for any state legislature to assume that authority would be—

1st. Blending together legislative and judicial powers;

2nd. Hazarding an interruption of the peace of the states by civil discord, in case of a diversity of opinions among the state legislatures; each state having, in that case, no resort for vindicating its own opinions but the strength of its own arm;

3rd. Submitting most important questions of law to less competent tribunals [legislatures]; and,

4th. An infraction of the Constitution of the United States, expressed in plain terms.

3. *Resolved,* That, although, for the above reasons, this legislature, in their public capacity, do not feel themselves authorized to consider and decide on the constitutionality of the Sedition and Alien laws (so called), yet they are called upon, by the exigency of this occasion, to declare that, in their private opinions, these laws are within the powers delegated to Congress, and promotive of the welfare of the United States.

4. *Resolved,* That the governor communicate these resolutions to the supreme executive of the state of Virginia, and at the same time express to him that this legislature cannot contemplate without extreme concern and regret the many evil and fatal consequences which may flow from the very unwarrantable resolutions aforesaid. . . .

[Vice President Jefferson, again collaborating secretly with James Madison, prepared two sets of resolutions that were adopted in 1798 and 1799 by the Kentucky legislature. Jefferson kept his authorship secret for twenty-three years, partly because it was improper for the vice president to be engaged in such activity, and partly because he feared Federalist prosecution for sedition. The second set of Kentucky resolutions reaffirmed the Virginia resolutions in protesting against violations of the Constitution, but went further in baldly approving nullification by the "sovereign" states as follows: "That a nullification, by those sovereignties, of all unauthorized acts done under color of that instrument [the Constitution] is the rightful remedy: That this commonwealth does, under the most deliberate reconsideration, declare, that the said Alien and Sedition Laws are, in their opinion, palpable violations of the said Constitution; and . . . in momentous regulations like the present . . . it would consider a silent acquiescence as highly criminal.". . .]

Thought Provokers

1. Which principles of Jefferson, the founder of the Democratic party, are upheld by Democrats today and which are not? Which principles of Hamilton, the godfather of the present Republican party, are upheld by Republicans today and which are not? Explain.

2. How credible is the testimony of a man like Jefferson, a bitter foe of Hamilton, as revised more than a quarter of a century after the event?

3. Hamilton had written in 1783: "The rights of government are as essential to be defended as the rights of individuals. The security of the one is inseparable from that of the other." Based on Hamilton's handling of the Whiskey Rebellion of 1794, comment on his statement.

4. Has the federal government become more or less Hamiltonian during the past two centuries?

5. In defending the bloody excesses of the French Revolution, Jefferson argued in effect that the end justified the means. Comment. After reviewing Franco-American relations during these years, assess Washington's observation that when a nation develops too great a fondness for another, it is in some degree its slave.

6. Massachusetts senator Henry Cabot Lodge once remarked that politics should stop at the water's edge. Comment with reference to foreign affairs in the 1790s.

7. Was Washington's Farewell Address necessary? What have been its most misunderstood parts, and why? Was it designed as a prescription for all future years? Which parts are still valid and which are not?

8. Can the Alien and Sedition Acts be justified, especially in view of the excesses of editors Bache and Cobbett? Assuming that free speech ought to be curbed, who should do the curbing? Why is free speech necessary for the workings of a free government? It has been said that many a minority has become a majority because its foes were unwise enough to persecute it. Comment with reference to the Jeffersonian Republicans of 1798.

11

The Triumphs and Travails of Jeffersonian Democracy, 1800–1812

We have a perfect horror at everything like connecting
ourselves with the politics of Europe.

Thomas Jefferson, 1801

Prologue: Jeffersonians and Federalists alike contributed to the process of nation
building as the nineteenth century opened. Jefferson's Federalist cousin, Supreme
Court Justice John Marshall, handed down a series of Court decisions that significantly strengthened the powers of the federal government at the expense of the individual states. Jefferson himself swallowed some of his constitutional scruples to
accomplish the boldest achievement of his presidency—the Louisiana Purchase—
which at a stroke doubled the size of the United States and guaranteed American
control of the Mississippi River and its crucial ocean port at New Orleans. Jefferson
proved less successful in his increasingly desperate efforts to keep the United States
out of the war then raging in Europe. Though sorely provoked by British impressment of American sailors, Jefferson consistently tried to avoid fighting. He resorted
finally to a self-denying trade embargo as the price he was willing to pay for peace.

A. John Marshall and the Supreme Court

1. Marshall Sanctions the Bank (1819)

*Jefferson and Hamilton had clashed over the constitutionality of the monopolistic
Bank of the United States in 1791 (see p. 183). Nearly three decades later, Chief Justice John Marshall, a die-hard Hamiltonian Federalist, settled the issue judicially
when he led a unanimous Supreme Court in a sweeping decision in the case of Mc-
Culloch v. Maryland. Certain branches of the Second Bank of the United States, guilty
of reckless speculation and even fraud, had incurred popular hatred. Consequently,
Maryland undertook to stamp out a branch of the Bank by a prohibitory tax. In upholding the constitutionality of the Bank and its branches, Marshall invoked the*

---

[1]Henry Wheaton, *Reports of Cases Argued and Adjudged in the Supreme Court of the United States,
1816–1827,* vol. 4 (Newark, N.Y.: The Lawyers' Co-operative Publishing Company, 1819), pp. 432–433,
436, 437.

"necessary and proper" clause of the Constitution to the advantage of the national government. In fact, he used almost the exact words of Hamilton in 1791. In denying the right of a state to destroy by taxation an arm of the federal government, Marshall ringingly reasserted the supremacy of the central regime over the states. What might have happened to the federal authority if the Court had upheld Maryland?

We admit, as all must admit, that the powers of the government are limited, and that its limits are not to be transcended. But we think the sound construction of the Constitution must allow to the national legislature that discretion, with respect to the means by which the powers it confers are to be carried into execution, which will enable that body to perform the high duties assigned to it, in the manner most beneficial to the people. Let the end be legitimate, let it be within the scope of the constitution, and all means which are appropriate, which are plainly adapted to that end, which are not prohibited, but consist with the letter and spirit of the constitution, are constitutional. . . .

That the power of taxation is one of vital importance; that it is retained by the states; that it is not abridged by the grant of a similar power to the government of the Union; that it is to be concurrently exercised by the two governments—are truths which have never been denied. But such is the paramount character of the Constitution that its capacity to withdraw any subject from the action of even this power is admitted. The states are expressly forbidden to lay any duties on imports or exports, except what may be absolutely necessary for executing their inspection laws. . . . The same paramount character would seem to restrain . . . a state from such other exercise of this power as is in its nature incompatible with, and repugnant to, the constitutional laws of the Union. A law absolutely repugnant to another, as entirely repeals that other as if express terms of repeal were used.

On this ground the counsel for the Bank place its claim to be exempted from the power of a state to tax its operations. There is no express provision for the case, but the claim has been sustained on a principle which so entirely pervades the Constitution, is so intermixed with the materials which compose it, so interwoven with its web, so blended with its texture, as to be incapable of being separated from it without rending it into shreds.

This great principle is that the Constitution, and the laws made in pursuance thereof, are supreme; that they control the constitutions and laws of the respective states, and cannot be controlled by them. From this, which may be almost termed an axiom, other propositions are deduced as corollaries. . . . These are: 1. That a power to create implies a power to preserve. 2. That a power to destroy, if wielded by a different hand, is hostile to, and incompatible with, these powers to create and preserve. 3. That where this repugnancy exists, that authority which is supreme must control, not yield to that over which it is supreme. . . .

That the power to tax involves the power to destroy; that the power to destroy may defeat and render useless the power to create; that there is a plain repugnance in conferring on one government a power to control the constitutional measures of another . . . are propositions not to be denied. . . .

If we apply the principle for which the state of Maryland contends, to the Constitution generally, we shall find it capable of changing totally the character of that instrument. We shall find it capable of arresting all the measures of the government, and of prostrating it at the foot of the states. The American people have declared their Constitution, and the laws made in pursuance thereof, to be supreme; and this principle would transfer the supremacy, in fact, to the states.

If the states may tax one instrument employed by the government in the execution of its powers, they may tax any and every other instrument. They may tax the mail; they may tax the mint; they may tax patent rights; they may tax the papers of the custom-house; they may tax judicial process; they may tax all the means employed by the government, to an excess which would defeat all the ends of government. This was not intended by the American people. They did not design to make their government dependent on the states. . . .

The question is, in truth, a question of supremacy. And if the right of the states to tax the means employed by the general government be conceded, the declaration that the Constitution, and the laws made in pursuance thereof, shall be the supreme law of the land, is empty and unmeaning declamation.

2. A Maryland Editor Dissents (1819)

Maryland hotheads reacted vehemently against their setback in the famous Bank case. Outspoken Hezekiah Niles of Baltimore, editor from 1811 to 1836 of the most influential weekly in the country, expressed grave concern. He did not believe that Congress, in 1791, had been empowered to charter the first Bank of the United States. What was the validity of his states' rights argument? Was he more concerned about the monopolistic power of the Bank or about the encroachment on states' rights?

. . . A deadly blow has been struck at the sovereignty of the states, and from a quarter so far removed from the people as to be hardly accessible to public opinion. It is needless to say that we allude to the decision of the Supreme Court in the case of McCulloch *versus* the State of Maryland, by which it is established that the states cannot tax the Bank of the United States.

We are yet unacquainted with the grounds of this alarming decision, but of this are resolved—that nothing but the tongue of an angel can convince us of its compatibility with the Constitution of the United States, in which a power to grant acts of incorporation is not delegated [to the federal government], and all powers not delegated are retained.

Far be it from us to be thought as speaking disrespectfully of the Supreme Court, or to subject ourselves to the suspicion of a "contempt" of it. We do not impute corruption to the judges, nor intimate that they have been influenced by improper feelings. They are great and learned men; but still, only men. And, feeling as we do—as if the very stones would cry out if we did not speak on this subject—we will exercise our right to do it, and declare that, if the Supreme Court is not mistaken in its construction of the Constitution of the United States, or that [if] another definition cannot be given to it by some act of the states, their sovereignty is at the mercy of their creature—Congress. It is not on account of the Bank of the United States

---

²*Niles' Weekly Register* 16 (1819): 41, 43.

that we speak thus . . . it is but a drop in the bucket compared with the principles established by the decision, which appear to us to be these:

1. That Congress has an unlimited right to grant acts of incorporation!
2. That a company incorporated by Congress is exempted from the common operation of the laws of the state in which it may be located!! . . .

We repeat it: it is not on account of the Bank of the United States that we are thus moved. Our sentiments are on record that we did not wish the destruction of that institution but, fearing the enormous power of the corporation, we were zealous that an authority to arrest its deleterious influence might be vested in responsible hands, for it has not got any soul. Yet this solitary institution may *not* subvert the liberties of our country, and command every one to bow down to it as Baal. It is the principle of it that alarms us, as operating against the unresigned rights of the states.

3. Marshall Asserts the Supremacy of the Constitution (1803)

No principle is more important to the system of constitutional democracy than the notion that the Constitution represents a higher level of law than that routinely enacted by legislatures. And no American jurist has been more instrumental in asserting that principle than the great Federalist justice John Marshall. Marshall also helped mightily to resolve the question—unclear in the early days of the republic—of where final authority to interpret the Constitution lay. In the following excerpt from his famous decision in the case of Marbury v. Madison, *how does he trace the linkages between the Constitution and the concept of limited government?*

The question, whether an act, repugnant to the constitution, can become the law of the land, is a question deeply interesting to the United States; but, happily, not of an intricacy proportioned to its interest. It seems only necessary to recognize certain principles, supposed to have been long and well established, to decide it.

That the people have an original right to establish, for their future government, such principles, as, in their opinion, shall most conduce to their own happiness is the basis on which the whole American fabric has been erected. The exercise of this original right is a very great exertion; nor can it, nor ought it, to be frequently repeated. The principles, therefore, so established, are deemed fundamental. And as the authority from which they proceed is supreme, and can seldom act, they are designed to be permanent.

This original and supreme will organizes the government, and assigns to different departments their respective powers. It may either stop here, or establish certain limits not to be transcended by those departments.

The government of the United States is of the latter description. The powers of the legislature are defined and limited; and that those limits may not be mistaken, or forgotten, the constitution is written. To what purpose are powers limited, and to what purpose is that limitation committed to writing, if these limits may, at any time,

---

[3]William Cranch, *Reports of Cases Argued and Adjudged in the Supreme Court of the United States, 1801–1815* (Newark, N.Y.: The Lawyers' Co-operative Publishing Company, 1804), vol. 1, p. 137.

be passed by those intended to be restrained? The distinction between a government with limited and unlimited powers is abolished, if those limits do not confine the persons on whom they are imposed, and if acts prohibited and acts allowed, are of equal obligation. It is a proposition too plain to be contested, that the constitution controls any legislative act repugnant to it; or, that the legislature may alter the constitution by an ordinary act.

Between these alternatives there is no middle ground. The constitution is either a superior paramount law, unchangeable by ordinary means, or it is on a level with ordinary legislative acts, and, like other acts, is alterable when the legislature shall please to alter it.

If the former part of the alternative be true, then a legislative act contrary to the constitution is not law: if the latter part be true, then written constitutions are absurd attempts, on the part of the people, to limit a power in its own nature illimitable.

Certainly all those who have framed written constitutions contemplate them as forming the fundamental and paramount law of the nation, and, consequently, the theory of every such government must be, that an act of the legislature, repugnant to the constitution, is void.

This theory is essentially attached to a written constitution, and, is consequently, to be considered, by this court, as one of the fundamental principles of our society. It is not therefore to be lost sight of in the further consideration of this subject. . . .

So if a law be in opposition to the constitution; if both the law and the constitution apply to a particular case, so that the court must either decide that case conformably to the law, disregarding the constitution; or conformably to the constitution, disregarding the law; the court must determine which of these conflicting rules governs the case. This is of the very essence of judicial duty.

If, then, the courts are to regard the constitution, and the constitution is superior to any ordinary act of the legislature, the constitution, and not such ordinary act, must govern the case to which they both apply.

Those, then, who controvert the principle that the constitution is to be considered, in court, as a paramount law, are reduced to the necessity of maintaining that courts must close their eyes on the constitution, and see only the law.

This doctrine would subvert the very foundation of all written constitutions. It would declare that an act which, according to the principles and theory of our government, is entirely void, is yet, in practice, completely obligatory. It would declare that if the legislature shall do what is expressly forbidden, such act, notwithstanding the express prohibition, is in reality effectual. It would be giving to the legislature a practical and real omnipotence, with the same breath which professes to restrict their powers within narrow limits. It is prescribing limits, and declaring that those limits may be passed at pleasure.

That it thus reduces to nothing what we have deemed the greatest improvements on political institutions, a written constitution, would of itself be sufficient, in America, where written constitutions have been viewed with so much reverence, for rejecting the construction. . . .

Thus, the particular phraseology of the constitution of the United States confirms and strengthens the principle, supposed to be essential to all written constitutions, that a law repugnant to the constitution is void; and that courts, as well as other departments, are bound by that instrument. . . .

B. The Louisiana Purchase

1. Thomas Jefferson Alerts Robert Livingston (1802)

Rumors of the secret treaty of 1800, under which Spain agreed to cede Louisiana to France, filled President Jefferson with apprehension. The extent of his concern is betrayed in this remarkable letter, addressed to the American minister in Paris, Robert R. Livingston. A distinguished lawyer and diplomat, Livingston was also famous as the financial backer of Robert Fulton's successful steamboat in 1807. Why did Jefferson feel that French occupancy of Louisiana would force the United States to reverse its "political relations"?

The cession of Louisiana . . . by Spain to France works most sorely on the United States. On the subject the Secretary of State has written to you fully. Yet I cannot forbear recurring to it personally, so deep is the impression it makes in my mind. It completely reverses all the political relations of the United States and will form a new epoch in our political course.

Of all nations of any consideration, France is the one which hitherto has offered the fewest points on which we could have any conflict of right, and the most points of a communion of interests. From these causes we have ever looked at her as our natural friend, as one with which we never could have an occasion of difference.* Her growth therefore we viewed as our own, her misfortunes ours.

There is on the globe one single spot, the possessor of which is our natural and habitual enemy. It is New Orleans, through which the produce of three-eighths of our territory must pass to market, and from its fertility it will ere long yield more than half of our whole produce and contain more than half our inhabitants. France, placing herself in that door, assumes to us the attitude of defiance.

Spain might have retained it quietly for years. Her pacific dispositions, her feeble state, would induce her to increase our facilities there, so that her possession of the place would be hardly felt by us. And it would not perhaps be very long before some circumstances might arise which might make the cession of it to us the price of something of more worth to her.

Not so can it ever be in the hands of France. The impetuosity of her temper, the energy and restlessness of her character . . . render it impossible that France and the United States can continue long friends when they meet in so irritable a position. They, as well as we, must be blind if they do not see this; and we must be very improvident if we do not begin to make arrangements on that hypothesis.

The day that France takes possession of New Orleans fixes the sentence which is to restrain her forever within her low-water mark. It seals the union of two nations who in conjunction can maintain exclusive possession of the ocean. From that moment we must marry ourselves to the British fleet and nation. We must turn all our attentions to a maritime force, for which our resources place us on very high grounds; and having formed and cemented together a power which may render reinforcement of her settlements here impossible to France, make the first cannon

---

[1]P. L. Ford, *Writings of Thomas Jefferson* (1897), vol. 8, pp. 144–146 (April 18, 1802).
*Jefferson conveniently overlooked the undeclared naval war of 1798–1800.

which shall be fired in Europe the signal for tearing up any settlement she may have made, and for holding the two continents of America in sequestration for the common purposes of the united British and American nations.

This is not a state of things we seek or desire. It is one which this measure, if adopted by France, forces on us, as necessarily as any other cause, by the laws of nature, brings on its necessary effect. It is not from a fear of France that we deprecate this measure proposed by her. For however greater her force is than ours compared in the abstract, it is nothing in comparison of ours when to be exerted on our soil. But it is from a sincere love of peace, and a firm persuasion that, bound to France by the interests and the strong sympathies still existing in the minds of our citizens, and holding relative positions which ensure their continuance, we are secure of a long course of peace. Whereas the change of friends, which will be rendered necessary if France changes that position, embarks us necessarily as a belligerent power in the first war of Europe. In that case, France will have held possession of New Orleans during the interval of a peace, long or short, at the end of which it will be wrested from her. . . .

She may say she needs Louisiana for the supply of her West Indies. She does not need it in time of peace. And in war she could not depend on them because they would be so easily intercepted [by the British navy]. . . .

If France considers Louisiana, however, as indispensable for her views, she might perhaps be willing to look about for arrangements which might reconcile it to our interests. If anything could do this, it would be the ceding to us the Island of New Orleans and the Floridas. This would certainly in a great degree remove the causes of jarring and irritation between us, and perhaps for such a length of time as might produce other means of making the measure permanently conciliatory to our interests and friendships.

2. Jefferson Stretches the Constitution to Buy Louisiana (1803)

In early 1803, Jefferson dispatched James Monroe to Paris to consummate the purchase of Louisiana for the United States. Monroe was instructed to pay up to $10 million for New Orleans and as much land to the east as he could obtain. To the surprise of Americans, Napoleon offered to sell all of Louisiana, including the vast territory to the west and north of New Orleans. The Americans readily agreed, though Jefferson worried that he was exceeding his constitutional mandate. When he had earlier opposed Hamilton's Bank (see p. 183), Jefferson had argued that powers not conferred on the central government were reserved to the states. The Constitution did not specifically empower the president—or the Congress, for that matter—to annex foreign territory, especially territory as large as the nation itself. But the bargain acquisition of Louisiana seemed too breathtaking an opportunity to pass up. In the following letter to Senate leader John Breckinridge, Jefferson defends his action. Is his "guardian" analogy sound?

---

[2]A. A. Lipscomb, ed., *Writings of Thomas Jefferson* (Washington, D.C.: Thomas Jefferson Memorial Association, 1904), vol. 10, pp. 410–411 (August 12, 1803).

This treaty must, of course, be laid before both Houses, because both have important functions to exercise respecting it. They, I presume, will see their duty to their country in ratifying and paying for it, so as to secure a good which would otherwise probably be never again in their power. But I suppose they must then appeal to the nation for an additional article [amendment] to the Constitution, approving and confirming an act which the nation had not previously authorized.

The Constitution has made no provision for our holding foreign territory, still less for incorporating foreign nations into our Union. The Executive, in seizing the fugitive occurrence which so much advances the good of their country, have done an act beyond the Constitution. The Legislature, in casting behind them metaphysical subtleties, and risking themselves like faithful servants, must ratify and pay for it, and throw themselves on their country for doing for them, unauthorized, what we know they would have done for themselves had they been in a situation to do it.

It is the case of a guardian, investing the money of his ward in purchasing an important adjacent territory; and saying to him when of age, "I did this for your good. I pretend to no right to bind you: you may disavow me, and I must get out of the scrape as I can. I thought it my duty to risk myself for you."

But we shall not be disavowed by the nation, and their act of indemnity will confirm and not weaken the Constitution, by more strongly marking out its lines.

3. Representative Roger Griswold Is Unhappy (1803)

Jefferson summoned Congress into special session because the Senate had to approve the Louisiana Purchase treaties, and the House and Senate had to vote the money. The New England Federalists fought the acquisition, largely because "the mixed race of Anglo-Hispano-Gallo-Americans" would ultimately outvote the charter-member states of the Union and, they feared, cause its dismemberment. Representative Griswold of Connecticut, perhaps the ablest Federalist spokesman in the House, had already attained notoriety in 1798 by caning Representative Matthew Lyon of Kentucky after the latter had spat in his face. On what terms would Griswold, in the following speech, have accepted Louisiana?

It is, in my opinion, scarcely possible for any gentleman on this floor to advance an opinion that the President and Senate may add to the members of the Union by treaty whenever they please, or, in the words of this treaty, may "incorporate in the union of the United States" a foreign nation who, from interest or ambition, may wish to become a member of our government. Such a power would be directly repugnant to the original compact between the states, and a violation of the principles on which that compact was formed.

It has been already well observed that the union of the states was formed on the principle of a co-partnership, and it would be absurd to suppose that the agents of the parties who have been appointed to execute the business of the compact, in behalf of the principals, could admit of a new partner without the consent of the parties themselves. . . .

---

[3]*Annals of Congress,* 8th Congress, 1st session, vol. 1, cols. 461–462, 463, 465.

The incorporation of a foreign nation into the Union, so far from tending to preserve the Union, is a direct inroad upon it. It destroys the perfect union contemplated between the original parties, by interposing an alien and a stranger to share the powers of government with them. . . .

A gentleman from Pennsylvania, however (Mr. Smilie), has said that it is competent for this government to obtain a new territory by conquest, and if a new territory can be obtained by conquest, he infers that it can be procured in the manner provided for by the treaty.

While I admit the premises of the gentleman from Pennsylvania, I deny his conclusion. A new territory and new subjects may undoubtedly be obtained by conquest and by purchase; but neither the conquest nor the purchase can incorporate them into the Union. They must remain in the condition of colonies, and be governed accordingly. The objection to the third article is not that the province of Louisiana could not have been purchased, but that neither this nor any other foreign nation can be incorporated into the Union by treaty or by a law. And as this country has been ceded to the United States only under the condition of an incorporation, it results that, if the condition is unconstitutional or impossible, the cession itself falls to the ground. . . .

This subject was much considered during the last session of Congress, but it will not be found . . . that any individual entertained the least wish to obtain the province of Louisiana. Our views were then confined to New Orleans and the Floridas, and, in my judgment, it would have been happy for the country if they were still confined within those limits. The vast and unmanageable extent which the accession of Louisiana will give to the United States; the consequent dispersion of our population; and the destruction of that balance which it is so important to maintain between the Eastern and the Western states, threatens, at no very distant day, the subversion of our Union.

4. Senator John Breckinridge Supports the Purchase (1803)

Virginia-born Senator John Breckinridge of Kentucky, then the ablest spokesman for the West, had sponsored Jefferson's secretly prepared Kentucky resolutions of 1798–1799 in his state legislature. Alert both to western interests and to partisan politics, he urged the Louisiana Purchase in this noteworthy speech. He took sharp issue with the Federalist senators, including Senator Samuel White of Delaware, who held that Louisiana would "be the greatest curse that could at present befall us. . . ." Breckinridge noted particularly the disagreement of the Federalists among themselves concerning the extravagance of the price, the validity of the title, and the unconstitutionality of acquiring foreign territory. He then launched into his argument, as follows. How effectively did he meet the Federalist objections, especially with reference to the problem of the westerners?

As to the enormity of price, I would ask that gentleman [Senator White], would his mode of acquiring it [by war] through 50,000 men have cost nothing? Is he so

⁴*Annals of Congress,* 8th Congress, 1st session, vol. 1, cols. 60–62, 65.

confident of this as to be able to pronounce positively that the price is enormous? Does he make no calculation on the hazard attending this conflict? Is he sure the God of battles was enlisted on his side? Were France and Spain, under the auspices of Bonaparte, contemptible adversaries? Good as the cause was, and great as my confidence is in the courage of my countrymen, sure I am that I shall never regret, as the gentleman seems to do, that the experiment was not made. . . .

To acquire an empire of perhaps half [once again] the extent of the one we possessed, from the most powerful and warlike nation on earth, without bloodshed, without the oppression of a single individual, without in the least embarrassing the ordinary operations of your finances, and all this through the peaceful forms of negotiation, and in despite too of the opposition of a considerable portion of the community, is an achievement of which the archives of the predecessors, at least, of those now in office cannot furnish a parallel.

The same gentleman has told us, that this acquisition will, from its extent, soon prove destructive to the confederacy [Union]. . . .

So far from believing in the doctrine that a republic ought to be confined within narrow limits, I believe, on the contrary, that the more extensive its dominion the more safe and more durable it will be. In proportion to the number of hands you entrust the precious blessings of a free government to, in the same proportion do you multiply the chances for their preservation. I entertain, therefore, no fears for the confederacy on account of its extent. . . .

The gentlemen from Delaware [White] and Massachusetts [Pickering] both contend that the third article of the treaty is unconstitutional, and our consent to its ratification a nullity, because the United States cannot acquire foreign territory. . . . Cannot the Constitution be so amended (if it should be necessary) as to embrace this territory? If the authority to acquire foreign territory be not included in the treatymaking power, it remains with the people; and in that way all the doubts and difficulties of gentlemen may be completely removed; and that, too, without affording France the smallest ground of exception to the literal execution on our part of that article of the treaty. . . .

What palliation can we offer to our Western citizens for a conduct like this? Will they be content with the redefined and metaphysical reasonings and constructions upon which gentlemen have bottomed their opposition today? Will it be satisfactory to them to be told that the title is good, the price low, the finances competent, and the authority, at least to purchase, constitutional; but that the country is too extensive, and that the admission of these people to all the privileges we ourselves enjoy is not permitted by the Constitution? It will not, sir.

5. Lewis and Clark Meet a Grizzly (1805)

Diplomacy done, the vast and uncharted wilderness that was the Louisiana territory remained to be explored. President Jefferson commissioned Meriwether Lewis and William Clark for the job, which took two years. The Lewis and Clark party of thirty-

---

[5]Reuben Gold Thwaites, ed., *Original Journals of the Lewis and Clark Expedition, 1804–1806* (Washington, D.C.: Government Printing Office, 1904), vol. 2, pp. 33–34.

four soldiers and ten civilians moved up the Missouri River from St. Louis in the autumn of 1804, wintered with the Mandan Indians in present-day North Dakota, and struck out for the Pacific Ocean again in the spring of 1805. They sighted the Pacific in November 1805 and eventually returned to St. Louis nearly a year later. Along the way they collected botanical and geological specimens and made preliminary maps of the country. They also had numerous adventures, such as this one, recounted in Lewis's diary, which took place in present-day eastern Montana. What does it suggest about the task of taming the nearly trackless territory Jefferson had acquired?

Tuesday May 14th 1805.

Some fog on the river this morning, which is a very rare occurrence; the country much as it was yesterday with this difference that the bottoms are somewhat wider; passed some high black bluffs. Saw immence herds of buffaloe today also Elk deer wolves and Antelopes. Passed three large creeks one on the Starboard and two others on the Larboard side, neither of which had any runing water. Capt Clark walked on shore and killed a very fine buffaloe cow. I felt an inclination to eat some veal and walked on shore and killed a very fine buffaloe calf and a large woolf, much the whitest I had seen, it was quite as white as the wool of the common sheep. One of the party wounded a brown bear very badly, but being alone did not think proper to pursue him. In the evening the men in two of the rear canoes discovered a large brown bear lying in the open grounds about 300 paces from the river, and six of them went out to attack him, all good hunters; they took the advantage of a small eminence which concealed them and got within 40 paces of him unperceived. Two of them reserved their fires as had been previously conscerted, the four others fired nearly at the same time and put each his bullet through him. Two of the balls passed through the bulk of both lobes of his lungs. In an instant this monster ran at them with open mouth. The two who had reserved their fir[e]s discharged their pieces at him as he came towards them. Boath of them struck him, one only slightly and the other fortunately broke his shoulder, this however only retarded his motion for a moment only. The men unable to reload their guns took to flight, the bear pursued and had very nearly overtaken them before they reached the river; two of the party betook themselves to a canoe and the others seperated an[d] concealed themselves among the willows, reloaded their pieces, each discharged his piece at him as they had an opportunity. They struck him several times again but the guns served only to direct the bear to them. In this manner he pursued two of the seperately so close that they were obliged to throw aside their guns and pouches and throw themselves into the river altho' the bank was nearly twenty feet perpendicular; so enraged was this anamal that he plunged into the river only a few feet behind the second man he had compelled [to] take refuge in the water, when one of those who still remained on shore shot him through the head and finally killed him; they then took him on shore and butch[er]ed him when they found eight balls had passed through him in different directions; the bear being old the flesh was indifferent, they therefore only took the skin and fleece, the latter made us several gallons of oil; . . .

EXPLORING THE LOUISIANA PURCHASE

BRITISH TERRITORY

OREGON COUNTRY *(In dispute)*

RETURN OF LEWIS

Columbia R.

Missouri R.

RETURN OF CLARK

Yellowstone R.

L O U I S I A N A

Missouri R.

Mississippi

St. Louis

Great Salt Lake

P U R C H A S E

SPANISH

Colorado R.

TERRITORY

Rio Grande R.

New Orleans

___ Louisiana Purchase

⟵⟶ Lewis and Clark's Route 1804–1806

⊗ Approximate location of encounter with Grizzly bear

0   100   200   300 MILES

C. The Issue of Sailors' Rights

1. A Briton (James Stephen) Recommends Firmness (1805)

The titanic struggle between France and Britain flared up anew in 1803. American shipping boomed, especially in carrying coffee and sugar from the French and Spanish West Indies to blockaded France and Spain. Yankee shipowners, shorthanded, used high wages to lure hundreds of sailors from the British merchant fleet and the Royal Navy, where pay was poor and flogging frequent. Some deserters became naturalized; others purchased faked naturalization papers for as little as one dollar.

---

[1]James Stephen, *War in Disguise,* 2nd ed. (London: C. Whittingham, 1805), pp. 120–124.

With firsthand knowledge of these tricks, James Stephen published a popular and potent pamphlet in England that stiffened the London government in its determination to stifle Yankee-carried traffic between Britain's enemies and the West Indies. Of the grievances mentioned by Stephen, which one did he regard as most serious? Why?

The worst consequences, perhaps, of the independence and growing commerce of America is the seduction of our seamen. We hear continually of clamors in that country on the score of its sailors being [im]pressed at sea by our frigates. But how have these sailors become subjects of the United States? By engaging in their merchant service during the last or the present war; or at most by obtaining that formal naturalization which they are entitled to receive by law after they have sailed two years from an American port, but the fictitious testimonials of which are to be bought the moment they land in the country, and for a price contemptible even in the estimate of a common sailor.

If those who by birth, and by residence and employment, prior to 1793, were confessedly British, ought still to be regarded as His Majesty's subjects, a very considerable part of the navigators [sailors] of American ships are such at this moment; though, unfortunately, they are not easily distinguishable from genuine American seamen. . . .

The unity of language and the close affinity of manners between English and American seamen are the strong inducements with our sailors for preferring the service of that country to any other foreign employment. Or, to speak more correctly, these circumstances remove from the American service, in the minds of our sailors, those subjects of aversion which they find in other foreign ships; and which formerly counteracted, effectually, the general motives to desert from, or avoid, the naval service of their country.

What these motives are, I need not explain. They are strong, and not easy to be removed; though they might perhaps be palliated by alterations in our naval system. . . . If we cannot remove the general causes of predilection for the American service, or the difficulty of detecting and reclaiming British seamen when engaged in it, it is, therefore, the more unwise to allow the merchants of that country, and other neutrals, to encroach on our maritime rights in time of war; because we thereby greatly, and suddenly, increase their demand for mariners in general; and enlarge their means, as well as their motives, for seducing the sailors of Great Britain. . . .

It is truly vexatious to reflect that, by this abdication of our belligerent rights, we not only give up the best means of annoying the enemy, but raise up, at the same time, a crowd of dangerous rivals for the seduction of our sailors, and put bribes into their hands for the purpose. We not only allow the trade of the hostile [French] colonies to pass safely, in derision of our impotent warfare, but to be carried on by the mariners of Great Britain. This illegitimate and noxious navigation, therefore, is nourished with the lifeblood of our navy.

2. A Briton (Basil Hall) Urges Discretion (1804)

British cruisers, hovering off New York harbor, blockaded French ships that had sought refuge there. They also visited and searched incoming and outgoing Ameri-

---

[2]Basil Hall, *Fragments of Voyages and Travels, First Series* (London: E. Moxon, 1840), pp. 47–49.

can merchantmen, and impressed British seamen (and sometimes Americans by mistake). Basil Hall, later both a captain and a distinguished author, entered the British navy as a midshipman in 1802, when he was only thirteen. Many years later he published these recollections of his early service on the fifty-gun frigate Leander *in American waters. Which was the most infuriating of the practices he describes?*

. . . It seems quite clear that, while we can hold it, we will never give up the right of search, or the right of impressment. We may and ought, certainly, to exercise so disagreeable a power with such temper and discretion as not to provoke the enmity of any friendly nation.

But at the time I speak of, and on board our good old ship the *Leander,* whose name, I was grieved, but not surprised, to find, was still held in detestation three or four and twenty years afterwards at New York, I am sorry to own that we had not much of this discretion in our proceedings; or, rather, we had not enough consideration for the feelings of the people we were dealing with. . . .

To place the full annoyance of these matters in a light to be viewed fairly by English people, let us suppose that the Americans and French were to go to war, and that England for once remained neutral—an odd case, I admit, but one which might happen. Next, suppose that a couple of French frigates were chased into Liverpool, and that an American squadron stationed itself off that harbor to watch the motions of these French ships, which had claimed the protection of our neutrality, and were accordingly received into "our waters." I ask, "Would this blockade of Liverpool be agreeable to us or not?"

Even if the blockading American frigates did nothing but sail backwards and forwards across the harbor's mouth, or occasionally run up and anchor abreast of the town, it would not, "I guess," be very pleasant to be thus superintended. If, however, the American ships, in addition to this legitimate surveillance of their enemy, were to detain off the port, with equal legitimacy of usage, and within a league or so of the lighthouse, every British vessel coming from France, or from a French colony; and if, besides looking over the papers of these vessels to see whether all was regular, they were to open every private letter, in the hope of detecting some trace of French ownership in the cargo, what should we say? And if, out of some twenty ships arrested daily in this manner, one or two of our own were to be completely diverted from their course, from time to time, and sent off under a prizemaster to New York for adjudication, I wonder how the Liverpool folks would like it? But if, in addition to this perfectly regular and usual exercise of a belligerent right on the part of the Americans, under such circumstances, we bring in that most awkward and ticklish of questions, the impressment of seamen, let us consider how much the feeling of annoyance on the part of the English neutral would be augmented.

Conceive, for instance, that the American squadron employed to blockade the French ships in Liverpool were shorthanded, but, from being in daily expectation of bringing their enemy to action, it had become an object of great consequence with them to get their ships manned. And suppose, likewise, that it were perfectly notorious to all parties that, on board every English ship arriving or sailing from the port in question, there were several American citizens, but calling themselves English, and having in their possession "protections," or certificates to that effect, sworn to in regular form, but well known to be false, and such as might be bought for 4s. 6d. any day. Things being in this situation, if the American men-of-war off the English port were then to fire at and stop every ship, and, besides overhauling her papers and cargo, were to take out any seamen, to work their own guns withal, whom they had reason, or supposed or said they had reason, to consider American citizens, or whose country they guessed, from dialect or appearance; I wish to know with what degree of patience this would be submitted to on the Exchange at Liverpool, or elsewhere in England. . . .

Suppose the blockading American ships off Liverpool, in firing a shot ahead of a vessel they wished to examine, had accidentally hit, not that vessel, but a small coaster, so far beyond her that she was not even noticed by the blockading ships. And suppose, further, this unlucky chance-shot to have killed one of the crew on board the said English ship. The vessel would, of course, proceed immediately to Liverpool with the body of their slaughtered countryman; and in fairness it may be asked, what would have been the effect of such a spectacle on the population of England . . . ?

This is not an imaginary case; for it actually occurred in 1804 [1806], when we were blockading the French frigates in New York. A consul-shot from the *Leander* hit an unfortunate sloop's mainboom; and the broken spar striking the mate, John Pierce by name, killed him instantly. The sloop sailed on to New York, where the mangled body, raised on a platform, was paraded through the streets, in order to augment the vehement indignation, already at a high pitch, against the English.

Now, let us be candid to our rivals; and ask ourselves whether the Americans would have been worthy of our friendship, or even of our hostility, had they tamely submitted to indignities which, if passed upon ourselves, would have roused not only one seaport, but the whole country, into a towering passion of nationality.

D. The Resort to Economic Coercion

1. A Federalist (Philip Barton Key) Attacks the Embargo (1808)

With the nation militarily weak, Jefferson decided to force respect for the nation's rights by an economic boycott. In 1807 Congress passed his embargo, which prohibited shipments from leaving American shores for foreign ports, including the West Indies. Paralysis gradually gripped American shipping and agriculture, except for illicit trade. Representative Philip Barton Key, uncle of Francis Scott Key and a former Maryland Loyalist who had fought under George III, here assails the embargo. Why, in his view, did it play into Britain's hands? Why did he regard his proposed alternative as more effective?

But, Mr. Chairman, let us review this [embargo] law and its effects. In a commercial point of view, it has annihilated our trade. In an agricultural point of view, it

---

[1]*Annals of Congress,* 10th Congress, 1st session, vol. 2, cols. 2122–2123.

has paralyzed industry. . . . Our most fertile lands are reduced to sterility, so far as it respects our surplus product. As a measure of political economics, it will drive (if continued) our seamen into foreign employ, and our fishermen to foreign sandbanks. In a financial point of view, it has dried up our revenue, and if continued will close the sales of Western lands, and the payment of installments of past sales. For unless produce can be sold, payments cannot be made. As a war measure, the embargo has not been advocated.

It remains then to consider its effects as a peace measure—a measure inducing peace. I grant, sir, that if the friends of the embargo had rightly calculated its effects—if it had brought the belligerents of Europe to a sense of justice and respect for our rights, through the weakness and dependence of their West India possessions—it would have been infinitely wise and desirable. . . . But, sir, the experience of near four months has not produced that effect. . . .

If that be the case, if such should be the result, then will the embargo, of all measures, be the most acceptable to Britain. By occluding [closing] our ports, you give to her ships the exclusive use of the ocean; and you give to her despairing West India planter the monopoly of sugar and rum and coffee to the European world. . . .

But, sir, who are we? What are we? A peaceable agricultural people, of simple and, I trust, virtuous habits, of stout hearts and willing minds, and a brave, powerful, and badly disciplined militia, unarmed, and without troops. And whom are we to come in conflict with? The master of continental Europe [Napoleon] in the full career of universal domination, and the mistress of the ocean [Britain] contending for self-preservation; nations who feel power and forget right.

What man can be weak enough to suppose that a sense of justice can repress or regulate the conduct of Bonaparte? We need not resort to other nations for examples. Has he not in a manner as flagrant as flagitious, directly, openly, publicly violated and broken a solemn treaty [of 1800] entered into with us? Did he not stipulate that our property should pass free even to enemy ports, and has he not burnt our ships at sea under the most causeless pretexts?

Look to England; see her conduct to us. Do we want any further evidence of what she will do in the hour of impending peril than the attack on Copenhagen?* That she prostrates all rights that come in collision with her self-preservation?

No, sir; let us pursue the steady line of rigid impartiality. Let us hold the scales of impartial neutrality with a high and steady hand, and export our products to, and bring back supplies from, all who will trade with us. Much of the world is yet open to us, and let us profit of the occasion.

At present we exercise no neutral rights. We have quit the ocean; we have abandoned our rights; we have retired to our shell. Sooner than thus continue, our merchantmen should arm to protect legitimate trade. Sir, I believe war itself, as we could carry it on, would produce more benefit and less cost than the millions lost by the continuance of the embargo.

---

*The British, seeking to forestall Napoleon, had bombarded and captured the neutral Danish capital in 1807.

2. A Jeffersonian (W. B. Giles) Upholds the Embargo (1808)

Stung by Federalist criticisms of the embargo, Senator W. B. Giles of Virginia sprang to its defense. A prickly personage but a brilliant debater, he had assailed or was to assail virtually every figure prominent in public life. Bitterly anti-Hamilton and anti-British, he was more Jeffersonian than Jefferson himself. Is his argument for the coercive role of the embargo as convincing as that for the precautionary role?

Sir, I have always understood that there were two subjects contemplated by the embargo laws. The first, precautionary, operating upon ourselves. The second, coercive, operating upon the aggressing belligerents. Precautionary, in saving our seamen, our ships, and our merchandise from the plunder of our enemies, and avoiding the calamities of war. Coercive, by addressing strong appeals to the interests of both the belligerents.

The first object has been answered beyond my most sanguine expectations. To make a fair and just estimate of this measure, reference should be had to our situation at the time of its adoption. At that time, the aggressions of both the belligerents were such as to leave the United States but a painful alternative in the choice of one of three measures, to wit, the embargo, war, or submission. . . .

It was found that merchandise to the value of one hundred millions of dollars was actually afloat, in vessels amounting in value to twenty millions more; that an amount of merchandise and vessels equal to fifty millions of dollars more was expected to be shortly put afloat; and that it would require fifty thousand seamen to be employed in the navigation of this enormous amount of property. The administration was informed of the hostile edicts of France previously issued, and then in a state of execution; and of an intention on the part of Great Britain to issue her orders [in Council], the character and object of which were also known. The object was to sweep this valuable commerce from the ocean. The situation of this commerce was as well known to Great Britain as to ourselves, and her inordinate cupidity could not withstand the temptation of the rich booty she vainly thought within her power. This was the state of information at the time this measure was recommended.

The President of the United States, ever watchful and anxious for the preservation of the persons and property of all our fellow citizens, but particularly of the merchants, whose property is most exposed to danger, and of the seamen, whose persons are also most exposed, recommended the embargo for the protection of both. And it has saved and protected both. . . . It is admitted by all that the embargo laws have saved this enormous amount of property and this number of seamen, which, without them, would have forcibly gone into the hands of our enemies, to pamper their arrogance, stimulate their injustice, and increase their means of annoyance.

---

[2]*Annals of Congress,* 10th Congress, 2d session, vol. 3, cols. 96–106, passim.

I should suppose, Mr. President, this saving worth some notice. But, sir, we are told that, instead of protecting our seamen, it has driven them out of the country, and into foreign service. I believe, sir, that this fact is greatly exaggerated. But, sir, suppose for a moment that it is so, the government has done all, in this respect, it was bound to do. It placed these seamen in the bosoms of their friends and families, in a state of perfect security. And if they have since thought proper to abandon these blessings and emigrate from their country, it was an act of choice, not of necessity. . . .

. . . But, sir, these are not the only good effects of the embargo. It has preserved our peace—it has saved our honor—it has saved our national independence. Are these savings not worth notice? Are these blessings not worth preserving . . . ?

The gentleman next triumphantly tells us that the embargo laws have not had their expected effects upon the aggressing belligerents. That they have not had their complete effects; that they have not caused a revocation of the British orders and French decrees, will readily be admitted. But they certainly have not been without some beneficial effects upon those nations. . . .

The first effect of the embargo upon the aggressing belligerents was to lessen their inducements to war, by keeping out of their way the rich spoils of our commerce, which had invited their cupidity, and which was saved by those laws. . . .

The second effect which the embargo laws have had on the aggressing belligerents is to enhance the prices of all American produce, especially articles of the first necessity to them, to a considerable degree; and, if it be a little longer persisted in, will either banish our produce (which I believe indispensable to them) from their markets altogether, or increase the prices to an enormous amount; and, of course, we may hope will furnish irresistible inducements for a relaxation of their hostile orders and edicts.

[The effects of the embargo ultimately proved disastrous. Confronted with anarchy and bankruptcy, Jefferson engineered its repeal in 1809 and the substitution of a more limited Non-Intercourse Act.]

Thought Provokers

1. Why was John Marshall's famous Bank decision so unpopular in many parts of the country? Did it strengthen or weaken nationalism? Is a highly centralized government necessarily antidemocratic? Since Marshall was a Federalist and the Federalist party had died out, was it consonant with democracy for him to be handing down Federalist decisions? Should he have been impeached?
2. To what extent did the Louisiana Purchase strengthen or weaken the no-alliance tradition? Did good diplomacy or good luck bring about the purchase?
3. Did it take more courage on Jefferson's part to accept Louisiana than to reject it? What becomes of the Constitution if the executive may resort to what he believes to be unconstitutional acts for the common good? What probably would have happened if, as the

Federalists argued, the thirteen original states had kept all the new territory in a permanently colonial status?

4. In the matter of impressment, were the Americans more sinned against than sinning? Why were the British so unwilling to give up the practice of impressment?

5. Was it inconsistent for the Americans, dedicated to the principle of freedom of the seas, to abandon their right to sail the high seas as a way of keeping out of war? Under what conditions should principle yield to expediency in foreign policy?

6. President Woodrow Wilson said in 1916: "The immortality of Jefferson does not lie in any one of his achievements, but in his attitude toward mankind." Comment.

12

The Second War of Independence and the Upsurge of Nationalism, 1812–1824

The war [of 1812] has renewed and reinstated the national feelings and character which the Revolution had given, and which were daily lessened.

Albert Gallatin, 1816

Prologue: The western war hawks in Congress, bitter about maritime grievances against Britain and the British-backed Indian raids on the frontier, engineered a declaration of war on Britain in 1812. But the pro-British Federalists of new England vehemently opposed "Mr. Madison's War" as a scheme of the Jeffersonian Republicans to ruin them economically and politically. With the nation thus dangerously divided, the war went badly for the Americans, and ended with the Treaty of Ghent (1814), which essentially restored the status quo. Yet partly as a result of Andrew Jackson's stirring victory over the British at the Battle of New Orleans, an outburst of nationalism followed the otherwise frustrating War of 1812. As time went on, the chief setback to nationalism was the ominous sectional quarrel over slavery in Missouri. The volatile issue of slavery was eventually contained for a period of years by the Missouri Compromise of 1820, but it smoldered on until it finally exploded in the Civil War in 1861. In foreign affairs, meanwhile, nationalism manifested itself in the Monroe Doctrine (1823), which warned the European powers to keep their hands off the two American continents.

A. The Cauldron of War

1. Tecumseh Challenges William Henry Harrison (1810)

The American frontiersmen blamed the British for egging the Native Americans on to attack them, but actually American greed was goad enough. William Henry Harri-

[1]C. M. Depew, ed., *The Library of Oratory* (New York: The Globe Publishing Company, 1902), vol. 4, pp. 363–364.

son, the aggressive governor of Indiana Territory, had negotiated a series of land-grabbing agreements with the Indians, culminating in the Treaty of Fort Wayne (1809). Two Indian tribes, ignoring the rights of all others, sold 3 million acres of their ancestral lands for a pittance. The gifted Shawnee chief Tecumseh, together with his visionary brother The Prophet, was then organizing the Indians against white encroachments. Absent when the Treaty of Fort Wayne was negotiated, Tecumseh journeyed angrily to Vincennes (Indiana), where, in a stormy scene, he confronted Governor Harrison and threatened to resist white occupancy of the ceded lands. How valid was his main grievance?

I would not then come to Governor Harrison to ask him to tear the treaty and to obliterate the landmark. But I would say to him: Sir, you have liberty to return to your own country.

The Being within, communing with past ages, tells me that . . . until lately there was no white man on this continent; that it then all belonged to red men, children of the same parents, placed on it by the Great Spirit that made them, to keep it, to traverse it, to enjoy its productions, and to fill it with the same race—once a happy race, since made miserable by the white people, who are never contented, but always encroaching. The way—and the only way—to check and to stop this evil is for all the red men to unite in claiming a common equal right in the land, as it was at first, and should be yet. For it never was divided, but belongs to all for the use of each. That no part has a right to sell, even to each other, much less to strangers; those who want all, and will not do with less.

The white people have no right to take the land from the Indians, because they had it first. It is theirs. They may sell, but all must join. Any sale not made by all is not valid. The late sale is bad. It was made by a part only. Part do not know how to sell. It requires all to make a bargain for all. All red men have equal rights to the unoccupied land. The right of occupancy is as good in one place as in another. There cannot be two occupations in the same place. The first excludes all others. It is not so in hunting or traveling; for there the same ground will serve many, as they may follow each other all day. But the camp is stationary, and that is occupancy. It belongs to the first who sits down on his blanket or skins which he has thrown upon the ground; and till he leaves it no other has a right.

2. Representative Felix Grundy Demands War (1811)

Following Tecumseh's speech and the subsequent Indian raids on the frontier, Governor Harrison led an army provocatively toward the headquarters of the Indians. On the night of November 7, 1811, at Tippecanoe near the Wabash River (Indiana), he succeeded in beating back an Indian attack. This hollow but costly victory further inflamed the West, from which came Henry Clay and other leaders of the war hawks to Congress in 1811. Among them was Felix Grundy of Tennessee, three of whose brothers had been killed by the Indians. As the most famous criminal lawyer

[2]*Annals of Congress,* 12th Congress, 1st session, vol. 1, cols. 424–426 (December 9, 1811).

in the Southwest, he had often cheated the gallows by reducing the jury to tears. In this eloquent speech in Congress, which grievances were peculiarly western and which ones were nationwide? What interest did westerners have in freedom of the seas?

I will now state the reasons which influenced the Committee [on Foreign Affairs] in recommending the [war] measures now before us.

It is not the [Atlantic] carrying trade properly so called about which this nation and Great Britain are at present contending. Were this the only question now under consideration, I should feel great unwillingness (however clear our claim might be) to involve the nation in war for the assertion of a right in the enjoyment of which the community at large are not more deeply concerned.

The true question in controversy is of a very different character; it involves the interest of the whole nation. It is the right of exporting the productions of our own soil and industry to foreign markets. Sir, our vessels are now captured when destined to the ports of France, and condemned by the British Courts of Admiralty, without even the pretext of having on board contraband of war, enemies' property, or having in any other respect violated the laws of nations.

These depredations on our lawful commerce, under whatever ostensible pretense committed, are not to be traced to any maxims or rules of public law, but to the maritime supremacy and pride of the British nation. This hostile and unjust policy of that country towards us is not to be wondered at, when we recollect that the United States are already the second commercial nation in the world. The rapid growth of our commercial importance has not only awakened the jealousy of the commercial interests of Great Britain, but her statesmen, no doubt, anticipate with deep concern the maritime greatness of this republic. . . .

What, Mr. Speaker, are we now called on to decide? It is whether we will resist by force the attempt, made by the [British] government, to subject our maritime rights to the arbitrary and capricious rule of her will. For my part I am not prepared to say that this country shall submit to have her commerce interdicted, or regulated, by any foreign nation. Sir, I prefer war to submission.

Over and above these unjust pretensions of the British government, for many years past they have been in the practice of impressing our seamen from merchant vessels. This unjust and lawless invasion of personal liberty calls loudly for the interposition of this government. To those better acquainted with the facts in relation to it, I leave it to fill up the picture.

My mind is irresistibly drawn to the West. Although others may not strongly feel the bearing which the late transactions in that quarter [Tippecanoe] have on this subject, upon my mind they have great influence. It cannot be believed, by any man who will reflect, that the savage tribes, uninfluenced by other powers, would think of making war on the United States. They understand too well their own weakness and our strength. They have already felt the weight of our arms; they know they hold the very soil on which they live as tenants in sufferance. How, then, sir, are we to account for their late conduct? In one way only: some powerful nation must have intrigued with them, and turned their peaceful dispositions towards us into hostilities. Great Britain alone has intercourse with those Northern tribes. I therefore infer that if British gold has not been employed, their baubles and

trinkets, and the promise of support and a place of refuge, if necessary, have had their effect.

If I am right in this conjecture, war is not to commerce by sea or land. It is already begun; and some of the richest blood of our country has already been shed. . . . The whole Western country is ready to march; they only wait for our permission. And, sir, war once declared, I pledge myself for my people—they will avenge the death of their brethren. . . .

Ask the Northern man, and he will tell you that any state of things is better than the present. Inquire of the Western people why their crops are not equal to what they were in former years; they will answer that industry has no stimulus left, since their surplus products have no markets. . . .

This war, if carried on successfully, will have its advantages. We shall drive the British from our continent. They will no longer have an opportunity of intriguing with our Indian neighbors and setting on the ruthless savage to tomahawk our women and children. That nation will lose her Canadian trade, and, by having no resting place in this country, her means of annoying us will be diminished.

3. Causes of the War (1812, 1813)

The "Second War for American Independence" was prompted by events on the frontier as well as on the high seas. The first print below, entitled A Scene on the Frontier as Practiced by the Humane British and Their Worthy Allies, *may have been inspired by the August 1812 "Massacre of Chicago" in which it was reported that British officers had purchased American scalps from Indians. The second scene,* The Tory Editor and His Apes Give Their Pitiful Advice to the American Sailors, *presum-*

---

[3]Library of Congress, #USZ62-5800; Lilly Library, Indiana University, Bloomington.

ably takes place in an Atlantic seaport, where American sailors are rejecting the counsel being offered. Why were the British depicted so differently in these two prints? What view of themselves would Americans get from these images? What do these views suggest about the relative importance of the various causes of the War of 1812?

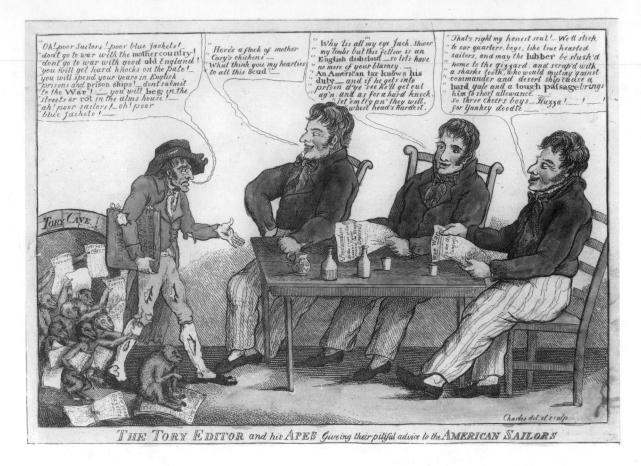

THE TORY EDITOR and his APES Giveing their pitiful advice to the AMERICAN SAILORS

4. President James Madison's Fateful War Message (1812)

Scholars once believed that Madison—mild-mannered and highly intellectual—was prodded into war by the purposeful war hawks from the West. The truth is that the president, unable to wring concessions from the British, worked hand in glove with the war hawks. In his following War Message, does he seem more concerned with purely western grievances than with national grievances? Which of his numerous charges against England carries the least conviction?

British cruisers have been in the continued practice of violating the American flag on the great highway of nations, and of seizing and carrying off persons sailing under it, not in the exercise of a belligerent right founded on the law of nations against an enemy, but of a municipal [internal] prerogative over British subjects. British jurisdiction is thus extended to neutral vessels. . . .

---

[4]J. D. Richardson, ed., *Messages and Papers of the Presidents* (1896), vol. 1, pp. 500–504.

The practice . . . is so far from affecting British subjects alone that, under the pretext of searching for these, thousands of American citizens, under the safeguard of public law and of their national flag, have been torn from their country and from everything dear to them; have been dragged on board ships of war of a foreign nation and exposed, under the severities of their discipline, to be exiled to the most distant and deadly climes, to risk their lives in the battles of their oppressors, and to be the melancholy instruments of taking away those of their own brethren.

Against this crying enormity, which Great Britain would be so prompt to avenge if committed against herself, the United States have in vain exhausted remonstrances and expostulations. And that no proof might be wanting of their conciliatory dispositions, and no pretext left for a continuance of the practice, the British government was formally assured of the readiness of the United States to enter into arrangements such as could not be rejected if the recovery of British subjects were the real and the sole object. The communication passed without effect.

British cruisers have been in the practice also of violating the rights and the peace of our coasts. They hover over and harass our entering and departing commerce. To the most insulting pretensions they have added the most lawless proceedings in our very harbors, and have wantonly spilt American blood within the sanctuary of our territorial jurisdiction. . . . [See Pierce case, p. 214.]

Under pretended blockades, without the presence of an adequate force and sometimes without the practicability of applying one, our commerce has been plundered in every sea, the great staples of our country have been cut off from their legitimate markets, and a destructive blow aimed at our agricultural and maritime interests. . . .

Not content with these occasional expedients for laying waste our neutral trade, the Cabinet of Britain resorted at length to the sweeping system of blockages, under the name of Orders in Council, which has been molded and managed as might best suit its political views, its commercial jealousies, or the avidity of British cruisers. . . .

It has become, indeed, sufficiently certain that the commerce of the United States is to be sacrificed, not as interfering with the belligerent rights of Great Britain; not as supplying the wants of her enemies, which she herself supplies; but as interfering with the monopoly which she covets for her own commerce and navigation. . . .

In reviewing the conduct of Great Britain toward the United States, our attention is necessarily drawn to the warfare just renewed by the savages on one of our extensive frontiers—a warfare which is known to spare neither age nor sex and to be distinguished by features peculiarly shocking to humanity. It is difficult to account for the activity and combinations which have for some time been developing themselves among tribes in constant intercourse with British traders and garrisons, without connecting their hostility with that influence, and without recollecting the authenticated examples of such interpositions heretofore furnished by the officers and agents of that government.

5. Federalist Congressmen Protest (1812)

A group of thirty-four antiwar Federalists, outvoted in the House, prepared the follow-ing remonstrance, which was widely circulated. One of its leading authors was the unbridled Josiah Quincy, who, the year before, had declared that if the Territory of Louisiana was admitted as a state, the Union was "virtually dissolved," and that like-minded men must "prepare definitely for a separation—amicably, if they can; vio-lently, if they must." The protest of the thirty-four congressmen was in effect a reply to Madison's War Message. After minimizing or partially justifying Britain's provocative maritime practices and Indian policy, the statement continued as follows. How plau-sibly does it make its points regarding the futility of the war and the folly of becoming a virtual ally of France? To what extent does it describe the war as immoral?

If our ills were of a nature that war would remedy, if war would compensate any of our losses or remove any of our complaints, there might be some alleviation of the suffering in the charm of the prospect. But how will war upon the land pro-tect commerce upon the ocean? What balm has Canada for wounded honor? How are our mariners benefited by a war which exposes those who are free, without promising release to those who are impressed?

But it is said that war is demanded by honor. Is national honor a principle which thirsts after vengeance, and is appeased only by blood? . . . If honor demands a war with England, what opiate lulls that honor to sleep over the wrongs done us by France? On land, robberies, seizures, imprisonments, by French authority; at sea, pillage, sinkings, burnings, under French orders. These are notorious. Are they unfelt because they are French? . . . With full knowledge of the wrongs inflicted by the French, ought the government of this country to aid the French cause by engaging in war against the enemy of France? . . .

It would be some relief to our anxiety if amends were likely to be made for the weakness and wildness of the project by the prudence of the preparation. But in no aspect of this anomalous affair can we trace the great and distinctive properties of wisdom. There is seen a headlong rushing into difficulties, with little calculation about the means, and little concern about the consequences. With a navy compara-tively nominal, we are about to enter into the lists against the greatest marine [sea power] on the globe. With a commerce unprotected and spread over every ocean, we propose to make a profit by privateering, and for this endanger the wealth of which we are honest proprietors. An invasion is threatened of the colonies of a power which, without putting a new ship into commission, or taking another soldier into pay, can spread alarm or desolation along the extensive range of our seaboard. . . .

The undersigned cannot refrain from asking, what are the United States to gain by this war? Will the gratification of some privateersmen compensate the nation for that sweep of our legitimate commerce by the extended marine of our enemy which this desperate act invites? Will Canada compensate the Middle states for New York; or the Western states for New Orleans?

Let us not be deceived. A war of invasion may invite a retort of invasion. When

---

[5]*Annals of Congress,* 12th Congress, 1st session, vol. 2, cols. 2219–2221.

we visit the peaceable, and as to us innocent, colonies of Great Britian with the horrors of war, can we be assured that our own coast will not be visited with like horrors? At a crisis of the world such as the present, and under impressions such as these, the undersigned could not consider the war, in which the United States have in secret been precipitated, as necessary, or required by any moral duty, or any political expediency.

6. The London Times *Cries Vengeance (1814)*

Congress had declared war on Britain in the confident expectation that Napoleon would pin down British forces in Europe. After his power crumbled in 1814, three veteran armies of redcoats were readied for invasions of the United States. The powerful London Times, *eager for a thrashing of the Yankees, thundered against any reasonable peace terms. Why did this journal believe that the Madison administration was untrustworthy and treacherous? Why was it willing to trust the Federalists?*

. . . Let us direct our attention to the situation of America. By a gradual but entire subversion of the Constitution, the faction who are impregnated with the most deep and rancorous hatred of Britain had possessed themselves of the supreme power in the United States. They abused that sacred trust, to put, as they fondly hoped, the last hand to our ruin.

Let the memorable era of June, 1812, be ever had in remembrance, when these wretches joined with the Corsican tyrant [Napoleon] to overwhelm Russia and Britain at once. Scepticism itself cannot doubt of the infamous pre-concert. Charity, that hopeth all things, and believeth all things, cannot persuade itself that the motive was not most black and malignant.

Let us follow up their attack on Canada, the real object of their hostilities. Let us recall to mind their insidious proclamations to the British subjects to revolt, and their invitation to the Indians to join them. Foiled and defeated in these views, let us not forget that with the most unblushing effrontery they turned round and accused us of inhumanity in accepting the proffered cooperation of the very Indians whom they first courted to their standard. . . .

It is possible that men who have carried on hostilities with so diabolical a spirit can have relaxed their whole system, and that so suddenly, from any other motive than fear? They are struck to the heart with terror for their impending punishment—and oh! may no false liberality, no mistaken lenity, no weak and cowardly policy interpose to save them from the blow! Strike. Chastise the savages; for such they are, in a much truer sense than the followers of Tecumseh or The Prophet.

Let us not be so foolishly confiding as to trust again to the honour or veracity of the Madisons, the Jeffersons, or any of the tribe, to whom we are well aware that those principles are altogether unknown. A real peace with them is impossible. But, as we predicted of Bonaparte, so, and with much more confidence, do we predict of them—their fall is at hand, if we do but persevere in a vigorous prosecution of hostilities. . . .

---

[6]*London Times,* May 24, 1814.

With Madison and his perjured set, no treaty can be made; for no oath can bind them. But his political antagonists are men not insensible of the many claims we have on their friendship, not unmindful of the common origin and common principles which they share with us.

7. The London Times *Bemoans Peace (1814)*

The British had expected to topple the United States by invading northern New York in 1814, but the redcoats were turned back at Plattsburgh by Thomas Macdonough's spectacular victory on Lake Champlain. The hard-pressed Americans, meanwhile, had completely abandoned their demands on impressment and other issues, and gladly accepted the stalemate Treaty of Ghent. The grim reality was that the British had begun the war with over eight hundred ships in their navy, the Americans with sixteen. When the war ended, the British still dominated the seas, whereas the Americans, although they had won a dozen or so single-ship duels, were down to two or three warships. But one would hardly have thought so from the following anguished outburst in the London Times, *which irresponsibly urged nonratification of the treaty. Why was this influential journal so unhappy? Did it present a false picture of British operations?*

. . . [The European powers] will reflect that we have attempted to force our principles on America, and have failed. Nay, that we have retired from the combat with the stripes yet bleeding on our backs—with the recent defeats at Plattsburg and on Lake Champlain unavenged. To make peace at such a moment, they will think, betrays a deadness to the feelings of honour, and shows a timidity of disposition, inviting further insult.

. . . "Two or three of our ships have struck to a force vastly superior!"—No, not two or three, but many on the ocean, and whole squadrons [to Perry and Macdonough] on the Lakes. And their numbers are to be viewed with relation to the comparative magnitude of the two navies. Scarcely is there one American ship of war which has not to boast a victory over the British flag; scarcely one British ship in thirty or forty that has beaten an American.

Our seamen, it is urged, have on all occasions fought bravely. Who denies it? Our complaint is that with the bravest seamen and the most powerful navy in the world, we retire from the contest when the balance of defeat is so heavily against us. Be it accident or be it misconduct, we enquire not now into the cause. The certain, the inevitable consequences are what we look to, and these may be summed up in a few words—the speedy growth of an American navy—and the recurrence of a new and much more formidable American war. . . .

The [American] people—naturally vain, boastful, and insolent—have been filled with an absolute contempt of our maritime power, and a furious eagerness to beat down our maritime pretensions. Those passions, which have been inflamed by success, could only have been cooled by what in vulgar and emphatic language has been termed "a sound flogging." But, unfortunately, our Christian meekness has in-

---

[7]*London Times*, December 30, 1814.

duced us rather to kiss the rod than to retaliate its exercise. Such false and feeble humanity is not calculated for the guidance of nations.

War is, indeed, a tremendous engine of justice. But when justice wields the sword, she must be inflexible. Looking neither to the right nor to the left, she must pursue her blow until the evil is clean rooted out. This is not blind rage, or blinder revenge; but it is a discriminating, a calm, and even a tender calculation of consequences. Better is it that we should grapple with the young lion when he is first fleshed with the taste of our flocks than wait until, in the maturity of his strength, he bears away at once both sheep and shepherd.

B. Disloyalty in New England.

1. A Boston Paper Obstructs the War (1813)

The antiwar bitterness of the New England Federalists found vigorous voice in Major Benjamin Russell's Columbian Centinel *(Boston). The editor, earlier fined twenty shillings for spitting in the face of a journalistic adversary, believed that a French-loving cabal of Virginia planter lordlings had provoked unnecessary hostilities. He charged that this Jeffersonian Republican group, headed by President Madison, was determined to ruin the Federalists by destroying their commerce and by carving new states out of Canada—states that would outvote the New England bloc. Considering that the United States had already been at war for six months, was this editorial treasonable? What was the validity of its charges? How far did it go toward secession?*

The sentiment is hourly extending, and in these Northern states will soon be universal, that we are in a condition no better in relation to the South than that of a conquered people. We have been compelled, without the least necessity or occasion, to renounce our habits, occupations, means of happiness, and subsistence. We are plunged into a war without a sense of enmity, or a perception of sufficient provocation; and obliged to fight the battles of a cabal which, under the sickening affectation of republican equality, aims at trampling into the dust the weight, influence, and power of commerce and her dependencies.

We, whose soil was the hotbed and whose ships were the nursery of sailors, are insulted with the hypocrisy of a devotedness to sailors' rights, and the arrogance of pretended skill in maritime jurisprudence, by those whose country furnishes no navigation beyond the size of a ferry boat or an Indian canoe. We have no more interest in waging this sort of war, at this period and under these circumstances, at the command of Virginia, than Holland in accelerating her ruin by uniting her destiny to France. . . .

We resemble Holland in another particular. The officer [offices] and power of government are engrossed [monopolized] by executive minions, who are selected

---

[1]*Columbian Centinel* (Boston), January 13, 1813.

on account of their known infidelity to the interest of their fellow citizens, to foment divisions and to deceive and distract the people whom they cannot intimidate. . . .

The consequence of this state of things must then be either that the Southern states must drag the Northern states farther into the war, or we must drag them out of it; or the chain will break. This will be the "imposing attitude" of the next year. We must no longer be deafened by senseless clamors about a separation of the states. It is an event we do not desire, not because we have derived advantages from the compact, but because we cannot foresee or limit the dangers or effects of revolution. But the states are separated in fact, when one section assumes an imposing attitude, and with a high hand perseveres in measures fatal to the interests and repugnant to the opinions of another section, by dint of a geographical majority.

2. The Hartford Convention Fulminates (1814)

As the war dragged on, the British extended their suffocating blockade to the coasts of New England. The New Englanders, forced to resort to costly defensive measures, complained bitterly that their federal tax payments were being used to fight the war elsewhere. Late in 1814, with Massachusetts and Connecticut as ringleaders, twenty-six delegates assembled secretly in a protest convention at Hartford, Connecticut. Although some of the Federalist extremists spoke brazenly of immediate secession, conservatives like the venerable George Cabot sat on the lid, saying, "We are going to keep you young hotheads from getting into mischief." The final resolutions, less treasonable than commonly supposed, were a manifesto of states' rights and sectionalism designed to revive New England's slipping national power, avert Jeffersonian embargoes, and keep new western states from outvoting the charter members. Which of these proposed amendments were most clearly sectional, and which one probably had the best chance of adoption at the time?

Resolved, That the following amendments of the Constitution of the United States be recommended to the states. . . .

First. Representatives and direct taxes shall be apportioned among the several states which may be included within this Union, according to their respective numbers of free persons, including those bound to serve for a term of years, and excluding Indians not taxed, and all other persons. [Aimed at reducing southern representation based on slaves.]

Second. No new state shall be admitted into the Union by Congress, in virtue of the power granted by the Constitution, without the concurrence of two-thirds of both Houses.

Third. Congress shall not have power to lay any embargo on the ships or vessels of the citizens of the United States, in the ports or harbors thereof, for more than sixty days.

Fourth. Congress shall not have power, without the concurrence of two-thirds of both Houses, to interdict the commercial intercourse between the United States and any foreign nation, or the dependencies thereof.

---

[2]Timothy Dwight, *History of the Hartford Convention* (1833), pp. 377–378.

Fifth. Congress shall not make or declare war, or authorize acts of hostility against any foreign nation, without the concurrence of two-thirds of both Houses, except such acts of hostility be in defense of the territories of the United States when actually invaded.

Sixth. No person who shall hereafter be naturalized shall be eligible as a member of the Senate or House of Representatives of the United States, nor capable of holding any civil office under the authority of the United States. [Aimed at men like Jefferson's Swiss-born secretary of the treasury, Albert Gallatin.]

Seventh. The same person shall not be elected President of the United States a second time; nor shall the President be elected from the same state two terms in succession. [Prompted by the successive two-term tenures of Jefferson and Madison, both from Virginia.]

Resolved, That if the application of these states to the government of the United States, recommended in a foregoing resolution, should be unsuccessful, and peace should not be concluded, and the defense of these states should be neglected, as it has been since the commencement of the war, it will, in the opinion of this convention, be expedient for the legislatures of the several states to appoint delegates to another convention, to meet at Boston . . . with such powers and instruction as the exigency of a crisis so momentous may require.

[The legislatures of Massachusetts and Connecticut enthusiastically approved the Hartford Resolutions. Three emissaries from Massachusetts departed for Washington with their demands, confidently expecting to hear at any moment of a smashing British victory at New Orleans, the collapse of the peace negotiations at Ghent, and the dissolution of the Union. Instead came news of the smashing British defeat at New Orleans and the signing of the peace treaty at Ghent. The Hartfordites were hooted off the stage of history, amid charges of treason that cling to this day.]

3. John Quincy Adams Reproaches the Hartfordites (1815)

Independent-minded John Quincy Adams, son of the second president and destined to be the sixth president, rose above the sectional prejudices of his native New England. Elected to the Senate by Massachusetts, he reluctantly voted for the Louisiana Purchase appropriation and subsequently supported Jefferson's unpopular embargo as preferable to war. The Federalists of New England now regarded him as a traitor. After serving as one of the five American negotiators of the Treaty of Ghent, he wrote the following spirited attack on the Hartford Convention. What, in his view, was the ultimate aim of the Hartfordites?

The [Hartford] Convention represented the extreme portion of the Federalism of New England—the party spirit of the school of Alexander Hamilton combined with the sectional Yankee spirit. . . .

---

[3]Henry Adams, ed., *Documents Relating to New England Federalism, 1800–1815* (Boston: 1877), pp. 283–284, 321–322.

This coalition of Hamiltonian Federalism with the Yankee spirit had produced as incongruous and absurd a system of politics as ever was exhibited in the vagaries of the human mind. It was compounded of the following prejudices:—

1. An utter detestation of the French Revolution and of France, and a corresponding excess of attachment to Great Britain, as the only barrier against the universal, dreaded empire of France.

2. A strong aversion to republics and republican government, with a profound impression that our experiment of a confederated republic had failed for want of virtue in the people.

3. A deep jealousy of the Southern and Western states, and a strong disgust at the effect of the slave representation in the Constitution of the United States.

4. A belief that Mr. Jefferson and Mr. Madison were servilely devoted to France, and under French influence.

Every one of these sentiments weakened the attachments of those who held them to the Union, and consequently their patriotism. . . .

It will be no longer necessary to search for the objects of the Hartford Convention. They are apparent from the whole tenor of their report and resolutions, compared with the journal of their proceedings. They are admitted in the first and last paragraphs of the report, and they were:

To wait for the issue of the negotiation at Ghent.

In the event of the continuance of the war, to take one more chance of getting into their own hands the administration of the general government.

On the failure of that, a secession from the Union and a New England confederacy.

To these ends, and not to the defense of this part of the country against the foreign enemy, all the measures of the Hartford Convention were adapted. . . .

C. The Missouri Statehood Controversy

1. Representative John Taylor Reviles Slavery (1819)

The slaveholding territory of Missouri applied to Congress for admission as a state in 1819. Representative James Tallmadge of New York touched off the fireworks when he proposed an amendment to the Missouri statehood bill (a) prohibiting any further introduction of slaves and (b) freeing at age twenty-five all children born to slave parents after the admission of the state. During the ensuing debates, a leading role was played by Representative John W. Taylor, a prominent antislavery leader from New York who was to serve for twenty consecutive years in the House. The South never forgave him, and later engineered his defeat for election as Speaker. In his speech for the Tallmadge amendment, what were the apparent contradictions in the attitude of the South toward blacks?

Having proved . . . our right to legislate in the manner proposed, I proceed to illustrate the propriety of exercising it. And here I might rest satisfied with reminding

---

[1]*Annals of Congress,* 15th Congress, 2d session, vol. 3, cols. 1174–1176.

THE MISSOURI
COMPROMISE

my [southern] opponents of their own declarations on the subject of slavery. How often, and how eloquently, have they deplored its existence among them! What willingness, nay, what solicitude have they not manifested to be relieved from this burden! How have they wept over the unfortunate policy that first introduced slaves into this country! How have they disclaimed the guilt and shame of that original sin, and thrown it back upon their ancestors!

I have with pleasure heard these avowals of regret and confided in their sincerity. I have hoped to see its effects in the advancement of the cause of humanity. Gentlemen now have an opportunity of putting their principles into practice. If they have tried slavery and found it a curse, if they desire to dissipate the gloom with which it covers their land, I call upon them to exclude it from the Territory in question. Plant not its seeds in this uncorrupt soil. Let not our children, looking back to the proceedings of this day, say of them, as they have been constrained to speak of their fathers, "We wish their decision had been different. We regret the existence of this unfortunate population among us. But we found them here; we know not what to do with them. It is our misfortune; we must bear it with patience."

History will record the decision of this day as exerting its influence for centuries to come over the population of half our continent. If we reject the amendment and suffer this evil, now easily eradicated, to strike its roots so deep in the soil that it can never be removed, shall we not furnish some apology for doubting our sincerity when we deplore its existence? . . .

Mr. Chairman, one of the gentlemen from Kentucky (Mr. Clay) has pressed into his service the cause of humanity. He has pathetically urged us to withdraw our amendment and suffer this unfortunate population to be dispersed over the country. He says they will be better fed, clothed, and sheltered, and their whole condition will be greatly improved. . . .

Sir, my heart responds to the call of humanity. I will zealously unite in any practicable means of bettering the condition of this oppressed people. I am ready to appropriate a territory to their use, and to aid them in settling it—but I am not willing, I never will consent, to declare the whole country west of the Mississippi a market overt for human flesh. . . .

To the objection that this amendment will, if adopted, diminish the value of a species of property in one portion of the Union, and thereby operate unequally, I reply that if, by depriving slaveholders of the Missouri market, the business of raising slaves should become less profitable, it would be an effect incidentally produced, but is not the object of the measure. The law prohibiting the importation of foreign slaves was not passed for the purpose of enhancing the value of those then in the country, but that effect has been incidentally produced in a very great degree. . . .

It is further objected that the amendment is calculated to disfranchise our brethren of the South by discouraging their emigration to the country west of the Mississippi. . . . The description of emigrants may be affected, in some measure, by the amendment in question. If slavery shall be tolerated, the country will be settled by rich planters, with their slaves. If it shall be rejected, the emigrants will chiefly consist of the poorer and more laborious classes of society. If it be true that the prosperity and happiness of a country ought to constitute the grand object of its legislators, I cannot hesitate for a moment which species of population deserves most to be encouraged by the laws we may pass.

2. Representative Charles Pinckney Upholds Slavery (1820)

Angered southerners spoke so freely of secession and "seas of blood" during the Missouri debate that the aging Thomas Jefferson likened the issue to "a fire bell in the night." The argument inevitably involved the general problem of slavery, and the view of the South was eloquently presented, in a justly famous speech, by Representative Charles Pinckney of South Carolina. Vain, demogogic, and of questionable morals, he was nevertheless touched with genius. As one of the few surviving members of the Philadelphia Convention that had framed the Constitution in 1787, and as South Carolina's former governor and U.S. senator, Pinckney was in a position to command attention. What is the most alarming aspect of the speech?

A great deal has been said on the subject of slavery: that it is an infamous stain and blot on the states that hold them, not only degrading the slave, but the master, and making him unfit for republican government; that it is contrary to religion and the law of God; and that Congress ought to do everything in their power to prevent its extension among the new states.

Now, sir, . . . is there a single line in the Old or New Testament either censuring or forbidding it [slavery]? I answer without hesitation, no. But there are hundreds speaking of and recognizing it. . . . Hagar, from whom millions sprang, was an

---

[2]*Annals of Congress,* 16th Congress, 1st session, vol. 2, cols. 1323–1328, passim.

African slave, brought out of Egypt by Abraham, the father of the faithful and the beloved servant of the Most High; and he had, besides, three hundred and eighteen male slaves. The Jews, in the time of the theocracy, and the Greeks and Romans, had all slaves; at that time there was no nation without them.

If we are to believe that this world was formed by a great and omnipotent Being, that nothing is permitted to exist here but by his will, and then throw our eyes throughout the whole of it, we should form an opinion very different indeed from that asserted, that slavery was against the law of God. . . .

It will not be a matter of surprise to anyone that so much anxiety should be shown by the slaveholding states, when it is known that the alarm, given by this attempt to legislate on slavery, has led to the opinion that the very foundations of that kind of property are shaken; that the establishment of the precedent is a measure of the most alarming nature. . . . For, should succeeding Congresses continue to push it, there is no knowing to what length it may be carried.

Have the Northern states any idea of the value of our slaves? At least, sir, six hundred millions of dollars. If we lose them, the value of the lands they cultivate will be diminished in all cases one half, and in many they will become wholly useless. And an annual income of at least forty millions of dollars will be lost to your citizens, the loss of which will not alone be felt by the non-slaveholding states, but by the whole Union. For to whom, at present, do the Eastern states, most particularly, and the Eastern and Northern, generally, look for the employment of their shipping, in transporting our bulky and valuable products [cotton], and bringing us the manufactures and merchandises of Europe?

Another thing, in case of these losses being brought on us, and our being forced into a division of the Union, what becomes of your public debt? Who are to pay this, and how will it be paid? In a pecuniary view of this subject, therefore, it must ever be the policy of the Eastern and Northern states to continue connected with us.

But, sir, there is an infinitely greater call upon them, and this is the call of justice, of affection, and humanity. Reposing at a great distance, in safety, in the full enjoyment of all their federal and state rights, unattacked in either, or in their individual rights, can they, with indifference, or ought they, to risk, in the remotest degree, the consequences which this measure may produce? These may be the division of this Union and a civil war. Knowing that whatever is said here must get into the public prints, I am unwilling, for obvious reasons, to go into the description of the horrors which such a war must produce, and ardently pray that none of us may ever live to witness such an event.

[Other southerners, so reported Representative William Plumer, Jr., of New Hampshire, "throw out many threats, and talk loudly of separation." Even "Mr. [Henry] Clay declares that he will go home and raise troops, if necessary, to defend the people of Missouri." But the Tallmadge amendment was rejected, and the famed Missouri Compromise was finally hammered out in 1820. The delicate sectional balance subsisting between the eleven free states and eleven slave states was cleverly preserved: Maine (then a part of Massachusetts) was to come in as a free state and Missouri as a slave state. But henceforth slavery was forbidden elsewhere in the Louisiana Purchase territory north of the line of 36° 30'—the southern border of Missouri. John

Quincy Adams wrote prophetically: "I take it for granted that the present question is a mere preamble—a title page to a great tragic volume."]

3. A Connecticut Antislavery Outcry (1820)

It would be erroneous to assume that the clash over Missouri was prompted solely by sectional and economic differences. The forebears of the extreme Garrisonian abolitionists in New England were deeply disturbed by the moral offensiveness of human bondage. The Boston Gazette *printed a "Black List" of the members of Congress from the free states who had supported the Missouri Compromise. A writer signing himself "Brutus," and attributing undue weight to three Connecticut members of Congress, published the following indictment in a New Haven newspaper. What does it reveal about abolitionism in New England eleven years before William Garrison launched his* Liberator?

Slavery is extended to Missouri, by a majority of three.

The deed is done. The galling chains of slavery are forged for myriads yet unborn. Humble yourselves in the dust, ye high-minded citizens of Connecticut. Let your cheeks be red as crimson. On *your* representatives rests the stigma of this foul disgrace. It is a stain of blood, which oceans of tears and centuries of repentance can never obliterate. The names of Lanman, Stevens, and Foot will go down to posterity with the name of Judas.* Their memory will be preserved in the execrations of the good, in the groans and sighs of the oppressed, and they will be remembered by the proud oppressor himself in *the day of retribution.* That day will surely come, for God is just. But for *their* vote future millions now destined to the whips and scourges of the inhuman slavedealer might have breathed the air of freedom and of happiness.

D. Launching the Monroe Doctrine

1. Thomas Jefferson Turns Pro-British (1823)

Stirred by the Napoleonic upheaval, most of Spain's colonies in the Americas threw off the monarchical yoke and set themselves up as independent republics. Late in 1823 rumors were afloat in Europe that the great powers—Russia, Austria, Prussia, and France (loosely called the Holy Alliance)—were planning to crush the upstart

---

[3]*New Haven Journal,* March 14, 1820; facsimile reproduction in Glover Moore, *The Missouri Controversy, 1819–1821* (Lexington, Ky.: University of Kentucky Press, 1953), p. 196.

*The writer does not mean to intimate that, like Judas, these men were *bribed*. The public will judge of their motives for themselves.

[1]P. L. Ford, ed., *Writings of Thomas Jefferson* (New York: G. P. Putnam's Sons, 1899), vol. 10, pp. 277–278 (October 24, 1823).

colonials and restore Spanish misrule. British Foreign Secretary George Canning, fearful that these newly opened markets would be lost to British merchants, proposed to the American minister in London, Richard Rush, that the United States and Britain issue a joint warning against foreign intervention in Spanish America. President Monroe sought the advice of ex-President Jefferson, the eighty-year-old Sage of Monticello. Remember that Jefferson had been anti-alliance, antiwar, and anti-British. What is curious about his response? Why did he take the stand that he did?

Dear Sir, The question presented by the letters you have sent me is the most momentous which has ever been offered to my contemplation since that of Independence. That made us a nation; this sets our compass and points the course which we are to steer through the ocean of time opening on us. And never could we embark on it under circumstances more auspicious.

Our first and fundamental maxim should be never to entangle ourselves in the broils of Europe. Our second, never to suffer Europe to intermeddle with cis-Atlantic affairs. America—North and South—has a set of interests distinct from those of Europe, and peculiarly her own. She should therefore have a system of her own, separate and apart from that of Europe. While the last is laboring to become the domicile of despotism, our endeavor should surely be to make our hemisphere that of freedom.

One nation, most of all, could disturb us in this pursuit. She now offers to lead, aid, and accompany us in it. By acceding to her proposition, we detach her from the bands, bring her mighty weight into the scale of free government, and emancipate a continent [South America] at one stroke, which might otherwise linger in doubt and difficulty.

Great Britain is the nation which can do us the most harm of any one, or all on earth. And with her on our side, we need not fear the whole world. With her, then, we should most sedulously cherish a cordial friendship; and nothing would tend more to knit our affections than to be fighting once more, side by side, in the same cause.

Not that I would purchase even her amity at the price of taking part in her wars. But the war in which the present proposition might engage us, should that be its consequence, is not her war, but ours. Its object is to introduce and establish the American system of keeping out of our land all foreign powers, of never permitting those of Europe to intermeddle with the affairs of our nations. It is to maintain our own principle, not to depart from it. And if, to facilitate this, we can effect a division in the body of the European powers, and draw over to our side its most powerful member, surely we should do it.

But I am clearly of Mr. Canning's opinion that it will prevent instead of provoking war. With Great Britain withdrawn from their scale and shifted into that of our two continents, all Europe combined would not undertake such a war. For how would they propose to get at either enemy without superior fleets? . . .

But we have first to ask ourselves a question. Do we wish to acquire to our own confederacy any one or more of the Spanish provinces?

I candidly confess that I have ever looked on Cuba as the most interesting addition which could ever be made to our system of states. The control which, with

Florida Point, this island would give us over the Gulf of Mexico . . . would fill up the measure of our political well-being. Yet, as I am sensible that this can never be obtained, even with her own consent, but by war; and its independence, which is our second interest (and especially its independence of England), can be secured without it, I have no hesitation in abandoning my first wish to future chances, and accepting its independence, with peace and the friendship of England, rather than its association at the expense of war and her enmity.

2. John Quincy Adams Rejects a Joint Declaration (1823)

John Quincy Adams, Monroe's stiff-backed and lone-wolf secretary of state, strongly suspected Canning's motives in approaching Minister Rush. Adams cleverly calculated that the potent British navy would not permit the newly opened Spanish-American markets to be closed, and he therefore concluded that the European monarchs were powerless to intervene, no matter what the United States did. He failed to share Secretary Calhoun's fear of the French army, which, acting as the avenging sword of the reactionary powers, was then crushing a republican uprising in Spain. Adams here records in his diary the relevant cabinet discussion. Of the arguments he advanced against cooperation with Canning, which was strongest? Why?

Washington, November 7th.—Cabinet meeting at the President's from half-past one till four. Mr. Calhoun, Secretary of War, and Mr. Southard, Secretary of the Navy, present. The subject for consideration was the confidential proposals of the British Secretary of State, George Canning, to Richard Rush, and the correspondence between them relating to the projects of the Holy Alliance upon South America. There was much conversation without coming to any definite point. The object of Canning appears to have been to obtain some public pledge from the government of the United States, ostensibly against the forcible interference of the Holy Alliance between Spain and South America, but really or especially against the acquisition to the United States themselves of any part of the Spanish-American possessions.

Mr. Calhoun inclined to giving a discretionary power to Mr. Rush to join in a declaration against the interference of the Holy Allies, if necessary, even if it should pledge us not to take Cuba or the province of Texas; because the power of Great Britain being greater than ours to seize upon them, we should get the advantage of obtaining from her the same declaration we should make ourselves.

I thought the cases not parallel. We have no intentions of seizing either Texas or Cuba. But the inhabitants of either or both may exercise their primitive rights, and solicit a union with us. They will certainly do no such thing to Great Britain. By joining with her, therefore, in her proposed declaration, we give her a substantial and perhaps inconvenient pledge against ourselves, and really obtain nothing in return.

---

[2]C. F. Adams, ed., *Memoirs of John Quincy Adams* (Philadelphia: J. B. Lippincott & Co., 1875), vol. 6, pp. 177–179.

Without entering now into the enquiry of the expediency of our annexing Texas or Cuba to our Union, we should at least keep ourselves free to act as emergencies may arise, and not tie ourselves down to any principle which might immediately afterwards be brought to bear against ourselves. . . .

I remarked that the communications recently received from the Russian minister, Baron Tuyl, afforded, as I thought, a very suitable and convenient opportunity for us to take our stand against the Holy Alliance, and at the same time to decline the overture of Great Britain. It would be more candid, as well as more dignified, to avow our principles explicitly to Russia and France than to come in as a cockboat in the wake of the British man-of-war.

3. James Monroe Warns the European Powers (1823)

Secretary Adams's cogent arguments helped turn President Monroe toward a go-it-alone policy. The president's annual message to Congress, surprisingly, contained several emphatic warnings. The Russians, who had caused some alarm by their push toward California, had privately shown a willingness to retreat to the southern bounds of present Alaska. But Monroe warned them and the other powers that there was now a closed season on colonizing in the Americas. On the other hand, the heroic struggle of the Greeks for independence from the Turks was creating some agitation in America for intervention, but Monroe made his "you stay out" warning seem fairer by volunteering a "we'll stay out" pledge. Did he aim his main warning at noncolonization on the northwest coast or at the nonextension of monarchical systems to Spanish America? To what extent did he tie America's hands regarding the acquisition of Cuba or intervention in Greece? Did he actually threaten the European powers?

In the discussions to which this interest [Russia's on the northwest coast] has given rise, the occasion has been judged proper for asserting, as a principle in which the rights and interests of the United States are involved, that the American continents, by the free and independent condition which they have assumed and maintain, are henceforth not to be considered as subjects for the future colonization by any European powers. . . .

The political system of the Allied Powers [Holy Alliance] is essentially different . . . from that of America. This difference proceeds from that which exists in their respective [monarchical] governments; and to the defense of our own . . . this whole nation is devoted. We owe it, therefore, to candor and to the amicable relations existing between the United States and those powers to declare that we should consider any attempt on their part to extend their system to any portion of this hemisphere as dangerous to our peace and safety.

With the existing colonies or dependencies of any European power, we have not interfered and shall not interfere. But with the governments [of Spanish America] who have declared their independence and maintained it, and whose independence

---

[3]J. D. Richardson, ed., *Messages and Papers of the Presidents* (1896), vol. 2, pp. 209, 218–219.

we have, on great consideration and on just principles, acknowledged, we could not view any interposition for the purpose of oppressing them, or controlling in any other manner their destiny, by any European power in any other light than as the manifestation of an unfriendly disposition toward the United States. . . .

Our policy in regard to Europe, which was adopted at an early stage of the wars which have so long agitated that quarter of the globe, nevertheless remains the same, which is, not to interfere in the internal concerns of any of its powers; to consider the government *de facto* as the legitimate government for us; to cultivate friendly relations with it, and to preserve those relations by a frank, firm, and manly policy, meeting in all instances the just claims of every power, submitting to injuries from none.

But in regard to those [American] continents, circumstances are eminently and conspicuously different. It is impossible that the Allied Powers should extend their political system to any portion of either continent without endangering our peace and happiness. Nor can anyone believe that our southern brethren, if left to themselves, would adopt it of their own accord. It is equally impossible, therefore, that we should behold such interposition in any form with indifference.

4. A Baltimore Editor Exults (1823)

Monroe's defiant pronouncement touched a patriotic chord and evoked near-unanimous acclaim. The Vermont Gazette, *with remarkable foresight, predicted that the message would "go down in our annals along with Washington's Farewell Address." Other journals guessed that the president must have had some secret information about a possible hostile move by the "crowned conspirators" of Europe. The Baltimore* Morning Chronicle *gave vent to the following editorial bombast. What role in the world did the writer envision for the United States?*

We can tell . . . further that this high-toned, independent, and dignified message will not be read by the crowned heads of Europe without a revolting stare of astonishment. The conquerors of Bonaparte, with their laurels still green and blooming on their brows, and their disciplined animal machines, called armies, at their backs, could not have anticipated that their united force would so soon be defied by a young republic, whose existence, as yet, cannot be measured with the ordinary life of man.

This message itself constitutes an era in American history, worthy of commemoration. . . . We are confident that, on this occasion, we speak the great body of American sentiment, such as exulting millions are ready to re-echo. . . . We are very far from being confident that, if Congress occupy the high and elevated ground taken in the Message, it may not, under the smiles of Divine Providence, be the means of breaking up the Holy Alliance.

Of this we are positively sure: that all timidity, wavering, imbecility, and backwardness on our part will confirm these detested tyrants in their confederacy; para-

---

[4]Baltimore *Morning Chronicle,* December 5, 1823, in *Daily National Intelligencer* (Washington, D.C.), December 8, 1823.

lyze the exertions of freedom in every country; accelerate the fall of those young sister republics whom we have recently recognized; and, perhaps, eventually destroy our own at the feet of absolute monarchy.

5. Prince Metternich Is Miffed (1824)

Only minor dissenting voices in the American press complained that the United States was not endangered and that the president had gone too far. A few surviving Federalist newspapers quibbled over the unwisdom of safeguarding the Patagonians and Eskimos from despotism. But the reaction in continental Europe was uniformly unfavorable. The monarchical powers were not frightened away by Monroe's paper pronouncement; they were painfully aware that the thundering broadsides of the British navy stood between them and Spanish America. In their anger and frustration, they vented their spleen against the upstart American republic, which had already given much unofficial aid and comfort to Spain's rebelling subjects. Prince Metternich, the Austrian chancellor and archpriest of post-Napoleonic reaction, boiled over. What seemed to bother him most, and why?

These United States of America, which we have seen arise and grow, and which during their too short youth already meditated projects which they dared not then avow, have suddenly left a sphere too narrow for their ambition, and have astonished Europe by a new act of revolt, more unprovoked, fully as audacious, and no less dangerous than the former. They have distinctly and clearly announced their intention to set not only power against power, but, to express it more exactly, altar against altar. In their indecent declarations they have cast blame and scorn on the institutions of Europe most worthy of respect, on the principles of its greatest sovereigns, on the whole of those measures which a sacred duty no less than an evident necessity has forced our government to adopt to frustrate plans most criminal.

In permitting themselves these unprovoked attacks, in fostering revolutions wherever they show themselves, in regretting those which have failed, in extending a helping hand to those which seem to prosper, they lend new strength to the apostles of sedition, and reanimate the courage of every conspirator.

If this flood of evil doctrines and pernicious examples should extend over the whole of America, what would become of our religious and political institutions, of the moral force of our governments, and of that conservative system which has saved Europe from complete dissolution?

Thought Provokers

1. Why did the United States go to war with Britain in 1812? Was there any single cause whose removal would have averted hostilities?
2. Why were the Federalists so bitterly opposed to the war? Were their grievances legitimate? Were they victims of the "tyranny of the majority," or simply poor losers?

---

[5]Quoted in Dexter Perkins *The Monroe Doctrine,* 1823–1826 (Cambridge, Mass.: Harvard University Press, 1927) p. 167.

3. If the peace of Ghent was so unpopular in England, and so popular in America, what conclusions might be drawn as to which side won the war? How is "victory" to be measured in a military contest?

4. If many leaders of the South acknowledged that slavery was a wicked institution, why did they fight its proposed abolition in Missouri?

5. Would the United States have been better off in the long run if Monroe had followed Jefferson's advice and joined hands with Britain to keep the other European powers out of the Americas?

6. Why did the American public react so favorably to the Monroe Doctrine, and why did the European governments, then and later, never show much enthusiasm for it?

13

The Rise
of Jacksonian Democracy,
1824–1830

The tendency of democracies is, in all things, to
mediocrity.

James Fenimore Cooper, 1838

Prologue: The explosive growth of the West, with its ocean of available land,
weakened the old property qualifications for voting and stimulated the New
Democracy of the "unwashed masses." General Andrew Jackson was the people's
choice for president in 1824, but a disputed election and a so-called corrupt bargain
with Speaker Henry Clay brought the austere John Quincy Adams to the White
House for four frustrating years. The Jacksonites finally swept their military hero
into the presidency in 1829. Although Jefferson had introduced the spoils system on
a minor scale, Jackson went much further in his efforts to reward supporters, oust
political enemies, and rid Washington of entrenched bureaucrats. Meanwhile, southern anger was boiling up over a tariff that had edged steadily upward in 1816, 1824,
and 1828. One resulting flare-up was the turn taken by the classic Webster–Hayne
debate of 1830 in the Senate. Webster immensely strengthened the ideal of Union
by touching a nationalistic chord that vibrated in harmony with America's call to
greatness.

A. Background of the New Democracy

1. A Disgusting Spirit of Equality (1807)

*Freedom of opportunity in America weakened class barriers and caused the "lower
orders" to be freer and easier with their "betters." Such behavior was highly offensive
to English visitors from a class-ridden society, especially to those who came in the
1830s and 1840s. C. W. Janson emigrated to America from England to make his fortune, lost his money, and vented his spleen in an ill-natured book that contained
numerous unpleasant truths. What specific American traits did he find annoying,*

[1]C. W. Janson, *The Stranger in America, 1793–1806* (London: J. Cundee, 1807), pp. 85–88.

and which one the most annoying? Do universal manhood suffrage and bad manners necessarily go together?

Arrived at your [New England] inn, let me suppose, like myself, you had fallen in with a landlord who at the moment would condescend to take the trouble to procure you refreshment after the family hour. . . . He will sit by your side and enter in the most familiar manner into conversation; which is prefaced, of course, with a demand of your business, and so forth. He will then start a political question (for here every individual is a politician), force your answer, contradict, deny, and, finally, be ripe for a quarrel, should you not acquiesce in all his opinions.

When the homely meal is served up, he will often place himself opposite to you at the table at the same time declaring that "though he thought he had eaten a hearty dinner, yet he will pick a bit with you."

Thus he will sit, drinking out of your glass, and of the liquor you are to pay for, belching in your face, and committing other excesses still more indelicate and disgusting. Perfectly inattentive to your accommodation, and regardless of your appetite, he will dart his fork into the best of the dish, and leave you to take the next cut.

If you arrive at the dinner hour, you are seated with "mine hostess" and her dirty children, with whom you have often to scramble for a plate, and even the servants of the inn. For liberty and equality level all ranks upon the road, from the host to the hostler.

The children, imitative of their free and polite papa, will also seize your drink, slobber in it, and often snatch a dainty bit from your plate. This is esteemed wit, and consequently provokes a laugh, at the expense of those who are paying for the board. . . .

The arrogance of domestics [servants] in this land of republican liberty and equality is particularly calculated to excite the astonishment of strangers. To call persons of this description servants, or to speak of their master or mistress, is a grievous affront.

Having called one day at the house of a gentleman of my acquaintance, on knocking at the door, it was opened by a servant-maid, whom I had never before seen, as she had not been long in his family. The following is the dialogue, word for word, which took place on this occasion:

"Is your master at home?"

"I have no master."

"Don't you live here?"

"I stay here."

"And who are you then?"

"Why, I am Mr. —'s help. I'd have you to know, man, that I am no sarvant. None but negers are sarvants."

2. A Plea for Nonproperty Suffrage (1841)

Until the days of Jacksonian democracy, property qualifications were generally demanded of all voters. In Virginia, where such restrictions discouraged immigration

---

[2]George S. Camp, *Democracy* (New York: Harper and Brothers, 1841), pp. 145–146.

and encouraged emigration, a memorable convention met at Richmond in 1829–1830 to revise the state constitution. The result was a widening of the suffrage, in accord with the New Democracy, but a retention of certain property qualifications. One of the strongest arguments against change—an argument repeated in other conservative states—was that possession of property provided the surest guarantee of a permanent stake in the community. Grave dangers would presumably be courted if political power were put into the hands of the irresponsible, propertyless "bipeds of the forest." A popular author, George S. Camp, took sharp issue with the advocates of property qualifications in a long-lived book on democracy. In the light of his argument, is it true that the propertyless have as much of a stake in the community as the propertied?

All should have an equal voice in the public deliberations of the state, however unequal in point of circumstances, since human rights, by virtue of which alone we are entitled to vote at all, are the attributes of the man, not of his circumstances.

Should the right to vote, the characteristic and the highest prerogative of a freeman, be at the mercy of a casualty? I am rich today, worth my hundred thousands. But my wealth consists in stock and merchandise; it may be in storehouses, it may be upon the ocean. I have been unable to effect an insurance, or there is some concealed legal defect in my policy. The fire or the storms devour my wealth in an hour: am I the less competent to vote? Have I less of the capacity of a moral and intelligent being? Am I the less a good citizen? Is it not enough that I have been deprived of my fortune—must I be disfranchised by community?

My having a greater or less amount of property does not alter my rights. Property is merely the subject on which rights are exercised; its amount does not alter rights themselves. If it were otherwise, every one of us would be in some degree subject to some wealthier neighbor. And, if the representation of property were consistently carried out, the affairs of every community, instead of being governed by the majority of rational and intelligent beings, would be governed by a preponderance of houses, lands, stocks, plate, jewelry, merchandise, and money!

It is not true that one man has more at stake in the commonwealth than another. We all have our rights, and no man has anything more. If we look at the subject philosophically, and consider how much superior man is by nature to what he is by external condition, how much superior his real attributes are to what he acquires from the accidents of fortune, we shall then view the distinctions of rank and wealth in their true comparative insignificance, and make as little difference on these accounts with the political as with the moral man.

3. Davy Crockett Advises Politicians (1836)

David Crockett—notorious Tennessee frontiersman, Indian scout, rifleman, bear hunter, and braggart—was a homespun product of the New Democracy. His scanty six months of schooling led him to scorn both grammar and "book larnin'," although he became a justice of the peace, an elected militia colonel, and a member of

---

[3]David Crockett, *Exploits and Adventures in Texas* . . . (1836), pp. 56–59 (a pseudo-autobiography generally ascribed to Richard Penn Smith).

the state legislature. When a joking remark prompted him to campaign for Congress, he overwhelmed his two opponents with a barrage of ridicule and humorous stories. Reelected for two additional terms, he attracted wide attention in Washington with his backwoods dress, racy language, homely wit, shrewd common sense, and presumed naiveté regarding the aristocratic East. Ruggedly independent, he delighted eastern conservatives by refusing to follow President Jackson on all issues. His advice to aspiring politicians, though offered in a jocular vein, reveals the debased tone of the new manhood-suffrage democracy. Which of his recommended devices are still employed by politicians today?

"Attend all public meetings," says I, "and get some friend to move that you take the chair. If you fail in this attempt, make a push to be appointed secretary. The proceedings of course will be published, and your name is introduced to the public. But should you fail in both undertakings, get two or three acquaintances, over a bottle of whisky, to pass some resolutions, no matter on what subject. Publish them, even if you pay the printer. It will answer the purpose of breaking the ice, which is the main point in these matters.

"Intrigue until you are elected an officer of the militia. This is the second step toward promotion, and can be accomplished with ease, as I know an instance of an election being advertised, and no one attending, the innkeeper at whose house it was to be held, having a military turn, elected himself colonel of his regiment." Says I, "You may not accomplish your ends with as little difficulty, but do not be discouraged—Rome wasn't built in a day.

"If your ambition or circumstances compel you to serve your country, and earn three dollars a day, by becoming a member of the legislature, you must first publicly avow that the constitution of the state is a shackle upon free and liberal legislation, and is, therefore, of as little use in the present enlightened age as an old almanac of the year in which the instrument was framed. There is policy in this measure, for by making the constitution a mere dead letter, your headlong proceedings will be attributed to a bold and unshackled mind; whereas, it might otherwise be thought they arose from sheer mulish ignorance. 'The Government' has set the example in his [Jackson's] attack upon the Constitution of the United States, and who should fear to follow where 'the Government' leads?

"When the day of election approaches, visit your constituents far and wide. Treat liberally, and drink freely, in order to rise in their estimation, though you fall in your own. True, you may be called a drunken dog by some of the clean-shirt and silk-stocking gentry, but the real roughnecks will style you a jovial fellow. Their votes are certain, and frequently count double.

"Do all you can to appear to advantage in the eyes of the women. That's easily done. You have but to kiss and slabber [slobber over] their children, wipe their noses, and pat them on the head. This cannot fail to please their mothers, and you may rely on your business being done in that quarter.

"Promise all that is asked," said I, "and more if you can think of anything. Offer to build a bridge or a church, to divide a county, create a batch of new offices, make a turnpike, or anything they like. Promises cost nothing; therefore, deny nobody who has a vote or sufficient influence to obtain one.

"Get up on all occasions, and sometimes on no occasion at all, and make long-winded speeches, though composed of nothing else than wind. Talk of your devotion to your country, your modesty and disinterestedness, or on any such fanciful subject. Rail against taxes of all kinds, officeholders, and bad harvest weather; and wind up with a flourish about the heroes who fought and bled for our liberties in the times that tried men's souls. To be sure, you run the risk of being considered a bladder of wind, or an empty barrel. But never mind that; you will find enough of the same fraternity to keep you in countenance.

"If any charity be going forward, be at the top of it, provided it is to be advertised publicly. If not, it isn't worth your while. None but a fool would place his candle under a bushel on such an occasion.

"These few directions," said I, "if properly attended to, will do your business. And when once elected—why, a fig for the dirty children, the promises, the bridges, the churches, the taxes, the offices, and the subscriptions. For it is absolutely necessary to forget all these before you can become a thoroughgoing politician, and a patriot of the first water."

B. John Quincy Adams and the "Corrupt Bargain"

1. Adams Confers with Henry Clay (1824–1825)

In the free-for-all presidential campaign of 1824, the popular vote pushed General Jackson well ahead. Strung out behind were Secretary of State J. Q. Adams, Secretary of the Treasury William Crawford, and Speaker of the House Henry Clay, in that order. Since no candidate had won a majority in the Electoral College, the issue was thrown into the House of Representatives, with fourth-place Henry Clay eliminated. After a long private conference with Adams, Clay, a former foe, threw his potent support to Adams, who consequently was declared elected, on February 9, 1825. Three days later President-elect Adams formally offered Clay the secretaryship of state. Angry and suspicious Jacksonites promptly proclaimed that the secretaryship was a part of the "corrupt bargain" by which Adams had purchased the presidency of the United States. Do the following relevant excerpts from Adams's diary suggest that some kind of deal was entered into for Clay's support?

[December 15, 1824] [Edward] Wyer [confidential informant] came also to the office [State Department], and told me that he had it from good authority that Mr. Clay was much disposed to support me, if he could at the same time be useful to himself. . . . I had conversation at dinner with Mr. Clay.

[December 17, 1824, conversation with R. P. Letcher, member of the House of Representatives of Kentucky, Clay's state.] Letcher wished to know what my sentiments towards Clay were, and I told him without disguise that I harbored no hostility against him; that whatever of difference there had been between us had arisen altogether from him, and not from me. . . . He was sure Clay felt now no hostility to

---

[1]C. F. Adams, ed., *Memoirs of John Quincy Adams,* vol. 6 (Philadelphia: J. B. Lippincott & Co., 1875), pp. 444, 447, 457, 464–465.

me. He had spoken respectfully of me, and was a man of sincerity. . . . The drift of all Letcher's discourse was much the same as Wyer had told me, that Clay would willingly support me if he could thereby serve himself, and the substance of his *meaning* was, that if Clay's friends could *know* that he would have a prominent share in the administration, that might induce them to vote for me, even in the face of instructions. But Letcher did not profess to have any authority from Clay for what he said and he made no definite propositions. He spoke of his interview with me as altogether confidential, and in my answers to him I spoke in more general terms.

[January 1, 1825, after a public dinner.] He [Clay] told me [in a whisper] that he should be glad to have with me soon some confidential conversation upon public affairs. I said I should be happy to have it whenever it might suit his convenience.

[January 9, 1825.] Mr. Clay came at six, and spent the evening with me in a long conversation explanatory of the past and prospective of the future. He said that the time was drawing near when the choice must be made in the House of Representatives of a President from the three candidates presented by the electoral colleges; that he had been much urged and solicited with regard to the part in that transaction that he should take, and had not been five minutes landed at his lodgings before he had been applied to by a friend of Mr. Crawford's, in a manner so gross that it had disgusted him; that some of my friends also, disclaiming, indeed, to have any authority from me, had repeatedly applied to him, directly or indirectly, urging considerations personal to himself as motives to his cause.

He had thought it best to reserve for some time his determination to himself first, to give a decent time for his own funeral solemnities as a candidate; and, secondly, to prepare and predispose all his friends to a state of neutrality between the three candidates who would be before the House, so that they might be free ultimately to take that course which might be most conducive to the public interest. The time had now come at which he might be explicit in his communication with me, and he had for that purpose asked this confidential interview. He wished me, as far as I might think proper, to satisfy him with regard to some principles of great public importance, but without any personal considerations for himself. In the question to come before the House between General Jackson, Mr. Crawford, and myself, he had no hesitation in saying that his preference would be for me.

[At this point in his diary Adams, who was usually most painstaking, left a blank space, as though he intended to fill in later the details of the conversation. Dr. Samuel Flagg Bemis, his ablest biographer, states that "he let his conscience slip." On January 23, 1825, two weeks after the secret conference, Clay wrote to a correspondent that he believed he could enter the cabinet "in any situation" he desired. Both parties to the so-called corrupt bargain denied that they had made any specific deal. But politics being politics, some kind of informal understanding was almost certainly reached in advance; and it brought to the presidency a man who was not the people's choice. Dr. Bemis concluded that the so-called corrupt bargain was "the least questionable of the several deals" that Adams made to secure his election.]

2. Clay Protests His Innocence (1825)

Henry Clay, hard bitten by the presidential bug, probably would have favored Adams in any event. He had quarreled bitterly with General Jackson, who remained his lifelong foe. Crawford was now a paralytic wreck, unable to walk normally or speak distinctly. Clay readily perceived that if Jackson, a fellow westerner, entered the White House, the country probably would not stomach another westerner as his successor. In passages from two letters, the first to Francis P. Blair and the second to Francis Brooke, Clay thus unburdened himself. What was his ostensible reason for opposing Jackson? What was his attitude toward Adams? Do these statements support the contention that there was no "corrupt bargain"?

[January 29, 1825] The friends of [Jackson?] have turned upon me, and with the most amiable unanimity agree to vituperate me. . . . The knaves cannot comprehend how a man can be honest. They cannot conceive that I should have solemnly interrogated my conscience and asked it to tell me seriously what I ought to do. That it should have enjoined me not to establish the dangerous precedent of elevating, in this early stage of the Republic, a military chieftain, merely because he has won a great victory. That it should have told me that a public man is undeserving his station who will not, regardless of aspersions and calumnies, risk himself for his country.

I am afraid that you will think me moved by these abuses. Be not deceived. I assure you that I never in my whole life felt more perfect composure, more entire confidence in the resolutions of my judgment, and a more unshakable determination to march up to my duty. And, my dear sir, is there an intelligent and unbiased man who must not, sooner or later, concur with me?

Mr. Adams, you know well, I should never have selected, if at liberty to draw from the whole mass of our citizens for a President. But there is no danger in his elevation now, or in time to come. Not so of his competitor, of whom I cannot believe that killing two thousand five hundred Englishmen at New Orleans qualifies for the various, difficult, and complicated duties of the Chief Magistracy.

[February 4, 1825.] I observe what you kindly tell me about the future Cabinet. My dear sir, I want no office. When have I shown an avidity for office? In rejecting the mission to Russia and the Department of War under one administration? In rejecting the same Department, the mission to England, or any other foreign mission under the succeeding administration? If Mr. Adams is elected, I know not who will be his Cabinet; I know not whether I shall be offered a place in it or not. If there should be an offer, I shall decide upon it, when it may be made, according to my sense of duty. But do you not perceive that this denunciation of me, by anticipation, is a part of the common system between the discordant confederates which I have above described? Most certainly, if an office should be offered to me under the new administration, and I should be induced to think that I ought to accept it, I shall not be deterred from accepting it, either by the denunciations of open or secret enemies, or the hypocrisy of pretended friends.

---

[2]Calvin Colton, ed., *The Works of Henry Clay* (New York and London: G. P. Putnam's Sons, 1904), vol. 4, pp. 112–114.

C. The Renewal of the Tariff Controversy

1. Representative James Strong Pleads for Wool (1828)

Tarred at the outset by the so-called corrupt bargain, President Adams floundered from one embarrassment to another in domestic and foreign affairs. Most ominous of all for the Union was the frightening sectional clash over the Tariff of 1828 (the "Tariff of Abominations"). Designed largely as a measure to protect the wool grow- ers, it was pushed up to ridiculous heights by the logrollers and political schemers in Congress. President Adams nevertheless signed it, thereby adding further to his over- flowing cup of woes. Representative James Strong, from the wool-producing state of New York, presented his case as follows on the floor of the House of Representatives. What were his weakest and strongest arguments? Did the wool producer as well as the manufacturer need tariff protection?

What, then does the farmer require? What does he need, to enable him to pro- duce and to continue the production of wool? He obviously needs, and must have, a market. Has he any abroad? None. He must therefore look, and can look only, to the home market. Who makes this market? The manufacturer of woolen goods. No one else can make it. How is this market to be secured? By protecting the fabric; by keeping the spindle and shuttle in motion. Is there any other, and is not this the only way? Destroy all the woolen factories, and what would your wool be worth? Where the market? Who would buy?

It has been assumed in the course of this debate—and much of the argument has rested upon the assumption—that the interests of the wool grower and of the woolen manufacturer are separate, at variance, not common to each other, and that a high degree of protection to the manufacturer is rather an injury than a benefit to the producer of the wool. Sir, I think this wholly erroneous. It is plain to the com- monest understanding that, without the aid of machinery, wool, essential as it is to human comfort, would be of little use and of less value. . . .

It is conceded, even by the advocates of the bill as reported, that the manufac- ture of woolen goods is valuable to the country; that the business is depressed, and needs further protection. . . .

England is our greatest competitor; and the existence of her power essentially depends upon the spindle and the anvil. Who, then, can doubt that she would sac- rifice much in order to command a market like ours, in which the whole annual consumption of woolens, exclusive of household manufactures, is not less than twenty or twenty-five millions of dollars? The prostration of our woolen factories would give her this market. How can she accomplish it, in case the impost duty on woolens be too low? Why, sir, by adapting her goods to these low minimum points—forcing them into the country, and underselling our own manufacturers. In this way, a great foreign capital will be constantly acting upon a small American capital. The difference will be nearly as five hundred to one. The odds are fearful. The competition will be manifestly unequal. . . .

---

[1]*Congressional Debates* (1827–1828), vol. 4, part 2, cols. 2269–2270, 2273–2274 (April 10, 1828).

But it is alleged that the proposed duties, which are intended for the protection of our capital and industry, will tax and oppress the poor. Sir, it is true that an impost on an article not produced in the country, as on tea, for example, is a charge upon both the producer and the consumer. But, when the home manufacturer can, and does, supply the home market with any given article, no amount of impost will enhance its price, because the domestic competition will always keep it at the lowest rate for which it can be made, allowing to the maker a reasonable profit. This is a law of human labor that never varies.

2. A Carolinian Condemns the Tariff (1828)

Representative (later Senator) George McDuffie of South Carolina, an air-pawing orator of the old school, customarily packed the galleries with expectant listeners. Already hostile to protective duties, he assailed the towering "Tariff of Abominations" of 1828. He went so far as to advocate a prohibitory tax on northern goods, and in 1830 propounded the "forty-bale" theory—namely, that each southern cotton planter indirectly contributed forty bales out of every hundred to northern manufacturers because of tariff inequities. In this speech in the House of Representatives, how convincing was he in arguing that the North should join the South in fighting a protective tariff? Why was free trade to the advantage of the cotton grower?

Mr. Speaker, it is distressing to witness the kind of aristocratic influence by which measures of this sort are obviously controlled. I have witnessed, with astonishment and regret, as a strong proof of the aristocratic tendency of every system of government, the melancholy fact that intelligent and honorable men upon this floor, in whose Congressional districts there is perhaps a single manufactory of iron, owned by perhaps the very wealthiest man in the county, will give their votes, without the least compunction, to impose an odious and oppressive tax upon the remaining thousands of their poor constituents, to increase the profits of one wealthy nabob.

And yet, sir, we hear gentlemen very gravely talking about promoting the interest of "a whole state," when they are in the very act of imposing a tax upon the great body of the people of that very state. Such, for example, was the language used by the gentleman from Missouri, when urging the expediency of increasing the duty on lead; when, I will venture to say, one hundred of his constituents would feel the tax, where one of them would realize the bounty of such an imposition. And yet, sir, we talk about a democratic government, and the responsibility of the representative to the people!

I speak not the language of the demagogue, but the grave and solemn language of historical and philosophical truth, when I say that it is the very genius of this system, as exhibited in this and every other country, to tax the many and the poor for the benefit of the few and the wealthy.

---

[2]*Congressional Debates* (1827–1828), vol. 4, part 2, cols. 2401–2403 (April 19, 1828).

Take up the articles embraced in the scheme of protection, one by one, and I defy any man to point out a single one of them that does not specifically prove and illustrate the proposition I have laid down. Salt, for example, is an article of first necessity, equally consumed by the poor and the rich. The people of the United States now pay about 100 percent on ever bushel of salt they consume, amounting in the aggregate to a tax of at least a million and a half dollars, paid by all classes, for the exclusive benefit of the owners of some one or two hundred salt works, at the most. The same remark is strictly applicable to the duty on iron. It imposes a universal tax, both heavy and permanent, for the benefit of not more than one or two hundred ironmasters in the United States. . . .

. . . I, sir, complain of the duty upon sugar as much as any other member of the House. It is obnoxious [open], in a peculiar manner, to the objection I have urged against the duties on salt and iron. It is a tax on the great body of the people, for the benefit of some two or three hundred sugar planters, who are men of immense wealth. For the fact is notorious that the business is almost exclusively confined to large capitalists. Every family in the United States that consumes 33⅓ pounds of sugar pays a tax of one dollar to these wealthy monopolists. And I know a single individual—he is a personal friend—worth between two and three millions of dollars, who receives annually about $30,000 as his dividend of this national bounty.

Can there be a more striking proof of the injustice, and impolicy, and antirepublican tendency of this system? It imposes a tax of at least four millions five hundred thousand dollars upon the mass of the people in every state in the Union, for the sole and exclusive benefit of the ironmasters, sugar planters, and owners of salt works, not amounting, in the whole Union, to more than from five hundred to one thousand persons. And if we add all the owners of cotton and woolen manufactories in the United States, it would not swell the number to two thousand. . . .

. . . But sir, I shall be probably asked how it happens that the capitalists of the South, the wealthy cotton planters, are arrayed on the side of the great mass of the people in the contest between capital and labor? Have they more knowledge or more honesty than other capitalists? Sir, I set up no such pretension for them. We lay claim to no other intelligence and honesty than such as enables us to understand, and prompts us to defend, our own rights. I will not undertake to say that we might not be tempted to join this plundering expedition, if a tariff could be so regulated as to increase the price of cotton. But such is our position in this contest that our interest throws us into a natural alliance with the great body of the people in the farming states.

The wealthy cotton planter of the South fights by the side of the small farmer, the mechanic, the merchant, and the laborer, in New York and Pennsylvania, because they all have a similar interest in opposing a system of which the burden falls upon them and the benefit on others. . . . The Southern states, depending on free trade for their prosperity, must always be opposed to any attempts on the part of this government to build up, by commercial prohibitions, an aristocracy of favored monopolists.

Sir, this is not a contest as some are anxious to represent it, between the Southern and Northern states. It is a contest of less than one hundred thousand manufacturers and farmers against all the other farmers and manufacturers in the Union, and against the whole population in the Southern states.

D. The New Spirit of Enterprise in Jacksonian America

1. Justice Joseph Story Defends the Rights of Contract (1837)

In 1785 the Massachusetts legislature gave to a corporation called the Proprietors of the Charles River Bridge the right to build a bridge between Boston and Charlestown (see map). When the legislature in 1828 allowed a group of Charlestown merchants to build the Warren Bridge, the Proprietors of the Charles River Bridge sought an injunction to halt the construction of the new, competing bridge. They alleged that the charter for the Warren Bridge breached their original contract with the state and violated the contracts clause of the Constitution (Article I, section 10, clause 1). Daniel Webster argued the case for the Proprietors of the Charles River Bridge, charging that the new charter destroyed the vested property right of the original bridge company. A majority of the U.S. Supreme Court eventually ruled in favor of the new bridge company, but in a minority opinion, Justice Joseph Story invoked Webster's arguments to support his dissenting views. What are his principal points?

But it has been argued, and the argument has been pressed in every form which ingenuity could suggest, that if grants of this nature are to be construed liberally, as conferring any exclusive rights on the grantees, it will interpose an effectual barrier against all general improvements of the country. For myself, I profess not to feel the cogency of this argument, either in its general application to the grant of franchises or in its special application to the present grant. This is a subject upon which different minds may well arrive at different conclusions, both as to policy and principle. Men may, and will, complexionally differ upon topics of this sort according to their natural and acquired habits of speculation and opinion. For my own part, I can conceive of no surer plan to arrest all public improvements founded on private capital and enterprise that to make the outlay of that capital uncertain and questionable, both as to security and as to productiveness. No man will hazard his capital in any enterprise in which, if there be a loss, it must be borne exclusively by himself, and if there be success, he has not the slightest security of enjoying the rewards of that success for a single moment. If the government means to invite its citizens to enlarge the public comforts and conveniences, to establish bridges, or turnpikes, or canals, or railroads, there must be some pledge that the property will be safe, that the enjoyment will be coextensive with the grant, and that success will not be the signal of a general combination to overthrow its rights and to take away its profits. The very agitation of a question of this sort is sufficient to alarm every stockholder in every public enterprise of this sort throughout the whole country. Already, in my native State [Massachusetts], the Legislature has found it necessary expressly to concede the exclusive privilege here contended against in order to insure the accomplishment of a railroad for the benefit of the public. And yet we are told that all such exclusive grants are to the detriment of the public. . . .

---

[1]*Charles River Bridge* v. *Warren Bridge,* 36 U.S. 420, in Richard Peters, *Reports of Cases Argued and Adjudged in the Supreme Court of the United States* (New York: Banks Law Publishing Company, 1903), 11: 451–452.

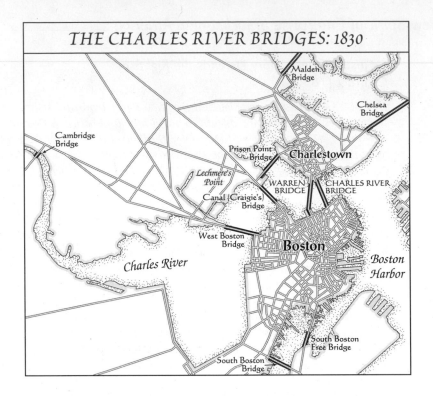

THE CHARLES RIVER BRIDGES: 1830

2. Chief Justice Roger B. Taney Supports "Creative Destruction" (1837)

Chief Justice Roger B. Taney, a Jackson appointee to the Supreme Court, wrote the majority opinion in the Charles River Bridge *case, basing his argument on legal, social, political, and economic principles that contrasted sharply with those of Justice Story. What are their major differences? What is the meaning of Taney's warning about the old corporations awakening from their sleep"? Taney's opinion is often said to have paved the way for the "creative destruction" of old businesses and old technologies. How might it have had that effect?*

And what would be the fruits of this doctrine of implied contracts, on the part of the states, and of property in a line of travel, by a corporation, if it would now be sanctioned by this court? To what results would it lead us? If it is to be found in the charter to this bridge, the same process of reasoning must discover it, in the various acts which have been passed, within the last forty years, for turnpike companies. And what is to be the extent of the privileges of exclusion on the different sides of

Map used by permission from Stanley I. Kutler, *Privilege and Creative Destruction.* Copyright © 1990 by Johns Hopkins University Press.
[2]*Charles River Bridge* v. *Warren Bridge,* 36 U.S. 420, in Richard Peters, Reports of Cases Argued and Adjudged in the Supreme Court of the United States (New York: Banks Law Publishing Company, 1903), 11: 552–553.

the road? The counsel who have so ably argued this case, have not attempted to define it by any certain boundaries. How far must the new improvement be distant from the old one? How near may you approach, without invading its rights in the privileged line? If this court should establish the principles now contended for, what is to become of the numerous railroads established on the same line of travel with turnpike companies; and which have rendered the franchises of the turnpike corporations of no value? Let it once be understood, that such charters carry with them these implied contracts, and give this unknown and undefined property in a line of travelling; and you will soon find the old turnpike corporations awakening from their sleep, and calling upon this court to put down the improvements which have taken their place. The millions of property which have been invested in railroads and canals, upon lines of travel which had been before occupied by turnpike corporations, will be put in jeopardy. We shall be thrown back to the improvements of the last century, and obliged to stand still, until the claims of the old turnpike corporations shall be satisfied; and they shall consent to permit these states to avail themselves of the lights of modern science, and to partake of the benefit of those improvements which are now adding to the wealth and prosperity, and the convenience and comfort, of every other part of the civilized world. Nor is this all. This court will find itself compelled to fix, by some arbitrary rule, the width of this new kind of property in a line of travel; for if such a right of property exists, we have no lights to guide us in marking out its extent, unless, indeed, we resort to the old feudal grants, and to the exclusive rights of ferries, by prescription, between towns; and are prepared to decide that when a turnpike road from one town to another, had been made, no railroad or canal, between these two points, could afterwards be established. This court are not prepared to sanction principles which must lead to such results. . . .

E. The Debate on Internal Improvements

1. Jackson Vetoes the Maysville Road Bill (1830)

Although Jackson generally looked favorably on internal improvements, he vetoed a bill in 1830 providing for a government subscription of stock, in the amount of $150,000, in a company that proposed to build a sixty-mile road near Maysville, Kentucky. Jackson's veto message offered some thoughtful commentary on the question of federal-state relationships and on the general role of government in society. His action also stung his political rival Henry Clay, whose home state of Kentucky would have benefited directly from the legislation. In the following excerpt from Jackson's veto message, how does he defend his states' rights philosophy?

May 27, 1830.

To the House of Representatives

Gentlemen: I have maturely considered the bill proposing to authorize "a subscription of stock in the Maysville, Washington, Paris, and Lexington Turnpike Road

---

[1]J. D. Richardson, ed., *Messages and Papers of the Presidents* (1897), vol. 3, pp. 1046–1055.

Company," and now return the same to the House of Representatives, in which it originated, with my objections to its passage. . . .

Although many of the States, with a laudable zeal and under the influence of an enlightened policy, are successfully applying their separate efforts to works of this character, the desired to enlist the aid of the General Government in the construction of such as from their nature ought to devolve upon it, and to which the means of the individual States are inadequate, is both rational and patriotic, and if that desire is not gratified now it does not follow that it never will be. The general intelligence and public spirit of the American people furnish a sure guaranty that at the proper time this policy will be made to prevail under circumstances more auspicious to its successful prosecution than those which now exist. But great as this object undoubtedly is, it is not the only one which demands the fostering care of the Government. The preservation and success of the republican principle rest with us. To elevate its character and extend its influence rank among our most important duties, and the best means to accomplish this desirable end are those which will rivet the attachment of our citizens to the Government of their choice by the comparative lightness of their public burthens and by the attraction which the superior success of its operations will present to the admiration and respect of the world. Through the favor of an overruling and indulgent Providence our country is blessed with general prosperity and our citizens exempted from the pressure of taxation, which other less favored portions of the human family are obliged to bear; yet it is true that many of the taxes collected from our citizens through the medium of imposts have for a considerable period been onerous. In many particulars these taxes have borne severely upon the laboring and less prosperous classes of the community, being imposed on the necessaries of life, and this, too, in cases where the burthen was not relieved by the consciousness that it would ultimately contribute to make us independent of foreign nations for articles of prime necessity by the encouragement of their growth and manufacture at home. They have been cheerfully borne because they were thought to be necessary to the support of Government and the payment of the debts unavoidably incurred in the acquisition and maintenance of our national rights and liberties. But have we a right to calculate on the same cheerful acquiescence when it is known that the necessity for their continuance would cease were it not for irregular, improvident, and unequal appropriations of the public funds? Will not the people demand, as they have a right to do, such a prudent system of expenditure as will pay the debts of the Union and authorize the reduction of every tax to as low a point as the wise observance of the necessity to protect that portion of our manufactures and labor whose prosperity is essential to our national safety and independence will allow? When the national debt is paid, the duties upon those articles which we do not raise may be repealed with safety, and still leave, I trust, without oppression to any section of the country, an accumulating surplus fund, which may be beneficially applied to some well-digested system of improvement.

Under this view the question as to the manner in which the Federal Government can or ought to embark in the construction of roads and canals, and the extent to which it may impose burthens on the people for these purposes, may be presented on its own merits, free of all disguise and of every embarrassment, except such as may arise from the Constitution itself. Assuming these suggestions to be correct, will not our constituents require the observance of a course by which they can be effected? Ought they not to require it? With the best disposition to aid, as far as I can conscientiously, in furtherance of works of internal improvement, my opinion is that the soundest views of national policy at this time point to such a course. Besides the avoidance of an evil influence upon the local concerns of the country, how solid is the advantage which the Government will reap from it in the elevation of its character! How gratifying the effect of presenting to the world the sublime spectacle of a Republic of more than 12,000,000 happy people, in the fifty-fourth year of her existence, after having passed through two protracted wars—the one for the acquisition and the other for the maintenance of liberty—free from debt and with all her immense resources unfettered! What a salutary influence would not such an exhibition exercise upon the cause of liberal principles and free government throughout the world! Would we not ourselves find in its effect an additional guaranty that our political institutions will be transmitted to the most remote posterity without decay? A course of policy destined to witness events like these can not be benefited by a legislation which tolerates a scramble for appropriations that have no relation to any general system of improvement, and whose good effects must of necessity be very limited. . . .

This subject has been one of much, and, I may add, painful, reflection to me. It has bearings that are well calculated to exert a powerful influence upon our hitherto prosperous system of government, and which, on some accounts, may even excite despondency in the breast of an American citizen. I will not detain you with professions of zeal in the cause of internal improvements. If to be their friend is a virtue which deserves commendation, our country is blessed with an abundance of it, for I do not suppose there is an intelligent citizen who does not wish to see them flourish. But though all are their friends, but few, I trust, are unmindful of the means by which they should be promoted; none certainly are so degenerate as to desire their success at the cost of that sacred instrument with the preservation of which is indissolubly bound our country's hopes. If different impressions are entertained in any quarter; if it is expected that the people of this country, reckless of their constitutional obligations, will prefer their local interest to the principles of the Union, such expectations will in the end be disappointed; or if it be not so, then indeed has the world but little to hope from the example of free government. When an honest observance of constitutional compacts can not be obtained from communities like ours, it need not be anticipated elsewhere, and the cause in which there has been so much martyrdom, and from which so much was expected by the friends of liberty, may be abandoned, and the degrading truth that man is unfit for self-government admitted. And this will be the case if *expediency* be made a rule of construction in interpreting the Constitution. Power in no government could desire a better shield for the insidious advances which it is ever ready to make upon the checks that are designed to restrain its action. . . .

If it be the desire of the people that the agency of the Federal Government should be confined to the appropriation of money in aid of such undertakings, in virtue of State authorities, then the occasion, the manner, and the extent of the appropriations should be made the subject of constitutional regulation. This is the more necessary in order that they may be equitable among the several States, promote harmony between different sections of the Union and their representatives, preserve other parts of the Constitution from being undermined by the exercise of doubtful powers or the too great extension of those which are not so, and protect the whole subject against the deleterious influence of combinations to carry by concert measures which, considered by themselves, might meet but little countenance.

That a constitutional adjustment of this power upon equitable principles is in the highest degree desirable can scarcely be doubted, nor can it fail to be promoted by every sincere friend to the success of our political institutions. In no government are appeals to the source of power in cases of real doubt more suitable than in ours. No good motive can be assigned for the exercise of power by the constituted authorities, while those for whose benefit it is to be exercised have not conferred it and may not be willing to confer it. It would seem to me that an honest application of the conceded powers of the General Government to the advancement of the common weal present a sufficient scope to satisfy a reasonable ambition. The difficult and supposed impracticability of obtaining an amendment of the Constitution in this respect is, I firmly believe, in a great degree unfounded. The time has never yet been when the patriotism and intelligence of the American people were not fully equal to the greatest exigency, and it never will when the subject calling forth their interposition is plainly presented to them. To do so with the questions involved in this bill, and to urge them to an early, zealous, and full consideration of their deep importance, is, in my estimation, among the highest of our duties.

Andrew Jackson

2. Clay Protests (1830)

Henry Clay blasted Jackson's veto message in the following speech. What were his principal points? To what extent was his dispute with Jackson a matter of principle, and to what extent was it a matter of politics?

If any thing could be considered as settled under the present Constitution of our Government, I had supposed that it was its authority to construct such internal improvements as may be deemed by Congress necessary and proper to carry into effect the power granted to it. For near twenty-five years the power has been asserted and exercised by the Government. For the last fifteen years it has been often controverted in Congress, but it has been invariably maintained in that body, by repeated decisions, pronounced after full and elaborate debate, and at intervals of time implying the greatest deliberation. Numerous laws attest the existence of the power, and no less than twenty-odd laws have been passed in relation to a single work. This power, necessary to all parts of the Union, is indispensable to the West. Without it, this section can never enjoy any part of the benefit of a regular disbursement of the vast revenues of the United States. . . .

If I could believe that the Executive message which was communicated to Congress, upon the application of the Veto to the Maysville Road, really expressed the opinion of the President of the United States, in consequence of the unfortunate re-

---

[2]Speech by Henry Clay before the Mechanics' Collation in the Apollonian Garden in Cincinnati, August 3, 1830. Recorded in the *Daily National Intelligencer,* September 1, 1830.

lations which have existed between us, I would forbear to make any observation upon it. It has his name affixed to it: but it is not every paper which bears the name of a distinguished personage, that is his own, or expresses his opinions. . . . It is impossible that the veto message should express the opinions of the President, and I prove it by evidence derived from himself. Not forty days before that message was sent to Congress, he approved a bill embracing appropriations to various objects of internal improvement, and among others, to improve the navigation of Conneaut Creek. Although somewhat acquainted with the geography of our country, I declare I did not know of the existence of such a stream until I read the bill. I have since made it an object of inquiry, and have been told that it rises in one corner of Pennsylvania, and is discharged into Lake Erie, in a corner of the State of Ohio; and that the utmost extent to which its navigation is suceptible of improvement is about seven miles! Is it possible that the President could conceive *that a National* object, and that the improvement of a great thoroughfare on which the mail is transported for some eight or ten States and Territories is not of National consideration? The power to improve the navigation of water courses, no where expressly recognized in the Constitution, is infinitely more doubtful than the establishment of mail roads, which is explicitly authorized in that instrument! . . .

The Veto Message is perfectly irreconcilable with the previous acts, votes, and opinions of General Jackson. It does not express *his* opinions, but those of his advisers and counsellors, and especially those of his Cabinet. . . .

Let us glance at a few only of the reasons, if reasons they can be called, of this piebald Message. The first is, that the exercise of the power has produced discord, and to restore harmony to the National Councils, it should be abandoned, or, which is tantamount, the Constitution must be amended. The President is therefore advised to throw himself into the minority. Well; did that revive harmony?—When the question was taken in the House of the people's Representatives, an obstinate majority still voted for the bill, the objections in the Message notwithstanding. And in the Senate, the Representatives of the States, a refractory majority stood unmoved. But does this Message mean to assert that no great measure about which public sentiment is much divided, ought to be adopted in consequence of that division? Then none can ever be adopted. . . . The principle is nothing more or less than a declaration that the right of the majority to govern, must be yielded to the perseverance, respectability, and numbers, of the minority. It is in keeping with the nullifying doctrines of South Carolina. . . .

The Veto Message proceeds to insist that the Maysville and Lexington Road is not a national but a local road of sixty miles in length, and confined within the limits of a particular State. If, as that document also asserts, the power can in *no case* be exercised until it shall have been explained and defined by an amendment of the Constitution, the discrimination of national and local roads would seem to be altogether unnecessary. What is or is not a national road the message supposes may admit of controversy, and is not susceptible of precise definition. The difficulty which its authors imagine, grows out of their attempt to substitute a rule, founded upon the extent and locality of the road, instead of the *use* and *purposes* to which it is applicable. If the road facilitates, in a considerable degree, the transportation of the mail to a considerable portion of the Union, and at the same time promotes internal commerce among the several States, and may tend to accelerate the movements of armies, and the distribution of the munitions of war, it is of national consideration. Tested by this, the true rule, the Maysville Road was undoubtedly national. It connects the largest body, perhaps, of fertile land in the Union, with the navigation of the Ohio and Mississippi rivers, and with the canals of the States of Ohio, Pennsylvania, and New York. It begins on the line which divides the States of Ohio and Kentucky, and of course, quickens trade and intercourse between them. Tested by the character of other works, for which the President, as a Senator, voted, or which were approved by him only about a month before he rejected the Maysville Bill, the road was undoubtedly national.

F. The Webster-Hayne Debate

1. Senator Robert Hayne Advocates Nullification (1830)

The restrictive "Tariff of Abominations" of 1828 had angered the South, especially the South Carolinians, who protested vehemently against an "unconstitutional" tax levied indirectly on them to support "greedy" Yankee manufacturers. An eruption finally occurred in the Senate when Senator Robert Y. Hayne of South Carolina—fluent, skillful, and personally attractive—attacked New England's inconsistency, greed, and selfishness, notably during the War of 1812. The only way to resist usurpations by the federal government, Hayne insisted, was for the states to nullify unauthorized acts of Congress, as foreshadowed by Jefferson in the Kentucky Resolutions of 1798–1799 (see page 198). In this peroration of his impressive speech, is Hayne a disunionist? Was he willing to let the Supreme Court rule on the unconstitutionality of acts of Congress?

Thus it will be seen, Mr. President, that the South Carolina doctrine [of nullification] is the [Jeffersonian] Republican doctrine of 1798; that it was first promulgated by the Fathers of the Faith; that it was maintained by Virginia and Kentucky in the worst of times; that it constituted the very pivot on which the political revolution of that day turned; that it embraces the very principles the triumph of which at that time saved the Constitution at its last gasp, and which New England statesmen were not unwilling to adopt [at Hartford in 1814] when they believed themselves to be the victims of unconstitutional legislation.

Sir, as to the doctrine that the federal government is the exclusive judge of the extent as well as the limitations of its powers, it seems to me to be utterly subversive of the sovereignty and independence of the states. It makes but little difference in my estimation whether Congress or the Supreme Court are invested with this power. If the federal government in all or any of its departments is to prescribe the limits of its own authority, and the states are bound to submit to the decision and are not allowed to examine and decide for themselves when the barriers of the Con-

---

[1]*Register of Debates in Congress* (1829–1830), vol. 6, part 1, p. 58 (January 25, 1830).

stitution shall be overleaped, this is practically "a government without limitation of powers." The states are at once reduced to mere petty corporations and the people are entirely at your mercy.

I have but one word more to add. In all the efforts that have been made by South Carolina to resist the unconstitutional [tariff] laws which Congress has extended over them, she has kept steadily in view the preservation of the Union by the only means by which she believes it can be long preserved—a firm, manly, and steady resistance against usurpation.

The [tariff] measures of the federal government have, it is true, prostrated her interests, and will soon involve the whole South in irretrievable ruin. But even this evil, great as it is, is not the chief ground of our complaints. It is the principle involved in the contest—a principle which, substituting the discretion of Congress for the limitations of the Constitution, brings the states and the people to the feet of the federal government and leaves them nothing they can call their own.

Sir, if the measures of the federal government were less oppressive, we should still strive against this usurpation. The South is acting on a principle she has always held sacred—resistance to unauthorized taxation.

These, sir, are the principles which induced the immortal [John] Hampden to resist the payment [in 1637] of a tax of twenty shillings [to the English government]. Would twenty shillings have ruined his fortune? No! but the payment of half twenty shillings on the principle on which it was demanded would have made him a slave.

Sir, if in acting on these high motives, if animated by that ardent love of liberty which has always been the most prominent trait in the Southern character, we should be hurried beyond the bounds of a cold and calculating prudence, who is there with one noble and generous sentiment in his bosom that would not be disposed, in the language of [Edmund] Burke, to exclaim, "You must pardon something to the spirit of liberty!"

2. Daniel Webster Pleads for the Union (1830)

Daniel Webster, native son of New Hampshire and adopted son of Massachusetts, sprang to the defense of New England and the Union in a running debate with Hayne that lasted two weeks and ranged over many subjects. The crowded Senate galleries thrilled to the eloquence of the two parliamentary gladiators, as the states' rightism of the South clashed head-on with the buoyant nationalism of the North. Webster's main points were that the people and not the states had formed the Constitution of 1787 (here he was historically shaky), that although the people were sovereign, the national government was supreme in its sphere and the state governments were supreme in their spheres; that if each of the twenty-four states could defy the laws of Congress at will, there would be no Union but only "a rope of sand"; and that there was a better solution than nullification if the people disapproved of their fundamental law. What was it? In Webster's magnificent peroration, memorized by countless nineteenth-century schoolchildren, are liberty and Union mutually incompatible? What objective did Webster and Hayne have in common?

---

[2]*The Works of Daniel Webster,* 20th ed. (Boston: Little, Brown and Company, 1890), vol. 3, pp. 340–342 (January 26, 1830).

If anything be found in the national Constitution, either by original provision or subsequent interpretation, which ought not to be in it, the people know how to get rid of it. If any construction be established, unacceptable to them, so as to become, practically, a part of the Constitution, they will amend it, at their sovereign pleasure. But while the people choose to maintain it as it is—while they are satisfied with it, and refuse to change it—who has given, or who can give, to the state legislatures a right to alter it, either by interference, construction, or otherwise? . . .

I profess, sir, in my career, hitherto, to have kept steadily in view the prosperity and honor of the whole country, and the preservation of our Federal Union. It is to that Union we owe our safety at home and our consideration and dignity abroad. It is to that Union that we are chiefly indebted for whatever makes us most proud of our country.

That Union we reached only by the discipline of our virtues in the severe school of adversity. It had its origin in the necessities of disordered finance, prostrate commerce, and ruined credit. Under its benign influence, these great interests immediately awoke us from the dead and sprang forth with newness of life. Every year of its duration has teemed with fresh proofs of its utility and its blessings; and although our territory has stretched out wider and wider, and our population spread farther and farther, they have not outrun its protection or its benefits. It has been to us all a copious fountain of national, social, and personal happiness.

I have not allowed myself, sir, to look beyond the Union to see what might lie hidden in the dark recess behind. I have not coolly weighed the chances of preserving liberty when the bonds that unite us together shall be broken asunder. I have not accustomed myself to hang over the precipice of disunion to see whether, with my short sight, I can fathom the depth of the abyss below. Nor could I regard him as a safe counselor in the affairs of this government whose thoughts should be mainly bent on considering not how the Union should be best preserved, but how tolerable might be the condition of the people when it shall be broken up and destroyed.

While the Union lasts we have high, exciting, gratifying prospects spread out before us—for us and our children. Beyond that, I seek not to penetrate the veil. God grant that in my day, at least, that curtain may not rise! God grant that, on my vision, never may be opened what lies behind!

When my eyes shall be turned to behold, for the last time, the sun in heaven, may I not see him shining on the broken and dishonored fragments of a once glorious Union; on states dissevered, discordant, belligerent; on a land rent with civil feuds, or drenched, it may be, in fraternal blood! Let their last feeble and lingering glance rather behold the gorgeous ensign of the Republic, now known and honored throughout the earth, still full high advanced, its arms and trophies streaming in their original luster, not a stripe erased or polluted, not a single star obscured, bearing for its motto no such miserable interrogatory as "What is all this worth?" nor those other words of delusion and folly, "Liberty first and Union afterward"; but everywhere, spread all over in characters of living light, blazing on all its ample folds, as they float over the sea and over the land, and in every wind under the whole heavens, that other sentiment, dear to every true American heart—Liberty *and* Union, now and forever, one and inseparable!

Thought Provokers

1. Is it true that the coming of universal manhood suffrage made for better government? Comment. Macaulay said, "The only way in which to fit a people for self-government is to entrust them with self-government." Comment. Metternich said, "Ten million ignorances do not constitute one knowledge." Comment.

2. In reference to the "corrupt bargain," is it possible to succeed in politics without stooping to unsavory deals?

3. How would subsequent American history have been changed if a protective tariff could have raised the price of cotton?

4. With reference to the New Democracy, it has been said that once we start counting heads, we have to educate them. Comment. Does democracy have more to fear from ingrown bureaucrats or from inexperienced zealots holding office? It has been said that ignorance is more of a menace to American democracy than corruption and graft. Comment. Jefferson said, "Whenever a man has cast a longing eye on offices, a rottenness begins in his conduct." Comment.

5. In what ways did Justice Taney's decision in the *Charles River Bridge* case reflect the economic philosophy of Jacksonian democracy?

6. Southern nullification did not succeed in the 1830s, yet it has been noted that informal nullification of unpopular federal laws, amendments, and court decisions has been going on for generations. Illustrate. What better or other safeguards have a minority of the states instituted against the "tyranny of the majority"?

14

Jacksonian Democracy at Flood Tide, 1830–1840

I consider, then, the power to annul a law of the
United States, assumed by one state, incompatible
with the existence of the Union, contradicted
expressly by the letter of the Constitution,
unauthorized by its spirit, inconsistent with every
principle on which it was founded, and destructive of
the great object for which it was formed.

Jackson's South Carolina Nullification Proclamation, 1832

Prologue: President Jackson, idol and champion of the Democratic masses, was
a direct-actionist. Resenting back talk from the states, he took a firm stand against
South Carolina during the anti-high-tariff nullification crisis of 1832–1833. The state
finally rescinded its nullification ordinance and gagged down the more reasonable
rates of the compromise tariff of 1833. Jackson engineered the brutal uprooting of
the southeastern Indian tribes to the western plains. Distrusting the monopolistic
Bank of the United States, he crippled it in 1832 with his scorching veto of a recharter bill, and then drove it to the wall. Ever popular with the poorer classes, Jackson
was triumphantly reelected over the Whig, Henry Clay, in 1832, with the bank issue
uppermost. Four years later "King Andrew" succeeded in enthroning his hand-
picked crown prince, the wire-pulling "American Talleyrand," Martin Van Buren. But
the paralyzing panic of 1837, triggered partly by Jackson's roughshod financial policies, blighted the unhappy four years of the Van Buren administration. Meanwhile,
mass-based, organized political parties had emerged (Democrats and Whigs)—
something new in American experience.

A. The Nullification Crisis

1. South Carolina Threatens Secession (1832)

*As if detonated by a delayed-action fuse, the tariff issue exploded during the Jackson-
Clay campaign. The recent tariff act of 1832, though watering down the "abom-*

---

[1]*Daily National Intelligencer* (Washington), December 7, 1832.

*inable" Tariff of 1828, aroused the South Carolinians by its reassertion of the pro-
tective principle. Excitedly summoning a special convention in Columbia, they
formally declared that the two tariff acts "are unauthorized by the Constitution
of the United States, and violate the true meaning and intent thereof, and are
null, void, and no law, nor binding upon this State, its officers or citizens. . . ." The
convention specifically forbade the enforcement of the federal tariff within the
borders of the state, and bluntly threatened secession if the federal government
employed force. Before adjourning, the delegates issued the following public appeal to the American people. Comment critically on the assumption that the other
southern states would have to follow South Carolina in dissolving the Union and
that the tariff law was unconstitutional. Were the South Carolinians acting in
earnest?*

If South Carolina should be driven out of the Union, all the other planting states,
and some of the Western states, would follow by an almost absolute necessity. Can
it be believed that Georgia, Mississippi, Tennessee, and even Kentucky, would
continue to pay a tribute of 50 percent upon their consumption to the Northern
states, for the privilege of being united to them, when they could receive all
their supplies through the ports of South Carolina without paying a single cent for
tribute?

The separation of South Carolina would inevitably produce a general dissolution of the Union, and, as a necessary consequence, the protecting system, with all
its pecuniary bounties to the Northern states, and its pecuniary burdens upon the
Southern states, would be utterly overthrown and demolished, involving the ruin of
thousands and hundreds of thousands in the manufacturing states. . . .

With them, it is a question merely of pecuniary interest, connected with no
shadow of right, and involving no principle of liberty. With us, it is a question involving our most sacred rights—those very rights which our common ancestors left
to us as a common inheritance, purchased by their common toils, and consecrated
by their blood. It is a question of liberty on the one hand, and slavery on the other.

If we submit to this system of unconstitutional oppression, we shall voluntarily
sink into slavery, and transmit that ignominious inheritance to our children. We will
not, we cannot, we dare not submit to this degradation; and our resolve is fixed and
unalterable that a protecting tariff shall be no longer enforced within the limits of
South Carolina. We stand upon the principles of everlasting justice, and no human
power shall drive us from our position.

We have not the slightest apprehension that the General Government will attempt to force this system upon us by military power. We have warned our brethren
of the consequences of such an attempt. But if, notwithstanding, such a course of
madness should be pursued, we here solemnly declare that this system of oppression shall never prevail in South Carolina, until none but slaves are left to submit to
it. We would infinitely prefer that the territory of the state should be the cemetery of
freemen than the habitation of slaves. Actuated by these principles, and animated by
these sentiments, we will cling to the pillars of the temple of our liberties, and, if it
must fall, we will perish amidst the ruins.

2. Andrew Jackson Denounces Nullification (1832)

South Carolina's defiance of the federal government, combined with its feverish military preparations, angered its most famous native son, Commander-in-Chief General Andrew Jackson. Privately he issued orders to strengthen federal forces in Charleston harbor. Five days after his resounding reelection over Clay, he issued the following proclamation (ghostwritten by Secretary of State Edward Livingston) appealing to the Carolinians to forsake the treacherous paths of nullification and disunion. Is his appeal to practicalities more convincing than that to patriotism? Was he prepared to negotiate with the South Carolinians?

For what would you exhange your share in the advantages and honor of the Union? For the dream of a separate independence—a dream interrupted by bloody conflicts with your neighbors and a vile dependence on a foreign power.

If your leaders could succeed in establishing a separation, what would be your situation? Are you united at home? Are you free from the apprehension of civil discord, with all its fearful consequences? Do our neighboring [Latin American] republics, every day suffering some new revolution or contending with some new insurrection, do they excite your envy?

But the dictates of a high duty oblige me solemnly to announce that you cannot succeed. The laws of the United States must be executed. I have no discretionary power on the subject; my duty is emphatically pronounced in the Constitution. Those who told you that you might peaceably prevent their execution deceived you; they could not have been deceived themselves. They know that a forcible opposition could alone prevent the execution of the laws, and they know that such opposition must be repelled. Their object is disunion.

But be not deceived by names. Disunion by armed force is treason. Are you really ready to incur its guilt? If you are, on the heads of the instigators of the act be the dreadful consequences; on their heads be the dishonor, but on yours may fall the punishment. On your unhappy state will inevitably fall all the evils of the conflict you force upon the government of your country. . . . The consequence must be fearful for you, distressing to your fellow citizens here and to the friends of good government throughout the world.

Its enemies have beheld our prosperity with a vexation they could not conceal. It was a standing refutation of their slavish doctrines, and they will point to our discord with the triumph of malignant joy. It is yet in your power to disappoint them. There is yet time to show that the descendants of the Pinckneys, the Sumters, the Rutledges, and of the thousand other names which adorn the pages of your Revolutionary history will not abandon that Union to support which so many of them fought and bled and died.

I adjure you, as you honor their memory, as you love the cause of freedom, to which they dedicated their lives, as you prize the peace of your country, the lives of its best citizens, and your own fair fame, to retrace your steps. Snatch from the archives of your state the disorganizing edict of its convention; bid its members to

---

[2]J. D. Richardson, ed., *Messages and Papers of the Presidents* (1896), vol. 2, pp. 654–655.

reassemble and promulgate the decided expressions of your will to remain in the path which alone can conduct you to safety, prosperity, and honor.

3. Jackson Fumes in Private (1832)

The Unionists of South Carolina, constituting perhaps two-fifths of the adult whites, were branded "submissionists, cowards, and Tories" by the nullifiers. But the Union men, undaunted, hanged John C. Calhoun and Governor James Hamilton, Jr. in effigy, held their own convention, and gathered weapons for their defense. One of their leaders in organizing the militia, Joel R. Poinsett, wrote of his activities to Jackson, even though the post office was infiltrated with nullifiers. The doughty general replied as follows in a letter whose original spelling, punctuation, and capitalization are here preserved as revealing of Jackson and his era. Article III, Section III of the Constitution states: "Treason against the United States shall consist only in levying war against them, or in adhering to their enemies, giving them aid and comfort." Was Jackson correct in branding the actions of the Carolinians treasonous? Was he more bellicose in this private letter than in his recently published proclamation?

Washington, December 9, 1832.

My D'r Sir, Your letters were this moment recd, from the hands of Col. Drayton, read and duly considered, and in haste I reply. The true spirit of patriotism that they breath fills me with pleasure. If the Union party unite with you, heart and hand in the text you have laid down, you will not only preserve the union, but save our native state, from that ruin and disgrace into which her treasonable leaders have attempted to plunge her. All the means in my power, I will employ to enable her own citizens, those faithful patriots, who cling to the Union to put it down.

The proclamation I have this day Issued, and which I inclose you, will give you my views, of the treasonable conduct of the convention and the Governors reccommendation to the assembly—it is not merely rebellion, but the act of raising troops, positive treason, and I am assured by all the members of congress with whom I have conversed that I will be sustained by congress. If so, I will meet it at the threshold, and have the leaders arrested and arraigned for treason—I am only waiting to be furnished with the acts of your Legislature, to make a communication to Congress, ask the means necessary to carry my proclamation into compleat affect, and by an exemplary punishment of those leaders for treason so unprovoked, put down this rebellion, and strengthen our happy government both at home and abroad.

My former letter and the communication from the Dept. of War, will have informed you of the arms and equipments having been laid in Deposit subject to your requisition, to aid the civil authority in the due execution of the law, *whenever called on as the posse comitatus,* etc. etc.

---

[3]J. S. Bassett, ed., *Correspondence of Andrew Jackson* (Washington, D.C.: The Carnegie Institution, 1929), Vol. 4, p. 39 (May 30, 1829). Reprinted by permission of the Carnegie Institution of Washington.

The vain threats of resistance by those who have raised the standard of rebellion shew their madness and folly. You may assure those patriots who cling to their country, and this union, which alone secures our liberty prosperity and happiness, that in forty days, I can have within the limits of So. Carolina fifty thousand men, and in forty days more another fifty thousand—However potant the threat of resistance with only a population of 250,000 whites and nearly that double in blacks with our ships in the port to aid in the execution of our laws?—The wickedness, madness and folly of the leaders and the delusion of their followers in the attempt to destroy themselves and our union has not its paralel in the history of the world. The Union will be preserved. The safety of the republic, the supreme law, which will be promptly obeyed by me.

I will be happy to hear from you often, thro' Col. Mason or his son, if you think the postoffice unsafe I am with sincere respect

yr mo. obdt. servt.

[Jackson's stern words, both public and private, no doubt shook the South Carolinians. Supported by no other state, and riven by a Unionist minority, they finally came down off their high horse and accepted the lower schedules of the compromise Tariff of 1833.]

B. The War on the Bank

1. Jackson Vetoes the Bank Recharter (1832)

The charter of the Second Bank of the United States was due to expire in 1836. Senator Henry Clay, seeking a surefire issue in the presidential campaign of 1832 against Jackson, arranged in Congress for a premature recharter. The assumption was that if the president vetoed the bill, he would incur the wrath of the voters. But Jackson, his ire aroused, wielded the veto pen. He denounced the Bank as monopolistic, as the tool of a favored few stockholders, as a gold mine for certain foreign investors, as a citadel of special privilege, as a menace to basic liberties, and as unconstitutional to boot (although John Marshall's Surpeme Court had decreed otherwise, p. 200). Jackson also complained that an incomplete investigation by a House committee had recently uncovered questionable practices that needed further probing. Is Jackson, in this veto message, resorting to electioneering demagoguery? To what extent was he Jeffersonian in his views toward states' rights and the rich?

As the [Bank] charter had yet four years to run, and as a renewal now was not necessary to the successful prosecution of its business, it was to have been expected that the Bank itself, conscious of its purity and proud of its character, would have

---

[1]J. D. Richardson, ed., *Messages and Papers of the Presidents* (1896), vol. 2, pp. 589–590 (July 10, 1832).

withdrawn its application for the present, and demanded the severest scrutiny into all its transactions. . . .

The Bank is professedly established as an agent of the Executive Branch of the government, and its constitutionality is maintained on that ground. Neither upon the propriety of present action nor upon the provisions of this act was the Executive consulted. It has had no opportunity to say that it neither ends nor wants an agent clothed with such powers and favored by such exemptions. There is nothing in its legitimate functions which makes it necessary or proper. Whatever interest or influence, whether public or private, has given birth to this act, it cannot be found either in the wishes or necessities of the Executive Department, by which present action is deemed premature, and the powers conferred upon its agent not only unnecessary but dangerous to the government and country.

It is to be regretted that the rich and powerful too often bend the acts of government to their selfish purposes. Distinctions in society will always exist under every just government. Equality of talents, of education, or of wealth cannot be produced by human institutions. In the full enjoyment of the gifts of heaven and the fruits of superior industry, economy, and virtue, every man is equally entitled to protection by law.

But when the laws undertake to add to these natural and just advantages artificial distinctions, to grant titles, gratuities, and exclusive privileges, to make the rich richer and the potent more powerful, the humble members of society—the farmers, mechanics, and laborers—who have neither the time nor the means of securing like favors to themselves, have a right to complain of the injustice of their government.

There are no necessary evils in government. Its evils exist only in its abuses. If it would confine itself to equal protection, and, as heaven does its rains, shower its favors alike on the high and the low, the rich and the poor, it would be an unqualified blessing. In the act before me there seems to be a wide and unnecessary departure from these just principles.

Nor is our government to be maintained or our Union preserved by invasions of the rights and powers of the several states. In thus attempting to make our General Government strong, we make it weak. Its true strength consists of leaving individuals and states as much as possible to themselves—in making itself felt, not in its power, but in its beneficence; not in its control, but in its protection; not in binding the states more closely to the center, but leaving each to move unobstructed in its proper orbit.

Experience should teach us wisdom. Most of the difficulties our government now encounters, and most of the dangers which impend over our Union, have sprung from an abandonment of the legitimate objects of government by our national legislation, and the adoption of such principles as are embodied in this act. Many of our rich men have not been content with equal protection and equal benefits, but have besought us to make them richer by act of Congress. By attempting to gratify their desires we have in the results of our legislation arrayed section against section, interest against interest, and man against man, in a fearful commotion which threatens to shake the foundations of our Union.

2. A Boston Journal Attacks Jackson (1832)

The Bank of the United States, as Jackson charged, had undoubtedly wielded its vast power ruthlessly, arrogantly, and at times unscrupulously. Its numerous "loans" to public men had often resembled bribes. The pro-Jackson men hated it as a despotism of wealth. The pro-Bank men suspected, especially after the veto message, that Jackson was trying to establish a despotism of the masses, with himself as chief despot. Senator Daniel Webster, a paid counsel for the Bank, shared these fears. The Boston Daily Atlas, *a pro-Webster journal that was rapidly becoming the most influential Whig newspaper in New England, reacted with the following counterblast against Jackson's veto message. Which charge in this editorial would be most likely to arouse the anti-Jackson Whigs in the campaign then being fought between the Democrat Jackson and the Whig Clay?*

The Bank veto . . . is the most wholly radical and basely Jesuitical document that ever emanated from any administration, in any country.

It violates all our established notions and feelings. It arraigns Congress for not asking permission of the Executive before daring to legislate on the matter, and fairly intimates a design to save the two Houses in future from all such trouble.

It impudently asserts that Congress have acted prematurely, blindly, and without sufficient examination.

It falsely and wickedly alleges that the rich and powerful throughout the country are waging a war of oppression against the poor and the weak; and attempts to justify the President on the ground of its being his duty thus to protect the humble when so assailed.

Finally, it unblushingly denies that the Supreme Court is the proper tribunal to decide upon the constitutionality of the laws!!

The whole paper is a most thoroughgoing electioneering missile, intended to secure the madcaps of the South, and as such deserves the execration of all who love their country or its welfare.

This veto seems to be the production of the whole Kitchen Cabinet [an informal group of advisors to Jackson]—of hypocrisy and arrogance; of imbecility and talent; of cunning, falsehood, and corruption—a very firebrand, intended to destroy their opponents, but which now, thanks to Him who can bring good out of evil, bids fair to light up a flame that shall consume its vile authors.

If the doctrines avowed in this document do not arouse the nation, we shall despair that anything will, until the iron hand of despotism has swept our fair land, and this glorious Republic, if not wholly annihilated, shall have been fiercely shaken to its very foundations.

3. Cartooning the Banking Crisis (1833, 1837)

Andrew Jackson believed that the Bank of the United States was a corrupt pillar of privilege that must be destroyed. Yet when a national depression occurred shortly

---

[2]*Boston Daily Atlas,* quoted in the *Daily National Intelligencer* (Washington, D.C.), August 9, 1832.
[3]The Granger Collection, New York; Library of Congress, #USZ62-8844.

after the charter of the bank was revoked, many observers blamed Jackson's bank policy. In the first image below, Nicholas Biddle, ex-president of the Bank of America and president of the Bank of Pennsylvania, is shown holding the head of a violently ill "Mother Bank," while supporters of the bank—Clay, Calhoun, and Webster—consult in the sickroom, and Jackson peers in through the window. Where are the cartoonist's sympathies? The second image, The Times, *was created during the height of the financial panic of 1837. What does it portray as the worst effects of the panic? What views of the causes and consequences of Jackson's bank policies do these images provide?*

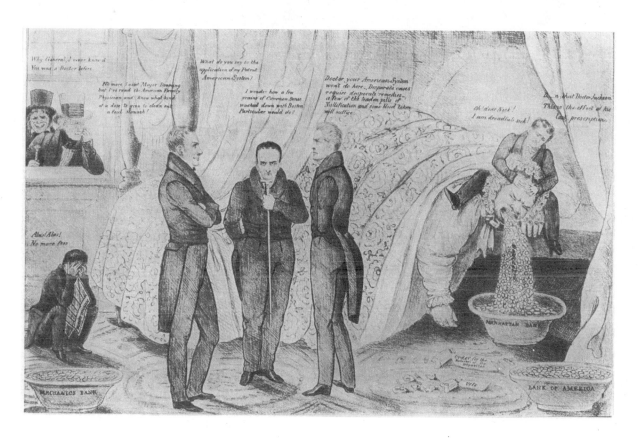

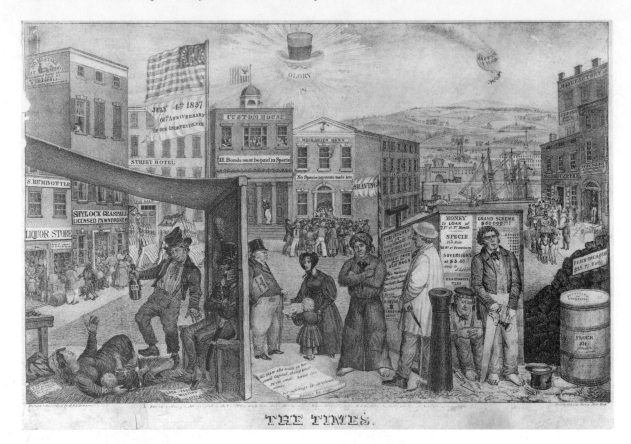

C. Transplanting the Tribes

1. Jackson Endorses the Indian Removal (1829)

By the 1820s the once "inexhaustible" land east of the Mississippi was filling up with white people, and the luckless Native Americans were being elbowed aside. In response to pressure to transplant the native tribes to a "permanent" home beyond the Mississippi River, Congress took under consideration the Indian Removal Bill. President Jackson threw his powerful weight behind the movement in the following section of his first annual message to Congress. What attitude toward Indians does Jackson's speech reveal?

The condition and ulterior destiny of the Indian tribes within the limits of some of our states have become objects of much interest and importance. It has long been the policy of government to introduce among them the arts of civilization, in the hope of gradually reclaiming them from a wandering life. This policy has, however,

---

[1]J. D. Richardson, ed., *Messages and Papers of the Presidents* (1896), vol. 2, pp. 456–459 (December 8, 1829).

been coupled with another wholly incompatible with its success. Professing a desire to civilize and settle them, we have at the same time lost no opportunity to purchase their lands and thrust them farther into the wilderness. By this means they have not only been kept in a wandering state, but been led to look upon us as unjust and indifferent to their fate. . . .

Our conduct toward these people is deeply interesting to our national character. Their present condition, contrasted with what they once were, makes a most powerful appeal to our sympathies. Our ancestors found them the uncontrolled possessors of these vast regions. By persuasion and force they have been made to retire from river to river and from mountain to mountain, until some of the tribes have become extinct and others have left but remnants to preserve for awhile their once terrible names. Surrounded by the whites with their arts of civilization, which, by destroying the resources of the savage, doom him to weakness and decay, the fate of the Mohegan, the Narragansett, and the Delaware is fast overtaking the Choctaw, the Cherokee, and the Creek. That this fate surely awaits them if they remain within the limits of the states does not admit of a doubt. Humanity and national honor demand that every effort should be made to avert so great a calamity. . . .

As a means of effecting this end, I suggest for your consideration the propriety of setting apart an ample district west of the Mississippi, and without [outside] the limits of any state or territory now formed, to be guaranteed to the Indian tribes as long as they shall occupy it, each tribe having a distinct control over the portion designated for its use. There they may be secured in the enjoyment of governments of their own choice, subject to no other control from the United States than such as may be necessary to preserve peace on the frontier and between the several tribes. There the benevolent may endeavor to teach them the arts of civilization, and, by promoting union and harmony among them, to raise up an interesting commonwealth, destined to perpetuate the race and to attest the humanity and justice of this government.

This emigration should be voluntary, for it would be as cruel as unjust to compel the aborigines to abandon the graves of their fathers and seek a home in a distant land. But they should be distinctly informed that if they remain within the limits of the states they must be subject to their laws.

2. Theodore Frelinghuysen Champions Justice (1830)

Senator Theodore Frelinghuysen, a distinguished New Jersey lawyer and later president of Rutgers College, shone so prominently as a lay leader as to be dubbed "the Christian statesman." Respected by both Whigs and Democrats in Congress, he gained nationwide recognition as a result of his magnificent six-hour speech opposing the Indian removal. To what extent were his arguments valid insofar as they related to law, justice, and humanity? Why did they not prevail?

I now proceed to the discussion of those principles which, in my humble judgment, fully and clearly sustain the claims of the Indians to all their political and civil

---

[2]*Register of Debates in Congress,* 21st Congress, 1st session, vol. 6, part 1, pp. 311–312, 318.

rights, as by them asserted. And here I insist that, by immemorial possession, as the original tenants of the soil, they hold a title beyond and superior to the British Crown and her colonies, and to all adverse pretensions of our Confederation and subsequent Union. God, in his Providence, planted these tribes on this western continent, so far as we know, before Great Britain herself had a political existence. . . .

In the light of natural law, can a reason for a distinction exist in the mode of enjoying that which is my own? If I use it for hunting, may another take it because he needs it for agriculture? I am aware that some writers have, by a system of artificial reasoning, endeavored to justify, or rather excuse, the encroachments made upon Indian territory; and they denominate these abstractions the law of nations, and in this ready way the question is despatched. Sir, as we trace the sources of this law, we find its authority to depend either upon the conventions or common consent of nations. And when, permit me to inquire, were the Indian tribes ever consulted on the establishment of such a law? . . .

Our ancestors found these people, far removed from the commotions of Europe, exercising all the rights and enjoying the privileges of free and independent sovereigns of this new world. . . . The white men, the authors of all their wrongs, approached them as friends . . . and, being then a feeble colony and at the mercy of the native tenants of the soil, by presents and profession propitiated their good will.

The Indian yielded a slow but substantial confidence; granted to the colonists an abiding place; and suffered them to grow up to man's estate beside him. He never raised the claim of elder title; as the white man's wants increased, he opened the hand of his bounty wider and wider.

By and by conditions are changed. His people melt away; his lands are constantly coveted; millions after millions [of acres] are ceded. The Indian bears it all meekly. He complains, indeed, as well he may, but suffers on. And now he finds that this neighbor, whom his kindness had nourished, has spread an adverse title over the last remains of his patrimony, barely adequate to his wants, and turns upon him and says, "Away! we cannot endure you so near us! These forests and rivers, these groves of your fathers, these firesides and hunting grounds are ours by the right of power and the force of numbers."

Sir, . . . I ask who is the injured and who is the aggressor? Let conscience answer, and I fear not the result. . . . Do the obligations of justice change with the color of the skin? Is it one of the prerogatives of the white man that he may disregard the dictates of moral principles when an Indian shall be concerned? No, sir. . . .

Sir, . . . if the contending parties were to exchange positions; place the white man where the Indian stands; load him with all these wrongs; and what path would his outraged feelings strike out for his career? . . . A few pence of duty on tea—that invaded no fireside, excited no fears, disturbed no substantial interest whatever— awakened in the American colonies a spirit of firm resistance. And how was the tea tax met, sir? Just as it should be. . . . We successfully and triumphantly contended for the very rights and privileges that our Indian neighbors now implore us to protect and to preserve to them.

Sir, this thought invests the subject under debate with most singular and momentous interest. We, whom God has exalted to the very summit of prosperity— whose brief career forms the brightest page in history; the wonder and praise of the world; freedom's hope and her consolation—we, about to turn traitors to our principles and our fame, about to become the oppressors of the feeble and to cast away our birthright! Sir, I hope for better things. . . .

The end, however, is to justify the means. "The removal of the Indian tribes to the west of the Mississippi is demanded by the dictates of humanity." This is a word of conciliating import. But it often makes its way to the heart under very doubtful titles, and its present claims deserve to be rigidly questioned. Who urges this plea? They who covet the Indian lands—who wish to rid themselves of a neighbor that they despise, and whose state pride is enlisted in rounding off their territories.

[The Indian Removal Bill passed Congress in 1830. The sequel was a sorry tale of greed, force, and fraud. Thousands of Indians of all ages and both sexes died on the tragic trek—perhaps as many as one-quarter of the sixty thousand from the South. Hostile tribes in the West often did not welcome the newcomers; and the new home lost its "permanency" as soon as unscrupulous whites found the land worth grabbing.]

D. The Van Buren Era

1. Davy Crockett Caricatures Martin Van Buren (1835)

Rifleman Davy Crockett, who perished at the Alamo early the next year (1836), permitted his name to be used by certain Whig politicians and ghost writers to cloak an anti-Jackson and anti-Van Buren campaign biography. A bitter foe of Jackson, Crockett feared that the "gin'ral," seeking vengeance against political foes, would "appoint" the "little gentleman" from New York as his successor. This, essentially, was what happened in the campaign of 1836. Which alleged trait of Van Buren did the Whigs seize upon most eagerly in this Crockett book?

Van Buren is as opposite to General Jackson as dung is to a diamond. Jackson is open, bold, warm-hearted, confiding, and passionate to a fault. Van Buren is secret, sly, selfish, cold, calculating, distrustful, treacherous; and if he could gain an object just as well by openness as intrigue, he would choose the latter. . . .

But there is one thing in which I think all will agree, that Martin Van Buren is not the man he is cracked up to be; and that if he is made President of the United States, he will have reached a place to which he is not entitled, either by sense or sincerity; and that he owes his good luck to the hangers-on of office, who, to serve themselves, have used the popularity of General Jackson to abuse the country with Martin Van Buren. . . .

A pleasant anecdote is related of him when he was quite young. It is truly like him, and planted the principle upon which he has acted ever since. A warmly con-

---

[1]David Crockett, *The Life of Martin Van Buren, Heir-Apparent to the "Government," and the Appointed Successor of General Andrew Jackson,* 16th ed. (Philadelphia: R. Wright, 1837), pp. 13, 20, 31–32.

tested election was coming on, and the friends on both sides, being men of influence, used great exertions, and became much excited; our hero applied to quite a knowing politician for his opinion as to the result. The answer expressing much doubt, young Martin, casting his eyes wishfully towards the ground, said, "I do wish I knew which party would succeed, as I want to take a side, but don't like to be in the minority."

2. Philip Hone Welcomes a Change (1837)

Balding little Martin Van Buren took the inaugural oath on March 4, 1837. Philip Hone, the wealthy New York Whig, though approving of Jackson's resolute stand against South Carolina, approved of little else done by "this terrible old man." Although he was a Whig, he expected better things of Van Buren's Democratic regime. In this diary entry, why does Hone have these expectations? What most appalled him (and other aristocratic Whigs) about the Jackson administration?

March 4 [1837].—This is the end of General Jackson's administration—the most disastrous in the annals of the country, and one which will excite "the special wonder" of posterity. That such a man should have governed this great country, with a rule more absolute than that of any hereditary monarch of Europe, and that the people should not only have submitted to it, but upheld and supported him in his encroachments upon their rights, and his disregard of the Constitution and the laws, will equally occasion the surprise and indignation of future generations. The people's indifference will prove that the love of liberty and independence is no longer an attribute of our people, and that the patriotic labors of the men of the Revolution have sunk like water in the sands, and that the vaunted rights of the people are considered by them as a "cunningly devised fable."

This is also the commencement of Mr. Van Buren's reign, the first New York President. He has said that it was "honor enough to have served [as vice-president] under such a chief," and will no doubt for a time speak with reverence of the ladder by which he has risen to the summit of ambitious hopes. But I do not despair of him. He will be a party President, but he is too much of a gentleman to be governed by the rabble who surrounded his predecessor and administered to his bad passions. As a man, a gentleman, and a friend, I have great respect for Mr. Van Buren. I hate the cause, but esteem the man, and, although I differ in my expectations from some of my political friends, I am disposed to give him a fair chance.

3. Van Buren Opposes Handouts (1837)

President Van Buren, once described by a foreign diplomat as the most perfect imitation of a gentleman he had ever seen, was left to face the post-Jackson whirlwind.

---

[2]Bayard Tuckerman, ed., *The Diary of Philip Hone, 1828–1851* (New York: Dodd, Mead and Company, 1889), vol. 1, pp. 245–246.

[3]J. D. Richardson, ed., *Messages and Papers of the Presidents* (1896), vol. 3, pp. 344–345.

The frightful panic of 1837, touched off in part by Jackson's bull-in-a-china-shop financial policies, brought bankruptcies, suicides, bank failures, shipping stagnation, mass unemployment, widespread hunger, and even food riots. In response to appeals for a helping hand from the federal government, Van Buren sent this Jeffersonian warning to Congress. Was his reasoning sound? Why, a century later, did the Democratic party (Van Buren's party) depart from it so conspicuously during the Great Depression of the 1930s?

Those who look to the action of this Government for specific aid to the citizen to relieve embarrassments, arising from losses by revulsions in commerce and credit, lose sight of the ends for which it was created, and the powers with which it is clothed.

It was established to give security to us all in our lawful and honorable pursuits, under the lasting safeguard of republican institutions. It was not intended to confer special favors on individuals or on any classes of them; to create systems of agriculture, manufactures, or trade; or to engage in them either separately or in connection with individual citizens or organized associations. If its operations were to be directed for the benefit of any one class, equivalent favors must in justice be extended to the rest, and the attempt to bestow such favors with an equal hand, or even to select those who should most deserve them, would never be successful.

All communities are apt to look to government for too much. Even in our own country, where its powers and duties are so strictly limited, we are prone to do so, especially at periods of sudden embarrassment and distress.

But this ought not to be. The framers of our excellent Constitution, and the people who approved it with calm and sagacious deliberation, acted at the time on a sounder principle. They wisely judged that the less government interferes with private pursuits, the better for the general prosperity. It is not its legitimate object to make men rich, or to repair, by direct grants of money or legislation in favor of particular pursuits, losses not incurred in the public service. This would be substantially to use the property of some for the benefit of others. But its real duty—that duty the performance of which makes a good government the most precious of human blessings—is to enact and enforce a system of general laws commensurate with, but not exceeding, the objects of its establishment, and to leave every citizen and every interest to reap under its benign protection the rewards of virtue, industry, and prudence.

I cannot doubt that, on this as on all similar occasions, the Federal Government will find its agency most conducive to the security and happiness of the people when limited to the exercise of its conceded powers. In never assuming, even for a well-meant object, such powers as were not designed to be conferred upon it, we shall in reality do most for the general welfare. To avoid every unnecessary interference with the pursuits of the citizen will result in more benefit than to adopt measures which could only assist limited interests, and are eagerly, but perhaps naturally, sought for under the pressure of temporary circumstances.

If, therefore, I refrain from suggesting to Congress any specific plan for regulating the [stock and mercantile] exchanges of the country, relieving mercantile embarrassments, or interfering with the ordinary operations of foreign or domestic commerce, it is from a conviction that such measures are not within the constitutional province of the General Government, and that their adoption would not promote the real and permanent welfare of those they might be designed to aid.

4. Charles Dickens Dislikes Yankee "Smartness" (1842)

Many British investors were hard hit by the Van Buren panic of 1837. More than a half-dozen states, after plunging too deeply into debt, openly repudiated their outstanding bonds or defaulted on them. The world-famous novelist Charles Dickens, smarting from his losses in the Cairo [Illinois] City & Canal Company, made a memorable tour of America in 1842. The criticisms in his resulting book stirred up a storm of resentment in the United States and contributed much ammunition to the verbal war with England discussed in the next chapter. Reconcile the American reputation for industry, morality, and churchgoing with the trait that, fairly or unfairly, Dickens here criticizes.

Another prominent feature [of America] is the love of "smart" dealing, which gilds over many a swindle and gross breach of trust, many a defalcation, public and private; and enables many a knave to hold his head up with the best, who well deserves a halter; though it has not been without its retributive operation, for this smartness has done more in a few years to impair the public credit, and to cripple the public resources, than dull honesty, however rash, could have effected in a century. The merits of a broken speculation, or a bankruptcy, or of a successful scoundrel, are not gauged by its or his observance of the golden rule, "Do as you would be done by," but are considered with reference to their smartness.

I recollect, on both occasions of our passing that ill-fated Cairo on the Mississippi, remarking on the bad effects such gross deceits must have when they exploded, in generating a want of confidence abroad, and discouraging foreign investment. But I was given to understand that this was a very smart scheme by which a deal of money had been made; and that its smartest feature was that they forgot these things abroad in a very short time, and speculated again, as freely as ever.

The following dialogue I have held a hundred times:

"Is it not a very disgraceful circumstance that such a man as So-and-so should be acquiring a large property by the most infamous and odious means, and, notwithstanding all the crimes of which he has been guilty, should be tolerated and abetted by your citizens? He is a public nuisance, is he not?"

"Yes, sir."

"A convicted liar?"

"Yes, sir."

"He has been kicked, and cuffed, and caned?"

"Yes, sir."

"And he is utterly dishonorable, debased, and profligate?"

---

[4]Charles Dickens, *American Notes,* chap. 18.

"Yes, sir."

"In the name of wonder, then, what is his merit?"

"Well, sir, he is a smart man."

E. The Emergence of Mass Political Parties

1. James Fenimore Cooper Castigates Parties (1838)

The Jacksonian Democrats, heirs of the manhood-suffrage New Democracy, had hurrahed Jackson and Van Buren into the presidential chair with frothy, slogan-filled campaigns. The more aristocratic Whigs, finally stealing the thunder of the Jacksonites, hurrahed Van Buren out of the presidential chair and William Henry Harrison into it in the frothy hard-cider campaign of 1840. The political boss had now come into his own, and the national nominating conventions had become his to manipulate. The famed author of the Leatherstocking Tales, *James Fenimore Cooper, after an extended sojourn abroad, returned to the United States and was shocked by what he found. The following blast, which he published in 1838, two years before the hard-cider campaign, illustrates the bitterness that involved him in protracted public controversy, including numerous libel suits. How much of his indictment seems sound? How much of it is true today?*

Party is known to encourage prejudice, and to lead men astray in the judgment of character. Thus it is we see one half the nation extolling those that the other half condemns, and condemning those that the other half extols. Both cannot be right, and as passions, interests, and prejudices are all enlisted on such occasions, it would be nearer the truth to say that both are wrong.

Party is an instrument of error, by pledging men to support its policy instead of supporting the policy of the state. Thus we see party-measures almost always in extremes, the resistance of opponents inducing the leaders to ask for more than is necessary.

Party leads to vicious, corrupt, and unprofitable legislation, for the sole purpose of defeating party. Thus have we seen those territorial divisions and regulations which ought to be permanent, as well as other useful laws, altered [gerrymandered], for no other end than to influence an election. . . .

The discipline and organization of party are expedients to defeat the intention of the institutions, by putting managers in the place of the people; it being of little avail that a majority elect, when the nomination rests in the hands of a few. . . .

Party pledges the representative to the support of the Executive, right or wrong, when the institutions intend that he shall be pledged only to justice, expediency, and the right, under the restrictions of the Constitution.

When party rules, the people do not rule, but merely such a portion of the people as can manage to get the control of party. The only method by which the peo-

---

[1]James F. Cooper, *The American Democrat* (Cooperstown, N.Y.: H. & E. Phinney, 1838), pp. 180–181.

ple can completely control the country is by electing representatives known to prize and understand the institutions; and who, so far from being pledged to support an administration, are pledged to support nothing but the right, and whose characters are guarantees that this pledge will be respected.

The effect of party is always to supplant established power. In a monarchy it checks the king; in a democracy it controls the people.

Party, by feeding the passions and exciting personal interests, overshadows truth, justice, patriotism, and every other public virtue, completely reversing the order of a democracy by putting unworthy motives in the place of reason.

It is a very different thing to be a democrat, and to be a member of what is called a Democratic Party; for the first insists on his independence and an entire freedom of opinion, while the last is incompatible with either.

The great body of the nation has no real interest in party. Every local election should be absolutely independent of great party divisions, and until this be done, the intentions of the American institutions will never be carried out, in their excellence. . . .

No freeman who really loves liberty and who has a just perception of its dignity, character, action, and objects will ever become a mere party man. He may have his preferences as to measures and men, may act in concert with those who think with himself, on occasions that require concert. But it will be his earnest endeavor to hold himself a free agent, and most of all to keep his mind untrammeled by the prejudices, frauds, and tyranny of factions.

2. Alexis de Tocqueville Defends Parties (1830s)

Permanently organized political parties were a novelty in the early-eighteenth-century Western world. This was especially true of the mass-based parties based on universal manhood suffrage that emerged in the United States. James Fenimore Cooper was not alone in regarding parties as dangerously disruptive of the consenus and harmony presumably essential to an orderly society. But Alexis de Tocqueville, among the shrewdest of all students of American democracy, appraised parties differently—especially in the American context of the 1830s. What did he identify as the beneficial effects of parties? What factors in the American setting did he portray as mitigating the possibly harmful effects of parties?

It must be admitted that unlimited freedom of association in the political sphere has not yet produced in America the fatal results that one might anticipate from it elsewhere. The right of association is of English origin and always existed in America. Use of this right is now an accepted part of customs and of mores.

In our own day freedom of association has become a necessary guarantee against the tyranny of the majority. In the United States, once a party has become predominant, all public power passes into its hands; its close supporters occupy all

[2]Excerpted from *Democracy in America* by Alexis de Tocqueville, edited by J. P. Mayer and Max Lerner. Translated by George Lawrence. English translation, copyright © 1965 by Harper & Row, Publishers, Inc. Copyright renewed. Reprinted by permission of HarperCollins Publishers, Inc.

offices and have control of all organized forces. The most distinguished men of the opposite party, unable to cross the barrier keeping them from power, must be able to establish themselves outside it; the minority must use the whole of its moral authority to oppose the physical power oppressing it. Thus the one danger has to be balanced against a more formidable one.

The omnipotence of the majority seems to me such a danger to the American republics that the dangerous expedient used to curb it is actually something good.

Here I would repeat something which I have put in other words when speaking of municipal freedom: no countries need associations more—to prevent either despotism of parties or the arbitrary rule of a prince—than those with a democratic social state. In aristocratic nations secondary bodies form natural associations which hold abuses of power in check. In countries where such associations do not exist, if private people did not artificially and temporarily create something like them, I see no other dike to hold back tyranny of whatever sort, and a great nation might with impunity be oppressed by some tiny faction or by a single man.

The meeting of a great political convention (for conventions are of all kinds), though it may often be a necessary measure, is always, even in America, a serious event and one that good patriots cannot envisage without alarm.

That came out clearly during the convention of 1831, when all the men of distinction taking part therein tried to moderate its language and limit its objective. Probably the convention of 1831 did greatly influence the attitude of the malcontents and prepared them for the open revolt of 1832 against the commercial laws of the Union.

One must not shut one's eyes to the fact that unlimited freedom of association for political ends is, of all forms of liberty, the last that a nation can sustain. While it may not actually lead it into anarchy, it does constantly bring it to the verge thereof. But this form of freedom, howsoever dangerous, does provide guarantees in one direction; in countries where associations are free, secret societies are unknown. There are factions in America, but no conspirators. . . .

The most natural right of man, after that of acting on his own, is that of combining his efforts with those of his fellows and acting together. Therefore the right of association seems to me by nature almost as inalienable as individual liberty. Short of attacking society itself, no lawgiver can wish to abolish it. However, though for some nations freedom to unite is purely beneficial and a source of prosperity, there are other nations who pervert it by their excesses and turn a fount of life into a cause of destruction. So I think it will be thoroughly useful both for governments and for political parties if I make a comparison between the different ways in which associations are used in those nations that understand what freedom is and in those where this freedom turns into license.

Most Europeans still regard association as a weapon of war to be hastily improvised and used at once on the field of battle.

An association may be formed for the purpose of discussion, but everybody's mind is preoccupied by the thought of impending action. An association is an army; talk is needed to count numbers and build up courage, but after that they march against the enemy. Its members regard legal measures as possible means, but they are never the only possible means of success.

The right of association is not understood like that in the United States. In America the citizens who form the minority associate in the first place to show their numbers and to lessen the moral authority of the majority, and secondly, by stimulating competition, to discover the arguments most likely to make an impression on the majority, for they always hope to draw the majority over to their side and then to exercise power in its name.

Political associations in the United States are therefore peaceful in their objects and legal in the means used; and when they say that they only wish to prevail legally, in general they are telling the truth.

There are several reasons for this difference between the Americans and ourselves. In Europe there are parties differing so much from the majority that they can never hope to win its support, and yet these parties believe themselves strong enough to struggle against it on their own. When such a party forms an association it intends not to convince but to fight. In America those whose opinions make a wide gap between them and the majority can do nothing to oppose its power; all others hope to win it over.

So the exercise of the right of association becomes dangerous when great parties see no possibility of becoming the majority. In a country like the United States, where differences of view are only matters of nuance, the right of association can remain, so to say, without limits.

It is our inexperience of liberty in action which still leads us to regard freedom of association as no more than a right to make war on the government. The first idea which comes into a party's mind, as into that of an individual, when it gains some strength is that of violence; the thought of persuasion only comes later, for it is born of experience. . . .

But perhaps universal suffrage is the most powerful of all the elements tending to moderate the violence of political associations in the United States. In a country with universal suffrage the majority is never in doubt, because no party can reasonably claim to represent those who have not voted at all. Therefore associations know, and everyone knows, that they do not represent the majority. The very fact of their existence proves this, for if they did represent the majority, they themselves would change the law instead of demanding reforms.

Thereby the moral strength of the government they attack is greatly increased and their own correspondingly weakened.

Thought Provokers

1. Should Jackson have taken a stronger position in public against South Carolina? Should he have used force? Who won in the struggle over nullification, especially in view of the forthcoming Civil War? Would a preventive war at this time have been wise policy for Jackson?

2. Why did Jackson's veto of the Bank recharter appeal so strongly to the masses? Was Jackson right? Should foreigners have been allowed to hold stock in the Bank? Is it bet-

ter to have aristocratically controlled financial institutions that are sound than democratically controlled financial institutions that are less sound?

3. Explain why the Indians and the whites appeared unable to live peacefully side by side.
   What are the moral implications of the argument that the Indians were not putting their
   land to good use?

4. Would Van Buren have approved federal unemployment relief and price supports as we
   now know them? What would probably have happened during the Great Depression of
   the 1930s if President Franklin Roosevelt had pursued Van Buren's philosophy?

5. Are political parties necessary in a democracy? How did the Republic get along without
   them from approximately 1815 until the 1830s? Why did they emerge when they did?

15

Forging the National Economy, 1790–1860

Take not from the mouth of labor the bread it has earned.

Thomas Jefferson, 1801

Prologue: The Industrial Revolution spawned the factory, and in turn the factory-magnet drew from the hallowed home countless men, women, and even tiny children. Alexander Hamilton himself had stressed the spiritual value of training "the little innocents" in honest habits of industry. But the exploitation of little innocents, as well as their elders, resulted in grave abuses. For more than a century, labor fought an uphill fight against employers for a gradual improvement of its lot. Meanwhile the spread of the factory was spurred by the canal network, by the river steamboat, and then by the railroad. The fast-growing states of the Ohio Valley and the Upper Mississippi Valley became less dependent on the mouth of the Mississippi as the outlet for their produce, because the new arteries of transportation carried their exports cheaply and swiftly to the cities of the eastern seaboard. The ties of the Union, conspicuously in an east-west direction, were thus greatly strengthened.

A. The Spread of the Factory

1. Wage Slavery in New England (1832)

Seth Luther, a poorly educated carpenter who helped construct New England textile factories, ranks as one of the most forceful of the early labor reformers. In numerous speeches and pamphlets he condemned such abuses as paternalistic control, "black-lists" of troublemakers, low wages, and overlong hours. He especially deplored the exploitation of children, who were sometimes dragged to "whipping rooms." His deadly earnestness and biting sarcasm were partly responsible for the United States' first law to control child labor, enacted by Massachusetts in 1842. It prohibited children under twelve from working more than ten hours a day. What were the most serious abuses that Luther here discusses? In what specific ways were they harmful?

[1]Seth Luther, *An Address to the Working-Men of New-England* . . . , 2nd ed. (Boston, 1833), pp. 17–21.

A [Western] member of the United States Senate seems to be extremely pleased with cotton mills. He says in the Senate, "Who has not been delighted with the clockwork movements of a large cotton manufactory? He had visited them often, and always with increased delight." He says the women work in large airy apartments, well warmed. They are neatly dressed, with ruddy complexions, and happy countenances. They mend the broken threads and replace the exhausted balls or broaches, and at stated periods they go to and return from their meals with light and cheerful step. (While on a visit to that pink of perfection, Waltham [Massachusetts], I remarked that the females moved with a very light step, and well they might, for the bell rang for them to return to the mill from their homes in nineteen minutes after it had rung for them to go to breakfast. Some of these females boarded the largest part of a half a mile from the mill.)

And the grand climax [says the western senator] is that at the end of the week, after working like slaves for thirteen or fourteen hours every day, "they enter the temples of God on the Sabbath, and thank him for all his benefits. . . ." We remark that whatever girls or others may do west of the Allegheny Mountains, we do not believe there can be a single person found east of those mountains who ever thanked God for permission to work in a cotton mill. . . .

We would respectfully advise the honorable Senator to travel incognito when he visits cotton mills. If he wishes to come at the truth, he must not be known. Let him put on a short jacket and trousers, and join the "lower orders" for a short time. . . . In that case we could show him, in some of the prisons in New England called cotton mills, instead of rosy cheeks, the pale, sickly, haggard countenance of the ragged child—haggard from the worse than slavish confinement in the cotton mill. He might see that child driven up to the "clockwork" by the cowskin [whip], in some cases. He might see, in some instances, the child taken from his bed at four in the morning, and plunged into cold water to drive away his slumbers and prepare him for the labors of the mill. After all this he might see that child robbed, yes, robbed of a part of his time allowed for meals by moving the hands of the clock backwards, or forwards, as would best accomplish that purpose. . . . He might see in some, and not infrequent, instances, the child, and the female child too, driven up to the "clockwork" with the cowhide, or well-seasoned strap of American manufacture.

We could show him many females who have had corporeal punishment inflicted upon them; one girl eleven years of age who had her leg broken with a billet of wood; another who had a board split over her head by a heartless monster in the shape of an overseer of a cotton mill "paradise."

We shall for want of time . . . omit entering more largely into detail for the present respecting the cruelties practiced in some of the American mills. Our wish is to show that education is neglected, . . . because if thirteen hours' actual labor is required each day, it is impossible to attend to education among children, or to improvement among adults.

2. The Abuse of Female Workers (1836)

The factory girls of Lowell, Massachusetts, were a showpiece for visitors, notably Charles Dickens in 1842. Having seen the miserable working conditions in England, he wrote almost ecstatically of the fresh air in the Lowell mills, and of the cheerful faces and blooming health of the "Lowell girls." He also took favorable note of the girls' cleanliness, clothes, thrift, morals, and educational and recreational facilities. Perhaps he was unduly impressed by the contrast with English factories; certainly he did not investigate as carefully the less savory mills. Six years earlier, a reformist writer in a contemporary American journal presented a strikingly different view. How, in the following account, does this writer evaluate the early factory system?

We have lately visited the cities of Lowell [Massachusetts] and Manchester [New Hampshire] and have had an opportunity of examining the factory system more closely than before. We had distrusted the accounts which we had heard from persons engaged in the labor reform now beginning to agitate New England. We could scarcely credit the statements made in relation to the exhausting nature of the labor in the mills, and to the manner in which the young women—the operatives—lived in their boardinghouses, six sleeping in a room, poorly ventilated.

We went through many of the mills, talked particularly to a large number of the operatives, and ate at their boardinghouses, on purpose to ascertain by personal inspection the facts of the case. We assure our readers that very little information is possessed, and no correct judgments formed, by the public at large, of our factory system, which is the first germ of the industrial or commercial feudalism that is to spread over our land. . . .

In Lowell live between seven and eight thousand young women, who are generally daughters of farmers of the different states of New England. Some of them are members of families that were rich in the generation before. . . .

The operatives work thirteen hours a day in the summer time, and from daylight to dark in the winter. At half past four in the morning the factory bell rings, and at five the girls must be in the mills. A clerk, placed as a watch, observes those who are a few minutes behind the time, and effectual means are taken to stimulate to punctuality. This is the morning commencement of the industrial discipline (should we not rather say industrial tyranny?) which is established in these associations of this moral and Christian community.

At seven the girls are allowed thirty minutes for breakfast, and at noon thirty minutes more for dinner, except during the first quarter of the year, when the time is extended to forty-five minutes. But within this time they must hurry to their boardinghouses and return to the factory, and that through the hot sun or the rain or the cold. A meal eaten under such circumstances must be quite unfavorable to digestion and health, as any medical man will inform us. At seven o'clock in the evening the factory bell sounds the close of the day's work.

Thus thirteen hours per day of close attention and monotonous labor are exacted from the young women in these manufactories. . . . So fatigued—we should

---

[2]*The Harbinger,* November 14, 1836, in H. R. Warfel et al., eds., *The American Mind* (New York and Cincinnati: The American Book Company, 1937), pp. 390–391. In 1847 this journal became the official organ of the Brook Farm colony.

say, exhausted and worn out, but we wish to speak of the system in the simplest language—are numbers of girls that they go to bed soon after their evening meal, and endeavor by a comparatively long sleep to resuscitate their weakened frames for the toil of the coming day.

When capital has got thirteen hours of labor daily out of a being, it can get nothing more. It would be a poor speculation in an industrial point of view to own the operative; for the trouble and expense of providing for times of sickness and old age would more than counterbalance the difference between the price of wages and the expense of board and clothing. The far greater number of fortunes accumulated by the North in comparison with the South shows that hireling labor is more profitable for capital than slave labor.

Now let us examine the nature of the labor itself, and the conditions under which it is performed. Enter with us into the large rooms, when the looms are at work. The largest that we saw is in the Amoskeag Mills at Manchester. . . . The din and clatter of these five hundred looms, under full operation, struck us on first entering as something frightful and infernal, for it seemed such an atrocious violation of one of the faculties of the human soul, the sense of hearing. After a while we became somewhat inured to it, and by speaking quite close to the ear of an operative and quite loud, we could hold a conversation and make the inquiries we wished.

The girls attend upon an average three looms; many attend four, but this requires a very active person, and the most unremitting care. However, a great many do it. Attention to two is as much as should be demanded of an operative. This gives us some idea of the application required during the thirteen hours of daily labor. The atmosphere of such a room cannot of course be pure; on the contrary, it is charged with cotton filaments and dust, which, we are told, are very injurious to the lungs.

On entering the room, although the day was warm, we remarked that the windows were down. We asked the reason, and a young woman answered very naïvely, and without seeming to be in the least aware that this privation of fresh air was anything else than perfectly natural, that "when the wind blew, the threads did not work well." After we had been in the room for fifteen or twenty minutes, we found ourselves, as did the persons who accompanied us, in quite a perspiration, produced by a certain moisture which we observed in the air, as well as by the heat. . . .

The young women sleep upon an average six in a room, three beds to a room. There is no privacy, no retirement, here. It is almost impossible to read or write alone, as the parlor is full and so many sleep in the same chamber. A young woman remarked to us that if she had a letter to write, she did it on the head of a bandbox, sitting on a trunk, as there was no space for a table.

So live and toil the young women of our country in the boardinghouses and manufactories which the rich and influential of our land have built for them.

3. The "Utopian" Lowell Looms (1844)

Charles Dickens recorded three facts about the Lowell girls that he was sure would startle his English readers. First, many of the boardinghouses had joint-stock pianos; second, "nearly all" of the young women subscribed to circulating libraries; third, the operatives—ultimately about seventy of the more literate—published a journal called The Lowell Offering. *The factory owners, no doubt conscious of its public-relations value, encouraged it—and probably censored it as well. Actually, the matrons of the boardinghouses went to great lengths to keep "fallen women" from entering this "paradise" and tainting the virginal farm girls. The following imaginary and stilted conversation, published in* The Lowell Offering, *is a piece of propaganda probably inspired by the employers and certainly representing the employers' point of view. What serious grievances does it omit mentioning?*

Miss S: I am very happy to see you this evening, Miss Bartlett, for I have something particular to say to you. Now do tell me if you still persist in your resolution to return to your factory employment?

Miss B: I do. I have no objection, neither have I heard any sufficiently strong to deter me.

Miss S: The idea that it is degrading, in the opinion of many, would be objection enough for me without taking into account its real tendency to promote ignorance and vice.

Miss B: By whom is factory labor considered degrading? It is by those who believe all labor degrading—by those who contemptuously speak of the farmer, the mechanic, the printer, the seamstress, and all who are obliged to toil as belonging to the lower orders—by those who seem to think the condition of labor excludes all the capacities of the mind and the virtues of humanity. They forget that circumstances, over which they have little or no control, place them above the necessity of labor; and that circumstances may yet compel them to engage in that at which they now scoff and spurn.

Miss S: There are objections to factory labor, which serve to render it degrading—objections which cannot be urged against any other kind of female employment. For instance, to be called and to be dismissed by the ringing of a bell savors of compulsion and slavery, and cannot cease to produce mortification without having been destructive to self-respect.

Miss B: In almost all kinds of employment it is necessary to keep regular established hours: more particularly so where there are so many connected as in the factories. Because we are reminded of those hours by the ringing of a bell, it is no argument against our employment, any more than it would be against going to church or to school. Our engagements are voluntarily entered into with our employers, with the understanding that they may be dissolved at our pleasure. However derogatory to our dignity and liberty you may consider factory labor, there is not a tinge of slavery existing in it, unless there be in every kind of labor that is urged upon us by the force of circumstances.

---

[3]From *American Issues,* vol. 1, *The Social Record, Revised,* edited by Willard Thorp, Merle Curti, and Carlos Baker (Chicago: J. B. Lippincott Company, 1955), pp. 410–411. Copyright, 1955 by J. B. Lippincott Company.

Miss S: Objections have been brought up against the boardinghouses, and, I think, with much plausibility. The large number of females who are there thrown together are, unavoidably, intimately connected with each other. It cannot be denied that some, guilty of immoralities, find their way into the factories and boardinghouses. The example and influence of such must be pernicious, and terminate in the increase of vice.

Miss B: It is true that the example and influence of immorality, wherever it exists, cannot be otherwise than evil. We know, also, that some exceptionable characters occasionally find a place among those employed in factories. We know it from the fact that dismissals do, now and then, occur as the consequence. But, my dear Miss S, did you ever know or hear of a class of people who could boast of perfection? among whom wrong of any description was never known?

Miss S: O, no! And, as I am no perfectionist, I never expect to know one.

Miss B: Then, if in one case the guilt of a few has not corrupted the whole, why should it in the other? Living in a factory boardinghouse, and working in a factory, changes not "human nature": it is susceptible of good, and also of evil, there, as it is elsewhere.

Miss S: I agree with you in thinking that among all classes, and in every condition in life, evil influences are at work. But in some situations in life is not the exposure to these influences much more extensive, and, therefore, more dangerous, especially to the young?

Miss B: I believe there are many kinds of female employment offered in our large towns and cities far more dangerous in this respect than factory employment, although they may be considered more desirable and respectable. . . .

Miss S: You will not acknowledge that factory labor is degrading, or that it is productive of vice, but you must own that it fosters ignorance. When there are so many hours out of each day devoted to labor, there can be no time for study and improvement.

Miss B: It is true that too large a portion of our time is confined to labor. But, first, let me remark that this is an objection which cannot be said to exist only in factory labor. . . . We have abundant proof that unremitted toil is not always derogatory to improvement. A factory girl's work is neither hard nor complicated. She can go on with perfect regularity in her duties while her mind may be actively employed on any other subject. There can be no better place for reflection, when there must be toil, than the factory. The patronage which newspapers and periodicals find in our city, our well-worn libraries, evening schools, crowded churches and sabbath schools, prove that factory operatives find leisure to use the means of improvement both in mind and heart.

4. "Slavers" for New England Girls (1846)

Many of the Lowell girls toiled only a few years—perhaps to help needy parents, to pay off a farm mortgage, to accumulate a dowry, or to send a brother through college. Dickens noted that 978 women workers had deposits in the Lowell Savings Bank

---

[4] *Voice of Industry,* January 2, 1846, in H. R. Warfel et al., eds., *The American Mind* (New York and Cincinnati: the American Book Company, 1937), p. 392.

totaling an estimated $100,000. But conditions in other factories were less wholesome, and the following account in a labor journal, though no doubt overdrawn, contains a large element of truth. How free were these New England women to quit their jobs? In what respects is the comparison with slavery plausible?

We were not aware, until within a few days, of the *modus operandi* of the factory powers in this village of forcing poor girls from their quiet homes to become their tools and, like the Southern slaves, to give up their life and liberty to the heartless tyrants and taskmasters.

Observing a singular-looking "long, low, black" wagon passing along the street, we made inquiries respecting it, and were informed that it was what we term a "slaver." She makes regular trips to the north of the state [Massachusetts], cruising around in Vermont and New Hampshire, with a "commander" whose heart must be as black as his craft, who is paid a dollar a head for all he brings to the market, and more in proportion to the distance—if they bring them from such a distance that they cannot easily get back.

This is done by "hoisting false colors," and representing to the girls that they can tend more machinery than is possible, and that the work is so very neat, and the wages such that they can dress in silks and spend half their time in reading. Now, is this true? Let those girls who have been thus deceived, answer.

Let us say a word in regard to the manner in which they are stowed in the wagon, which may find a similarity only in the manner in which slaves are fastened in the hold of a vessel. It is long, and the seats so close that it must be very inconvenient.

Is there any humanity in this? Philanthropists may talk of Negro slavery, but it would be well first to endeavor to emancipate the slaves at home. Let us not stretch our ears to catch the sound of the lash on the flesh of the oppressed black while the oppressed in our very midst are crying out in thunder tones, and calling upon us for assistance.

5. Disaster in a Massachusetts Mill (1860)

The lot of women factory workers in New England seemed less idyllic after an appalling accident in the five-story Pemberton textile mill, described next. George T. Strong, a prominent New York lawyer and public-spirited citizen, poured his indignation into his diary. Who was at fault? Why might the South have taken some secret satisfaction in the tragedy?

January 11 [1860]. News today of a fearful tragedy at Lawrence, Massachusetts, one of the wholesale murders commonly known in newspaper literature as accident or catastrophe. A huge factory, long notoriously insecure and ill-built, requiring to be patched and bandaged up with iron plates and braces to stand the introduction of its machinery, suddenly collapsed into a heap of ruins yesterday afternoon without the smallest provocation. Some five or six hundred operatives went down with

[5]Reprinted with the permission of Simon & Schuster from *The Diary of George Templeton Strong,* edited by Allan Nevins and Milton Halsey Thomas. Copyright © 1956 by John Tracy Ellis.

it—young girls and women mostly. An hour or two later, while people were working frantically to dig out some two hundred still under the ruins, many of them alive and calling for help, some quite unhurt, fire caught in the great pile of debris, and these prisoners were roasted. It is too atrocious and horrible to think of.

Of course, nobody will be hanged. Somebody has murdered about two hundred people, many of them with hideous torture, in order to save money, but society has no avenging gibbet for the respectable millionaire and homicide. Of course not. He did not want to or mean to do this massacre; on the whole, he would have preferred to let these people live. His intent was not homicidal. He merely thought a great deal about making a large profit and very little about the security of human life. He did not compel these poor girls and children to enter his accursed mantrap. They could judge and decide for themselves whether they would be employed there. It was a matter of contract between capital and labor; they were to receive cash payment for their services.

No doubt the legal representatives of those who have perished will be duly paid the fractional part of their week's wages up to the date when they became incapacitated by crushing or combustion, as the case may be, from rendering further service. Very probably the wealthy and liberal proprietor will add (in deserving cases) a gratuity to defray funeral charges. It becomes us to prate about the horrors of slavery! What Southern capitalist trifles with the lives of his operatives as do our philanthropes of the North?

B. The Flocking of the Immigrants

1. An English Radical Praises America (1818)

Economic hardship, begotten by the Industrial Revolution and the Napoleonic wars, laid a withering hand on England. Political reaction under the Tories was hardly less blighting; the Reform Bills of 1832 and 1867 lay in the future. Of the 24 million souls in the British Isles in 1831, only 400,000 were qualified voters. "Pocket boroughs," controlled by the crown or by aristocratic landowners, sent members to Parliament, while newly mushroomed industrial cities, like Manchester and Birmingham, enjoyed no direct representation. The tax supported state Church of England rode high. Thomas Hulme, an English radical, here tells his story. Despairing of parliamentary reform and chafing under the rule of "the great insolent" families, he decided to bring his children to America before he should die and leave them "the slaves of such a set of beings." What were his most violent prejudices, and what features of America appealed to him most?

I was well pleased with America, over a considerable part of which I traveled. I saw an absence of human misery. I saw a government taking away a very, very small portion of men's earnings. I saw ease and happiness and a fearless utterance of thought everywhere prevail. I saw laws like those of the old laws of England, everywhere obeyed with cheerfulness and held in veneration. I heard of no mobs,

[1]In William Cobbett, *A Year's Residence in America* (Boston: Small, Maynard, 1819), pp. 201–204 (Part 3).

no riots, no spies, no [penal] transportings, no hangings. I saw those very Irish, to keep whom in order such murderous laws exist in Ireland, here good, peaceable, industrious citizens. I saw no placemen and pensioners riding the people under foot. I saw no greedy Priesthood fattening on the fruits of labor in which they had never participated, and which fruits they seized in despite of the people. I saw a debt, indeed, but then it was so insignificant a thing; and, besides, it had been contracted for the people's use, and not for that of a set of tyrants who had used the money to the injury of the people. In short, I saw a state of things precisely the reverse of that in England, and very nearly what it would be in England if the Parliament were reformed. . . .

During the spring and early part of the summer of 1817, I made preparations for the departure of myself and family, and when all was ready, I bid an everlasting adieu to boroughmongers, sinecure placemen and placewomen, pensioned lords and ladies, standing armies in time of peace, and (rejoice, oh! my children) to a hireling, tithe-devouring Priesthood.

We arrived safe and all in good health, and which health has never been impaired by the climate. We are in a state of ease, safety, plenty; and how can we help being so happy as people can be? The more I see of my adopted country, the more gratitude do I feel towards it for affording me and my numerous offspring protection from the tyrants of my native country. There I should have been in constant anxiety about my family. Here I am in none at all. Here I am in fear of no spies, no false witnesses, no blood-money men. Here no fines, irons, no gallowses await me, let me think or say what I will about the government. Here I have to pay no people to be ready to shoot at me, or run me through the body, or chop me down. Here no vile priest can rob me and mock me in the same breath. . . .

I could mention numerous instances of Englishmen, coming to this country with hardly a dollar in their pocket, and arriving at a state of ease and plenty and even riches in a few years. And I explicitly declare that I have never known or heard of an instance of one common laborer who, with common industry and economy, did not greatly better his lot. Indeed, how can it otherwise be, when the average wages of agricultural labor is double what it is in England, and when the average price of food is not more than half what it is in that country? These two facts, undeniable as they are, are quite sufficient to satisfy any man of sound mind.

As to the manners of the people, they are precisely to my taste: unostentatious and simple. Good sense I find everywhere, and never affectation; kindness, hospitality, and never-failing civility. I traveled more than four thousand miles about this country, and I have never met with one single insolent or rude native American.

2. The Coming of the Irish (1836)

Charles J. Latrobe was a Londoner who achieved some fame as a minor poet, a travel writer, and a mountain climber in Switzerland. On his two extensive trips to America in 1832 and 1834, he observed the "swarming" of the Irish even in those pre–potato famine days. How did their situation resemble that of later immigrant groups?

[2]C. J. Latrobe, *The Rambler in North America* (London: R. B. Seeley and W. Burnside, 1836), vol. 2, pp. 222–223.

Here comes a shipload of Irish. They land upon the wharfs of New York in rags and open-knee'd breeches, with their raw looks and bare necks. They flourish their cudgels, throw up their torn hats, and cry, "Hurrah for Gineral Jackson!" They get drunk and kick up a row, lend their forces to any passing disturbance, and make early acquaintance with the interior of the lock-ups [jails].

From New York they go in swarms to the canals, railroads, and public works, where they perform that labor which the Americans are not inclined to do. Now and then they get up a fight among themselves in the style of old Ireland, and perhaps kill one another, expressing great indignation and surprise when they find that they must answer for it though they are in a free country. By degrees, the more thrifty get and keep money, and diving deeper into the continent, purchase lands; while the intemperate and irreclaimable vanish from the surface.

The Americans complain, and justly, of the disorderly population which Ireland throws into the bosom of the Union, but there are many reasons why they should be borne with. They, with the poor Germans, do the work which without them could hardly be done. Though the fathers may be irreclaimable, the children become good citizens—and there is no finer race in the world, both for powers of mind and body, than the Irish, when favored by education and under proper control.

In one thing the emigrant Irish of every class distinguish themselves above the people of other nations, and that is in the love and kindly feeling which they cherish towards their native land, and towards those whom they have left behind—a fact proved by the large sums which are yearly transmitted from them to the mother country, in aid of their poverty-stricken relatives.

3. The Burning of a Convent School (1834)

The swelling tide of Irish-Catholic immigrants in the Boston area intensified a long-festering prejudice against the Catholic church. A half-dozen riots occurred before public indignation vented itself against an Ursuline convent school at Charlestown, outside Boston. Responding to ill-founded tales of abuse suffered by incarcerated nuns, a well-organized mob of about fifty men sacked and burned the four-story brick building on August 11, 1834. (Ironically, more than half of the fifty-seven pupils were Protestant girls.) Neither the authorities nor the hundreds of approving spectators made any attempt to restrain the mob. In retaliation, angry Irish laborers began to mobilize, but were restrained by Bishop Fenwick. The following editorial from the Boston Atlas *expresses the widespread condemnation voiced in the press and among responsible citizens. What did this journal find most disturbing about the outrage?*

From all we can learn, the violence was utterly without cause. The institution was in its very nature unpopular, and a strong feeling existed against it. But there was nothing in the vague rumors that have been idly circulating to authorize or account for any the least act of violence. We should state, perhaps, that during the violent scenes that were taking place before the convent—while the mob were

---

[3]Quoted in *Niles' Weekly Register* 46 (August 23, 1834): 437.

breaking the windows and staving in the doors of the institution—and while the fire was blazing upon the hill as a signal to the mob—one or two muskets were discharged from the windows of the nunnery, or some of the buildings in the vicinity.

What a scene must this midnight conflagration have exhibited—lighting up the inflamed countenances of an infuriated mob of demons—*attacking a convent of women, a seminary for the instruction of young females;* and turning them out of their beds half naked in the hurry of their flight, and half dead with confusion and terror. And this drama, too, to be enacted on the very soil that afforded one of the earliest places of refuge to the Puritans of New England—themselves flying from religious persecution in the Old World—that their descendants might wax strong and mighty, and in their turn be guilty of the same persecution in the New!

We remember no parallel to this outrage in the whole course of history. Turn to the bloodiest incidents of the French Revolution . . . and point us to its equal in unprovoked violence, in brutal outrage, in unthwarted iniquity. It is in vain that we search for it. In times of civil commotion and general excitement . . . there was some palliation for violence and outrage—in the tremendously excited state of the public mind. But here there was no such palliation. The courts of justice were open to receive complaints of any improper confinement, or unauthorized coercion. The civil magistrates were, or ought to be, on the alert to detect any illegal restraint, and bring its authors to the punishment they deserve. But nothing of the kind was detected. The whole matter was a cool, deliberate, systematized piece of brutality—unprovoked—under the most provoking circumstances totally unjustifiable—and visiting the citizens of the town, and most particularly its magistrates and civil officers, with indelible disgrace.

[Local sentiment undoubtedly supported the mobsters. The subsequent trial of the ringleaders was a farce: insults were showered on the prosecution, the nuns, and the Catholic church. Only one culprit was convicted, and he was pardoned following a petition by forgiving Catholics. The Massachusetts legislature, bowing to intimidation, dropped all efforts to provide financial recompense. Catholic churches in the area were forced to post armed guards, and for a time insurance companies refused to insure Catholic buildings built of inflammable materials. The Ursuline sisters of Charlestown finally moved to Canada, and for thirty-five years the blackened brick ruins of the school remained a momument to religious bigotry.]

4. A Southerner Defends the Catholics (1854)

The great flood of Irish Catholics, uprooted by the potato famine of the mid-1840s, further aroused many "native Americans." The newcomers not only worsened already stinking slums but became willing voting tools of the corrupt political machines. "Nativist" resentment found vent in the powerful Know-Nothing (American) party, which undertook to elect only "natives" to office; to raise the residence requirement for naturalization from five to twenty-one years; and to exclude Roman

[4]*Congressional Globe,* 33rd Congress, 2d session, Appendix, pp. 58–59.

Catholics from office, on the popular assumption that orders from the Pope took precedence over their oath to support the Constitution. Yet Know-Nothingism found little support in the South. Relatively few Catholic immigrants went there; and in addition the Catholic church did not cry out against slavery, as did the leading Protestant denominations of the North. Representative William T. S. Barry of Mississippi, a Presbyterian with Episcopalian leanings and one of the South's great orators, here defends the Catholics in a justly famous speech. In the light of his remarks, assess the following statements: persecution strengthens the persecuted; proscriptionists become the proscribed; intolerance has no logical halfway stopping point.

The last purpose to be achieved by the Know-Nothings is the exclusion of all Catholics from office. . . . How dare we talk of freedom of conscience, when more than a million of our citizens are to be excluded from office for conscience sake!

Yesterday, to have argued in favor of religious toleration in this country would have been absurd, for none could have been found to deny or question it. But today there is a sect [Know-Nothings] boasting that it can control the country, avowing the old Papist and monarchical doctrine of political exclusion for religious opinions' sake. The arguments by which they sustain themselves are those by which the Inquisition justified their probing the consciences and burning the bodies of men five hundred years ago, and against which Protestantism has struggled since the days of Luther.

You, sir, and I, and all of us, owe our own right to worship God according to our consciences to that very doctrine which this new [Know-Nothing] order abjures; and if the right of the Catholic is first assailed and destroyed, you, sir, or another member who believes according to a different Protestant creed, may be excluded from this House, and from other preferment, because of your religious faith.

The security of all citizens rests upon the same broad basis of universal right. Confederates who disfranchise one class of citizens soon turn upon each other. The strong argument of general right is destroyed by their united action, and the proscriptionist of yesterday is the proscribed of tomorrow. Human judgment has recognized the inexorable justice of the sentence which consigned Robespierre and his accomplices [of the French Revolution] to the same guillotine to which they had condemned so many thousand better men.

No nation can content itself with a single act of persecution; either public intelligence will reject that as unworthy of itself, or public prejudice will add others to it. If the Catholic be untrustworthy as a citizen, and the public liberty is unsafe in his keeping, it is but a natural logical consequence that he shall not be permitted to disseminate a faith which is adjudged hostile to national independence; that he shall not be allowed to set the evil example of the practice of his religion before the public; that it shall not be preached from the pulpit; that it shall not be taught in the schools; and that, by all the energy of the law, it shall be utterly exterminated.

If this [Catholic] faith be incompatible with good citizenship, and you set about to discourage it—destroy it utterly, uproot it from the land. Petty persecution will but irritate a sect which the Know-Nothings denounce as so powerful and so dangerous. This was the course which England pursued when she entertained the same fears of the Catholics three hundred years ago, and which she has lived to see the absurdity of, and has removed almost, if not quite, every disability imposed. Perhaps, however, this new [Know-Nothing] sect will not startle the public mind by proposing too much at once, and holds that it will be time enough to propose further and more minute persecution when the national sentiment is debauched enough to entertain favorably this first great departure from the unbounded toleration of our fathers.

It is the experience of this country that persecution strengthens a new creed. . . . Perhaps it is true of all times and countries. . . . In my judgment, this attempt at proscription will do more to spread Catholicism here than all the treasures of Rome, or all the Jesuitism of the Cardinals.

C. Mounting Labor Unrest

1. A One-Sided Labor Contract (c. 1832)

The plight of the factory worker in the 1830s was such as to justify the term wage slavery. *Work contracts—often a precondition of employment—gave the employer blank-check power. The following contract was used by a textile company in Dover, New Hampshire. What feature of it would be most offensive to an active trade unionist today?*

We, the subscribers [the undersigned], do hereby agree to enter the service of the Cocheco Manufacturing Company, and conform, in all respects, to the regulations which are now, or may hereafter be adopted, for the good government of the institution.

We further agree to work for such wages per week, and prices by the job, as the Company may see fit to pay, and be subject to the fines as well as entitled to the premiums paid by the Company.

We further agree to allow two cents each week to be deducted from our wages for the benefit of the sick fund.

We also agree not to leave the service of the Company without giving two weeks' notice of our intention, without permission of an agent. And if we do, we agree to forfeit to the use of the Company two weeks' pay.

We also agree not to be engaged in any combination [union] whereby the work may be impeded or the Company's interest in any work injured. If we do, we agree to forfeit to the use of the Company the amount of wages that may be due to us at the time.

We also agree that in case we are discharged from the service of the Company for any fault, we will not consider ourselves entitled to be settled with in less than two weeks from the time of such discharge.

Payments for labor performed are to be made monthly.

---

[1]Seth Luther, *An Address to the Working-Men of New-England* . . . (Boston, 1833), p. 36.

2. Agitation for the Ten-Hour Day (1835)

A reduction of daily working hours from thirteen or more was a primary goal of labor in the 1830s. During a third unsuccessful strike for the ten-hour day, the Boston artisans issued the following circular. It led to the successful general strike in Philadelphia on the coal wharves. What was the employers' main objection to the ten-hour day, and how did the workers try to meet it?

. . . In the name of the Carpenters, Masons, and Stone Cutters [we] do respectfully represent—

That we are now engaged in a cause which is not only of vital importance to ourselves, our families, and our children, but is equally interesting and equally important to every mechanic in the United States and the whole world. We are contending for the recognition of the natural right to dispose of our own time in such quantities as we deem and believe to be most conducive to our own happiness and the welfare of all those engaged in manual labor.

The work in which we are now engaged is neither more nor less than a contest between money and labor. Capital, which can only be made productive by labor, is endeavoring to crush labor, the only source of all wealth.

We have been too long subjected to the odious, cruel, unjust, and tyrannical system which compels the operative mechanic to exhaust his physical and mental powers by excessive toil, until he has no desire to eat and sleep, and in many cases he has no power to do either from extreme debility. . . .

It is for the rights of humanity we contend. Our cause is the cause of philanthropy. Our opposers resort to the most degrading obloquy to injure us—not degrading to us, but to the authors of such unmerited opprobrium which they attempt to cast upon us. They tell us, "We shall spend all our hours of leisure in drunkenness and debauchery if the hours of labor are reduced." We hurl from us the base, ungenerous, ungrateful, detestable, cruel, malicious slander, with scorn and indignation. . . .

To show the utter fallacy of their idiotic reasoning, if reasoning it may be called, we have only to say they employ us about eight months in the year during the longest and the hottest days, and in short days hundreds of us remain idle for want of work for three or four months, when our expenses must of course be the heaviest during winter. When the long days again appear, our guardians set us to work, as they say, "to keep us from getting drunk." No fear has ever been expressed by these benevolent employers respecting our morals while we are idle in short days, through their avarice. . . . Further, they threaten to starve us into submission to their will. Starve us to prevent us from getting drunk!! Wonderful wisdom!! Refined benevolence!! Exalted philanthropy!!

---

[2]Quoted in Irving Mark and E. I. Schwaab, *The Faith of Our Fathers* (1952), pp. 342–343.

3. The Tailors Strike in New York (1836)

Under existing laws, a strike for higher wages was a criminal conspiracy. The courts dealt harshly with strikers, especially before the pro-labor decision in Massachusetts in the case of Commonwealth *v.* Hunt *(1842). Philip Hone, a wealthy and conservative New York businessman, approved of keeping laborers in their place, particularly the New York tailors, as the following diary entry reveals. In the light of present-day standards, who expresses the more extreme views—Hone or the strikers?*

June 6 [1836].—In corroboration of the spirit of faction and contempt of the laws which pervades the community at this time is the conduct of the journeymen tailors, instigated by a set of vile foreigners (principally English), who, unable to endure the restraints of wholesome law well administered in their own country, take refuge here, establish trades-unions, and vilify Yankee judges and juries. Twenty odd of these were convicted at the Oyer and Terminer [Court] of a conspiracy to raise their wages and to prevent any of the craft from working at prices less than those for which they struck. Judge Edwards gave notice that he would proceed to sentence them this day. But, in consequence of the continuance of Robinson's trial, the Court postponed the sentence until Friday.

This, however, being the day on which it was expected, crowds of people have been collected in the park, ready for any mischief to which they may have been instigated, and a most diabolical and inflammatory hand-bill was circulated yesterday, headed by a coffin. The Board of Aldermen held an informal meeting this evening, at which a resolution was adopted authorizing the Mayor to offer a reward for the discovery of the author, printer, publisher, or distributor of this incendiary publication. The following was the hand-bill:

The Rich Against the Poor!

Judge Edwards, the tool of the aristocracy, against the people! Mechanics and working men! A deadly blow has been struck at your liberty! The prize for which your fathers fought has been robbed from you! The freemen of the North are now on a level with the slaves of the South! with no other privilege than laboring, that drones may fatten on your lifeblood! Twenty of your brethren have been found guilty for presuming to resist a reduction of their wages! And Judge Edwards has charged an American jury, and, agreeably to that charge, they have established the precedent that workingmen have no right to regulate the price of labor, or, in other words, the rich are the only judges of the wants of the poor man. On Monday, June 6, 1836, at ten o'clock, these freemen are to receive their sentence, to gratify the hellish appetites of the aristocrats!

On Monday, the liberty of the workingmen will be interred! Judge Edwards is to chant the requiem! Go! Go! Go! every freeman, every workingman, and hear the hollow and melancholy sound of the earth on the coffin of equality! Let the courtroom, the City Hall, yea! the whole park, be filled with mourners. But remember, offer no violence to Judge Edwards, bend meekly, and receive the chain wherewith you are to be bound! Keep the peace! Above all things, keep the peace!

[Judge Edwards fined the president of the "unlawful club" of tailors $150, the other defendants $50 or $100. In passing sentence, he scolded them for having "craftily" entered into "a conspiracy" to "injure trade," and declared: "The law

---

[3]Bayard Tuckerman, ed., *Diary of Philip Hone* (New York: Dodd, Mead and Company, 1889), pp. 210–211.

leaves every individual [the] master of his own individual acts. But it will not suffer him to encroach upon the rights of others. He may work or not, as suits his pleasure, but he shall not enter into a confederacy with a view of controlling others, and take measures to carry it into effect." Contrary to this dictum, the tailors had not only resorted to a strike but had also harassed the employers with picketing and other demonstrations, and had brought various kinds of pressures to bear on the strike-breakers.]

4. Chattel Slavery Versus Wage Slavery (1840)

Orestes A. Brownson, a self-taught Vermonter, made his mark as a preacher, magazine editor, lecturer, reformer, socialist, transcendentalist, and writer (twenty volumes). Fearless and uncompromising, he began as a Presbyterian minister and wound up as a convert to Catholicism. While preaching to groups of workers, he had become deeply interested in labor reform, and his blast, given here, was music to the ears of southern slaveowners. What are his most obvious exaggerations? Was the slaveowner or the mill owner the greater hypocrite?

In regard to labor, two systems obtain: one that of slave labor, the other that of free labor. Of the two, the first is, in our judgment, except so far as the feelings are concerned, decidedly the least oppressive. If the slave has never been a free man, we think, as a general rule, his sufferings are less than those of the free laborer at wages. As to actual freedom, one has just about as much as the other. The laborer at wages has all the disadvantages of freedom and none of its blessings, while the slave, if denied the blessings, is freed from the disadvantages.

We are no advocates of slavery. We are as heartily opposed to it as any modern abolitionist can be. But we say frankly that, if there must always be a laboring population distinct from proprietors and employers, we regard the slave system as decidedly preferable to the system at wages.

It is no pleasant thing to go days without food; to lie idle for weeks, seeking work and finding none; to rise in the morning with a wife and children you love, and know not where to procure them a breakfast; and to see constantly before you no brighter prospect than the almshouse.

Yet these are no infrequent incidents in the lives of our laboring population. Even in seasons of general prosperity, when there was only the ordinary cry of "hard times," we have seen hundreds of people in a not very populous village, in a wealthy portion of our common country, suffering for the want of the necessaries of life, willing to work and yet finding no work to do. Many and many is the application of a poor man for work, merely for his food, we have seen rejected. These things are little thought of, for the applicants are poor; they fill no conspicuous place in society, and they have no biographers. But their wrongs are chronicled in heaven.

It is said there is no want in this country. There may be less in some other countries. But death by actual starvation in this country is, we apprehend, no uncommon

---

[4]*Boston Quarterly Review* 3 (1840): 368–370.

occurrence. The sufferings of a quiet, unassuming but useful class of females in our cities, in general seamstresses, too proud to beg or to apply to the almshouse, are not easily told. They are industrious; they do all that they can find to do. But yet the little there is for them to do, and the miserable pittance they receive for it, is hardly sufficient to keep soul and body together.

And yet there is a man who employs them to make shirts, trousers, etc., and grows rich on their labors. He is one of our respectable citizens, perhaps is praised in the newspapers for his liberal donations to some charitable institution. He passes among us as a pattern of morality and is honored as a worthy Christian. And why should he not be, since our Christian community is made up of such as he, and since our clergy would not dare question his piety lest they should incur the reproach of infidelity and lose their standing and their salaries? . . .

The average life—working life, we mean—of the girls that come to Lowell, for instance, from Maine, New Hampshire, and Vermont, we have been assured, is only about three years. What becomes of them then? Few of them ever marry; fewer still ever return to their native places with reputations unimpaired. "She has worked in a factory" is almost enough to damn to infamy the most worthy and virtuous girl. . . .

Where go the proceeds of their labors? The man who employs them, and for whom they are toiling as so many slaves, is one of our city nabobs, reveling in luxury; or he is a member of our legislature, enacting laws to put money in his own pocket; or he is a member of Congress, contending for a high tariff to tax the poor for the benefit of the rich; or in these times he is shedding crocodile tears over the deplorable condition of the poor laborer, while he docks his wages 25 percent. . . . And this man too would fain pass for a Christian and a republican. He shouts for liberty, stickles for equality, and is horrified at a Southern planter who keeps slaves.

One thing is certain: that, of the amount actually produced by the operative, he retains a less proportion than it costs the master to feed, clothe, and lodge his slave. Wages is a cunning device of the devil, for the benefit of tender consciences who would retain all the advantages of the slave system without the expense, trouble, and odium of being slaveholders.

5. Regulations at the Lowell Mills (1830s)

Factory life was a novelty to all involved in the early nineteenth century, employers as well as employees. Manufacturers often worried about both the efficiency and the moral character of their workers. At the Lawrence Manufacturing Company in Lowell, Massachusetts, the following regulations were designed to guide the work and the very lives of the mill workers. Why did the company lay such emphasis on the religious practices of its workers? What do these regulations suggest were the employer's greatest concerns? What can be inferred from these rules of conduct about the backgrounds from which the workers came?

---

[5]Smithsonian Institution.

D. Steamboats and Canals

1. The First "Fire Canoe" in the West (1811)

Less well known than Robert Fulton's epochal steamboat trip up the Hudson in 1807, but hardly less significant, was the first steamboat on the Mississippi. The New Orleans *was built at Pittsburgh by Nicholas J. Roosevelt, an associate of Fulton and a distant relative of two future presidents. The vessel made the historic voyage from Pittsburgh to New Orleans in fourteen days, despite low water at the falls of the Ohio, a fire on board, the birth of a baby, and a series of tremendous earthquakes that changed the course of the river in places and so destroyed landmarks as to confuse*

---

[1]J. H. B. Latrobe, *The First Steamboat Voyage on the Western Waters* (Baltimore: J. Murphy, 1871), pp. 13–28, passim.

the pilot. The story is here told by J. H. B. Latrobe, whose eldest sister, married to Roosevelt, made the trip. What does this account reveal about the conditions of early steamboat travel?

As the *New Orleans* approached completion, and when it came to be known that Mrs. Roosevelt intended to accompany her husband on the voyage, the numerous friends she had made in Pittsburgh united in endeavoring to dissuade her from what they regarded as utter folly, if not absolute madness. Her husband was appealed to. The criticisms that had been freely applied to the boat by the crowds of visitors to the shipyard were now transferred to the conduct of the builder. He was told that he had no right to peril his wife's life, however reckless he might be of his own. Mrs. Roosevelt, too, expected before long to become a mother; and this was held to enhance the offense which the good people of Pittsburgh fancied he was committing. But the wife believed in her husband; and in the latter part of September, 1811, the *New Orleans,* after a short experimental trip up the Monongahela, commenced her voyage . . . the voyage which changed the relations of the West— which may almost be said to have changed its destiny. . . .

On the second day after leaving Pittsburgh, the *New Orleans* rounded to opposite Cincinnati, and cast anchor in the stream. Levees and wharf boats were things unknown in 1811. Here, as at Pittsburgh, the whole town seemed to have assembled on the bank, and many of the acquaintances of the former visit came off in small boats. "Well, you are as good as your word; you have visited us in a steamboat," they said; "but we see you for the last time. Your boat may go *down* the river; but, as to coming up it, the very idea is an absurd one." This was one of those occasions on which seeing was not believing. . . .

The morning after the arrival of the vessel at Louisville, Mr. Roosevelt's acquaintances and others came on board, and here the same things were said that had been said at Cincinnati. Congratulations at having descended the river were, without exception, accompanied by regrets that it was the first and last time a steamboat would be seen above the Falls of the Ohio. Still, so far, certainly, Mr. Roosevelt's promises had been fulfilled; and there was a public dinner given to him a few days after his arrival. . . .

Not to be outdone in hospitality, Mr. Roosevelt invited his hosts to dine on board the *New Orleans,* which still lay anchored opposite the town. The company met in the forward or gentlemen's cabin, and the feast was at its height when suddenly there were heard unwonted rumblings, accompanied by a very perceptible motion in the vessel. The company had but one idea. The *New Orleans* had escaped from her anchor, and was drifting towards the Falls, to the certain destruction of all on board. There was an instant and simultaneous rush to the upper deck, when the company found that, instead of drifting towards the Falls of the Ohio, the *New Orleans* was making good headway up the river and would soon leave Louisville in the distance downstream. As the engine warmed to its work, and the steam blew off at the safety valve, the speed increased. Mr. Roosevelt, of course, had provided this mode of convincing his incredulous guests, and their surprise and delight may readily be imagined. After going up the river for a few miles, the *New Orleans* returned to her anchorage. . . .

Hitherto the voyage had been one of pleasure. Nothing had marred the enjoyment of the travelers. The receptions at Louisville and Cincinnati had been great events. But now were to come, to use the words of the letter already referred to, "those days of horror." The comet of 1811 had disappeared, and was followed by the earthquake of that year . . . , and the earthquake accompanied the *New Orleans* far on her way down the Mississippi. . . .

Sometimes the Indians attempted to approach the steamboat; and, again, fled on its approach. The Chickasaws still occupied that part of the state of Tennessee lying below the mouth of the Ohio. On one occasion, a large canoe, fully manned, came out of the woods abreast of the steamboat. The Indians, outnumbering the crew of the vessel, paddled after it. There was at once a race, and for a time the contest was equal. The result, however, was what might have been anticipated. Steam had the advantage of endurance; and the Indians with wild shouts, which might have been shouts of defiance, gave up the pursuit, and turned into the forest from whence they had emerged. . . .

Sometimes Indians would join the wood choppers [seeking fuel]; and occasionally one would be able to converse in English with the men. From these it was learned that the steamboat was called the "Penelore" or "Fire Canoe" and was supposed to have some affinity with the comet that had preceded the earthquake—the sparks from the chimney of the boat being likened to the train of the celestial visitant. Again, they would attribute the smoky atmosphere of the steamer and the rumbling of the earth to the beating of the waters by the fast-revolving paddles.

To the native inhabitants of the boundless forest that lined the river banks, the coming of the first steamboat was an omen of evil; and as it was the precursor of their own expulsion from their ancient homes, no wonder they continued for years to regard all steamboats with awe. As late as 1834, when the emigration of the Chickasaws to their new homes, west of the river, took place, hundreds refused to trust themselves in such conveyances but preferred making their long and weary pilgrimage on foot.

2. The Impact of the Erie Canal (1853)

The Erie Canal, completed in 1825, wrote epochal new chapters in the history of American transportation and industry. Projected by western-minded New Yorkers, it was bitterly opposed by New York City, which shortsightedly clung to its seaboard orientation. When the issue was debated in the state legislature, and the question arose of filling the canal with water, one eastern member exclaimed, "Give yourself no trouble—the tears of our constituents will fill it!" The most immediate result of the canal was to reduce sharply the cost of moving bulk shipments. Further results were analyzed as follows in a graphic report by the secretary of the treasury in 1853. Why did other cities lose out in competition with New York? Which section gained the most from the canal?

[2]*Senate Executive Documents,* 32d Congress, 1st session, no. 112, pp. 278–279.

Although the rates of transportation over the Erie Canal, at its opening, were nearly double the present charges . . . it immediately became the convenient and favorite route for a large portion of the produce of the Northwestern states, and secured to the City of New York the position which she now holds as the emporium of the Confederacy [Union].

Previous to the opening of the Canal, the trade of the West was chiefly carried on through the cities of Baltimore and Philadelphia, particularly the latter, which was at that time the first city of the United States in population and wealth, and in the amount of its internal commerce.

As soon as the [Great] Lakes were reached, the line of navigable water was extended through them nearly one thousand miles farther into the interior. The Western states immediately commenced the construction of similar works, for the purpose of opening a communication, from the more remote portions of their territories, with this great water-line. All these works took their direction and character from the Erie Canal, which in this manner became the outlet for almost the greater part of the West.

It is difficult to estimate the influence which this Canal has exerted upon the commerce, growth, and prosperity of the whole country, for it is impossible to imagine what would have been the state of things without it.

But for this work, the West would have held out few inducements to the settler, who would have been without a market for his most important products, and consequently without the means of supplying many of his most essential wants. That portion of the country would have remained comparatively unsettled up to the present time; and, where now exist rich and populous communities, we should find an uncultivated wilderness.

The East would have been equally without the elements of growth. The Canal has supplied it with cheap food, and has opened an outlet and created a market for the products of its manufactures and commerce.

The increase of commerce, and the growth of the country, have been very accurately measured by the growth of the business of the Canal. It has been one great bond of strength, infusing life and vigor into the whole. Commercially and politically, it has secured and maintained to the United States the characteristics of a homogeneous people.

3. Steamboats Lose to the Railroads (c. 1857)

Samuel Clemens, whose pen name, "Mark Twain," was a depth measurement, became apprenticed as a Mississippi pilot in 1857, when he was only twenty-two. Emerging as a full-fledged pilot, he remained on the river until the Civil War interrupted traffic in 1861. In 1883, at the height of his powers, he published his classic Life on the Mississippi, *in which he described the spectacular races between river queens that foamed perilously against the current at an average of more than fourteen miles an hour. What does the following brief episode, as related by Clemens, reveal about the pace of technological change?*

---

[3]Mark Twain, *Life on the Mississippi* (London: Chatto & Windus, 1883), chap. 58.

The locomotive is in sight from the deck of the steamboat almost the whole way from St. Louis to St. Paul—eight hundred miles. These railroads have made havoc with the steamboat commerce. The clerk of our boat was a steamboat clerk before these roads were built. In that day the influx of population was so great, and the freight business so heavy, that the boats were not able to keep up with the demands made upon their carrying capacity; consequently the captains were very independent and airy—pretty "biggity," as Uncle Remus would say. The clerk nutshelled the contrast between the former time and the present, thus:

"Boat used to land—captain on hurricane roof—mighty stiff and straight—iron ramrod for a spine—kid gloves, plug tile [hat], hair parted behind—man on shore takes off hat and says:

"'Got twenty-eight tons of wheat, cap'n—be great favor if you can take them.'

"Captain says:

"'I'll take two of them'—and don't even condescend to look at him.

"But nowadays the captain takes off his old slouch [hat], and smiles all the way around to the back of his ears, and gets off a bow which he hasn't got any ramrod to interfere with, and says:

"'Glad to see you, Smith, glad to see you—you're looking well—haven't seen you looking so well for years—what you got for us?'

"'Nuth'n,' says Smith; and keeps his hat on, and just turns his back and goes to talking with somebody else.

"Oh, yes! eight years ago the captain was on top; but it's Smith's turn now. Eight years ago a boat used to go up the river with every stateroom full, and people piled five and six deep on the cabin floor; and a solid deckload of immigrants and harvesters down below, into the bargain. To get a first class stateroom, you'd got to prove sixteen quarterings of nobility and four hundred years of descent, or be personally acquainted with the nigger that blacked the captain's boots. But it's all changed now; plenty staterooms above, no harvesters below—there's a patent self-binder now, and they don't have harvesters any more; they've gone where the woodbine twineth—and they didn't go by steamboat, either; they went by the train."

E. The Coming of the Iron Horse _____

1. A Canal Stockholder's Outburst (1830)

New methods of transportation naturally alarmed entrenched interests. Turnpike investors fought the canals; canal investors and teamsters fought the railroads; railroad investors were later to fight the motor trucks and airlines. In particular, teamsters objected to "the damned railroad" because it cut up farms; ruined the horse and hay market; deprived wheelwrights, blacksmiths, and mechanics of their employment; and brought in hordes of pick-and-shovel Irishmen, with ready fists, to work on the roadbeds. Canal boatmen and canal investors voiced similar grievances. What real substance is there in these obviously overdrawn objections that appeared in an Indiana newspaper?

_____
[1]*Vincennes* [Indiana] *Western Sun,* July 24, 1830.

The following humorous argument was advanced by a canal stockholder, for the purpose of putting down railways:

"He saw what would be the effect of it; that it would set the whole world a-gadding. Twenty miles an hour, sir.—Why, you will not be able to keep an apprentice boy at his work! Every Saturday evening he must have a trip to Ohio to spend a Sunday with his sweetheart. Grave, plodding citizens will be flying about like comets. All local attachments will be at an end. It will encourage flightiness of intellect. Veracious people will turn into the most immeasurable liars: all conceptions will be exaggerated by the magnificent notions of distance.—Only a hundred miles off!—Tut, nonsense, I'll step across, madam and bring your fan! 'Pray, sir, will you dine with me today, at my little box on the Allegheny?' 'Why indeed I don't know— I shall be there, but you must let me off in time for the theater.'

"And then, sir, there will be barrels of pork, cargoes of flour, chaldrons of coal, and even lead and whiskey, and such-like sober things that have always been used to slow traveling—whisking away like a sky rocket. It will upset all the gravity of the nation. If a couple of gentlemen have an affair of honor, it is only to steal off to the Rocky Mountains and there is no jurisdiction that can touch them. And then, sir; think of it—flying for debt! A set of bailiffs mounted on bombshells would never overtake an absconding debtor, only give him a fair start.

"Upon the whole, sir, it is a pestilential, topsy-turvy, harum-scarum whirligig. Give me the old, solemn, straightforward, regular Dutch canal—three miles an hour for expresses, and two-rod jogtrot journeys—with a yoke of oxen for heavy loads! I go for beasts of burden, it is more firmative and scriptural, and suits a moral and religious people better. None of your hop-skip-and-jump whimsies for me."

2. Railroads Link East and West (1849)

Alexander Mackay, a gifted British journalist and barrister, published in 1849 a three-volume description of his American travels. It ranks as the finest work of its kind for the era. Liberal, sympathetic, and friendly, Mackay struck up enlightening conversations with the Americans, as the following passage attests. How much logic was there in his prognosis of an East-West split? Why did such a division not occur in actual practice?

"It is a common thing in Europe," said I [Mackay], "to speculate upon the probabilities of a speedy dissolution between the Northern and Southern divisions of the Union. But I confess that, for myself, I have for some time back been of opinion that, should a disseverance ever take place, the danger is that it will be between the East and the West."

"On what do you base such an opinion?" inquired my [American] companion.

"On referring to the map," replied I, "it will be found that fully one-third of the members [states] of the Confederation are situated in the same great basin, having one great interest in common between them, being irrigated by the same system of

---

[2]Alexander Mackay, *The Western World, or Travels in the United States in 1846–1847* (London: R. Bentley, 1849), vol. 1, pp. 236–240.

navigable rivers, and all united together into one powerful belt by their common artery, the Mississippi."

"Admitting this," observed my friend, "what danger arises therefrom to the stability of the Union?"

"Only that arising from a probable conflict of interests," replied I. "The great region drained by the Mississippi is pre-eminently agricultural, whilst much of the seaboard is manufacturing and commercial. The first-named region is being rapidly filled with an adventurous and energetic population, and its material resources are being developed at a ratio unexampled in the annals of human progress. The revolution [passing] of a very few years will find it powerful enough to stand by itself, should it feel so inclined. And then nothing can prevent a fatal collision of interests between it and the different communities on the seaboard but the recognition and adoption of a commercial policy which will afford it an ample outlet for its vast and varied productions." . . .

"I am free to admit," cried my friend, "the necessity for such an adjustment as an essential condition to the stability of the Union. . . . Antagonistic as they are in many respects in their interests, were the East and the West to be left physically isolated from each other, the difficulties in the way of a compromise of interests would indeed be insurmountable. Had the East no direct hold upon the West, and had the West no communication with the rest of the world but through the Mississippi, one might well despair of a permanent reconciliation. It is in obviating the physical obstructions . . . that the great barrier to a permanent good understanding between the East and the West has been broken down. It is by rendering each more necessary to the other that the foundation has been laid for that mutual concession which alone can ensure future harmony and give permanence to the Union."

"And how have you done this?" inquired I.

"We have tapped the West," replied he. . . .

"By tapping the West, then, you mean opening direct communications between the East and the West?"

"Exactly so," said he. "Had matters been left as nature arranged them, the whole traffic of the Mississippi valley would have been thrown upon the Gulf of Mexico. . . ."

"When I consider," said I, "the many parallel lines of artificial communication which you have established between the East and the West, I must say that, in tapping the latter, you have tapped it liberally."

"We have taken, or are taking, advantage of all our opportunities in this respect," replied he [referring to the East-West network of canals and railroads]. . . .

"And to these you look," observed I, "as your securities for the integrity of the republic?"

"As bonds," said he, "the existence of which renders improbable the severance of the East from the West. These four great parallel lines of intercommunication have effectually counteracted the political tendencies of the Mississippi. . . . Everything, too, which improves the position of the West, as regards the Atlantic seaports, renders the mutual dependence between the two sections of the Union, as respects their home trade, more intimate and complete. In addition to this, it strengthens more and more the sentiment of nationality, by bringing the denizens of the West and the East in constant communication with each other. They freely traverse each other's fields, and walk each other's streets, and feel equally at home, whether they are on the Wabash, the Arkansas, the Potomac, the Susquehanna, the Genesee, or the St. John's.

"This is what we have effected by tapping the West. We have united it to us by bonds of iron, which it cannot, and which, if it could, it would not, break. By binding it to the older states by the strong tie of material interests, we have identified its political sentiment with our own. We have made the twain one by our canals, our railroads, and our electric telegraphs, by making the Atlantic more necessary to the West than the Gulf; in short," said he, "by removing the Alleghenies."

Thought Provokers

1. What were the principal effects of industrialization on women and the family?
2. Compare the ways in which anti-foreignism manifests itself in the United States today with those of the 1850s and 1860s. Has the nation grown more tolerant?
3. Were the rich of the 1830s really exploiting the workers, or were they providing them with job opportunities? Would you rather have been a black slave in the South or a wage slave in a New England factory? Argue both sides. In what noteworthy respects is labor better off today than it was in the 1830s, and why?
4. Compare and contrast the advantages and disadvantages of canals, river waterways, and railroads, and draw conclusions. Why could some canals, including the Erie Canal, continue to compete with the railroads?
5. Why can it be asserted with plausibility that the Erie Canal won the Civil War for the North? Would there have been a Civil War if there had been no Erie Canal? Do contrasting economies tend to divide sections or to unite them because of their dependence on one another?

16

The Ferment
of Reform and Culture,
1790–1860

I could readily see in Emerson, notwithstanding his
merit, a gaping flaw. It was the insinuation that, had
he lived in those days when the world was made, he
might have offered some valuable suggestions.

Herman Melville, 1849

Prologue: The War of Independence, the War of 1812, and the astonishing physical mobility of westward-pushing Americans disrupted the traditional churches and
undermined cultural conventions of all sorts. Beginning in the early nineteenth century, a wave of religious revivals swept across the country, checking backsliding and
summoning the people back to the hellfire religion of colonial days. The revivals of
this "Second Great Awakening" inspired a host of humanitarian crusades—including
campaigns for prison reform, temperance, women's rights, and, eventually, the abolition of slavery. The combined effects of industrialism and democracy initiated far-
reaching changes in the character of the family and in the roles of women.
Meanwhile, an impressive group of writers, based mainly in New England, laid the
foundations of a distinctively American literary tradition, which contained (perhaps
paradoxically) healthy doses of social utopianism and unbridled individualism.

A. Religious Ferment

1. A Catholic Views Camp Meetings (c. 1801)

*Kentucky-born Martin J. Spalding was an eminent Catholic prelate who died as the
archbishop of Baltimore. He won many friends with his merry laugh, attractive
speaking voice, and frank manner. Drawing on memoirs and oral testimony, he described some forty years later the great Protestant camp meetings in Kentucky, where*

---

[1]M. J. Spalding, *Sketches of the Early Catholic Missions of Kentucky* . . . (Louisville, Ky.: Webb & Brother;
Baltimore: J. Murphy, 1844), pp. 104–106.

thousands assembled for a week or so to repent of their sins and to find emotional re-
lease from a grinding, monotonous frontier life. The camp meeting, though not con-
fined to the frontier, was a typically frontier phenomenon, and attracted camp
followers who purveyed alcohol and sex. Who were the main participants in the
meeting here described? How is the writer's own religious sensibility evident?

To understand more fully how very "precious and astonishing" this great revival was, we must farther reflect: 1st, that it produced, not a mere momentary excitement, but one that lasted for several successive years. 2ndly, that it was not confined to one particular denomination, but, to a greater or less extent, pervaded all. 3rdly, that men of sense and of good judgment in other matters were often carried away by the same fanaticism which swayed the mob. 4thly, that this fanaticism was as widespread as it was permanent—not being confined to Kentucky, but pervading most of the adjoining states and territories. And 5thly, that though some were found who had good sense enough to detect the imposture, yet they were comparatively few in number, and wholly unable to stay the rushing torrent of fanaticism, even if they had had the moral courage to attempt it.

Such are some of the leading features of a movement in religion (!) which is perhaps one of the most extraordinary recorded in history, and to which we know of but few parallels, except in some of the fanatical doings of the Anabaptists in Germany during the first years of their history. The whole matter furnishes one more conclusive evidence of the weakness of the human mind when left to itself; and one more sad commentary on the Protestant rule of faith.

Here we see whole masses of population, spread over a vast territory, boasting too of their enlightenment and Bible-learning, swayed for years by a fanaticism as absurd as it was blasphemous; and yet believing all this to be the work of the Holy Spirit! Let Protestants after this talk about Catholic ignorance and superstition! Had Catholics ever played the "fantastic tricks" which were played off by Protestants during these years, we would perhaps never hear the end of it. . . .

Besides the "exercises" [described earlier] . . . there was also the jumping exercise. Spasmodic convulsions, which lasted sometimes for hours, were the usual sequel to the falling exercise. Then there were the "exercises" of screaming and shouting and crying. A camp meeting during that day exhibited the strangest bodily feats, accompanied with the most Babel-like sounds. An eyewitness of undoubted veracity stated to us that, in passing one of the camp-grounds, he noticed a man in the "barking exercise," clasping a tree with his arms, and dashing his head against it until it was all besmeared with blood, shouting all the time that he had "treed his Saviour"!! Another eyewitness stated that in casually passing by a camp in the night, while the exercises were at the highest, he witnessed scenes of too revolting a character even to be alluded to here.

One of the most remarkable features, perhaps, of these "exercises" is the apparently well-authenticated fact that many fell into them by a kind of sympathy, almost in spite of themselves, and some even positively against their own will! Some who visited the meetings to laugh at the proceedings, sometimes caught the contagion themselves. There seems to have then existed in Kentucky a kind of mental and moral epidemic—a sort of contagious frenzy—which spread rapidly from one to another.

Yet the charm was not so strong that it could not be broken, as the following incident, related to us by a highly intelligent Protestant gentleman, clearly proves. Some young ladies of his acquaintance came from one of those meetings to pass the night at this father's house. They were laboring under great nervous excitement, and, in the course of the evening, began to jerk most violently. The father, one of the most intelligent men in Kentucky, severely rebuked them, and told them bluntly that he would "have no such behavior as this in his house." The reproof was effectual, and the jerking spirit was exorcised! . . .

2. Joseph Smith Has a Vision (1820)

Joseph Smith, prophet and first president of the Church of Jesus Christ of Latter-Day Saints (Mormons), was born in Vermont and moved as a young boy with his family to the town of Manchester, in western New York. The region was at that time pulsating with religious fervor and denominational rivalry. Pious but confused, the fourteen-year-old Smith prayed for guidance. The result, he later wrote, was a vision that led him to shun the contending existing churches and move toward the establishment of the Mormon religion. In his account of the episode, which follows, what is revealed about the religious temper of the age?

Some time in the second year after our removal to Manchester, there was in the place where we lived an unusual excitement on the subject of religion. It commenced with the Methodists, but soon became general among all the sects in that region of country. Indeed, the whole district of country seemed affected by it, and great multitudes united themselves to the different religious parties, which created no small stir and division amongst the people, some crying, "Lo here!" and others, "Lo, there!" Some were contending for the Methodist faith, some for the Presbyterian, and some for the Baptist. . . .

I was at this time in my fifteenth year. My father's family was proselyted to the Presbyterian faith, and four of them joined that church, namely—my mother Lucy; my brothers Hyrum and Samuel Harrison; and my sister Sophronia. During this time of great excitement, my mind was called up to serious reflection and great uneasiness; but though my feelings were deep and often poignant, still I kept myself aloof from all these parties, though I attended their several meetings as often as occasion would permit. In process of time my mind became somewhat partial to the Methodist sect, and I felt some desire to be united with them; but so great were the confusion and strife among the different denominations, that it was impossible for a person young as I was, and so unacquainted with men and things, to come to any certain conclusion who was right and who was wrong. My mind at times was greatly excited, the cry and tumult were so great and incessant. The Presbyterians were most decided against the Baptists and Methodists, and used all the powers of both reason and sophistry to prove their errors, or, at least, to make the people think they were in error. On the other hand, the Baptists and Methodists in their turn were equally zealous in endeavoring to establish their own tenets and disprove all others.

---

[2]From Joseph Smith, *The Pearl of Great Price* (Salt Lake City: Deseret Book Co., 1920) chap. 1, verses 5, 7–24, 26.

In the midst of this war of words and tumult of opinions, I often said to myself, what is to be done? Who of all these parties are right; or, are they all wrong together? If any one of them be right, which is it, and how shall I know it? While I was laboring under the extreme difficulties caused by the contests of these parties of religionists, I was one day reading the Epistle of James, first chapter and fifth verse, which reads: "If any of you lack wisdom, let him ask of God, that giveth to all men liberally, and upbraideth not; and it shall be given him."

Never did any passage of Scripture come with more power to the heart of man than this did at this time to mine. It seemed to enter with great force into every feeling of my heart. I reflected on it again and again, knowing that if any person needed wisdom from God, I did; for how to act I did not know and unless I could get more wisdom than I then had, I would never know; for the teachers of religion of the different sects understood the same passage of Scripture so differently as to destroy all confidence in settling the question by an appeal to the Bible. At length I came to the conclusion that I must either remain in darkness and confusion, or else I must do as James directs, that is, ask of God. I at length came to the determination to "ask of God," concluding that if He gave wisdom to them that lacked wisdom, and would give liberally, and not upbraid, I might venture. So, in accordance with this, my determination to ask God, I returned to the woods to make the attempt. It was on the morning of a beautiful, clear day, early in the spring of eighteen hundred and twenty. It was the first time in my life I had made such an attempt, for amidst all my anxieties I had never as yet made the attempt to pray vocally.

After I had retired to the place where I had previously designed to go, having looked around me, and finding myself alone, I kneeled down and began to offer up the desires of my heart to God. I had scarcely done so, when immediately I was seized upon by some power which entirely overcame me, and had such an astonishing influence over me as to bind my tongue so that I could not speak. Thick darkness gathered around me, and it seemed to me for a time as if I were doomed to sudden destruction. But, exerting all my powers to call upon God to deliver me out of the power of this enemy which had seized upon me, and at the very moment when I was ready to sink into despair and abandon myself to destruction—not to an imaginary ruin, but to the power of some actual being from the unseen world, who had such marvelous power as I had never before felt in any being—just at this moment of great alarm, I saw a pillar of light exactly over my head, above the brightness of the sun, which descended gradually until it fell upon me.

It no sooner appeared than I found myself delivered from the enemy which held me bound. When the light rested upon me I saw two personages, whose brightness and glory defy all description, standing above me in the air. One of them spake unto me, calling me by name, and said—pointing to the other—"This is my beloved Son. Hear Him."

My object in going to inquire of the Lord was to know which of all the sects was right, that I might know which to join. No sooner, therefore, did I get possession of myself, so as to be able to speak, than I asked the personages who stood above me in the light, which of all the sects was right—and which I should join. I was answered that I must join none of them, for they were all wrong, and the personage who addressed me said that all their creeds were an abomination in His sight: that those professors were all corrupt; that "they draw near to me with their lips, but their hearts are far from me; they teach for doctrines the commandments of men: having a form of godliness, but they deny the power thereof." He again forbade me to join with any of them: and many other things did he say unto me, which I cannot write at this time. When I came to myself again, I found myself lying on my back, looking up into heaven. When the light had departed, I had no strength; but soon recovering in some degree, I went home. And as I leaned up to the fireplace, mother inquired what the matter was. I replied, "Never mind, all is well—I am well enough off." I then said to my mother, "I have learned for myself that Presbyterianism is not true."

It seems as though the adversary was aware, at a very early period of my life, that I was destined to prove a disturber and an annoyer of his kingdom; else why should the powers of darkness combine against me? Why the opposition and persecution that arose against me, almost in my infancy? Some few days after I had this vision, I happened to be in company with one of the Methodist preachers, who was very active in the before-mentioned religious excitement, and, conversing with him on the subject of religion, I took occasion to give him an account of the vision which I had had. I was greatly surprised at his behavior; he treated my communication not only lightly, but with great contempt, saying, it was all of the devil, that there were no such things as visions or revelations in these days; that all such things had ceased with the Apostles, and that there would never be any more of them. I soon found, however, that my telling the story had excited a great deal of prejudice against me among professors of religion, and was the cause of great persecution, which continued to increase; and though I was an obscure boy, only between fourteen and fifteen years of age, and my circumstances in life such as to make a boy of no consequence in the world, yet men of high standing would take notice sufficient to excite the public mind against me, and create a bitter persecution; and this was common among all the sects—all united to persecute me.

It caused me serious reflection then, and often has since, how very strange it was that an obscure boy, of a little over fourteen years of age, and one, too, who was doomed to the necessity of obtaining a scanty maintenance by his daily labor, should be thought a character of sufficient importance to attract the attention of the great ones of the most popular sects of the day, and in a manner to create in them a spirit of the most bitter persecution and reviling. But strange or not, so it was, and it was often the cause of great sorrow to myself. However, it was nevertheless a fact that I had beheld a vision. . . .

I had now got my mind satisfied so far as the sectarian world was concerned; that it was not my duty to join with any of them, but to continue as I was until further directed. I had found the testimony of James to be true, that a man who lacked wisdom might ask of God, and obtain, and not be upbraided.

B. Social and Humanitarian Reformers

1. William Ellery Channing Preaches Reformism (c. 1831)

The famed Boston minister William Ellery Channing (1780-1842) was a leading light in the Unitarian movement, which criticized Calvinistic Puritanism for its emphasis on human depravity. Channing, in contrast, preached a gospel of human goodness, dignity, and even perfectibility. Such doctrines gave powerful impetus to the reform crusades of the early nineteenth century. In the following sermon, entitled "The Perfect Life: The Essence of the Christian Religion," how does Channing support his arguments for perfectionism? How does he portray the relationship of religious belief to worldly actions?

I believe that Christianity has one great principle, which is central, around which all its truths gather, and which constitutes it the glorious gospel of the blessed God. I believe that no truth is so worthy of acceptance and so quickening as this. In proportion as we penetrate into it, and are penetrated by it, we comprehend our religion, and attain to a living faith. This great principle can be briefly expressed. It is the doctrine that "God purposes, in his unbounded fatherly love, to perfect the human soul; to purify it from all sin; to create it after his own image; to fill it with his own spirit; to unfold it for ever; to raise it to life and immortality in heaven—that is, to communicate to it from himself a life of celestial power, virtue, and joy." The elevation of men above the imperfections, temptations, sins, sufferings, of the present state, to a diviner being,—this is the great purpose of God, revealed and accomplished by Jesus Christ; this it is that constitutes the religion of Jesus Christ,—glad tidings to all people: for it is a religion suited to fulfill the wants of every human being.

In the New Testament I learn that God regards the human soul with unutterable interest and love; that in an important sense it bears the impress of his own infinity, its powers being germs, which may expand without limit or end; that he loves it, even when fallen, and desires its restoration; that he has sent his Son to redeem and cleanse it from all iniquity; that he for ever seeks to communicate it to a divine virtue which shall spring up, by perennial bloom and fruitfulness, into everlasting life. In the New Testament I learn that what God wills is our perfection; by which I understand the freest exercise and perpetual development of our highest powers,— strength and brightness of intellect, unconquerable energy of moral principle, pure and fervent desire for truth, unbounded love of goodness and greatness, benevolence free from every selfish taint, the perpetual consciousness of God and of his immediate presence, co-operation and friendship with all enlightened and disinterested spirits, and radiant glory of divine will and beneficent influence, of which we have an emblem—a faint emblem only—in the sun that illuminates and warms so many worlds. Christianity reveals to me this moral perfection of man, as the great purpose of God.

---

[1]William Ellery Channing, *Channing's Works* (Boston: American Unitarian Association, 1895), pp. 1001–1005.

When I look into man's nature, I see that moral perfection is his only true and enduring good; and consequently the promise of this must be the highest truth which any religion can contain. The loftiest endowment of our nature is the moral power,—the power of perceiving and practising virtue, of discerning and seeking goodness. . . .

At this period, we see a mighty movement of the civilized world. Thrones are tottering, and the firmest establishments of former ages seem about to be swept away by the torrent of revolution. In this movement I rejoice, though not without trembling joy. But I rejoice, only because I look at it in the light of the great truth which I have this day aimed to enforce; because I see, as I think, in the revolutionary spirit of our times, the promise of a freer and higher action of the human mind,—the pledge of a state of society more fit to perfect human beings. I regard the present state of the world in this moral light altogether. The despotisms, which are to be prostrated, seem to be evils, chiefly as they have enslaved men's faculties, as they have bowed and weighed down the soul. The liberty, after which men aspire, is to prove a good only so far as it shall give force and enlargement to the mind; only so far as it shall conspire with Christianity in advancing human nature. Men will gain little by escaping outward despotism, if the soul continues enthralled. Men must be subjected to some law; and unless the law in their own breast, the law of God, of duty, of perfection, be adopted by their free choice as the supreme rule, they will fall under the tyranny of selfish passion, which will bow their necks for an outward yoke.

I have hope in the present struggle of the world, because it seems to me more spiritual, more moral, in its origin and tendencies, than any which have preceded it. It differs much from the revolts of former times, when an oppressed populace or peasantry broke forth into frantic opposition to government, under the goading pressure of famine and misery. Men are now moved, not merely by physical wants and sufferings, but by ideas, by principles, by the conception of a better state of society, under which the rights of human nature will be recognized, and greater justice be done to the mind in all classes of the community. There is then an element—spiritual, moral, and tending towards perfection—in the present movement; and this is my great hope. When I see, however, the tremendous strength of unsubdued passions, which mix with and often overpower this conception of a better order of society; when I consider the success with which the selfish, crafty, and ambitious have turned to their own purposes the generous enthusiasm of the people; when I consider the darkness which hangs over the nations, the rashness with which they have rushed into infidelity and irreligion, as the only refuge from priestcraft and superstition; and when I consider how hard it is for men, in seasons of tumult and feverish excitement, to listen to the mild voice of wisdom teaching that moral perfection alone constitutes glory and happiness,—I fear. I fear not for the final results; not for the *ultimate* triumphs of truth, right, virtue, piety; not for the gradual melioration of men's lot: but for those nearer results, those immediate effects, which the men of this generation are to witness and to feel.

2. Dorothea Dix Succors the Insane (1843)

In 1840 there were only eight insane asylums in the twenty-six states. The overflow, regarded as perverse, were imprisoned or chained in poorhouses, jails, and houses of correction. Schoolteacher Dorothea Dix—a frail, soft-spoken spinster from New England who lived to be eighty-five despite incipient tuberculosis—almost single-handedly wrought a revolution. Filled with infinite compassion for these outcasts, she journeyed thousands of wearisome miles to investigate conditions and to appeal to state legislatures. Despite the powerful prejudice against women who were outspoken in public, she succeeded in securing modern facilities with trained attendants. Her horrifying report to the Massachusetts legislature is a classic. In the following excerpt, where does she lay the blame for the existing conditions?

I must confine myself to few examples, but am ready to furnish other and more complete details, if required. If my pictures are displeasing, coarse, and severe, my subjects, it must be recollected, offer no tranquil, refined, or composing features. The condition of human beings, reduced to the extremest states of degradation and misery, cannot be exhibited in softened language, or adorn a polished page.

I proceed, gentlemen, briefly to call your attention to the present state of insane persons confined within this Commonwealth, in cages, closets, cellars, stalls, pens! Chained, naked, beaten with rods, and lashed into obedience!

As I state cold, severe facts, I feel obliged to refer to persons, and definitely to indicate localities. But it is upon my subject, not upon localities or individuals, I desire to fix attention. And I would speak as kindly as possible of all wardens, keepers, and other responsible officers, believing that most of these have erred not through hardness of heart and willful cruelty so much as want of skill and knowledge, and want of consideration.

Familiarity with suffering, it is said, blunts the sensibilities, and where neglect once finds a footing, other injuries are multiplied. This is not all, for it may justly and strongly be added that, from the deficiency of adequate means to meet the wants of these cases, it has been an absolute impossibility to do justice to this matter. Prisons are not constructed in view of being converted into county hospitals, and almshouses are not founded as receptacles for the insane. And yet, in the face of justice and common sense, wardens are by law compelled to receive, and the masters of almshouses not to refuse, insane and idiotic subjects in all stages of mental disease and privation.

It is the Commonwealth, not its integral parts, that is accountable for most of the abuses which have lately [existed] and do still exist. I repeat it, it is defective legislation which perpetuates and multiplies these abuses. . . .

Danvers. November. Visited the almshouse. A large building, much out of repair. Understand a new one is in contemplation. Here are fifty-six to sixty inmates, one idiotic, three insane, one of the latter in close confinement at all times.

Long before reaching the house, wild shouts, snatches of rude songs, imprecations and obscene language, fell upon the ear, proceeding from the occupant of a low building, rather remote from the principal building to which my course was di-

---

²*Old South Leaflets* (1904), vol. 6, pp. 490–491, 493–494, 513, 518–519.

rected. Found the mistress, and was conducted to the place which was called "the home" of the forlorn maniac, a young woman, exhibiting a condition of neglect and misery blotting out the faintest idea of comfort, and outraging every sentiment of decency. She had been, I learned, "a respectable person, industrious and worthy. Disappointments and trials shook her mind, and, finally, laid prostrate reason and self-control. She became a maniac for life. She had been at Worcester Hospital for a considerable time, and had been returned as incurable." The mistress told me she understood that, "while there, she was comfortable and decent."

Alas, what a change was here exhibited! She had passed from one degree of violence to another, in swift progress. There she stood, clinging to or beating upon the bars of her caged apartment, the contracted size of which afforded space only for increasing accumulations of filth, a foul spectacle. There she stood with naked arms and disheveled hair, the unwashed frame invested with fragments of unclean garments, the air so extremely offensive though ventilation was afforded on all sides save one, that it was not possible to remain beyond a few moments without retreating for recovery to the outward air. Irritation of body, produced by utter filth and exposure, incited her to the horrid process of tearing off her skin by inches. Her face, neck, and person were thus disfigured to hideousness. She held up a fragment just rent off. To my exclamation of horror, the mistress replied: "Oh, we can't help it. Half the skin is off sometimes. We can do nothing with her; and it makes no difference what she eats, for she consumes her own filth as readily as the food which is brought her." . . .

The conviction is continually deepened that hospitals are the only places where insane persons can be at once humanely and properly controlled. Poorhouses converted into madhouses cease to effect the purposes for which they were established, and instead of being asylums for the aged, the homeless, and the friendless, and places of refuge for orphaned or neglected childhood, are transformed into perpetual bedlams. . . .

Injustice is also done to the convicts. It is certainly very wrong that they should be doomed day after day and night after night to listen to the ravings of madmen and madwomen. This is a kind of punishment that is not recognized by our statutes, and is what the criminal ought not to be called upon to undergo. The confinement of the criminal and of the insane in the same building is subversive of the good order and discipline which should be observed in every well-regulated prison. . . .

Gentlemen, I commit to you this sacred cause. Your action upon this subject will affect the present and future condition of hundreds and of thousands.

3. T. S. Arthur's Ten Nights in a Barroom (1854)

T. S. Arthur, an ill-educated New Yorker, became the moralistic author of seventy books and countless articles. His lurid Ten Nights in a Barroom *was the* Uncle Tom's Cabin *of the temperance crusade, and second only to* Uncle Tom's Cabin *as the best-seller of the 1850s. Endorsed by the clergy, it was put on the stage for an incredible run. Although the author was a foe of saloons, he was not a teetotaler, and he consistently advocated temperance by education rather than prohibition by legislation.*

---

[3]T. S. Arthur, *Ten Nights in a Barroom,* "Night the Sixth" (Boston: L. P. Crown, 1854).

In his famous novel, Simon Slade's tavern ("Sickle and Sheaf") is portrayed as the ruination of quiet Cedarville. After numerous heart-tugging tragedies, the climax comes when the drunken tavern owner is murdered with a brandy bottle by his drunken son. Earlier in the book the followng conversation takes place. Enumerate and assess the arguments on both sides, and evaluate this interchange as propaganda in the battle against the bottle.

The man, who had until now been sitting quietly in a chair, started up, exclaiming as he did so—

"Merciful heavens! I never dreamed of this! Whose sons are safe?"

"No man's," was the answer of the gentleman in whose office we were sitting; "no man's—while there are such open doors to ruin as you may find at the 'Sickle and Sheaf.' Did not you vote the anti-temperance ticket at the last election?"

"I did," was the answer, "and from principle."

"On what were your principles based?" was inquired.

"On the broad foundations of civil liberty."

"The liberty to do good or evil, just as the individual may choose?"

"I would not like to say that. There are certain evils against which there can be no legislation that would not do harm. No civil power in this country has the right to say what a citizen shall eat or drink."

"But may not the people, in any community, pass laws, through their delegated lawmakers, restraining evil-minded persons from injuring the common good?"

"Oh, certainly—certainly."

"And are you prepared to affirm that a drinking shop, where young men are corrupted—ay, destroyed, body and soul—does not work an injury to the common good?"

"Ah! but there must be houses of public entertainment."

"No one denies this. But can that be a really Christian community which provides for the moral debasement of strangers, at the same time that it entertains them? Is it necessary that, in giving rest and entertainment to the traveler, we also lead him into temptation?"

"Yes—but—but—it is going too far to legislate on what we are to eat and drink. It is opening too wide a door for fanatical oppression. We must inculcate temperance as a right principle. We must teach our children the evils of intemperance, and send them out into the world as practical teachers of order, virtue, and sobriety. If we do this, the reform becomes radical, and in a few years there will be no barrooms, for none will crave the fiery poison.

"Of little value, my friend, will be, in far too many cases, your precepts, if temptation invites our sons at almost every step of their way through life. Thousands have fallen, and thousands are now tottering, soon to fall. Your sons are not safe, nor are mine. We cannot tell the day nor the hour when they may weakly yield to the solicitation of some companion, and enter the wide-open door of ruin. . . . Sir! while you hold back from the work of staying the flood that is desolating our fairest homes, the black waters are approaching your own doors."

There was a startling emphasis in the tones with which this last sentence was uttered, and I did not wonder at the look of anxious alarm that it called to the face of him whose fears it was meant to excite.

"What do you mean, sir?" was inquired.

"Simply, that your sons are in equal danger with others."

"And is that all?"

"They have been seen of late in the barroom of the 'Sickle and Sheaf.'"

"Who says so?"

"Twice within a week I have seen them going in there," was answered.

"Good heavens! No!"

"It is true, my friend. But who is safe? If we dig pits and conceal them from view, what marvel if our own children fall therein?"

"My sons going to a tavern!" The man seemed utterly confounded. "How can I believe it? You must be in error, sir."

"No. What I tell you is the simple truth."

4. Dr. William Morton Administers Ether (1846)

After Sydney Smith sneered in 1820, "What does the world yet owe to American physicians and surgeons?" he finally got his answer in a dramatic form. Whiskey, opium, and mesmerism having failed as anesthetics, Dr. Crawford Long of Georgia performed the first known surgical operation with ether in 1842, when he removed a tumor from the back of a patient's neck. Unfortunately for his fame, his exploits were not publicized until 1849. Meanwhile Dr. William T. G. Morton, a Boston dentist working with Professor Charles T. Jackson of Harvard, independently experimented on patients seeking extractions. In 1846 he performed the "miracle" here described—the first public feat of its kind. Dr. Morton's health ultimately broke down, and he died in poverty while trying to monopolize his discovery. In this latter day account, what is remarkable about the skepticism shown?

Meanwhile, within, all necessary preparations for the operation had been made. The patient selected for the trial was Gilbert Abbott, who was suffering from a congenital but superficial vascular tumor just below the jaw on the left side of the neck. The announcement that the operation was to furnish a test of some preparation for which the astounding claim had been made that it would render the person treated with it temporarily incapable of feeling pain, had attracted a large number of medical men to the theater. It was inevitable that nearly all of those present should be skeptical as to the result. As the minutes slipped by without any sign of Dr. Morton, the incredulous gave vent to their suspicions concerning him and his discovery.

"As Dr. Morton has not yet arrived," said Dr. Warren, after waiting fifteen minutes, "I presume that he is otherwise engaged."

The response was a derisive laugh, clearly implying the belief that Dr. Morton was staying away because he was afraid to submit his discovery to a critical test.

Dr. Warren grasped the knife. At that critical moment Dr. Morton entered. No outburst of applause, no smiles of encouragement, greeted him. Doubt and suspicion were depicted on the faces of those who looked down upon him from the tiers

---

[4]E. L. Snell, "Dr. Morton's Discovery of Anesthesia," *Century Illustrated Monthly Magazine* 48 (1894): 589–591.

of seats that encircled the room. No actor about to assume a new role ever received a more chilling reception.

"Well, sir," exclaimed Dr. Warren abruptly, "your patient is ready."

Thus aroused from the bewilderment into which the novelty of his position had thrown him, he [Dr. Morton] spoke a few words of encouragement to the young man about to be operated on, adjusted the inhaler, and began to administer the ether. As the subtle vapor gradually took possession of the citadel of consciousness, the patient dropped off into a deep slumber.

Dr. Warren seized the bunch of veins and made the first incision with his knife.

Instead of awakening with a cry of pain, the patient continued to slumber peacefully, apparently as profoundly unconscious as before.

Then the spectators underwent a transformation. All signs of incredulity and indifference vanished. Not a whisper was uttered. As the operation progressed, men began to realize that they were witnessing something the like of which had never been seen before.

When the operation was over, and while the patient still lay like a log on the table, Dr. Warren, addressing the spectators, said, with solemn emphasis, "Gentlemen, this is no humbug."

But notwithstanding that Dr. Morton had thus demonstrated that a patient could be rendered completely insensible to suffering while undergoing an operation, yet for three weeks the employment of the ether at the hospital was discontinued, and surgery and agony still went hand in hand. In fact, instead of being hailed as a public benefactor, Dr. Morton found himself, for a short period immediately following the public announcement of his discovery, the target for indignant scorn and contempt. He was pilloried in the public prints by medical men and laymen as a charlatan.

C. The Changing Role of Women

1. The Seneca Falls Manifesto (1848)

Lucretia C. Mott, a militant antislavery Quaker, received her first harsh lesson in feminism when, as a teacher, she was paid half a man's salary. Elizabeth C. Stanton, also a temperance and antislavery reformer, insisted on leaving the word "obey" out of her marriage ceremony. Both were aroused when, attending the World Anti-Slavery Convention in London in 1840, they were denied seats because of their sex. These two women sparked the memorable convention at Seneca Falls, New York, which formally launched the modern women's rights movement. The embattled women issued a flaming pronouncement in the manner of the Declaration of Independence ("all men and women are created equal"). They not only proclaimed their grievances but also passed eleven resolutions designed to improve their lot. Which of the grievances listed here remain unresolved today?

[1]Elizabeth Cady Stanton, Susan B. Anthony, and Matilda Joslyn Gage, eds., *History of Woman Suffrage* (New York: Fowler & Wells, 1881), vol. 1, pp. 70–71.

Declaration of Sentiments

When, in the course of human events, it becomes necessary for one portion of the family of man to assume among the people of the earth a position different from that which they have hitherto occupied, but one to which the laws of nature and of nature's God entitle them, a decent respect to the opinions of mankind requires that they should declare the causes that impel them to such a course.

We hold these truths to be self-evident: that all men and women are created equal; that they are endowed by their Creator with certain inalienable rights; that among these are life, liberty, and the pursuit of happiness; that to secure these rights governments are instituted, deriving their just powers from the consent of the governed. Whenever any form of government becomes destructive of these ends, it is the right of those who suffer from it to refuse allegiance to it, and to insist upon the institution of a new government, laying its foundation on such principles, and organizing its powers in such form, as to them shall seem most likely to effect their safety and happiness. Prudence, indeed, will dictate that governments long established should not be changed for light and transient causes; and accordingly all experience hath shown that mankind are more disposed to suffer, while evils are sufferable, than to right themselves by abolishing the forms to which they were accustomed. But when a long train of abuses and usurpations, pursuing invariably the same object, evinces a design to reduce them under absolute despotism, it is their duty to throw off such government, and to provide new guards for their future security. Such has been the patient sufferance of the women under this government, and such is now the necessity which constrains them to demand the equal station to which they are entitled.

The history of mankind is a history of repeated injuries and usurpations on the part of man toward woman, having in direct object the establishment of an absolute tyranny over her. To prove this, let facts be submitted to a candid world.

He has never permitted her to exercise her inalienable right to the elective franchise.

He has compelled her to submit to laws, in the formation of which she had no voice.

He has withheld from her rights which are given to the most ignorant and degraded men—both natives and foreigners.

Having deprived her of this first right of a citizen, the elective franchise, thereby leaving her without representation in the halls of legislation, he has oppressed her on all sides.

He has made her, if married, in the eye of the law, civilly dead.

He has taken from her all right in property, even to the wages she earns.

He has made her, morally, an irresponsible being, as she can commit many crimes with impunity, provided they be done in the presence of her husband. In the covenant of marriage, she is compelled to promise obedience to her husband, he becoming, to all intents and purposes, her master—the law giving him power to deprive her of her liberty, and to administer chastisement.

He has so framed the laws of divorce, as to what shall be the proper causes, and in case of separation, to whom the guardianship of the children shall be given, as to be wholly regardless of the happiness of women—the law, in all cases, going upon the false supposition of the supremacy of man, and giving all power into his hands.

After depriving her of all rights as a married woman, if single, and the owner of property, he has taxed her to support a government which recognizes her only when her property can be made profitable to it.

He has monopolized nearly all the profitable employments, and from those she is permitted to follow, she receives but a scanty remuneration. He closes against her all the avenues to wealth and distinction which he considers most honorable to himself. As a teacher of theology, medicine, or law, she is not known.

He has denied her the facilities for obtaining a thorough education, all colleges being closed against her.

He allows her in Church, as well as State, but a subordinate position, claiming Apostolic authority for her exclusion from the ministry, and, with some exceptions, from any public participation in the affairs of the Church.

He has created a false public sentiment by giving to the world a different code of morals for men and women, by which moral delinquencies which exclude women from society, are not only tolerated, but deemed of little account in man.

He has usurped the prerogative of Jehovah himself, claiming it as his right to assign for her a sphere of action, when that belongs to her conscience and to her God.

He has endeavored, in every way that he could, to destroy her confidence in her own powers, to lessen her self-respect, and to make her willing to lead a dependent and abject life.

Now, in view of this entire disfranchisement of one-half the people of this country, their social and religious degradation—in view of the unjust laws above mentioned, and because women do feel themselves aggrieved, oppressed, and fraudulently deprived of their most sacred rights, we insist that they have immediate admission to all the rights and privileges which belong to them as citizens of the United States.

In entering upon the great work before us, we anticipate no small amount of misconception, misrepresentation, and ridicule; but we shall use every instrumentality within our power to effect our object. We shall employ agents, circulate tracts, petition the State and National legislatures, and endeavor to enlist the pulpit and the press in our behalf. We hope this Convention will be followed by a series of Conventions embracing every part of the country.

Resolutions

WHEREAS, The great precept of nature is conceded to be, that "man shall pursue his own true and substantial happiness." Blackstone in his Commentaries remarks, that this law of Nature being coeval with mankind, and dictated by God himself, is of course superior in obligation to any other. It is binding over all the globe, in all countries and at all times; no human laws are of any validity if contrary to this, and such of them as are valid, derive all their force, and all their validity, and all their authority, mediately and immediately, from this original; therefore,

Resolved, That such laws as conflict, in any way, with the true and substantial happiness of woman, are contrary to the great precept of nature and of no validity, for this is "superior in obligation to any other."

Resolved, That all laws which prevent woman from occupying such a station in society as her conscience shall dictate, or which place her in a position inferior to that of man, are contrary to the great precept of nature, and therefore of no force or authority.

Resolved, That woman is man's equal—was intended to be so by the Creator, and the highest good of the race demands that she should be recognized as such.

Resolved, That the women of this country ought to be enlightened in regard to the laws under which they live, that they may no longer publish their degradation by declaring themselves satisfied with their present position, nor their ignorance, by asserting that they have all the rights they want.

Resolved, That inasmuch as man, while claiming for himself intellectual superiority, does accord to woman moral superiority, it is pre-eminently his duty to encourage her to speak and teach, as she has an opportunity, in all religious assemblies.

Resolved, That the same amount of virtue, delicacy, and refinement of behavior that is required of woman in the social state, should also be required of man, and the same transgressions should be visited with equal severity on both man and woman.

Resolved, That the objection of indelicacy and impropriety, which is so often brought against woman when she addresses a public audience, comes with a very ill-grace from those who encourage, by their attendance, her appearance on the stage, in the concert, or in feats of the circus.

Resolved, That woman has too long rested satisfied in the circumscribed limits which corrupt customs and a perverted application of the Scriptures have marked out for her, and that it is time she should move in the enlarged sphere which her great Creator has assigned her.

Resolved, That it is the duty of the women of this country to secure to themselves their sacred right to the elective franchise.

Resolved, That the equality of human rights results necessarily from the fact of the identity of the race in capabilities and responsibilities.

Resolved, therefore, That, being invested by the Creator with the same capabilities, and the same consciousness of responsibility for their exercise, it is demonstrably the right and duty of woman, equally with man, to promote every righteous cause by every righteous means; and especially in regard to the great subjects of morals and religion, it is self-evidently her right to participate with her brother in teaching them, both in private and in public, by writing and by speaking, by any instrumentalities proper to be used, and in any assemblies proper to be held; and this being a self-evident truth growing out of the divinely implanted principles of human nature, any custom or authority adverse to it, whether modern or wearing the hoary sanction of antiquity, is to be regarded as a self-evident falsehood, and at war with mankind.

Resolved, That the speedy success of our cause depends upon the zealous and untiring efforts of both men and women, for the overthrow of the monopoly of the pulpit, and for the securing to woman an equal participation with men in the various trades, professions, and commerce.

2. New Yorkers Ridicule Feminists (1856)

Male opponents of feminism claimed that the female crusaders were frustrated old maids (many, in fact, were married); that women would become coarsened and de-feminized by entering the cutthroat arena of politics; that their husbands (if they were lucky enough to have husbands) would look after their rights; and that women, like black slaves, were divinely ordained to be inferior and would be happier in that status. An editorial in the New York Herald *wondered what would happen if pregnant sea captains, generals, members of Congress, physicians, and lawyers were suddenly seized with birth pangs in critical situations. The following official report reveals the joking condescension with which the New York legislature approached the problem. How might feminists have answered these jibes?*

Mr. Foote, from the Judiciary Committee, made a report on Women's Rights that set the whole House in roars of laughter:

"The Committee is composed of married and single gentlemen. The bachelors on the Committee, with becoming diffidence, have left the subject pretty much to the married gentlemen. They have considered it with the aid of the light they have before them and the experience married life has given them. Thus aided, they are enabled to state that the ladies always have the best place and choicest tidbit at the table. They have the best seat in the cars, carriages, and sleighs; the warmest place in the winter, and the coolest place in the summer. They have their choice on which side of the bed they will lie, front or back. A lady's dress costs three times as much as that of a gentleman; and, at the present time, with the prevailing fashion, one lady occupies three times as much space in the world as a gentleman.

"It has thus appeared to the married gentlemen of your Committee, being a majority (the bachelors being silent for the reason mentioned, and also probably for the further reason that they are still suitors for the favors of the gentler sex), that, if there is any inequality or oppression in the case, the gentlemen are the sufferers. They, however, have presented to petitions for redress; having, doubtless, made up their minds to yield to an inevitable destiny.

"On the whole, the Committee have concluded to recommend no measure, except that as they have observed several instances in which husband and wife have both signed the same petition. In such case, they would recommend the parties to apply for a law authorizing them to change dresses, so that the husband may wear petticoats, and the wife the breeches, and thus indicate to their neighbors and the public the true relation in which they stand to each other."

3. Lucy Stone Protests Traditional Marriage (1855)

Lucy Stone graduated from Oberlin College (America's first coeducational institution of higher learning) in 1847 and launched herself on a lifelong career as a reformer. She was an outspoken abolitionist and advocate of women's rights. Traditionalists were so irritated with her that they rudely repeated a poem published

---

[2]E. C. Stanton et al., eds., *History of Woman Suffrage* (1881), vol. 1, pp. 629–630.

[3]E. C. Stanton et al., eds., *History of Woman Suffrage* (1881), vol. 1, pp. 260–261.

by a Boston newspaper promising "fame's loud trumpet shall be blown" for the man who "with a wedding kiss shuts up the mouth of Lucy Stone." When she did marry Henry B. Blackwell in 1855, she hardly fell silent. Instead, with her new husband, she used the occasion to dramatize the plight of women. In her wedding declaration, which follows, what aspects of women's condition are most condemned? In what ways does this document suggest the relationship between the abolitionist and feminist crusades?

Protest

While acknowledging our mutual affection by publicly assuming the relationship of husband and wife, yet in justice to ourselves and a great principle, we deem it a duty to declare that this act on our part implies no sanction of, nor promise of voluntary obedience to such of the present laws of marriage, as refuse to recognize the wife as an independent, rational being, while they confer upon the husband an injurious and unnatural superiority, investing him with legal powers which no honorable man would exercise, and which no man should possess. We protest especially against the laws which give to the husband:

1. The custody of the wife's person.

2. The exclusive control and guardianship of their children.

3. The sole ownership of her personal, and use of her real estate, unless previously settled upon her, or placed in the hands of trustees, as in the case of minors, lunatics, and idiots.

4. The absolute right to the product of her industry.

5. Also against laws which give to the widower so much larger and more permanent an interest in the property of his deceased wife, than they give to the widow in that of the deceased husband.

6. Finally, against the whole system by which "the legal existence of the wife is suspended during marriage," so that in most States, she neither has a legal part in the choice of her residence, nor can she make a will, nor sue or be sued in her own name, nor inherit property.

We believe that personal independence and equal human rights can never be forfeited, except for crime; that marriage should be an equal and permanent partnership, and so recognized by law; that until it is so recognized, married partners should provide against the radical injustice of present laws, by every means in their power.

We believe that where domestic difficulties arise, no appeal should be made to legal tribunals under existing laws, but that all difficulties should be submitted to the equitable adjustment of arbitrators mutually chosen.

Thus reverencing law, we enter our protest against rules and customs which are unworthy of the name, since they violate justice, the essence of law.

(Signed) *Henry B. Blackwell,*
Lucy Stone.

4. Orestes Brownson Explores the Woman Question (1869)

Not all reformers favored the changes in women's status that Lucy Stone and other feminists advocated. Orestes A. Brownson championed abolition and the Working-men's party, and participated in the transcendantalist utopian experiment at Brook Farm in Massachusetts. But he stopped well short of supporting women's suffrage. Variously a Presbyterian, a Unitarian, and a Universalist, he converted to Catholicism in 1844. In the following passages from two of his articles in 1869, he bases his opposition to women's suffrage, in part, on religious arguments. What specific arguments does he cite? What was his view of women, and of the "feminine character"? What important differences did he see between men and women? Did he exalt women or insult them?

The conclusive objection to the political enfranchisement of women is, that it would weaken and finally break up and destroy the Christian family. The social unit is the family, not the individual; and the greatest danger to American society is, that we are rapidly becoming a nation of isolated individuals, without family ties or affections. The family has already been much weakened, and is fast disappearing. We have broken away from the old homestead, have lost the restraining and purifying associations that gathered around it, and live away from home in hotels and boarding-houses. We are daily losing the faith, the virtues, the habits, and the manners without which the family cannot be sustained; and when the family goes, the nation goes too, or ceases to be worth preserving. . . .

Extend now to women suffrage and eligibility; give them the political right to vote and to be voted for; render it feasible for them to enter the arena of political strife, to become canvassers in elections and candidates for office, and what remains of family union will soon be dissolved. The wife may espouse one political party, and the husband another, and it may well happen that the husband and wife may be rival candidates for the same office, and one or the other doomed to the mortification of defeat. Will the husband like to see his wife enter the lists against him, and triumph over him? Will the wife, fired with political ambition for place or power, be pleased to see her own husband enter the lists against her, and succeed at her expense? Will political rivalry and the passions it never fails to engender increase the mutual affection of husband and wife for each other, and promote domestic union and peace, or will it not carry into the bosom of the family all the strife, discord, anger, and division of the political canvas? . . .

Woman was created to be a wife and a mother; that is her destiny. To that destiny all her instincts point, and for it nature has specially qualified her. Her proper sphere is home, and her proper function is the care of the household, to manage a family, to take care of children, and attend to their early training. For this she is endowed with patience, endurance, passive courage, quick sensibilities, a sympathetic nature, and great executive and administrative ability. She was born to be a queen in her own household, and to make home cheerful, bright, and happy.

---

[4]Henry F. Brownson, ed., *The Works of Orestes A. Brownson* (Detroit: T. Nourse, 1885), vol. 18, pp. 388–389, 403.

We do not believe women, unless we acknowledge individual exceptions, are fit to have their own head. The most degraded of the savage tribes are those in which women rule, and descent is reckoned from the mother instead of the father. Revelation asserts, and universal experience proves that the man is the head of the woman, and that the woman is for the man, not the man for the woman; and his greatest error, as well as the primal curse of society is that he abdicates his headship, and allows himself to be governed, we might almost say, deprived of his reason, by woman. It was through the seductions of the woman, herself seduced by the serpent, that man fell, and brought sin and all our woe into the world. She has all the qualities that fit her to be a help-meet of man, to be the mother of his children, to be their nurse, their early instructress, their guardian, their life-long friend; to be his companion, his comforter, his consoler in sorrow, his friend in trouble, his ministering angel in sickness; but as an independent existence, free to follow her own fancies and vague longings, her own ambition and natural love of power, without masculine direction or control, she is out of her element, and a social anomaly, sometimes, a hideous monster, which men seldom are, excepting through a woman's influence. This is no excuse for men, but it proves that women need a head, and the restraint of father, husband, or the priest of God.

5. The Beecher Sisters Defend the Home (1869)

Catharine and Harriet Beecher were but two of the eleven remarkable children of the equally remarkable Lyman Beecher. He was a powerful preacher who presided for nearly two decades over Cincinnati's Lane Theological Seminary, a notorious nursery of reformist and abolitionist ideas. Harriet, writing under her married name of Harriet Beecher Stowe, won worldwide fame in the 1850s as the author of Uncle Tom's Cabin. *Catharine founded the Hartford Female Seminary in Connecticut, and, later, the Western Female Institute in Cincinnati. Opposed to women's suffrage, she crusaded ceaselessly for women's education in the domestic arts, and became perhaps the foremost spokesperson for the idea that a woman's place was in the home. How, precisely, did the Beecher sisters define that place? Did they see the domestic sphere as confining or ennobling? In what ways, if any, did they depreciate women? In what ways might their position, in the mid-nineteenth century, have marked a positive, progressive advance in ideas about women's role?*

The authors of this volume, while they sympathize with every honest effort to relieve the disabilities and sufferings of their sex, are confident that the chief cause of these evils is the fact that the honor and duties of the family state are not duly appreciated, that women are not trained for these duties as men are trained for their trades and professions, and that, as the consequence, family labor is poorly done, poorly paid, and regarded as menial and disgraceful.

To be the nurse of young children, a cook, or a housemaid, is regarded as the lowest and last resort of poverty, and one which no woman of culture and position can assume without loss of caste and respectability.

---

[5]Catharine Beecher and Harriet Beecher Stowe, *The American Women's Home* (New York: J. B. Ford and Company, 1869), pp. 13–19.

It is the aim of this volume to elevate both the honor and the remuneration of all the employments that sustain the many difficult and sacred duties of the family state, and thus to render each department of woman's true profession as much desired and respected as are the most honored professions of men.

When the other sex are to be instructed in law, medicine, or divinity, they are favored with numerous institutions richly endowed, with teachers of the highest talents and acquirements, with extensive libraries, and abundant and costly apparatus. With such advantages they devote nearly ten of the best years of life to preparing themselves for their profession; and to secure the public from unqualified members of these professions, none can enter them until examined by a competent body, who certify to their due preparation for their duties.

Woman's profession embraces the care and nursing of the body in the critical periods of infancy and sickness, the training of the human mind in the most impressible period of childhood, the instruction and control of servants, and most of the government and economies of the family state. These duties of woman are as sacred and important as any ordained to man; and yet no such advantages for preparation have been accorded to her, nor is there any qualified body to certify the public that a woman is duly prepared to give proper instruction in her profession. . . .

During the upward progress of the age, and the advance of a more enlightened Christianity, the writers of this volume have gained more elevated views of the true mission of woman—of the dignity and importance of her distinctive duties, and of the true happiness which will be the reward of a right appreciation of this mission, and a proper performance of these duties. . . .

What, then, is the end designed by the family state which Jesus Christ came into this world to secure?

It is to provide for the training of our race to the highest possible intelligence, virtue, and happiness, by means of the self-sacrificing labors of the wise and good, and this with chief reference to a future immortal existence.

The distinctive feature of the family is self-sacrificing labor of the stronger and wiser members to raise the weaker and more ignorant to equal advantages. The father undergoes toil and self-denial to provide a home, and then the mother becomes a self-sacrificing laborer to train its inmates. The useless, troublesome infant is served in the humblest offices; while both parents unite in training it to an equality with themselves in every advantage. Soon the older children become helpers to raise the younger to a level with their own. When any are sick, those who are well become self-sacrificing ministers. When the parents are old and useless, the children become their self-sacrificing servants.

Thus the discipline of the family state is one of daily self-devotion of the stronger and wiser to elevate and support the weaker members. Nothing could be more contrary to its first principles than for the older and more capable children to combine to secure to themselves the highest advantages, enforcing the drudgeries on the younger, at the sacrifice of their equal culture.

Jesus Christ came to teach the fatherhood of God and consequent brotherhood of man. He came as the "firstborn Son" of God and the Elder Brother of man, to teach by example the self-sacrifice by which the great family of man is to be raised to equality of advantages as children of God. For this end, he "humbled himself" from the highest to the lowest place. He chose for his birthplace the most despised village; for his parents the lowest in rank; for his trade, to labor with his hands as a carpenter being "subject to his parents" thirty years. And, what is very significant, his trade was that which prepares the family home, as if he would teach that the great duty of man is labor—to provide for and train weak and ignorant creatures. Jesus Christ worked with his hands nearly thirty years, and preached less than three. And he taught that his kingdom is exactly opposite to that of the world, where all are striving for the highest positions. "Whoso will be great shall be your minister, and whoso will be chiefest shall be servant of all."

The family state, then, is the aptest earthly illustration of the heavenly kingdom, and in it woman is its chief minister. Her great mission is self-denial, in training its members to self-sacrificing labors for the ignorant and weak: if not her own children, then the neglected children of her Father in heaven. She is to rear all under her care to lay up treasures, not on earth, but in heaven. All the pleasures of this life end here; but those who train immortal minds are to reap the fruit of their labor through eternal ages.

To man is appointed the out-door labor—to till the earth, dig the mines, toil in the foundries, traverse the ocean, transport merchandise, labor in manufactories, construct houses, conduct civil, municipal, and state affairs, and all the heavy work, which, most of the day, excludes him from the comforts of a home. But the great stimulus to all these toils, implanted in the heart of every true man, is the desire for a home of his own, and the hopes of paternity. Every man who truly lives for immortality responds to the beatitude, "Children are a heritage from the Lord: blessed is the man that hath his quiver full of them!" The more a father and mother live under the influence of that "immortality which Christ had brought to light," the more is the blessedness of rearing a family understood and appreciated. Every child trained aright is to dwell forever in exalted bliss with those that gave it life and trained it for heaven.

D. Transcendentalism and Earthly Utopias

1. Ralph Waldo Emerson Chides the Reformers (1844)

Dissatisfied Europeans let off steam in the 1840s in a series of armed revolts; dissatisfied Americans let off steam in various reformist protests. Every brain was seemingly gnawed by a "private maggot." Ralph Waldo Emerson—poet, essayist, transcendentalist, and ever-popular lyceum lecturer—delivered this famous discourse on the New England reformers in 1844. A nonconformist himself, he had resigned his Unitarian pastorate in Boston after disagreeing with his congregation over the sacrament of the Lord's Supper. What might have linked the phenomena that

---

[1]R. W. Emerson, *Complete Works* (Boston: Houghton, Mifflin and Company, 1884), vol. 3, pp. 240–243.

Emerson describes and the southern spirit of political nullification? Did Emerson oppose all reform?

What a fertility of projects for the salvation of the world!

One apostle thought all men should go to farming, and another that no man should buy or sell, that the use of money was the cardinal evil; another that the mischief was in our diet, that we eat and drink damnation. These made unleavened bread and were foes to the death to fermentation.

It was in vain urged by the housewife that God made yeast as well as dough, and loves fermentation just as dearly as he loves vegetation; that fermentation develops the saccharine element in the grain, and makes it more palatable and more digestible. No; they wish the pure wheat, and will die but it shall not ferment. Stop, dear nature, these incessant advances of thine; let us scotch these ever-rolling wheels!

Others attacked the system of agriculture, the use of animal manures in farming, and the tyranny of man over brute nature [animals]. These abuses polluted his food. The ox must be taken from the plow, and the horse from the cart; the hundred acres of the farm must be spaded. And the man must walk, wherever boats and locomotives will not carry him.

Even the insect world was to be defended—that had been too long neglected, and a society for the protection of ground-worms, slugs, and mosquitoes was to be incorporated without delay.

With these, appeared the adepts of homoeopathy, of hydropathy, of mesmerism, of phrenology, and their wonderful theories of the Christian miracles! Others assailed particular vocations, as that of the lawyer, that of the merchant, of the manufacturer, of the clergyman, of the scholar. Others attacked the institution of marriage as the fountain of social evils. Others devoted themselves to the worrying of churches and meetings for public worship, and the fertile forms of antinomianism* among the elder Puritans seemed to have their match in the plenty of the new harvest of reform.

With this din of opinion and debate, there was a keener scrutiny of institutions and domestic life than any we had known. There was sincere protesting against existing evils, and there were changes of employment dictated by conscience. . . .

In politics, for example, it is easy to see the progress of dissent. The country is full of rebellion; the country is full of kings. Hands off! Let there be no control and no interference in the administration of the affairs of this kingdom of me. Hence the growth of the doctrine and of the party of Free Trade, and the willingness to try that experiment in the face of what appear incontestable facts.

I confess the motto of the *Globe* newspaper is so attractive to me that I can seldom find much appetite to read what is below it in its columns: "The world is governed too much." So the country is frequently affording solitary examples of resistance to the government, solitary nullifiers who throw themselves on their reserved rights; nay, who have reserved all their rights; who reply to the [tax] assessor and to the clerk of the court that they do not know the state, and embarrass the

---

*The belief that Christian faith alone, not obedience to moral law, ensures salvation.

courts of law by nonjuring [refusing to take an oath] and the commander-in-chief of the militia by nonresistance.

2. The "Paradise" at Brook Farm (c. 1846)

Of the numerous communal schemes of the 1840s, Brook Farm (1841–1847) attractively combined "plain living with high thinking." Pooling their poverty, the members were to share the intellectual feast, while contributing enough manual labor to keep the enterprise going. But the sandy soil, combined with inexperience in farming, contributed to their undoing. Nathaniel Hawthorne, who extracted a perceptive novel from the adventure (The Blithedale Romance), *recorded in his diary: "Mr. Ripley put a four-pronged instrument into my hands, which he gave me to understand was called a pitchfork, and he and Mr. Farley being armed with similar weapons, we all commenced a gallant attack upon a heap of manure." The following description was written some years later by Robert Carter, a well-known writer who enjoyed the friendship of nearly all the literary giants of his generation. How does Carter explain the purposes of Brook Farm and the general causes of its failure?*

At Brook Farm the disciples of the "Newness" [transcendentalism] gathered to the number, I think, of about a hundred. Among them were [George] Ripley, the founder of the institution, Charles A. Dana, W. H. Channing, J. S. Dwight, Warren Burton, Nathaniel Hawthorne, G. W. Curtis, and his brother Burrill Curtis. The place was a farm of two hundred acres of good land, eight miles from Boston, in the town of West Roxbury, and was of much natural beauty, with a rich and varied landscape. The avowed object of the association was to realize the Christian ideal of life by making such industrial, social, and educational arrangements as would promote economy, combine leisure for study with healthful and honest toil, avert collisions of caste, equalize refinements, diffuse courtesy, and sanctify life more completely than is possible in the isolated household mode of living.

It is a remarkable feature of this establishment that it was wholly indigenous, a genuine outgrowth of the times in New England, and not at all derived from Fourierism [French cooperative socialism], as many supposed. Fourier was, in fact, not known to its founders until Brook Farm had been a year or two in operation. They then began to study him, and fell finally into some of his fantasies, to which in part is to be ascribed the ruin of the institution.

Of the life of Brook Farm I do not intend to say much, for I was there only one day, though I knew nearly all the members. It was a delightful gathering of men and women of superior cultivation, who led a charming life for a few years, laboring in its fields and philandering in its pleasant woods. It was a little too much of a picnic for serious profit, and the young men and maidens were rather unduly addicted to moonlight wanderings in the pine-grove, though it is creditable to the sound moral training of New England that little or no harm came of these wanderings—at least not to the maidens. So far as the relation of the sexes is concerned, the Brook Farmers, in spite of their free manners, were as pure, I believe, as any other people.

The enterprise failed pecuniarily, after seeming for some years to have succeeded. Fourierism brought it into disrepute, and finally a great wooden phalanstery [main building], in which the members had invested all their means, took fire, and burned to the ground just as it was completed. Upon this catastrophe the association scattered (in 1847, I think), and Brook Farm became the site of the town poorhouse.

3. Henry David Thoreau Praises Spiritual Wealth (1854)

Henry David Thoreau, a leading transcendentalist, had worn a green coat to the Harvard chapel because the rules required black. He tried his hand at teaching, but when the authorities criticized his use of moral suasion, he whipped a dozen surprised pupils, just to show the absurdity of flogging, and forthwith resigned. While the Brook Farmers sought stimulation in association, he sought it in solitude. Building a hut on the shore of Walden Pond, near Concord, Massachusetts, he spent over two years in philosophical introspection and in communion with the wildlife, including fish and moles. His experiences unfold in his classic Walden, *which was socialistic enough to become a textbook of the British Labour party. James Russell Lowell accused Thoreau of trying to make a virtue out of his indolence and other defects of character. Which of Thoreau's observations in* Walden *have been weakened or strengthened by the passage of over a hundred years? Which ones would we regard as absurd today?*

For more than five years I maintained myself thus solely by the labor of my hands, and I found that by working about six weeks in a year, I could meet all the expenses of living. The whole of my winters, as well as most of my summers, I had free and clear for study.

I have thoroughly tried schoolkeeping, and found that my expenses were in proportion, or rather out of proportion, to my income, for I was obliged to dress and train, not to say think and believe, accordingly, and I lost my time into the bargain. As I did not teach for the good of my fellow-men, but simply for a livelihood, this was a failure.

I have tried trade. But I found that it would take ten years to get under way in that, and that then I should probably be on my way to the devil. I was actually afraid that I might by that time be doing what is called a good business.

When formerly I was looking about to see what I could do for a living, . . . I thought often and seriously of picking huckleberries. That surely I could do, and its small profits might suffice—for my greatest skill has been to want but little—so little capital it required, so little distraction from my wonted moods, I foolishly thought. While my acquaintances went unhesitantly into trade or the professions, I contemplated this occupation as most like theirs; ranging the hills all summer to pick the berries which came in my way, and thereafter carelessly dispose of them. . . . But I have since learned that trade curses everything it handles; and

---

[3]H. D. Thoreau, *Walden* (Boston: Houghton, Mifflin and Company, 1893), pp. 110–111, 112, 498, 505–506, 510.

though you trade in messages from heaven, the whole curse of trade attaches to the business. . . .

For myself, I found that the occupation of a day-laborer was the most independent of any, especially as it required only thirty or forty days in a year to support one. The laborer's day ends with the going down of the sun, and he is then free to devote himself to his chosen pursuit, independent of his labor. But his employer, who speculates from month to month, has no respite from one end of the year to the other. . . .

I left the woods for as good a reason as I went there. Perhaps it seemed to me that I had several more lives to live, and could not spare any more time for that one. It is remarkable how easily and insensibly we fall into a particular route, and make a beaten track for ourselves. I had not lived there a week before my feet wore a path from my door to the pond side; and though it is five or six years since I trod it, it is still quite distinct. It is true, I fear, that others may have fallen into it, and so helped to keep it open.

The surface of the earth is soft and impressible by the feet of men; and so with the paths which the mind travels. How worn and dusty, then, must be the highways of the world, how deep the ruts of tradition and conformity! I did not wish to take a cabin passage, but rather to go before the mast and on the deck of the world, for there I could best see the moonlight amid the mountains. I do not wish to go below now. . . .

However mean your life is, meet it and live it; do not shun it and call it hard names. It is not so bad as you are. It looks poorest when you are richest. The fault-finder will find faults even in Paradise. Love your life, poor as it is. You may perhaps have some pleasant, thrilling, glorious hours even in a poorhouse. The setting sun is reflected from the windows of the almshouse as brightly as from the rich man's abode; the snow melts before its door as early in the spring. I do not see but a quiet mind may live as contentedly there, and have as cheering thoughts, as in a palace.

The town's poor seem to me often to live the most independent lives of any. Maybe they are simply great enough to receive without misgiving. Most think that they are above being supported by the town; but it oftener happens that they are not above supporting themselves by dishonest means, which should be more disreputable.

Cultivate poverty like a garden herb, like sage. Do not trouble yourself much to get new things, whether clothes or friends. Turn the old; return to them. Things do not change; we change. Sell your clothes and keep your thoughts. God will see that you do not want society. If I were confined to a corner of a garret all my days, like a spider, the world would be just as large to me while I had my thoughts about me. . . .

Rather than love, than money, than fame, give me truth.

4. Emersonisms and Thoreauisms

The following pithy sayings are culled from the writings of Emerson and Thoreau, who were close transcendentalist friends and nonconformists. In what areas does there seem to be a close similarity in thinking? How many of these observations have been borne out by personalities or experiences in American history?

Government

The less government we have, the better—fewer laws, and the less confided power. *(Emerson)*

I heartily accept the motto "That government is best which governs least." . . . . Carried out, it finally amounts to this, which I also believe: "That government is best which governs not at all"; and when men are prepared for it, that will be the kind of government which they will have. *(Thoreau)*

Under a government which imprisons any unjustly, the true place for a just man is also a prison.* *(Thoreau)*

Of all debts men are least willing to pay the taxes. What a satire this [is] on government! *(Emerson)*

Reform

We are reformers in spring and summer; in autumn and winter we stand by the old; reformers in the morning, conservers at night. Reform is affirmative, conservatism negative; conservatism goes for comfort, reform for truth. *(Emerson)*

Every reform was once a private opinion. *(Emerson)*

Beware when the Great God lets loose a thinker on this planet. *(Emerson)*

There is no strong performance without a little fanaticism in the performer. *(Emerson)*

Every burned book enlightens the world. *(Emerson)*

Every reform is only a mask under cover of which a more terrible reform, which dares not yet name itself, advances. *(Emerson)*

If anything ail a man so that he does not perform his functions, if he have a pain in his bowels . . . he forthwith sets about reforming—the world. *(Thoreau)*

Wealth

The greatest man in history [Jesus] was the poorest. *(Emerson)*

If a man own land, the land owns him. *(Emerson)*

Poverty consists in feeling poor. *(Emerson)*

I would rather sit on a pumpkin, and have it all to myself, than to be crowded on a velvet cushion. *(Thoreau)*

They take their pride in making their dinner cost much; I take my pride in making my dinner cost little. *(Thoreau)*

Men have become the tools of their tools. *(Thoreau)*

---

*In 1845 Thoreau was jailed for one night for refusing to pay his poll tax to a state (Massachusetts) that supported slavery. The tax, much to his disgust, was paid by an aunt. Legend has it that Emerson visited him in jail, saying, "Why are you here?" Thoreau allegedly replied, "Why are you not here?"

To inherit property is not to be born—it is to be stillborn, rather. *(Thoreau)*

That man is the richest whose pleasures are the cheapest. *(Thoreau)*

Great Men

To be great is to be misunderstood. *(Emerson)*

Shallow men believe in luck. *(Emerson)*

Every hero becomes a bore at last. *(Emerson)*

If the single man plant himself indomitably on his instincts, and there abide, the huge world will come around to him. *(Emerson)*

Great men are they who see that spiritual is stronger than any material force; that thoughts rule the world. *(Emerson)*

The true test of civilization is, not the census, nor the size of cities, nor the crops—no, but the kind of man the country turns out. *(Emerson)*

An institution is the lengthened shadow of one man. *(Emerson)*

There are men too superior to be seen except by a few, as there are notes too high for the scale of most ears. *(Emerson)*

If a man does not keep pace with his companions, perhaps it is because he hears a different drummer. Let him step to the music he hears, however measured or far away. *(Thoreau)*

Living

Nothing can bring you peace but yourself. *(Emerson)*

The only gift is a portion of thyself. *(Emerson)*

Hitch your wagon to a star. *(Emerson)*

Nothing is so much to be feared as fear.* *(Thoreau)*

We do not quite forgive a giver. *(Emerson)*

Do not be too moral. You may cheat yourself out of much life so. Aim above morality. Be not simply good; be good for something. *(Thoreau)*

I never found the companion that was so companionable as solitude. *(Thoreau)*

The mass of men lead lives of quiet desperation. *(Thoreau)*

E. Three Views of the Indians

1. Alexis de Tocqueville Predicts the Indians' Future (1835)

Alexis de Tocqueville (1805–1859), the remarkable French commentator whose observations of American life in the 1830s inspired his classic Democracy in America *(1835), speculated in that book on "the present and probable future condition of the*

---

*Perhaps Franklin D. Roosevelt's most famous saying, uttered in his inaugural address in 1933, was: "The only thing we have to fear is fear itself."

Indian tribes." Near present-day Memphis, be actually witnessed the westward migration of some Choctaw Indians in the year immediately following the Indian Removal Act of 1830, as described in the selection that follows. What feature of white civilization did de Tocqueville find most injurious to the traditional ways of Indian life? How accurate were his predictions about the Native Americans' future?

When the Indians were the sole inhabitants of the wilds whence they have since been expelled, their wants were few. Their arms were of their own manufacture, their only drink was the water of the brook, and their clothes consisted of the skins of animals, whose flesh furnished them with food.

The Europeans introduced among the savages of North America firearms, ardent spirits, and iron; they taught them to exchange for manufactured stuffs the rough garments that had previously satisfied their untutored simplicity. Having acquired new tastes, without the arts by which they could be gratified, the Indians were obliged to have recourse to the workmanship of the whites; but in return for their productions the savage had nothing to offer except the rich furs that still abounded in his woods. Hence the chase became necessary, not merely to provide for his subsistence, but to satisfy the frivolous desires of Europeans. He no longer hunted merely to obtain food, but to procure the only objects of barter which he could offer. While the wants of the natives were thus increasing, their resources continued to diminish.

From the moment when a European settlement is formed in the neighborhood of the territory occupied by the Indians, the beasts of chase take the alarm. Thousands of savages, wandering in the forests and destitute of any fixed dwelling, did not disturb them; but as soon as the continuous sounds of European labor are heard in their neighborhood, they begin to flee away and retire to the West, where their instinct teaches them that they will still find deserts of immeasurable extent. "The buffalo is constantly receding," say Messrs. Clarke and Cass in their *Report* of the year 1829; "a few years since they approached the base of the Allegheny; and a few years hence they may even be rare upon the immense plains which extend to the base of the Rocky Mountains." I have been assured that this effect of the approach of the whites is often felt at two hundred leagues' distance from their frontier. Their influence is thus exerted over tribes whose name is unknown to them, and who suffer the evils of usurpation long before they are acquainted with the authors of their distress.

Bold adventurers soon penetrate into the country the Indians have deserted, and when they have advanced about fifteen or twenty leagues from the extreme frontiers of the whites, they begin to build habitations for civilized beings in the midst of the wilderness. This is done without difficulty, as the territory of a hunting nation is ill defined; it is the common property of the tribe and belongs to no one in particular, so that individual interests are not concerned in protecting any part of it.

A few European families, occupying points very remote from one another, soon drive away the wild animals that remain between their places of abode. The Indians, who had previously lived in a sort of abundance, then find it difficult to subsist, and still more difficult to procure the articles of barter that they stand in need of. To drive away their game has the same effect as to render sterile the fields of our agriculturists; deprived of the means of subsistence, they are reduced, like famished wolves, to prowl through the forsaken woods in quest of prey. Their instinctive love of country attaches them to the soil that gave them birth, even after it has ceased to yield anything but misery and death. At length they are compelled to acquiesce and depart; they follow the traces of the elk, the buffalo, and the beaver and are guided by these wild animals in the choice of their future country. Properly speaking, therefore, it is not the Europeans who drive away the natives of America; it is famine, a happy distinction which had escaped the casuists [moralists] of former times and for which we are indebted to modern discovery!

It is impossible to conceive the frightful sufferings that attend these forced migrations. They are undertaken by a people already exhausted and reduced; and the countries to which the newcomers betake themselves are inhabited by other tribes, which receive them with jealous hostility. Hunger is in the rear, war awaits them, and misery besets them on all sides. To escape from so many enemies, they separate, and each individual endeavors to procure secretly the means of supporting his existence by isolating himself, living in the immensity of the desert like an outcast in civilized society. The social tie, which distress had long since weakened, is then dissolved; they have no longer a country, and soon they will not be a people; their very families are obliterated; their common name is forgotten; their language perishes; and all traces of their origin disappear. Their nation has ceased to exist except in the recollection of the antiquaries of America and a few of the learned of Europe.

I should be sorry to have my reader suppose that I am coloring the picture too highly; I saw with my own eyes many of the miseries that I have just described, and was the witness of sufferings that I have not the power to portray.

At the end of the year 1831, while I was on the left bank of the Mississippi, at a place named by Europeans Memphis, there arrived a numerous band of Choctaws (or Chactas, as they are called by the French in Louisiana). These savages had left their country and were endeavoring to gain the right bank of the Mississippi, where they hoped to find an asylum that had been promised them by the American government. It was then the middle of winter, and the cold was unusually severe; the snow had frozen hard upon the ground, and the river was drifting huge masses of ice. The Indians had their families with them, and they brought in their train the wounded and the sick, with children newly born and old men upon the verge of death. They possessed neither tents nor wagons, but only their arms and some provisions. I saw them embark to pass the mighty river, and never will that solemn spectacle fade from my remembrance. No cry, so sob, was heard among the assembled crowd; all were silent. Their calamities were of ancient date, and they knew them to be irremediable. The Indians had all stepped into the bark that was to carry them across, but their dogs remained upon the bank. As soon as these animals perceived that their masters were finally leaving the shore, they set up a dismal howl and, plunging all together into the icy waters of the Mississippi, swam after the boat.

The expulsion of the Indians often takes place at the present day in a regular and, as it were, a legal manner. When the European population begins to approach the limit of the desert inhabited by a savage tribe, the government of the United States usually sends forward envoys who assemble the Indians in a large plain and, having first eaten and drunk with them, address them thus: "What have you to do in the land of your fathers? Before long, you must dig up their bones in order to live. In what respect is the country you inhabit better than another? Are there no woods, marshes, or prairies except where you dwell? And can you live nowhere but under your own sun? Beyond those mountains which you see at the horizon, beyond the lake which bounds your territory on the west, there lie vast countries where beasts of chase are yet found in great abundance; sell us your lands, then, and go to live happily in those solitudes." After holding this language, they spread before the eyes of the Indians firearms, woolen garments, kegs of brandy, glass necklaces, bracelets of tinsel, ear-rings, and looking-glasses. If, when they have beheld all these riches, they still hesitate, it is insinuated that they cannot refuse the required consent and that the government itself will not long have the power of protecting them in their rights. What are they to do? Half convinced and half compelled, they go to inhabit new deserts, where the importunate whites will not let them remain ten years in peace. In this manner do the Americans obtain, at a very low price, whole provinces, which the richest sovereigns of Europe could not purchase.

These are great evils; and it must be added that they appear to me to be irremediable. I believe that the Indian nations of North America are doomed to perish, and that whenever the Europeans shall be established on the shores of the Pacific Ocean, that race of men will have ceased to exist. The Indians had only the alternative of war or civilization; in other words, they must either destroy the Europeans or become their equals. . . .

The Spaniards pursued the Indians with bloodhounds, like wild beasts; they sacked the New World like a city taken by storm, with no discernment or compassion; but destruction must cease at last and frenzy has a limit: the remnant of the Indian population which had escaped the massacre mixed with its conquerors and adopted in the end their religion and their manners. The conduct of the Americans of the United States towards the aborigines is characterized, on the other hand, by a singular attachment to the formalities of law. Provided that the Indians retain their barbarous condition, the Americans take no part in their affairs; they treat them as independent nations and do not possess themselves of their hunting-grounds without a treaty of purchase; and if an Indian nation happens to be so encroached upon as to be unable to subsist upon their territory, they kindly take them by the hand and transport them to a grave far from the land of their fathers.

The Spaniards were unable to exterminate the Indian race by those unparalleled atrocities which brand them with indelible shame, nor did they succeed even in wholly depriving it of its rights; but the Americans of the United States have accomplished this twofold purpose with singular felicity, tranquilly, legally, philanthropically, without shedding blood, and without violating a single great principle of morality in the eyes of the world. It is impossible to destroy men with more respect for the laws of humanity.

2. George Catlin Dreams of a National Park to Preserve the Indian Way of Life (1832)

George Catlin (1796–1872), a Pennsylvanian who gave up the practice of law to study art, joined an American Fur Company expedition to the upper Missouri River in 1832. He made detailed observations of the landscape and of the Indian way of life. His descriptions and paintings of Native American culture and individual Indians are among the richest sources for understanding the antebellum West, though Catlin has been criticized for inaccuracies, especially for romanticizing Indian ways. While camped in present-day South Dakota in 1832, Catlin witnessed the slaughter of hundreds of buffaloes (bison) by Native Americans who sold the animals' tongues to white traders for liquor. Disgusted by this spectacle, Catlin proposed a vast national refuge for both buffaloes and Native Americans—an idea that eventually blossomed into the distinctive American system of national parks, including Yellowstone Park. How does Catlin assess the buffalo's importance to Indian life? How realistic—or romantic—was his proposal for a "nation's park"? To what extent did the eventual national park system realize Catlin's dream?

Letter—No. 31
Mouth of Teton River, Upper Missouri

. . . Nature has no where presented more beautiful and lovely scenes, than those of the vast prairies of the West; and of *man* and *beast,* no nobler specimens than those who inhabit them—the *Indian* and the *buffalo*—joint and original tenants of the soil, and fugitives together from the approach of civilized man; they have fled to the great plains of the West, and there, under an equal doom, they have taken up their *last abode,* where their race will expire, and their bones will bleach together. . . .

It is not enough in this polished and extravagant age, that we get from the Indian his lands, and the very clothes from his back, but the food from their mouths must be stopped, to add a new and useless article to the fashionable world's luxuries. The ranks must be thinned, and the race exterminated, of this noble animal, and the Indians of the great plains left without the means of supporting life, that white men may figure a few years longer, enveloped in buffalo robes—that they may spread them, for their pleasure and elegance, over the backs of their sleighs, and trail them ostentatiously amidst the busy throng, as things of beauty and elegance that had been made for them!

Reader! listen to the following calculations, and forget them not. The buffaloes (the quadrupeds from whose backs your beautiful robes were taken, and whose myriads were once spread over the whole country, from the Rocky Mountains to the Atlantic Ocean) have recently fled before the appalling appearance of civilized man, and taken up their abode and pasturage amid the almost boundless prairies of the West. An instinctive dread of their deadly foes, who made an easy prey of them whilst grazing in the forest, has led them to seek the midst of the vast and treeless

---

²George Catlin, *Letters and Notes on the Manners, Customs, and Conditions of the North American Indians* (New York: 1841), pp. 260–264.

plains of grass, as the spot where they would be least exposed to the assaults of their enemies; and it is exclusively in those desolate fields of silence (yet of beauty) that they are to be found—and over these vast steppes, or prairies, have they fled, like the Indian, towards the "setting sun"; until their bands have been crowded together, and their limits confined to a narrow strip of country on this side of the Rocky Mountains.

This strip of country, which extends from the province of Mexico to lake Winnepeg on the North, is almost one entire plain of grass, which is, and ever must be, useless to cultivating man. It is here, and here chiefly, that the buffaloes dwell; and with, and hovering about them, live and flourish the tribes of Indians, whom God made for the enjoyment of that fair land and its luxuries.

It is a melancholy contemplation for one who has travelled as I have, through these realms, and seen this noble animal in all its pride and glory, to contemplate it so rapidly wasting from the world, drawing the irresistible conclusion too, which one must do, that its species is soon to be extinguished, and with it the peace and happiness (if not the actual existence) of the tribes of Indians who are joint tenants with them, in the occupancy of these vast and idle plains.

And what a splendid contemplation too, when one (who has travelled these realms, and can duly appreciate them) imagines them as they *might* in future be seen, (by some great protecting policy of government) preserved in their pristine beauty and wildness, in a *magnificent park,* where the world could see for ages to come, the native Indian in his classic attire, galloping his wild horse, with sinewy bow, and shield and lance, amid the fleeting herds of elks and buffaloes. What a beautiful and thrilling specimen for America to preserve and hold up to the view of her refined citizens and the world, in future ages! A *nation's Park,* containing man and beast, in all the wild and freshness of their nature's beauty!

I would ask no other monument to my memory, nor any other enrolment of my name amongst the famous dead, than the reputation of having been the founder of such an institution.

Such scenes might easily have been preserved, and still could be cherished on the great plains of the West, without detriment to the country or its borders; for the tracts of country on which the buffaloes have assembled, are uniformly sterile, and of no available use to cultivating man.

It is on these plains, which are stocked with buffaloes, that the finest specimens of the Indian race are to be seen. It is here, that the savage is decorated in the richest costume. It is here, and here only, that his wants are all satisfied, and even the luxuries of life are afforded him in abundance. And here also is he the proud and honourable man (before he has had teachers or laws), above the imported wants, which beget meanness and vice; stimulated by ideas of honour and virtue, in which the God of Nature has certainly not curtailed him.

There are, by a fair calculation, more than 300,000 Indians, who are now subsisted on the flesh of the buffaloes, and by those animals supplied with all the luxuries of life which they desire, as they know of none others. The great variety of uses to which they convert the body and other parts of that animal, are almost incredible to the person who has not actually dwelt amongst these people, and closely studied their modes and customs. Every part of their flesh is converted into food, in one shape or another, and on it they entirely subsist. The robes of the animals are worn by the Indians instead of blankets—their skins when tanned, are used as coverings for their lodges, and for their beds; undressed, they are used for constructing canoes—for saddles, for bridles—l'arrêts, lasos, and thongs. The horns are shaped into ladles and spoons—the brains are used for dressing the skins—their bones are used for saddle trees—for war clubs, and scrapers for graining the robes—and others are broken up for the marrow-fat which is contained in them. Their sinews are used for strings and backs to their bows—for thread to string their beads and sew their dresses. The feet of the animals are boiled, with their hoofs, for the glue they contain, for fastening their arrow points, and many other uses. The hair from the head and shoulders, which is long, is twisted and braided into halters, and the tail is used for a fly brush. In this wise do these people convert and use the various parts of this useful animal, and with all these luxuries of life about them, and their numerous games, they are happy (God bless them) in the ignorance of the disastrous fate that awaits them.

Yet this interesting community, with its sports, its wildnesses, its languages, and all its manners and customs, could be perpetuated, and also the buffaloes, whose numbers would increase and supply them with food for ages and centuries to come, if a system of non-intercourse could be established and preserved. But such is not to be the case—the buffalo's doom is sealed, and with their extinction must assuredly sink into real despair and starvation, the inhabitants of these vast plains, which afford for the Indians, no other possible means of subsistence; and they must at last fall a prey to wolves and buzzards, who will have no other bones to pick.

It seems hard and cruel, (does it not?) that we civilized people with all the luxuries and comforts of the world about us, should be drawing from the backs of these useful animals the skins for our luxury, leaving their carcasses to be devoured by the wolves—that we should draw from that country, some 150 or 200,000 of their robes annually, the greater part of which are taken from animals that are killed expressly for the robe, at a season when the meat is not cured and preserved, and for each of which skins the Indian has received but a pint of whiskey!

3. John James Audubon Is Pessimistic About the Indians' Fate (1843)

The great naturalist and ornithologist John James Audubon (1785–1851) followed Catlin's route on the upper Missouri a decade later, on a hunting trip. How does his assessment of the Native Americans differ from Catlin's? What factors might account for their differing appraisals?

May 17, Wednesday [1843] . . . We have seen floating eight Buffaloes, one Antelope, and one Deer; how great the destruction of these animals must be during high freshets! The cause of their being drowned in such extraordinary numbers might not astonish one acquainted with the habits of these animals, but to one who is not, it may be well enough for me to describe it. Some few hundred miles above us, the river becomes confined between high bluffs or cliffs, many of which are nearly perpendicular, and therefore extremely difficult to ascend. When the Buffaloes have

---

[3]Maria Audubon, *Audubon and His Journals* (New York: 1877).

leaped or tumbled down from either side of the stream, they swim with ease across, but on reaching these walls, as it were, the poor animals try in vain to climb them, and becoming exhausted by falling back some dozens of times, give up the ghost, and float down the turbid stream; their bodies have been known to pass, swollen and putrid, the city of St. Louis. The most extraordinary part of the history of these drowned Buffaloes is, that the different tribes of Indians on the shores, are ever on the lookout for them, and no matter how putrid their flesh may be, provided the hump proves at all fat, they swim to them, drag them on shore, and cut them to pieces; after which they cook and eat this loathsome and abominable flesh, even to the marrow found in the bones. In some instances this has been done when the whole of the hair had fallen off, from the rottenness of the Buffalo. Ah! Mr. Catlin, I am now sorry to see and to read your accounts of the Indians you saw—how very different they must have been from any that I have seen! . . .

June 7, Wednesday . . . We reached Fort Clark and the Mandan Villages at half-past seven this morning. Great guns were fired from the fort and from the "Omega," as our captain took the guns from the "Trapper" at Fort Pierre. The site of this fort appears a good one, though it is placed considerably below the Mandan Village. We saw some small spots cultivated, where corn, pumpkins, and beans are grown. The fort and village are situated on the high bank, rising somewhat to the elevation of a hill. The Mandan mud huts are very far from looking poetical, although Mr. Catlin has tried to render them so by placing them in regular rows, and all of the same size and form, which is by no means the case. But different travellers have different eyes! We saw more Indians than at any previous time since leaving St. Louis; and it is possible that there are a hundred huts, made of mud, all looking like so many potato winter-houses in the Eastern States. As soon as we were near the shore, every article that could conveniently be carried off was placed under lock and key, and our division door was made fast, as well as those of our own rooms. Even the axes and poles were put by. Our captain told us that last year they stole his cap and his shot-pouch and horn, and that it was through the interference of the first chief that he recovered his cap and horn; but that a squaw had his leather belt, and would not give it up. The appearance of these poor, miserable devils, as we approached the shore, was wretched enough. There they stood in the pelting rain and keen wind, covered with Buffalo robes, red blankets, and the like, some partially and most curiously besmeared with mud; and as they came on board, and we shook hands with each of them, I felt a clamminess that rendered the ceremony most repulsive. Their legs and naked feet were covered with mud. They looked at me with apparent curiosity, perhaps on account of my beard, which produced the same effect at Fort Pierre. They all looked very poor; and our captain says they are the *ne plus ultra* of thieves. It is said there are nearly three thousand men, women, and children that, during winter, cram themselves into these miserable hovels. . . .

After this, Mr. Chardon asked one of the Indians to take us into the village, and particularly to show us the "Medicine Lodge." We followed our guide through mud and mire, even into the Lodge. We found this to be, in general terms, like all the other lodges, only larger, measuring twenty-three yards in diameter, with a large squarish aperture in the centre of the roof, some six or seven feet long by about four wide. We had entered this curiosity shop by pushing aside a wet Elk skin stretched on four sticks. Looking around, I saw a number of calabashes [gourds], eight or ten Otter skulls, two very large Buffalo skulls with the horns on, evidently of great age, and some sticks and other magical implements with which none but a "Great Medicine Man" is acquainted. During my survey there sat, crouched down on his haunches, an Indian wrapped in a dirty blanket, with only his filthy head peeping out. Our guide spoke to him; but he stirred not. Again, at the foot of one of the posts that support the central portion of this great room, lay a parcel that I took for a bundle of Buffalo robes; but it moved presently, and from beneath it half arose the emaciated body of a poor blind Indian, whose skin was quite shrivelled; and our guide made us signs that he was about to die. We all shook both hands with him; and he pressed our hands closely and with evident satisfaction. He had his pipe and tobacco pouch by him, and soon lay down again. We left this abode of mysteries, as I was anxious to see the interior of one of the common huts around; and again our guide led us through mud and mire to his own lodge, which we entered in the same way as we had done the other. All these lodges have a sort of portico that leads to the door, and on the tops of most of them I observed Buffalo skulls. This lodge contained the whole family of our guide—several women and children, and another man, perhaps a son-in-law or a brother. All these, except the man, were on the outer edge of the lodge, crouching on the ground, some suckling children; and at nearly equal distances apart were placed berths, raised about two feet above the ground, made of leather, and with square apertures for the sleepers or occupants to enter. The man of whom I have spoken was lying down in one of these, which was all open in front. I walked up to him, and, after disturbing his happy slumbers, shook hands with him; he made signs for me to sit down; and after Harris and I had done so, he rose, squatted himself near us, and, getting out a large spoon made of boiled Buffalo horn, handed it to a young girl, who brought a great rounded wooden bowl filled with pemmican, mixed with corn and some other stuff. I ate a mouthful or so of it, and found it quite palatable; and Harris and the rest then ate of it also. Bell was absent; we had seen nothing of him since we left the boat. This lodge, as well as the other, was dirty with water and mud; but I am told that in dry weather they are kept cleaner, and much cleaning do they need, most truly. A round, shallow hole was dug in the centre for the fire; and from the roof descended over this a chain, by the aid of which they do their cooking, the utensil being attached to the chain when wanted. . . .

After dinner we went up the muddy bank again to look at the corn-fields, as the small patches that are meanly cultivated are called. We found poor, sickly looking corn about two inches high, that had been represented to us this morning as full six inches high. We followed the prairie, a very extensive one, to the hills, and there found a deep ravine, sufficiently impregnated with saline matter to answer the purpose of salt water for the Indians to boil their corn and pemmican, clear and clean; but they, as well as the whites at the fort, resort to the muddy Missouri for their drinking water, the only fresh water at hand. Not a drop of spirituous liquor has been brought to this place for the last two years; and there can be no doubt that on this account the Indians have become more peaceable than heretofore, though now and then a white man is murdered, and many horses are stolen. As we walked over the plain, we saw heaps of earth thrown up to cover the poor Mandans who died of the small-pox. These mounds in many instances appear to contain the remains of several bodies and, perched on the top, lies, pretty generally, the rotting skull of a Buffalo. Indeed, the skulls of the Buffaloes seem as if a kind of relation to these most absurdly superstitious and ignorant beings. . . .

June 11, Sunday. . . . We have seen many Elks swimming the river, and they look almost the size of a well-grown mule. They stared at us, were fired at, at an enormous distance, it is true, and yet stood still. These animals are abundant beyond belief hereabouts. We have seen much remarkably handsome scenery, but nothing at all comparing with Catlin's descriptions; his book must, after all, be altogether a humbug. Poor devil! I pity him from the bottom of my soul; . . .

July 21, Friday. We were up at sunrise, and had our coffee, after which Lafleur a mulatto, Harris, and Bell went off after Antelopes, for we cared no more about bulls; where the cows are, we cannot tell. Cows run faster than bulls, yearlings faster than cows, and calves faster than any of these. Squires felt sore, and his side was very black, so we took our guns and went after Black-breasted Lark Buntings, of which we saw many, but could not near them. I found a nest of them, however, with five eggs. The nest is planted in the ground, deep enough to sink the edges of it. It is formed of dried fine grasses and roots, without any lining of hair or wool. By and by we saw Harris sitting on a high hill about one mile off, and joined him; he said the bulls they had killed last evening were close by, and I offered to go and see the bones, for I expected that the Wolves had devoured it during the night. We travelled on, and Squires returned to the camp. After about two miles of walking against a delightful strong breeze, we reached the animals; Ravens or Buzzards had worked at the eyes, but only one Wolf, apparently, had been there. They were bloated, and smelt quite unpleasant. We returned to the camp and saw a Wolf cross our path, and an Antelope looking at us. We determined to stop and try to bring him to us; I lay on my back and threw my legs up, kicking first one and then the other foot, and sure enough the Antelope walked towards us, slowly and carefully, however. In about twenty minutes he had come two or three hundred yards; he was a superb male, and I looked at him for some minutes; when about sixty yards off I could see his eyes, and being loaded with buck-shot pulled the trigger without rising from my awkward position. Off he went; Harris fired, but he only ran the faster for some hundred yards, when he turned, looked at us again, and was off. When we reached camp we found Bell there; he had shot three times at Antelopes without killing; Lafleur had also returned, and had broken the foreleg of one, but an Antelope can run fast enough with three legs, and he saw no more of it. We now broke camp, arranged the horses and turned our heads towards the Missouri, and in four and three-quarter hours reached the landing. On entering the wood we again broke branches of service-berries, and carried a great quantity over the river. I much enjoyed the trip; we had our supper, and soon to bed in our hot room, where Sprague says the thermometer has been at 99° most of the day. I noticed it was warm when walking. I must not forget to notice some things which happened on our return. First, as we came near Fox River, we thought of the horns of our bulls, and Mr. Culbertson, who knows the country like a book, drove us first to Bell's, who knocked the horns off, then to Harris's, which was served in the same manner; this bull had been eaten entirely except the head, and a good portion of mine had been devoured also; it lay immediately under "Audubon's Bluff" (the name Mr. Culbertson gave the ridge on which I stood to see the chase), and we could see it when nearly a mile distant. Bell's horns were the handsomest and largest, mine next best, and Harris's the smallest, but we are all contented. Mr. Culbertson tells me that Harris and Bell have done wonders, for persons who have never shot at Buffaloes from on horseback. Harris had a fall too, during his second chase, and was bruised in the manner of Squires, but not so badly. I have but little doubt that Squires killed his bull, as he says he shot it three times, and Mr. Culbertson's must have died also. What a terrible destruction of life, as it were for nothing, or next to it, as the tongues only were brought in, and the flesh of these fine animals was left to beasts and birds of prey, or to rot on the spots where they fell. The prairies are literally covered with the skulls of the victims, and the roads the Buffalo make in crossing the prairies have all the appearance of heavy wagon tracks. . . .

August 4, Friday. . . . We saw, after we had travelled ten miles, some Buffalo bulls; some alone, others in groups of four or five, a few Antelopes, but more shy than ever before. I was surprised to see how careless the bulls were of us, as some actually gave us chances to approach them within a hundred yards, looking stead-fastly, as if not caring a bit for us. At last we saw one lying down immediately in our road, and determined to give him a chance for his life. Mr. C. had a white horse, a runaway, in which he placed a good deal of confidence; he mounted it, and we looked after him. The bull did not start till Mr. C. was within a hundred yards, and then at a gentle and slow gallop. The horse galloped too, but only at the same rate. Mr. C. thrashed him until his hands were sore, for he had no whip, the bull went off without even a shot being fired, and the horse is now looked upon as forever disgraced. . . .

August 5, Saturday. . . . The white horse, which had gone out as a *hunter*, re-turned as a *pack-horse*, loaded with the entire flesh of a Buffalo cow; and our two mules drew three more and the heads of all four. This morning at daylight, when we were called to drink our coffee, there was a Buffalo feeding within twenty steps of our tent, and it moved slowly towards the hills as we busied ourselves making preparations for our departure. We reached the fort at noon; Squires, Provost, and LaFleur had returned; they had wounded a Bighorn, but had lost it. Owen and Bell returned this afternoon; they had seen no Cocks of the plains, but brought the skin of a female Elk, a Porcupine, and a young White-headed Eagle. Provost tells me that Buffaloes become so very poor during hard winters, when the snows cover the ground to the depth of two or three feet, that they lose their hair, become covered with scabs, on which the Magpies feed, and the poor beasts die by hundreds. One can hardly conceive how it happens, notwithstanding these many deaths and the immense numbers that are murdered almost daily on these boundless wastes called prairies, besides the hosts that are drowned in the freshets, and the hundreds of young calves who die in early spring, so many are yet to be found. Daily we see so many that we hardly notice them more than the cattle in our pastures about our homes. But this cannot last; even now there is a perceptible difference in the size of the herds, and before many years the Buffalo, like the Great Auk, will have disap-peared; surely this should not be permitted. Bell has been relating his adventures, our boat is going on, and I wish I had a couple of Bighorns. God bless you all.

Thought Provokers

1. How might a skeptical secular critic explain the religious revivalism of the early nineteenth century?

2. Article VIII of the Bill of Rights of the Constitution requires that "cruel and unusual punishments" shall not be "inflicted." In what respects did Dorothea Dix find the Constitution being widely violated? Why do reformers invariably encounter difficulties?

3. In what ways was it a man's world in the nineteenth century? How much has changed today? In what ways did the changes in women's role in the early nineteenth century represent an improvement or a deterioration from earlier conditions?

4. Is there less reformism in America today than there was in the 1840s? Assess the soundness of Emerson's remark: "Men are conservative when they are least vigorous, or when they are most luxurious. They are conservatives after dinner." It has been said that the wise man reduces his wants; the fool increases his income. Comment in the light of Thoreau's philosophy. What would happen to our economic and social structure if large numbers of people literally followed Thoreau's teachings?

5. By what means did the arrival of white pioneers transform the environment and the Native American cultures of the trans-Appalachian West?

17

The South and the Slavery Controversy, 1793–1860

Whenever I hear anyone arguing for slavery, I feel a
strong impulse to see it tried on him personally.

Abraham Lincoln, 1865

Prologue: In slavery, the Southerners had a bear by the tail: to hang on was embarrassing; to let go would be costly and seemingly dangerous. So situated, they put
the best face they could on their "peculiar institution," and freely quoted the Bible
to defend an archaic practice that both God and Jesus had tolerated, if not sanctioned. The abolitionists, especially the Garrisonians, harped on the evils of slavery;
the white Southerners stressed its benefits. The truth lay somewhere between. Certainly most slaveowners were not sadists. Self-interest, if not humanity, was a strong
though not infallible deterrent to mayhem. Yet slavery was a grave moral offense,
especially in a "free" society, even if the slaves did sometimes preserve their dignity
and if some masters were kind. The slaves were seldom beaten to death, and as a
rule families were not needlessly separated. Slaves were discouraged from learning
to read and encouraged to embrace the Christian religion, which is often the solace
of the oppressed. Despite the manifest immorality of slavery, countless Northerners,
with a financial stake in slave-grown cotton, deplored the boat-rocking tactics of the
abolitionists.

A. The Face of Slavery

1. A Slave Boy Learns a Lesson (c. 1827)

*The amazing Frederick Douglass, sired by an unknown white father, was born in
Maryland to a slave woman. He learned to read and write; and after suffering much
cruel usage he escaped to the North, where, despite mobbings and beatings, he became a leading abolitionist orator and journalist. A commanding figure of a man,
he raised black regiments during the Civil War, and in 1889 became U.S. minister to
the republic of Haiti. He showed impartiality in his two marriages: his first wife, he*

[1]*Life and Times of Frederick Douglass* (Hartford, Conn.: Park, 1882), pp. 94–97.

quipped, was the color of his mother and his second (despite a storm of criticism) was that of his father. From the following passage in his autobiography, ascertain why the slaveholders were willing to have their slaves know the Bible but not read it.

The frequent hearing of my mistress reading the Bible aloud—for she often read aloud when her husband was absent—awakened my curiosity in respect to this mystery of reading, and roused in me the desire to learn. Up to this time I had known nothing whatever of this wonderful art, and my ignorance and inexperience of what it could do for me, as well as my confidence in my mistress, emboldened me to ask her to teach me to read.

With an unconsciousness and inexperience equal to my own, she readily consented, and in an incredibly short time, by her kind assistance, I had mastered the alphabet and could spell words of three or four letters. My mistress seemed almost as proud of my progress as if I had been her own child, and supposing that her husband would be as well pleased, she made no secret of what she was doing for me. Indeed, she exultingly told him of the aptness of her pupil, and of her intention to persevere in teaching me, as she felt her duty to do, at least to read the Bible. . . .

Master Hugh was astounded beyond measure, and probably for the first time proceeded to unfold to his wife the true philosophy of the slave system, and the peculiar rules necessary in the nature of the case to be observed in the management of human chattels. Of course, he forbade her to give me any further instruction, telling her in the first place that to do so was unlawful, as it was also unsafe. "For," said he, "if you give a nigger an inch, he will take an ell. Learning will spoil the best nigger in the world. If he learns to read the Bible, it will forever unfit him to be a slave. He should know nothing but the will of his master, and learn to obey it. As to himself, learning will do him no good, but a great deal of harm, making him disconsolate and unhappy. If you teach him how to read, he'll want to know how to write, and this accomplished, he'll be running away with himself."

2. A Former Slave Exposes Slavery (1850)

Flogged without effect by his master, Douglass was hired out for one year to a notorious "slave breaker," who also professed to be a devout Methodist. Worked almost to death in all kinds of weather, allowed five minutes or less for meals, and brutally whipped about once a week, Douglass admitted that "Mr. Covey succeeded in breaking me—in body, soul, and spirit. My natural elasticity was crushed; my intellect languished, the disposition to read departed, the cheerful spark that lingered about my eye died out; the dark night of slavery closed in upon me; and behold a man transformed to a brute!" In this abolitionist speech in Rochester, New York, Douglass spoke from bitter experience. In what respects were the nonphysical abuses of slaves worse than the physical ones? Where was the system most unjust?

[2]Quoted in Irving Mark and E. L. Schwaab, eds., *The Faith of Our Fathers* (New York: Alfred A. Knopf, Inc., 1952), pp. 157–159.

More than twenty years of my life were consumed in a state of slavery. My childhood was environed by the baneful peculiarities of the slave system. I grew up to manhood in the presence of this hydra-headed monster not as a master—not as an idle spectator—not as the guest of the slaveholder; but as A SLAVE, eating the bread and drinking the cup of slavery with the most degraded of my brother bondmen, and sharing with them all the painful conditions of their wretched lot. In consideration of these facts, I feel that I have a right to speak, and to speak strongly. Yet, my friends, I feel bound to speak truly. . . .

First of all, I will state, as well as I can, the legal and social relation of master and slave. A master is one (to speak in the vocabulary of the Southern states) who claims and exercises a right of property in the person of a fellow man. This he does with the force of the law and the sanction of Southern religion.

The law gives the master absolute power over the slave. He may work him, flog him, hire him out, sell him, and in certain contingencies kill him with perfect impunity.

The slave is a human being, divested of all rights—reduced to the level of a brute—a mere "chattel" in the eye of the law—placed beyond the circle of human brotherhood—cut off from his kind. His name, which the "recording angel" may have enrolled in heaven among the blest, is impiously inserted in a master's ledger with horses, sheep, and swine.

In law a slave has no wife, no children, no country, and no home. He can own nothing, possess nothing, acquire nothing, but what must belong to another. To eat the fruit of his own toil, to clothe his person with the work of his own hands, is considered stealing.

He toils, that another may reap the fruit. He is industrious, that another may live in idleness. He eats unbolted meal, that another may eat the bread of fine flour. He labors in chains at home, under a burning sun and biting lash, that another may ride in ease and splendor abroad. He lives in ignorance, that another may be educated. He is abused, that another may be exalted. He rests his toil-worn limbs on the cold, damp ground, that another may repose on the softest pillow. He is clad in coarse and tattered raiment, that another may be arrayed in purple and fine linen. He is sheltered only by the wretched hovel, that a master may dwell in a magnificent mansion. And to this condition he is bound down by an arm of iron.

From this monstrous relation there springs an unceasing stream of most revolting cruelties. The very accompaniments of the slave system stamp it as the offspring of hell itself. To ensure good behavior, the slaveholder relies on the whip. To induce proper humility, he relies on the whip. To rebuke what he is pleased to term insolence, he relies on the whip. To supply the place of wages, as an incentive to toil, he relies on the whip. To bind down the spirit of the slave, to imbrute and destroy his manhood, he relies on the whip, the chain, the gag, the thumb-screw, the pillory, the bowie knife, the pistol, and the bloodhound. . . .

There is a still deeper shade to be given to this picture. The physical cruelties are indeed sufficiently harassing and revolting; but they are as a few grains of sand on the sea shore, or a few drops of water in the great ocean, compared with the stupendous wrongs which it inflicts upon the mental, moral, and religious nature of its hapless victims. It is only when we contemplate the slave as a moral and intellectual being that we can adequately comprehend the unparalleled enormity of slavery, and the intense criminality of the slaveholder.

3. Human Cattle for Sale (c. 1850)

Slave auctions, ugly affairs at best, received top billing in abolitionist propaganda. Here is an account, less sensational than many, by Solomon Northup, a free black of New York State. Kidnapped in Washington, D.C., and enslaved on a Louisiana plantation, he luckily managed to regain his freedom. His narrative, edited and perhaps ghostwritten by a New York lawyer, bears the earmarks of credibility. What aspect of this New Orleans slave auction, held by a Mr. Freeman, would be most likely to wound Northern sensibilities?

Next day many customers called to examine Freeman's "new lot" [of slaves]. The latter gentleman was very loquacious, dwelling at much length upon our several good points and qualities. He would make us hold up our heads, walk briskly back and forth, while customers would feel of our hands and arms and bodies, turn us about, ask us what we could do, make us open our mouths and show our teeth, precisely as a jockey examines a horse which he is about to barter for or purchase.

Sometimes a man or woman was taken back to the small house in the yard, stripped, and inspected more minutely. Scars upon a slave's back were considered evidence of a rebellious or unruly spirit, and hurt his sale.

One old gentleman, who said he wanted a coachman, appeared to take a fancy to me. From his conversation with Freeman, I learned he was a resident of the city [New Orleans]. I very much desired that he would buy me, because I conceived it would not be difficult to make my escape from New Orleans on some Northern vessel. Freeman asked him $1,500 for me. The old gentleman insisted it was too much, as times were very hard. Freeman, however, declared that I was sound and healthy, of a good constitution, and intelligent. He made it a point to enlarge upon my musical attainments. The old gentleman argued quite adroitly that there was nothing extraordinary about the nigger, and finally, to my regret, went out, saying he would call again.

During the day, however, a number of sales were made. David and Caroline were purchased together by a Natchez planter. They left us, grinning broadly, and in the most happy state of mind, caused by the fact of their not being separated. Lethe was sold to a planter of Baton Rouge, her eyes flashing with anger as she was led away.

The same man also purchased Randall. The little fellow was made to jump, and run across the floor, and perform many other feats, exhibiting his activity and condition. All the time the trade was going on, Eliza [the mother] was crying aloud, and wringing her hands. She besought the man not to buy him unless he also bought herself and Emily. She promised, in that case, to be the most faithful slave that ever lived. The man answered that he could not afford it, and then Eliza burst into a paroxysm of grief, weeping plaintively.

[3]Solomon Northup, *Twelve Years a Slave* (New York: Miller, Orton & Mulligan, 1853), pp. 79–82.

Freeman turned round to her, savagely, with his whip in his uplifted hand, ordering her to stop her noise, or he would flog her. He would not have such work—such sniveling; and unless she ceased that minute, he would take her to the yard and give her a hundred lashes. Yes, he would take the nonsense out of her pretty quick—if he didn't, might he be d———d.

Eliza shrunk before him, and tried to wipe away her tears, but it was all in vain. She wanted to be with her children, she said, the little time she had to live. All the frowns and threats of Freeman could not wholly silence the afflicted mother. She kept on begging and beseeching them, most piteously, not to separate the three. Over and over again she told them how she loved her boy. A great many times she repeated her former promises—how very faithful and obedient she would be; how hard she would labor day and night, to the last moment of her life, if he would only buy them all together.

But it was of no avail; the man could not afford it. The bargain was agreed upon, and Randall must go alone. Then Eliza ran to him; embraced him passionately; kissed him again and again; told him to remember her—all the while her tears falling in the boy's face like rain.

4. Cohabitation in the Cabins (c. 1834)

As the once-fertile lands of Maryland and Virginia petered out, the producing of slaves often proved more profitable than the producing of tobacco. Blacks were bred for export to the newly opened cotton lands of the booming Southwest. Frederick Douglass, in his reminiscences, here recounts how his Maryland slave-breaker, Mr. Covey, laid the foundations of riches. What does Douglass find most objectionable?

In pursuit of this object [wealth], pious as Mr. Covey was, he proved himself as unscrupulous and base as the worst of his neighbors. In the beginning he was only able—as he said—"to buy one slave"; and scandalous and shocking as is the fact, he boasted that he bought her simply "as a breeder." But the worst of this is not told in this naked statement. This young woman (Caroline was her name) was virtually compelled by Covey to abandon herself to the object for which he had purchased her; and the result was the birth of twins at the end of the year. At this addition to his human stock Covey and his wife were ecstatic with joy. No one dreamed of reproaching the woman or finding fault with the hired man, Bill Smith, the father of the children, for Mr. Covey himself had locked the two up together every night, thus inviting the result.

But I will pursue this revolting subject no farther. No better illustration of the unchaste, demoralizing, and debasing character of slavery can be found than is furnished in the fact that this professedly Christian slaveholder, amidst all his prayers and hymns, was shamelessly and boastfully encouraging and actually compelling, in his own house, undisguised and unmitigated fornication, as a means of increasing his stock. It was the system of slavery which made this allowable, and which condemned the slaveholder for buying a slave woman and devoting her to this life no

---

[4]*Life and Times of Frederick Douglass* (Hartford, Conn.: Park, 1882), pp. 150–151.

more than for buying a cow and raising stock from her; and the same rules were observed, with a view to increasing the number and quality of the one as of the other.

5. From Slavery to Freedom (1835)

African-born James L. Bradley was one of many slaves who purchased their freedom out of their own hard-gained, meager earnings. Bradley eventually made his way to the Lane Seminary in Cincinnati, a hotbed of abolitionist sentiment presided over by Lyman Beecher, father of the novelist Harriet Beecher Stowe. There he wrote the following short account of his life. What did he see as the worst aspects of slavery? What did his ability to purchase his freedom imply about the character of the slave system? What was his attitude toward Christianity?

I will try to write a short account of my life, as nearly as I can remember; though it makes me sorrowful to think of my past days; for they have been very dark and full of tears. I always longed and prayed for liberty, and had at times hopes that I should obtain it. I would pray, and try to study out some way to earn money enough to buy myself, by working in the night-time. But then something would happen to disappoint my hopes, and it seemed as though I must live and die a slave, with none to pity me.

I will begin as far back as I can remember. I think I was between two and three years old when the soul-destroyers tore me from my mother's arms, somewhere in Africa, far back from the sea. They carried me a long distance to a ship; all the way I looked back, and cried. The ship was full of men and women loaded with chains; but I was so small, they let me run about on deck.

After many long days, they brought us into Charleston, South Carolina. A slaveholder bought me, and took me up into Pendleton County. I suppose that I staid with him about six months. He sold me to a Mr. Bradley, by whose name I have ever since been called. This man was considered a wonderfully kind master; and it is true that I was treated better than most of the slaves I knew. I never suffered for food, and never was flogged with the whip; but oh, my soul! I was tormented with kicks and knocks more than I can tell. My master often knocked me down, when I was young. Once, when I was a boy, about nine years old, he struck me so hard that I fell down and lost my senses. I remained thus some time, and when I came to myself, he told me he thought he had killed me. At another time, he struck me with a currycomb, and sunk the knob into my head. I have said that I had food enough; I wish I could say as much concerning my clothing. But I let that subject alone, because I cannot think of any suitable words to use in telling you.

I used to work very hard. I was always obliged to be in the field by sunrise, and I labored till dark, stopping only at noon long enough to eat dinner. When I was about fifteen years old, I took what was called the cold plague, in consequence of being over-worked, and I was sick a long time. My master came to me one day, and hearing me groan with pain, he said, "This fellow will never be of any more use to

---

[5]*Fourth Annual Report of the Trustees of the Cincinnati Lane Seminary,* Lane Seminary, Ohio (1834), p. 27.

me—I would as soon knock him in the head, as if he were an opossum." His children sometimes came in, and shook axes and knives at me, as if they were about to knock me on the head. But I have said enough of this. The Lord at length raised me up from the bed of sickness, but I entirely lost the use of one of my ankles. Not long after this, my master moved to Arkansas Territory, and died. Then the family let me out; but after [line illegible] the plantation, saying she could not do with me. My master had kept me ignorant of everything he could. I was never told anything about God, or my own soul. Yet from the time I was fourteen years old, I used to think a great deal about freedom. It was my heart's desire; I could not keep it out of my mind. Many a sleepless night I have spent in tears, because I was a slave. I looked back on all I had suffered—and when I looked ahead, all was dark and hopeless bondage. My heart ached to feel within me the life of liberty. After the death of my master, I began to contrive how I might buy myself. After toiling all day for my mistress, I used to sleep three or four hours, and then get up and work for myself the remainder of the night. I made collars for horses, out of plaited husks. I could weave one in about eight hours; and I generally took time enough from my sleep to make two collars in the course of a week. I sold them for fifty cents each. One summer, I tried to take two or three hours from my sleep every night; but I found that I grew weak, and I was obliged to sleep more. With my first money I bought a pig. The next year I earned for myself about thirteen dollars; and the next about thirty. There was a good deal of wild land in the neighborhood that belonged to Congress. I used to go out with my hoe, and dig up little patches, which I planted with corn, and got up in the night to tend it. My hogs were fattened with this corn, and I used to sell a number every day. Besides this, I used to raise small patches of tobacco, and sell it to buy more corn for my pigs. In this way I worked for five years, at the end of which time, after taking out my losses, I found that I had earned one hundred and sixty dollars. With this money I hired my own time for two years. During this period, I worked almost all the time night and day. The hope of liberty strung my nerves, and braced up my soul so much, that I could do with very little sleep or rest. I could do a great deal more work than I was ever able to do before. At the end of the two years, I had earned three hundred dollars, besides feeding and clothing myself. I now bought my time for eighteen months longer, and went two hundred and fifty miles west, nearly into Texas, where I could make more money. Here I earned enough to buy myself; which I did in 1833, about one year ago. I paid for myself, including what I gave for my time, about seven hundred dollars.

As soon as I was free, I started for a free State. When I arrived in Cincinnati, I heard of Lane Seminary, about two miles out of the city. I had for years been praying to God that my dark mind might see the light of knowledge. I asked for admission into the Seminary. They pitied me, and granted my request, though I knew nothing of the studies which were required for admission. I am so ignorant, that I suppose it will take me two years to get up with the lowest class in the institution. But in all respects I am treated just as kindly, and as much like a brother by the students, as if my skin were as white, and my education as good as their own. Thanks to the Lord, prejudice against colour does not exist in Lane Seminary! If my life is spared, I shall probably spend several years here, and prepare to preach the gospel.

I will now mention a few things, that I could not conveniently bring in, as I was going along with my story.

In the year 1828, I saw some Christians, who talked with me concerning my soul, and the sinfulness of my nature. They told me I must repent, and live to do good. This led me to the cross of Christ;—and then, oh, how I longed to be able to read the Bible! I made out to get an old spelling-book, which I carried in my hat for many months, until I could spell pretty well, and read easy words. When I got up in the night to work, I used to read a few minutes, if I could manage to get a light. Indeed, every chance I could find, I worked away at my spelling-book. After I had learned to read a little, I wanted very much to learn to write; and I persuaded one of my young masters to teach me. But the second night, my mistress came in, bustled about, scolded her son, and called him out. I overheard her say to him, "You fool! what are you doing? If you teach him to write, he will write himself a pass and run away." That was the end of my instruction in writing; but I persevered, and made marks of all sorts and shapes I could think of. By turning every way, I was, after a long time, able to write tolerably plain.

I have said a good deal about my desire for freedom. How strange it is that anybody should believe any human being *could* be a slave, and yet be contented! I do not believe there ever was a slave, who did not long for liberty. I know very well that slave-owners take a great deal of pains to make the people in the free States believe that the slaves are happy; but I know, likewise, that I was never acquainted with a slave, however well he was treated, who did not long to be free. There is one thing about this, that people in the free States do not understand. When they ask slaves whether they wish for their liberty, they answer, "No;" and very likely they will go so far as to say they would not leave their masters for the world. But at the same time, they desire liberty more than anything else, and have, perhaps, all along been laying plans to get free. The truth is, if a slave shows any discontent, he is sure to be treated worse, and worked the harder for it; and every slave knows this. This is why they are careful not to show any uneasiness when white men ask them about freedom. When they are alone by themselves, all their talk is about liberty— liberty! It is the great thought and feeling that fills the mind full all the time.

6. A Slave Woman's Tale

Though the slave system was cruel and oppressive, the African-American bonds-men and -women could sometimes succeed in asserting their dignity, and could find the means to wed and to worship, to love and to laugh. In the following interview, conducted in the 1930s, ex-slave Annie Coley tells her life story. What areas of freedom, however limited, does she identify within the slave system? How does she describe the situation of women in slavery? What does her account imply about the relationship between masters and slaves? What differences did she see between slavery and freedom?

---

[6]George P. Rawick, ed., *The American Slave: A Composite Autobiography* (Westport, Conn.: Greenwood Publishing Company, 1972), Supplement, Series 1, vol. 7, Mississippi Narratives, Part 2, pp. 438–446. (The interview, originally recorded in dialect, is here rendered in standard English.)

My mammy told me I was a slave going on five years. I don't remember myself, I have to go by what my mammy and pappy say. I was born twenty miles above Camden, South Carolina. My pappy was Ben Jones, but after Big Boss Truesler bought him, he was called Ben Truesler. Rhody was my mammy's name.

All of us colored folks lived in loghouses in the quarters then. We didn't have any beds and mattresses like we have now. There were just bunks built in the wall with sacks filled with hay to lay on. All of us children slept on the floor.

Boss lived in a big white house, two story, with big white posts in front. He could look out from the upstairs windows and see what all the niggers were doing in the fields.

We worked in the fields in the cotton and the corn, from early morning till sundown. Saturdays, all day, just the same. Sundays we could rest. Big Boss gave each colored man a piece of ground to make a crop of corn and cotton for himself. Sundays each nigger worked out his own crop.

After the crop was laid by, we went with Big Boss to his church and sat in the back seats. We couldn't any of us read the Bible, so that was why Boss made us go to church, so that we could hear it read.

One Sunday, there was a mighty good preacher, and one old religious-hearted colored man got happy and rose up and shouted till he disturbed the preacher. At dinner Boss said, "Uncle, you must sit still this evening and not do no shoutin'! If you sit still, I will buy you a brand new pair of boots."

That evening the old man sat still as long as he could. But when the preacher began to tell about heaven and farewell to this world, the old colored man went wild. He rose up in his seat and yelled, "Boss, boots or no boots, I'm going to shout."

We bought Sunday clothes with our cotton money. Boss gave us plenty good work clothes. We got to rest three days at Christmas. We had a big dinner, but Boss gave us that out of his smokehouse. . . .

My mammy had a heap of children in slavery time, one every other year. She had them so fast that they took her out of the field and put her to weaving cloth, ten yards a day. She kept on having them until she had twelve head, and then she never did have any more. She had a heap of them before me, I was the seventh child.

My Boss's overseer was a poor white man, but he was good to us colored folks. Once some nigger women got to fighting in the cotton field. Boss brought them all to the gallery of the big house, and gave them all a lick or two with a whip, then sent them back to the field and told them to behave themselves.

But old Boss Jones had a mean overseer who took advantage of the women in the fields. One time he slammed a nigger woman down that was heavy, and caused her to have her baby—dead. The nigger women in the quarters jumped on him and said they were going to take him to a brushpile and burn him up. But their men hollered for them to turn him loose. Then Big Boss Jones came and made the women go back to the quarters. He said, "I ain't whipped these wretches for a long time, and I aim to whip them this evening." But all the women hid in the woods that evening, and Boss never said any more about it. He sent the overseer away and never did have any more overseers. He and his little boys looked over the work in the fields.

Yes, I saw a nigger in chains once. He was my mammy's brother. He stole the house girl and ran off with her to Camden. Big Boss brought him back, whipped him, and kept him chained in the kitchen for two weeks. Every morning Boss would go in the kitchen and whip him again.

His daddy, old Mike, who was my grandpa, was a wagon and buggy maker. He stayed in the shop all the time, and never did work in the fields. He made wagons and buggies for the white folks, and made big money for Boss, over a hundred dollars a month. Old Mike kept getting madder and madder about the way Boss treated his boy. He went plum crazy, and ran after Boss in the big house, yelling "This day, my Boss and I are both going to die." Boss, he ran upstairs, and old Missus locked him in a closet and then locked herself in the room.

Then old Mike ran to the kitchen and turned his boy loose. They both went back to the quarters, and Mike went on awhile for two or three days. Then he went back to the shop and went to work. But Boss was afraid of him and never did talk to him no more. Old Missus tended to the business in the shop and collected the money. The white men told Boss, "You should have whipped that nigger and sent him back to the field. Now you have driven your best nigger crazy. . . ."

There weren't any schools for the niggers in slavery days. After freedom, I went to night school in Camden and learned out of the old Blue Back Speller. The teacher was a white lady—there weren't any colored folks then who could teach us.

I never joined church until I was grown and married; let me see, I was twenty-two. I don't want to live no other life but a Christian life, so I'll be saved and go home to rest, for the Bible says the wicked will be left here and burned up. . . .

We didn't have any weddings on our plantation in those days. Boss just gave us a script saying we were man and wife. If a man wanted a girl from another plantation, Boss bought her or traded for her. . . .

My mammy told me when a slave was sick, the Boss man dosed her with medicine. If she didn't get any better, he had a doctor come. If a slave died, he was laid out, locked up in the house, and all the other niggers had to go back to the field. Slaves weren't allowed any time off for buryings, so the colored folks had to bury their dead at night.

Yes, we sang at the buryings, and at church, and while we were at work. Those old black folks just studied up their songs in their heads. How did we do it? I heard a Bishop say that God gave the black folks wisdom to study out those songs. . . .

Let me say one word about slavery. When we were under the white folks, there was none of this killing and murdering like there is now. There weren't any hangings because there wasn't anybody to hang.

I asked my ma, after freedom, were there the same laws in slavery time as there are now. And she said, "Yes, honey, we had the same laws, but there wasn't anybody to use them on in those days."

7. The Sundering of Families (1874)

The brutality of whip and branding iron was monstrous, but slavery's greatest psychological horror was the cruel separation of family members. In the following account Lorenzo Ivy, the son of a slave cobbler on a Virginia plantation, describes his family's efforts, not always successful, to stay together. How did the spread of the cotton economy (what Ivy refers to as the "cotton fever") increase the suffering of the slaves?

Times have changed so fast in the last ten years, that I often ask myself who am I, and why am I not on my master's plantation, working under an overseer, instead of being here in this institution [Hampton Institute, in Virginia, founded as a school for freed slaves after the Civil War], under the instruction of a school-teacher. I was born in 1849. My master was very good to his slaves, and they thought a great deal of him. But all of our happy days were over when he went South and caught the cotton fever. He was never satisfied till he moved out there. He sold the house before any of the black people knew anything about it, and that was the beginning of our sorrow. My father belonged to another man, and we knew not how soon we would be carried off from him. Two of my aunts were married, and one of them had ten children, and both of their husbands belonged to another man. Father and my uncles went to their masters and asked them to buy their families. They tried to, but our master wouldn't sell, and told [them] how many hundred dollars' worth of cotton he could make off us every year, and that we little chaps were just the right size to climb cotton-stalks and pick cotton. But our master and father's master had once agreed that if either one of them ever moved away, he would sell out to the other. So father's master sent for the other gentlemen who heard the conversation, and they said it was true. After a day or two's consideration, he agreed to let him have mother and the seven children for $12,000. That released us from sorrow. But it was not so with my aunts; they had lost all hope of being with their husbands any longer; the time was set for them to start; it was three weeks from the time we were sold. Those three weeks did not seem as long as three days to us who had to shake hands for the last time with those bound together with the bands of love.

Father said he could never do enough for his master for buying us. They treated us very well for the first three or four years—as the saying was with the black people, they fed us on soft corn at first and then choked us with the husk. When I was large enough to use a hoe, I was put under the overseer to make tobacco-hills. I worked under six overseers, and they all gave me a good name to my master. I only got about three whippings from each of them. The first one was the best; we did not know how good he was till he went away to the war. Then times commenced getting worse with us. I worked many a day without any thing to eat but a tin cup of buttermilk and a little piece of corn-bread, and then walk two miles every night or so to carry the overseer his dogs; if we failed to bring them, he would give us a nice flogging.

---

[7]Mrs. M. F. Armstrong and Helen W. Ludlow, *Hampton and Its Students* (New York: G. P. Putnam, 1874), pp. 78–80.

When the war closed, our master told all the people, if they would stay and get in the crop, he would give them part of it. Most of them left; they said they knew him too well. Father made us all stay, so we all worked on the remainder of the year, just as if Lee hadn't surrendered. I never worked harder in my life, for I thought the more we made, the more we would get. We worked from April till one month to Christmas. We raised a large crop of corn and wheat and tobacco, shucked all the corn and put it in the barn, stripped all the tobacco, and finished one month before Christmas. Then we went to our master for our part he had promised us, but he said he wasn't going to give us any thing, and he stopped giving us any thing to eat, and said we couldn't live any longer on his land. Father went to an officer of the Freedmen's Bureau, but the officer was like Isaac said to Esau: "The voice is like Jacob's voice, but the hands are the hands of Esau." So that was the way with the officer—he had on Uncle Sam's clothes, but he had Uncle Jeff's [Jefferson Davis's] heart. He said our master said we wasn't worth any thing, and he couldn't get any thing for us, so father said no more about it.

We made out to live that winter—I don't know how. In April, 1866, father moved to town where he could work at his trade. He hired all of us boys that were large enough to work in a brick-yard for from three to six dollars a month. That was the first time I had tasted the sweet cup of freedom. . . .

B. The White Southern View of Slavery

1. William Harper's Apology (1837)

William Harper was a distinguished South Carolina jurist, an antitariff zealot, and a nullification advocate who early predicted civil war. He is perhaps best remembered as the author of the memorable ordinance of nullification voted by South Carolina in 1832, and also of the Memoir on Slavery. *This remarkable apology, a part of which is presented here, ranks as one of the most vigorous defenses of the "peculiar institution." In what respects did Harper's defense turn out to be an indictment? What was the weakness in the argument that cotton could not be grown without slaves?*

Slavery was forced upon us by the extremest exigency of circumstances in a struggle for very existence. Without it, it is doubtful whether a white man would be now existing on this continent—certain that, if there were, they would be in a state of the utmost destitution, weakness, and misery. I neither deprecate nor resent the gift of slavery.

The Africans brought to us had been slaves in their own country and only underwent a change of masters.

---

[1]Quoted in A. C. McLaughlin et al., eds., *Source Problems in United States History* (New York and London: Harper & Brothers, 1918), pp. 419–424.

That there are great evils in a society where slavery exists, and that the institution is liable to great abuse, I have already said. But the whole of human life is a system of evils and compensations. The free laborer has few real guarantees from society, while security is one of the compensations of the slave's humble position.* There have been fewer murders of slaves than of parents, children, and apprentices in society where slavery does not exist. The slave offers no temptation to the murderer, nor does he really suffer injury from his master. Who but a driveling fanatic has thought of the necessity of protecting domestic animals from the cruelty of their owners?

. . . It is true that the slave is driven to labor by stripes [lashes]; and if the object of punishment be to produce obedience or reformation with the least permanent injury, it is the best method of punishment. Men claim that this is intolerable. It is not degrading to a slave, nor is it felt to be so. Is it degrading to a child?

Odium has been cast upon our legislation on account of its forbidding the elements of education to be communicated to slaves. But in truth what injury has been done them by this? He who works during the day with his hands does not read in intervals of leisure for his amusement or the improvement of his mind—or the exception is so rare as scarcely to need the being provided for. If there were any chance of elevating their rank, the denial of the rudiments of education might be a matter of hardship. But this they know cannot be and that further attainments would be useless to them. . . .

It has been said that marriage does not exist among our slaves. But we know that marriages among slaves are solemnized; but the law does not make them indissoluble, nor could it do so. . . . Some suppose that a slaveholding country is one wide stew [brothel] for the indulgence of unbridled lust, and there are particular instances of brutal and shameless debauches in every country. It is even true that in this respect the morals of this class [slave women] are very loose and that the passions of men of the superior caste tempt and find gratification in the easy chastity of the females. . . .

[In countries where free labor prevails] the unmarried woman who becomes a mother is an outcast from society—and though sentimentalists lament the hardship of the case, it is justly and necessarily so. But with us this female slave has a different status. She is not a less useful member of society than before. She has not impaired her means of support nor materially impaired her character or lowered her station in society; she has done no great injury to herself or any other human being. Her offspring is not a burden but an acquisition to her owner. . . .

Supposing finally that the abolitionists should effect their purpose. What would be the result? The first and most obvious effect would be to put an end to the cultivation of our great Southern staple [cotton]. . . . The cultivation of the great staple crops cannot be carried on in any portion of our own country where there are not slaves. . . . Even if it were possible to procure laborers at all, what planter would venture to carry on his operations? Imagine an extensive rice or cotton plantation cultivated by free laborers who might perhaps strike for an increase of wages at a season when the neglect of a few days would insure the destruction of the whole

---

*For the evils of "wage slavery," see p. 299.

crop. I need hardly say that these staples cannot be produced to any extent where the proprietor of the soil cultivates it with his own hands.

And what would be the effect of putting an end to the cultivation of these staples and thus annihilating, at a blow, two-thirds or three-fourths of our foreign commerce? Can any sane mind contemplate such a result without terror? Our slavery has not only given existence to millions of slaves within our own territories; it has given the means of subsistence, and therefore of existence, to millions of freemen in our Confederate [United] States, enabling them to send forth their swarms to overspread the plains and forests of the West and appear as the harbingers of civilization. Not only on our continent but on the other it has given existence [in textile mills] to hundreds of thousands and the means of comfortable subsistence to millions. A distinguished citizen of our state has lately stated that our great staple, cotton, has contributed more than anything else of later times to the progress of civilization. By enabling the poor to obtain cheap and becoming clothing, it has inspired a taste for comfort, the first stimulus to civilization.

2. The "Blessings" of the Slave (1849)

Connecticut-born and Puritan-descended Solon Robinson became a Yankee peddler at eighteen. After he moved to Indiana, he attained prominence as a trader and agriculturist. During the course of his extensive travels through practically every state, he wrote a series of discerning sketches for the foremost agricultural magazines. The following contribution to a leading Southern trade journal is hardly what one would expect from a Connecticut Yankee. In what respects did Robinson appear to be too soft on slavery, and in what respects did he disagree with the abolitionists?

A greater punishment could not be devised or inflicted upon the Southern slave at this day than to give him that liberty which God in his wisdom and mercy deprived him of. . . .

Free them from control, and how soon does poverty and wretchedness overtake them! . . . I boldly and truly assert that you may travel Europe over—yea, you may visit the boasted freemen of America—aye, you may search the world over—before you find a laboring peasantry who are more happy, more contented, as a class of people, or who are better clothed and fed and better provided for in sickness, infirmity, and old age, or who enjoy more of the essential comforts of life, than these so-called miserable, oppressed, abused, starved slaves. . . .

I doubt whether one single instance can be found among the slaves of the South where one has injured himself at long and excessive labor. Instead of a cruel and avaricious master being able to extort more than a very reasonable amount of labor from him, his efforts will certainly produce the contrary effect. This is a well-known fact, so much so indeed that an overseer of this character cannot get employment among masters, who know that over-driving a Negro, as well as a mule, is the poorest way to get work out of either of them. These facts are well understood

---

[2]*De Bow's Review,* vol. 7 (n.s., vol. 1, 1849), pp. 217–221, 383–384.

by all observant masters and overseers: that neither mule nor Negro can be made to do more than a certain amount of work; and that amount so small in comparison to the amount done by white laborers at the North that it is a universal observation at the South. Northern men are always the hardest masters, in the vain attempt they make to force the Negro to do even half as much as a hireling in New England is compelled to do, or lose his place and wages. . . .

It is true that some men abuse and harshly treat their slaves. So do some men abuse their wives and children and apprentices and horses and cattle. . . .

The fact is notorious that slaves are better treated now than formerly, and that the improvement in their condition is progressing; partly from their masters becoming more temperate and better men, but mainly from the greatest of all moving causes in human actions—self-interest. For masters have discovered in the best of all schools—experience—that their true interest is inseparably bound up with the humane treatment, comfort, and happiness of their slaves.

And many masters have discovered, too, that their slaves are more temperate, more industrious, more kind to one another, more cheerful, more faithful, and more obedient under the ameliorating influences of religion than under all the driving and whipping of all the tyrannical taskmasters that have existed since the day when the children of Israel were driven to the task of making Egyptian brick without straw.

And I do most fearlessly assert, and defy contradiction, that in no part of this Union, even in Puritan New England, is the Sabbath better kept by master and slave, by employer and hireling, or by all classes, high and low, rich and poor, than in the state of Mississippi, where I have often been told that that thing so accursed of God [slavery] existed in all its most disgusting deformity, wretchedness, and sinful horror. From the small plantations, the slaves go more regularly, and better dressed and behaved, to church, often a distance of five or six miles, than any other class of laborers that I have ever been acquainted with. Upon many of the large plantations, divine service is performed more regularly, and to larger and more orderly audiences, than in some county towns. . . .

In all my tour during the past winter, I did not see or hear of but two cases of flogging: one of which was for stealing, and the other for running away from as good a master as ever a servant need to have, which is proved by the appearance and general good conduct of his Negroes. And that they are well fed I know from many days' personal observation; and I have seen some of them with better broadcloth suits on than I often wear myself; and more spare money than their master, as he will freely acknowledge. . . .

But I do seriously say that I did not see or hear of one place where the Negroes were not well fed; and I did not see a ragged gang of Negroes in the South. And I could only hear of one plantation where the Negroes were overworked or unjustly flogged, and on that plantation the master was a drunken, abusive wretch, as heartily despised by his neighbors as he was hated by his Negroes. And were it not for the consequences to themselves if they should rise upon and pull him limb from limb, his brother planters would rejoice that he had met the fate that cruelty to slaves, they are free to say, justly merits.

The two things that are most despised and hated in the South are masters that abuse and starve and ill-treat their slaves, and abolitionists, who seize upon every isolated case of the kind, and trumpet it through the land as evidence of the manner that all slaves are treated, and then call upon the people of the free states to aid the Negroes to free themselves from such inhuman bondage, peaceably if they can, forcibly if they must, no matter whose or how much blood shall flow.

3. Slaves Don't Strike (1846)

The South invested its capital in human muscle, not machinery; in the lash system, not the cash system. The slaveowners had one ace-in-the-hole argument against emancipation: it would wipe out that reliable supply of labor without which Southern agriculture (and Northern textile factories) would perish. These fears were not groundless, as the economic chaos that followed the Civil War amply demonstrated. Sir Charles Lyell, the distinguished British geologist and world traveler, was exposed to the Southern viewpoint. How does he explain the fact that the South clung to slavery while white day labor was admittedly cheaper?

An intelligent Louisianian said to me, "Were we to emancipate our Negroes as suddenly as your government did the West Indians, they would be a doomed race. But there can be no doubt that white labor is more profitable even in this climate."

"Then, why do you not encourage it?" I asked.

"It must be the work of time," he replied. "The prejudices of owners have to be overcome, and the sugar and cotton crop is easily lost if not taken in at once when ripe; the canes being damaged by a slight frost, and the cotton requiring to be picked dry as soon as mature, and being ruined by rain. Very lately a planter, five miles below New Orleans, having resolved to dispense with slave labor, hired one hundred Irish and German emigrants at very high wages. In the middle of the harvest they all struck for double pay. No others were to be had, and it was impossible to purchase slaves in a few days. In that short time he lost produce to the value of $10,000."

4. Comparing Slave Labor and Wage Labor (1850)

In response to abolitionist attacks in the 1840s, supporters of slavery became more aggressive. Instead of simply defending the "peculiar institution," they began to argue that slavery benefited slaveowners and slaves alike. Proslavery propagandists frequently compared Northern and Southern institutions in the light of this argument. This cartoon published in Boston is an example of such a comparison. Why would an attack on conditions in England be an effective way to respond to criticism of slavery in America? Were there advantages of slave labor, and if so, to whom did they accrue? In what sense was wage labor really "free"?

[3]Charles Lyell, *A Second Visit to the United States of North America* (New York: Harper & Brothers; London: J. Murray, 1849), vol. 2, pp. 126–127.
[4]Library of Congress #USZ62-1285.

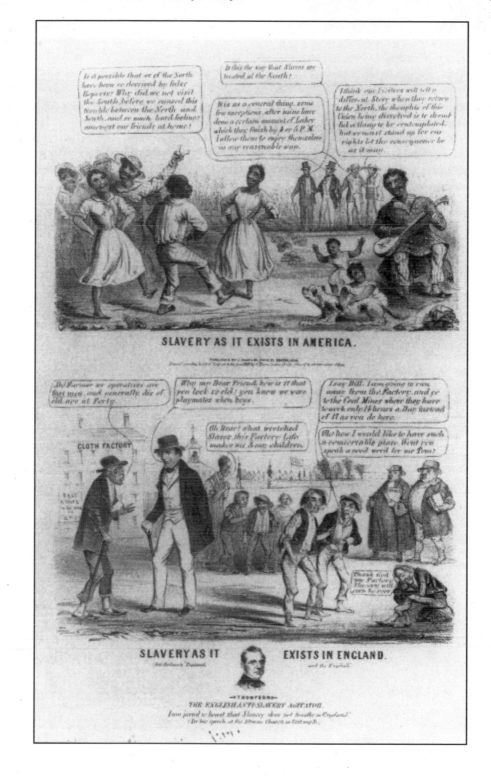

C. The Abolitionist Crusade

1. William Lloyd Garrison Launches The Liberator (1831)

Mild-appearing William Lloyd Garrison, the most impassioned of the abolitionists, began publication of his incendiary weekly newspaper, The Liberator, *with the following trumpet blast. Despite a subscription list of not more than three thousand and embarrassing annual deficits, he continued the journal for thirty-five years—until slavery was legally ended. The rude woodcut at the top of the front page showing a slave auction near the Capitol infuriated the South; the state of Georgia offered $5,000 for Garrison's arrest and conviction. Jailed in Baltimore for libel, mobbed in Boston, and jeered at while on the lecture platform, he not only outraged the South but also angered Northern conservatives and even moderate abolitionists. What specific measures did he advocate? Did he address his appeal exclusively to the South? Has posterity vindicated him, as he claimed it would?*

During my recent tour for the purpose of exciting the minds of the people by a series of discourses on the subject of slavery, every place that I visited gave fresh evidence of the fact that a greater revolution in public sentiment was to be effected in the free states—*and particularly in New England*—than at the South. I found contempt more bitter, opposition more active, detraction more relentless, prejudice more stubborn, and apathy more frozen, than among slaveowners themselves. Of course, there were individual exceptions to the contrary.

This state of things afflicted but did not dishearten me. I determined, at every hazard, to lift up the standard of emancipation in the eyes of the nation, *within sight of Bunker Hill and in the birthplace of liberty.* That standard is now unfurled; and long may it float, unhurt by the spoliations of time or the missiles of a desperate foe—yea, till every chain be broken, and every bondman set free! Let Southern oppressors tremble—let their secret abettors tremble—let their Northern apologists tremble—let all the enemies of the persecuted blacks tremble. . . .

Assenting to the "self-evident truth" maintained in the American Declaration of Independence "that all men are created equal, and endowed by their Creator with certain inalienable rights—among which are life, liberty, and the pursuit of happiness," I shall strenuously contend for the immediate enfranchisement of our slave population. . . . In Park Street Church, on the Fourth of July, 1829, in an address on slavery, I unreflectingly assented to the popular but pernicious doctrine of *gradual* abolition. I seize this opportunity to make a full and unequivocal recantation, and thus publicly to ask pardon of my God, of my country, and of my brethren the poor slaves, for having uttered a sentiment so full of timidity, injustice, and absurdity. . . .

I am aware that many object to the severity of my language; but is there not cause for severity? I *will be* as harsh as truth, and as uncompromising as justice. On

---

[1]*The Liberator* (Boston), January 1, 1831.

this subject I do not wish to think, or speak, or write, with moderation. No! No! Tell a man whose house is on fire to give a moderate alarm; tell him to moderately rescue his wife from the hands of the ravisher; tell the mother to gradually extricate her babe from the fire into which it has fallen—but urge me not to use moderation in a cause like the present. I am in earnest—I will not equivocate—I will not excuse—I will not retreat a single inch—AND I WILL BE HEARD. The apathy of the people is enough to make every statue leap from its pedestal, and to hasten the resurrection of the dead.

It is pretended that I am retarding the cause of emancipation by the coarseness of my invective and the precipitancy of my measures. *The charge is not true.* On this question my influence—humble as it is—is felt at this moment to a considerable extent, and shall be felt in coming years—not perniciously, but beneficially—not as a curse, but as a blessing. And posterity will bear testimony that I was right.

2. Manifesto of the Anti-Slavery Society (1833)

About fifty abolitionist idealists, meeting in Philadelphia, launched the American Anti-Slavery Society with the following declaration. William L. Garrison, who would be its president twenty-two times, was chief architect of this manifesto. Later becoming more insistent and impatient, he denounced the churches as "cages of unclean birds" (because they tolerated slavery), denied the full inspiration of the Bible (because it sanctioned slavery), publicly burned a copy of the Constitution (because it upheld slavery), and as early as 1841 advocated the disruption of the Union (because it legalized slavery). The following is an edict by the American Anti-Slavery Society. Why does it demand immediate and uncompensated emancipation? What concessions does it make at this early date to the South? Which of its proposals were most (and least) politically feasible?

We further maintain that no man has a right to enslave or imbrute his brother—to hold or acknowledge him, for one moment, as a piece of merchandise—to keep back his hire by fraud—or to brutalize his mind by denying him the means of intellectual, social, and moral improvement.

The right to enjoy liberty is inalienable. To invade it is to usurp the prerogative of Jehovah. Every man has a right to his own body—to the products of his own labor—to the protection of law—and to the common advantages of society. It is piracy to buy or steal a native African and subject him to servitude. Surely, the sin is as great to enslave an American as an African.

Therefore we believe and affirm that there is no difference, in principle, between the African slave trade and American slavery;

That every American citizen who retains a human being in involuntary bondage as his property is, according to Scripture (Exodus 21:16), a mansteaacler;

---

[2]W. P. Garrison and F. J. Garrison, *William Lloyd Garrison, 1805–1879* (New York: The Century Co., 1885), vol. 1, pp. 410–411.

That the slaves ought instantly to be set free and brought under the protection of law; . . .

That all those laws which are now in force admitting the right of slavery are therefore, before God, utterly null and void. . . .

We further believe and affirm that all persons of color who possess the qualifications which are demanded of others ought to be admitted forthwith to the enjoyment of the same privileges, and the exercise of the same prerogatives, as others; and that the paths of preferment, of wealth, and of intelligence should be opened as widely to them as to persons of a white complexion.

We maintain that no compensation should be given to the planters emancipating their slaves:

Because it would be a surrender of the great fundamental principle that man cannot hold property in man;

Because slavery is a crime, and therefore [the slave] is not an article to be sold;

Because the holders of slaves are not the just proprietors of what they claim; freeing the slave is not depriving them of property, but restoring it to its rightful owner; it is not wronging the master, but righting the slave—restoring him to himself;

Because immediate and general emancipation would only destroy nominal, not real, property; it would not amputate a limb or break a bone of the slaves, but, by infusing motives into their breasts, would make them doubly valuable to the masters as free laborers; and

Because, if compensation is to be given at all, it should be given to the outraged and guiltless slaves, and not to those who have plundered and abused them.

We regard as delusive, cruel, and dangerous any scheme of expatriation [to Liberia] which pretends to aid, either directly or indirectly, in the emancipation of the slaves, or to be a substitute for the immediate and total abolition of slavery.

We fully and unanimously recognize the sovereignty of each state to legislate exclusively on the subject of the slavery which is tolerated within its limits; we concede that Congress, under the present national compact, has no right to interfere with any of the slave states in relation to this momentous subject;

But we maintain that Congress has a right, and is solemnly bound, to suppress the domestic trade between the several states, and to abolish slavery in those portions of our territory which the Constitution has placed under its exclusive jurisdiction [District of Columbia].

3. *Theodore Dwight Weld Pillories Slavery (1839)*

Theodore Dwight Weld assumed leadership of the New York abolitionist group, which objected to the anticonstitutional tactics of Garrison's New England following. He was one of the most influential of the abolitionists, and certainly one of the great men of his era. Preacher, lecturer (until he ruined his voice), pamphleteer, organ-

---

[3]T. D. Weld, *American Slavery As It Is* (New York: American Anti-Slavery Society, 1839), p. 9.

izer, and inspirational genius, he founded numerous local abolitionist societies and won countless converts to abolition, including congressmen and other public figures. His documented compilation of horror tales, published in 1839 in American Slavery As It Is, *not only became the bible of the cause but greatly influenced the writing of* Uncle Tom's Cabin. *The following statements in his Introduction have been criticized as grossly overdrawn. How exaggerated or accurate are they?*

We will prove that the slaves in the United States are treated with barbarous inhumanity; that they are overworked, underfed, wretchedly clad and lodged, and have insufficient sleep; that they are often made to wear round their necks iron collars armed with prongs, to drag heavy chains and weights at their feet while working in the field, and to wear yokes, and bells, and iron horns; that they are often kept confined in the stocks day and night for weeks together, made to wear gags in their mouths for hours or days, have some of their front teeth torn out or broken off, that they may be easily detected when they run away; that they are frequently flogged with terrible severity, have red pepper rubbed into their lacerated flesh, and hot brine, spirits of turpentine, etc., poured over the gashes to increase the torture; that they are often stripped naked, their backs and limbs cut with knives, bruised and mangled by scores and hundreds of blows with the paddle, and terribly torn by the claws of cats, drawn over them by their tormentors; that they are often hunted with bloodhounds and shot down like beasts, or torn in pieces by dogs; that they are often suspended by the arms and whipped and beaten till they faint, and when revived by restoratives beaten again till they faint, and sometimes till they die; that their ears are often cut off, their eyes knocked out, their bones broken, their flesh branded with red-hot irons; that they are maimed, mutilated, and burned to death over slow fires.

All these things, and more, and worse, we shall prove. . . . We shall show, not merely that such deeds are commited, but that they are frequent; not done in corners, but before the sun; not in one of the slave states, but in all of them; not perpetrated by brutal overseers and drivers merely, but by magistrates, by legislators, by professors of religion, by preachers of the Gospel, by governors of states, by "gentlemen of property and standing," and by delicate females moving in the "highest circles of society."

We know, full well, the outcry that will be made by multitudes at these declarations; the multiform cavils, the flat denials, the charges of "exaggeration" and "falsehood" so often bandied; the sneers of affected contempt at the credulity that can believe such things; and the rage and imprecations against those who give them currency.

We know, too, the threadbare sophistries by which slaveholders and their apologists seek to evade such testimony. If they admit that such deeds are committed, they tell us that they are exceedingly rare, and therefore furnish no grounds for judging of the general treatment of slaves; that occasionally a brutal wretch in the free states barbarously butchers his wife, but that no one thinks of inferring from that the general treatment of wives at the North and West.

They tell us, also, that the slaveholders of the South are proverbially hospitable, kind, and generous, and it is incredible that they can perpetrate such enormities upon human beings; further, that it is absurd to support that they would thus injure their own property, that self-interest would prompt them to treat their slaves with kindness, as none but fools and madmen wantonly destroy their own property; further, that Northern visitors at the South come back testifying to the kind treatment of the slaves, and that the slaves themselves corroborate such representations. . . . We are not to be turned from our purpose by such vapid babblings.

4. Slavery and the Family (1840)

This illustration depicts what was probably the abolitionists' most telling argument against slavery: the violence it wrought upon the integrity of family life. Harriet Beecher Stowe would later make that argument the central motif of her epochal antislavery novel, Uncle Tom's Cabin. *Why was this argument so powerful? Did it appeal differently to men and women? How did the illustrator here make special appeal to women's sentiments?*

1840.]   *Anti-Slavery Almanac.*   15

SELLING A MOTHER FROM HER CHILD.
" ' Do you *often* buy the wife without the husband?' 'Yes, *very often;* and *frequently*, too, they sell me the mother while they keep her children. I have often known them take away the infant from its mother's breast, and keep it, while they sold her.' "—*Prof. Andrews, late of the University*

---

[4]*Anti-Slavery Almanac,* 1840.

D. Judgments on the Abolitionists

1. Daniel Webster Is Critical (1850)

The thunderously eloquent Daniel Webster was no abolitionist, though the abolitionists liked to think of him as in their camp. He sadly disillusioned them in his famous Seventh of March speech about the Compromise of 1850 (see later, p. 401). Pleading passionately for North-South harmony, he turned upon the antislaveryites. Their pained outcry rent the heavens. At a public meeting in Faneuil Hall in Boston, the Reverend Theodore Parker declared, "I know of no deed in American history done by a son of New England to which I can compare this but the act of Benedict Arnold. . . ." In this portion of Webster's speech, is he convincing about the harm done by the abolitionists?

Then, sir, there are those abolition societies, of which I am unwilling to speak, but in regard to which I have very clear notions and opinions. I do not think them useful. I think their operations for the last twenty years have produced nothing good or valuable.

At the same time, I know thousands of them are honest and good men; perfectly well-meaning men. They have excited feelings; they think they must do something for the cause of liberty. And in their sphere of action, they do not see what else they can do than to contribute to an abolition press, or an abolition society, or to pay an abolition lecturer.

I do not mean to impute gross motives even to the leaders of these societies, but I am not blind to the consequences. I cannot but see what mischiefs their interference with the South has produced.

And is it not plain to every man? Let any gentleman who doubts of that recur to the debates in the Virginia House of Delegates in 1832, and he will see with what freedom a proposition made by Mr. Randolph for the gradual abolition of slavery was discussed in that body. Everyone spoke of slavery as he thought; very ignominious and disparaging names and epithets were applied to it.

The debates in the House of Delegates on that occasion, I believe, were all published. They were read by every colored man who could read, and if there were any who could not read, those debates were read to them by others. At that time Virginia was not unwilling nor afraid to discuss this question, and to let that part of her population know as much of it as they could learn.

That was in 1832. . . . These abolition societies commenced their course of action in 1835. It is said—I do not know how true it may be—that they sent incendiary publications into the slave states. At any event, they attempted to arouse, and did arouse, a very strong feeling. In other words, they created great agitation in the North against Southern slavery.

Well, what was the result? The bonds of the slaves were bound more firmly than before; their rivets were more strongly fastened. Public opinion, which in Virginia had begun to be exhibited against slavery, and was opening out for the discussion of the question, drew back and shut itself up in its castle.

---

[1]*Congressional Globe,* 31st Congress, 1st session, Appendix, vol. 22, part 1, p. 275.

I wish to know whether anybody in Virginia can, now, talk openly as Mr. Randolph, Gov. McDowell, and others talked there, openly, and sent their remarks to the press, in 1832.

We all know the fact, and we all know the cause. And everything that this agitating people have done, has been, not to enlarge, but to restrain, not to set free, but to bind faster, the slave population of the South. That is my judgment.

2. Abraham Lincoln Appraises Abolitionism (1854)

Abolitionism and crackpotism were, for a time, closely associated in the public mind, and the taint of abolitionism was almost fatal to a man aspiring to public office. Southerners commonly regarded Abraham Lincoln as an abolitionist, even though his wife's family in Kentucky were slaveholders. Lincoln set forth his views at some length in this memorable speech at Peoria, Illinois, in 1854. On the basis of these remarks, did he deserve to be called an abolitionist? In what respects might the South have resented his position?

Before proceeding, let me say that I have no prejudice against the Southern people. They are just what we would be in their situation. If slavery did not now exist among them, they would not introduce it. If it did now exist amongst us, we should not instantly give it up. This I believe of the masses North and South.

Doubtless there are individuals, on both sides, who would not hold slaves under any circumstances, and others who would gladly introduce slavery anew, if it were out of existence. We know that some Southern men do free their slaves, go North, and become tiptop abolitionists; while some Northern ones go South and become most cruel slave-masters.

When Southern people tell us they are no more responsible for the origin of slavery than we, I acknowledge the fact. When it is said that the institution exists, and that it is very difficult to get rid of it in any satisfactory way, I can understand and appreciate the saying. I surely will not blame them for not doing what I should not know how to do myself.

If all earthly power were given me, I should not know what to do as to the existing institution. My first impulse would be to free all the slaves and send them to Liberia—to their native land. But a moment's reflection would convince me that whatever of high hope (as I think there is) there may be in this in the long run, its sudden execution is impossible. If they all landed there in a day, they would all perish in the next ten days; and there are not surplus shipping and surplus money enough to carry them there in many times ten days.

What then? Free them all and keep them among us as underlings? Is it quite certain that this betters their condition? I think I would not hold one in slavery at any rate; yet the point is not clear enough for me to denounce people upon.

What next? Free them, and make them politically and socially our equals? My own feelings will not admit of this; and if mine would, we well know that those of

---

[2]R. P. Basler, ed., *The Collected Works of Abraham Lincoln* (New Brunswick, N.J.: Rutgers University Press, 1953), vol. 2, pp. 255–256.

the great mass of white people would not. Whether this feeling accords with justice and sound judgment is not the sole question, if indeed it is any part of it. A universal feeling, whether well or ill founded, cannot be safely disregarded. We cannot then make them equals.

It does seem to me that systems of gradual emancipation might be adopted; but for their tardiness in this I will not undertake to judge our brethren of the South.

When they remind us of their constitutional rights, I acknowledge them, not grudgingly but fully and fairly. And I would give them any legislation for the reclaiming of their fugitives which should not, in its stringency, be more likely to carry a free man into slavery than our ordinary criminal laws are to hang an innocent one.

3. The Abolitionists Provoke War (1882)

The abolitionists were often accused of having precipitated the Civil War. In his memoirs Frederick Douglass, the remarkable ex-slave and abolitionist agitator, pleads partly guilty to the indictment. How correct was his assumption as to who were the aggressors?

The abolitionists of this country have been charged with bringing on the war between the North and South, and in one sense this is true. Had there been no anti-slavery agitation at the North, there would have been no active anti-slavery anywhere to resist the demands of the Slave Power at the South, and where there is no resistance there can be no war. Slavery would then have been nationalized, and the whole country would then have been subjected to its power. Resistance to slavery and the extension of slavery invited and provoked secession and war to perpetuate and extend the slave system.

Thus, in the same sense, England is responsible for our Civil War. The abolition of slavery in the West Indies gave life and vigor to the abolition movement in America. Clarkson of England gave us Garrison of America; Granville Sharpe of England gave us our Wendell Phillips; and Wilberforce of England gave us our peerless Charles Sumner.*

These grand men and their brave co-workers here took up the moral thunderbolts which had struck down slavery in the West Indies, and hurled them with increased zeal and power against the gigantic system of slavery here, till, goaded to madness, the traffickers in the souls and bodies of men flew to arms, rent asunder the Union at the center, and filled the land with hostile armies and the ten thousand horrors of war. Out of this tempest, out of this whirlwind and earthquake of war, came the abolition of slavery, came the employment of colored troops, came colored citizens, came colored jurymen, came colored Congressmen, came colored schools in the South, and came the great amendments of our national Constitution.

---

[3] *The Life and Times of Frederick Douglass* (Hartford, Conn.: Park, 1882), p. 607.

*Thomas Clarkson (1760–1846), Granville Sharp (1735–1813), and William Wilberforce (1759–1833) were English abolitionists whose efforts persuaded Parliament to end the slave trade within the British empire in 1807. William Lloyd Garrison (1805–1879), Wendell Phillips (1811–1884), and Charles Sumner (1811–1874), were leading American abolitionists—all of them, interestingly, from Massachusetts.

E. The Rising White Southern Temper

1. Hinton Helper's Banned Book (1857)

Hinton R. Helper, an impoverished North Carolinian who hated blacks, published a sensational book in 1857 in which he statistically contrasted the rapid economic growth of the North with the slower progress of the South. Concluding that the slave-less whites were the chief victims of the slave system, he urged upon them various means, some incendiary, to overthrow both slavery and the grip of the white oligarchy. Unable to find a publisher in the South, he aired his views in the North under the title The Impending Crisis of the South. *The Southern aristocracy reacted violently, banning the book and roughly handling a few daring souls who had obtained smuggled copies. Tens of thousands of copies in one form or another were distributed. Why was it to the advantage of the slaveowners to treat the poor whites as Helper alleged they did?*

Notwithstanding the fact that the white non-slaveholders of the South are in the majority as five to one, they have never yet had any part or lot in framing the laws under which they live. There is no legislation except for the benefit of slavery and slaveholders.

As a general rule, poor white persons are regarded with less esteem and attention than Negroes, and though the condition of the latter is wretched beyond description, vast numbers of the former are infinitely worse off. A cunningly devised mockery of freedom is guaranteed to them, and that is all. To all intents and purposes, they are disfranchised and outlawed, and the only privilege extended to them is a shallow and circumscribed participation in the political movements that usher slaveholders into office.

We have not breathed away seven and twenty years in the South without becoming acquainted with the demagogical maneuverings of the oligarchy. . . . To the illiterate poor whites—made poor and ignorant by the system of slavery—they hold out the idea that slavery is the very bulwark of our liberties, and the foundation of American independence! . . .

The lords of the lash are not only absolute masters of the blacks, who are bought and sold, and driven about like so many cattle, but they are also the oracles and arbiters of all non-slaveholding whites, whose freedom is merely nominal, and whose unparalleled illiteracy and degradation is purposely and fiendishly perpetuated. How little the "poor white trash"—the great majority of the Southern people—know of the real condition of the country is, indeed, sadly astonishing.

The truth is they know nothing of public measures, and little of private affairs, except what their imperious masters, the slave-drivers, condescend to tell—and that is but precious little. And even that little, always garbled and one-sided, is never told except in public harangues. For the haughty cavaliers of shackles and handcuffs will not degrade themselves by holding private converse with those who have neither dimes nor hereditary rights in human flesh.

---

[1]H. R. Helper, *The Impending Crisis of the South* (New York: A. C. Bundick, 1860), pp. 42–45.

Whenever it pleases . . . a slaveholder to become communicative, poor whites may hear with fear and trembling, but not speak.

Non-slaveholders are not only kept in ignorance of what is transpiring at the North, but they are continually misinformed of what is going on even in the South. Never were the poorer classes of a people, and those classes so largely in the majority, and all inhabiting the same country, so basely duped, so adroitly swindled, or so damnably outraged.

It is expected that the stupid and sequacious [servile] masses, the white victims of slavery, will believe—and, as a general thing, they do believe—whatever the slaveholders tell them. And thus it is that they are cajoled into the notion that they are the freest, happiest, and most intelligent people in the world, and are taught to look with prejudice and disapprobation upon every new principle or progressive movement. Thus it is that the South, woefully inert and inventionless, has lagged behind the North, and is now weltering in the cesspool of ignorance and degradation.

2. The South Condemns Helperites (1859)

Helper's appeal to the poor whites of the South fell on barren ground; most of them were illiterate or apathetic, while others could not get the book. But the free-soil Republicans of the North seized upon it for political purposes, and sixty-eight members of the House of Representatives signed an appeal for funds to distribute free 100,000 copies of a paperbacked abridgment. Following John Brown's fear-inspiring raid into Virginia in 1859, the Southerners were determined to keep from the Speakership of the House any endorser of Helper's book. For two months they filibustered successfully against Republican John Sherman, who had ill-advisedly signed the appeal, while the flames of sectional conflict roared higher and higher. What does the following speech by Representative James Bullock Clark of Missouri [later a member of the Confederate Congress] presage about the preservation of the Union?

These [Helperite] gentlemen come in and say that the riches of the South are neglected by the bad management of the South; that the accursed plague of slavery does it; and that, therefore, non-slaveholders at the South should rise in their majesty—peaceably if they can, forcibly if they must—take their arms, subdue the slaveholders, drive out the plague of slavery, take possession of the country, and dedicate it to free labor.

That is the sentiment in the book which these gentlemen recommend to have circulated gratuitously all over the South. Are such men fit to preside over the destinies of our common country? Can the South expect from such men the maintenance of the integrity of the Constitution? Our slave property is as much our property under the Constitution, and under the guarantees of this government, as any property held at the North. Whether it is sinful to hold slaves, whether slavery is a plague and a loss, and whether it will affect our future destiny, is our own business. We suffer for that, and not they.

---

[2]*Congressional Globe,* 36th Congress, 1st session (December 8, 1859), p. 17.

We ask none of their prayers. We need none of them. If we were in need of them, and if the only way to escape future punishment and misery were to receive benefit from the prayers of those [sixty-eight] who signed that recommendation, I should expect, after death, to sink into the nethermost Hell. [Laughter.]

Do gentlemen expect that they can distribute incendiary books, give incendiary advice, advise rebellion, advise non-intercourse in all the relations of life, spread such works broadcast over the country, and not be taken to task for it? I presume that the South has sufficient self-respect; that it understands the effect of its institutions well enough; that it has its rights, and dares to maintain them.

3. James Hammond Proclaims Cotton King (1858)

As the resentment of the South rose, so did its confidence in its ability to stand alone as a Confederacy, if need be. It rode through the panic of 1857 with flying colors; its enormous exports of "King Cotton" overshadowed all others from America. But the North might well have responded with the cry "Grass is King!" For, as Helper pointed out in his banned book, the value of the North's hay crop, though consumed at home, was greater than that of the South's cotton crop. Yet Senator Hammond of South Carolina, a bombastic owner of some three hundred slaves, voiced the cry "Cotton is King!" in this famous Senate speech. He referred to the dangerous dependence of the enormous English textile industry on the huge imports from the South. What were the problems with his argument?

Why, sir, the South has never yet had a just cause of war. Every time she has seized her sword it has been on the point of honor, and that point of honor has been mainly loyalty to her sister colonies and sister states, who have ever since plundered and calumniated her.

But if there were no other reason why we should never have a war, would any sane nation make war on cotton? Without firing a gun, without drawing a sword, when they make war on us we can bring the whole world to our feet.

The South is perfectly competent to go on, one, two, or three years, without planting a seed of cotton. I believe that if she was to plant but half her cotton, it would be an immediate advantage to her. I am not so sure but that after three years' cessation she would come out stronger than ever she was before and better prepared to enter afresh upon her great career of enterprise.

What would happen if no cotton was furnished for three years? I will not stop to depict what everyone can imagine, but this is certain: old England would topple headlong and carry the whole civilized world with her. No, sir, you dare not make war on cotton. No power on earth dares make war upon it. Cotton is King!

[It is not surprising that cotton should have deluded the South when the British themselves conceded their fatal dependence. A writer in Blackwood's Edinburgh Magazine *(February 1851, p. 216) confessed: ". . . We rest almost entirely on the supplies obtained from a single state [nation]. No one need be told that five-sixths, often nine-tenths, of the supply of cotton consumed in our manufactures come from*

---

[3]*Congressional Globe,* 35th Congress, 1st session (March 3, 1858), p. 961.

America, and that seven or eight thousand persons are directly or indirectly employed in the operations which take place upon it. Suppose America wishes to bully us, to make us abandon Canada or Jamaica for example, she has no need to go to war. She has only to stop the export of cotton for six months, and the whole of our manufacturing counties are starving or in rebellion; while a temporary cessation of profit is the only inconvenience they experience on the other side of the Atlantic. Can we call ourselves independent in such circumstances?"]

Thought Provokers

1. A favorite argument of the South was that the black slave was better off than the wage slave of the North or England. (See also earlier, p. 299.) In what respects was this true? false? J. Q. Adams said, "Misery is not slavery." Comment.
2. Why could persons who had eyewitnessed slavery in the South offer such radically differing accounts? What would have been the future of slavery if it had been left alone?
3. It has been said that the Garrison abolitionists were right in principle but wrong in method. Comment. Garrison advocated disunion as a means of ending slavery. Explain the logic or illogic of his position. Explain how you would have dealt with slavery if given "all earthly power."
4. Why did so many people in the North deplore the boat-rocking tactics of the abolitionists and often despise them? Did the abolitionists do more harm or good?
5. In what respects did Hinton R. Helper help to cause the Civil War? In what respects did the "Cotton is King" complex cause the Civil War? It has been said that cotton was a king who enslaved his subjects. Comment.

18

Manifest Destiny and Its Legacy, 1841–1848

If you will take all the theft, all the assaults, all the cases of arson, ever committed in time of peace in the United States since the settlement of Jamestown in 1608 [1607], and add to them all the cases of violence offered to woman, with all the murders, they will not amount to half the wrongs committed in this war for the plunder of Mexico.

Theodore Parker, Abolitionist Clergyman, 1848

Prologue: Hereditary British-American antipathy came to a head in 1846 over extreme American demands for the boundary line of 54° 40' in the Oregon Country. The dispute was settled later that year by a compromise on the line of 49°. Meanwhile the overconfident Mexicans, not unwilling to fight and encouraged by the prospect of an Anglo-American conflict over Oregon, were threatening the United States with war over the annexation of the revolted province of Texas. President James K. Polk, unable to buy coveted California from the Mexicans or to adjust other disputes with them, forced a showdown in 1846 by moving U.S. troops provocatively close to the Mexican border. In the ensuing war the Americans were everywhere victorious—General Zachary Taylor in northern Mexico at Monterrey and Buena Vista, General Winfield Scott at Cerro Gordo and elsewhere in his spectacular drive toward Mexico City. By the terms of peace, Polk finally secured California—and an aggravated slavery problem to boot.

A. The Debate over Oregon

1. Senator George McDuffie Belittles Oregon (1843)

British critics aimed their shafts at alleged Yankee land grabbing, which was highlighted by the Anglo-American dispute over the vast Oregon Country. The controversy came to a boil in 1843, when Congress heatedly debated but finally rejected a

---

[1]*Congressional Globe,* 27th Congress, 3d session, vol. 12, 199–200.

bill to fortify the overland route to Oregon and grant land to the Americans settling there. Senator George McDuffie of South Carolina, an impassioned pro-slavery orator (see p. 251), vehemently opposed the acquisition of free-soil Oregon, although he had favored the annexation of slave-soil Texas. In what respects were his foresight and his geographical knowledge faulty? Or was he just overstating his case?

What do we want with this [Oregon] territory? What are we to do with it? What is to be the consequence of our taking possession of it? What is the act we are called on now to do? Why, it is neither more nor less than an act of colonization, for the first time proposed since the foundation of this government?

If this were a question of gradual, and continuous, and progressive settlement— if the territory to which our citizens are invited were really to become a part of the Union, it would present a very different question. But, sir, does any man seriously suppose that any state which can be formed at the mouth of the Columbia River, or any of the inhabitable parts of that territory, would ever become one of the states of the Union?

I have great faith . . . in the power of the representative principle to extend the sphere of government. But I confess that, even in the most sanguine days of my youth, I never conceived the possibility of embracing within the same government people living five thousand miles apart.

But, sir, the worthy Senator from New Hampshire [Mr. Woodbury] seems to have discovered a principle much more potent than the representative principle. He refers you to steam, far more potent. I should doubt very much whether the elements or powers, or organization of the principles of government, will ever be changed by steam.

Steam! How are you to apply steam in this case? Has the Senator examined the character of the country? What is the character of the country?

Why, as I understand it, that about seven hundred miles this side of the Rocky Mountains is uninhabitable, where rain scarcely ever falls—a barren sandy soil. On the other side—we have it from a very intelligent gentleman [John Frémont?], sent to explore that country by the State Department, that there are three successive ridges of mountains extending towards the Pacific, and running nearly parallel; which mountains are totally impassable, except in certain parts, where there are gaps or depressions, to be reached only by going one hundred miles out of the direct course.

Well, now, what are we to do in such a case as this? How are we going to apply steam? Have you made anything like an estimate of the cost of a railroad running from here to the mouth of the Columbia? Why, the wealth of the Indies would not be sufficient. You would have to tunnel through mountains five hundred or six hundred miles in extent. It is true they [the British] have constructed a tunnel beneath the Thames, but at a vast expenditure of capital. With a bankrupt Treasury and a depressed and suffering people, to talk about constructing a railroad to the western shore of the continent manifests a wild spirit of adventure which I never expected to hear broached in the Senate of the United States. . . .

Why, sir, of what use will this be for agricultural purposes? I would not for that purpose give a pinch of snuff for the whole territory. I wish to God we did not own it. I wish it was an impassable barrier to secure us against the intrusion of others.

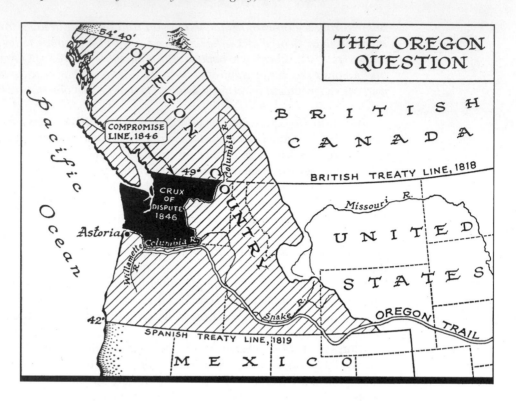

2. Senator Edward Hannegan Demands 54° 40' (1846)

The Democratic party, when nominating Polk for the presidency at Baltimore in 1844, had demanded the annexation of the Republic of Texas and the acquisition of Oregon all the way to 54° 40'. Texas entered the Union as a slave state in 1845. A year later Congress, before acquiescing in the Oregon compromise line of 49°, was debating resolutions proclaiming U.S. ownership of all the territory to the line of 54° 40'. Senator Hannegan, an intemperate orator (and drinker) from Indiana, was the most bellicose spokesman for the free-soil Northwest. How does his Senate speech—reported in the third person—help to explain the existing upsurge of nationalism?

Now, if the adoption of the [Oregon] resolutions, which contained the immutable principles of truth, should bring war on us, let war come! What American was there who, through fear of war, would hesitate to declare the truth in this Chamber? He [Hannegan] also was for peace. He shrunk back from the thought of war as much as could the Senator from South Carolina [John Calhoun]. He loved peace; but if it were only to be maintained on degrading and dishonorable terms, war, even of extermination, would be far preferable. . . .

There had been a singular course pursued on this Oregon question, and with reference to which he must detain the Senate a moment. It contrasted so strangely, so wonderfully, with a precisely similar question—the annexation of Texas. Texas

---

[2]*Congressional Globe,* 29th Congress, 1st session, vol. 15, part 1, pp. 109–110.

and Oregon were born the same instant, nursed and cradled in the same cradle—the Baltimore Convention—and they were at the same instant adopted by the Democracy throughout the land. There was not a moment's hesitation, until Texas was admitted. But the moment she was admitted, the peculiar friends of Texas turned, and were doing all they could to strangle Oregon!

But the country were not blind or deaf. The people see, they comprehend, and he trusted they would speak. It was a most singular state of things. We were told that we must be careful not to involve ourselves in a war with England on a question of disputed boundary. There was a question of disputed boundary between us and Mexico. But did we hear, from the same quarter, any warning against a collision with Mexico when we were about to consummate the annexation of Texas? We were told by those who knew something of these matters that the Nueces [River] was the proper boundary of Texas! And how did they find the friends of Texas moving on that occasion? Did we, for a single instant, halt on the banks of the Nueces? No; at a single bound we crossed the Nueces, and the blasts of our trumpets, and the prancing of our war-horses, were heard on the banks of the Rio del Norte [Rio Grande], one hundred miles beyond. Nearly one hundred miles of disputed territory gives no cause for a moment's hesitation!

There was no negotiation then, so far as Mexico was concerned: we took all. But when Oregon is brought into question, we are called on, as an act proper and right, to give away a whole empire on the Pacific, if England desire it. He never would consent to a surrender of any portion of the country north of 49°, nor one foot, by treaty or otherwise, under 54° 40'.

3. Two Pioneers Describe Oregon (1847)

While statesmen debated, settlers continued to pour into the Oregon Country. They did not all have the same reaction to the virgin wilderness they encountered. In these two descriptions of the new territory, what observations are made by both writers? On what do they disagree? How might their different perceptions be explained?

Hezekiah Packingham to his Brother,
Willamette Valley, March 1, 1847

I arrived in the Wallamette Valley on the 30th of September, and my calculations are all defeated about Oregon. I found it a mean, dried up, and drowned country. The Yam Hill is a small valley, destitute of timber. I soon got sick of this place, and then went to the mouth of the Columbia river. I can give Oregon credit for only one or two things, and these are, good health and plenty of salmon, and Indians; as for the farming country there is none here—wheat grows about the same as in Illinois; corn, potatoes, and garden vegetables cannot grow here without watering. The nights are too cold here in summer. The soil is not as good as in Illinois—the face of the country is hilly, and high mountains covered with snow all summer, and small valleys—the mountains and hills are covered with the heaviest timber that I ever

---

[3]From Dale Morgan, ed., *Overland in 1846: Diaries and Letters of the California-Oregon Trail* (1963), vol. II, pp. 685–686, 691–692. Reprinted by permission of the Talisman Press.

saw. We have had a very hard winter here, snow fell two feet deep, and lay three weeks, by reason of which hundreds of cattle have died of starvation. The thermometer fell to three degrees above zero.—Prairie grass here is the same as in Illinois. There is no timothy nor clover. Mechanics are very numerous here. Of the ships that sailed from New York last April, but one arrived, and she was ice bound for 50 days, in latitude 50 1-2. It is supposed the other has gone to her long home. A United States man-of-war [*Shark*] was recently wrecked at the mouth of the Columbia. Money is very scarce here—and they have a kind of currency here (orders on stores and scrip)—they value property very high, but if they would put things at cash prices, they would be about the same as they are in the States. Oregon is rapidly filling up with young men, (but no girls,) of whom two-thirds are dissatisfied and many would return to the States if they were able, but the road is long and tedious, and it is hard for families to get back; my trip was pleasant until I got to the South Pass—after that the country was rugged, and bad roads. Tell young men if they intend coming to Oregon, to drive no teams unless it is their own. We were uninjured by the Indians, though they were very saucy—they have no manners; they worship idols [totem poles?], and I saw one of their gods at the mouth of the river. There is no society here except the Camelites [Campbellites]. I shall return to the States next spring. Don't believe all that is said about Oregon, as many falsehoods are uttered respecting the country.

Hezekiah Packingham

Richard R. Howard to a Friend in Illinois, "Oregon Territory," April 6, 1847

We arrived safe in Oregon City on the 12th of September last. We reached Fort Laramie in 42 days from Independence; Fort Hall in 33 days more; the Dalles in 37 days more; and Oregon City in 16 days more—making in all 128 days. Our journey was two weeks longer than necessary had we lost no time. We met with no serious obstructions on our journey. We had to raise the front of our wagon beds two or three inches in crossing the Larimie Fork to keep the water out; sometimes we had long drives to find a good place for camping, with water and grass. [The writer gives a long detail of the necessary outfit for the journey and cautions to be used on the road—which we omit. *Illinois Journal*] No single man should come to this country. One third of the men in Oregon at this time are without wives. Nothing but men of families are wanted here to till the soil, to make this one of the greatest countries in the world. This country does not get so muddy as Illinois. There is no dust in summer here. The good land in this country is more extensive than I expected to find it. The hills are not so high as represented. From the Cascade mountains to the Pacific, the whole country can be cultivated. The natural soil of the country, especially in the bottoms, is a black loam, mixed with gravel and clay. We have good timber; but there appears to be a scarcity of good building rock. The small streams furnish us with trout the year round.

My wife to the old lady—Greeting; says she was never more satisfied with a move in her life before; that she is fast recovering her health; and she hopes you will come to Oregon, where you can enjoy what little time you have remaining in health.

The roads to Oregon are not as bad as represented. Hastings in his history* speaks of the Falls of Columbia being 50 feet and roaring loud, making the earth tremble, &c. The falls are about like that of a mill-dam. Every thing in this country now is high, except molasses, sugar and salt; but when we raise our wheat crop to trade on, we will make them pay for their high charges. I think no place where a living is to be made out of the earth can be preferable to Oregon for that purpose— and let people say what they may—all agree that it is healthy. It is certainly the healthiest country in the world, disease is scarcely known here, except among the late emigrants, ninety-nine out of a hundred of them get well the first season. I have heard of only two deaths since I have been in Oregon; one of them was a man who came here diseased and in one year died; the other was a woman who it is said was near dead ten years before she came here.

Richard R. Howard

4. A British View of the Oregon Controversy (1846)

Many Britons were bemused that the upstart Yankees were in such a bellicose mood over Oregon. This cartoon, entitled "What? You Young Yankee-Noodle, Strike Your Own Father!" is from the British magazine Punch, *and pokes fun at the Americans. What did the cartoonist find most amusing about the American position? Why is the American figure rendered as a southerner, with a slave driver's whip in his pocket?*

"WHAT? YOU YOUNG YANKEE-NOODLE, STRIKE YOUR OWN FATHER!"

---

*The reference is to L. W. Hastings, *Emigrants' Guide to Oregon and California* (1845), a standard guidebook for travelers on the Oregon and California trails.

[4]*Punch* [London], 1846.

B. Provoking War with Mexico

1. Charles Sumner Assails the Texas Grab (1847)

Boston-bred and Harvard-polished Charles Sumner, soon to be a U.S. senator, was one of the most impressive orators of his day. Six feet four inches in height and blessed with a powerful voice, he could sway vast audiences. An earnest foe of war, he preached arbitration; an impassioned enemy of slavery, he demanded abolition; a devoted champion of race equality, he fought the Massachusetts law forbidding marriages between whites and blacks. In 1847, in the midst of the war with Mexico, the Massachusetts legislature adopted this document, which Sumner had prepared, blasting the annexation of Texas. Although he overplayed the slave conspiracy accusation, he made a number of telling points. Assuming that his facts are correct, how many genuine grievances did Mexico have against the United States?

The history of the annexation of Texas cannot be fully understood without reverting to the early settlement of that province by citizens of the United States.

Mexico, on achieving her independence of the Spanish Crown, by a general ordinance worthy of imitation by all Christian nations, had decreed the abolition of human slavery within her dominions, embracing the province of Texas. . . .

At this period, citizens of the United States had already begun to remove into Texas, hardly separated, as it was, by the River Sabine from the slaveholding state of Louisiana. The idea was early promulgated that this extensive province ought to become a part of the United States. Its annexation was distinctly agitated in the Southern and Western states in 1829; and it was urged on the ground of the strength and extension it would give to the "Slave Power," and the fresh market it would open for the sale of slaves.

The suggestion of this idea had an important effect. A current of emigration soon followed from the United States. Slaveholders crossed the Sabine with their slaves, in defiance of the Mexican ordinance of freedom. Restless spirits, discontented at home, or feeling the restraint of the narrow confines of our country, joined them; while their number was swollen by the rude and lawless of all parts of the land, who carried to Texas the love of license which had rendered a region of justice no longer a pleasant home to them. To such spirits, rebellion was natural.

It soon broke forth. At this period the whole [Texan] population, including women and children, did not amount to twenty thousand; and, among these, most of the older and wealthier inhabitants still favored peace. A Declaration of Independence, a farcical imitation of that of our fathers, was put forth, not by persons acting in a Congress or in a representative character, but by about ninety individuals—all, except two, from the United States—acting for themselves, and recommending a similar course to their fellow citizens. In a just cause the spectacle of this handful of adventurers, boldly challenging the power of Mexico, would excite our sympathy, perhaps our admiration. But successful rapacity, which seized broad and fertile

---

[1]*Old South Leaflets* (Boston, 1904), vol. 6, no. 132, pp. 2–4.

lands while it opened new markets for slaves, excites no sentiment but that of abhorrence.

The work of rebellion sped. Citizens of the United States joined its fortunes, not singly, but in numbers, even in armed squadrons. Our newspapers excited the lust of territorial robbery in the public mind. Expeditions were openly equipped within our own borders. Advertisements for volunteers summoned the adventurous, as to patriotic labors. Military companies, with officers and standards, directed their steps to the revolted province.

During all this period the United States were at peace with Mexico. A proclamation from our government, forbidding these hostile preparations within our borders, is undeniable evidence of their existence, while truth compels us to record its impotence in upholding the sacred duties of neutrality between Mexico and the insurgents. . . .

The Texan flag waved over an army of American citizens. Of the six or eight hundred who won the [decisive] battle of San Jacinto, scattering the Mexican forces and capturing their general [Santa Anna], not more than fifty were citizens of Texas having grievances of their own to redress on that field.

The victory was followed by the recognition of the independence of Texas by the United States; while the new state took its place among the nations of the earth. . . .

Certainly our sister republic [Mexico] might feel aggrieved by this conduct. It might justly charge our citizens with disgraceful robbery, while, in seeking extension of slavery, they repudiated the great truths of American freedom.

Meanwhile Texas slept on her arms, constantly expecting new efforts from Mexico to regain her former power. The two combatants regarded each other as enemies. Mexico still asserted her right to the territory wrested from her, and refused to acknowledge its independence.

Texas turned for favor and succor to England. The government of the United States, fearing it might pass under the influence of this power, made overtures for its annexation to our country. This was finally accomplished by joint resolutions of Congress, in defiance of the Constitution [?], and in gross insensibility to the sacred obligations of amity with Mexico, imposed alike by treaty and by justice, "both strong against the deed." The Mexican minister regarded it as an act offensive to his country, and, demanding his passport, returned home.

2. President James Polk Justifies the Texas Coup (1845)

The United States had tried to wrest Texas from Spain under the vague terms of the Louisiana Purchase, but had at last abandoned such claims in the swap that netted the Floridas in 1819. The Texan-Americans finally staged a successful revolt against Mexico in 1835–1836, but for nine years thereafter lived in constant apprehension of a renewed Mexican invasion. Three days before President Polk took office on

---

[2]J. D. Richardson, ed., *Messages and Papers of the Presidents* (1897), vol. 4; pp. 379–381.

March 4, 1845, President John Tyler had signed a joint resolution of Congress offering the Republic of Texas annexation to the United States. All that remained was for the Texans to accept the terms, and they formally did so on June 23, 1845. The tension was heightened by the keen interest of Britain and France in making Texas a satellite, with the consequent dangers of involving the United States in war. Polk, a purposeful and persistent expansionist, justified the annexation as follows in his inaugural address. Which of his arguments was the most convincing from the standpoint of the United States? Which was the least convincing from the standpoint of Mexico? Did he handle the slavery issue persuasively?

The Republic of Texas has made known her desire to come into our Union, to form a part of our Confederacy and enjoy with us the blessings of liberty secured and guaranteed by our Constitution. Texas was once a part of our country—was unwisely ceded away to a foreign power [in 1819]—is now independent, and possesses an undoubted right to dispose of a part or the whole of her territory, and to merge her sovereignty as a separate and independent state in ours. . . .

I regard the question of annexation as belonging exclusively to the United States and Texas. They are independent powers, competent to contract; and foreign nations have no right to interfere with them or to take exception to their reunion. . . . Foreign powers should therefore look on the annexation of Texas to the United States, not as the conquest of a nation seeking to extend her dominions by arms and violence, but as the peaceful acquisition of a territory once her own, by adding another member to our Confederation, with the consent of that member, thereby diminishing the chances of war and opening to them new and ever-increasing markets for their products.

To Texas, the reunion is important because the strong protecting arm of our government would be extended over her, and the vast resources of her fertile soil and genial climate would be speedily developed, while the safety of New Orleans and of our whole southwestern frontier against hostile aggression, as well as the interests of the whole Union, would be promoted by it. . . .

None can fail to see the danger to our safety and future peace if Texas remains an independent state, or becomes an ally or dependency of some foreign nation more powerful than herself. Is there one among our citizens who would not prefer perpetual peace with Texas to occasional wars, which so often occur between bordering independent nations? Is there one who would not prefer free intercourse with her, to high duties on all our products and manufactures which enter her ports or cross her frontiers? Is there one who would not prefer an unrestricted communication with her citizens, to the frontier obstructions which must occur if she remains out of the Union?

Whatever is good or evil in the local [slave] institutions of Texas will remain her own, whether annexed to the United States or not. None of the present states will be responsible for them any more than they are for the local institutions of each other. They have confederated together for certain specific objects. Upon the same principle that they would refuse to form a perpetual union with Texas because of her local institutions, our forefathers would have been prevented from forming our present Union.

3. The Cabinet Debates War (1846)

The expansionist Polk, fearing that so-called British land grabbers would forestall him, was eager to purchase California from Mexico. But the proud Mexicans, though bankrupt, refused to sell. They also threatened war over the annexation of Texas and defaulted on their payment of claims to Americans for damages during their recent revolutionary disturbances. Polk made a last-hope effort to buy California and adjust other disputes when he sent John Slidell to Mexico as a special envoy late in 1845, but the Mexicans refused to negotiate with Slidell. Polk then ordered General Taylor to move his small army from Corpus Christi on the Nueces River (the traditional southwest border of Texas) to the Rio Grande del Norte (which the Texans extravagantly claimed as their new boundary). Still the Mexicans did not attack the provocative Yankee invader. Polk thereupon recommended to his cabinet a declaration of war, presumably on the basis of (1) unpaid damage claims and (2) Slidell's rejection. Both were rather flimsy pretexts. From this passage in his diary, was the president really trying to avoid a fight? Were his grounds for war valid, even after sixteen American soliders were killed or wounded?

Saturday, 9th May, 1846.—The Cabinet held a regular meeting today; all the members present.

I brought up the Mexican question, and the question of what was the duty of the administration in the present state of our relations with that country. The subject was very fully discussed.

All agreed that if the Mexican forces at Matamoros committed any act of hostility on Gen'l Taylor's forces, I should immediately send a message to Congress recommending an immediate declaration of war.

I stated to the Cabinet that up to this time, as they knew, we had heard of no open act of aggression by the Mexican army, but that the danger was imminent that such acts would be committed. I said that in my opinion we had ample cause of war, and that it was impossible that we could stand *in statu quo,* or that I could remain silent much longer; that I thought it was my duty to send a message to Congress very soon and recommend definitive measures. I told them that I thought I ought to make such a message by Tuesday next; that the country was excited and impatient on the subject; and if I failed to do so, I would not be doing my duty.

I then propounded the distinct question to the Cabinet, and took their opinions individually, whether I should make a message to Congress on Tuesday, and whether in that message I should recommend a declaration of war against Mexico.

All except the Secretary of the Navy [George Bancroft] gave their advice in the affirmative. Mr. Bancroft dissented, but said if any act of hostility should be committed by the Mexican forces, he was then in favor of immediate war. Mr. Buchanan [Secretary of State] said he would feel better satisfied in his course if the Mexican forces had or should commit any act of hostility, but that as matters stood we had ample cause of war against Mexico, and he gave his assent to the measure.

---

[3]M. M. Quaife, ed., *The Diary of James K. Polk* (A. C. McClurg, 1910), vol. 1, 384–386.

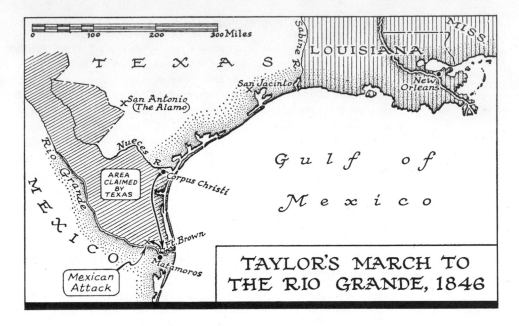

TAYLOR'S MARCH TO THE RIO GRANDE, 1846

It was agreed that the message should be prepared and submitted to the Cabinet in their meeting on Tuesday. . . .

About 6 o'clock P.M. Gen'l R. Jones, the Adjutant General of the Army, called and handed to me despatches received from Gen'l Taylor by the Southern mail which had just arrived, giving information that a part of [the] Mexican army had crossed . . . the [Rio Grande] Del Norte, and attacked and killed and captured two companies of dragoons of Gen'l Taylor's army, consisting of 63 officers and men. . . .

I immediately summoned the Cabinet to meet at 7½ o'clock this evening. The Cabinet accordingly assembled at that hour; all the members present. The subject of the despatch received this evening from Gen'l Taylor, as well as the state of our relations with Mexico, were fully considered. The Cabinet were unanimously of opinion, and it was so agreed, that a message should be sent to Congress on Monday laying all the information in my possession before them, and recommending vigorous and prompt measure[s] to enable the Executive to prosecute the war.

4. The President Blames Mexico (1846)

The hundred-mile-wide expanse between the Nueces River and the Rio Grande, virtually uninhabited except for tens of thousands of wild horses, was clearly in dispute between the United States and Mexico, although the Mexicans still claimed all of re-

---

[4]J. D. Richardson, ed., *Messages and Papers of the Presidents* (1897), vol. 4, pp. 441–442.

volted Texas. The blunt truth is that the Mexican title to the disputed area was then the stronger. The Whigs and other antislavery foes of the Democratic Polk, regarding him as a willing tool of the expansionist southern "slavocracy," condemned him as a liar ("Polk the Mendacious") for his allegations that Mexico, rather than the United States, had provoked the war. In the president's war message to Congress, given here with italics added by the present editors, what grounds are there to support this accusation? Did the United States have just grounds for war?

The grievous wrongs perpetrated by Mexico upon our citizens throughout a long period of years remain unredressed, and solemn [claims] treaties pledging her public faith for this redress have been disregarded. A government either unable or unwilling to enforce the execution of such treaties fails to perform one of its plainest duties.

Our commerce with Mexico has been almost annihilated. It was formerly highly beneficial to both nations, but our merchants have been deterred from prosecuting it by the system of outrage and extortion which the Mexican authorities have pursued against them, while their appeals through their own government for indemnity have been made in vain. Our forbearance has gone to such an extreme as to be mistaken in its character. Had we acted with vigor in repelling the insults and redressing the injuries inflicted by Mexico at the commencement, we should doubtless have escaped all the difficulties in which we are now involved.

Instead of this, however, we have been exerting our best efforts to propitiate her good will. Upon the pretext that Texas, a nation as independent as herself, thought proper to unite its destinies with our own, she has affected to believe that we have severed her rightful territory, and in official proclamations and manifestoes has repeatedly threatened to make war upon us for the purpose of reconquering Texas. In the meantime, we have tried every effort at reconciliation.

The cup of forbearance had been exhausted even before the recent information from the frontier of the [Rio Grande] Del Norte. But now, after reiterated menaces, Mexico has passed the boundary of the United States, has *invaded our territory,* and *shed American blood upon the American soil.* She has proclaimed that hostilities have commenced, and that the two nations are now at war.

As war exists, and, *notwithstanding all our efforts* to avoid it, exists by the act of Mexico herself, we are called upon by every consideration of duty and patriotism to vindicate with decision the honor, the rights, and the interests of our country.

5. A British View of the Mexican War (1847)

This cartoon criticizes America's imperial ambitions in the war against Mexico. In what ways did the British artist agree with opponents of the war in the United States?

---

[5]*Punch,* December 4, 1847.

THE LAND OF LIBERTY.

RECOMMENDED TO THE CONSIDERATION OF "BROTHER JONATHAN."

C. Opposition to the War

1. Massachusetts Voices Condemnation (1847)

The killing or wounding of sixteen American soldiers on American (?) soil precipitated war with Mexico. But the abolitionists and the free-soil Whigs of the North, resenting an alleged grab for more slave territory, gradually increased their clamor for peace. The following mid-war resolution, drafted by the orator Charles Sumner and passed by the Massachusetts legislature in 1847, betrayed an ugly frame of mind. In what respects is this statement sound in describing the outbreak of war? In what respects is it unsound? In what respects does it verge on treason?

---

[1]*Old South Leaflets* (1904), vol. 6, no. 132, pp. 10–11, 30–31.

This was the state of things when . . . General Taylor was directed, by the President of the United States, to occupy the east bank of the Rio Grande, being the extreme western part of the territory claimed by Texas, the boundaries of which had been designated as an "open question," to be determined by "negotiation." General Taylor broke up his quarters at Corpus Christi on the 11th March, and, proceeding across this disputed territory, established his post, and erected a battery, directly opposite the Mexican city of Matamoros, and, under his directions, the mouth of the Rio Grande was blockaded, so as to cut off supplies from the Mexican army at Matamoros. . . .

These were acts of war, accomplished without bloodshed. But they were nevertheless acts of unquestioned hostility against Mexico. Blockade! and military occupation of a disputed territory! These were the arbiters of the "open question" of boundary. These were the substitutes for "negotiation."

It is not to be supposed that the Mexican army should quietly endure these aggressive measures, and regard with indifference cannon pointed at their position. . . . On the 26th of April a small body of American troops, under the command of Captain Thornton, encountered Mexican troops at a place twenty miles north of General Taylor's camp. Here was the first collision of arms. The report of this was hurried to Washington. Rumor, with a hundred tongues, exaggerated the danger of the American army under General Taylor, and produced an insensibility to the aggressive character of the movement. . . .

It was under the influence of this feeling that the untoward act of May 13th was pressed through Congress, by which it was declared that "war exists by the act of Mexico". . . . The passage of this act placed the whole country in hostile array against Mexico, and impressed upon every citizen of the United States the relation of enemy of every citizen of Mexico. This disastrous condition still continues. War is still waged; and our armies, after repeated victories achieved on Mexican soil, are still pursuing the path of conquest. . . .

Resolves. Concerning the Mexican War, and the Institution of Slavery.

Resolved, That the present war with Mexico has its primary origin in the unconstitutional annexation to the United States of the foreign state of Texas while the same was still at war with Mexico; that it was unconstitutionally commenced by the order of the President, to General Taylor, to take military possession of territory in dispute between the United States and Mexico, and in the occupation of Mexico; and that it is now waged ingloriously—by a powerful nation against a weak neighbor—unnecessarily and without just cause, at immense cost of treasure and life, for the dismemberment of Mexico, and for the conquest of a portion of her territory, from which slavery has already been excluded, with the triple object of extending slavery, of strengthening the "Slave Power," and of obtaining the control of the Free States, under the Constitution of the United States.

Resolved, That such a war of conquest, so hateful in its objects, so wanton, unjust, and unconstitutional in its origin and character, must be regarded as a war against freedom, against humanity, against justice, against the Union, against the Constitution, and against the Free States; and that a regard for the true interests and the highest honor of the country, not less than the impulses of Christian duty, should arouse all good citizens to join in efforts to arrest this gigantic crime, by withholding supplies, or other voluntary contributions, for its further prosecution; by calling for the withdrawal of our army within the established limits of the United States; and in every just way aiding the country to retreat from the disgraceful position of aggression which it now occupies towards a weak, distracted neighbor and sister republic.

Resolved, That our attention is directed anew to the wrong and "enormity" of slavery, and to the tyranny and usurpation of the "Slave Power," as displayed in the history of our country, particularly in the annexation of Texas and the present war with Mexico. . . .

2. Abolitionists Libel General Zachary Taylor (1848)

One of the foulest murders of the century occurred in 1830. Captain Joseph White, a wealthy merchant of Salem, Massachusetts, was found dead in his bed with a fractured skull and thirteen stab wounds. The murderer was Dick Crowningshield, who had been offered $1,000 by two expectant heirs. Henry C. Wright, an abolitionist and pacifist, compared the current war hero, General Zachary Taylor, to Crowningshield. After reading Wright's tirade, entitled "The Assassin and the Soldier," what conclusions can you draw about the nature of the opposition to the Mexican War by the pacifist-abolitionist extremists? Is this attack too overdrawn to be effective?

Zachary had millions of employers; the assassin had but two.

Zachary killed thousands; the assassin killed one.

Zachary's sword, balls, and bombshells were accounted Christian weapons to slay men; the assassin's bludgeon and dirk were considered un-Christian.

Zachary broke the limbs and tore the flesh of his victims, and left them to die in protracted agony; the assassin killed his instantly and without protracted pain.

Zachary's deeds are said by the priest and churches to be God-approved and Christlike; the assassin's are denounced by them as evil and only evil.

Zachary is hailed as a Christian patriot; Dick is shunned by all.

Zachary, as he returns from Monterrey, his face, his hands, and garments dripping with the blood of innocent women and children, is welcomed "by the smiles and kisses of his countrywomen"; they shrink from Dick with horror.

Zachary is held up by mothers, by teachers, by priests, and politicians, as an example of piety and patriotism; Dick is held up by them to execration.

Zachary is made a life-member of a Missionary Society; Dick is cast out as a heathen.

Zachary is counted worthy of all honor by a professedly enlightened, civilized republican and Christian people, and is by them elevated to the Presidency; Dick, by the same people, is elevated to the gallows.

Such are the different results of killing one at the bidding and for the benefit of two, and killing thousands for the benefit and at the bidding of millions.

---

[2]H. C. Wright, *Dick Crowningshield the Assassin and Zachary Taylor the Soldier: The Difference Between Them* (Hopedale, Mass.: Non-resistant and Practical Christian Office, 1848), pp. 11–12.

D. Peace with Mexico

I. Polk Submits the Trist Treaty (1848)

Hoping to win California with a minimum of bloodshed, President Polk sent special envoy Nicholas Trist to Mexico. There he was to join General Scott's army driving toward Mexico City. Trist bungled an attempt to bribe Santa Anna, the slippery Mexican dictator, and Polk recalled his negotiator in disgust. But Trist, who now saw a temporary opening, concluded a treaty anyhow. Polk, though furious at such defiance, finally decided to submit Trist's Treaty of Guadalupe-Hidalgo to the Senate. By its terms Mexico formally yielded Texas, California, and the intervening territory; the United States bound itself to pay $18,250,000, including $3,250,000 in the damage claims owing to U.S. citizens. In Polk's diary account, what argument for the treaty seems strongest? Which one seems to carry the most weight with him?

Monday, 21st February, 1848.—I saw no company this morning. At 12 o'clock the Cabinet met; all the members present. I made known my decision upon the Mexican Treaty, which was that under all the circumstances of the case, I would submit it [to] the Senate for ratification. . . .

I assigned my reasons for my decision. They were, briefly, that the treaty conformed on the main question of limits and boundary to the instructions given to Mr. Trist in April last; and that though, if the treaty was now to be made, I should demand more territory, perhaps to make the Sierra Madre* the line, yet it was doubtful whether this could be ever obtained by the consent of Mexico.

I looked, too, to the consequences of its rejection. A [Whig] majority of one branch of Congress [the House] is opposed to my administration; they have falsely charged that the war was brought on and is continued by me with a view to the conquest of Mexico. And if I were now to reject a treaty made upon my own terms, as authorized in April last, with the unanimous approbation of the Cabinet, the probability is that Congress would not grant either men or money to prosecute the war. Should this be the result, the army now in Mexico would be constantly wasting and diminishing in numbers, and I might at last be compelled to withdraw them, and thus lose the two provinces of New Mexico and Upper California, which were ceded to the United States by this treaty.

Should the opponents of my administration succeed in carrying the next presidential election, the great probability is that the country would lose all the advantages secured by this treaty. I adverted to the immense value of Upper California and concluded by saying that if I were now to reject my own terms, as offered in April last, I did not see how it was possible for my administration to be sustained.

---

[1]M. M. Quaife, ed., *The Diary of James K. Polk* (A. C. McClurg, 1910), vol. 3, 347–348.
*A mountain range bordering the central plateau of Mexico.

2. A Whig Journal Accepts the Pact (1848)

The Washington Daily National Intelligencer, an opposition Whig newspaper, wry-facedly supported the Trist draft as an unsatisfactory way out of a bad mess. One reason for a speedy acceptance was the mounting popular clamor for all of Mexico, rather than the one-half actually taken. What were the main objections to annexing still more Mexican territory?

We regard with distrust and apprehension the proposed vast acquisition of territory by the United States. So far from paying twenty millions of dollars for it, we have not the smallest doubt that the acquisition of it will entail mischiefs upon this country which no supposed advantages to be derived from it will compensate, now or ever. Were these territories to be whelmed in the Pacific Ocean, instead of being incorporated in our Union, far better, in our opinion, would it be for the welfare and prosperity of the present population of the United States. . . .

That the annexation of *the whole* of Mexico to the United States would be fatal to this government, whoever may doubt it, we are well convinced. Add to our Senate the representation of some fifteen or twenty Mexican states, and the conservative character of that body will be destroyed. The increased representation in the other branch of the national legislature might, at first, be less injurious; but its evils cannot now be computed. Would our commercial, manufacturing, and agricultural states be content to be governed by Mexican generals, who are ignorant of civil government, and who could not understand the principles of our Constitution? *Pronunciamentos* at the head of a military array constitute the basis of their political knowledge. The Union of these states has withstood the shocks of war and of internal excitement, but it would be dissolved by the annexation of Mexico.

We would take the treaty, then, as it is, to avoid a greater national evil. We cannot reject it and continue our opposition to the war. Payment of the debts which Mexico owed our citizens at the commencement of the war is now hopeless; her means are exhausted. Her territory with its population will entail upon us increased expenditures, and evils moral and political. But it is all that Mexico can give. There can be no indemnity for the war expenses. We had better, then, as we have said, stop where we are; for if we go further, we shall only increase the evil.

The crisis should be met with firmness. By the continued prosecution of the war, we should in three months expend a larger sum than the treaty requires us to pay to our own citizens and to the Mexican government. And where is the individual so lost to a sense of justice and to the common sympathies of our nature who would not rather pay the money than to expend even that much (more likely ten times as much) in prosecuting the war to the annihilation of the Mexican government and name?

3. Democrats Hail a Glorious Achievement (1848)

A staunch pro-Polk newspaper, the Democratic Washington Daily Union, *took sharp issue with its rival, the* Whig Daily National Intelligencer. *It hailed the outcome of the*

[2]*Daily National Intelligencer* (Washington), February 28, 1848.
[3]*Washington Daily Union,* March 16, 1848.

war as a magnificent triumph. What does it seem to regard as the greatest intangible gain? the greatest tangible gain? How would the treaty benefit both the security and the commerce of the United States?

It is true that the war has cost us millions of money, and, what is far more precious, the lives of some of our noblest citizens. But what great advantages has it not obtained for us? It has covered us with glory. It has extended our fame to the remotest corners of the earth. If the treaty be ratified, it will extend the area of freedom to the Southern Pacific.

The *National Intelligencer,* indeed, denies that it has "accomplished any one of the ostensible objects of the war." Yet surely nothing but the blindest party spirit could have made this extravagant assertion.

Have we not driven back the insolent enemy, who invaded Texas and shed the blood of our citizens upon our own soil? Have we not pursued him into the heart of his own country, seized all his strongholds upon the coast, and occupied his capital? Have we not subdued that vainglorious and arrogant spirit which has been productive of so many insults and so many aggressions? What has become of all those idle threats to drive us from Texas—of the silly boast of Santa Anna that he would gather his laurels upon the banks of the Sabine [River]!*

The London *Times,* in 1845, flattered the national vanity of the Mexicans with the hope that we should not be able to send men enough to encounter their troops. They were under the impression that our army dared not enter Mexico, or, if we made the attempt, that we should be driven back like chaff before the whirlwind. Their vanity deceived them; but their government flattered their arrogance and increased their infatuation.

Now they are tamed. Now they have consented to negotiate for peace, without requiring our ships to leave their coast and our troops to desert their territory. These changes in the popular sentiment have been produced by the brilliant achievements of Buena Vista and of Cerro Gordo, the capture of their castle and of their capital. Does anyone now believe that their spirit is not humbled, and that the sense of their own inferiority will not induce them to refrain from a repetition of the insults and aggressions which they had so repeatedly perpetrated upon us?

They will be stripped, too, of a large portion of their territory. They may be stripped of more, if they should wantonly insult us again. Will not the lessons they have learned operate as a "security for the future"? Will not the moral force we have gained, and the military genius we have exhibited, go beyond Mexico, and produce their impression upon the other nations of the earth?

With ample "indemnity for the past," then, and with such "security for the future"—with achievements in arms which any nation might envy—with an extension of territory to the Pacific, which gives us some of the finest harbors in the world (for one of which alone—the bay of San Francisco—Gen. Jackson was willing to give five millions of dollars)—with an immense commerce opening upon us with the richest nations of Asia—with every facility secured for our whalers in the Pacific, and with the other advantages which we will have secured—with all these, we can

*The southwestern border of Louisiana.

truly say that we have every reason to be proud of the war, and proud of the peace which it has obtained us.

4. Mexico Remembers the Despoilers (1935)

Patriotic Mexicans can never forget the catastrophe that cost them about half of their country. Their resistance was weakened by internal political turmoil, amounting almost to civil war. The teenage boys of the military academy of Chapultepec, near Mexico City, perished heroically; legend has several throwing themselves suicidally from the battlements. In 1935, after some of the bitterness had subsided, the Ministry of Education in Mexico City published an elementary survey of Mexican history in which there appears the following account of the war and the treaty—with a before-and-after map. What is revealed of the weakness of Mexican resistance, and the grievances against the United States? Which one seems to rankle most deeply?

In the war with the United States, and in the military operations incidental thereto, we are unable to find a single outstanding figure to represent the defense of Mexico, in the form of a hero or military leader. Invasion first of all took place from the north, and the American troops defeated our armies, not beneath them in courage, but due to interior organization, armaments, and high command. The classes that controlled material resources, and the groups at the head of the political situation, failed to rise to the occasion in that desperate situation.

A chronicle of the march of invasion makes painful reading. Our soldiers were defeated at Matamoros, at Resaca de Guerrero, and Monterrey, in spite of the sacrifices of the troops. . . .

When one follows, event by event, the military operations and the political happenings of this period, one's feelings are harrowed by the details.

In this swift historical sketch, we shall be content to mention, if no great captain representative of defense, the youthful heroes who saved the honor of Mexico: the cadets of the Military College [at Chapultepec], who fell on September 13, 1847, when the school was stormed by the invading troops, then on the point of occupying the capital of the Republic. The glorious deaths of Francisco Marquez, Agustin Melgar, Juan Escutia, Fernando Montes de Oca, Vicente Suarez, and Juan de la Barrera, in an unequal contest, without hope, crushed by an overwhelming force, are as it were a symbol and image of this unrighteous war.

To Mexico, the American invasion contains a terrible lesson. In this war we saw that right and justice count but little in contests between one people and another, when material force, and organization, are wanting.

A great portion of Mexico's territory was lost because she had been able to administer and settle those regions, and handed them over to alien colonization [Texas].

There is no principle nor law that can sanction spoliation. Only by force was it carried out, and only by force or adroit negotiation could it have been avoided. That

---

[4]Alfonso Teja Zabre, *Guide to the History of Mexico* (Mexico: Ministry of Foreign Affairs, 1935), pp. 299–304, passim.

which Spain had been unable to colonize, and the [Mexican] Republic to settle, was occupied by the stream of Anglo-American expansion.

The war of 1847 is not, so far as Mexico is concerned, offset by anything but the courage of her soldiers. At Matamoros, at Resaca de Guerrero, at La Angostura [Buena Vista], at Vera Cruz, at Cerro Gordo, at Padierna, at Churubusco, and at Chapultepec, victory was won by a well-organized and instructed General Staff; by longer-range rifles and cannon, better-fed soldiers, abundance of money and ammunition, and of horses and wagons. . . .

The American invasion cost Mexico the total loss of Texas, whose boundaries were, without the slightest right, brought down to the Rio Grande; the Province of New Mexico and Upper California; and an outpouring of blood, energy, and wealth, offset only by material compensation in the amount of fifteen million pesos, by way of indemnity.

Thought Provokers

1. Why should Britain and America have been on friendly terms in the 1830s and 1840s, and why were they not?
2. Why was there such a lack of interest in Oregon during the early 1840s?
3. Polk claimed that no other power similarly situated would have refused the annexation of Texas. Do you agree or disagree? Explain how each side, at the outbreak of the Mexican War, could claim that the other was the aggressor. Were the annexation of Texas and the sending of General Taylor to the Rio Grande unconstitutional, as the abolitionists claimed? If England had held Mexico, as it did Canada, how would matters have been worked out differently?
4. Should a democratic government permit the kind of criticism that was indulged in by the Whigs and the abolitionists during the Mexican War? Compare the attitude of Massachusetts toward the War of 1812 with its attitude toward the Mexican War.
5. Did the advantages to the United States from the Mexican War outweigh the ultimate disadvantages? Emerson remarked that victory would be a dose of arsenic. Comment. Mexicans claim they would now be a rich nation if they had not been robbed of the oil and other riches of California and Texas. Comment.

19

Renewing the Sectional Struggle, 1848–1854

There is a higher law than the Constitution.

William H. Seward, in the Senate, 1850

Prologue: The electrifying discovery of gold in California in 1848 brought a frantic inrush of population, a demand for statehood, and a showdown in Congress over the future of slavery in the territories. The fruit of these debates was the great Compromise of 1850, which purchased an uneasy truce between North and South. It left the Southerners unhappy over the gains of free soil, and the Northerners unhappy over being drafted as slave catchers under the new Fugitive Slave Act of 1850. The short-lived truce was ruptured by the Kansas-Nebraska Act of 1854, which threw open the free soil of Kansas to possible slavery. To many Northerners this repeal of the time-sanctified Missouri Compromise line of 1820 seemed like bad faith on the part of the South; to many Southerners the open flouting of the Fugitive Slave Act, especially after 1854, seemed like bad faith on the part of the North. With distrust rapidly mounting on both sides, the days of the Union seemed numbered.

A. The Wilmot Proviso Issue

1. David Wilmot Appeals for Free Soil (1847)

While the Mexican War was still being fought, President Polk, his eye on California, asked Congress for $2 million with which to negotiate a peace. Representative David Wilmot of Pennsylvania proposed adding to the appropriation bill an amendment or proviso designed to bar slavery forever from any territory to be wrested from Mexico. Angry Southerners sprang to their feet; and the so-called Wilmot Proviso, though twice passing the House, was blocked in the Senate. But it became the cradle of the yet unborn Republican party, and it precipitated a debate that continued until silenced by the guns of civil war. In the following speech in Congress by Wilmot, what does he conceive the moral issue to be? How effectively does he meet the argu-

[1]*Congressional Globe,* 29th Congress, 2d session, Appendix, p. 315 (February 8, 1847).

ment regarding "joint blood and treasure"? Could he properly be regarded as an abolitionist?

But, sir, the issue now presented is not whether slavery shall exist unmolested where it now is, but whether it shall be carried to new and distant regions, now free, where the footprint of a slave cannot be found. This, sir, is the issue. Upon it I take my stand, and from it I cannot be frightened or driven by idle charges of abolitionism.

I ask not that slavery be abolished. I demand that this government preserve the integrity of free territory against the aggressions of slavery—against its wrongful usurpations.

Sir, I was in favor of the annexation of Texas. . . . The Democracy [Democratic Party] of the North, almost to a man, went for annexation. Yes, sir, here was an empire larger than France given up to slavery. Shall further concessions be made by the North? Shall we give up free territory, the inheritance of free labor? Must we yield this also? Never, sir, never, until we ourselves are fit to be slaves. . . .

But, sir, we are told that the joint blood and treasure of the whole country being expended in this acquisition, therefore it should be divided, and slavery allowed to take its share. Sir, the South has her share already; the instalment for slavery was paid in advance. We are fighting this war for Texas and for the South. I affirm it—every intelligent man knows it—Texas is the primary cause of this war. For this, sir, Northern treasure is being exhausted, and Northern blood poured upon the plains of Mexico. We are fighting this war cheerfully, not reluctantly—cheerfully fighting this war for Texas; and yet we seek not to change the character of her institutions. Slavery is there; there let it remain. . . .

Now, sir, we are told that California is ours, that New Mexico is ours—won by the valor of our arms. They are free. Shall they remain free? Shall these fair provinces be the inheritance and homes of the white labor of freemen or the black labor of slaves? This, sir, is the issue—this the question. The North has the right, and her representatives here have the power. . . .

But the South contend that, in their emigration to this free territory, they have the right to take and hold slaves, the same as other property. Unless the amendment I have offered be adopted, or other early legislation is had upon this subject, they will do so. Indeed, they unitedly, as one man, have declared their right and purpose so to do, and the work has already begun.

Slavery follows in the rear of our armies. Shall the war power of our government be exerted to produce such a result? Shall this government depart from its neutrality on this question, and lend its power and influence to plant slavery in these territories?

There is no question of abolition here, sir. Shall the South be permitted, by aggression, by invasion of the right, by subduing free territory and planting slavery upon it, to wrest these provinces from Northern freemen, and turn them to the accomplishment of their own sectional purposes and schemes?

This is the question. Men of the North, answer. Shall it be so? Shall we of the North submit to it? If we do, we are coward slaves, and deserve to have the manacles fastened upon our own limbs.

2. Southerners Threaten Secession (1849)

After the Mexican War officially brought rich territorial plums, the Northern anti-slaveryites became more persistent. They introduced measures in Congress for abolishing slavery in the District of Columbia and for organizing California and New Mexico as territories without slavery—that is, on the basis of the unpassed Wilmot Proviso. Outraged Southerners responded with cries of disunion. The following incendiary outbursts all occurred on the floor of the House on December 13, 1849. The most famous speaker was hale and hearty Robert Toombs of Georgia, a brilliant orator and one of the more moderate Southern planters. (He later became secretary of state for the Confederacy.) Why was the South so bitterly aroused over the question of slavery in the territories?

Mr. Meade [of Virginia]—But, sir, if the organization of this House is to be followed by the passage of these bills—if these outrages are to be committed upon my people—I trust in God, sir, that my eyes have rested upon the last Speaker of the House of Representatives. . . .

Mr. Toombs [of Georgia]—I do not, then, hesitate to avow before this House and the country, and in the presence of the living God, that if by your legislation you [Northerners] seek to drive us from the territories of California and New Mexico, purchased by the common blood and treasure of the whole people, and to abolish slavery in this District [of Columbia], thereby attempting to fix a national degradation upon half the states of this Confederacy, *I am for disunion.* And if my physical courage be equal to the maintenance of my convictions of right and duty, I will devote all I am and all I have on earth to its consummation.

From 1787 to this hour, the people of the South have asked nothing but justice—nothing but the maintenance of the principles and the spirit which controlled our fathers in the formation of the Constitution. Unless we are unworthy of our ancestors, we will never accept less as a condition of union. . . .

The Territories are the common property of the people of the United States, purchased by their common blood and treasure. You [the Congress] are their common agents. It is your duty, while they are in a territorial state, to remove all impediments to their free enjoyment by all sections and people of the Union, the slaveholder and the non-slaveholder. . . .

Mr. Colcock [of South Carolina]— . . . I here pledge myself that if any bill should be passed at this Congress abolishing slavery in the District of Columbia, or incorporating the Wilmot Proviso in any form, I will introduce a resolution in this House declaring, in terms, *that this Union ought to be dissolved.*

---

[2]*Congressional Globe,* 31st Congress, 1st session, part 1, pp. 26, 28, 29.

B. The Compromise Debates of 1850

1. John Calhoun Demands Southern Rights (1850)

Two burning questions brought the sectional controversy to a furious boil in 1850. The first was the failure of Northerners loyally to uphold both the Constitution and the Fugitive Slave Law of 1793 regarding runaway slaves. The second was the effort of California to win admission as a free state, thus establishing a precedent for the rest of the Mexican Cession territory. The subsequent debate over the compromise measures of 1850 featured a galaxy of forensic giants: Henry Clay, John C. Calhoun, Daniel Webster, Thomas H. Benton, William H. Seward, Stephen A. Douglas, Jefferson Davis, and many others. Highly revealing was the following swan-song speech of Senator Calhoun. On the verge of death from tuberculosis, he authorized a colleague to read it for him. What were his views on the Constitution, the Union, and secession? How successfully did he place the onus of insincerity and aggression on the North? How practicable were his remedies for preserving the Union?

. . . How can the Union be saved? To this I answer, there is but one way by which it can be, and that is by adopting such measures as will satisfy the states belonging to the Southern section that they can remain in the Union consistently with their honor and their safety. There is, again, only one way by which this can be effected, and that is by removing the causes by which this belief [that the South cannot honorably and safely remain in the Union] has been produced. Do that and discontent will cease, harmony and kind feelings between the sections be restored, and every apprehension of danger to the Union removed. The question, then, is, By what can this be done? But, before I undertake to answer this question, I propose to show by what the Union cannot be saved.

It cannot, then, be saved by eulogies on the Union, however splendid or numerous. The cry of "Union, Union, the glorious Union!" can no more prevent disunion than the cry of "Health, health, glorious health!" on the part of the physician can save a patient lying dangerously ill. So long as the Union, instead of being regarded as a protector, is regarded in the opposite character by not much less than a majority of the states, it will be in vain to attempt to conciliate them by pronouncing eulogies on it.

Besides, this cry of Union comes commonly from those whom we cannot believe to be sincere. It usually comes from our assailants. But we cannot believe them to be sincere; for, if they loved the Union, they would necessarily be devoted to the Constitution. It made the Union, and to destroy the Constitution would be to destroy the Union. But the only reliable and certain evidence of devotion to the Constitution is to abstain, on the one hand, from violating it, and to repel, on the other, all attempts to violate it. It is only by faithfully performing these high duties that the Constitution can be preserved, and with it the Union. . . .

---

[1]*Congressional Globe,* 31st Congress, 1st session (March 4, 1850) pp. 453, 455.

Having now shown what cannot save the Union, I return to the question with which I commenced, How can the Union be saved? There is but one way by which it can, with any certainty; and that is by a full and final settlement, on the principle of justice, of all the questions at issue between the two sections.

The South asks for justice, simple justice, and less she ought not to take. She has no compromise to offer but the Constitution; and no concession or surrender to make. She has already surrendered so much that she has little left to surrender. Such a settlement would go to the root of the evil, and remove all cause of discontent by satisfying the South she could remain honorably and safely in the Union, and thereby restore the harmony and fraternal feelings between the sections which existed anterior to the Missouri [Compromise] agitation [1820]. Nothing else can, with any certainty, finally and forever settle the questions at issue, terminate agitation, and save the Union.

But can this be done? Yes, easily; not by the weaker party [the South], for it can of itself do nothing—not even protect itself—but by the stronger. The North has only to will it to accomplish it—to do justice by conceding to the South an equal right in the acquired territory, and to do her duty by causing the stipulations relative to fugitive slaves to be faithfully fulfilled—to cease the agitation of the slave question, and to provide for the insertion of a provision in the Constitution, by an amendment, which will restore to the South, in substance, the power she possessed of protecting herself, before the equilibrium between the sections was destroyed by the action of this government. There will be no difficulty in devising such a provision*—one that will protect the South, and which, at the same time, will improve and strengthen the government instead of impairing and weakening it.

But will the North agree to this? It is for her to answer the question. But, I will say, she cannot refuse if she has half the love of the Union which she professes to have, or without justly exposing herself to the charge that her love of power and aggrandizement is far greater than her love of the Union.

At all events, the responsibility of saving the Union rests on the North, and not the South. The South cannot save it by any act of hers, and the North may save it without any sacrifice whatever, unless to do justice, and to perform her duties under the Constitution, should be regarded by her as a sacrifice. . . .

If you, who represent the stronger portion, cannot agree to settle . . . [the question at issue] on the broad principle of justice and duty, say so; and let the states we both represent agree to separate and part in peace. If you are unwilling we should part in peace, tell us so; and we shall know what to do, when you reduce the question to submission or resistance.

If you remain silent, you will compel us to infer by your acts what you intend. In that case, California will become the test question. If you admit her, under all the difficulties that oppose her admission, you compel us to infer that you intend to exclude us from the whole of the acquired territories, with the intention of destroying, irretrievably, the equilibrium between the two sections. We would be blind not to perceive, in that case, that your real objects are power and aggrandizement, and infatuated not to act accordingly.

---

*Calhoun evidently had in mind two presidents: one Northern, one Southern, each with crippling veto power.   ·

2. Daniel Webster Urges Concessions (1850)

On the anvil of congressional debate was forged the great Compromise of 1850. California was admitted as a free state; the fate of slavery in the rest of the Mexican Cession territory was left to the inhabitants. The major sop to the south was the enactment of a more stringent Fugitive Slave Law. As a concession to the North, slave trade was abolished in the District of Columbia; as a concession to the South, slavery in the District was retained. Texas received $10 million for yielding a disputed chunk of its territory to New Mexico.

Senator Daniel Webster's Seventh of March speech during these congressional debates emphasized concession, compromise, moderation, and Union. He attacked the abolitionists (see earlier, p. 369) and deplored the agitation over the extension of slavery to the territories. A slave economy was geographically impossible there, he felt, and no legislative body should reenact the law of God. Finally, he took sharp issue with Calhoun's threat of secession. How good a prophet was Webster? Which of his arguments on the impracticability of peaceful secession probably carried the most weight in the North?

Mr. President, I wish to speak today, not as a Massachusetts man, nor as a Northern man, but as an American, and a member of the Senate of the United States. . . . I speak today for the preservation of the Union. "Hear me for my cause." . . .

Mr. President, I should much prefer to have heard, from every member on this floor, declarations of opinion that this Union should never be dissolved, than the declaration of opinion that in any case, under the pressure of circumstances, such a dissolution was possible. I hear with pain, and anguish, and distress, the word *secession,* especially when it falls from the lips of those who are eminently patriotic, and known to the country, and known all over the world, for their political services.

Secession! Peaceable secession! Sir, your eyes and mine are never destined to see that miracle. The dismemberment of this vast country without convulsion! The breaking up of the fountains of the great deep without ruffling the surface! Who is so foolish—I beg everybody's pardon—as to expect to see any such thing? . . .

There can be no such thing as a peaceable secession. Peaceable secession is an utter impossibility. Is the great Constitution under which we live here—covering this whole country—is it to be thawed and melted away by secession, as the snows on the mountain melt under the influence of a vernal sun—disappear almost unobserved, and die off? No, sir! No, sir! No, sir! I will not state what might produce the disruption of the states; but, sir, I see it as plainly as I see the sun in heaven—I see that disruption must produce such a war as I will not describe, in its twofold characters.

Peaceable secession! Peaceable secession! The concurrent agreement of all the members of this great Republic to separate! A voluntary separation, with alimony on one side and on the other! Why, what would be the result? Where is the line to be drawn? What states are to secede?—What is to remain American? What am I to be?—

[2]*Congressional Globe,* 31st Congress, 1st session (March 7, 1850), pp. 276, 482–483.

an American no longer? Where is the flag of the Republic to remain? Where is the eagle still to tower? or is he to cower, and shrink, and fall to the ground? . . .

What is to become of the army? What is to become of the navy? What is to become of the public lands? How is each of the thirty states to defend itself? I know, although the idea has not been stated distinctly, there is to be a Southern Confederacy. I do not mean, when I allude to this statement, that anyone seriously contemplates such a state of things. I do not mean to say that it is true, but I have heard it suggested elsewhere, that that idea has originated in a design to separate. I am sorry, sir, that it has ever been thought of, talked of, or dreamed of, in the wildest flights of human imagination. But the idea must be of a separation, including the slave states upon one side and the free states on the other.

Sir, there is not—I may express myself too strongly perhaps—but some things, some moral things, are almost as impossible as other natural or physical things. And I hold the idea of a separation of these states—those that are free to form one government, and those that are slaveholding to form another—as a moral impossibility.

We could not separate the states by any such line, if we were to draw it. We could not sit down here today and draw a line of separation that would satisfy any five men in the country. There are natural causes that would keep and tie us together, and there are social and domestic relations which we could not break if we would, and which we should not if we could. . . .

And now, Mr. President, instead of speaking of the possibility of utility of secession . . . let our comprehension be as broad as the country for which we act, our aspirations as high as its certain destiny. Let us not be pigmies in a case that calls for men.

Never did there devolve on any generation of men higher trusts than now devolve upon us for the preservation of this Constitution and the harmony and peace of all who are destined to live under it. Let us make our generation one of the strongest and brightest links in that golden chain which is destined, I fully believe, to grapple the people of all the states to this Constitution for ages to come.

3. Free-Soilers Denounce Webster (1850)

The new and more merciless Fugitive Slave Act of 1850 was the keystone of the Compromise of 1850, and Senator Webster's eloquent support of it scandalized the abolitionists. "The fame of Webster ends in this nasty law," wrote Ralph Waldo Emerson. But conservative-minded Northerners were well aware, as Emerson himself had recorded, that "Cotton thread holds the Union together." Bankers, shippers, and manufacturers—holding Southern mortgages, transporting cotton, or using it in their factories—praised Webster's course as statesmanlike. Indeed, the abolitionists cried, the "Lords of the Loom" were joining hands with the "Lords of the Lash." A New Hampshire newspaper editor here assails the New England "cotton lords." Judging from this criticism, what were the political reactions to Webster's stand?

---

[3]*Independent Democrat* (Concord, N.H.), in *The Liberator* (Boston), April 19, 1850.

Some eight hundred of the "cotton lords" of State Street [Boston], with a few . . . Doctors of Divinity . . . of the Andover Theological Seminary, have signed a letter of thanks to Daniel Webster for his recent apostasy to freedom.

This was to be expected. There are, and always have been, men at the North whose habits, associations, and interests all lead them to love whatever degrades labor, and the man who lives by labor. Wherever Mammon is the great god, there flourishes the spirit of slavery. Wealth and luxury are ever the handmaids of oppression. The fastnesses of liberty have always been in the homes of the untilted masses. And hence the antagonism between capital and labor, which marks so strongly modern civilization.

In thanking Mr. Webster for his efforts in behalf of slavery, the "cotton" men of Boston are but signing a certificate of his servility to themselves. No such certificate, however, will commend him to the people of New England, nor of Massachusetts. Instead, it will have the very opposite effect. It is already doing a work far different from that intended.

The honest anti-slavery masses, upon whom Webster has heretofore relied, see at once that it cannot be for any good thing done for freedom and humanity that such men praise him. To the representative of freemen, the "well done" of the enemies of freedom is the breath of infamy. That "well done" Daniel Webster has received, not only from the "cotton lords" of Massachusetts, but from the prince of cotton lords [Calhoun?] of South Carolina. He is doomed, withered, blasted; and the "thanks" of all the worshipers of Mammon and Wrong in the universe cannot save him.

[Southerners, as indicated, were generally pleased by the unexpected show of support from the Yankee Webster, but their praise was a political kiss of death to the Senator. The Richmond Enquirer remarked that the Massachusetts abolitionists— "the miserable peddlers for notoriety"—would "defame and abuse him." It further stated that his "selfish and penurious constituency"—"the moneyed men and manufacturers of New England"—were finally "aroused to the dangers that threaten the Union and their interests . . . ." (quoted in The Liberator, *April 5, 1850).]*

C. Reactions to the Fugitive Slave Law

1. Joshua Giddings Rejects Slave Catching (1850)

If the South had a grievance against Northern abettors of runaway slaves, the North had a grievance against the harsh Fugitive Slave Act of 1850. No single irritant of the 1850s proved to be more persistently galling. Among the numerous features of the law, federal officers could summon bystanders to form a posse to chase the fugitive. Citizens who prevented an arrest or aided the escapee were liable to six months' im-

---

[1]*Congressional Globe,* 31st Congress, 2d session (December 9, 1850), p. 15.

prisonment and a fine of $1,000. Few were more deeply outraged by these stipulations than fiery Joshua R. Giddings, who served for twenty years as an uncompromising antislavery congressman from Ohio. In his speech in Congress against the Fugitive Slave Act, what parts were most offensive to the South? Does the accessory-to-murder analogy hold water? What were the sources of Giddings's outrage?

Sir, what protection does this law lend to the poor, weak, oppressed, degraded slave, whose flesh has often quivered under the lash of his inhuman owner? whose youth has been spent in labor for another? whose intellect has been nearly blotted out? When he seeks an asylum in a land of freedom, this worse than barbarous law sends the officers of government to chase him down. The people are constrained to become his pursuers. Famishing, fainting, and benumbed with the cold, he drags his weary limbs forward, while the whole power of the government under the President's command, the army and navy, and all the freemen of the land, organized into a constabulary force, are on his track to drag him back to bondage, under this law. . . .

Sir, there is not a man in this body—there is not an intelligent man in the free states—but knows, if he delivers a fugitive into the custody of his pursuers, that he will be carried to the South and sold to the sugar and cotton plantations. And his life will be sacrificed in five years if employed on the sugar plantations, and in seven years on the cotton plantations. The men of the North, who look upon this as murder, would as soon turn out and cut the throats of the defenseless Negro as to send him back to a land of chains and whips. As soon would they do this as comply with a law which violates every principle of common justice and humanity.

The [common] law, sir, holds him who aids in a murder as guilty as he who strikes the knife to the heart of the victim. Under our law, a man is hanged if he fails to prevent a murder when it is plainly in his power to do so. Such man is held guilty of the act, and he is hanged accordingly. The man who should assist in the capture of a fugitive would be regarded by us as guilty as he under whose lash the victim expires.

I have compared this capture of a fugitive to a common murder. In doing that, I do injustice to the common murderer. To capture a slave and send him to the South, to die under a torture of five years, is far more criminal than ordinary murder.

Sir, we will not commit this crime. Let me say to the President, no power of government can compel us to involve ourselves in such guilt. No! The freemen of Ohio will never turn out to chase the panting fugitive—they will never be metamorphosed into bloodhounds, to track him to his hiding-place, and seize and drag him out, and deliver him to his tormentors. Rely upon it, they will die first. They may be shot down, the cannon and bayonet and sword may do their work upon them; they may drown the fugitives in their blood, but never will they stoop to such degradation.

Let no man tell me there is no higher law than this fugitive bill. We feel there is a law of right, of justice, of freedom, implanted in the breast of every intelligent human being, that bids him look with scorn upon this libel upon all that is called law.

2. Robert Rhett Resents a Hoax (1851)

When Northerners began to obstruct the enforcement of the Fugitive Slave Law, the Southerners heatedly cried betrayal. Their only real gain from the Compromise of 1850 had presumably been this trouble-brewing statute. One of the loudest Southern voices was that of the impassioned Senator Robert B. Rhett, who had opposed the compromise measures of 1850 and who had fallen heir to the seat of Senator Calhoun of South Carolina. Sometimes referred to as the "Father of Secession," Rhett resigned from the Senate after two years because his state would not take an extreme position on withdrawal from the Union. In this Senate speech, was he sound in his view of the relationship of law to public opinion? Was he justified in his belief that the Fugitive Slave Law was a deliberate hoax?

Sir, the law is not always a law. . . . A law to have its practical effect must move in harmony with the opinions and feelings of the community where it is to operate. In this case, no one can doubt that the feeling of the whole and entire North—whatever may be their submission to what they may consider to be the supreme law of the land—is opposed to the institution of slavery, and opposed to this law.

Now, you may multiply officers as much as you please; you may make every ship a prison; you may make every custom-house a guard-room; you may, in all your great central points, make every effort you can for the purpose honestly of enforcing the law; nay, you may have a large majority in all the free states in favor of its enforcement. And yet, if there be a formidable minority that determine upon the defeat of the operation of the law, they can defeat it, and they will defeat it.

The recovery of the fugitive slave is not merely the case of a person coming into court. It is not merely a case in which the law should be enforced by courts. The fugitive slave may be concealed or sworn out of court; a thousand artifices and expedients may be resorted to, by which the slaveholder will be unable to recapture his slave, or the slave, when regained, will be rescued. Although the government may be perfectly honest in its determination to enforce the law, although you may legislate with the utmost rigor, yet, after all, the statutes may be nothing more than so much waste paper, of no use but to deceive those who are willing to be deceived.

As my honorable colleague very correctly said the other day, out of fifteen thousand slaves at the North—and I have seen a statement myself putting the number at thirty thousand—how many have been recaptured? Some fifteen have been taken in eight or nine months; and in every case in which there was any dispute it cost the master more than the worth of the slave.

I know of a case which has been communicated to me very recently. Several gentlemen in Maryland, on the Eastern Shore, knowing that they had fugitive slaves in Philadelphia, agreed that one should go and endeavor to recapture his slave, and, if he succeeded, the rest would endeavor to do so likewise. The gentleman went armed with the proof of the identity of his slave by the presence of several of his neighbors, but when he got to Philadelphia, embarrassments of one kind and an-

---

[2]*Congressional Globe,* 31st Congress, 2d session (February 24, 1851), Appendix, pp. 317–318.

other were thrown in his way—false swearing as to the identity of the person was resorted to, and he was defeated. . . .

It is on an examination of these facts that I have come to the conclusion that this law cannot and will not be so enforced as practically to secure the rights of the South. With this conviction, I have looked most carefully into this matter since it arose here in debate. And I have come to the conclusion that, from the beginning of the legislation of Congress on this whole subject to this day, we of the South have been wronged, and have been made to abandon a better and more efficient remedy [secession?], which the Constitution provides.

3. The South Threatens Retaliation (1855)

The Fugitive Slave Act of 1850 prompted a number of Northern states to strengthen their old "personal liberty laws" or enact new ones. Ostensibly these statutes were designed to protect the bona-fide free black from the ever-present danger of being kidnapped and reenslaved. Actually they operated to hamper or nullify the Fugitive Slave Act. Slaveholders who entered free states risked being sued for false arrest, jailed for kidnapping, or mobbed. Some states denied their jails to slave catchers. Numerous attempts by Northern mobs to rescue black fugitives from the authorities led to riots and some loss of life. In 1854 angry abolitionists in Boston stormed the courthouse and shot Deputy Marshal Batchelder in a vain attempt to rescue the escaped slave Anthony Burns. In the following New Orleans editorial, what merit is there in the arguments that the North had consistently violated the Constitution; that retaliation in kind would be justified; and that one section of the nation had already seceded?

Under the Massachusetts "personal liberty law," no open action as yet has taken place. . . . Our people are scattered for the summer, hundreds spending their money in pleasure excursions or purchases in Massachusetts. No, my good friends of Bunker Hill and Lexington (and long may I be permitted to address you as such), there has been as yet no open action. Some of our [social] bees and butterflies have fluttered off among you, but we who are toiling here at home consult together about your "liberty law," and other movements, and I have leave to tell you some things which are more than hinted at, if such laws are to be enforced.

First.—Excluding your ships.

Second.—Excluding your manufactures.

Third.—Ceasing our visits to your borders, already unsafe and more or less unpleasant.

Fourth.—Requiring your citizens trading here at least to take out licenses, perhaps to furnish bond for good behavior.

How will such laws suit you? Of course not at all. They trench on that provision of the Constitution [Art. IV, Sec. II] which declares that the citizens of each state shall be entitled to all the privileges and immunities of citizens in the several states. They certainly do, my conscientious friends, and such laws operate against all other rights

---

[3]*New Orleans Bulletin,* July, 1855, in Allan Nevins, ed., *American Press Opinion* (Boston and New York: D. C. Heath and Company, 1928), pp. 205–206.

the people of the several states have in other states under the Federal Constitution. . . . We know it! But we also know that this is precisely our objection to this "liberty law," which has made all the trouble, and that its unconstitutionality has been pronounced by our highest tribunals.

All your reasoning would have done very well, so long as you held to your bargain—so long as you yourselves submitted to the paramount law, and recognized our rights under its guarantees—so long as Massachusetts held to her obligations and place in the great American family. But now you have repudiated a right of vital importance to us, and passed a law to fine and imprison as felons our citizens who may claim their rights under that Constitution.

Why wait for a formal rupture and separation from you? You have not done so. Our compact is broken by you. There is little obligation on us to respect the rights of your citizens or their property, when you openly trample on ours. There is as little to restrain a [New Orleans] mob from taking possession of one or more of your ships as there was to restrain your [Boston] mob in the case of the Negro Burns from their assaults on the court and its officers, and from murdering the marshal Batchelder.

D. The Debate over the Kansas-Nebraska Bill

1. Stephen Douglas's Popular-Sovereignty Plea (1854)

The Kansas-Nebraska Act of 1854 shattered the uneasy sectional truce. Senator Stephen Arnold Douglas of Illinois—a bouncy, stumpy, real estate booster and transcontinental railroad enthusiast—undertook to organize Nebraska into a territory. Hoping to enlist Southern support, he held out the bait of making Kansas a slave state by the operation of "squatter" or "popular" sovereignty. In short, he would let the people of the territories themselves democratically decide whether they wanted slaves or no slaves. But this meant an outright repeal, by means of the Kansas-Nebraska Act, of the time-hallowed Compromise of 1820—the compromise that had banned slavery in the Louisiana Purchase territory north of 36° 30' (see earlier, p. 236). Whatever his motives, Douglas infuriated Northern abolitionists and free-soilers by driving the Kansas-Nebraska bill through the Senate with relentless energy. In this portion of his Senate speech, how does he define the merits of "popular sovereignty"?

. . . When the people of the North shall all be rallied under one banner, and the whole South marshaled under another banner, and each section excited to frenzy and madness by hostility to the institutions of the other, then the patriot may well tremble for the perpetuity of the Union. Withdraw the slavery question from the political arena, and remove it to the states and territories, each to decide for itself, such a catastrophe can never happen. Then you will never be able to tell, by any Senator's vote for or against any measure, from what state or section of the Union he comes.

---

[1]*Congressional Globe,* 33d Congress, 1st session (March 3, 1854), Appendix, p. 338.

Why, then, can we not withdraw this vexed question from politics? Why can we not adopt the [popular sovereignty] principle of this [Kansas-Nebraska] bill as a rule of action in all new territorial organizations? Why can we not deprive these agitators of their vocation, and render it impossible for Senators to come here upon bargains on the slavery question? I believe that the peace, the harmony, and perpetuity of the Union require us to go back to the doctrines of the Revolution, to the principles of the Constitution, to the principles of the Compromise of 1850, and leave the people, under the Constitution, to do as they may see proper in respect to their own internal affairs.

Mr. President, I have not brought this question forward as a Northern man or as a Southern man. I am unwilling to recognize such divisions and distinctions. I have brought it forward as an American Senator, representing a state which is true to this principle, and which has approved of my action in respect to the Nebraska bill. I have brought it forward not as an act of justice to the South more than to the North. I have presented it especially as an act of justice to the people of those territories, and of the states to be formed therefrom, now and in all time to come.

I have nothing to say about Northern rights or Southern rights. I know of no such divisions or distinctions under the Constitution. The bill does equal and exact justice to the whole Union, and every part of it; it violates the rights of no state or territory, but places each on a perfect equality, and leaves the people thereof to the free enjoyment of all their rights under the Constitution. . . .

I say frankly that, in my opinion, this measure will be as popular at the North as at the South, when its provisions and principles shall have been fully developed and become well understood.

2. Salmon Chase Upholds Free Soil (1854)

Senator Salmon P. Chase of Ohio—later Lincoln's secretary of the treasury, and still later Chief Justice of the Supreme Court—was an ardent free-soiler. So active was he in defense of runaway slaves that he was dubbed "attorney general for the fugitive slaves." Pathologically ambitious for the presidency, he was so handsome as to be "a sculptor's ideal of a president." He vehemently opposed both the Compromise of 1850 and the Kansas-Nebraska Act of 1854. These two measures, particularly the second, aroused so much ill feeling between the sections as to make future compromise improbable, and led to the spontaneous formation of the Republican party. In the light of Chase's remarks, was he justified in considering the slave power the aggressor? Was all future compromise now impossible? Was he a better prophet than Douglas?

Now, sir, who is responsible for this renewal of strife and controversy? Not we [free-soilers], for we have introduced no question of territorial slavery into Congress—not we who are denounced as agitators and factionists. No, sir; the quietists and the finalists have become agitators; they who told us that all agitation was quieted, and that the resolutions of the political conventions put a final period to the discussion of slavery.

---

[2]*Congressional Globe,* 33d Congress, 1st session (February 3, 1854), Appendix, pp. 134, 140.

This will not escape the observation of the country. It is slavery that renews the strife. It is slavery that again wants room. It is slavery, with its insatiate demands for more slave territory and more slave states.

And what does slavery ask for now? Why, sir, it demands that a time-honored and sacred compact [Missouri Compromise] shall be rescinded—a compact which has endured through a whole generation—a compact which has been universally regarded as inviolable, North and South—a compact the constitutionality of which few have doubted, and by which all have consented to abide. . . .

You may pass it here. You may send it to the other House. It may become law. But its effect will be to satisfy all thinking men that no compromises with slavery will endure, except so long as they serve the interests of slavery; and that there is no safe and honorable ground for non-slaveholders to stand upon, except that of restricting slavery within state limits, and excluding it absolutely from the whole sphere of federal jurisdiction.

The old questions between political parties are at rest. No great question so thoroughly possesses the public mind as this of slavery. This discussion will hasten the inevitable reorganization of parties upon the new issues which our circumstances suggest. It will light up a fire in the country which may, perhaps, consume those who kindle it.

I cannot believe that the people of this country have so far lost sight of the maxims and principles of the Revolution, or are so insensible to the obligations which those maxims and principles impose, as to acquiesce in the violation of this compact. Sir, the Senator from Illinois [Douglas] tells us that he proposes a final settlement of all territorial questions in respect to slavery, by the application of the principle of popular sovereignty. What kind of popular sovereignty is that which allows one portion of the people to enslave another portion? Is that the doctrine of equal rights? Is that exact justice? Is that the teaching of enlightened, liberal, progressive democracy?

No, sir; no! There can be no real democracy which does not fully maintain the rights of man, as man.

3. Northwestern Support for Douglas (1854)

Critics have frequently maintained that the whole controversy over slavery in the territories rang hollow. It concerned a nonexistent slave in an area where he could not exist—thanks to geography and climate. The ideal of popular sovereignty received some support in Douglas's own Northwest, as indicated by this editorial in the Detroit Free Press. *What evidence does it offer that slavery would not go into the territories? Why should the Northwest in particular favor popular sovereignty?*

Slavery, in this country, is the creature of statutory law. It exists, and can exist, nowhere except by positive enactment. It cannot go to Nebraska, or Kansas, or any other new territory, until it is established by the legislative power.

Now, is there a man in the whole country who supposes that the legislatures of either the territories of Nebraska or Kansas will legalize slavery? Under Mr. Douglas's

---

[3]*Detroit Free Press,* March 16, 1854, in *Daily National Intelligencer* (Washington, D.C.), March 21, 1854.

bill, as it passed the Senate, those legislatures will have the sole and unlimited control of the subject. Is there the most distant probability that they will exercise that control in favor of slavery? Have Utah and New Mexico, both further south than Nebraska, so exercised it? Did California, over which no restriction existed, so exercise it? In Utah and New Mexico, although they have been four years organized, no slavery has been established, or attempted to be established. In California, the convention which formed her state constitution voted unanimously for a slavery-prohibition clause.

Mr. Douglas's bill is the greatest advance movement in the direction of human freedom that has been made since the adoption of the Constitution. Never before has the right of all American communities to self-government been fully recognized. The people of the territories have hitherto been held to a species of vassalage not less humiliating to them than it was inconsistent with popular rights. They have not been permitted to make their own laws or to manage their own domestic concerns. They have been treated as minors, incompetent to take care of themselves. Mr. Douglas's bill changes all this. The territories have the same privileges in respect to domestic legislation as the states, and their citizens are recognized as American freemen.

Ought not this bill to receive universal commendation? We believe it ought. And it would, were it not for the delusion that prevails in the minds of some, encouraged and excited by Whig and abolition demagogues, that there is danger of slavery extension.

4. The South Is Lukewarm (1854)

The antislavery North, as might have been expected, reacted violently against the gain for slavery (on paper) under the Kansas-Nebraska Act. Ominously, most of the opposition came not from already-committed abolitionists but from citizens who had reluctantly accepted the Compromise of 1850 but had now lost all confidence in the good faith of the South. "The day of compromise is over," warned the Hartford [Connecticut] Courant. *Horace Greeley, editor of the potent* New York Tribune, *declared that Douglas and his co-conspirators had "made more abolitionists than Garrison and Phillips could have made in half a century." Even the South, though on the whole mildly favorable, had its misgivings. The Columbia* South Carolinian *conceded that "practically" the Kansas-Nebraska Act would "scarcely ever benefit the South," but it would "render justice to the South" and serve as a "triumph" over abolitionism. A more realistic view was taken by an editorial in the slaveholding state of Kentucky. Why did the editor, with uncanny insight, regard the Kansas-Nebraska Act as a thing of unmitigated evil?*

The Nebraska Bill is advocated and denounced upon grounds the most opposite and for reasons the most diverse. There is the greatest contrariety of opinion as to what effect its passage will have upon the question of slavery. Southern men, of course, support it upon the ground that it will give slavery a chance to get into the

---

[4]*Western Citizen* (Kentucky), April 21, 1854, in *Daily National Intelligencer* (Washington, D.C.), April 24, 1854.

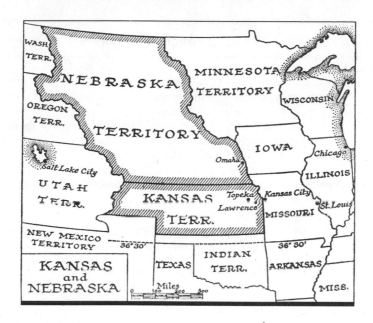

territory from which it has hitherto been excluded; whilst others, with quite as much show of reason, take the ground occupied by the President, that the effect will be to prevent the admission of slave states into the Union forever.

A measure whose effects, in matters of so much consequence, are so uncertain; which proposes to violate and disannul a compact [Missouri Compromise] regarded by one section of our common country as sacred, and acquiesced in for a third of a century by the other—a compact the advantages of which the South has fully received on her part—should at least promise some decided practical good as the result of its passage, and should be chargeable with the production of as few evils as possible.

We believe that the adoption of the measure will be productive of evil, and only evil, continually. Even supposing that the Missouri Compromise is not a bargain that we of the slave states are bound to respect and stand to, and that we may declare it void without a breach of faith, what do we gain by its repeal? What but a revival, in a wilder and intenser and more dangerous form, of that agitation of the slavery question which was but yesterday allayed by the all but superhuman efforts of our noblest statesmen [in the Compromise of 1850]? The North regards the Missouri Compromise as a sacred compact, to the preservation of which the honor and faith of the South was pledged. If we now violate that pledge, what right have we to expect the North to respect any compromise that has been or may be made for our advantage? . . .

And what should we gain? A mere right to carry slaves into Nebraska, which we can never exercise; the mere gratification of having an old law [Missouri Compromise] repealed which the South now chooses to consider unjust to her, but which her wisest statesmen at the time of its passage regarded as highly advantageous to her—a law carried by Southern votes, and heretofore looked upon as one of the noblest achievements of Southern statesmanship.

Thought Provokers

1. If the Wilmot Proviso issue had not come up during the Mexican war, was it probable that the question of slavery in the territories would have been raised in an acute form?

2. It has been said that by the 1850s each side distrusted the other so greatly that disunion was inevitable: the North because of Southern grasping for more slave territory; the South because of Northern nullification of the Constitution and federal laws. Comment critically. Webster in 1850 was condemned as an appeaser or compromiser and hence not a statesman. Is compromise essential to statecraft?

3. Are a people ever justified in openly violating laws (like the Fugitive Slave Act) that they disapprove of and think immoral? What has been the fate of such laws in U.S. history? Should the majority always rule?

4. Was it immoral, as abolitionists alleged, for Congress to repeal the Missouri Compromise line of 1820? Why was further compromise between North and South impossible after 1854? Was the North or the South the aggressor in the 1850s with regard to the slavery issue? Which side was constitutionally right?

20

Drifting Toward Disunion, 1854–1861

It is an irrepressible conflict between opposing and
enduring forces.

William H. Seward, 1858

Prologue: Popular sovereignty in Kansas degenerated into unpopular savagery. Embattled free-soilers fought embittered proslaveryites, as the complaisant pro-Southern administrations of Presidents Franklin Pierce and James Buchanan continued to drift. Irate Northerners, resenting the Kansas-Nebraska grab, increasingly turned the Fugitive Slave Act into a dead letter. At the same time the newly born Republican party, sired by the same Kansas-Nebraska Act, gathered such amazing momentum in the North as to give the Democrats a real scare in the presidential election of 1856. The sectional tension was heightened by a series of inflammatory incidents, including Representative Preston Brooks's brutal beating of Senator Charles Sumner, the proslavery Dred Scott decision, and John Brown's fantastic raid at Harpers Ferry. Southerners also reacted angrily against the overwhelming approval in the North of such antislavery propaganda as *Uncle Tom's Cabin* and Helper's *Impending Crisis of the South* (see earlier, p. 372). And the imminent election of the Republican Lincoln in 1860 foreshadowed both secession and shooting.

A. The Impact of Uncle Tom's Cabin

1. Tom Defies Simon Legree (1852)

Harriet Beecher Stowe, a busy mother and housewife then living in Maine, was aroused by the recent gains of slavery to write—partly on old wrapping paper—her heart-tugging novel Uncle Tom's Cabin. *Reared in New England as the daughter of famed preacher Lyman Beecher, and having lived for seventeen years in Ohio on the route of the Underground Railroad, she had developed an abhorrence of the "peculiar institution." Oddly enough, her firsthand observations of slavery were limited to a brief visit to Kentucky. In her best-selling book she sought to mollify the South to some extent by representing the saintly slave Uncle Tom as having two kind masters;*

---

[1]Harriet B. Stowe, *Uncle Tom's Cabin* (Boston: J. P. Jewett, 1852), chap. 33.

*by featuring the whimsical Topsy and the angelic little Eva (who died); and by por-
traying the monster Simon Legree, who finally ordered Uncle Tom beaten to death, as
a Yankee from Vermont. In the following scene, the cotton-picking slaves have just
returned from the fields, and Legree orders Tom to flog one of the sickly women for
not having picked enough. What details of this episode would most offend the anti-
slavery North? the proslavery South?*

"And now," said Legree, "come here, you Tom. You see, I telled ye I didn't buy
ye jest for the common work. I mean to promote ye, and make a driver of ye; and
tonight ye may jest as well begin to get yer hand in. Now, ye jest take this yer gal
and flog her; ye've seen enough on't [of it] to know how."

"I beg Mas'r's pardon," said Tom; "hopes Mas'r won't set me at that. It's what I
an't used to—never did—and can't do, no way possible."

"Ye'll larn a pretty smart chance of things ye never did know, before I've done
with ye!" said Legree, taking up a cowhide and striking Tom a heavy blow across
the cheek, and following up the infliction by a shower of blows.

"There!" he said, as he stopped to rest; "now, will ye tell me ye can't do it?"

"Yes, Mas'r," said Tom, putting up his hand, to wipe the blood that trickled
down his face. "I'm willin' to work, night and day, and work while there's life and
breath in me. But this yer thing I can't feel it right to do; and, Mas'r, I never shall do
it—*never!*"

Tom had a remarkably smooth, soft voice, and a habitually respectful manner
that had given Legree an idea that he would be cowardly and easily subdued. When
he spoke these last words, a thrill of amazement went through everyone. The poor
woman clasped her hands and said, "O Lord!" and everyone involuntarily looked at
each other and drew in their breath, as if to prepare for the storm that was about to
burst.

Legree looked stupefied and confounded; but at last burst forth:

"What! ye blasted black beast! tell *me* ye don't think it *right* to do what I tell ye!
What have any of you cussed cattle to do with thinking what's right? I'll put a stop
to it! Why, what do ye think ye are? May be ye think ye're a gentleman, master Tom,
to be a telling your master what's right, and what an't! So you pretend it's wrong to
flog the gal!"

"I think so, Mas'r," said Tom; "the poor crittur's sick and feeble; 'twould be
downright cruel, and it's what I never will do, nor begin to. Mas'r, if you mean to kill
me, kill me; but, as to my raising my hand agin any one here, I never shall—I'll die
first!"

Tom spoke in a mild voice, but with a decision that could not be mistaken.
Legree shook with anger; his greenish eyes glared fiercely, and his very whiskers
seemed to curl with passion. But, like some ferocious beast, that plays with its victim before he devours it, he kept back his strong impulse to proceed to immediate
violence, and broke out into bitter raillery.

"Well, here's a pious dog, at least, let down among us sinners!—a saint, a gentleman, and no less, to talk to us sinners about our sins! Powerful holy crittur, he
must be! Here, you rascal, you make believe to be so pious—didn't you never hear,
out of yer Bible, 'Servants, obey yer masters'? An't I yer master? Didn't I pay down

twelve hundred dollars, cash, for all there is inside yer old cussed black shell? An't yer mine, now, body and soul?" he said, giving Tom a violent kick with his heavy boot; "tell me!"

In the very depth of physical suffering, bowed by brutal oppression, this question shot a gleam of joy and triumph through Tom's soul. He suddenly stretched himself up, and, looking earnestly to heaven, while the tears and blood that flowed down his face mingled, he exclaimed,

"No! no! no! my soul an't yours, Mas'r! You haven't bought it—ye can't buy it! It's been bought and paid for by One that is able to keep it. No matter, no matter, you can't harm me!"

"I can't!" said Legree, with a sneer; "we'll see—we'll see! Here, Sambo, Quimbo, give this dog such a breakin' in as he won't get over this month!"

The two gigantic Negroes that now laid hold of Tom, with fiendish exultation in their faces, might have formed no unapt personification of powers and darkness. The poor woman screamed with apprehension, and all rose, as by a general impulse, while they dragged him unresisting from the place.

2. The South Scorns Mrs. Stowe (1852)

Northern abolitionists naturally applauded Mrs. Stowe's powerful tale; the poet John Greenleaf Whittier now thanked God for the Fugitive Slave Act, which had inspired the book. The few Northern journals that voiced criticism were drowned out by the clatter of the printing presses running off tens of thousands of new copies. Southern critics cried that this "wild and unreal picture" would merely arouse the "fanaticism" of the North while exciting the "indignation" of the South. They insisted that the slave beatings were libelously overemphasized; that the worst slave drivers were imported Northerners (like Legree); that the Southern black slave was better off than the Northern wage slave; and that relatively few families were broken up—fewer, in fact, than among soldiers on duty, Irish immigrants coming to America, sailors going to sea, or pioneers venturing West. Why did the Southern Literary Messenger *of Richmond find it important to refute Mrs. Stowe's "slanders" as follows?*

There are some who will think we have taken upon ourselves an unnecessary trouble in exposing the inconsistencies and false assertions of *Uncle Tom's Cabin.* It is urged by such persons that in devoting so much attention to abolition attacks we give them an importance to which they are not entitled. This may be true in general. But let it be borne in mind that this slanderous work has found its way to every section of our country, and has crossed the water to Great Britain, filling the minds of all who know nothing of slavery with hatred for that institution and those who uphold it. Justice to ourselves would seem to demand that it should not be suffered to circulate longer without the brand of falsehood upon it.

---

[2]*Southern Literary Messenger* 18 (1852): 638, 731.

Let it be recollected, too, that the importance Mrs. Stowe will derive from Southern criticism will be one of infamy. Indeed she is only entitled to criticism at all as the mouthpiece of a large and dangerous faction which, if we do not put down with the pen, we may be compelled one day (God grant that day may never come!) to repel with the bayonet.

There are questions that underlie the story of *Uncle Tom's Cabin* of far deeper significance than any mere false coloring of Southern society. . . . We beg to make a single suggestion to Mrs. Stowe—that, as she is fond of referring to the Bible, she will turn over, before writing her next work of fiction, to the twentieth chapter of Exodus and there read these words—"Thou shalt not bear false witness against thy neighbor." . . .

We have not had the heart to speak of an erring woman as she deserved, though her misconduct admitted of no excuse and provoked the keenest and most just reprobation. We have little inclination—and, if we had much, we have not the time—to proceed with our disgusting labor, to anatomize minutely volumes as full of poisonous vermin as of putrescence, and to speak in such language as the occasion would justify, though it might be forbidden by decorum and self-respect.

We dismiss *Uncle Tom's Cabin* with the conviction and declaration that every holier purpose of our nature is misguided, every charitable sympathy betrayed, every loftier sentiment polluted, every moral purpose wrenched to wrong, and every patriotic feeling outraged, by its criminal prostitution of the high functions of the imagination to the pernicious intrigues of sectional animosity, and to the petty calumnies of willful slander.

3. Mrs. Stowe Inflames the Southern Imagination (1853)

Uncle Tom's Cabin *touched the imaginations of millions of readers. Few Americans, North or South, could regard slavery calmly; the "peculiar institution" inflamed the hearts and even the dreams of Americans on all sides of the issue. For Southerners, Mrs. Stowe's novel could unleash frightful images. This print, first published in Louisville, Kentucky, illustrated a dream supposedly "caused by the perusal" of Mrs. Stowe's novel. Why would a novel critical of slavery prompt such a vision? Was this nightmarish vision confirmed by events? What do the images here suggest were the South's deepest fears about slavery and abolitionism? What is the artist's view of Mrs. Stowe?*

---

[3]Library of Congress, #USZ62-15058.

A. DREAM

Caused by the perusal of Mrs. H. Beecher Stowe's popular work "Uncle Tom's Cabin."

4. The London Times Demurs (1852)

Uncle Tom's Cabin *was also a sensational success abroad, even prompting some Russian noblemen to free their serfs. Lord Palmerston, who had not read a novel in thirty years, devoured this one three times. But the lordly* London Times, *reputedly the semiofficial mouthpiece of the government, was one of the few important journals in England to express strong reservations. In this portion of the lengthy review in the* Times, *how sound is the argument that the book was self-defeating because it would hinder the peaceful abolition of slavery?*

The gravest fault of the book has, however, to be mentioned. Its object is to abolish slavery. Its effect will be to render slavery more difficult than ever of abolishment. Its very popularity constitutes its greatest difficulty. It will keep ill-blood at boiling point, and irritate instead of pacifying those whose proceedings Mrs. Stowe is anxious to influence on behalf of humanity.

---

[4]*London Times,* September 3, 1852.

Uncle Tom's Cabin was not required to convince the haters of slavery of the abomination of the "institution"; of all books, it is the least calculated to weigh with those whose prejudices in favour of slavery have yet to be overcome, and whose interests are involved in the perpetuation of the system. If slavery is to cease in America, and if the people of the United States, who fought and bled for their liberty and nobly won it, are to remove the disgrace that attaches to them for forging chains for others which they will not tolerate on their own limbs, the work of enfranchisement must be a movement, not forced upon slaveowners, but voluntarily undertaken, accepted, and carried out by the whole community.

There is no federal law which can compel the slave states to resign the "property" which they hold. The states of the South are as free to maintain slavery as are the states of the North to rid themselves of the scandal. Let the attempt be made imperiously and violently to dictate to the South, and from that hour the Union is at an end.

We are aware that to the mind of the "philanthropist" the alternative brings no alarm, but to the rational thinkers, to the statesman, and to all men interested in the world's programs, the disruption of the bond that holds the American states together is fraught with calamity, with which the present evil of slavery—a system destined sooner or later to fall to pieces under the weight of public opinion and its own infamy—bears no sensible comparison.

The writer of *Uncle Tom's Cabin* and similar well-disposed authors have yet to learn that to excite the passions of their readers in favour of their philanthropic schemes is the very worst mode of getting rid of a difficulty which, whoever may be to blame for its existence, is part and parcel of the whole social organization of a large proportion of the states, and cannot be forcibly removed without instant anarchy, and all its accompanying mischief.

B. Bleeding Kansas and "Bully" Brooks

1. Charles Sumner Assails the Slavocracy (1856)

The erasing of the Missouri Compromise line in 1854 touched off a frantic tug-of-war between South and North to make Kansas either a slave or a free state. "Border ruffians," pouring into Kansas from slaveholding Missouri by the hundreds, set up a fraudulent but legal government. Resolute pioneers from the North, some of them assisted by the New England Emigrant Aid Company, countered by founding Lawrence, by setting up an extralegal free-soil government, and by seeking admission as a free state. Aroused by the resulting civil war, Senator Charles Sumner of Massachusetts—a handsome, egotistical, and flamingly outspoken abolitionist—assailed the slavery men in a savage two-day speech ("The Crime against Kansas"). He singled out the slaveholding state of South Carolina, and in particular her well-liked Senator Andrew P. Butler, who, declared Sumner, had taken as his "mistress" "the harlot, slavery." What aspects of the speech would be most offensive to a South Carolina "gentleman"?

---

[1]*Congressional Globe,* 34th Congress, 1st session (May 19–20, 1856), Appendix, pp. 530, 543.

If the slave states cannot enjoy what, in mockery of the great Fathers of the Republic, he [Butler] misnames equality under the Constitution—in other words, the full power in the national territories to compel fellow men to unpaid toil, to separate husband and wife, and to sell little children at the auction block—then, sir, the chivalric Senator will conduct the state of South Carolina out of the Union! Heroic knight! Exalted Senator! A second Moses come for a second exodus!

But not content with this poor menace . . . the Senator, in the unrestrained chivalry of his nature, has undertaken to apply opprobrious words to those who differ from him on this floor. He calls them "sectional and fanatical"; and opposition to the usurpation in Kansas he denounces as "an uncalculating fanaticism." To be sure, these charges lack all grace of originality, and all sentiment of truth; but the adventurous Senator does not hesitate. He is the uncompromising, unblushing representative on this floor of a flagrant sectionalism, which now domineers over the Republic. . . .

With regret, I come again upon the Senator from South Carolina [Butler], who, omnipresent in this debate, overflowed with rage at the simple suggestion that Kansas had applied for admission as a state; and, with incoherent phrases, discharged the loose expectoration of his speech,* now upon her representative, and then upon her people. There was no extravagance of the ancient parliamentary debate which he did not repeat. Nor was there any possible deviation from truth which he did not make, with so much of passion, I am glad to add, as to save him from the suspicion of intentional aberration.

But the Senator touches nothing which he does not disfigure—with error, sometimes of principle, sometimes of fact. He shows an incapacity of accuracy, whether in stating the Constitution or in stating the law, whether in the details of statistics or the diversions of scholarship. He cannot ope his mouth but out there flies a blunder. . . .

[Sumner next attacks South Carolina, with its "shameful imbecility" of slavery, for presuming to sit in judgment over free-soil Kansas and block the latter's admission as a free state.]

South Carolina is old; Kansas is young. South Carolina counts by centuries; where Kansas counts by years. But a beneficent example may be born in a day; and I venture to say that against the two centuries of the older state may be already set the two years of trial, evolving corresponding virtue, in the younger community. In the one is the long wail of Slavery; in the other, the hymns of Freedom. And if we glance at special achievements, it will be difficult to find anything in the history of South Carolina which presents so much of heroic spirit in an heroic cause as appears in that repulse of the Missouri invaders by the beleaguered town of Lawrence, where even the women gave their efforts to Freedom. . . .

Were the whole history of South Carolina blotted out of existence, from its very beginning down to the day of the last election of the Senator to his present seat on this floor, civilization might lose—I do not say how little; but surely less than it has already gained by the example of Kansas, in its valiant struggle against oppression, and in the development of a new science of emigration. Already in Lawrence alone there are newspapers and schools, including a high school, and throughout this infant territory there is more mature scholarship far, in proportion to its inhabitants,

---

*Butler suffered from a slight paralysis of the mouth.

than in all South Carolina. Ah, sir, I tell the Senator that Kansas, welcomed as a free state, will be a "ministering angel" to the Republic when South Carolina, in the cloak of darkness which she hugs, "lies howling."

2. The South Justifies Yankee-Beaters (1856)

Southern fire-eaters had already used abusive language in Congress, but Sumner's epithets infuriated Congressman Brooks of South Carolina. Resenting the insults to his state and to his cousin (Senator Butler), he entered the Senate chamber and broke his cane over the head of Sumner, then sitting at his desk. The senator fell bleeding to the floor, while several other members of Congress, perhaps thinking that he was getting his just desserts, made no effort to rescue him. His nervous system shattered, Sumner was incapacitated for about three years; Brooks resigned his seat and was unanimously reelected. A resolution passed by the citizens of his district applauded his exhibition of "the true spirit of Southern chivalry and patriotism" in "chastising, coolly and deliberately, the vile and lawless Sumner." The same group sent him a new cane inscribed, "Use knock-down arguments." What does the following editorial in an Alabama newspaper suggest about the general attitude of the white South and what it portended for the Union?

There are but two papers in the state that we have seen that denounce the chastisement of Sumner by Mr. Brooks as a shameful outrage. One of them is the *Mobile Tribune,* one of the editors of which is a Yankee, and the other is a sheet, the name of which we shall not mention.

With the exception of the papers alluded to, the press of the entire state have fully approved of the course Mr. Brooks pursued, under the circumstances, and recommended that other Southern members of Congress adopt the same method of silencing the foul-mouthed abolition emissaries of the North. Indeed, it is quite apparent, from recent developments, that the shillalah [club] is the best argument to be applied to such low-bred mongrels.

More than six years ago, the abolitionists were told that if they intended to carry out their principles, they must fight. When the Emigrant Aid Societies began to send their [Yankee] tools to Kansas, they were told that if their object was to establish a colony of thieves under the name of "Free State Men," on the border of Missouri, for the purpose of keeping out Southerners and destroying slavery, they must fight. And let them understand that if they intend to carry their abolitionism into Congress, and pour forth their disgusting obscenity and abuse of the South in the Senate Chamber, and force their doctrines down the throats of Southerners, they must fight.

Let [editor Horace] Greeley be severely cowhided, and he will cease to publish his blackguardism about Southern men. Let [Senators] Wilson and Sumner and Seward, and the whole host of abolition agitators in Congress, be chastised to their heart's content, and, our word for it, they will cease to heap abuse upon our citizens.

We repeat, let our Representative in Congress use the cowhide and hickory stick (and, if need be, the bowie knife and revolver) more frequently, and we'll bet our old hat that it will soon come to pass that Southern institutions and Southern men will be respected.

---

[2]*Autauga* (Alabama) *Citizen,* in *The Liberator* (Boston), July 4, 1856.

3. The Delicate Balance (1856)

This chart was prepared for the 1856 presidential election. In what ways does it re-flect growing tension over the slavery controversy?

C. The Dred Scott Decision

1. The Pro-Southern Court Speaks (1857)

Dred Scott, an illiterate Missouri slave, was taken by his master for several years (1834–1838) to the free state of Illinois and then to a portion of Wisconsin Territory now located in the state of Minnesota. The Minnesota area was then free territory, since it lay north of the line of 36° 30''established by the Missouri Compromise of 1820 (subsequently repealed in 1854). Scott, taken in hand by interested abolition-

---

[3]Chicago Historical Society, #Chi-06440.

[1]B. C. Howard, *Reports of Cases Argued and Adjusted in the Supreme Court of the United States* (Newark, N.Y.: The Lawyers Co-operative Publishing Company, 1857).

ists, sued for his freedom on the grounds of residence on free soil. The case was appealed from the circuit court to the Supreme Court, which grappled with several basic questions: Was a slave a citizen under the Constitution? (If not, he was not entitled to sue in the federal courts.) Was Dred Scott rendered free by residence in Wisconsin Territory, under the terms of the Missouri Compromise? The Court, headed by the pro-Southern Chief Justice Roger Taney of the slaveholding state of Maryland, ruled as follows. How were the basic questions answered? What were their implications for the future?

Now . . . the right of property in a slave is distinctly and expressly affirmed in the Constitution. The right to traffic in it, like an ordinary article of merchandise and property, was guaranteed to the citizens of the United States, in every state that might desire it, for twenty years. And the government in express terms is pledged to protect it in all future time, if the slave escapes from his owner. This is done in plain words—too plain to be misunderstood. And no word can be found in the Constitution which gives Congress a greater power over slave property, or which entitles property of that kind to less protection, than property of any other description. The only power conferred is the power coupled with the duty of guarding and protecting the owner in his rights.

Upon these considerations, it is the opinion of the Court that the Act of Congress [Missouri Compromise] which prohibited a citizen from holding and owning property of this kind in the territory of the United States north of the line [of 36° 30'] therein mentioned is not warranted by the Constitution, and is therefore void; and that neither Dred Scott himself, nor any of his family, were made free by being carried into this territory; even if they had been carried there by the owner with the intention of becoming a permanent resident. . . .

Upon the whole, therefore, it is the judgment of this Court that it appears by the record before us that the plaintiff in error [Dred Scott] is not a citizen of Missouri, in the sense in which that word is used in the Constitution; and that the Circuit Court of the United States for that reason had no jurisdiction in the case, and could give no judgment in it.

2. A Virginia Newspaper Gloats (1857)

The South was overjoyed at the Dred Scott decision. The sanctity of slave property was ringingly reaffirmed. A slave could be taken with impunity into the territories and perhaps also into the free states. Even if the territory of Kansas should vote slavery down under popular sovereignty, slaveowners could still keep their slaves. Also pleasing to the South was Chief Justice Taney's observation that in 1776 the blacks were "so far inferior that they had no rights which the white man was bound to respect. . . ." This dictum, torn out of context and applied to the present, enraged the abolitionists. What did the following editorial in a Virginia newspaper portend for an amicable solution of the slave-race problem?

---

[2]*Southside* (Virginia) *Democrat,* in *The Liberator* (Boston), April 3, 1857.

The highest judicial tribunal in the land has decided that the blackamoors, called by the extreme of public courtesy the colored population, are not citizens of the United States. This decision must be followed by other decisions and regulations in the individual states themselves. Negro suffrage must, of course, be abolished everywhere.

Negro nuisances, in the shape of occupying promiscuous seats in our rail-cars and churches with those who are citizens, must be abated. Negro insolence and domineering arrogance must be rebuked; the whole tribe must be taught to fall back into their legitimate position in human society—the position that Divine Providence intended they should occupy. Not being citizens, they can claim none of the rights or privileges belonging to a citizen. They can neither vote, hold office, nor occupy any other position in society than an inferior and subordinate one—the only one for which they are fitted, the only one for which they have the natural qualifications which entitle them to enjoy or possess.

3. The North Breathes Defiance (1857)

The antislavery North was shocked by the Dred Scott decision. If slavery could not be barred from the territories, then the constitutional basis of popular sovereignty was in doubt, and the already unpopular Kansas-Nebraska Act of 1854 was a gigantic hoax. Especially galling was the presence of several slaveholders on the Supreme Court. Various Northern spokesmen denounced the decision as no more binding than that of a Southern debating society. Horace Greeley, editor of the influential New York Tribune, insisted that the Court's findings had no more "moral weight" than the judgment of "a Washington barroom." The rising politician Abraham Lincoln, referring to the "apparent partisan bias" and the numerous dissenting opinions of the Court, branded the decision "erroneous." Judging from the following reaction in a Boston religious journal, was the South justified in feeling that the North was determined to break up the Union?

Shall this decision be submitted to? It need not be. A most righteous decision of the Supreme Court (as we believe), regarding the rights of the Cherokee nation, was made of none effect by the state of Georgia, with the connivance of President Jackson.

The people are mightier than courts or Presidents. The acts of Congress, though declared void, are not repealed. The acts of the free states, though pronounced invalid, still exist. If the people will, they can be maintained and enforced.

Is it said that this is revolutionary counsel? We answer, it is the Southern judges of the Supreme Court who are the authors of revolution. They have enacted a principle contrary to the most plain and obvious sense of the Constitution they pretend to interpret. . . . The most explicit allusion to slaves, in that instrument, describes them as held to service in the states "under the laws thereof," plainly deriving the rights of the master from local, not from common law.

---

[3]*Christian Watchman and Reflector* (Boston), in *The Liberator* (Boston), March 27, 1857.

The decision is also opposed to the unanimous judgment of the statesmen and jurists by whom the Constitution was formed, and to the amplest recorded testimony as to their intentions. It is a doctrine not twenty years old, which those judges, conspiring with the most desperate school of Southern politicians, the men who have been for the space of a generation plotting against the Union, have dared to foist upon the Constitution. It is a sacrilege, against which the blood of our fathers cries from the ground. No man who has in his veins a drop kindred to the blood that bought our liberties can actively submit to their decree.

But if the free states will sit down in the dust, without an effort to vindicate their sovereign rights, if the majority of the people are so fallen away from the spirit of their fathers as to yield their birthright without a struggle, then it becomes the solemn duty of every conscientious freeman to regard the Union of these states as stripped henceforth of all title to his willing allegiance. If the Constitution is a charter to protect slavery, everywhere, then it is a sin against God and man to swear allegiance to it. Every man will be forced to choose between disunion and the guilt of an accomplice in the crime of slavery. May God avert such an alternative!

D. The Lincoln-Douglas Debates

1. Stephen Douglas Opposes Black Citizenship (1858)

With the Illinois senatorship at stake, "Honest Abe" Lincoln boldly challenged Senator Douglas—the "Little Giant"—to a series of joint debates, presumably on current issues. He lost the ensuing election but placed his feet squarely on the path to the White House. The first forensic encounter occurred at Ottawa, Illinois, where the gladiators exchanged the following verbal blows before some twelve thousand partisans. How did Douglas's remarks on this occasion both please and offend the South?

We are told by Lincoln that he is utterly opposed to the Dred Scott decision, and will not submit to it, for the reason that he says it deprives the Negro of the rights and privileges of citizenship. (Laughter and applause.) That is the first and main reason which he assigns for his warfare on the Supreme Court of the United States and its decision.

I ask you, are you in favor of conferring upon the Negro the rights and privileges of citizenship? ("No, no.") Do you desire to strike out of our state constitution that clause which keeps slaves and free Negroes out of the state, and allow the free Negroes to flow in ("Never.") and cover your prairies with black settlements? Do you desire to turn this beautiful state into a free Negro colony ("No, no.") in order that when Missouri abolishes slavery she can send one hundred thousand emancipated slaves into Illinois, to become citizens and voters, on an equality with yourselves? ("Never," "No.")

---

[1]R. P. Basler, ed., *The Collected Works of Abraham Lincoln* (New Brunswick, N.J.: Rutgers University Press, 1953), vol. 3, pp. 9–11.

If you desire Negro citizenship, if you desire to allow them to come into the state and settle with the white man, if you desire them to vote on an equality with yourselves, and to make them eligible to office, to serve on juries, and to adjudge your rights, then support Mr. Lincoln and the Black [pro-Negro] Republican Party, who are in favor of the citizenship of the Negro. ("Never, never.")

For one, I am opposed to Negro citizenship in any and every form. (Cheers.) I believe this government was made on the white basis. ("Good.") I believe it was made by white men for the benefit of white men and their posterity for ever, and I am in favor of confining citizenship to white men, men of European birth and descent, instead of conferring it upon Negroes, Indians, and other inferior races. ("Good for you," "Douglas forever.")

Mr. Lincoln, following the example and lead of all the little abolition orators who go around and lecture in the basements of schools and churches, reads from the Declaration of Independence that all men were created equal, and then asks how can you deprive a Negro of that equality which God and the Declaration of Independence awards to him. He and they maintain that Negro equality is guaranteed by the laws of God, and that it is asserted in the Declaration of Independence. If they think so, of course they have a right to say so, and so vote. I do not question Mr. Lincoln's conscientious belief that the Negro was made his equal, and hence is his brother (Laughter.), but for my own part, I do not regard the Negro as my equal, and positively deny that he is my brother or any kin to me whatever. ("Never," "Hit him again," and cheers.) . . .

Now, I do not believe that the Almighty ever intended the Negro to be the equal of the white man. ("Never, never.") If he did, he has been a long time demonstrating the fact. (Cheers.) . . . He belongs to an inferior race, and must always occupy an inferior position. ("Good," "That's so," etc.)

I do not hold that because the Negro is our inferior that therefore he ought to be a slave. By no means can such a conclusion be drawn from what I have said. On the contrary, I hold that humanity and Christianity both require that the Negro shall have and enjoy every right, every privilege, and every immunity consistent with the safety of the society in which he lives. ("That's so.") On that point, I presume, there can be no diversity of opinion. . . . This is a question which each state and each territory must decide for itself—Illinois has decided it for herself. . . .

Now, I hold that Illinois had a right to abolish and prohibit slavery as she did, and I hold that Kentucky has the same right to continue and protect slavery that Illinois had to abolish it. I hold that New York had as much right to abolish slavery as Virginia has to continue it, and that each and every state of this Union is a sovereign power, with the right to do as it pleases upon this question of slavery, and upon all its domestic institutions.

2. Abraham Lincoln Denies Black Equality (1858)

Lincoln, in his high-pitched voice, parried Douglas's charges, to the delight of his noisy Ottawa supporters, who outnumbered the Douglasites about two to one. When this particular debate ended, the Republicans bore their awkward hero in triumph

---

[2]R. P. Basler, ed., *The Collected Works of Abraham Lincoln* (1953), vol. 3, pp. 13, 16.

from the platform—with his drawn-up trousers, said one observer, revealing the edges of his long underwear. Douglas later claimed that his opponent, beaten and exhausted, was unable to leave under his own power—a charge that angered Lincoln. In the following portion of Lincoln's contribution to the interchange at Ottawa, what portion of his stand was most offensive to Northern abolitionists? to the white South?

My Fellow Citizens: When a man hears himself somewhat misrepresented, it provokes him—at least, I find it so with myself. But when the misrepresentation becomes very gross and palpable, it is more apt to amuse him. (Laughter.) . . .

. . . Anything that argues me into his [Douglas's] idea of perfect social and political equality with the Negro is but a specious and fantastic arrangement of words, by which a man can prove a horse chestnut to be a chestnut horse. (Laughter.)

I will say here, while upon this subject, that I have no purpose directly or indirectly to interfere with the institution of slavery in the states where it exists. I believe I have no lawful right to do so, and I have no inclination to do so. I have no purpose to introduce political and social equality between the white and the black races. There is a physical difference between the two, which in my judgment will probably forever forbid their living together upon the footing of perfect equality, and inasmuch as it becomes a necessity that there must be a difference, I, as well as Judge Douglas, am in favor of the race to which I belong having the superior position.

I have never said anything to the contrary, but I hold that, notwithstanding all this, there is no reason in the world why the Negro is not entitled to all the natural rights enumerated in the Declaration of Independence, the right to life, liberty, and the pursuit of happiness. (Loud cheers.) I hold that he is as much entitled to these as the white man. I agree with Judge Douglas he is not my equal in many respects—certainly not in color, perhaps not in moral or intellectual endowment. But in the right to eat the bread, without leave of anybody else, which his own hand earns, *he is my equal and the equal of Judge Douglas, and the equal of every living man.* (Great applause.)

E. John Brown at Harpers Ferry

1. The Richmond Enquirer Is Outraged (1859)

The fanatical abolitionist John Brown plotted a large slave insurrection at Harpers Ferry in western Virginia. Puchasing arms with about $3,000 provided by sympathetic Northern abolitionists, he launched his abortive enterprise with a score of men, including two of his own sons. Wounded and captured, after the loss of several innocent lives, he was given every opportunity to pose as a martyr while being tried. He was found guilty of three capital offenses: conspiracy with slaves, murder, and treason. Most of the abolitionists who had financed his enterprise ran for cover, although

---

[1]*Richmond Enquirer,* October 25, 1859, in Edward Stone, ed., *Incident at Harpers Ferry* (Englewood Cliffs, N.J.: Prentice-Hall, 1956), p. 177.

many of them had evidently not known of his desperate plan to attack a federal arsenal and bring down on himself the Washington government. The Southerners were angered by the widespread expressions of sympathy for Brown in the North. A week after the raid, the influential Richmond Enquirer *wrote as follows. What is the most alarming aspect of this editorial?*

The Harper's Ferry invasion has advanced the cause of Disunion more than any other event . . . since the formation of the government; it has rallied to that standard men who formerly looked upon it with horror; it has revived, with tenfold strength, the desire of a Southern Confederacy. The heretofore most determined friends of the Union may now be heard saying, "If under the form of a Confederacy [Union] our peace is disturbed, our state invaded, its peaceful citizens cruelly murdered . . . by those who should be our warmest friends, . . . and the people of the North sustain the outrage, then let disunion come."

2. Governor J. A. Wise Refuses Clemency (1859)

It is perhaps surprising that Brown was not lynched instead of being hanged after an orderly, if hurried, trial. Ten of his own men had been killed; six more were tried and hanged. Other casualties that his raid inflicted included seven dead and ten wounded. Pressures of various kinds converged on Governor Wise to extend clemency, and he explained to the legislature as follows why he could not do so. What was the basis for his reasoning?

During the trial of . . . [the Harpers Ferry raiders] and since, appeals and threats of every sort . . . have been made to the Executive. I lay before you the mass of these, it being impossible to enter into their details.

Though the laws do not permit me to pardon in cases of treason, yet pardons and reprieves have been demanded on the grounds of, 1st, insanity; 2nd, magnanimity; 3rd, the policy of not making martyrs.

As to the first, the parties themselves or counsel put in no plea of insanity. No insanity was feigned even; the prisoner Brown spurned it. . . .

As to the second ground . . . : I know of no magnanimity which is inhumane, and no inhumanity could well exceed that to our society, our slaves as well as their masters, which would turn felons like these . . . loose again on a border already torn by a fanatical and sectional strife. . . .

As to the third ground . . . : to hang would be no more martyrdom than to incarcerate the fanatic. The sympathy would have asked on and on for liberation, and to nurse and soothe him, while life lasted, in prison. His state of health would have been heralded weekly, as from a palace . . . ; the work of his hands would have been sought as holy relics. . . .

There is no middle ground of mitigation. To pardon or reprieve at all was to proclaim a licensed impunity to the thousand fanatics who are mad only in the guilt and folly of setting up their individual supremacy over life, law, property, and civil

---

[2]*Richmond Enquirer,* December 6, 1859, in Edward Stone, ed., *Incident at Harpers Ferry* (Englewood Cliffs, N.J.: Prentice-Hall, 1956), p. 177.

liberty itself. The sympathy with the leader was worse than the invasion itself. The appeal was: it is policy to make no martyrs, but disarm murderers, traitors, robbers, insurrectionists, by free pardon for wanton, malicious, unprovoked felons!

3. Horace Greeley Hails a Martyr (1859)

Reactions in the North to Brown's incredible raid ranged from execration to adulation. The most devoted abolitionists, who believed that slavery was so black a crime as to justify violence, defended Brown. The orator Wendell Phillips cried (amid cheers), "John Brown has twice as much right to hang Governor Wise as Governor Wise has to hang him." Ralph Waldo Emerson and Henry David Thoreau publicly likened the execution to the crucifixion of Jesus. Eccentric Horace Greeley, the influential antislavery editor of the New York Tribune, *was denounced by Southerners for having given editorial aid and comfort to John Brown. Greeley replied as follows in an editorial that no doubt reflected the views of countless moderate antislavery people, who deplored the method while applauding the goal. How effectively did Greeley make the point that Brown's crime was no ordinary felony, and to what extent was he anti-Brown?*

John Brown knew no limitations in his warfare on slavery—why should slavery be lenient to John Brown, defeated and a captive?

War has its necessities, and they are sometimes terrible. We have not seen how slavery could spare the life of John Brown without virtually confessing the iniquity of its own existence. We believe Brown himself has uniformly taken this view of the matter, and discountenanced all appeals in his behalf for pardon or commutation, as well as everything savoring of irritation or menace. There are eras in which death is not merely heroic but beneficent and fruitful. Who shall say that this was not John Brown's fit time to die?

We are not those who say, "If slavery is wrong, then John Brown was wholly right." There are fit and unfit modes of combating a great evil; we think Brown at Harper's Ferry pursued the latter. . . . And, while we heartily wish every slave in the world would run away from his master tomorrow and never be retaken, we should not feel justified in entering a slave state to incite them to do so, even if we were sure to succeed in the enterprise. Of course, we regard Brown's raid as utterly mistaken and, in its direct consequences, pernicious.

But his are the errors of a fanatic, not the crimes of a felon. It were absurd to apply to him opprobrious epithets or wholesale denunciations. The essence of crime is the pursuit of selfish gratification in disregard of others' good; and that is the precise opposite of Old Brown's impulse and deed. He periled and sacrificed not merely his own life—that were, perhaps, a moderate stake—but the lives of his beloved sons, the earthly happiness of his family and theirs, to benefit a despised and downtrodden race—to deliver from bitter bondage and degradation those whom he had never seen.

Unwise, the world will pronounce him. Reckless of artificial yet palpable obligations he certainly was, but his very errors were heroic—the faults of a brave, im-

---

[3]*New York Tribune,* December 3, 1859.

pulsive, truthful nature, impatient of wrong, and only too conscious that "resistance to tyrants is obedience to God." Let whoever would first cast a stone ask himself whether his own noblest act was equal in grandeur and nobility to that for which John Brown pays the penalty of a death on the gallows.

And that death will serve to purge his memory of any stain which his errors might otherwise have cast upon it. Mankind are proverbially generous to those who have suffered all that can here be inflicted—who have passed beyond the portals of the life to come. John Brown dead will live in millions of hearts—will be discussed around the homely hearth of toil and dreamed of on the couch of poverty and trial. . . .

Admit that Brown took a wrong way to rid his country of the curse, his countrymen of the chains of bondage, what is the right way? And are we pursuing that way as grandly, unselfishly, as he pursued the wrong one? If not, is it not high time we were? Before censuring severely his errors, should we not abandon our own?

4. Lincoln Disowns Brown (1860)

The South quickly seized upon the John Brown raid as a club with which to belabor the fast-growing Republican party, which allegedly had connived with the conspirators. Rough-hewn Abraham Lincoln, Republican presidential aspirant, came east from Illinois for his make-or-break speech before a sophisticated eastern audience at Cooper Union in New York City. During the course of his address, which was a smashing success, he dealt with the Brown raid. How convincingly did he meet the accusation of Republican complicity, and to what extent was he both pro-Brown and anti-Brown?

You [Southerners] charge that we [Republicans] stir up insurrections among your slaves. We deny it; and what is your proof? Harper's Ferry! John Brown!!

John Brown was no Republican; and you have failed to implicate a single Republican in his Harper's Ferry enterprise. If any member of our party is guilty in that matter, you know it, or you do not know it. If you do know it, you are inexcusable for not designating the man and proving the fact. If you do not know it, you are inexcusable for asserting it, and especially for persisting in the assertion after you have tried and failed to make the proof. You need not be told that persisting in a charge which one does not know to be true is simply malicious slander.

Some of you admit that no Republican designedly aided or encouraged the Harper's Ferry affair, but still insist that our doctrines and declarations necessarily lead to such results. We do not believe it. . . .

Slave insurrections are no more common now than they were before the Republican Party was organized. What induced the Southampton [Nat Turner's] insurrection, twenty-eight years ago, in which at least three times as many lives were lost as at Harper's Ferry? You can scarcely stretch your very elastic fancy to the conclusion that Southampton was "got up by Black Republicanism." In the present state of things in the United States, I do not think a general, or even a very extensive, slave insurrection is possible. . . .

---

[4]J. G. Nicolay and John Hay, eds., *Complete Works of Abraham Lincoln* (New York: The Century Co., 1894), vol. 5, pp. 314–319, passim.

John Brown's effort was peculiar. It was not a slave insurrection. It was an attempt by white men to get up a revolt among slaves, in which the slaves refused to participate. In fact, it was so absurd that the slaves, with all their ignorance, saw plainly enough it could not succeed. That affair, in its philosophy, corresponds with the many attempts, related in history, at the assassination of kings and emperors. An enthusiast broods over the oppression of a people till he fancies himself commissioned by Heaven to liberate them. He ventures the attempt, which ends in little else than his own execution.

F. The Presidential Campaign of 1860 _____

1. Fire-Eaters Urge Secession (1860)

The surprise nomination of Abraham Lincoln for president on the Republican ticket in 1860 precipitated a crisis. Many Southern spokesmen served notice that the election of this backwoods "ape," whose opposition to slavery was grossly exaggerated, would prove that the North no longer wanted the South in the Union. The vitriolic Charleston Mercury, *which had championed nullification as early as 1832, was perhaps the foremost newspaper advocating secession. What grievances does the following editorial cite? Did they justify secession?*

The leaders and oracles of the most powerful party in the United States [Republican] have denounced us as tyrants and unprincipled heathens, through the civilized world. They have preached it from their pulpits. They have declared it in the halls of Congress and in their newspapers. In their schoolhouses they have taught their children (who are to rule this government in the next generation) to look upon the slaveholder as the special disciple of the devil himself. They have published books and pamphlets in which the institution of slavery is held up to the world as a blot and a stain upon the escutcheon of America's honor as a nation.

They have established abolition societies among them for the purpose of raising funds—first to send troops to Kansas to cut the throats of all the slaveholders there, and now to send emissaries among us to incite our slaves to rebellion against the authority of their masters, and thereby endanger the lives of our people and the destruction of our property.

They have brought forth an open and avowed enemy to the most cherished and important institution of the South, as candidate for election to the Chief Magistracy of this government—the very basis of whose political principles is an uncompromising hostility to the institution of slavery under all circumstances.

They have virtually repealed the Fugitive Slave Law, and declare their determination not to abide by the decision of the Supreme Court guaranteeing to us the right to claim our property wherever found in the United States.

And, in every conceivable way, the whole Northern people, as a mass, have shown a most implacable hostility to us and our most sacred rights; and this, too, without the slightest provocation on the part of the South. . . .

_____

[1]*Charleston* (South Carolina) *Mercury,* Sept. 18, 1860.

Has a man's own brother, born of the same parents, a right to invade the sacred precincts of his fireside, to wage war upon him and his family, and deprive him of his property? And if he should do so, the aggrieved brother has not only a right, but it is his duty, sanctioned by every principle of right, to cut off all communication with that unnatural brother, to drive him from the sanctuary of his threshold, and treat him as an enemy and a stranger. Then why should we any longer submit to the galling yoke of our tyrant brother—the usurping, domineering, abolition North!

The political policy of the South demands that we should not hesitate, but rise up with a single voice and proclaim to the world that we will be subservient to the North no longer, but that we will be a free and an independent people. . . .

All admit that an ultimate dissolution of the Union is inevitable, and we believe the crisis is not far off. Then let it come now; the better for the South that it should be today; she cannot afford to wait.

2. The North Resents Threats (1860)

Outstanding among Northern newspapers was the Springfield (Massachusetts) Re-publican. *Edited by the high-strung Samuel Bowles, who was known at times to drive himself forty-eight hours without sleep, it featured straightforward reporting and concise writing. Can you determine, from the following editorial, the extent to which the issue of majority rule was legitimately involved in the North-South dispute?*

The South, through the mouth of many of its leading politicians and journals, defies the North to elect Abraham Lincoln to the Presidency. It threatens secession in case he shall be elected. It arrogantly declares that he shall never take his seat. It passes resolutions of the most outrageous and insolent character, insulting every man who dares to vote for what they call a "Black Republican." To make a long matter very short and plain, they claim the privilege of conducting the government in all the future, as they have in all the past, for their own benefit and their own way, with the alternative of dissolving the Union of the States.

Now, if the non-slaveholding people have any spirit at all, they will settle this question at once and forever. Look at the history of the last two administrations, in which the slave interest has had undisputed sway. This sway, the most disgraceful and shameless of anything in the history of the government, we are told must not be thrown off, else the Union will be dissolved. Let's try it! Are we forever to be governed by a slaveholding minority? Will the passage of four years more of misrule make it any easier for the majority to assume its legitimate functions?

There are many reasons why we desire to see this experiment tried this fall. If the majority cannot rule the country without the secession of the minority, it is time the country knew it. If the country can only exist under the rule of an oligarchy [of slaveowners], let the fact be demonstrated at once, and let us change our institutions. We desire to see the experiment tried, because we wish to have the Southern people, who have been blinded and cheated by the politicians, learn that a "Black Republican" respects the requirements of the Constitution and will protect their in-

---

[2]*Springfield Republican,* August 25, 1860.

terests. Harmony between the two sections of this country can never be secured until the South has learned that the North is not its enemy, but its best friend.

[The "Black Republican" Lincoln was elected president on November 6, 1860. Three days later a New Orleans newspaper declared, "The Northern people, in electing Mr. Lincoln, have perpetrated a deliberate, cold-blooded insult and outrage upon the people of the slaveholding states. . . ." On December 20, a special convention in South Carolina led the secessionist parade by voting 169 to 0 to leave the Union.]

Thought Provokers

1. Why did the fictional *Uncle Tom's Cabin* have more success, as propaganda, than the countless factual accounts published by abolitionists?
2. Compare the reaction of the North to the Dred Scott decision of 1857 with that of the South to the Supreme Court decision of 1954 ordering desegregation. To what extent is it true, as Republicans insisted in 1857, that the people are the court of last resort in this country?
3. Were both Douglas and Lincoln segregationists? Was Douglas more pro–popular sovereignty than he was proslavery? Was Lincoln, as often charged, an abolitionist?
4. In what ways may John Brown's raid be regarded as one of the causes of the Civil War? Since John Brown in Kansas had murdered proslavery men and run off their horses and slaves, how could he be rationally compared to Jesus? Was slavery such a grievous crime, as extreme abolitionists charged, as to justify theft and murder in fighting it?
5. Was Lincoln's election an excuse or a reason for secession? Did the white Southerners have solid grounds for fearing a Republican administration?

21

Girding for War:
The North and the South,
1861–1865

It has long been a grave question whether any
government not too strong for the liberties of its
people can be strong enough to maintain its existence
in great emergencies.

Abraham Lincoln, 1864

Prologue: The seven seceding states formed a provisional government about a
month before the firing on Fort Sumter forced the remaining four laggard sisters into
their camp. In the ensuing conflict the civilian front, both at home and abroad, was
no less important than the fighting front. Northern diplomats strove to keep the European powers out; Southern diplomats strove to drag them in. Britain, the key nation, remained officially neutral because of self-interest. Meanwhile, in America, with
dollars pouring into the maw of the war machine, conscienceless grafters and profiteers on each side grew fat. The Washington and Richmond regimes were both
forced to override constitutional guarantees and deal harshly with critics.

A. Lincoln and the Secession Crisis

1. A Marylander Rejects Disunion (1861)

*By early February 1861, seven Southern states had seceded, taking over most of the
federal forts, arsenals, mints, and other public property. Many Northerners were demanding that "in God's name" the "wayward sisters" be allowed to depart in peace.
At this juncture a stirring cry of protest arose from Henry Winter Davis, a handsome,
eloquent, and ambitious Maryland congressman. He was especially provoked by the
action of the South Carolinians in firing on and driving off from Charleston harbor
an unarmed merchant ship,* Star of the West, *sent to reinforce beleaguered Fort
Sumter. His speech had a profound effect in slaveholding Maryland, and although it
probably cost him his seat in the next election, it helped hold the state in the Union.
What arguments did he make against secession?*

---

[1]*Congressional Globe,* 36th Congress, 2d session (February 7, 1861), Appendix, p. 182.

Mr. Speaker, we are driven to one of two alternatives. We must recognize what we have been told more than once upon this floor is an accomplished fact—the independence of the rebellious states—or we must refuse to acknowledge it, and accept all the responsibilities that attach to that refusal.

Recognize them! Abandon the Gulf and coast of Mexico; surrender the forts of the United States; yield the privilege of free commerce and free intercourse; strike down the guarantees of the Constitution for our fellow citizens in all that wide region; create a thousand miles of interior frontier to be furnished with internal customhouses, and armed with internal forts, themselves to be a prey to the next caprice of state sovereignty; organize a vast standing army, ready at a moment's warning to resist aggression; create upon our southern boundary a perpetual foothold for foreign powers, whenever caprice, ambition, or hostility may see fit to invite the despot of France [Napoleon III] or the aggressive power of England to attack us upon our undefended frontier; sever that unity of territory which we have spent millions, and labored through three generations, to create and establish; pull down the flag of the United States and take a lower station among the nations of the earth; abandon the high prerogative of leading the march of freedom, the hope of struggling nationalities, the terror of frowning tyrants, the boast of the world, the light of liberty—to become the sport and prey of despots whose thrones we consolidate by our fall—to be greeted by Mexico with the salutation: "Art thou also become weak as we? Art thou become like unto us?" This is recognition.

Refuse to recognize! We must not coerce a state in the peaceful process of secession. We must not coerce a state engaged in the peaceful process of secession. We must not coerce a state engaged in the peaceful process of firing into a United States vessel [*Star of the West*] to prevent the reinforcement of a United States fort. We must not coerce states which, without any declaration of war, or any act of hostility of any kind, have united, as have Mississippi, Florida, and Louisiana, their joint forces to seize a public fortress. We must not coerce a state which has planted cannon upon its shores to prevent the free navigation of the Mississippi. We must not coerce a state which has robbed the United States Treasury. This is peaceful secession!

Mr. Speaker, I do not design to quarrel with gentlemen about words. I do not wish to say one word which will exasperate the already too much inflamed state of the public mind. But I say that the Constitution of the United States and the laws made in pursuance thereof must be enforced; and they who stand across the path of that enforcement must either destroy the power of the United States or it will destroy them.

2. Fort Sumter Inflames the North (1861)

Fort Sumter, in Charleston harbor, still flew the Stars and Stripes when Lincoln took office in March 1861. Unwilling either to goad the South into war or to see the garrison starved out, he compromised by announcing that he would send provisions but

---

[2]Morgan Dix, *Memoirs of John Adams Dix* (New York: Harper and Brothers, 1883), vol. 2, p. 9.

not reinforcements. The Southerners, who regarded provisioning as aggression, opened fire. The North rose in instant resentment. Especially important was the reaction of New York City, where the merchants and bankers involved in the cotton trade were plotting treacherous courses. What do the following recollections of a contemporary Episcopal clergyman suggest about the patriotism of the financial world, and about the importance of retaining New York's loyalty?

On Sunday, April 14 [1861], the fact became known that Fort Sumter had surrendered. The excitement created by the bombardment of that fortress and its magnificent defense by Anderson* was prodigious. The outrage on the government of the United States thus perpetrated by the authorities of South Carolina sealed the fate of the new-born Confederacy and the institution of slavery.

Intelligent Southerners at the North were well aware of the consequences which must follow. In the city of New York a number of prominent gentlemen devoted to the interests of the South, and desirous to obtain a bloodless dissolution of the Union, were seated together in anxious conference, studying with intense solicitude the means of preserving the peace. A messenger entered the room in breathless haste with the news: "General Beauregard has opened fire on Fort Sumter!" The persons whom he thus addressed remained a while in dead silence, looking into each other's pale faces; then one of them, with uplifted hands, cried, in a voice of anguish, "My God, we are ruined!"

The North rose as one man. The question had been asked by those who were watching events, "How will New York go?" There were sinister hopes in certain quarters of a strong sympathy with the secession movements; dreams that New York might decide on cutting off from the rest of the country and becoming a free city. These hopes and dreams vanished in a day. The reply to the question how New York would go was given with an energy worthy of herself.

3. Fort Sumter Inspirits the South (1861)

If the Southern attack on Fort Sumter angered the North, it had an exhilarating effect on the South. Gala crowds in Charleston harbor cheered their cannonading heroes. "The Star-Spangled Banner" was rewritten to read:

> *The Star-Spangled Banner in disgrace shall wave*
> *O'er the land of the tyrant, and the home of the knave.*

The Virginia "Submissionists," who had resisted secession, were overwhelmed by the popular clamor. What does the following account from the Daily Richmond Examiner *reveal about the mood of the people? What does it portend for the secession of Virginia and the prolongation of the war?*

---

*Major Robert Anderson, commander of U.S. troops in Charleston harbor.

[3]*Daily Richmond Examiner,* April 15, 1861, in W. J. Kimball, *Richmond in Time of War* (Boston: Houghton Mifflin, 1960), p. 4.

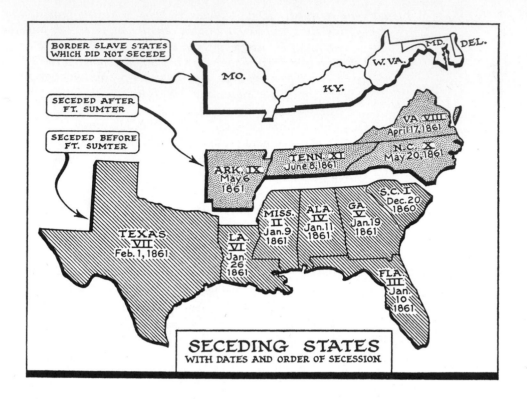

The news of the capture of Fort Sumter was greeted with unbounded enthusiasm in this city. Everybody we met seemed to be perfectly happy. Indeed, until the occasion we did not know how happy men could be. Everybody abuses war, and yet it has ever been the favorite and most honored pursuit of men; and the women and children admire and love war ten times as much as the men. The boys pulled down the stars and stripes from the top of the Capitol (some of the boys were sixty years old), and very properly run [*sic*] up the flag of the Southern Confederacy in its place. What the women did we don't precisely know, but learned from rumor that they praised South Carolina to the skies, abused Virginia, put it to the Submissionists hot and heavy with their two-edged swords, and wound up the evening's ceremonies by playing and singing secession songs until fifteen minutes after twelve on Saturday night.—The boys exploded an infinite number of crackers; the price of tar has risen 25 percent, and sky-rockets and Roman candles can be had at no price, the whole stock in trade having been used up Saturday night. We had great firing of cannon, all sorts of processions, an infinite number of grandiloquent, hifaluting speeches, and some drinking of healths, which has not improved healths; for one half the people we have met since are hoarse from long and loud talking, and the other half have a slight headache, it may be, from long and patriotic libations.

B. Framing a New Government

1. Alexander Hamilton Stephens's Cornerstone Speech (1861)

The same convention that met at Montgomery, Alabama, in February 1861 to frame the Confederate Constitution chose Jefferson Davis as president and Alexander Hamilton Stephens of Georgia, an ex-congressman, as vice president. Stephens was a sallow-complexioned, emaciated figure (seldom weighing more than one hundred pounds) with a piping voice and a fighting spirit. Although opposing secession, he loyally (or disloyally) went along with his state. In this famous speech at Savannah, three weeks before the blowup at Fort Sumter, he spelled out the philosophical basis of the Confederate Constitution. What do his remarks reveal about the white Southern attitude toward the future of slavery?

The new Constitution has put at rest forever all the agitating questions relating to our peculiar institution, African slavery, as it exists amongst us—the proper status of the Negro in our form of civilization. This was the immediate cause of the late rupture and present revolution. Jefferson, in his forecast, had anticipated this as the "rock upon which the old Union would split." He was right. What was conjecture with him is now a realized fact. But whether he fully comprehended the great truth upon which that rock stood and stands may be doubted. The prevailing ideas entertained by him and most of the leading statesmen at the time of the formation of the old Constitution were that the enslavement of the African was in violation of the laws of nature; that it was wrong in principle, socially, morally, and politically.

It was an evil they knew not well how to deal with, but the general opinion of the men of that day was that, somehow or other, in the order of Providence, the institution would be evanescent and pass away. This idea, though not incorporated in the Constitution, was the prevailing idea at the time. . . .

Our new government is founded upon exactly the opposite idea; its foundations are laid, as its cornerstone rests, upon the great truth that the Negro is not equal to the white man; that slavery—subordination to the superior race—is his natural and normal condition. [Applause.]

This, our new government, is the first, in the history of the world, based upon this great physical, philosophical, and moral truth.

2. The New York Times Dissents (1861)

The unabashed prominence that Stephens gave to slavery, though applauded by his audience, was probably a mistaken tactic. Determine why from this direct editorial

---

[1]Henry Cleveland, *Alexander H. Stephens* (Philadelphia and Chicago: National Publishing Company, 1866), p. 721 (March 21, 1861).

[2]*New York Times,* March 27, 1861.

response in the New York Times. *How had Stephens misled this journal with regard to the general motives for secession?*

Mr. Stephens is quite right in saying that this is the *first* government in the history of the world based upon slavery. This present year is the first time in the history of the world when a great community has overthrown a free Constitution, not because of its oppressions, but in order to perpetuate the abject slavery of four millions of its people.

Mr. Stephens apparently sees nothing in this fact of evil omen to the success of his experiment. Indeed, he makes it the chief glory of the new nation that its cornerstone is slavery. He may rest assured the civilized world will take a very different view of this matter. He will find in that declaration a barrier mountain-high against the sympathies of every nation on earth. There is no power so utterly dead to all the impulses of humanity, and to all the influences of Christian civilization, as to look with anything but horror and detestation upon a nation commencing its career for such a motive and with such an aim.

C. British Involvement

I. The London Times *Breathes Easier (1862)*

The British government tried to preserve a cold neutrality during the Civil War. The landed aristocracy, however, with a kindred feeling for the plantation aristocracy of the South, generally hoped for a Confederate victory. Some Britons even argued that their Christian duty required them to intervene and stop the senseless bloodshed. The pontifical London Times *on the whole supported the official policy of nonintervention, and the North could rejoice that it did. So influential was this journal that when it took snuff, the quipsters said, the rest of England sneezed. What does this* Times *editorial suggest about why, as between humanitarian intervention and realistic nonintervention, the British government chose nonintervention?*

The prevalent expectation is that both North and South will suffer unexampled injury, and finally settle down into two or more states, much the wiser and sadder for their bitter experience. Many politicians are only too content to see things take this course.

Indeed, people are breathing more freely, and talking more lightly of the United States, than they have done any time these thirty years. We don't now hear once a twelvemonth that England has complied with some ridiculous demand, or endured some high-flying specimen of American impudence, or allowed them to draw their boundary lines [Maine, Oregon?] as they please. We are no longer stunned every quarter of a year with the tremendous totals of American territory, population, and wealth, computed to come due thirty, sixty, a hundred years hence; when, of course, the tallest empire of the Old World will easily walk between the legs of the American colossus.

---

[1]*London Times,* August 15, 1862.

Nevertheless, the riddance of a nightmare is purchased very dearly at the cost of present suffering. Great as that suffering is, we have assured the Americans over and over again that we have no intention of interfering. If there is any fault to be found with this country, it is that we are too well resigned to the suicidal work of which we are the safe, but not unconcerned, witnesses. It is the old story of the traveller frightened by the tiger and relieved by seeing him immediately afterwards in deadly conflict with some other monster.

2. Britons Hail Democracy's Collapse (1862)

Many British aristocrats derived satisfaction from recalling 1776. Then thirteen colonies, struggling for freedom against King George III, were trying to secede from the British Empire. Now eleven states, struggling for freedom against King Abraham I, were trying to secede from the American Empire. Why did the London Times *believe that the South, in these weeks before Emancipation, had the better moral (if not legal) case? Why could this newspaper maintain that democracy had broken down?*

In this respect, as in others, the South has an immense advantage over the North. The Confederates are fighting in a cause which is at once plain and popular, which they have always avowed, and of which they have never despaired. They are fighting for independence—for possession and enjoyment of their own territories under their own laws, apart from any connection with a people from whom they always differed, and whom they now most cordially detest. . . .

But with the Northerners all is different. They are not content with their own. They are fighting to coerce others, and to retain millions of people in political union with them against their will. This, too, they are doing in spite of the principles on which all American institutions have been notoriously based—principles inculcating the most extreme doctrines of freedom, and deriving all governments from the mere will and assent of the governed. . . .

The principles on which the President and the majority, perhaps, of his coadjutors undertook the war are in themselves by no means indefensible. Mr. Lincoln held that the Constitution of the Union, which he was bound to preserve, did not permit the secession of any of its states, and, though the point is not very clear, it may be allowed that this view of the legal merits of the case was shared in England. We were of opinion that South Carolina had no title, under the provisions of the American Constitution, to proclaim her own independence, and it follows, therefore, that the Supreme Government was entitled to restrain her in such a proceeding.

But when South Carolina was followed by other states, when nine millions of people asserted their claims to self-government, and when it became evident that these claims were based, if not upon law, at any rate upon facts, we were unable to see how the Northerners could with any consistency resist the demand. That they did resist it, and even made an appeal to the sword, was simply a proof that democracies, in this respect, are influenced by the same passions as the most despotic monarchies.

---

[2]*London Times,* September 13, 1862.

Here, in fact, it was that republicanism broke down. The real collapse was not in the secession of the South, but in the resistance of the North. If the Northerners, on ascertaining the resolution of the South, had peaceably allowed the seceders to depart, the result might fairly have been quoted as illustrating the advantages of democracy. But when republicans put empire above liberty, and resorted to political oppression and war rather than suffer any abatement of national power, it was clear that nature at Washington was precisely the same as nature at St. Petersburg.

There was not, in fact, a single argument advanced in defense of the war against the South which might not have been advanced with exactly the same force for the subjugation of Hungary or Poland [by Russia].

Democracy broke down, not when the Union ceased to be agreeable to all its constituent states, but when it was upheld, like any other empire, by force of arms.

3. Southern Resentment Against England (1862)

"Cotton is King!" the Southern fire-eaters had exulted before secession. England was so heavily dependent on the Southern fiber for its vast textile industry that in the event of a North-South clash the British would presumably be forced to intervene on the side of the Confederacy. To the annoyance of Britishers, the Confederates even tried to hasten that day by burning cotton. Late in the second year of the Civil War, England was in the grip of a cotton famine; but, much to the disappointment of the South, the London regime refused even to extend recognition to the Confederates. President Davis openly condemned British partiality toward the North. Why, in the view of the Southern journal quoted here, did Britain want the Union to break up but nevertheless refuse to intervene? Which of the arguments seems most farfetched?

The Confederate States are the only new power she [England] has refused to recognize, and yet they have manifested a degree of strength greater than all those we have enumerated [e.g., Belgium] put together. We have, under these circumstances, we think, some right to be indignant. We have not the smallest right to be astonished.

Great Britain has been trying to bring about the very state of things now existing here ever since the United States became a recognized power of the earth. She never could find it in her heart to forgive the successful revolt of the colonies. . . . In latter days England has been jealous of the growing power of the United States to an inordinate degree. She has clearly foreseen that, if they continue united, they must become, before the close of this century, the first nation of the world, with an invincible army, a navy that must assume the empire of the seas, and a commerce that must swallow up all the commerce of the Old World.

Thus, in addition to the old grudge, she has been stimulated by the fear of losing her position among the powers of the earth. Cost what it might, she has felt that for her the greatest of all objects has been to destroy the Union. She has succeeded at last, and it is not wonderful that she should desire to see the war carried on as long as both parties may have the strength to maintain themselves. She feels that in-

---

[3]*Southern Illustrated News,* October 4, 1862.

tervention would follow recognition, and this she is by no means disposed to undertake, because it might have the effect of shortening the war.

The war in question, besides removing a powerful rival from her path, is useful to her in another respect. If it should last long enough, it may be the means of getting her cotton from India into demand, and it may stimulate the production in Australia. When we consider that cotton constitutes the very basis upon which her enormous power is built, we shall see at once the importance of having it all under her own control. This she hopes to accomplish by destroying the culture in this country, which can only be done by destroying the labor which produces it. The abolition of slavery in her West India possessions was but the preliminary step to the abolition of slavery in this country. . . .

In addition to these causes, it may be that the British Government feels itself in no condition to intervene, because of the present condition in Europe. Affairs are far from satisfactory in Italy, and any moment may witness the outbreak of a general war. As we have already observed, recognition might bring on intervention as a necessary consequence, and intervention would be sure to bring on war. This the British Government will avoid if it can. It already has a most exaggerated opinion of the strength of the Yankee Government, and is evidently very unwilling—we might almost say afraid—to come into collision with it. A late debate in Parliament plainly revealed an extraordinary degree of alarm on the subject of Canada. . . .

These, we think, are the reasons why Great Britain—meaning the British Government—is averse to recognize us. That the majority of the people sympathize with us, while they detest the Yankees, we do not doubt.

4. A Northerner Lambastes Britain (1863)

The South was disillusioned because England did not seem sympathetic enough; the North was angered because England seemed too sympathetic to the South. Several diplomatic crises between London and Washington were narrowly surmounted—the Trent *affair, the building of the cruiser* Alabama, *the Laird rams threat—but the construction of destructive Confederate commerce raiders in England rankled most deeply. Despite the serious shortage of cotton, the British prospered from an enormously expanded two-way trade with the North. George T. Strong, a prominent New York lawyer, here expresses a common view. Was his assessment of England's alleged unneutrality fair? Why was he more bitter toward England than his Southern counterpart in the preceding article?*

April 14 [1863]. We drift fast toward war with England, but I think we shall not reach that point. The shopkeepers who own England want to do us all the harm they can and to give all possible aid and comfort to our slave-breeding and woman-flogging adversary, for England has degenerated into a trader, manufacturer, and banker, and has lost all the instincts and sympathies that her name still suggests. She would declare war against us fast enough if she dared follow her sordid impulses, but there are dirty, selfish considerations on the other side.

[4]Reprinted with the permission of Simon & Schuster from *The Diary of George Templeton Strong,* edited by Allan Nevins and Milton Halsey Thomas. Copyright © 1956 by John Tracy Ellis.

She cannot ally herself with slavery, as she inclines to do, without closing a profitable market, exposing her commerce to [Yankee] privateers, and diminishing the supply of [Northern] breadstuffs on which her operatives depend for life. On the other side, however, is the consideration that by allowing piratical *Alabamas* to be built, armed, and manned in her ports to prey on our commerce, she is making a great deal of money.

It's fearful to think that the sympathies of England—the England of Shakespeare and Hooker, Cowper, Milton, Somers, Erskine, and others—with North or South, freedom or slavery, in this great continental battle of her children, are guided by mere considerations of profit and loss. Anglo-maniac [pro-English] Americans, like myself, are thoroughly "disillusioned."

D. Graft and Shortages North and South

1. Shoddy Wool in Yankeeland (1861–1865)

Great wars invariably inspire devotion and self-sacrifice; they also spawn grafters and chiselers. The Civil War, with all its noble ideals, was no exception. The orgy of greed, which begot the "shoddy millionaires," is here described by General Régis de Trobriand, a French émigré and New York newspaper editor who served as a volunteer officer in the U.S. Army for four years. What gave rise to the conditions he describes?

But besides the army formed to act against the enemy, there was another army—of lobbyists, contractors, speculators—which was continually renewed and never exhausted. These hurried to the assault on the Treasury, like a cloud of locusts alighting down upon the capital to devour the substance of the country. They were everywhere; in the streets, in the hotels, in the offices, at the Capitol, and in the White House. They continually besieged the bureaus of administration, the doors of the Senate and House of Representatives, wherever there was a chance to gain something.

Government, obliged to ask the aid of private industry for every kind of supply that the army and navy must have without delay, was really at the mercy of these hungry spoilers, who combined with one another to make the law for the government. From this arose contracts exceedingly burdensome, which impoverished the Treasury to enrich a few individuals.

As a matter of course, these latter classes, strangers to every patriotic impulse, saw in the war only an extraordinary opportunity of making a fortune. Every means of obtaining it was a good one to them; so that corruption played a great part in the business of contracting. Political protection was purchased by giving an interest in the contracts obtained. . . .

The government . . . was, then, fleeced by the more moderate and robbed by the more covetous. The army suffered from it directly, as the supplies, which were

---

[1]Régis de Trobriand, *Four Years with the Army of the Potomac* (Boston: Tichnor and Company, 1889), pp. 134–136.

furnished at a price which was much above their value if they had been of a good quality, were nearly all of a fraudulent inferiority. For example, instead of heavy woolen blankets, the recruits received, at this time, light, open fabrics, made I do not know of what different substances, which protected them against neither the cold nor the rain. A very short wear changed a large part of the uniform to rags, and during the winter spent at Tenallytown the ordinary duration of a pair of shoes was not longer than twenty or thirty days.

This last fact, well attested in my regiment, was followed by energetic remonstrances, on account of which the general commanding the brigade appointed, according to regulations, a special Board of Inspection, with the object of obtaining the condemnation of the defective articles. Amongst the members of the board was an officer expert in these matters, having been employed, before the war, in one of the great shoe factories of Massachusetts. The report was very precise. It showed that the shoes were made of poor leather, not having been properly tanned; that the inside of the soles was filled with gray paper; and that the heels were so poorly fastened that it needed only a little dry weather following a few days of rain to have them drop from the shoes. In fine, the fraud was flagrant in every way.

The report was duly forwarded to the superior authorities. Did it have any consideration? I never knew. However, it was necessary to exhaust the stock in hand before obtaining a new supply, and the price charged the soldier was not altered.

2. Chiselers in the South (1862–1863)

The myth that the Southern "Cavaliers" gave their all with selfless dedication must be discarded. There was magnificent devotion to the lost cause, but human nature did not change at the Mason and Dixon line. In proportion to numbers, desertion was about as rampant in the South as in the North, especially after Yankee invaders burned the homes of absent soldiers. And in proportion to the amount of graft obtainable, the number of grafters was probably about the same. John B. Jones, a prolific and popular Maryland novelist, worked as a clerk for the Confederate government in Richmond and recorded some bitter observations. What does he reveal about the South's capacity to resist?

[December 1, 1862] God speed the day of peace! Our patriotism is mainly in the army and among the ladies of the South. The avarice and cupidity of the men at home could only be excelled by ravenous wolves; and most of our sufferings are fully deserved. Where a people will not have mercy on one another, how can they expect mercy? They depreciate the Confederate notes [currency] by charging from $20 to $40 per bbl. for flour; $3.50 per bushel for meal; $2 per lb. for butter; $20 per cord for wood, etc. When we shall have peace, let the extortionists be remembered! Let an indelible stigma be branded upon them.

A portion of the people look like vagabonds. We see men and women and children in the streets in dingy and dilapidated clothes; and some seem gaunt and pale with hunger—the speculators, and thieving quartermasters and commissaries only, looking sleek and comfortable. If this state of things continue a year or so longer,

[2]E. S. Miers, ed., *A Rebel War Clerk's Diary* [John B. Jones] (1958), pp. 126, 257, 296.

they will have their reward. There will be governmental bankruptcy, and all their gains will turn to dust and ashes, dust and ashes! . . .

[February 11, 1863] Some idea may be formed of the scarcity of food in this city from the fact that, while my youngest daughter was in the kitchen today, a young rat came out of its hole and seemed to beg for something to eat; she held out some bread, which it ate from her hand, and seemed grateful. Several others soon appeared, and were as tame as kittens. Perhaps we shall have to eat them! . . .

[October 22, 1863] A poor woman yesterday applied to a merchant in Carey Street to purchase a barrel of flour. The price he demanded was $70.

"My God!" exclaimed she, "how can I pay such prices? I have seven children; what shall I do?"

"I don't know, madam," said he, coolly, "unless you eat your children."

3. The Pinch of the Blockade (1861–1865)

The Yankee blockade, which created acute shortages, played into the hands of Southern profiteers. Not all the blockade runners carried munitions of war exclusively. Dr. Paul Barringer, then a small boy in North Carolina, later recalled that an ornately bound copy of Samuel Johnson's Rasselas *came through to his family early in 1865. What do these recollections, edited after his death in 1941, suggest about the effect of the blockade on Southern armies and civilian morale?*

Almost at once we began to feel the pinch of war. White sugar disappeared immediately; not only were there no more lumps for gun-shy horses, but there was no sugar for the table. There was, however, an unlimited quantity of sorghum syrup, and around the barrels of sorghum a thick crust of brown sugar often formed. This was carefully scraped off to be served with coffee and berries, the fluid product going to the servants [slaves]. . . .

In a very short time I noticed that matches had disappeared, and I have learned that at the outbreak of the war there was not one match factory in the South. However, flint and steel had passed out of use so recently that many of these old relics, which were sticking around in closets and hidden recesses in attics, were taken out and returned to use. . . .

Other shortages threatened of which I, as a child, saw only the signs and could not realize the seriousness. Paper was getting so scarce that my elders feared that even the dreaded death lists might cease to come. Then it was discovered that wallpaper could be used, and if properly removed from the walls and bleached, it could be printed on both sides. At the last, they used wallpaper that could not be bleached, printing on one side only. I still have one of these old journals. Framed under glass, it shows pink flowers on one side, while the bloody harvest of war is recorded on the other. . . .

The Federal Government declared all drugs contraband of war, and almost no morphine or quinine came through the blockade. As a substitute for the latter, as I

[3]From *The Natural Bent: The Memoirs of Dr. Paul B. Barringer,* by Paul B. Barringer, pp. 48–53. Copyright (c) 1949, renewed 1977 by The University of North Carolina Press. Reprinted by permission of the publisher.

have already stated, we used boneset tea, which helped but did not cure malaria. To supply opiate we grew our own poppies, making incisions into the sides of the ovaries of these plants and with the flat of a case knife scraping up the exuded gum. The knife was then scraped off on the edge of a glass jar, and thus we found that we could raise gum opium that was 10 or 12 percent morphine.

There was a poppy bed in every garden planted for this purpose, and when I was seven years old I worked daily for the soldiers, scraping the inspissated juice of the poppy from the bulbar ovaries which had been punctured a few days before, and, like everyone else, I worked under the eternal mandate, "Don't taste it!" On some fifty poppy heads it was a morning's work to get a mass about as big as a small peanut.

The time came when no more Chilean nitre could run the blockade, and the South must depend on its own resources for this essential element of explosives. It was then that the urine cart began to make its rounds, collecting the night's urine and hauling it to the boiling vats, where the urea and other nitrogenous constituents were extracted and shipped to Augusta, Georgia, for the manufacture of gunpowder. That plant was never more than a few days ahead of the needs of the firing line.

Later on the need became so great that many old cabins which stood up on four corner posts were raised by levers, so that men could crawl under them to scrape the ground for the thin layer of nitrogen-charged clay at the top. As wondering children, we saw men crawling under old barns to scrape up the dry dust, and we saw old plaster taken from the walls and leached in the ash hopper. We heard that in Virginia and Kentucky searching parties invaded the caves where bats roosted, to scrape the bat manure from the floor. All such gleanings were likewise sent to the plant in Augusta.

Looking back at it now, I can see the reason for that persistent and unceasing call to save and extend every natural resource in every section of the South. The need was desperate, and the toil in the homes, the fields, and the improvised factories was unceasing.

E. Civil Liberties North and South

1. Clement Vallandigham Flays Despotism (1863)

To preserve the Constitution, Lincoln was forced to take liberties with it. His arbitrary acts included a suspension of the writ of habeas corpus, *and a consequent imprisonment without trial of scores of Southern sympathizers. Many Democrats in the North—dubbed Copperheads—condemned such highhanded action. The most notorious of these was Clement L. Vallandigham, an eloquent and outspoken critic of this "wicked and cruel" war. He regarded it as a diabolical attempt to end slavery and inaugurate a Republican despotism. Convicted by a military tribunal in Cincinnati of treasonable utterances, he was banished by Lincoln to the Confederacy. After a*

[1]C. L. Vallandigham, *Speeches, Arguments, Addresses, and Letters* (1864), pp. 486–489.

short stay, he made his way by ship to Canada. From there he ran for the governor-ship of Ohio in 1863 and, though defeated, polled a heavy vote. Some two months before his arrest in 1863 he delivered this flaming speech in New York to a Democratic group, assailing the recent act of Congress that authorized the president to suspend habeas corpus *during the war. Is this speech treasonable? Should* habeas corpus *have been suspended?*

. . . [The Habeas Corpus Act] authorizes the President whom the people made, whom the people had chosen by the ballot box under the Constitution and laws, to suspend the writ of *habeas corpus* all over the United States; to say that because there is a rebellion in South Carolina, a man shall not have freedom of speech, freedom of the press, or any of his rights untrammeled in the state of New York, or a thousand miles distant. That was the very question upon which the people passed judgment in the recent [congressional] elections, more, perhaps, than any other question. . . .

The Constitution gives the power to Congress, and to Congress alone, to suspend the writ of *habeas corpus,* but it can only be done in case of invasion or rebellion, and then only when the public safety requires it. And in the opinion of the best jurists of the land, and indeed of every one previous to these times, Congress could only suspend this writ in places actually in rebellion or actually invaded. That is the Constitution. [Cheers.] And whenever this question shall be tried before a court in the state of New York, or Ohio, or Wisconsin, or anywhere else, before honest and fearless judges worthy of the place they occupy, the decision will be that it is unconstitutional.* [Loud applause.] . . .

Was it this which you were promised in 1860, in that grand [Lincoln] "Wide Awake" campaign, when banners were borne through your streets inscribed "Free speech, free press, and free men"? And all this has been accomplished, so far as the forms of the law go, by the Congress which has just expired. Now, I repeat again that if there is anything wanting to make up a complete and absolute despotism, as iron and inexorable in its character as the worst despotisms of the old world, or the most detestable of modern times, . . . I am unable to comprehend what it is.

All this, gentlemen, infamous and execrable as it is, is enough to make the blood of the coldest man who has one single appreciation in his heart of freedom, to boil with indignation. [Loud applause.] Still, so long as they leave to us free assemblages, free discussion, and a free ballot, I do not want to see, and will not encourage or countenance, any other mode of ridding ourselves of it. ["That's it," and cheers.] We are ready to try these questions in that way. But . . . when the attempt is made to take away those other rights, and the only instrumentalities peaceably of reforming and correcting abuses—free assemblages, free speech, free ballot, and free elections—THEN THE HOUR WILL HAVE ARRIVED WHEN IT WILL BE THE DUTY OF FREE MEN TO FIND SOME OTHER AND EFFICIENT MODE OF DEFENDING THEIR LIBERTIES. [Loud and protracted cheering, the whole audience rising to their feet.]

Our fathers did not inaugurate the Revolution of 1776, they did not endure the sufferings and privations of a seven years' war to escape from the mild and moderate control of a constitutional monarchy like that of England, to be at last, in the

---

*The Supreme Court did not hold the Habeas Corpus Act unconstitutional.

third generation, subjected to a tyranny equal to that of any upon the face of the globe. [Loud applause.]

2. William Brownlow Scolds the Secessionists (1861)

If President Lincoln had his pro-Confederate Copperheads, President Davis had his pro-Union "Tories," chiefly among the mountain whites. If Lincoln had his Vallandigham, Davis had his William G. ("Parson") Brownlow, the fiery and fearless Methodist preacher with a foghorn voice who had become editor of the Knoxville Whig. *This journal was the most influential paper in East Tennessee, and the last Union paper in the South. Though not antislavery, Brownlow was antisecession. His newspaper was suppressed late in 1861, his press was destroyed, and he was imprisoned for treason. The Confederates banished him to the Federal lines—a Vallandigham case in reverse—but he returned to be elected Reconstruction governor of Tennessee in 1865. His defiant flying of a United States flag over his home led him to publish the following statement in his paper on May 25, 1861, two weeks before Tennessee seceded by a popular vote of 104,913 to 47,238. Considering the time of the incident, who acted treasonably—Brownlow or those who displayed the Confederate flag? What does this episode reveal of the strength of Unionism in Tennessee during those anxious weeks?*

It is known to this community and to the people of this county that I have had the Stars and Stripes, in the character of a small flag, floating over my dwelling, in East Knoxville, since February. This flag has become very offensive to certain leaders of the Secession party in this town, and to certain would-be leaders, and the more so as it is about the only one of the kind floating in the city. Squads of troops, from three to twenty, have come over to my house within the last several days, cursing the flag in front of my house, and threatening to take it down, greatly to the annoyance of my wife and children. No attack has been made upon it, and consequently we have had no difficulty.

It is due to the Tennessee troops to say that they have never made any such demonstrations. Other troops from the Southern states, passing on to Virginia, have been induced to do so by certain cowardly, sneaking, white-livered scoundrels residing here, who have not the melt [guts] to undertake what they urge strangers to do. One of the Louisiana squads proclaimed in front of my house, on Thursday, that they were told to take it down by citizens of Knoxville.

Now, I wish to say a few things to the public in connection with this subject. This flag is private property, upon a private dwelling, in a state that has never voted herself out of the Union or into the Southern Confederacy, and it is therefore lawfully and constitutionally under these same Stars and Stripes I have floating over my house. Until the state, by her citizens, through the ballot box, changes her federal relations, her citizens have a right to fling this banner to the breeze. Those who are in rebellion against the government represented by the Stars and Stripes have up the

---

[2]W. G. Brownlow, *Sketches of the Rise, Progress, and Decline of Secession* (Philadelphia: G. W. Childs; Cincinnati: Applegate & Co., 1862), pp. 55–58, passim.

Rebel flag, and it is a high piece of work to deny loyal citizens of the Union the privilege of displaying their colors! . . .

If these God-forsaken scoundrels and hell-deserving assassins want satisfaction [a duel] out of me for what I have said about them—and it has been no little—they can find me on these streets every day of my life but Sunday. I am at all times prepared to give them satisfaction. I take back nothing I have ever said against the corrupt and unprincipled villains, but reiterate all, cast it in their dastardly faces, and hurl down their lying throats their own infamous calumnies.

Finally, the destroying of my small flag or of my town property is a small matter. The carving out of the state upon the mad wave of secession is also a small matter, compared with the great PRINCIPLE involved. Sink or swim, live or die, survive or perish, I am a Union man, and owe my allegiance to the Stars and Stripes of my country. Nor can I, in any possible contingency, have any respect for the government of the Confederate States, originating as it did with, and being controlled by, the worst men in the South. And any man saying—whether of high or low degree—that I am an abolitionist or a Black Republican, is a LIAR and SCOUNDREL.

3. A North Carolinian Is Defiant (1863)

States' rights proved about as harmful to the South as Yankee bayonets. Many Southerners, with their strong tradition of localism, resented or resisted the arbitrary central government in Richmond. William W. Holden, who attacked conscription and other harsh measures, was the recklessly outspoken editor of the Raleigh North Carolina Standard. Probably the most influential paper in the state, it allegedly inspired wholesale desertions. In 1863, when a Georgia regiment destroyed Holden's office, he and his associates retaliated by wrecking the headquarters of a rival secessionist organ. (Scores of similar mob demonstrations occurred in the North against Copperhead journals.) What is ironical and fantastic about the extreme remedy that Holden here proposes, and what extraordinary conditions was he overlooking?

We were told, when the government was broken up by the states south of us, that the contest was to be for liberty; that the civil power was to prevail over the military; that the common government was to be the agent of the states, and not their master; and that free institutions, not an imperial despotism, were to constitute the great object of our toils and sufferings. But the official paper [the Richmond *Enquirer*] has declared otherwise. That paper is opposed to a nobility to be established by law, but it favors a military despotism like that of France. . . .

We know that a military despotism is making rapid strides in these [Confederate] states. We know that no people ever lost their liberties at once, but step by step, as some deadly disease steals upon the system and gradually but surely saps the fountain of life. . . . The argument now is, we hate Lincoln so bitterly that in order to resist him successfully we must make slaves of ourselves. The answer of our people is, we will be slaves neither to Lincoln, nor Davis, nor France, nor England.

North Carolina is a state, not a province, and she has eighty thousand of as brave troops as ever trod the earth. When she calls them they will come. If the worst

---

[3]*North Carolina Standard* (Raleigh), May 6, 1863.

should happen that can happen, she will be able to take care of herself as an independent power. She will not submit, in any event, to a law of [the Confederate] Congress, passed in deliberate violation of the Constitution, investing Mr. Davis with dictatorial powers; but will resist such a law by withdrawing, if necessary, from the Confederation, and she will fight her way out against all comers. . . . For one, we are determined not to exchange one despotism for another.

F. Abraham Lincoln Defines the Purposes of the War

I. The War to Preserve the Union (1863)

In his 1863 Gettysburg Address, President Lincoln defined the war's purpose with unmatched eloquence. What were his principal arguments?

Four score and seven years ago our fathers brought forth on this continent, a new nation, conceived in Liberty, and dedicated to the proposition that all men are created equal.

Now we are engaged in a great civil war, testing whether that nation or any nation so conceived and so dedicated, can long endure. We are met on a great battlefield of that war. We have come to dedicate a portion of that field, as a final resting place for those who here gave their lives that that nation might live. It is altogether fitting and proper that we should do this.

But, in a larger sense, we can not dedicate—we can not consecrate—we can not hallow—this ground. The brave men, living and dead, who struggled here, have consecrated it, far above our poor power to add or detract. The world will little note, nor long remember what we say here, but it can never forget what they did here. It is for us the living, rather, to be dedicated here to the unfinished work which they who fought here have thus far so nobly advanced. It is rather for us to be here dedicated to the great task remaining before us—that from these honored dead we take increased devotion to that cause for which they gave the last full measure of devotion—that we here highly resolve that these dead shall not have died in vain—that this nation, under God, shall have a new birth of freedom—and that government of the people, by the people, for the people, shall not perish from the earth.

2. The War to End Slavery (1865)

Near the war's end, in his Second Inaugural Address, Lincoln again returned to the theme of the war's purpose, but on this occasion he offered a different explanation of the war's goals and meaning than he had two years earlier at Gettysburg. What are

[1]*The Writings of Abraham Lincoln.* Consitutional ed., Vol. VII, p. 20.
[2]James D. Richardson, *A Compilation of the Messages and Papers of the Presidents* (Washington, D.C.: Bureau of National Literature, 1911), 5: 3477–3478.

the major differences? Which considerations do you think weighed most heavily in Lincoln's mind as the war progressed? Did his war aims change over time?

Fellow-Countrymen: At this second appearing to take the oath of the Presidential office there is less occasion for an extended address than there was at the first. Then a statement somewhat in detail of a course to be pursued seemed fitting and proper. Now, at the expiration of four years, during which public declarations have been constantly called forth on every point and phase of the great contest which still absorbs the attention and engrosses the energies of the nation, little that is new could be presented. The progress of our arms, upon which all else chiefly depends, is as well known to the public as to myself, and it is, I trust, reasonably satisfactory and encouraging to all. With high hope for the future, no prediction in regard to it is ventured.

On the occasion corresponding to this four years ago all thoughts were anxiously directed to an impending civil war. All dreaded it, all sought to avert it. While the inaugural address was being delivered from this place, devoted altogther to *saving* the Union without war, insurgent agents were in the city seeking to *destroy* it without war—seeking to dissolve the Union and divide effects by negotiation. Both parties deprecated war, but one of them would *make* war rather than let the nation survive, and the other would *accept* war rather than let it perish, and the war came.

One-eighth of the whole population were colored slaves, not distributed generally over the Union, but localized in the southern part of it. These slaves constituted a peculiar and powerful interest. All knew that this interest was somehow the cause of the war. To strengthen, perpetuate, and extend this interest was the object for which the insurgents would rend the Union even by war, while the Government claimed no right to do more than to restrict the territorial enlargement of it. Neither party expected for the war the magnitude or the duration which it has already attained. Neither anticipated that the *cause* of the conflict might cease with or even before the conflict itself should cease. Each looked for an easier triumph, and a result less fundamental and astounding. Both read the same Bible and pray to the same God, and each invokes His aid against the other. It may seem strange that any men should dare to ask a just God's assistance in wringing their bread from the sweat of other men's faces, but let us judge not, that we be not judged. The prayers of both could not be answered. That of neither has been answered fully. The Almighty has His own purposes. "Woe unto the world because of offenses; for it must needs be that offenses come, but woe to that man by whom the offense cometh." If we shall suppose that American slavery is one of those offenses which, in the providence of God, must needs come, but which, having continued through His appointed time, He now wills to remove, and that He gives to both North and South this terrible war as the woe due to those by whom the offense came, shall we discern therein any departure from those divine attributes which the believers in a living God always ascribe to Him? Fondly do we hope, fervently do we pray, that this mighty scourge of war may speedily pass away. Yet, if God wills that it continue until all the wealth piled by the bondsman's two hundred and fifty years of unrequited toil shall be sunk, and until every drop of blood drawn with the lash shall be paid by another drawn with the sword, as was said three thousand years ago, so still it must be said "the judgments of the Lord are true and righteous altogether."

With malice toward none, with charity for all, with firmness in the right as God gives us to see the right, let us strive on to finish the work we are in, to bind up the nation's wounds, to care for him who shall have borne the battle and for his widow and his orphan, to do all which may achieve and cherish a just and lasting peace among ourselves and with all nations.

Thought Provokers

1. Why did the South secede? Would the North have acquiesced in peaceful coexistence if the South had not fired on Fort Sumter? Which side was the aggressor in starting the war?
2. What were the most distinctive principles of the new Confederate government? Could a government founded on such principles long endure?
3. Why did both North and South regard Britain as unduly partial to the other side? What would probably have happened if the British fleet had intervened to break the blockade? To what extent was democracy an issue in the Civil War?
4. Why were the governments on both sides unable to stop profiteering, graft, and corruption? What special circumstances during the Civil War encouraged such practices?
5. Explain why, in all of the United States' major wars, constitutional guarantees of freedom have suffered infringement. What conditions during the Civil War caused them to be more endangered than during other wars?
6. Lincoln's two speeches—the Gettysburg Address and his Second Inaugural—are inscribed on facing walls of the Lincoln Memorial in Washington, D.C. In what ways do they constitute a fitting summmation of Lincoln's views on the war?

22

The Furnace of Civil War, 1861–1865

Among freemen there can be no successful appeal
from the ballot to the bullet, and . . . they who take
such appeal are sure to lose their case and pay the cost.

Abraham Lincoln, 1863

Prologue: At first Lincoln's sole proclaimed war aim was to preserve the Union—
to squelch secession without necessarily ending slavery. But the failure to end the
war quickly by capturing Richmond in the Peninsula Campaign in the summer of
1862 turned Lincoln toward total war against the South's political, economic, and social order—including slavery. The narrow Union victory at the Battle of Antietam in
September 1862 enabled Lincoln to issue the Emancipation Proclamation on January 1, 1863. The Proclamation changed the character of the war into a struggle for
the preservation of the Union *and* the abolition of slavery. Many white people in the
North greeted this new war aim with indignation, but the cause of antislavery added
luster to the North's moral image abroad. Meanwhile, the North proceeded to drag
the South back into the Union by brute force. The process was slow and frustrating,
until Lincoln finally found in Ulysses S. Grant a general "who fights." General William
Sherman campaigned relentlessly in Georgia and the Carolinas by warring on civilian morale as well as on uniformed armies. Lincoln, who had still not achieved military victory, was in grave danger of being unhorsed in the presidential election of
1864 by dissatisfied Democrats, but his ultimate triumph ensured a bitter-end prosecution of the war. The Confederates, finally forced to their knees by Grant's sledgehammer blows in Virginia, surrendered in the spring of 1865. Lincoln's assassination
just days later brought deification in the North and grave forebodings in the South.

A. Northern War Aims

1. Congress Voices Its Views (1861)

*John J. Crittenden of Kentucky—at various times a cabinet member, a senator, and
a congressman—achieved renown in 1860 by his efforts to work out a last-ditch*

---

[1]*House Journal,* 37th Congress, 1st session (July 22, 1861), p. 123.

compromise over slavery in the territories. After war broke out, one of his sons became a general in the Union army, another (to his father's sorrow) a general in the Confederate army. The older Crittenden, determined not to force slaveholding Kentucky and the other border states out of the Union by a crusade against slavery, shepherded the following new resolution through the House of Representatives in 1861. How was this statement designed to quiet the fears of Confederates, Southern Unionists, and border staters?

Resolved by the House of Representatives of the Congress of the United States, That the present deplorable civil war has been forced upon the country by the disunionists of the Southern states, now in arms against the constitutional government, and in arms around the capital; that in this national emergency, Congress, banishing all feelings of mere passion or resentment, will recollect only its duty to the whole country; that this war is not waged on their part in any spirt of oppression, or for any purpose of conquest or subjugation, or purpose of overthrowing or interfering with the rights or established institutions of those states, but to defend and maintain the supremacy of the Constitution, and to preserve the Union with all the dignity, equality, and rights of the several states unimpaired; and that as soon as these objects are accomplished the war ought to cease.

2. Abolitionists View the War (1863)

Lincoln at first described the Civil War as a struggle to preserve the Union, but many abolitionists had additional war aims; they saw the outbreak of the war as a divine opportunity to extinguish the evil of slavery once and for all. (Before the war began, some antislaveryites had even demanded that the North *secede from the Union, to be rid of the slaveholding South.) The illustration that follows,* The House That Jeff Built, *first published in Massachusetts, depicts the war aims of the abolitionists. How does the illustrator treat the issue of Union? If Lincoln at the start of the conflict had accepted the views advocated in this illustration, would the war have been fought differently? (The text that accompanies the illustration is reprinted on pages 456–457.)*

---

[2]Library of Congress, #USZ62-12963.

THE HOUSE TH

This is the House that Jeff built.

This is the cotton, by rebels call'd king,
(Tho call'd by loyalists no such thing)
That lay in the house that Jeff built

This is the thing by some call'd a man,
Whose trade is to sell all the chattels he can,
From yearlings to adults of life's longest span,
In and out of the house that Jeff built.

These are the shackles, for slaves who suppose
Their limbs are their own, from fingers to toes,
And are prone to believe lies as you can,
That they should n't be sold by that thing call'd a man,
Whose trade is to sell all the chattels he can
From yearlings to adults, of life's longest span,
In and out of the house that Jeff built.

This is the scourge by some call'd the cat.
Smit in the handle, and nine tails to that
'Tis joyous to think that the time's drawing near
When the cat will no longer cause chattels to fear
Nor the ping pong gang of that thing call'd a man
Whose trade is to sell all the chattels he can
From yearlings to adults of life's longest span
In and out of the house that Jeff built

Here the slave driver in transport applies.
Nine tails to his victim, nor heeds her shrill cries.
Alas! that a driver with nine tails his own,
Should be slave to a driver who owns only one.
Allied to some vile thing call'd a man
Whose trade is to sell all the chattels he can.
From yearlings to adults of life's longest span
In and out of the house that Jeff built

Deposited July 3d 1863
Recorded Vol. 38. Page 302.

No 3

FF BUILT

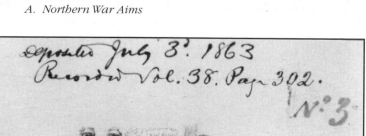

These are field-chattels that made cotton king.
Oh call'd by loyalists no such thing)
The boy in the house that Jeff built

These are the chattels babes, mothers, and men,
To be sold by the head in the slave pen—
A part of the house that Jeff built

These buy the slaves, both male and female
Who sell their own souls to a boss with a tail
Who owns the small soul of that thing call'd a man
Whose trade is to sell all the chattels he can.
From yearlings to adults of life's longest span
In and out of the house that Jeff built

Here the slave breeder parts with heaven first
To a trader down south, in the heart of secesh
Thus trader and breeder secure without fail
The lasting attachment of him with a tail,
Who owns the small soul of that thing called a man
Whose trade is to sell all the chattels he can
From yearlings to adults of life's longest span
In and out of the house that Jeff built

Here's the arch rebel Jeff whose infamous course
Has bro't rest to the plow, and made active the hearse,
And smoked on his head every patriot's curse
Spread ruin and famine, to stock the slave pen.
And furnish employment to that thing among men.
Whose trade is to sell all the chattels he can.
From yearlings to adults of life's longest span;
In and out of the house that Jeff built

But Jeff's infamous house, it doom'd to come down.
So says uncle Sam, and so said John Brown—
With slave pen, and auction, shackles, driver and cat,
Together with seller and buyer and breeder and that
Mean sort of bipeds by some call'd a men.
Whose trade is to sell all the chattels he can.
From yearlings to adults of life's longest span
In and out of the house that Jeff built

The House That Jeff Built*

This is the House that Jeff built.

This is the cotton, by rebels called king,
(Tho' call'd by loyalists no such thing)
That lay in the house that Jeff built.

These are the field chattels that made cotton king,
(Tho' call'd by loyalists no such thing)
That lay in the house that Jeff built.

These are the chattels, babes, mothers, and men,
To be sold by the head, in the slave pen:
A part of the house that Jeff built.

This is the thing by some call'd a man,
Whose trade is to sell all the chattels he can,
From yearlings to adults of life's longest span:
In and out of the house that Jeff built.

These are the shackles, for slaves who suppose
Their limbs are their own, from fingers to toes;
And are prone to believe say all that you can,
That they shouldn't be sold by that thing call'd a man:
Whose trade is to sell all the chattels he can,
From yearlings to adults of life's longest span:
In and out of the house that Jeff built.

These buy the slaves, both male and female,
And sell their own souls to a boss with a tail
Who owns the small soul of that thing called a man:
Whose trade is to sell all the chattels he can,
From yearlings to adults of life's longest span:
In and out of the house that Jeff built.

Here the slave breeder parts with his own flesh
To a trader down south in the heart of secesh
Thus trader and breeder secure without fail
The lasting attachment of him with a tail
Who owns the small soul of that thing called a man
Whose trade is to sell all the chattels he can,
From yearlings to adults of life's longest span:
In and out of the house that Jeff built.

*This is the text that accompanies the illustrations on pp. 454–455.

This is the scourge that some call's the cat
Stout in the handle and nine tails to that
Tis joyous to think that the time's drawing near
When the cat will no longer cause chattels fear
Nor the going, going, gone of that thing call'd a man
Whose trade is to sell all the chattels he can,
From yearlings to adults of life's longest span:
In and out of the house that Jeff built.

Here the slave driver in transport applies
Nine tails to his victim nor heeds her shrill cries
Alas! that a driver with nine tails of his own,
Should be slave to a driver who owns only one:
Albeit he owns that thing call'd a man,
Whose trade is to sell all the chattels he can,
From yearlings to adults of life's longest span:
In and out of the house that Jeff built.

Here's the arch rebel Jeff whose infamous course
Has bro't rest in the plow, and made active the hearse,
And invoked on his head every patriot's curse.
Spread ruin and famine to stock the slave pen,
And furnish employment to that thing among men,
Whose trade is to sell all the chattels he can,
From yearlings to adults of life's longest span:
In and out of the house that Jeff built.

But Jeff's infamous house is doom'd to come down
So says uncle Sam and so said John Brown
With slave pen and auction, shackles, driver, and cat,
Together the seller and buyer and breeder and that
Most loathsome of bipeds by some call'd a man,
Whose trade is to sell all the chattels he can,
From yearlings to adults of life's longest span:
In and out of the house that Jeff built.

2. Abraham Lincoln Answers Horace Greeley's Prayer (1862)

Bespectacled little Horace Greeley, editor of the widely read New York Tribune, *reached the heights of arrogance when he published an open letter to President Lincoln entitled "The Prayer of Twenty Millions." Professing to speak for virtually the entire population of the North, he thundered against the administration for hampering*

---

[2]R. P. Basler, ed., *The Collected Works of Abraham Lincoln* (New Brunswick, N.J.: Rutgers University Press, 1953), vol. 5, 388–389 (August 22, 1862).

the war effort by not coming out bluntly for the emancipation of slaves. Lincoln replied as follows in a public letter. Analyze the qualities of his character that shine through this remarkable statement. Was Lincoln putting expediency above morality? What would he have done if the South had been willing to surrender, subject only to the retention of its slaves?

Dear Sir: I have just read yours of the 19th, addressed to myself through the New York *Tribune.* If there be in it any statements, or assumptions of fact, which I may know to be erroneous, I do not, now and here, controvert them. If there be in it any inferences which I may believe to be falsely drawn, I do not now and here argue against them. If there be perceptible in it an impatient and dictatorial tone, I waive it in deference to an old friend, whose heart I have always supposed to be right.

As to the policy I "seem to be pursuing," as you say, I have not meant to leave anyone in doubt.

I would save the Union. I would save it the shortest way under the Constitution. The sooner the National authority can be restored, the nearer the Union will be "the Union as it was."

If there be those who would not save the Union unless they could at the same time save Slavery, I do not agree with them. If there be those who would not save the Union unless they could at the same time destroy Slavery, I do not agree with them. My paramount object in this struggle is to save the Union, and is not either to save or destroy Slavery.

If I could save the Union without freeing any slave, I would do it; and if I could save it by freeing all the slaves, I would do it; and if I could do it by freeing some and leaving others alone, I would also do that. What I do about Slavery and the colored race, I do because I believe it helps to save this Union; and what I forbear, I forbear because I do not believe it would help to save the Union.

I shall do less whenever I shall believe what I am doing hurts the cause, and I shall do more whenever I shall believe doing more will help the cause. I shall try to correct errors when shown to be errors; and I shall adopt new views so fast as they shall appear to be true views.

I have here stated my purpose according to my view of official duty; and I intend no modification of my oft-expressed personal wish that all men, everywhere, could be free.

B. Lincoln and His Generals

1. George McClellan Snubs the President (1861)

Stocky and well-built General George B. McClellan, a red-mustached West Pointer who sat his horse superbly, was given command of the Union army of the Potomac in 1861, at the unusually young age of thirty-four. A well-trained engineer and tacti-

[1]From *Lincoln and the Civil War in the Diaries and Letters of John Hay,* ed. Tyler Dennett, pp. 34–35.

cian, he was immensely popular with his men, who cheered and waved their caps as he galloped by. But the wine of responsibility and adulation went to his head. Youthful John Hay, Lincoln's private secretary, who later became a world-famous secretary of state, recorded in his diary the following astounding incident. What does it reveal about the characters of McClellan and Lincoln, as well as the general atmosphere of the time?

November 13 [1861]. I wish here to record what I consider a portent of evil to come. The President [Lincoln], Governor Seward, and I went over to McClellan's house tonight. The servant at the door said the General . . . would soon return. We went in, and after we had waited about an hour, McC. came in and without paying any particular attention to the porter, who told him the President was waiting to see him, went upstairs, passing the door of the room where the President and Secretary of State were seated. They waited about half an hour, and sent once more a servant to tell the General they were there, and the answer coolly came that the General had gone to bed.*

I merely record this unparalleled insolence of epaulettes without comment. It is the first indication I have yet seen of the threatened supremacy of the military authorities.

Coming home I spoke to the President about the matter but he seemed not to have noticed it specially, saying it was better at this time not to be making points of etiquette and personal dignity.

[Although Lincoln remarked, "I will hold McClellan's horse, if he will only bring us success," thereafter the president summoned McClellan to the White House whenever he wanted to see him.]

2. McClellan Upbraids His Superior (1862)

General McClellan, though a superb drillmaster and organizer of the Army of the Potomac, suffered from perfectionism and overcaution—"the slows," Lincoln once said. Relying on Pinkerton's Detective Agency, he habitually overestimated the number of his foes, and perceived difficulties more readily than possibilities. Finally prodded by Lincoln into moving, he assaulted the defenses of Richmond in the clumsily roundabout Peninsular Campaign. When he was driven back in bloody fighting by inferior forces (he reported "vastly superior numbers"), he blamed everybody but himself for his failures. He was particularly critical of the Lincoln administration for having failed to provide expected troops. What does his report to Secretary of War William Stanton reveal about his character? To what extent, if any, was he guilty of insubordination, and what may be said in his defense?

. . . My regulars were superb, and I count upon what are left to turn another battle, in company with their gallant comrades of the volunteers. Had I 20,000, or even

---

*It is possible that McClellan had been drinking too heavily at a party.

[2]G. B. McClellan, *McClellan's Own Story* (New York: C. L. Webster & Company, 1887), pp. 424–425 (June 28, 1862).

10,000, fresh troops to use tomorrow, I could take Richmond. But I have not a man in reserve, and shall be glad to cover my retreat and save the material and personnel of the army.

If we have lost the day, we have yet preserved our honor; and no one need blush for the army of the Potomac. I have lost this battle because my force was too small.

I again repeat that I am not responsible for this, and I say it with the earnestness of a general who feels in his heart the loss of every brave man who has been needlessly sacrificed today. I still hope to retrieve our fortunes; but to do this the government must view the matter in the same earnest light that I do. You must send me very large reinforcements, and send them at once. I shall draw back to this side of the Chickahominy [River], and think I can withdraw all our material. Please understand that in this battle we have lost nothing but men, and those the best we have.

In addition to what I have already said, I only wish to say to the President that I think he is wrong in regarding me as ungenerous when I said that my force was too weak. I merely intimated a truth which today has been too plainly proved. If, at this instant, I could dispose of 10,000 fresh men, I could gain the victory tomorrow.

I know that a few thousand more men would have changed this battle from a defeat to a victory. As it is, the government must not and cannot hold me responsible for the result.

I feel too earnestly tonight. I have seen too many dead and wounded comrades to feel otherwise than that the government has not sustained this army. If you do not do so now, the game is lost.

If I save the army now, I tell you plainly that I owe no thanks to you or to any other persons in Washington.

You have done your best to sacrifice this army.

[The supervisor of military telegrams ordered this message toned down before it was shown to the secretary of war. President Lincoln wrote to McClellan that the charge of withholding troops "pains me very much. I give you all I can, and act on the presumption that you will do the best you can with what you have, while you continue, ungenerously I think, to assume that I could give you more if I would. I have omitted, and shall omit, no opportunity to send you reënforcements whenever I possibly can." (J. G. Nicolay and John Hay, eds., Complete Works of Abraham Lincoln *[1894], vol. 7, p. 235.)]*

3. Lincoln Warns General Joseph Hooker (1863)

General McClellan was forced to yield the driver's seat to General John Pope, whom General Lee vanquished at the Second Battle of Bull Run (1862). This setback caused McClellan to look better, and he was now restored to his active command. After holding General Robert E. Lee to only a draw at Antietam, he was replaced by General Ambrose E. Burnside. Lee crushed his new adversary on the battlefield of Fredericksburg late in 1862. "Fighting Joe" Hooker now succeeded Burnside. Tall, robust, bronze-haired, and affable, this energetic West Pointer had already won lau-

---

[3]R. P. Basler, ed., *The Collected Works of Abraham Lincoln* (New Brunswick, N.J.: Rutgers University Press, 1953), vol. 6, pp. 78–79 (January 26, 1863).

rels for his dash and courage amid hailstorms of bullets. Perhaps he was the dictatorial "man on horseback" who, many critics thought, was necessary for victory. Yet this army of 138,000 men was defeated by Lee's 62,500 at the Battle of Chancellorsville, May 2–4, 1863. During much of the fray Hooker was in a daze from a near hit by a cannonball. The letter of appointment that Lincoln had earlier addressed to this ambitious general is one of the most remarkable ever written. What does it reveal of Lincoln's character? What did he most fear from Hooker, and what did he regard as Hooker's greatest disservice to the army?

General:—I have placed you at the head of the Army of the Potomac. Of course I have done this upon what appear to me to be sufficient reasons. And yet I think it best for you to know that there are some things in regard to which I am not quite satisfied with you.

I believe you to be a brave and skillful soldier, which, of course, I like. I also believe you do not mix politics with your profession, in which you are right. You have confidence in yourself, which is a valuable, if not an indispensable, quality. You are ambitious, which, within reasonable bounds, does good rather than harm. But I think that, during General Burnside's command of the army, you have taken counsel of your ambition, and thwarted him as much as you could, in which you did a great wrong to the country, and to a most meritorious and honorable brother officer.

I have heard, in such way as to believe it, of your recently saying that both the army and the government needed a dictator. Of course, it was not for this, but in spite of it, that I have given you the command. Only those generals who gain successes can set up dictators. What I now ask of you is military success, and I will risk the dictatorship. The government will support you to the utmost of its ability—which is neither more nor less than it has done and will do for all commanders.

I much fear that the spirit which you have aided to infuse into the army, of criticizing their commander [Burnside], and withholding confidence from him, will now turn upon you. I shall assist you, as far as I can, to put it down. Neither you nor Napoleon, if he were alive again, could get any good out of an army while such a spirit prevails in it.

And now, beware of rashness. Beware of rashness, but, with energy and sleepless vigilance, go forward and give us victories.

C. The Proclaiming of Emancipation

1. Lincoln Expresses Misgivings (1862)

Preserving the Union was the officially announced war aim of the North. But to many Northern abolitionists and free-soilers the unshackling of the slave was more important. An edict of emancipation would presumably quiet their clamor while strengthening the nation's moral position abroad. Yet such a stroke would antago-

---

[1] J. G. Nicolay and John Hay, eds., *Complete Works of Abraham Lincoln* (1894), vol. 8, pp. 30–33.

nize the slaveholding but still loyal border states, as well as countless Northern Democrats who were fighting for the Union and not for "a passel of slaves." The issuance of an emancipation proclamation after the current series of Northern defeats would, moreover, seem like a last-chance act of desperation. On September 13, 1862, four days before the crucial battle of Antietam and nine days before he issued his preliminary Emancipation Proclamation, Lincoln explained his position to a visiting delegation of Northern Christians from Chicago. What arguments did he give for and against an emancipation proclamation? Was Lincoln concerned with moral considerations primarily? What were his misgivings regarding the constitutionality of emancipation, and to what extent did he regard slavery as the cause of the war?

What good would a proclamation of emancipation from me do, especially as we are now situated? I do not want to issue a document that the whole world will see must necessarily be inoperative, like the Pope's bull against the comet.* Would my word free the slaves, when I cannot even enforce the Constitution in the rebel states? Is there a single court, or magistrate, or individual that would be influenced by it there? And what reason is there to think it would have any greater effect upon the slaves than the late law of Congress, which I approved, and which offers protection and freedom to the slaves of rebel masters who come within our lines? Yet I cannot learn that that law has caused a single slave to come over to us.

And suppose they could be induced by a proclamation of freedom from me to throw themselves upon us, what should we do with them? How can we feed and care for such a multitude? General Butler [in New Orleans] wrote me a few days since that he was issuing more rations to the slaves who have rushed to him than to all the white troops under his command. They eat, and that is all; though it is true General Butler is feeding the whites also by the thousand, for it nearly amounts to a famine there.

If, now, the pressure of the war should call off our forces from New Orleans to defend some other point, what is to prevent the masters from reducing the blacks to slavery again? For I am told that whenever the rebels take any black prisoners, free or slave, they immediately auction them off. They did so with those they took from a boat that was aground in the Tennessee River a few days ago. And then I am very ungenerously attacked for it! For instance, when, after the late battles at and near Bull Run, an expedition went out from Washington under a flag of truce to bury the dead and bring in the wounded, and rebels seized the blacks who went along to help, and sent them into slavery, Horace Greeley said in his paper [*New York Tribune*] that the government would probably do nothing about it. What could I do?

Now, then, tell me, if you please, what possible result of good would follow the issuing of such a proclamation as you desire? Understand, I raise no objections against it on legal or constitutional grounds; for, as commander-in-chief of the army and navy, in time of war I suppose I have a right to take any measure which may

---

*The tale that a terrified Pope Calixtus III excommunicated Halley's comet by a papal bull in 1456 is baseless, but he did decree "several days of prayer for averting the wrath of God . . ." (A. D. White, *A History of the Warfare of Science with Theology* [New York: D. Appleton & Company, 1896], p. 177).

best subdue the enemy. Nor do I urge objections of a moral nature, in view of possible consequences of insurrection and massacre at the South.

I view this matter as a practical war measure, to be decided on according to the advantages or disadvantages it may offer to the suppression of the rebellion.

I admit that slavery is the root of the rebellion, or at least its *sine qua non* [the factor without which it could not exist]. The ambition of politicians may have instigated them to act, but they would have been impotent without slavery as their instrument. I will also concede that emancipation would help us in Europe, and convince them that we are incited by something more than ambition. I grant, further, that it would help somewhat at the North, though not so much, I fear, as you and those you represent imagine. Still some additional strength would be added in that way to the war, and then, unquestionably, it would weaken the rebels by drawing off their laborers, which is of great importance; but I am not so sure we could do much with the blacks. If we were to arm them, I fear that in a few weeks the arms would be in the hands of the rebels; and, indeed, thus far we have not had arms enough to equip our white troops.

I will mention another thing, though it meet only your scorn and contempt. There are fifty thousand bayonets in the Union armies from the border slave states. It would be a serious matter if, in consequence of a proclamation such as you desire, they go over to the rebels. I do not think they all would—but so many, indeed, as a year ago, or six months ago—not so many today as yesterday. Every day increases their Union feeling. They are also getting their pride enlisted, and want to beat the rebels.

Let me say one thing more: I think you should admit that we already have an important principle to rally and unite the people, in the fact that constitutional government [Union] is at stake. This is a fundamental idea going down about as deep as anything.

2. Jefferson Davis Deplores Emancipation (1863)

Seeking to improve the military and moral position of the North, and taking advantage of the recent (limited) Union success at Antietam, Lincoln finally issued his preliminary Emancipation Proclamation on September 22, 1862, nine days after giving such excellent reasons for not doing so. Declaring anew that the preservation of the Union was still his primary goal, he announced that as of January 1, 1863, the slaves would be "forever free" in all areas still in rebellion—areas, in fact, where Lincoln was then powerless to free anybody. He further proclaimed that the Washington government would "do no act or acts to repress" the slaves "in any efforts they may make for their actual freedom." To Southerners, this seemed like an invitation to wholesale insurrection. They upbraided Lincoln "the Fiend," while seriously discussing the advisability of shooting all Yankee prisoners of war, wounded or able-bodied. President Jefferson Davis reacted bitterly as follows in his message to the Confederate Congress. How did his views compare with those of Lincoln, expressed in the preceding section?

[2]J. D. Richardson, comp., *Messages and Papers of the Confederacy* (1904), vol. 1, pp. 290–293, passim (January 12, 1863).

We may well leave it to the instincts of that common humanity which a beneficent Creator has implanted in the breasts of our fellow men of all countries to pass judgment on a measure by which several millions of human beings of an inferior race, peaceful and contented laborers in their sphere, are doomed to extermination, while at the same time they are encouraged to a general assassination of their masters by the insidious recommendation "to abstain from violence unless in necessary self-defense." Our own detestation of those who have attempted the most execrable measure recorded in the history of guilty man is tempered by profound contempt for the impotent rage which it discloses. . . .

In its political aspect this measure possesses great significance, and to it in this light I invite your attention. It affords to our whole people the complete and crowning proof of the true nature of the designs of the party which elevated to power the present occupant of the presidential chair at Washington, and which sought to conceal its purpose by every variety of artful device and by the perfidious use of the most solemn and repeated pledges on every possible occasion. I extract in this connection as a single example the following declaration, made by President Lincoln under the solemnity of his oath of Chief Magistrate of the United States, on the 4th of March, 1861: . . .

"I declare that I have no purpose, directly or indirectly, to interfere with the institution of slavery in the states where it exists. I believe I have no lawful right to do so; and I have no inclination to do so. . . ."

Nor was this declaration of the want of power or disposition to interfere with our social system confined to a state of peace. Both before and after the actual commencement of hostilities the President of the United States repeated in formal official communication to the Cabinets of Great Britain and France that he was utterly without constitutional power to do the act which he has just committed. . . .

This proclamation is also an authentic statement by the Government of the United States of its ability to subjugate the South by force of arms, and as such must be accepted by neutral nations, which can no longer find any justification in withholding our just claims to formal recognition.

3. Border Staters Are Alarmed (1862)

Lincoln did not dare issue his Emancipation Proclamation until he was reasonably sure that the crucial border states would not be driven into the welcoming arms of the Confederacy. Even so, he was careful to exempt from his edict the slaves held in these states, and to hold out to their owners the hope of compensated emancipation. But the border states were quick to perceive that the days of their own slave property were numbered. The fearless editor of the Louisville Journal, *George D. Prentice, a South-adopted Connecticut Yankee who had two sons in the Confederate army, had labored mightily to keep Kentucky in the Union, but even he voiced strong dissent. In his editorial, is he fair in his appraisal of the proclamation, especially its moral implications? Why did he not advocate joining the Confederacy?*

---

[3]Quoted in the *Daily National Intelligencer* (Washington, D.C.), October 8, 1862.

It [the Proclamation] is evidently an arbitrary act of the President as Commander-in-Chief of the army and navy of the Union. In short, it is a naked stroke of military necessity.

We shall not stop now to discuss the character and tendency of this measure. Both are manifest. The one is as unwarrantable as the other is mischievous. The measure is wholly unauthorized and wholly pernicious. Though it cannot be executed in fact, and though its execution probably will never be seriously attempted, its moral influence will be decided, and purely hurtful. So far as its own purpose is concerned, it is a mere *brutum fulmen* [futile display of force], but it will prove only too effectual for the purposes of the enemy [the South]. It is a gigantic usurpation, unrelieved by the promise of a solitary advantage, however minute and faint, but on the contrary aggravated by the menace of great and unmixed evil.

Kentucky cannot and will not acquiesce in this measure. Never! As little will she allow it to chill her devotion to the cause thus cruelly imperiled anew. The government our fathers framed is one thing, and a thing above price; Abraham Lincoln, the temporary occupant of the Executive chair, is another thing, and a thing of comparatively little worth. The one is an individual, the sands of whose official existence are running fast, and who, when his official existence shall end, will be no more or less than any other individual. The other is a grand political structure, in which is contained the treasures and the energies of civilization, and upon whose lofty and shining dome, seen from the shores of all climes, center the eager hopes of mankind.

What Abraham Lincoln, as President, does or fails to do may exalt or lower our estimate of himself, but not of the great and beneficent government of which he is but the temporary servant. The temple is not the less sacred and precious because the priest lays an unlawful sacrifice upon the altar. The loyalty of Kentucky is not to be shaken by any mad act of the President. If necessary, she will resist the act, and aid in holding the actor to a just and lawful accountability, but she will never lift her own hand against the glorious fabric because he has blindly or criminally smitten it. She cannot be so false to herself as this. She is incapable of such guilt and folly.

4. Racist Anxieties (1864)

Jefferson Davis focused on the "political aspects" of emancipation. But Lincoln's liberating manifesto stirred other fears as well. Prior to the Civil War, many critics of slavery, including Thomas Jefferson, had worried about how eventual emancipation might affect social and even sexual relations between the races. The Emancipation Proclamation compelled all Americans to confront this question, and even opponents of slavery expressed anxiety on this score. The anti-Republican illustration on page 466, The Miscegenation Ball, *purported to depict a social event that followed a meeting of the Lincoln Central Campaign Club in New York City in September 1864. Why might readers have found this scene disturbing? How is the typical interracial couple here portrayed?*

---

[3]Library of Congress, #USZ62-14828.

POLITICAL CARICATURE. Nº 4.

UNIVERSAL FREEDOM
ONE CONSTITUTION
ONE DESTINY
ABRAHAM LINCOLN PRE.ST

THE MISCEGENATION BALL

at the Headquarters of the Lincoln Central Campaign Club, Corner of Broadway and Twenty Third Street New York Sept. 22.d 1864 being a perfect fac simile of the room &c. &c. (From the New York World Sept. 23.d 1864) No sooner were the formal proceedings and speeches hurried through with, than the room was cleared for a "negro ball," which then and there took place. Some members of the 'Central Lincoln Club' left the room before the mystical and circling rites of languishing glance and warm dance commenced. But that MANY remained is also true. This fact WE CERTIFY, that on the floor during the progress of the ball were many of the accredited leaders of the Black Republican party, thus testifying their faith by their works in the hall and headquarters of their political gathering. There were Republican OFFICE-HOLDERS, and prominent men of various degrees, and at least one PRESIDENTIAL ELECTOR ON THE REPUBLICAN TICKET."

5. Lincoln's Home Town Applauds (1862)

Northern responses to the Emancipation Proclamation varied. Garrison's abolition-ist Liberator, *though complaining that Lincoln had not gone far enough fast enough, conceded that he had taken a major step in the right direction. Republican journals like the* New York Times *rejoiced that the Union cause was now strong enough to risk this act of military necessity. "God bless Abraham Lincoln!" cried the New York* Christian Inquirer. *Democratic critics were prone to condemn the unconstitutional-ity of the stroke and its shift of war aims to include freeing of the slaves. Others pointed out that Lincoln had indeed issued a "bull against a comet": in those areas where he had no control, he was freeing the slaves; in those others (the border states) where he had control, he refused to do so for reasons of expediency. Lincoln himself confessed keen disappointment over the public reaction. But his home-town newspa-*

---

[4]*Illinois State Journal* (Springfield), September 24, 1862, in Herbert Mitgang, *Lincoln as They Saw Him* (New York: Rinehart, 1956), p. 306.

per, the Illinois State Journal *of Springfield, printed a resounding endorsement. On what legal grounds did it justify this drastic action?*

President Lincoln has at last hurled against rebellion the bolt which he has so long held suspended. The act is the most important and the most memorable of his official career—no event in the history of this country since the Declaration of Independence itself has excited so profound attention either at home or abroad.

While its justice is indisputable, we may well suppose that the step has been taken reluctantly. A people waging a causeless and unholy war against a mild and just government has forfeited the right to protection by that government. No principle is clearer. Yet the President has repeatedly warned the people of the rebellious states to return to their allegiance without effect. He now employs the power with which Congress and the Constitution have clothed him.

There can be but one opinion among all true friends of the country. The President must and will be sustained. That extremists will condemn—one class because emancipation is not immediate and unconditional; the other because it is proclaimed even prospectively—is to be expected. But those who refuse to support the government in the exercise of its necessary and just authority are traitors and should be so treated, whatever name they may wear. True patriots of every name rally around the President, determined that the Union shall be preserved and the laws enforced.

D. The Emancipation Proclamation in England

1. Blackwood's *Blasts Servile War (1862)*

President Jefferson Davis, seeking both the moral support and the active intervention of neutral Europe, predicted that the Emancipation Proclamation would aid the South. He was correct insofar as the ruling class of England was concerned. The London Times *regarded the proclamation as "an incitement to assassination": Lincoln would abolish slavery to punish the rebellious and preserve it to reward the loyal. A member of Parliament branded the president's edict "one of the most devilish acts of fiendish malignity which the wickedness of men could have conceived." The Tory* Blackwood's Edinburgh Magazine, *after letting go the following salvo, vainly besought the London government to intervene by force of arms. Why did the magazine regard the proclamation as an act of bafflement and desperation beyond the pale of civilized warfare?*

The past month has brought us to the veritable crisis of the great Civil War in America. Brought to bay upon their own soil, the Federals in desperation have invoked to their aid the unutterable horrors of a servile war. With their armies baffled and beaten, and with the standards of the rebel army again within sight of Washington, the President has at length owned the impossibility of success in fair warfare, and seeks to paralyze the victorious armies of the South by letting loose upon their hearths and homes the lust and savagery of four million Negroes.

---

[1]*Blackwood's Edinburgh Magazine* 92 (1862): 637.

The die is cast. Henceforth it is a war of extermination. The North seeks to make of the South a desert—a wilderness of bloodshed and misery; for thus only, now, does it or can it hope to overcome the seceding Confederacy. Monstrous, reckless, devilish as the project is, we believe it will not succeed. But it at least marks the crisis and turning point of the war. It shows that the North has shot its last bolt—the effects of which we do not yet see, but beyond which there is no other. It proves what everyone in this country was loath to believe, that rather than let the Southern states be independent, rather than lose their trade and custom, the North would league itself with Beelzebub [the Devil], and seek to make a hell of half a continent.

In return, this atrocious act justifies the South in hoisting the black flag, and in proclaiming a war without quarter against the Yankee hosts. And thus, within the bosom of civilization, we are called upon to contemplate a war more full of horrors and wickedness than any which stands recorded in the world's history.

2. English Working Classes Cheer (1863)

The working class of England, deeply concerned with the dignity of human labor, favored emancipation, despite heavy unemployment caused by the cotton famine. They hailed the proclamation with spontaneous mass meetings. The city of Birmingham alone sent Lincoln a congratulatory address containing ten thousand signatures. Conspicuous among the British friends of the North was a wealthy low-tariff liberal and member of Parliament, Richard Cobden, who had twice visited the United States. He wrote privately to his abolitionist friend, Senator Charles Sumner, as follows. Why did Cobden regard the proclamation as an obstacle to possible British intervention?

You know how much alarmed I was from the first lest our government should interpose in your affairs. The disposition of our ruling class, and the necessities of our cotton trade, pointed to some act of intervention; and the indifference of the great mass of our population to your struggle, the object of which they did not foresee and understand, would have made intervention easy, indeed popular, if you had been a weaker naval power.

This state of feeling existed up to the announcement of the President's emancipation policy. From that moment our old anti-slavery feeling began to arouse itself, and it has been gathering strength ever since. The great rush of the public to all the public meetings called on the subject shows how wide and deep the sympathy for personal freedom still is in the hearts of our people. I know nothing in my political experience so striking as a display of spontaneous public action as that of the vast gathering at Exeter Hall when, without one attraction in the form of a popular orator, the vast building, its minor rooms and passages, and the streets adjoining were crowded with an enthusiastic audience. That meeting has had a powerful effect on our newspapers and politicians. It has closed the mouths of those who have been advocating the side of the South.

And now I write to assure you that any unfriendly act on the part of our government, no matter which of our aristocratic parties is in power, towards your cause

---

[2]Cobden to Sumner, February 13, 1863, in *American Historical Review* 2 (1897): 308–309.

is not to be apprehended. If an attempt were made by the government in any way to commit us to the South, a spirit would be instantly aroused which would drive our government from power. . . .

So much for the influence which your emancipation policy has had on the public opinion of England. But judging from the tone of your press in America, it does not seem to have gained the support of your masses. About this, however, I do not feel competent to offer an opinion. . . .

When I met [John C.] Frémont in Paris two years ago, just as you commenced this terrible war, I remarked to him that the total abolition of slavery in your northern continent was the only issue which could justify the war to the civilized world. Every symptom seems to point to this result. But at what a price is the Negro to be emancipated! I confess that if then I had been the arbiter of his fate, I should have refused him freedom at the cost of so much white men's blood and women's tears. I do not, however, blame the North. The South fired the first shot, and on them righteously falls the malediction that "they who take the sword shall perish by the sword."

E. The Uncivil War

1. A Report from Antietam (1862)

"War is at best barbarism," General William T. Sherman reportedly told a group of military academy graduates. "Its glory is all moonshine. It is only those who have neither fired a shot nor heard the shrieks and groans of the wounded who cry aloud for blood, more vengeance, more desolation. War is hell." What were the most diabolical aspects of the Battle of Antietam, as described by a sixteen-year-old Union soldier in the following account?

The next morning we had our Second battle—it was rather Strange music to hear the balls Scream within an inch of my head. I had a bullett strike me on the top of the head just as I was going to fire and a piece of Shell struck my foot—a ball hit my finger and another hit my thumb. I concluded they ment me. The rebels played the mischief with us by raising a U.S. flag. We were ordered not to fire and as soon as we went forward they opened an awful fire from their batteries on us we were ordered to fall back about ½ miles, I staid behind when our regiment retreated and a line of Skirmishers came up—I joined them and had a chance of firing about 10 times more— . . . Our Generals say they (the rebels) had as strong a position as could *possibly* be and we had to pick into them through an old chopping all grown up with bushes so thick that we couldent hardly get through—but we were so excited that the "old scratch" himself couldent have stopt us.* We rushed onto them every man for himself—all loading & firing as fast as he could see a rebel to Shoot at—at last the rebels began to get over the wall to the rear and run for the woods. The firing encreased tenfold, then it sounded like the rolls of thunder—and all the

[1]Bell Irvin Wiley, *The Life of Billy Yank* (Indianapolis. Bobbs-Merrill, (1952), pp. 84–85.

*[Perhaps a reference to General Zachary Taylor, the hero of the war against Mexico, who was popularly known as "Old Zach."—Ed.]

time evry man shouting as loud as he could—I got rather more excited than I wish to again. I dident *think* of getting hit but it was almost a miricle that I wasent. The rebels that we took prisoners said that they never before encountered a regiment that fought so like "Devils" (so they termed it) as we did—every one praised our regiment—one man in our company was Shot through the head no more than 4 feet from me; he was killed instantly. After the Sunday battle I took care of the wounded until 11 P.M. I saw some of the horidest sights I ever saw—one man had both eyes shot out—and they were wounded in all the different ways you could think of—the most I could do was to give them water—they were all very thirsty— . . . Our Colonel (Withington) was formerly a captain of the Mich 1st—he is just as cool as can be, he walked around amongst us at the battle the bullets flying all around him—he kept shouting to us to fire low and give it to them—

2. The Hell of Andersonville Prison (1864)

Andersonville was the biggest and most infamous of the Confederate stockades for Union prisoners of war. It was hastily erected in Georgia in early 1864, at a time when the South was reeling and desperately short of food, clothing, and medicine. The compound held up to thirty-two thousand prisoners in twenty-six fetid, disease-breeding acres. As many as half of them died. Union military authorities later tried the camp commander, German-born Confederate Captain Henry Wirz, and executed him for murder. Charles Ferren Hopkins was a twenty-year-old soldier with the First New Jersey Volunteers when he was captured at the Battle of the Wilderness in May 1864. Then began his ordeal at Andersonville. What were the worst conditions he had to tolerate? How did he find the will to survive? Was Wirz justly convicted of murder?

The prison was a parallelogram of about two to one as to its length and breadth, about eighteen acres at this time—it was enlarged July 1st to about twenty-seven acres—and one-third of this not habitable, being a swamp of liquid filth. This was enclosed by wooden walls of hewn pine logs, from eight to ten inches square, four feet buried in the ground, eighteen feet above, braced on the outside, cross-barred to make one log sustain the other, and a small platform making comfortable standing room for the guards, every one hundred feet, with above waist-high space below the top of stockade, reached by a ladder. A sloping roof to protect the guards from the sun and rain had been placed over them. Later in 1864 the second line of stockade was built and a third was partly built for protection if attacked by Federal troops, it was said, but we knew it was to discourage us from "tunneling"—the distance being too great. The Florida Artillery had cannon stationed at each corner of the stockade, thus commanding a range from any direction; four guns were so placed near the south gate and over the depressed section of stockade at which point the little stream entered the enclosure.

The "dead line" so much talked of and feared was a line of pine, four-inch boards on posts about three feet high. This line was seventeen feet from the stockade walls, thus leaving the distance all around the enclosure an open space, and in-

---

[2]From Charles F. Hopkins, "Hell and the Survivor," in *American Heritage* (October–November 1982): 78–93. Reprinted by permission of Gerald F. Hopkins.

cidentally reducing the acreage inside and giving the guards a clear view all about the stockade or "bull pen," the name given it by its inventor—the infamous General Winder. . . . To intrude inside this dead line was instant death, or wounds that would cause death, by the rifle of a watchful, ready, willing, murderous guard.

Inside the camp death stalked on every hand. Death at the hand of the guards, though murder in cold blood, was merciful beside the systematic, absolute murder inside, by slow death, inch by inch! As before stated, one-third of the original enclosure was swampy—a mud of liquid filth, voidings from the thousands, seething with maggots in full activity. This daily increased by the necessities of the inmates, being the only place accessible for the purpose. Through this mass of pollution passed the only water that found its way through the Bull Pen. It came to us between the two sources of pollution, the Confederate camp and the cook house; first the seepage of sinks; second, the dirt and filth emptied by the cook house; then was our turn to use it. I have known over three thousand men to wait in line to get water, and the line was added to as fast as reduced, from daylight to dark, yes, even into the night; men taking turns of duty with men of their mess, in order to hold their place in line, as no one man could stand it alone, even if in the "pink" of physical condition; the heat of the sun, blistering him, or drenching rains soaking him, not a breath of fresh air, and we had no covering but Heaven's canopy. The air was loaded with unbearable, fever-laden stench from that poison sink of putrid mud and water, continually in motion by the activity of the germs of death. We could not get away from the stink—we ate it, drank it and slept in it (when exhaustion compelled sleep).

What wonder that men died, or were so miserable as to prefer instant death to that which they had seen hourly taking place, and so preferring, deliberately stepping within the dead line and looking their willing murderer in the eye, while a shot was sent crashing into a brain that was yet clear.

The month of June gave us twenty-seven days of rain—not consecutively, but so frequently that no one was dry in all that time. Everything was soaked—even the sandy soil. Still, this watery month was a blessing in disguise as it gave water, plenty of which was pure to drink. The boost of Winder was that the selection of this spot for his Bull Pen was the place where disease and death would come more quickly by "natural causes," when a removal of two hundred feet east would have placed us upon a living, pure, deep and clear stream of water, properly named "Sweetwater Creek," which had we been allowed to utilize would have saved thousands of lives—but no, that was not the intent of its inventor. To kill by "natural causes" was made more possible by this location.

The average deaths per day for seven and half months were 85. But during the months of July, August, September, and October the average was 100 per day. One day in August, following the great freshet, I counted 235 corpses laying at the south gate and about. Many of those had been smothered in their "burrows" made in the side hill in which they crawled to shield themselves from sun and storm; the soil, being sandy, became rain soaked and settled down upon the occupant and became his grave instead of a protection. Others, who had no shelter, in whom life was barely existing, were rain-soaked, chilling blood and marrow, and life flitted easily away, and left but little to return to clay. These holes or burrows in both the flats and up the north slope were counted by thousands; no doubt there were some that never gave up their dead, the men buried in their self-made sepulcher. No effort was made to search unless the man was missed by a friend.

Such were Winder's "natural causes"!! These were murders committed by most "unnatural causes" and methods—systematic causes! Orders were issued that all should be vaccinated, and yet in all that den of filth, dirt, starvation, polluted water, vermin, flies, reeking with the filth of the open sinks, and polluted swamp mosquitoes ever at hand, smallpox cut no figure whatever, to October at least. Squads of ninety were ordered up to the gate for their possible death warrant, vaccination. Some were fortunate enough not to "take"; others, the moment they were treated and could turn aside, wiped the vaccine off and cleansed the spot by sucking the blood from it in order that no vaccine virus be left to work its destruction; some evaded by tricks and lies. The writer did his own "scratching" and covered the wound with mucous from his mouth—which may have been as dangerous had it been left to work its "scurvy" destiny—and bared his arm for inspection, which was no trouble, as my shirt was armless. The inspector passed me as "done." By this deception we perhaps escaped a death that hundreds found at the hands of those who had used impure vaccine matter.

The famous Providence Spring, so much read of, was made possible by the great storm and freshet of August 9, 1864. It broke in the stockade near the south gate, inside the dead line, and swept to the lower side and broke through there also. Near the north gate, some fifty to sixty feet south on the slope, the heavy downpour of rain rushed down the slope inside the dead line and under the strata of sand, found a clay bottom, and struck a small thread of pure water, and food-famished prisoners feasted their eyes on it for days. It grew a little larger and promised hope to those who might be able to drink of its purity. Being out of reach, all sorts of devices were invented to get some of it. The coy little life-giving stream persistently wriggled its way inside the dead line, though we were glad to welcome it to our side of death's border. Small it was but to that camp would have been like drinking diamonds—so precious were its drops to the minds of those that knew not pure water for months.

Wirz, the helpmate of the devil, concluded that even those precious drops of nature's nectar, so hardly and dangerously earned, were entirely too good for the "damned Yankees," and would in a measure defeat his "natural causes" system of death, and right here is where Providence Spring comes to our rescue. Wirz sent a force of Negroes into camp to stop the flow of water of this Providence Spring. Their efforts were in vain—fruitless, but ho! how fruitful to us poor wretches as the stream of life resented the brutal interference of Wirz, and in its wrath burst forth a torrent compared to its original flow. All the curses and demoniacal ravings of Wirz availed him nothing—he could not stop it or turn it away, being located so that it reached us eventually. We now could get water from near the dead line—pure as crystal. Wirz went so far as to lead it out of reach, yet its flow of pure water into the former reekings and seepings of the Rebel sinks was still a vast improvement, for it purified the stream and increased the flow.

3. General William Sherman Dooms Atlanta (1864)

General William T. Sherman, a tall, red-bearded West Pointer from Ohio, under-stood and liked the South better than most other Northerners did. He was in fact teaching in a military academy in Louisiana when war erupted. Yet he became one of the earliest practitioners of "total war"—that is, breaking the morale of the civilians in order to break the backbone of the military. Before leaving captured Atlanta on his spectacular march to the sea, he ordered the inhabitants to evacuate the city, pending its destruction as a military measure. In response to an appeal from the city fathers that he would work a cruel hardship on pregnant women, invalids, widows, orphans, and others in an area already overflowing with refugees, he sent the following reply. Was his position ethical?

Gentlemen: I have your letter of the 11th, in the nature of a petition to revoke my orders removing all the inhabitants from Atlanta. I have read it carefully, and give full credit to your statements of the distress that will be occasioned, and yet shall not revoke my orders, because they were not designed to meet the humanities of the case, but to prepare for the future struggles in which millions of good people outside of Atlanta have a deep interest.

We must have peace, not only at Atlanta, but in all America. To secure this, we must stop the war that now desolates our once happy and favored country. To stop war, we must defeat the rebel armies which are arrayed against the laws and Constitution that all must respect and obey. To defeat those armies, we must prepare the way to reach them in their recesses, provided with the arms and instruments which enable us to accomplish our purpose.

Now, I know the vindictive nature of our enemy, that we may have many years of military operations from this quarter; and, therefore, deem it wise and prudent to prepare in time. The use of Atlanta for warlike purposes is inconsistent with its character as a home for families. There will be no manufactures, commerce, or agriculture here for the maintenance of families, and sooner or later want will compel the inhabitants to go. Why not go now, when all the arrangements are completed for the transfer, instead of waiting till the plunging shot of contending armies will renew the scenes of the past month? Of course, I do not apprehend any such thing at this moment, but you do not suppose this army will be here until the war is over. I cannot discuss this subject with you fairly, because I cannot impart to you what we propose to do, but I assert that our military plans make it necessary for the inhabitants to go away, and I can only renew my offer of services to make their exodus in any direction as easy and comfortable as possible.

You cannot qualify war in harsher terms than I will. War is cruelty, and you cannot refine it; and those who brought war into our country deserve all the curses and maledictions a people can pour out. I know I had no hand in making this war, and I know I will make more sacrifices today than any of you to secure peace. But you cannot have peace and a division of our country. If the United States submits to a di-

[3]*Memoirs of General William T. Sherman* (New York: D. Appleton and Company, 1887), vol. 2, pp. 125–127 (letter of September 12, 1864).

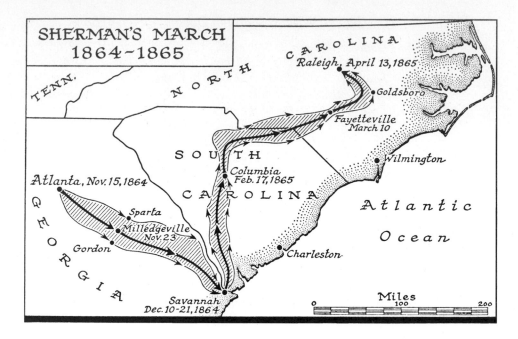

vision now, it will not stop, but will go on until we reap the fate of Mexico, which is eternal war.

The United States does and must assert its authority, wherever it once had power; for, if it relaxes one bit to pressure, it is gone, and I believe that·such is the national feeling. This feeling assumes various shapes, but always comes back to that of Union. Once admit the Union, once more acknowledge the authority of the national Government, and, instead of devoting your houses and streets and roads to the dread uses of war, I and this army become at once your promoters and supporters, shielding you from danger, let it come from what quarter it may. I know that a few individuals cannot resist a torrent of error and passion, such as swept the South into rebellion, but you can point out, so that we may know those who desire a government, and those who insist on war and its desolation.

You might as well appeal against the thunderstorm as against these terrible hardships of war. They are inevitable, and the only way the people of Atlanta can hope once more to live in peace and quiet at home, is to stop the war, which can only be done by admitting that it began in error and is perpetuated in pride.

We don't want your Negroes, or your horses, or your houses, or your lands, or anything you have, but we do want and will have a just obedience to the laws of the United States. That we will have, and, if it involves the destruction of your improvements, we cannot help it.

You have heretofore read public sentiment in your newspapers, that live by falsehood and excitement; and the quicker you seek for truth in other quarters, the better. I repeat then that, by the original compact of government, the United States had certain rights in Georgia, which have never been relinquished and never will be; that the South began war by seizing forts, arsenals, mints, custom-houses, etc., etc., long before Mr. Lincoln was installed, and before the South had one jot or tittle of provocation.

I myself have seen in Missouri, Kentucky, Tennessee, and Mississippi, hundreds of thousands of women and children fleeing from your armies and desperadoes, hungry and with bleeding feet. In Memphis, Vicksburg, and Mississippi, we fed thousands upon thousands of the families of rebel soldiers left on our hands, and whom we could not see starve.

Now that war comes home to you, you feel very different. You deprecate its horrors, but did not feel them when you sent carloads of soldiers and ammunition, and molded shells and shot, to carry war into Kentucky and Tennessee, to desolate the homes of hundreds and thousands of good people who only asked to live in peace at their old homes, and under the government of their inheritance.

But these comparisons are idle. I want peace, and believe it can only be reached through union and war, and I will ever conduct war with a view to perfect and early success.

But, my dear sirs, when peace does come, you may call on me for anything. Then will I share with you the last cracker, and watch with you to shield your homes and families against danger from every quarter.

Now you must go, and take with you the old and feeble, feed and nurse them, and build for them, in more quiet places, proper habitations to shield them against the weather until the mad passions of men cool down, and allow the Union and peace once more to settle over your old homes at Atlanta. Yours in haste,

W. T. Sherman, Major-General commanding

4. Georgia Damns the Yankees (1864)

After burning much of Atlanta, General Sherman daringly cut loose from his base of supplies, and headed for the sea. Forced to live off the country, he detailed soldiers (loosely called "bummers") to round up poultry, livestock, and other provisions. This type of foraging degenerated at times into pillaging, which was aggravated by bands of lawless civilians from both North and South. What light does this passage from the diary of a returning Georgia woman cast on the effectiveness of Sherman's methods, the state of Southern morale, and the prospect of North-South harmony after the war?

December 24, 1864.—About three miles from Sparta [Georgia] we struck the "Burnt Country," as it is well named by the natives, and then I could better understand the wrath and desperation of these poor people. I almost felt as if I should like to hang a Yankee myself. There was hardly a fence left standing all the way from Sparta to Gordon. The fields were trampled down and the road was lined with carcasses of horses, hogs, and cattle that the invaders, unable either to consume or to carry away with them, had wantonly shot down, to starve out the people and prevent them from making their crops. The stench in some places was unbearable; every few hundred yards we had to hold our noses or stop them with the cologne Mrs. Elzey had given us, and it proved a great boon.

The dwellings that were standing all showed signs of pillage, and on every plantation we saw the charred remains of the gin-house and packing-screw, while

---

[4]Eliza F. Andrews, *The War-Time Journal of a Georgia Girl* (New York: D. Appleton and Company, 1908), pp. 32–33.

here and there lone chimney-stacks, "Sherman's sentinels," told of homes laid in ashes. The infamous wretches! I couldn't wonder now that these poor people should want to put a rope round the neck of every red-handed "devil of them" they could lay their hands on.

Hay ricks and fodder stacks were demolished, corn-cribs were empty, and every bale of cotton that could be found was burnt by the savages. I saw no grain of any sort, except little patches they had spilled when feeding their horses and which there was not even a chicken left in the country to eat. A bag of oats might have lain anywhere along the road without danger from the beasts of the fields, though I cannot say it would have been safe from the assaults of hungry man.

Crowds of [Confederate] soldiers were tramping over the road in both directions; it was like traveling through the streets of a populous town all day. They were mostly on foot, and I saw numbers seated on the roadside greedily eating raw turnips, meat skins, parched corn—anything they could find, even picking up the loose grains that Sherman's horses had left. I felt tempted to stop and empty the contents of our provision baskets into their laps, but the dreadful accounts that were given of the state of the country before us made prudence get the better of our generosity.

Before crossing the Oconee [River] at Milledgeville we ascended an immense hill, from which there was a fine view of the town, with Governor Brown's fortifications in the foreground and the river rolling at our feet. The Yankees had burnt the bridge; so we had to cross on a ferry. There was a long train of vehicles ahead of us, and it was nearly an hour before our turn came; so we had ample time to look about us. On our left was a field where thirty thousand Yankees had camped hardly three weeks before. It was strewn with the debris they had left behind, and the poor people of the neighborhood were wandering over it, seeking anything they could find to eat, even picking up grains of corn that were scattered around where the Yankees had fed their horses. We were told that a great many valuables were found there at first, plunder that the invaders had left behind, but the place had been picked over so often by this time that little now remained except tufts of loose cotton, piles of half-rotted grain, and the carcasses of slaughtered animals, which raised a horrible stench. Some men were plowing in one part of the field, making ready for next year's crop.

5. General Ulysses S. Grant Displays Generosity (1865)

While Sherman was ravaging Georgia and the Carolinas, General Grant was slowly grinding his way into Virginia. Superior Union forces finally drove General Lee into a corner, and at Appomattox the sloppily dressed General Grant met with the handsomely attired General Lee to discuss terms of surrender. The following version is taken from Grant's Memoirs, *which he completed on his deathbed in 1885 while suffering agony from cancer of the throat. (Although he did not live to see the two volumes published, they netted his indebted widow more than $400,000 in royalties.) At the time of the surrender negotiations there were still several Confederate armies in the field, and there was a real possibility that the Civil War would degenerate into*

---

[5]*Personal Memoirs of U.S. Grant* (New York: C. L. Webster and Co., 1886), vol. 2, pp. 492–493.

a protracted guerilla war. In the light of these circumstances, comment on Grant's generosity, described in his Memoirs *as follows.*

Then, after a little further conversation, General Lee remarked to me again that their army was organized a little differently from the army of the United States (still maintaining by implication that we were two countries); that in their army the cavalrymen and artillerists owned their own horses; and he asked if he was to understand that the men who so owned their horses were to be permitted to retain them. I told him that as the terms were written they would not; that only the officers were permitted to take their private property. He then, after reading over the terms a second time, remarked that that was clear.

I then said to him that I thought this would be about the last battle of the war—I sincerely hoped so; and I said further I took it that most of the men in the ranks were small farmers. The whole country had been so raided by the two armies that it was doubtful whether they would be able to put in a crop to carry themselves and their families through the next winter without the aid of the horses they were then riding. The United States did not want them and I would, therefore, instruct the officers I left behind to receive the paroles of his troops to let every man of the Confederate army who claimed to own a horse or mule take the animal to his home. Lee remarked again that this would have a happy effect.

[On the day that Lee asked Grant for surrender terms (April 7, 1865), the Richmond Evening Whig *published the following obituary notice:*

DIED: CONFEDERACY, SOUTHERN.—At the late residence of his father, J. Davis, Richmond, Virginia, Southern Confederacy, aged 4 years. Death caused by strangulation. No funeral.]

6. An Abolitionist Officer Commands Black Troops (1869)

In late 1861 Union forces seized Port Royal, a heavily slave-populated sea island off the South Carolina coastal town of Beaufort. For the remainder of the war, Port Royal served as a kind of laboratory for abolitionist experiments in how to deal with freed slaves. Among the most striking developments at Port Royal was the raising of the first black regiment mustered into the Union forces. Thomas Wentworth Higginson (1823–1911), a Harvard-educated Unitarian minister and outspoken abolitionist, sailed south in 1862 to take up his new command as a colonel in the black First South Carolina Volunteers. After the war he published a remarkable book about his experiences, from which the following excerpt is taken. What did Higginson find most gratifying about the character and behavior of his troops? Is he ever condescending about them? What do his reflections suggest about the abolitionist temperament? about the freed slaves' aspirations?

Thanksgiving-Day; it is the first moment I have had for writing during these three days, which have installed me into a new mode of life so thoroughly that they

[6]Thomas Wentworth Higginson, *Army Life in a Black Regiment* (Boston: Lee and Shepard, 1882), pp. 8–10, 247–258.

seem three years. Scarcely pausing in New York or in Beaufort, there seems to have been for me but one step from the camp of a Massachusetts regiment to this, and that step over leagues of waves. . . .

Numerous plantation-buildings totter around, all slovenly and unattractive, while the interspaces are filled with all manner of wreck and refuse, pigs, fowls, dogs, and omnipresent Ethiopian infancy. All this is the universal Southern panorama; but five minutes' walk beyond the hovels and the live-oaks will bring one to something so unSouthern that the whole Southern coast at this moment trembles at the suggestion of such a thing,—the camp of a regiment of freed slaves. . . .

Already I am growing used to the experience, at first so novel, of living among five hundred men, and scarce a white face to be seen,—of seeing them go through all their daily processes, eating, frolicking, talking, just as if they were white. Each day at dress-parade I stand with the customary folding of the arms before a regimental line of countenances so black that I can hardly tell whether the men stand steadily or not; black is every hand which moves in ready cadence as I vociferate, "Battalion! Shoulder arms!" nor is it till the line of white officers moves forward, as parade is dismissed, that I am reminded that my own face is not the color of coal. . . .

It needs but a few days to show the absurdity of distrusting the military availability of these people. They have quite as much average comprehension as whites of the need of the thing, as much courage (I doubt not), as much previous knowledge of the gun, and, above all, a readiness of ear and of imitation, which, for purposes of drill, counterbalances any defect of mental training. To learn the drill, one does not want a set of college professors; one wants a squad of eager, active, pliant school-boys; and the more childlike these pupils are the better. There is no trouble about the drill; they will surpass whites in that. As to camp-life, they have little to sacrifice; they are better fed, housed, and clothed than ever in their lives before, and they appear to have few inconvenient vices. They are simple, docile, and affectionate almost to the point of absurdity. The same men who stood fire in open field with perfect coolness, on the late expedition, have come to me blubbering in the most irresistibly ludicrous manner on being transferred from one company in the regiment to another. . . .

[After describing his life with the First South Carolina Volunteers, Higginson in his concluding chapters tells some of the life stories of his individual troops and reflects on the meaning of their life in slavery and under arms.]

There was another family of brothers in the regiment named Miller. Their grandmother, a fine-looking old woman, nearly seventy, I should think, but erect as a pine-tree, used sometimes to come and visit them. She and her husband had once tried to escape from a plantation near Savannah. They had failed, and had been brought back; the husband had received five hundred lashes, and while the white men on the plantation were viewing the punishment, she was collecting her children and grandchildren, to the number of twenty-two, in a neighboring marsh, preparatory to another attempt that night. They found a flat-boat which had been rejected as unseaworthy, got on board,—still under the old woman's orders,—and drifted forty miles down the river to our lines. Trowbridge happened to be on board the gunboat which picked them up, and he said that when the "flat" touched the side of the vessel, the grandmother rose to her full height, with her youngest grandchild in her arms, and said only, "My God! are we free?" By one of those coincidences of which life is full, her husband escaped also, after his punishment, and was taken up by the same gunboat.

I hardly need point out that my young lieutenants did not have to teach the principles of courage to this woman's grandchildren.

I often asked myself why it was that, with this capacity of daring and endurance, they had not kept the land in a perpetual flame of insurrection; why, especially since the opening of the war, they had kept so still. The answer was to be found in the peculiar temperament of the races, in their religious faith, and in the habit of patience that centuries had fortified. The shrewder men all said substantially the same thing. What was the use of insurrection, where everything was against them? They had no knowledge, no money, no arms, no drill, no organization,— above all, no mutual confidence. It was the tradition among them that all insurrections were always betrayed by somebody. . . .

It always seemed to me that, had I been a slave, my life would have been one long scheme of insurrection. But I learned to respect the patient self-control of those who had waited till the course of events should open a better way. When it came they accepted it. Insurrection on their part would at once have divided the Northern sentiment; and a large part of our army would have joined with the Southern army to hunt them down. By their waiting till we needed them, their freedom was secured.

Two things chiefly surprised me in their feeling toward their former masters,— the absence of affection and the absence of revenge. I expected to find a good deal of the partriarchal feeling. It always seemed to me a very ill-applied emotion, as connected with the facts and laws of American slavery,—still I expected to find it. I suppose that my men and their families and visitors may have had as much of it was the mass of freed slaves; but certainly they had not a particle. I never could cajole one of them, in his most discontented moment, into regretting "ole mas'r time" for a single instant. I never heard one speak of the masters except as natural enemies. Yet they were perfectly discriminating as to individuals; many of them claimed to have had kind owners, and some expressed great gratitude to them for particular favors received. It was not the individuals, but the ownership, of which they complained. That they saw to be a wrong which no special kindnesses could right. On this, as on all points connected with slavery, they understood the matter as clearly as Garrison or Phillips; the wisest philosophy could teach them nothing as to that, nor could any false philosophy befog them. After all, personal experience is the best logician.

Certainly this indifference did not proceed from any want of personal affection, for they were the most affectionate people among whom I had ever lived. They attached themselves to every officer who deserved love, and to some who did not; and if they failed to show it to their masters, it proved the wrongfulness of the mastery. On the other hand, they rarely showed one gleam of revenge, and I shall never forget the self-control with which one of our best sergeants pointed out to me, at Jacksonville, the very place where one of his brothers had been hanged by the whites for leading a party of fugitive slaves. He spoke of it as a historic matter, without any bearing on the present issue.

But side by side with this faculty of patience, there was a certain tropical element in the men, a sort of fiery ecstasy when aroused, which seemed to link them by blood with the French Turcos, and made them really resemble their natural enemies, the Celts, far more than the Anglo-Saxon temperament. To balance this there were great individual resources when alone,—a sort of Indian wiliness and subtlety of resource. Their gregariousness and love of drill made them more easy to keep in hand than white American troops, who rather like to straggle or go in little squads, looking out for themselves, without being bothered with officers. The blacks prefer organization.

The point of inferiority that I always feared, though I never had occasion to prove it, was that they might show less fibre, less tough and dogged resistance, than whites, during a prolonged trial,—a long, disastrous march, for instance, or the hopeless defence of a besieged town. I should not be afraid of their mutinying or running away, but of their drooping and dying. It might not turn out so; but I mention it for the sake of fairness, and to avoid overstating the merits of these troops. As to the simple general fact of courage and reliability I think no officer in our camp ever thought of there being any difference between black and white. And certainly the opinions of these officers, who for years risked their lives every moment on the fidelity of their men, were worth more than those of all the world beside.

No doubt there were reasons why this particular war was an especially favorable test of the colored soldiers. They had more to fight for than the whites. Besides the flag and the Union, they had home and wife and child. They fought with ropes round their necks, and when orders were issued that the officers of colored troops should be put to death on capture, they took a grim satisfaction. It helped their *esprit de corps* immensely. With us, at least, there was to be no play-soldier. Though they had begun with a slight feeling of inferiority to the white troops, this compliment substituted a peculiar sense of self-respect. And even when the new colored regiments began to arrive from the North my men still pointed out this difference,— that in case of ultimate defeat, the Northern troops, black or white, would go home, while the First South Carolina must fight it out or be re-enslaved. . . .

I cannot conceive what people at the North mean by speaking of the negroes as a bestial or brutal race. Except in some insensibility to animal pain, I never knew of an act in my regiment which I should call brutal. In reading Kay's "Condition of the English Peasantry" I was constantly struck with the unlikeliness of my men to those therein described. This could not proceed from my prejudices as an abolitionist, for they would have led me the other way, and indeed I had once written a little essay to show the brutalizing influences of slavery. I learned to think that we abolitionists had underrated the suffering produced by slavery among the negroes, but had overrated the demoralization. Or rather, we did not know how the religious temperament of the negroes had checked the demoralization. Yet again, it must be admitted that this temperament, born of sorrow and oppression, is far more marked in the slave than in the native African. . . .

The point of greatest laxity in their moral habits—the want of a high standard of chastity—was not one which affected their camp life to any great extent, and it therefore came less under my observation. But I found to my relief that, whatever their deficiency in this respect, it was modified by the general quality of their temperament, and indicated rather a softening and relaxation than a hardening and brutalizing of their moral natures. Any insult or violence in this direction was a thing unknown. I never heard of an instance. It was not uncommon for men to have two or three wives in different plantations,—the second, or remoter, partner being called a "'broad wife,"—i.e. wife abroad. But the whole tendency was toward marriage, and this state of things was only regarded as a bequest from "mas'r time."

I knew a great deal about their marriages, for they often consulted me, and took my counsel as lovers are wont to do,—that is, when it pleased their fancy. Sometimes they would consult their captains first, and then come to me in despairing appeal. "Cap'n Scroby [Trowbridge] he acvise me not for marry dis lady, 'cause she hab seben chil'en. What for use? Cap'n Scroby can't lub for me. I mus' lub for myself, and I lub he." I remember that on this occasion "he" stood by, a most attractive woman, jet black, with an old pink muslin dress, torn white cotton gloves, and a very flowery bonnet, that must have descended through generations of tawdry mistresses.

I felt myself compelled to reaffirm the decision of the inferior court. The result was as usual. They were married the next day, and I believe that she proved an excellent wife, though she had seven children, whose father was also in the regiment. If she did not, I know many others who did, and certainly I have never seen more faithful or more happy marriages than among that people.

F. Lincoln's Reelection and Assassination

1. The South Bemoans Lincoln's Election (1864)

President Lincoln, though savagely criticized by many, was renominated in 1864. His opponent was slow-moving General McClellan, the deposed war hero, whom the Democrats nominated on a peace-at-almost-any-price platform, and for whose election the Confederates were praying. Leaving nothing to chance, the Republicans rounded up the soldier vote and, aided by timely military success, swept Lincoln to victory. Northern newspapers hailed the result as a triumph for the democratic processes. Southern journals reacted differently—notably the jaundiced Richmond Dispatch, *which had branded Lincoln "the Ape." Can you account for this newspaper's extreme bitterness, and for its conviction that the election had not been a free one?*

Yesterday [election day] will be long remembered in the annals of mankind. On yesterday, twenty millions of human beings, but four years ago esteemed the freest population on earth, met at various points of assemblage for the purpose of making a formal surrender of their liberties . . . to a vulgar tyrant who has never seen a shot fired in anger; who has no more idea of statesmanship than as a means of making money; whose career has been one of unlimited and unmitigated disaster, whose personal qualities are those of a low buffoon, and whose most noteworthy conversation is a medley of profane jests and obscene anecdotes—a creature who has squandered the lives of millions without remorse and without even the decency of pretending to feel for their misfortunes; who still cries for blood and for money in the pursuit of his atrocious designs. . . .

It seems strange to us that he should have condescended to submit to an election at all; and we are convinced he would never have done so had he not been convinced beforehand that it would result in his favor. How McClellan could ever have been so infatuated as to thrust himself in his way, we are unable to conceive. The

---

[1]*Richmond Dispatch,* November 9, 1864.

light punishment he had to expect was to be crushed, for he might have felt assured that, even had he been elected, he would not have been allowed to take his seat.

All the preparations of Lincoln indicate a determination to take possession of the government by force—his military arrangements; the stationing of soldiers about the polls; the arrest of the New York commissioners; the prohibition against any tickets but his own in the fleet; his jealous supervision of the voting in the army— all these indicate a determination to conquer by the ballot box if possible, but, in any event, to conquer. How could McClellan expect to weather such a storm as his adversary had it in his power to raise at any moment of the day? . . .

We are prone to believe that every nation enjoys the exact proportion of free-dom to which it is entitled. If the Yankees have lost their liberties, therefore, we think it self-evident that it is because they never deserved to have them. If they are slaves, it is because they are fit for the situation. Slaves they have been for years to all the base passions that are indicative of a profligate and degenerate race; and when na-tions advance to that point, the transition to material bondage costs but a single step.

2. Davis Deplores Lincoln's Murder (1881)

On Good Friday, April 14, 1865, Lincoln was shot in the head at close range by a half-crazed actor, John Wilkes Booth. The North was outraged. Frenzied mobs wrecked the headquarters of a number of Copperhead newspapers that displayed unconvincing grief or unconcealed satisfaction. Many unthinking Southerners ex-pressed secret or open joy. But others had sobering second thoughts. Jefferson Davis, who was then fleeing and who was falsely suspected of plotting the foul deed, recorded his impressions some sixteen years later. Why did Davis regard the assassi-nation as a great misfortune?

We arrived at Charlotte [North Carolina] on April 18, 1865, and I there received, at the moment of dismounting, a telegram from General Breckinridge announcing, on information received from General Sherman, that President Lincoln had been assassinated.

An influential citizen of the town, who had come to welcome me, was standing near me, and, after remarking to him in a low voice that I had received sad intelli-gence, I handed the telegram to him. Some troopers encamped in the vicinity had collected to see me; they called to the gentleman who had the dispatch in his hand to read it, no doubt supposing it to be army news. He complied with their request, and a few, only taking in the fact but not appreciating the evil it portended, cheered, as was natural at news of the fall of one they considered their most powerful foe. The man who invented the story of my having read the dispatch with exultation had free scope for his imagination, as he was not present, and had no chance to know whereof he bore witness, even if there had been any foundation of truth for his fiction.

For an enemy so relentless in the war for our subjugation, we could not be ex-pected to mourn; yet, in view of its political consequences, it could not be regarded otherwise than as a great misfortune to the South. He had power over the Northern

---

[2]Jefferson Davis, *The Rise of the Confederate Government* (New York: D. Appleton and Company, 1881), vol. 2, p. 683.

people, and was without personal malignity toward the people of the South. His successor [Andrew Johnson of Tennessee] was without power in the North, and the embodiment of malignity toward the Southern people, perhaps the more so because he had betrayed and deserted them in the hour of their need.

3. The British Press Recants (1865)

The British journals, which had been highly critical of Lincoln, were shocked by his assassination into substituting commendation for criticism. A conspicuous exception was the Tory London Standard, *which ungraciously declared, "He was not a hero while he lived, and therefore his cruel murder does not make him a martyr." The magisterial* London Times, *which had referred to the president as "Lincoln the Last," ate crow in generous amounts. Was Britain's concern wholly sentimental?*

. . . A space of twenty-four hours has sufficed not only to fill the country with grief and indignation, but to evoke almost unprecedented expression of feeling from constituted bodies. . . . In the House of Lords the absence of precedent for such a manifestation was actually made the subject of remark.

That much of this extraordinary feeling is due to the tragical character of the event and the horror with which the crime is regarded is doubtless true, nor need we dissemble the fact that the loss which the Americans have sustained is also thought our own loss is so far as one valuable guarantee for the amity of the two nations may have been thus removed.

But, upon the whole, it is neither the possible embarrassment of international relations nor the infamous wickedness of the act itself which has determined public feeling. The preponderating sentiment is sincere and genuine sympathy—sorrow for the chief of a great people struck down by an assassin, and sympathy for that people in the trouble which at a crisis of their destinies such a catastrophe must bring.

Abraham Lincoln was as little of a tyrant as any man who ever lived. He could have been a tyrant had he pleased, but he never uttered so much as an ill-natured speech. . . . In all America there was, perhaps, not one man who less deserved to be the victim of this revolution than he who has just fallen.

4. A Kentucky Editor Laments (1865)

The border state of Kentucky, precariously loyal during the Civil War, reacted to the murder of its most famous son with mixed emotions. Some seventy miles from the site of the log cabin in which the infant Lincoln had first seen the light of day, the editor of the Frankfort Commonwealth *penned the following sad tribute to "our noble and beloved President," stricken down, unarmed, defenceless and unwarned, by the hand of a rebel assassin." Why did this newspaper regard the tragedy as a calamity for the South?*

---

[3]*London Times,* April 29, 1865.
[4]*Frankfort Commonwealth,* April 18, 1865, in Herbert Mitgang, Lincoln as They Saw Him (New York: Rinehart, 1956), pp. 474–475.

LINCOLN IS DEAD. The awful fact which these few words convey has filled the land with mourning. How suddenly had it turned our joy to sadness, our gladness to grief. In the very midst of our rejoicing over the late triumph of the Union over the rebellion, of our joy in view of the ending of our civil strife, and of our thoughts and purposes of love towards those who have brought all these troubles upon us at whose hands we have so greatly suffered, this crushing blow has come upon us, turning the light to darkness, our happiness to misery, our laughter to tears. God in mercy grant it may not, too, turn our thoughts of peace and love towards our enemies into purposes of deadly hate and implacable revenge.

LINCOLN IS DEAD. They have conspired against his life, have sought and taken it, towards whom he had not one thought of hate, to whom he had again and again made most gracious offers of peace and pardon, and for whose kind and merciful reception back to their old places in the Union, his last thoughts and work were given. Truly they knew not what they did—when Abraham Lincoln fell, the South lost its best and truest friend.

LINCOLN IS DEAD. He has fallen at his post, working for the restoration of the Union to its old harmony and prosperity. And in this work there was an earnest desire to serve his whole country. In his heart there was no hate of the rebellious South, no feeling of revenge on account of the terrible wrongs it had inflicted upon our happy land, no bitterness of spirit towards those who continually maligned and traduced him. By the bands of love he would draw back those of rebellion to their old allegiance. Thus have they rewarded him.

LINCOLN IS DEAD. He has given his life a sacrifice for ours. That the Union might be preserved and the enjoyment of life, liberty and property be insured to us and our posterity, he called the people to arms after the blow struck at Sumter. For that, and for all that he has done well and wisely for the suppression of the rebellion, he has incurred the hatred of rebels in arms and their sympathizers in our midst. This hatred has bred vengeance, and vengeance has done its base, cowardly work in the assassination of our President. Thus he has laid down his life for ours—he has fallen a martyr to his country's cause, and in his country's memory his praise shall ever live.

Thought Provokers

1. Why did Lincoln believe that the ideal of Union was more important than that of freeing the slave? Which had the greater emotional appeal, and why?
2. Was there danger of a military dictatorship in the North during the Civil War?
3. In what respects did the Emancipation Proclamation prove to be statesmanlike? Why was it so late in coming?
4. In view of the earlier British emancipation of slaves, why should Britain's ruling class have criticized Lincoln's Emancipation Proclamation?
5. It has been argued that Sherman was a humane general because in the long run he reduced civilian suffering by bringing the war to a more speedy end. Comment.
6. During his lifetime Lincoln was widely regarded in the South and among many Northern Democrats as an inept, joke-telling buffoon. Account for his ranking today as perhaps our greatest president. Is he overrated?

23

The Ordeal
of Reconstruction,
1865–1877

The years of war tried our devotion to the Union;
the time of peace may test the sincerity of our faith
in democracy.

Herman Melville, c. 1866

Prologue: President Johnson, a rough-hewn Tennessean, favored reconstruction of the seceded states on a "soft" basis. But he soon ran afoul of the congressional Republicans. Though divided into hard-line ("radical") and more accommodating ("moderate") factions, Republicans agreed that the seceding states should not be readmitted until they had adopted the Fourteenth Amendment. This amendment (ratified in 1868) would guarantee civil rights to the blacks while reducing congressional representation in states where the ex-slave was denied a vote. But such terms were spurned by ten of the eleven high-spirited Southern states. The Republicans in Congress thereupon passed the drastic military reconstruction acts of 1867, under which black suffrage was forced upon the white South. The Congress also came within a hairsbreadth, in 1868, of removing the obstructive President Johnson by impeachment. Meanwhile the partly black Southern legislatures, despite grievous excesses, passed stacks of long-overdue social and economic legislation. The whites struck back through secret terrorist organizations, and ultimately secured control of their state governments by fraud, fright, and force.

A. The Status of the South

1. Carl Schurz Reports Southern Defiance (1865)

President Johnson sent Carl Schurz—the lanky, bewhiskered, and bespectacled German-American reformer—into the devastated South to report objectively on conditions there. But Schurz was predisposed to see continued defiance. He was on intimate terms with the radical Republican leaders, who favored a severe reconstruction of the South, and in addition he was financially obligated to the radical Charles

[1]*Georgia Historical Quarterly* 35 (1951), pp. 244–247 (July 31, 1865). Reprinted by permission.

Sumner. President Johnson, evidently hoping for evidence that would support his le-
nient policies, brushed aside Schurz's elaborate report with ill-concealed annoyance.
Schurz partially financed his trip by selling a series of letters under an assumed
name to the Boston Advertiser, *which presumably welcomed his pro-radical bias. In*
the following letter, which he wrote from Savannah to the newspaper, what class of
people does he deem responsible for the trouble? What motivated them? Why were
their outbursts not more serious?

But there is another class of people here [in Savannah], mostly younger men, who are still in the swearing mood. You can overhear their conversations as you pass them on the streets or even sit near them on the stoop of a hotel. They are "not conquered but only overpowered." They are only smothered for a time. They want to fight the war over again, and they are sure in five years they are going to have a war bigger than any we have seen yet. They are meaning to get rid of this d——d military despotism. They will show us what stuff Southern men are made of. They will send their own men to Congress and show us that we cannot violate the Constitution with impunity.

They have a rope ready for this and that Union man when the Yankee bayonets are gone. They will show the Northern interlopers that have settled down here to live on their substance the way home. They will deal largely in tar and feathers. They have been in the country and visited this and that place where a fine business is done in the way of killing Negroes. They will let the Negro know what freedom is, only let the Yankee soldiers be withdrawn.

Such is their talk. You can hear it every day, if you have your ears open. You see their sullen, frowning faces at every street corner. Now, there may be much of the old Southern braggadocio in this, and I do not believe that such men will again re-sort to open insurrection. But they will practice private vengeance whenever they can do it with impunity, and I have heard sober-minded Union people express their apprehension of it. This spirit is certainly no evidence of true loyalty.

It was this spirit which was active in an occurrence which disgraced this city on the Fourth of July. Perhaps you have heard of it. The colored firemen of this city de-sired to parade their engine on the anniversary of our independence. If nobody else would, they felt like celebrating that day. A number will deny that it was a legitimate desire. At first the engineer of the fire department, who is a citizen of this town, re-fused his permission. Finally, by an interposition of an officer of the "Freedmen's Bureau,"* he was prevailed upon to give his consent, and the parade took place. In the principal street of the city the procession was attacked with clubs and stones by a mob opposed to the element above described, and by a crowd of boys all swear-ing at the d——d niggers. The colored firemen were knocked down, some of them severely injured, their engine was taken away from them, and the peaceable procession dispersed. Down with the d——d niggers. A northern gentleman who loudly expressed his indignation at the proceedings was in danger of being mobbed, and had to seek safety in a house. . . .

To return to the "unconquered" in Savannah—the occurrence of the Fourth of July shows what they are capable of doing even while the Yankee bayonets are still

*A federal agency designed to help the ex-slaves adjust to freedom.

here. If from this we infer what they will be capable of doing when the Yankee bayonets are withdrawn, the prospect is not altogether pleasant, and Union people, white and black, in this city and neighborhood may well entertain serious apprehensions. . . .

Unfortunately, this spirit receives much encouragement from the fair sex. We have heard so much of the bitter resentment of the Southern ladies that the tale becomes stale by frequent repetition, but when inquiring into the feelings of the people, this element must not be omitted. There are certainly a good many sensible women in the South who have arrived at a just appreciation of the circumstances with which they are surrounded. But there is a large number of Southern women who are as vindictive and defiant as ever, and whose temper does not permit them to lay their tongues under any restraint. You can see them in every hotel, and they will treat you to the most ridiculous exhibitions, whenever an occasion offers.

A day or two ago a Union officer, yielding to an impulse of politeness, handed a dish of pickles to a Southern Lady at the dinner-table of a hotel in this city. A look of unspeakable scorn and indignation met him. "So you think," said the lady, "a Southern woman will take a dish of pickles from a hand that is dripping with the blood of her countrymen?"

It is remarkable upon what trifling material this female wrath is feeding and growing fat. In a certain district in South Carolina, the ladies were some time ago, and perhaps are now, dreadfully exercised about the veil question. You may ask me what the veil question is. Formerly, under the old order of things, Negro women were not permitted to wear veils. Now, under the new order of things, a great many are wearing veils. This is an outrage which cannot be submitted to; the white ladies of the neighborhood agree in being indignant beyond measure. Some of them declare that whenever they meet a colored woman wearing a veil they will tear the veil from her face. Others, mindful of the consequences which such an act of violence might draw after it, under this same new order of things, declare their resolve never to wear veils themselves as long as colored women wear veils. This is the veil question, and this is the way it stands at present.

Such things may seem trifling and ridiculous. But it is a well-known fact that a silly woman is sometimes able to exercise a powerful influence over a man not half as silly, and the class of "unconquered" above described is undoubtedly in a great measure composed of individuals that are apt to be influenced by silly women. It has frequently been said that had it not been for the spirit of the Southern women, the rebellion would have broken down long ago, and there is, no doubt, a grain of truth in it.

2. General Ulysses S. Grant Is Optimistic (1865)

President Johnson, hoping to capitalize on Grant's enormous prestige, also sent the general on a fact-finding trip to the South. Grant spent less than a week hurriedly visiting leading cities in four states. Schurz had ranged far more widely over a longer period, from July to September 1865. But just as Schurz was predisposed to see

---

[2]*Senate Executive Documents*, 39th Cong., 1st sess., I, no. 2, pp. 106–107.

defiance, Grant was predisposed to see compliance. Bear in mind also that Schurz was an idealist, strongly pro-black, and a leading Republican politician closely in touch with the radicals. Grant was none of these. Which of their reports is more credible?

I am satisfied that the mass of thinking men of the South accept the present situation of affairs in good faith. The questions which have heretofore divided the sentiment of the people of the two sections—slavery and state rights, or the right of a state to secede from the Union—they regard as having been settled forever by the highest tribunal—arms—that man can resort to. I was pleased to learn from the leading men whom I met that they not only accepted the decision arrived at as final, but, now that the smoke of battle has cleared away and time has been given for reflection, that this decision has been a fortunate one for the whole country, they receiving like benefits from it with those who opposed them in the field and in council.

Four years of war, during which law was executed only at the point of the bayonet throughout the states in rebellion, have left the people possibly in a condition not to yield that ready obedience to civil authority the American people have generally been in the habit of yielding. This would render the presence of small garrisons throughout those states necessary until such time as labor returns to its proper channel, and civil authority is fully established. I did not meet anyone, either those holding places under the government or citizens of the Southern states, who think it practicable to withdraw the military from the South at present. The white and the black mutually require the protection of the general government.

There is such universal acquiescence in the authority of the general government throughout the portions of country visited by me that the mere presence of a military force, without regard to numbers, is sufficient to maintain order. . . .

My observations lead me to the conclusion that the citizens of the Southern states are anxious to return to self-government, within the Union, as soon as possible; that whilst reconstructing they want and require protection from the government; that they are in earnest in wishing to do what they think is required by the government, not humiliating to them as citizens, and that if such a course were pointed out they would pursue it in good faith.

3. The Former Slaves Confront Freedom (1901)

The reactions of the freed slaves to their new liberty ran the gamut of human emotions from jubilation to anxiety. Attitudes toward former masters—and toward whites generally—ranged from resentment and fear to pity. Booker T. Washington was a young boy no more than eight years of age when the day of freedom came. What was his response? From what he describes as the first reactions of his family members and other freed slaves, what might one conclude were the worst deprivations suffered in slavery?

---

[3]Booker T. Washington, *Up from Slavery* (New York: A. L. Burt, 1901), pp. 224–227.

Finally the war closed, and the day of freedom came. It was a momentous and eventful day to all upon our plantation. We had been expecting it. Freedom was in the air, and had been for months. Deserting soldiers returning to their homes were to be seen every day. Others who had been discharged, or whose regiments had been paroled, were constantly passing near our place. The "grape-vine telegraph" was kept busy night and day. The news and mutterings of great events were swiftly carried from one plantation to another. In the fear of "Yankee" invasions, the silverware and other valuables were taken from the "big house," buried in the woods, and guarded by trusted slaves. Woe be to any one who would have attempted to disturb the buried treasure. The slaves would give the Yankee soldiers food, drink, clothing—anything but that which had been specifically intrusted to their care and honour. As the great day drew nearer, there was more singing in the slave quarters than usual. It was bolder, had more ring, and lasted later into the night. Most of the verses of the plantation songs had some reference to freedom. True, they had sung those same verses before, but they had been careful to explain that the "freedom" in these songs referred to the next world, and had no connection with life in this world. Now they gradually threw off the mask, and were not afraid to let it be known that the "freedom" in their songs meant freedom of the body in this world. The night before the eventful day, word was sent to the slave quarters to the effect that something unusual was going to take place at the "big house" the next morning. There was little, if any, sleep that night. All was excitement and expectancy. Early the next morning word was sent to all the slaves, old and young, to gather at the house. In company with my mother, brother, and sister, and a large number of other slaves, I went to the master's house. All of our master's family were either standing or seated on the veranda of the house, where they could see what was to take place and hear what was said. There was a feeling of deep interest, or perhaps sadness, on their faces, but not bitterness. As I now recall the impression they made upon me, they did not at the moment seem to be sad because of the loss of property, but rather because of parting with those whom they had reared and who were in many ways very close to them. The most distinct thing that I now recall in connection with the scene was that some man who seemed to be a stranger (a United States officer, I presume) made a little speech and then read a rather long paper— the Emancipation Proclamation, I think. After the reading we were told that we were all free, and could go when and where we pleased. My mother, who was standing by my side, leaned over and kissed her children, while tears of joy ran down her cheeks. She explained to us what it all meant, that this was the day for which she had been so long praying, but fearing that she would never live to see.

For some minutes there was great rejoicing, and thanksgiving, and wild scenes of ecstasy. But there was no feeling of bitterness. In fact, there was pity among the slaves for our former owners. The wild rejoicing on the part of the emancipated coloured people lasted but for a brief period, for I noticed that by the time they returned to their cabins there was a change in their feelings. The great responsibility of being free, or having charge of themselves, of having to think and plan for themselves and their children, seemed to take possession of them. It was very much like suddenly turning a youth of ten or twelve years out into the world to provide for himself. In a few hours the great questions with which the Anglo-Saxon race had been grappling for centuries had been thrown upon these people to be solved. These were the questions of a home, a living, the rearing of children, education, citizenship, and the establishment and support of churches. Was it any wonder that within a few hours the wild rejoicing ceased and a feeling of deep gloom seemed to pervade the slave quarters? To some it seemed that, now that they were in actual possession of it, freedom was a more serious thing than they had expected to find it. Some of the slaves were seventy or eighty years old; their best days were gone. They had no strength with which to earn a living in a strange place and among strange people, even if they had been sure where to find a new place of abode. To this class the problem seemed especially hard. Besides, deep down in their hearts there was a strange and peculiar attachment to "old Marster" and "old Missus," and to their children, which they found it hard to think of breaking off. With these they had spent in some cases nearly a half-century, and it was no light thing to think of parting. Gradually, one by one, stealthily at first, the older slaves began to wander from the slave quarters back to the "big house" to have whispered conversation with their former owners as to the future. . . .

After the coming of freedom there were two points upon which practically all the people on our place were agreed, and I find that this was generally true throughout the South: that they must change their names, and that they must leave the old plantation for at least a few days or weeks in order that they might really feel sure that they were free.

In some way a feeling got among the coloured people that it was far from proper for them to bear the surname of their former owners, and a great many of them took other surnames. This was one of the first signs of freedom. When they were slaves, a coloured person was simply called "John" or "Susan." There was seldom occasion for more than the use of the one name. If "John" or "Susan" belonged to a white man by the name of "Hatcher," sometimes he was called "John Hatcher," or as often "Hatcher's John." But there was a feeling that "John Hatcher" or "Hatcher's John" was not the proper title by which to denote a freeman; and so in many cases "John Hatcher" was changed to "John S. Lincoln" or "John S. Sherman," the initial "S" standing for no name, it being simply a part of what the coloured man proudly called his "entitles."

As I have stated, most of the coloured people left the old plantation for a short while at least, so as to be sure, it seemed, that they could leave and try their freedom on to see how it felt. After they had remained away for a time, many of the older slaves, especially, returned to their old homes and made some kind of contact with their former owners by which they remained on the estate.

My mother's husband, who was the stepfather of my brother John and myself, did not belong to the same owners as did my mother. In fact, he seldom came to our plantation. I remember seeing him there perhaps once a year, that being about Christmas time. In some way, during the war, by running away and following the Federal soldiers, it seems, he found his way into the new state of West Virginia. As soon as freedom was declared, he sent for my mother to come to the Kanawha Valley, in West Virginia. At that time a journey from Virginia over the mountains to West Virginia was rather a tedious and in some cases a painful undertaking. What little clothing and few household goods we had were placed in a cart, but the children walked the greater portion of the distance, which was several hundred miles.

4. Emancipation Violence in Texas (c. 1865)

In the following recollection by a former slave woman in Texas, what is revealed about the response of some slaveowners to emancipation? What implications did such responses have for the future of the freed slaves? for federal policy during Reconstruction?

I heard about freedom in September and they were picking cotton and a white man rode up to master's house on a big, white horse and the houseboy told master a man wanted to see him and he hollered, "Light, stranger." It was a government man and he had the big book and a bunch of papers and said why hadn't master turned the niggers loose. Master said he was trying to get the crop out and he told master to have the slaves in. Uncle Steven blew the cow horn that they used to call to eat and all the niggers came running, because that horn meant, "Come to the big house, quick." The man read the paper telling us we were free, but master made us work several months after that. He said we would get 20 acres of land and a mule but we didn't get it.

Lots of niggers were killed after freedom, because the slaves in Harrison County were turned loose right at freedom and those in Rusk County weren't. But they heard about it and ran away to freedom in Harrison County and their owners had them bushwhacked, then shot down. You could see lots of niggers hanging from trees in Sabine bottom right after freedom, because they caught them swimming across Sabine River and shot them. There sure are going to be lots of souls crying against them in judgment!

B. The Debate on Reconstruction Policy

1. Southern Blacks Ask for Help (1865)

As the smoke of war cleared, blacks throughout the South gathered in "Conventions of Freedmen" to determine the best strategies for protecting their fragile freedom. Several of these conventions formally petitioned the Congress for help. In the following petition from a convention meeting in Alexandria, Virginia, in August 1865, what forms of support are deemed most essential? What is the freedmen's greatest fear?

We, the undersigned members of a Convention of colored citizens of the State of Virginia, would respectfully represent that, although we have been held as slaves, and denied all recognition as a constituent of your nationality for almost the entire period of the duration of your Government, and that by *your permission* we have been denied either home or country, and deprived of the dearest rights of human nature; yet when you and our immediate oppressors met in deadly conflict upon the

---

[4]George P. Rawick, ed., *The American Slave: A Composite Autobiography* (Westport, Conn.: Greenwood Publishing Company, 1972), vol. 5, Texas Narratives, part 3, p. 78.

[1]"Proceedings of the Convention of the Colored People of Virginia, Held in the City of Alexandria, August 2, 3, 4, 5, 1865" (Alexandria, Va., 1865), in W. L. Fleming, ed., *Documentary History of Reconstruction* (Cleveland, Ohio, 1906), vol. 1, pp. 195–196.

field of battle—the one to destroy and the other to save your Government and nationality, *we,* with scarce an exception, in our inmost souls espoused your cause, and watched, and prayed, and waited, and labored for your success. . . .

When the contest waxed long, and the result hung doubtfully, you appealed to us for help, and how well we answered is written in the rosters of the two hundred thousand colored troops now enrolled in your service; and as to our undying devotion to your cause, let the uniform acclamation of escaped prisoners, "whenever we saw a black face we felt sure of a friend," answer.

Well, the war is over, the rebellion is "put down," and we are *declared* free! Four fifths of our enemies are paroled or amnestied, and the other fifth are being pardoned, and the President has, in his efforts at the reconstruction of the civil government of the States, late in rebellion, left us entirely at the mercy of these subjugated but unconverted rebels, in *everything* save the privilege of bringing us, our wives and little ones, to the auction block. . . . We *know* these men—know them *well*— and we assure you that, with the majority of them, loyalty is only "lip deep," and that their professions of loyalty are used as a cover to the cherished design of getting restored to their former relations with the Federal Government, and then, by all sorts of "unfriendly legislation," to render the freedom you have given us more intolerable than the slavery they intended for us.

We warn you in time that our only safety is in keeping them under Governors of the *military persuasion* until you have so amended the Federal Constitution that it will prohibit the States from making any distinction between citizens on account of race or color. In one word, the only salvation for us besides the power of the Government, is in the *possession of the ballot.* Give us this, and we will protect ourselves. . . . But, 'tis said we are ignorant. Admit it. Yet who denies we *know* a traitor from a loyal man, a gentleman from a rowdy, a friend from an enemy? . . . All we ask is an *equal chance* with the white *traitors* varnished and japanned with the oath of amnesty. Can you deny us this and still keep faith with us? . . .

We are "sheep in the midst of wolves," and nothing but the military arm of the Government prevents us and all the *truly* loyal white men from being driven from the land of our birth. Do not then, we beseech you, give to one of these "wayward sisters" the rights they abandoned and forfeited when they rebelled until you have secured *our* rights by the aforementioned amendment to the Constitution. . . .

2. The White South Asks for Unconditional Reintegration into the Union (1866)

The Joint Committee on Reconstruction, composed of nine congressional representatives and six senators, held extensive hearings in the spring of 1866 about the condition of the South and various proposals for reintegrating the Southern states into the Union. One leading proposal was the legislation that eventually became the Fourteenth Amendment to the Constitution. It was designed to reduce the representation in Congress of any state that denied the freedmen the right to vote. Congressional Republicans wanted to make any state's restoration to the Union conditional on its rat-

---

[2]*Report of the Joint Committee on Reconstruction* (Washington, D.C., 1866), Part III, pp. 163ff.

ification of the amendment. In the following testimony, former Confederate Vice President Alexander Stephens comments on the congressional plan. What are his main objections to it? What alternatives does he propose? Does his statement confirm or cast doubt on the concerns of blacks presented in the preceding selection?

I think the people of the State would be unwilling to do more than they have done for restoration. Restricted or limited suffrage would not be so objectionable as general or universal. But it is a matter that belongs to the State to regulate. The question of suffrage, whether universal or restricted, is one of State policy exclusively, as they believe. Individually I should not be opposed to a proper system of restricted or limited suffrage to this class of our population. . . . The only view in their opinion that could possibly justify the war that was carried on by the federal government against them was the idea of the indissolubleness of the Union; that those who held the administration for the time were bound to enforce the execution of the laws and the maintenance of the integrity of the country under the Constitution. . . . They expected as soon as the confederate cause was abandoned that immediately the States would be brought back into their practical relations with the government as previously constituted. That is what they looked to. They expected that the States would immediately have their representatives in the Senate and in the House; and they expected in good faith, as loyal men, as the term is frequently used—loyal to law, order, and the Constitution—to support the government under the Constitution. . . . Towards the Constitution of the United States the great mass of our people were always as much devoted in their feelings as any people ever were towards any laws or people . . . they resorted to secession with a view of more securely maintaining these principles. And when they found they were not successful in their object in perfect good faith, as far as I can judge from meeting with them and conversing with them, looking to the future development of their country . . . their earnest desire and expectation was to allow the past struggle . . . to pass by and to co-operate with . . . those of all sections who earnestly desire the preservation of constitutional liberty and the perpetuaion of the government in its purity. They have been . . . disappointed in this, and are . . . patiently waiting, however, and believing that when the passions of the hour have passed away this delay in representation will cease. . . .

My own opinion is, that these terms ought not to be offered as conditions precedent. . . . It would be best for the peace, harmony, and prosperity of the whole country that there should be an immediate restoration, an immediate bringing back of the States into their original practical relations; and let all these questions then be discussed in common council. Then the representatives from the south could be heard, and you and all could judge much better of the tone and temper of the people than you could from the opinions given by any individuals. . . . My judgment, therefore, is very decided, that it would have been better as soon as the lamentable conflict was over, when the people of the south abandoned their cause and agreed to accept the issue, desiring as they do to resume their places for the future in the Union, and to look to the arena of reason and justice for the protection of their rights in the Union—it would have been better to have allowed that result to take place, to follow under the policy adopted by the administration, than to delay or hinder it by propositions to amend the Constitution in respect to suffrage. . . . I think the people of all the southern States would in the halls of Congress discuss these questions calmly and deliberately, and if they did not show that the views they entertained were just and proper, such as to control the judgment of the people of the other sections and States, they would quietly . . . yield to whatever should be constitutionally determined in common council. But I think they feel very sensitively the offer to them of propositions to accept while they are denied all voice . . . in the discussion of these propositions. I think they feel very sensitively that they are denied the right to be heard.

3. The Radical Republicans Take a Hard Line (1866)

After weeks of testimony, the Joint Committee on Reconstruction made its report. With only three Democrats among its fifteen members, and dominated by the imperious Thaddeus Stevens, the committee reflected radical Republican views on Reconstruction policy. What were its principal conclusions? In the light of the evidence provided in the previous two selections, were the committee's views justified?

A claim for the immediate admission of senators and representatives from the so-called Confederate States has been urged, which seems to your committee not to be founded either in reason or in law, and which cannot be passed without comment. Stated in a few words, it amounts to this: That inasmuch as the lately insurgent States had no legal right to separate themselves from the Union, they still retain their position as States, and consequently the people thereof have a right to immediate representation in Congress without the interposition of any conditions whatever. . . . It has even been contended that until such admission all legislation affecting their interests is, if not unconstitutional, at least unjustifiable and oppressive.

It is believed by your Committee that these propositions are not only wholly untenable, but, if admitted, would tend to the destruction of the government. . . . It cannot, we think, be denied that the war thus waged was a civil war of the greatest magnitude. The people waging it were necessarily subject to all the rules which, by the law of nations, control a contest of that character, and to all the legitimate consequences following it. One of these consequences was that, within the limits prescribed by humanity, the conquered rebels were at the mercy of the conquerors. . . .

It is moreover contended . . . that from the peculiar nature and character of our government . . . from the moment rebellion lays down its arms and actual hostilities cease all political rights of rebellious communities are at once restored; that because the people of a state of the Union were once an organized community within the Union, they necessarily so remain, and their right to be represented in Congress at any and all times, and to participate in the government of the country under all circumstances, admits of neither question nor dispute. If this is indeed true, then is the government of the United States powerless for its own protection, and flagrant rebellion, carried to the extreme of civil war, is a pastime which any state may play at, not only certain that it can lose nothing in any event, but may even be the gainer by defeat?

It is the opinion of your committee—

---

[3]*Report of the Joint Committee on Reconstruction* (Washington, D.C., 1866), pp. 4ff.

I. That the States lately in rebellion were, at the close of the war, disorganized communities, without civil government, and without constitutions or other forms, by virtue of which political relation could legally exist between them and the federal government.

II. That Congress cannot be expected to recognize as valid the election of representatives from disorganized communities, which, from the very nature of the case, were unable to present their claim to representation under those established and recognized rules, the observance of which has been hitherto required.

III. That Congress would not be justified in admitting such communities to a participation in the government of the country without first providing such constitutional or other guarantees as will tend to secure the civil rights of all citizens of the republic; a just equality of representation; protection against claims founded in rebellion and crime; a temporary restoration of the right of suffrage to those who have not actively participated in the efforts to destroy the Union and overthrow the government, and the exclusion from position of public trust of, at least, a portion of those whose crimes have proved them to be enemies of the Union, and unworthy of public confidence. . . .

The necessity of providing adequate safeguards for the future, before restoring the insurrectionary States to a participation in the direction of public affairs, is apparent from the bitter hostility to the government and people of the United States yet existing throughout the conquered territory. . . .

The conclusion of your committee therefore is, that the so-called Confederate States are not, at present, entitled to representation in the Congress of the United States. . . .

4. President Andrew Johnson Tries to Restrain Congress (1867)

Alarmed by the outbreak of race riots in several Southern cities, and frustrated by the South's rejection of the Fourteenth Amendment, Congress passed the First Reconstruction Act on March 2, 1867. The act divided the South into military districts subject to martial law. It also stipulated that the seceding states could be restored to the Union only when they had called constitutional conventions, on the basis of universal manhood suffrage, which must guarantee black voting rights and ratify the Fourteenth Amendment. President Johnson promptly vetoed the bill, which just as promptly was passed over his veto. In his veto message, which follows, what reasons does he offer for his action? Are his arguments sound? Why might they have especially provoked the Republicans in Congress?

Washington, March 2, 1867

To the House of Representatives:

I have examined the bill "to provide for the more efficient government of the rebel States" with the care and anxiety which its transcendent importance is calcu-

[4]J. D. Richardson, ed., *Messages and Papers of the Presidents* (New York: Bureau of National Literature, 1911), vol. 5, pp. 3690–3696.

lated to awaken. I am unable to give it my assent, for reasons so grave that I hope a statement of them may have some influence on the minds of the patriotic and enlightened men with whom the decision must ultimately rest.

The bill places all the people of the ten States therein named under the absolute domination of military rulers; and the preamble undertakes to give the reason upon which the measure is based and the ground upon which it is justified. It declares that there exists in those States no legal governments and no adequate protection for life or property, and asserts the necessity of enforcing peace and good order within their limits. Is this true as matter of fact? . . .

Have we the power to establish and carry into execution a measure like this? I answer, Certainly not, if we derive our authority from the Constitution and if we are bound by the limitations which it imposes.

This proposition is perfectly clear, that no branch of the Federal Government—executive, legislative, or judicial—can have any just powers except those which it derives through and exercises under the organic law of the Union. Outside of the Constitution we have no legal authority more than private citizens, and within it we have only so much as that instrument gives us. This broad principle limits all our functions and applies to all subjects. It protects not only the citizens of States which are within the Union, but it shields every human being who comes or is brought under our jurisdiction. We have no right to do in one place more than in another that which the Constitution says we shall not do at all. If, therefore, the Southern States were in truth out of the Union, we could not treat their people in a way which the fundamental law forbids.

Some persons assume that the success of our arms in crushing the opposition which was made in some of the States to the execution of the Federal laws reduced those States and all their people—the innocent as well as the guilty—to the condition of vassalage and gave us a power over them which the Constitution does not bestow or define or limit. No fallacy can be more transparent than this. Our victories subjected the insurgents to legal obedience, not to the yoke of an arbitrary despotism. . . .

Invasion, insurrection, rebellion, and domestic violence were anticipated when the Government was framed, and the means of repelling and suppressing them were wisely provided for in the Constitution; but it was not thought necessary to declare that the States in which they might occur should be expelled from the Union. Rebellions, which were invariably suppressed, occurred prior to that out of which these questions grow; but the States continued to exist and the Union remained unbroken. In Massachusetts, in Pennsylvania, in Rhode Island, and in New York, at different periods in our history, violent and armed opposition to the United States was carried on; but the relations of those States with the Federal Government were not supposed to be interrupted or changed thereby after the rebellious portions of their population were defeated and put down. It is true that in these earlier cases there was no formal expression of a determination to withdraw from the Union, but it is also true that in the Southern States the ordinances of secession were treated by all the friends of the Union as mere nullities and are now acknowledged to be so by the States themselves. If we admit that they had any force or validity or that they did in fact take the States in which they were passed out of the Union, we sweep from under our feet all the grounds upon which we stand in justifying the use of Federal force to maintain the integrity of the Government. . . .

The United States are bound to guarantee to each State a republican form of government. Can it be pretended that this obligation is not probably broken if we carry out a measure like this, which wipes away every vestige of republican government in ten States and puts the life, property, liberty, and honor of all the people in each of them under the domination of a single person clothed with unlimited authority?

The purpose and object of the bill—the general intent which pervades it from beginning to end—is to change the entire structure and character of the State governments and to compel them by force to the adoption of organic laws and regulations which they are unwilling to accept if left to themselves. The negroes have not asked for the privilege of voting; the vast majority of them have no idea what it means. This bill not only thrusts it into their hands, but compels them, as well as the whites, to use it in a particular way. If they do not form a constitution with prescribed articles in it and afterwards elect a legislature which will act upon certain measures in a prescribed way, neither blacks nor whites can be relieved from the slavery which the bill imposes upon them. Without pausing here to consider the policy or impolicy of Africanizing the southern part of our territory, I would simply ask the attention of Congress to that manifest, well-known, and universally acknowledged rule of constitutional law which declares that the Federal Government has no jurisdiction, authority, or power to regulate such subjects for any State. To force the right of suffrage out of the hands of the white people and into the hands of the negroes is an arbitrary violation of this principle. . . .

The bill also denies the legality of the governments of ten of the States which participated in the ratification of the amendment to the Federal Constitution abolishing slavery forever within the jurisdiction of the United States [the Thirteenth Amendment] and practically excludes them from the Union. If this assumption of the bill be correct, their concurrence can not be considered as having been legally given, and the important fact is made to appear that the consent of three-fourths of the States—the requisite number—has not been constitutionally obtained to the ratification of that amendment, thus leaving the question of slavery where it stood before the amendment was officially declared to have become a part of the Constitution.

That the measure proposed by this bill does violate the Constitution in the particulars mentioned and in many other ways which I forbear to enumerate is too clear to admit of the least doubt. . . .

It is part of our public history which can never be forgotten that both Houses of Congress, in July, 1861, declared in the form of a solemn resolution that the war was and should be carried on for no purpose of subjugation, but solely to enforce the Constitution and laws, and that when this was yielded by the parties in rebellion the contest should cease, with the constitutional rights of the States and of individuals unimpaired. This resolution was adopted and sent forth to the world unanimously by the Senate and with only two dissenting voices in the House. It was accepted by the friends of the Union in the South as well as in the North as expressing honestly and truly the object of the war. On the faith of it many thousands of persons in both sections gave their lives and their fortunes to the cause. To repudiate it now by refusing to the States and to the individuals within them the rights which the Constitution and laws of the Union would secure to them is a breach of our plighted honor for which I can imagine no excuse and to which I can not voluntarily become a party. . . .

5. The Controversy over the Fifteenth Amendment (1866, 1870)

The Fifteenth Amendment guaranteed all adult males, regardless of race, the right to vote, and the campaign to have it ratified produced bitter arguments between the radical Republicans and their opponents. The first illustration below, entitled The Constitutional Amendment, *was first published during a heated election campaign in Pennsylvania in 1866. Supporters of the Democratic candidate for governor circulated this image in an attempt to defeat the Republican gubernatorial nominee. What are its most pointed arguments? The second image,* The Fifteenth Amendment and Its Results, *appeared in Baltimore in 1870 to celebrate the enactment of the Fifteenth Amendment. What does it find most praiseworthy about the new law? How are blacks depicted in the two prints? Were there any principled arguments against the Fifteenth Amendment?*

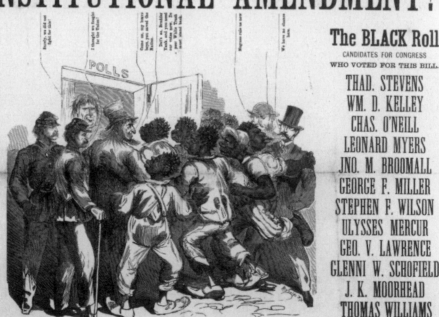

[5]Library of Congress #USZ62-40761; Library of Congress, #USZ62-22396.

C. Impeaching the President

1. Johnson's Cleveland Speech (1866)

A tactless and stubborn President Johnson clashed openly with the Republicans in Congress, including the embittered Thaddeus Stevens, when he vetoed a series of reconstruction bills. Two of the measures designed to help the former slaves—the Civil Rights Bill and the New Freedmen's Bureau Bill—were speedily repassed over his veto. Undaunted, Johnson embarked on a speech making tour to urge the election of

[1]Edward McPherson, *The Political History of the United States of America during the Period of Reconstruction,* 3rd ed. (Washington, D.C.: Philip and Salomons, 1871), pp. 134–136.

congressmen favorable to his policies. But the public was in an ugly mood. Former President Jefferson Davis, though still in prison, was untried and unhanged, as were other former Confederates. A recent antiblack riot in New Orleans had resulted in some two hundred casualties. Johnson had earlier distinguished himself as a rough-and-ready stump speaker in Tennessee, but, as Secretary Seward remarked, the president of the United States should not be a stump speaker. Johnson's undignified harangue in Cleveland contained passages (here italicized) that formed the basis of some of the impeachment charges later brought by the House. What criticisms can be legitimately leveled against this speech? Which one is the most serious?

Notwithstanding the subsidized gang of hirelings and traducers [in Congress?], I have discharged all my duties and fulfilled all my pledges, and I say here tonight that if my predecessor had lived, the vials of wrath would have been poured out upon him. [Cries of "Never!" "Three cheers for the Congress of the United States!"]

. . . Where is the man or woman who can place his finger upon one single act of mine deviating from any pledge of mine or in violation of the Constitution of the country? [Cheers.] . . . Who can come and place his finger on one pledge I ever violated, or one principle I ever proved false to? [A voice, "How about New Orleans?" Another voice, "Hang Jeff Davis."] Hang Jeff Davis, he says. [Cries of "No," and "Down with him!"] . . . Hang Jeff Davis. Why don't you hang him? [Cries of "Give us the opportunity."] Have not you got the court? Have not you got the Attorney General? . . .

I will tell you what I did do. I called upon your Congress that is trying to break up the government. [Emphasis added.] [Cries, "You be d———d!" and cheers mingled with hisses. Great confusion. "Don't get mad, Andy!"] Well, I will tell you who is mad. "Whom the gods wish to destroy, they first make mad." Did your Congress order any of them to be tried? ["Three cheers for Congress."] . . .

You pretend now to have great respect and sympathy for the poor brave fellow who has left an arm on the battlefield. [Cries, "Is this dignified?"] I understand you. . . . I care not for dignity. . . . [A voice, "Traitor!"] I wish I could see that man. I would bet you now that if the light fell on your face, cowardice and treachery would be seen in it. Show yourself. Come out here where I can see you. [Shouts of laughter.] If you ever shoot a man you will do it in the dark, and pull the trigger when no one is by to see you. [Cheers.]

I understand traitors. I have been fighting them at the south end of the line, and we are now fighting them in the other direction. [Laughter and cheers.] I come here neither to criminate or recriminate, but when attacked, my plan is to defend myself. [Cheers.] . . . As Chief Magistrate, I felt so after taking the oath to support the Constitution, and when I saw encroachments upon your Constitution and rights, as an honest man I dared to sound the tocsin of alarm. ["Three cheers for Andrew Johnson."] . . .

I love my country. Every public act of my life testifies that is so. Where is the man that can put his finger upon any one act of mine that goes to prove the contrary? And what is my offending? [A voice, "Because you are not a Radical," and cry of "Veto."] Somebody says veto. Veto of what? What is called the Freedmen's Bureau bill? . . . I might refer to the Civil Rights Bill, the results of which are very similar. I tell you, my countrymen, that though the powers of hell and Thad Stevens and his gang were by, they could not turn me from my purpose. . . .

In conclusion, beside that, Congress had taken such pains to poison their constituents against him.* But what had Congress done? Had they done anything to restore the Union of these states? No; on the contrary, they had done everything to prevent it; and because he stood now where he did when the rebellion commenced, he had been denounced as a traitor. Who had run greater risks or made greater sacrifices than himself? But Congress, factious and domineering, had [under]taken to poison the minds of the American people. [Emphasis added.]

2. Senator Lyman Trumbull Defends Johnson (1868)

Johnson's unrestrained oratory backfired, and at the polls in November the Republicans won control of a two-thirds majority in both houses of Congress. They proceeded to pass the Tenure of Office Act, which was designed to entrap Johnson. Doubting its constitutionality (by indirection it was later judged unconstitutional) and seeking to bring a test case, he deliberately challenged it by removing Secretary William Stanton. The House thereupon impeached Johnson for "high crimes and misdemeanors." Most of its indictment related to Johnson's alleged violation of the Tenure of Office Act; other charges related to his "scandalous harangues." Particularly objectionable was a speech at the White House in which the president had declared that acts of Congress were not binding upon him because the South did not enjoy proper representation in it. One of the ablest of those who spoke for Johnson was Senator Lyman Trumbull of Illinois, a brilliant constitutional lawyer and a former associate of Lincoln. As one who followed principle rather than partisanship, he changed parties three times during his career. In the following speech, what is his main reason for thinking that Johnson's removal would be unfortunate?

In coming to the conclusion that the President is not guilty of any of the high crimes and misdemeanors with which he stands charged, I have endeavored to be governed by the case made, without reference to other acts of his not contained in the record, and without giving the least heed to the clamor of intemperate zealots who demand the conviction of Andrew Johnson as a test of party faith, or seek to identify with and make responsible for his acts those who from convictions of duty feel compelled, on the case made, to vote for his acquittal.

His speeches and the general course of his administration have been as distasteful to me as to anyone, and I should consider it the great calamity of the age if the disloyal element, so often encouraged by his measures, should gain political ascendancy. If the question was, Is Andrew Johnson a fit person for President? I should answer, no; but it is not a party question, nor upon Andrew Johnson's deeds and acts, except so far as they are made to appear in the record, that I am to decide.

---

*The reporter now lapses into the third person.
[2]*Congressional Globe,* 40th Cong., 2d sess. (May 7, 1868), Supplement, p. 420.

Painful as it is to disagree with so many political associates and friends whose conscientious convictions have led them to a different result, I must, nevertheless, in the discharge of the high responsibility under which I act, be governed by what my reason and judgment tell me is the truth, and the justice and law of this case. . . .

Once set the example of impeaching a President for what, when the excitement of the hour shall have subsided, will be regarded as insufficient causes, as several of those now alleged against the President were decided to be by the House of Representatives only a few months since, and no future President will be safe who happens to differ with a majority of the House and two-thirds of the Senate on any measure deemed by them important, particularly if of a political character. Blinded by partisan zeal, with such an example before them, they will not scruple to remove out of the way any obstacle to the accomplishment of their purposes, and what then becomes of the checks and balances of the Constitution, so carefully devised and so vital to its perpetuity? They are all gone.

In view of the consequences likely to flow from this day's proceedings, should they result in conviction on what my judgment tells me are insufficient charges and profits, I tremble for the future of my country. I cannot be an instrument or produce such a result; and at the hazard of the ties even of friendship and affection, till calmer times shall do justice to my motives, no alternative is left me but the inflexible discharge of duty.

[President Johnson escaped removal by the margin of a single vote, and only because seven conscientious Republican senators, including Trumbull, risked political suicide by refusing to go along with the majority.]

D. "Black Reconstruction"

1. Thaddeus Stevens Demands Black Suffrage (1867)

The most influential radical Republican in the House, crippled and vindictive Thaddeus Stevens of Pennsylvania, loathed slavery, slaveholders, and slave breeders. He felt a deep compassion for blacks and, in fact, arranged to be buried in a black cemetery. But in his demands for black suffrage he was motivated, like many other Republicans, by a mixture of idealism and opportunism. Of the arguments for black voting that he set forth in the following speech in the House, which ones were the most selfish? the most idealistic?

There are several good reasons for the passage of this bill [for reconstructing the South].

---

[1]*Congressional Globe,* 39th Cong., 2d sess. (January 3, 1867), p. 252.

In the first place, it is just. I am now confining my argument to Negro suffrage in the rebel states. Have not loyal blacks quite as good a right to choose rulers and make laws as rebel whites?

In the second place, it is a necessity in order to protect the loyal white men in the seceded states. The white Union men are in a great minority in each of those states. With them the blacks would act in a body; and it is believed that in each of said states, except one, the two united would form a majority, control the states, and protect themselves. Now they are the victims of daily murder. They must suffer constant persecution, or be exiled. . . .

Another good reason is, it would insure the ascendancy of the Union [Republican] Party. "Do you avow the party purpose?" exclaims some horror-stricken demagogue. I do. For I believe, on my conscience, that on the continued ascendancy of that party depends the safety of this great nation.

If impartial suffrage is excluded in the rebel states, then every one of them is sure to send a solid rebel representative delegation to Congress, and cast a solid rebel electoral vote. They, with their kindred Copperheads of the North, would always elect the President and control Congress. While Slavery sat upon her defiant throne, and insulted and intimidated the trembling North, the South frequently divided on questions of policy between Whigs and Democrats, and gave victory alternately to the sections. Now, you must divide them between loyalists, without regard to color, and disloyalists, or you will be the perpetual vassals of the free-trade, irritated, revengeful South.

For these, among other reasons, I am for Negro suffrage in every rebel state. If it be just, it should not be denied; if it be necessary, it should be adopted; if it be a punishment to traitors, they deserve it.

2. Black and White Legislatures (c. 1876)

Black suffrage was finally forced on the Southern whites by their new state constitutions and by the Fifteenth Amendment to the federal Constitution (1870). Tension grew worse as designing Northern "carpetbaggers" and Unionist Southern whites ("scalawags") moved in to exploit the inexperienced former slaves. J. W. Leigh, an English clergyman turned Georgia rice planter, recorded the following observations in a personal letter. What conditions were most galling to the former Confederates?

The fact is, the poor Negro has since the war been placed in an entirely false position, and is therefore not to be blamed for many of the absurdities he has committed, seeing that he has been urged on by Northern "carpetbaggers" and Southern "scalawags," who have used him as a tool to further their own nefarious ends.

The great mistake committed by the North was giving the Negroes the franchise so soon after their emancipation, when they were not the least prepared for it. In

---

[2]Frances B. Leigh, *Ten Years on a Georgia Plantation since the War* (London: R. Bentley and Sons, 1883), pp. 268–292 (Appendix).

1865 slavery was abolished, and no one even among the Southerners, I venture to say, would wish it back. In 1868 they [Negroes] were declared citizens of the United States, and in 1870 they had the right of voting given them, and at the same time persons concerned in the rebellion were excluded from public trusts by what was called the "iron-clad" oath. And as if this was not enough, last year [1875] the Civil Rights Bill was passed, by which Negroes were to be placed on a perfect equality with whites, who were to be compelled to travel in the same cars with them, and to send their children to the same schools.

The consequence of all this is that where there is a majority of Negroes, as is the case in the states of Louisiana, Mississippi, and South Carolina, these states are placed completely under Negro rule, and scenes occur in the state legislatures which baffle description.

I recollect at the beginning of 1870 being at Montgomery, the capital of Alabama, and paying a visit to the State House there, when a discussion was going on with respect to a large grant which was to be made for the building of the Alabama and Chattanooga Railway, the real object of which was to put money into the pockets of certain carpetbaggers, who, in order to gain their object, had bribed all the Negroes to vote for the passing of the bill.

The scene was an exciting one. Several Negro members were present, with their legs stuck up on the desks in front of them, and spitting all about them in free and independent fashion. One gentleman having spoken for some time against the bill, and having reiterated his condemnation of it as a fraudulent speculation, a stout Negro member from Mobile sprung up and said, "Mister Speaker, when yesterday I spoke, I was not allowed to go on because you said I spoke twice on the same subject. Now what is sauce for the goose is sauce for the gander. Dis Member is saying over and over again de same thing; why don't you tell him to sit down? for what is sauce for," etc. To which the Speaker said, "Sit down yourself, sir." Another member (a carpetbagger) jumped up and shook his fist in the speaking member's face, and told him he was a liar, and if he would come outside he would give him satisfaction.

This is nothing, however, to what has been going on in South Carolina this last session. Poor South Carolina, formerly the proudest state in America, boasting of her ancient families, remarkable for her wealth, culture, and refinement, now prostrate in the dust, ruled over by her former slaves, an old aristocratic society replaced by the most ignorant democracy that mankind ever saw invested with the functions of government. Of the 124 representatives, there are but 23 representatives of her old civilization, and these few can only look on at the squabbling crowd amongst whom they sit as silent enforced auditors. Of the 101 remaining, 94 are colored, and 7 their white allies. The few honest amongst them see plundering and corruption going on on all sides, and can do nothing. . . .

The Negroes have it all their own way, and rob and plunder as they please. The Governor of South Carolina lives in luxury, and treats his soldiers to champagne, while the miserable planters have to pay taxes amounting to half their income, and if they fail to pay, their property is confiscated.

Louisiana and Mississippi are not much better off. The former has a Negro barber for its Lieutenant-governor, and the latter has just selected a Negro steamboat porter as its United States Senator, filling the place once occupied by Jefferson Davis.

3. W. E. B. Du Bois Justifies Black Legislators (1910)

W. E. B. Du Bois, a Massachusetts-born black of French Huguenot extraction, received his Ph.D. from Harvard University in 1895. Distinguished as a teacher, lecturer, historian, economist, sociologist, novelist, poet, and propagandist, he became a militant advocate of equal rights. A founder of the National Association for the Advancement of Colored People (NAACP), he served for twenty-four years as editor of its chief organ. Du Bois, who was born the day before the House impeached Johnson, here writes as a scholar. In what important respects does he argue that Reconstruction legislatures have been unfairly represented? In what ways were these bodies responsible for significant achievements?

Undoubtedly there were many ridiculous things connected with Reconstruction governments: the placing of ignorant field-hands who could neither read nor write in the legislature, the gold spittoons of South Carolina, the enormous public printing bill of Mississippi—all these were extravagant and funny; and yet somehow, to one who sees, beneath all that is bizarre, the real human tragedy of the upward striving of downtrodden men, the groping for light among people born in darkness, there is less tendency to laugh and jibe than among shallower minds and easier consciences. All that is funny is not bad.

Then, too, a careful examination of the alleged stealing in the South reveals much. First, there is repeated exaggeration. For instance, it is said that the taxation in Mississippi was fourteen times as great in 1874 as in 1869. This sounds staggering until we learn that the state taxation in 1869 was only ten cents on one hundred dollars, and that the expenses of government in 1874 were only twice as great as in 1860, and that too with a depreciated currency. . . .

The character of the real thieving shows that white men must have been the chief beneficiaries. . . . The frauds through the manipulation of state and railway bonds and of banknotes must have inured chiefly to the benefit of experienced white men, and this must have been largely the case in the furnishing and printing frauds. . . .

That the Negroes, led by astute thieves, became tools and received a small share of the spoils is true. But . . . much of the legislation which resulted in fraud was represented to the Negroes as good legislation, and thus their votes were secured by deliberate misrepresentation. . . .

Granted, then, that the Negroes were to some extent venal but to a much larger extent ignorant and deceived, the question is: Did they show any signs of a disposition to learn better things? The theory of democratic governments is not that the will of the people is always right, but rather that normal human beings of average intelligence will, if given a chance, learn the right and best course by bitter experience. This is precisely what Negro voters showed indubitable signs of doing. First, they strove for schools to abolish ignorance, and, second, a large and growing number of them revolted against the carnival of extravagance and stealing that marred the beginning of Reconstruction, and joined with the best elements to institute reform. . . .

---

[3]*American Historical Review* 15 (1910): 791–799, passim.

We may recognize three things which Negro rule gave to the South:

1. Democratic government.
2. Free public schools.
3. New social legislation. . . .

In South Carolina there was before the war a property qualification for office-holders, and, in part, for voters. The [Reconstruction] constitution of 1868, on the other hand, was a modern democratic document . . . preceded by a broad Declaration of Rights which did away with property qualifications and based representation directly on population instead of property. It especially took up new subjects of social legislation, declaring navigable rivers free public highways, instituting homestead exemptions, establishing boards of county commissioners, providing for a new penal code of laws, establishing universal manhood suffrage "without distinction of race or color," devoting six sections to charitable and penal institutions and six to corporations, providing separate property for married women, etc. Above all, eleven sections of the Tenth Article were devoted to the establishment of a complete public-school system.

So satisfactory was the constitution thus adopted by Negro suffrage and by a convention composed of a majority of blacks that the state lived twenty-seven years under it without essential change. And when the constitution was revised in 1895, the revision was practically nothing more than an amplification of the constitution of 1868. No essential advance step of the former document was changed except the suffrage article. . . .

There is no doubt but that the thirst of the black man for knowledge—a thirst which has been too persistent and durable to be mere curiosity or whim—gave birth to the public free-school system of the South. It was the question upon which black voters and legislators insisted more than anything else, and while it is possible to find some vestiges of free schools in some of the Southern states before the war, yet a universal, well-established system dates from the day that the black man got political power. . . .

Finally, in legislation covering property, the wider functions of the state, the punishment of crime, and the like, it is sufficient to say that the laws on these points established by Reconstruction legislatures were not only different from and even revolutionary to the laws in the older South, but they were so wise and so well suited to the needs of the new South that in spite of a retrogressive movement following the overthrow of Negro governments, the mass of this legislation, with elaboration and development, still stands on the statute books of the South.

4. Benjamin Tillman's Antiblack Tirade (1907)

Reared in a slaveowning family, Senator Benjamin R. Tillman of South Carolina had participated in antiblack outrages during Reconstruction days. His face contorted, his one good eye glowing like a live coal, and his voice rising to a whine, "Till-

---

[4]*Congressional Record,* 59th Cong., 2d sess. (January 21, 1907), p. 1440.

man the Terrible" shocked the Senate and the nation with wild speeches in which he boasted that "we took the government away [from blacks]," we "stuffed the ballot boxes," we used "tissue ballots," "we shot them," "we are not ashamed of it," and "we will do it again." Whom does he blame most for the alleged conditions to which he refers?

It was in 1876, thirty years ago, and the people of South Carolina had been living under Negro rule for eight years. There was a condition bordering upon anarchy. Misrule, robbery, and murder were holding high carnival. The people's substance was being stolen, and there was no incentive to labor. Our legislature was composed of a majority of Negroes, most of whom could neither read nor write. They were the easy dupes and tools of as dirty a band of vampires and robbers as ever preyed upon a prostrate people. . . . Life ceased to be worth having on the terms under which we were living, and in desperation we determined to take the government away from the Negroes.

We reorganized the Democratic party [of South Carolina] with one plank, and only one plank, namely, that "this is a white man's country, and white men must govern it." Under that banner we went to battle.

We had 8000 Negro militia organized by carpetbaggers. . . . They used to drum up and down the roads with their fifes and their gleaming bayonets, equipped with new Springfield rifles and dressed in the regulation uniform. It was lawful, I suppose, but these Negro soldiers—or this Negro militia, for they were never soldiers—growing more and more bold, let drop talk among themselves where the white children might hear their purpose, and it came to our ears. This is what they said: "The President [Grant] is our friend. The North is with us. We intend to kill all the white men, take the land, marry the white women, and then these white children will wait on us." . . .

We knew—who knew better—that the North then was a unit in its opposition to Southern ideas, and that it was their purpose to perpetuate Negro governments in those states where it could be done by reason of their being a Negro majority. Having made up our minds, we set about it as practical men. . . .

Clashes came. The Negro militia grew unbearable and more and more insolent. I am not speaking of what I have read; I am speaking of what I know, of what I saw. There were two militia companies in my township and a regiment in my county. We had clashes with these Negro militiamen. The Hamburg riot was one clash, in which seven Negroes and one white man were killed. A month later we had the Ellenton riot, in which no one ever knew how many Negroes were killed, but there were forty or fifty or a hundred. It was a fight between barbarism and civilization, between the African and the Caucasian, for mastery.

It was then that "we shot them"; it was then that "we killed them"; it was then that "we stuffed ballot boxes." After the [federal] troops came and told us, "You must stop this rioting," we had decided to take the government away from men so debased as were the Negroes. . . .

[President] Grant sent troops to maintain the carpetbag government in power and to protect the Negroes in the right to vote. He merely obeyed the law. . . . Then it was that "we stuffed ballot boxes," because desperate diseases require desperate remedies, and having resolved to take the state away, we hesitated at nothing. . . .

I want to say now that we have not shot any Negroes in South Carolina on account of politics since 1876. We have not found it necessary. Eighteen hundred and seventy-six happened to be the hundredth anniversary of the Declaration of Independence, and the action of the white men of South Carolina in taking the state away from the Negroes we regard as a second declaration of independence by the Caucasian from African barbarism.

E. The Ku Klux Klan's Reign of Terror

1. Alfred Richardson Testifies about Reconstruction-Era Georgia (1871)

In 1871, a special congressional committee took testimony, in hearings conducted in both Washington and the South, about the mounting violence that was being visited upon the newly freed blacks, especially by the Ku Klux Klan. The extensive record of the committee's investigation provides grisly evidence of the dangerous situation in which black men and women found themselves in the post–Civil War South. The testimony excerpted below was given by Alfred Richardson. He was born a slave in Georgia in about 1837 and supported his wife and three children after emancipation by working as a carpenter. He was also politically active in the Republican party, an affiliation that brought down upon him the savage wrath of his white neighbors, virtually all of them Democrats. What does his testimony suggest about the political situation in the Reconstruction-era South? about the situation of black women? By what means did whites assert political and economic control over blacks? In the light of this testimony, how should the success or failure of Reconstruction policy be judged?

Washington, D.C., July 7, 1871

Alfred Richardson (colored) sworn and examined.

Question. Since you became a freeman have you voted?
Answer. Yes, sir.
Question. With what party have you voted?
Answer. The republican party.
Question. State to the committee whether you have been attacked in any way by anybody; if so, when and how. Tell us the whole story about it.
Answer. Yes, sir; I was attacked twice. The first time was just before last Christmas; I cannot recollect exactly what day.
Question. Tell us all the particulars.
Answer. There was a set of men came down to about a quarter of a mile of where I live. They were all disguised. They had taken out an old man by the name of

---

[1]Alfred Richardson, in *Testimony Taken by the Joint Select Committee to Inquire into the Condition of Affairs in the Late Insurrectionary States; Georgia, Volume I*, pp. 1–2, 12–13. *Report* No. 41, Part 6, 42d Cong., 2d sess. Senate (Washington, D.C.: Government Printing Office, 1872).

Charles Watson. They commenced beating him. His wife and children all ran out, and screamed and hallooed for help to stop the men from beating him to death. We, who were in town, came out to see what was the matter.

Question. You heard the outcry?

Answer. Yes, sir, and came out to see what was the matter. We went up the street a piece, out on the edge of the town, and heard a great parcel of men talking beside the fence. It was the Ku-Klux, who had this old man down in the corner of the fence, knocking him and telling him he had to tell where Alfred Richardson was, and had to go with them to his house and show how he was fixed up. The old man seemed to be sort of dilatory in telling them, and they rapped him over the head again and told him he had to go.

Question. They wanted him to tell where you were?

Answer. Yes, sir; they wanted him to tell where I was, and how I was fixed up; they said he had to go and get me out. In the mean time, while they were telling him this, a crowd of boys came on behind me, and we all ran up, after we heard what they were up to. They all broke and ran, and carried this old man with them. We followed them to the forks of the road, about three hundred yards from where we met them. They all stopped and got over into the field, taking the old man with them. I ran up, and looked first up one road and then the other, to see which way they had gone. I could not see anybody for a long time; a cloud had got over the moon. After a while I saw one fellow slipping alongside the fence. He had a pistol in his hand, as if to shoot me. When I saw him doing that, I took my pistol, and shot at him. When I shot at him there were three or four men who shot me from through the fence. I did not see them. They shot about twenty shots into my leg and hip. I went off home, and went to the doctor's office. The doctor examined me, and fixed my wounds up. In three or four days I got so that I could travel very well. Things went on till after Christmas. On the 18th of January a man by the name of John O. Thrasher came to me———

Question. Was he a white man?

Answer. Yes, sir; a very wealthy man. He came to me. My brother was keeping a family grocery; and I was in with him. I did not stay in the store; I worked at my trade.

Question. Were you a partner in the concern?

Answer. Yes, sir. This man told me, "There are some men about here that have something against you; and they intend to kill you or break you up. They say you are making too much money; that they do not allow any nigger to rise that way; that you can control all the colored votes; and they intend to break you up, and then they can rule the balance of the niggers when they get you off." He said, "They said they wanted me to join their party, but I told them I did not want to do it; I never knew you to do anything wrong, and these are a parcel of low-down men, and I don't want to join any such business; but I tell you, you had better keep your eyes open, for they are after you." He talked to me about it that evening for three or four hours. I told him I didn't know why they had anything against me. I talked to the ordinary, and the clerk of the court, and several other citizens. They said they didn't see why anybody wanted to interrupt me; that I had always kept the peace between the colored and the white people; that when there was a fuss I was the only man that could break it up and make the colored people behave themselves; that they hated to let me go away. I talked with all the citizens, and they told me they did not see why anybody had anything against me. I said, "I am told that some men are coming to kill me or run me off, and I think I had better go away. I don't know whether I can stay safely." They told me, "No, don't move away; they are just talking that way to scare you, I reckon." The same night this man was telling me that, I went to bed about 9 o'clock. Between 12 and 1 o'clock these men came; there were about twenty or twenty-five of them, I reckon. About eight or ten of them got abreast and ran against my door. I sort of expected them, and had my door barred very tight; I had long staples at the side, and scantling across the door. They ran against the door and tried to burst it in. They could not do it. One fellow had a new patent ax with him; and he commenced cutting down the door. One lit a candle and put it down in the piazza; the other man cut the door till he cut it down. I stood and looked at him until he cut it spang through. Then I thought I had better go up-stairs. I did so. I thought I would stand at the head of the stair-steps and shoot them as they came up. But they broke in the lower door and came up-stairs firing in every direction. I could not stand in the stairway to shoot at them. I had some small arms back in the garret. There was a door up there about large enough for one man to creep in. I thought I had better go in there, and maybe they would not find me—probably they would miss me, and I could make my escape. They all came up-stairs. My wife opened the window to call out for help, and a fellow shot at her some twelve or fifteen times through that window while she was hallooing. A whole crowd came up, and when they saw that window open, they said, "He has jumped out of the window," and they hallooed to the fellows on the ground to shoot on top of the house. Thinking I had gone out of the window, they all went down-stairs except one man. He went and looked in the cuddy-hole where I was, and saw me there. He hallooed to the rest of the fellows that he had found me; but they had got down-stairs, and some of them were on the piazza. Then he commenced firing, and shot me three times. He lodged two balls in my side, and one in the right arm. That weakened me pretty smartly. After he had shot his loads all out, he said to the rest of them, "Come back up here; I have got him; and I have shot him, but he is not quite dead; let us go up and finish him." I crept from the door of the little room where I was to the stairway; they came up-stairs with their pistols in their hands, and a man behind with a light. I shot one of them as he got on the top step. They gathered him up by the legs; and then they all ran and left me. I never saw any more of them that night; and I have not seen them since. . . .

Question. Do these bands of men ever whip women?

Answer. Yes, sir.

Question. Why do they whip women? They do not vote.

Answer. Many times, you know, a white lady has a colored lady for cook or waiting in the house, or something of that sort. They have some quarrel, and sometimes probably the colored women gives the lady a little jaw. In a night or two a crowd will come in and take her out and whip her.

Question. For talking saucily to her mistress?

Answer. Yes, sir.

Question. Does that state of things control colored labor down there? Do these bands make the negroes work for whomever they please?

Answer. Do you mean the Ku-Klux?

Question. Yes, sir.

Answer. Well, they go sometimes so far as this: When a man is hired, if he and his employer have any dispute about the price, and there are hard words between them about the amount of money to be paid, they whip the colored man for disputing the white man's word, or having any words with him.

Question. They whip the colored man for having any dispute with his employer about what shall be paid him?

Answer. Yes, sir.

Question. Is that common?

Answer. Yes, sir; that has been done several times. Sometimes colored people are working for a part of the crop. They work on till the crop is nearly completed and ready for gathering. Then a fuss arises between them and the employer, and they are whipped off—whipped off by these men in disguise. If they do not whip a man, they come and knock his door down and run him out, and he gets scared and moves away, leaving his share of the crop. He will sometimes go to the employer, and the man will say, "Your crop in the field is worth such and such a price, and that is all I will give you." The man will have to take what he can get and move off. Some of the colored people swear that they do not intend to farm any more, excepting they can have peace to gather what they plant. Now, they work a part of the year and then get run off and make nothing. So they conclude it is best to go to some city and work by the day for what they can get. Every town in our State where there is any protection is overrun with colored people. Many of the farm hands are there; and there is a great mass of loafers who stand round town because they have got no work to do. Yet people's fields around in the country are running away with grass. Some men go to town and try to get hands. The colored men will ask, "In what part of the country do you live?" The man will mention such and such a place. They will say, "We can't go down there; the Ku-Klux is down there. If it wasn't for the Ku-Klux we would go down and work for you."

Question. Are there many white republicans in your county?

Answer. No, sir; I do not supose there are over four or five. In the city of Athens the man who attends the post office, I think, is a republican; then he has got two or three sons who are clerks in the post office; then there is the tax collector. They are republicans; they vote the republican ticket. . . .

2. Maria Carter Describes an Encounter with the Klan (1871)

Maria Carter, a twenty-eight-year-old slave from South Carolina, lived in Georgia at the time she gave the following testimony to the Joint Select Committee at its hearing

---

[2]Maria Carter, in *Testimony Taken by the Joint Select Committee to Inquire into the Condition of Affairs in the Late Insurrectionary States; Georgia, Volume I*. pp. 411–412. *Report* No. 41, Part 6, 42d Cong., 2d sess. Senate (Washington, D.C.: Government Printing Office, 1872).

in Atlanta. She describes a Klan raid on her house and that of a neighbor, John Walthall. What was Walthall's alleged offense? How might one account for the ferocity of the assault on Carter's family and Walthall?

Atlanta, Georgia, October 21, 1871

Maria Carter (colored) sworn and examined.

Question. How old are you, where were you born, and where do you now live?

Answer. I will be twenty-eight years old on the 4th day of next March; I was born in South Carolina; and I live in Haralson County now.

Question. Are you married or single?

Answer. I am married.

Question. What is your husband's name?

Answer. Jasper Carter.

Question. Where were you on the night that John Walthall was shot?

Answer. In my house, next to his house; not more than one hundred yards from his house.

Question. Did any persons come to your house that night?

Answer. Yes, sir, lots of them; I expect about forty or fifty of them.

Question. What did they do at your house?

Answer. They just came there and called; we did not get up when they first called. We heard them talking as they got over the fence. They came hollering and knocking at the door, and they scared my husband so bad he could not speak when they first came. I answered them. They hollered, "Open the door," I said, "Yes, sir." They were at the other door, and they said, "Kindle a light." My husband went to kindle a light, and they busted both doors open and ran in—two in one door and two in the other. I heard the others coming on behind them, jumping over the fence in the yard. One put his gun down to him and said, "Is this John Walthall?" They had been hunting him a long time. They had gone to my brother-in-law's hunting him, and had whipped one of my sisters-in-law powerfully and two more men on account of him. They said they were going to kill him when they got hold of him. They asked my husband if he was John Walthall. He was so scared he could not say anything. I said, "No." I never got up at all. They asked where he was, and we told them he was up to the next house. They jerked my husband up and said that he had to go up there. I heard them up there hollering "Open the door," and I heard them break the door down. While they were talking about our house, just before they broke open our door, I heard a chair fall over in John Walthall's house. He raised a plank then and tried to get under the house. A parcel of them ran ahead and broke the door down and jerked his wife out of the bed. I did not see them, for I was afraid to go out of doors. They knocked his wife about powerfully. I heard them cursing her. She commenced hollering, and I heard some of them say, "God damn her, shoot her." They struck her over the head with a pistol. The house looked next morning as if somebody had been killing hogs there. Some of them said, "Fetch a light here, quick;" and some of them said to her, "Hold a light." They said she held it, and they put their guns down on him and shot him. I heard him holler, and some of them said, "Pull him out, pull him out." When they pulled him out the hole was too small, and I heard them jerk a plank part off the house and I heard it fly back. At that time four men came in my house and drew a gun on me; I was sitting in my bed and the baby was yelling. They asked, "Where is John Walthall?" I said, "Up yonder." They said, "Who lives here?" I said, "Jasper Carter." They said, "Where is John Walthall?" I said, "Them folks have got him." They said, "What folks?" I said, "Them folks up there." They came in and out all the time. I heard John holler when they commenced whipping him, They said, "Don't holler, or we'll kill you in a minute." I undertook to try and count, but they scared me so bad that I stopped counting; but I think they hit him about three hundred licks after they shot him. I heard them clear down to our house ask him if he felt like sleeping with some more white women; and they said, "You steal, too, God damn you." John said, "No, sir." They said, "Hush your mouth, God damn your eyes, you do steal." I heard them talking, but that was all I heard plain. They beat him powerfully. She said they made her put her arms around his neck and then they whipped them both together. I saw where they struck her head with a pistol and bumped her head against the house, and the blood is there yet. They asked me where my husband's gun was; I said he had no gun, and they said I was a damned liar. One of them had a sort of gown on, and he put his gun in my face and I pushed it up. The other said, "Don't you shoot her." He then went and looked in a trunk among the things. I allowed they were hunting for a pistol. My husband had had one, but he sold it. Another said, "Let's go away from here." They brought in old Uncle Charlie and sat him down there. They had a light at the time, and I got to see some of them good. I knew two of them, but the others I could not tell. There was a very large light in the house, and they went to the fire and I saw them. They came there at about 12 o'clock and staid there until 1. They went on back to old Uncle Charley's then, to whip his girls and his wife. They did not whip her any to hurt her at all. They jabbed me on the head with a gun, and I heard the trigger pop. It scared me and I throwed my hand up. He put it back again, and I pushed it away again.

Question. How old was your baby?

Answer. Not quite three weeks old.

Question. You were still in bed?

Answer. Yes, sir; I never got up at all.

Question. Did they interrupt your husband in any way?

Answer. Yes, sir; they whipped him mightily; I do not know how much. They took him away up the road, over a quarter, I expect. I saw the blood running down when he came back. Old Uncle Charley was in there. They did not carry him back home. They said, "Old man, you don't steal." He said, "No." They sat him down and said to him, "You just stay here." Just as my husband got back to one door and stepped in, three men came in the other door. They left a man at John's house while they were ripping around. As they came back by the house they said, "By God, good-bye, hallelujah!" I was scared nearly to death, and my husband tried to keep it hid from me. I asked him if he had been whipped much. He said, "No." I saw his clothes were bloody, and the next morning they stuck to him, and his shoulder was almost like jelly.

3. Henry Lowther Falls Victim to the Klan (1871)

Forty-one-year-old Henry Lowther was jailed on a charge of conspiring to kill a black man by the name of Rack Bell, who allegedly collaborated with the Ku Klux Klan. What does his gruesome account reveal about the Ku Klux Klan's tactics? What role do you think the physician played?

Atlanta, Georgia, October 20, 1871

Henry Lowther (colored) sworn and examined.

I was put in jail Saturday evening; my son was put in there with me. They said they had a warrant for him, but they did not have any. . . . I said, "Tell Captain Cummins to come here." A gentleman came with him by the name of Beaman. Captain Cummins sat down and talked with me about an hour, but there was nothing he said that I thought had any substance in it, only when he went to leave he said, "Harry, are you willing to give up your stones to save your life?" I sat there for a moment, and then I told him, "Yes." Said he, "If they come for you will you make fight?" I said "No." He said, "No fuss whatever?" I said, "No." That was about an hour by sun. I lay right down then and went to sleep, and did not wake up until 2 o'clock in the morning. Then I saw one Ku-Klux in jail with a light. I raised up, and he caught my arm and told me to come out. I came out and looked around, and the whole town was covered with them.

Question. Covered with what?

Answer. Ku-Klux. There were supposed to be one hundred and eighty of them. When they first took me out they tied me and carried me off from the jail-house about a hundred yards; they then divided into four parties, and about twenty of them carried me off into a swamp about two miles. Well, within a hundred yards of the swamp they all stopped and called numbers, began with number one, and went up as high as number ten. When they got to number ten they went for a rope, and I was satisfied they were going to hang me. I begged for my life. They told me if they did not kill me I would shoot into the Ku-Klux again. I told them I had not done it. They asked me who it was; I told them who I heard it was, but I did not know. One of them who was standing by told the other who was talking to me to hush up and ask no questions, because he knew more about it than I did. They went on then into the swamp, and came to a halt again, and stood there and talked awhile. There were eight men walking with me—one hold of each arm, three in front of me with guns, and three right behind me. After some conversation, just before they were ordered to march, or something was said, every man cocked his gun and looked right at me. I thought they were going to shoot me, and leave me right there. The moon was shining bright, and I could see them. I was satisfied they were going to kill me, and I did not care much then. They asked me whether I preferred to be altered [castrated] or to be killed. I said I preferred to be altered. After laying me down

---

[3]Henry Lowther, in *Testimony Taken by the Joint Select Committee to Inquire into the Condition of Affairs in the Late Insurrectionary States; Georgia, Volume I.* pp. 356–358. *Report* No. 41, Part 6, 42d Cong., 2d sess. Senate (Washington, D.C.: Government Printing Office, 1872).

and getting through they said: "Now, as soon as you can get to a doctor go to one; you know the doctors in this country, and as soon as you are able to leave do it, or we will kill you next time." I asked how long it would take to get well, and they said five or six weeks. I was naked and bleeding very much. It was two miles and a quarter to a doctor's. The first man's house I got to was the jailer's. I called him up and asked him to go to the jail-house and get my clothes. He said he could not go; I said, "You must; I am naked and nearly froze to death." That was about 3 o'clock in the night. He had a light in the house, and there was a party of men standing in the door. I told him I wanted him to come out and give me some attention. He said he could not come. I could hardly walk then. I went on about ten steps further and I met the jailer's son-in-law. I asked him to go and get my clothes; and he said, "No," and told me to go up and lie down. I went right on and got up to a store; there were a great many men sitting along on the store piazza; I knew some of them, but I did not look at them much. They asked me what I wanted; I said I wanted a doctor. They told me to go on and lie down. I had then to stop and hold on to the side of the house to keep from falling. I staid there a few minutes, and then went on to a doctor's house, about a quarter of a mile, and called him aloud twice. He did not answer me. The next thing I knew I was lying on the sidewalk in the street—seemed to have just waked up out of a sleep. I thought to myself, "Did I lie down here and go to sleep?" I wanted some water; I had to go about a quarter of a mile to get some water; I was getting short of breath, but the water helped me considerably. I went to a house about fifty yards further. I called to a colored woman to wake my wife up; she was in town. I happened to find my son there, and he went back for a doctor. When he got there the doctor answered the first time he called him. The reason he did not answer me was that he was off on this raid. I asked the doctor where he was when I was at his house, and he said he was asleep. I said, "I was at your house." The men kept coming in and saying to me that I did not get to the doctor's house, and I said that I did. After two or three times I took the hint, and said nothing more about that. But I told my son the next morning to go there and see if there was not a large puddle of blood at the gate. They would not let him go. But some colored women came to see me and told me that the blood was all over town; at the doctor's gate, and everywhere else. It was running a stream all the time I was trying to find the doctor, and I thought I would bleed to death. My son tended me until I got so I could travel. Doctor Cummins came there to my house on Tuesday evening, between sunset and dark, and said, "I am told you say the reason I did not come to you was that I was out on the raid with the Ku-Klux." I said, "I did not say so." He said, "That is what I heard;" and he seemed to be mad about it. He said, "I am a practicing physician, and am liable to be called at night, and must go; I was in my horse-lot then." He talked a long while, and then he said he was in his stable. He kept talking, and after awhile he said he was in his drug-store. So I never knew where he was. He said the reason he was hiding about so was he was afraid of the Ku-Klux. In a day or two he came to the house and said, "The white people have got up a story here, and say I am the man who castrated you; now, this talk must stop." I said, "Doctor, I can't help it; I don't know who did it; I didn't start the story." He said it had to be stopped; and then he began to tell me where he was; that the Ku-Klux came in, and he went right off to hide. In a few days his brother, Captain Cummins, came in and said, "Harry, I am told you make a threat of what you are going to do when you get well." I said, "What can I do?" He shook his head. I said, "Do the people believe it?" He said, "Yes, some of the most responsible people in town do believe it." I said, "I am very sorry." I then said, "Do you think the Ku-Klux will bother me any more?" He said, "If this talk dies out, I do not think they will pester you any more." I had been in the house about seventeen days; I was not able to walk, but I was uneasy; they came to me so many times that I began to be uneasy, and I left there. Just before I left they sent old man Bush and Mr. Hatfield to me to know if I would stay here and turn state's evidence against them. I said, "I am in a close place; the Ku-Klux have ordered me to leave; but I reckon I will try and stay." When I got so I could travel—I believe I lay there twenty-one days—I think it was the 22d of September, I left there. Now, I want you to understand that there was a man by the name of Lavender, who got up a company of men after they came to my house on a Monday night. I had run away. They told my wife to tell me that they would give me five days to leave in. . . .

F. The Legacy of Reconstruction

1. Editor E. L. Godkin Grieves (1871)

Irish-born E. L. Godkin, a fearless liberal, founded the distinguished and long-lived New York Nation *in 1865. So biting were his criticisms that the magazine was dubbed "the weekly day of judgment." His views on the blunders of Reconstruction were aired with incisiveness. He argued that there were two ways of dealing with the postwar South: (1) reorganize the section "from top to bottom" or (2) treat the whole community as made up of "unfortunate Americans, equally entitled to care and protection, demoralized by an accursed institution for which the whole Union was responsible, and which the whole Union had connived at, and, down to 1860, had profited by. . . ." But the North, wrote Godkin, followed neither course. Which aspects of Reconstruction does he regard as the most regrettable?*

The condition of the Negro after emancipation . . . attracted the carpetbagger as naturally as a dead ox attracts the buzzard. The lower class of demagogue scents an unenlightened constituency at an almost incredible distance, and travels towards it over mountain, valley, and river with the certainty of the mariner's compass.

But then we hastened his coming by our legislation. We deliberately, and for an indefinite period, excluded all the leading Southern men from active participation in the management of their local affairs, by a discrimination not unlike that which would be worked in this city [New York], but very much worse, if every man who

---

[1]*The Nation* (New York) 13 (December 7, 1871): 364.

had not at some time belonged to the Tammany Society were declared incapable of holding office.

It was before the war the time-honored custom of the Southern states, and a very good custom too, to put their ablest men, and men of the highest social standing and character, in office. The consequence was that it was these men who figured most prominently in the steps which led to the rebellion, and in the rebellion itself. When the war was over, we singled these men out, and not unnaturally, for punishment by the 14th Amendment and other legislation.

But we forgot that, as the President points out, they were no worse, so far as disloyalty went, than the rest of the community. They broke their oaths of allegiance to the United States, but the other white men of the South would have done the same thing if they had got the chance of doing it by being elevated to office, either under the United States or under the Confederacy. We forgot, too, that when putting a mutinous crew in irons, the most justly indignant captain leaves at liberty enough able-bodied seamen to work the ship. . . .

The results . . . have been positively infernal. In the idea that we were befriending the Negroes, we gave them possession of the government, and deprived them of the aid of all the local capacity and experience in the management of it, thus offering the states as a prey to Northern adventurers, and thus inflicting on the freedmen the very worst calamity which could befall a race newly emerged from barbarism— that is, familiarity, in the very first movements of enfranchisement, with the process of a corrupt administration, carried on by gangs of depraved vagabonds, in which the public money was stolen, the public faith made an article of traffic, the legislature openly corrupted, and all that the community contained of talent, probity, and social respectability put under a legal ban as something worthless and disreputable.

We do not hesitate to say that a better mode of debauching the freedmen, and making them permanently unfit for civil government, could hardly have been hit on had the North had such an object deliberately in view. Instead of establishing equal rights for all, we set up the government of a class, and this class the least competent, the most ignorant and inexperienced, and a class, too, whose history and antecedents made its rule peculiarly obnoxious to the rest of the community.

Out of this state of things Ku-Kluxing has grown . . . naturally. . . . We cannot gainsay anything anybody says of the atrocity of riding about the country at night with one's face blackened, murdering and whipping people. But we confess we condemn Ku-Kluxing very much as we condemn the cholera. . . . There is no more use in getting in a rage with Ku-Kluxery, and sending cavalry and artillery after it, than of legislating against pestilence, as long as nothing is done to remove the causes.

2. Frederick Douglass Complains (1882)

The incredible former slave Frederick Douglass (see p. 347) raised two famous black regiments in Massachusetts during the Civil War. Among the first recruits were his

---

[2]*Life and Times of Frederick Douglass* (Hartford Park Publishing Company, 1881), pp. 458–459.

own sons. Continuing his campaign for civil rights and suffrage for the freedmen, he wrote the following bitter commentary in his autobiography. One of his keenest regrets was that the federal government, despite the urgings of Thaddeus Stevens and others, failed to provide land for the freed slaves. In the light of his observations, how would free land have alleviated the conditions he describes? Why did the former slaveowners make life extremely difficult for the former slaves?

Though slavery was abolished, the wrongs of my people were not ended. Though they were not slaves, they were not yet quite free. No man can be truly free whose liberty is dependent upon the thought, feeling, and action of others, and who has himself no means in his own hands for guarding, protecting, defending, and maintaining that liberty. Yet the Negro after his emancipation was precisely in this state of destitution.

The law on the side of freedom is of great advantage only where there is power to make that law respected. I know no class of my fellow men, however just, enlightened, and humane, which can be wisely and safely trusted absolutely with the liberties of any other class. Protestants are excellent people, but it would not be wise for Catholics to depend entirely upon them to look after their rights and interests. Catholics are a pretty good sort of people (though there is a soul-shuddering history behind them); yet no enlightened Protestants would commit their liberty to their care and keeping.

And yet the government had left the freedmen in a worse condition than either of these. It felt that it had done enough for him. It had made him free, and henceforth he must make his own way in the world, or, as the slang phrase has it, "root, pig, or die." Yet he had none of the conditions for self-preservation or self-protection.

He was free from the individual master, but the slave of society. He had neither money, property, nor friends. He was free from the old plantation, but he had nothing but the dusty road under his feet. He was free from the old quarter that once gave him shelter, but a slave to the rains of summer and the frosts of winter. He was, in a word, literally turned loose, naked, hungry, and destitute, to the open sky.

The first feeling toward him by the old master classes was full of bitterness and wrath. They resented his emancipation as an act of hostility toward them, and, since they could not punish the emancipator, they felt like punishing the object which that act had emancipated. Hence they drove him off the old plantation, and told him he was no longer wanted there. They not only hated him because he had been freed as a punishment to them, but because they felt that they had been robbed of his labor.

An element of greater bitterness still came into their hearts: the freedman had been the friend of the government, and many of his class had borne arms against them during the war. The thought of paying cash for labor that they could formerly extort by the lash did not in any wise improve their disposition to the emancipated slave, or improve his own condition.

Now, since poverty has, and can have, no chance against wealth, the landless against the landowner, the ignorant against the intelligent, the freedman was powerless. He had nothing left him but a slavery-distorted and diseased body, and lame and twisted limbs, with which to fight the battle of life.

3. Booker T. Washington Reflects (1901)

Booker T. Washington was reared in a one-room, dirt-floored shanty, and never slept on a bed until after emancipation. Obtaining an education under grave hardships, he ultimately became the head of the famed industrial institute at Tuskegee, Alabama. The acknowledged leader of his race after Frederick Douglass died in 1895, he won additional fame as an orator and as an apostle of "gradualism" in achieving equality with the whites. He believed that blacks should acquire manual skills and otherwise prove themselves worthy of a place beside whites. Black intellectuals like W. E. B. Du Bois (see p. 505) criticized this conservative "Uncle Tomism" as condemning the race to permanent inferiority. In the following selection from Washington's justly famous autobiography, what does the author regard as the chief mistakes made by both whites and blacks in Reconstruction?

Though I was but little more than a youth during the period of Reconstruction, I had the feeling that mistakes were being made, and that things could not remain in the condition that they were in then very long. I felt that the Reconstruction policy, so far as it related to my race, was in a large measure on a false foundation, was artificial and forced. In many cases it seemed to me that the ignorance of my race was being used as a tool with which to help white men into office, and that there was an element in the North which wanted to punish the Southern white men by forcing the Negro into positions over the heads of the Southern whites. I felt that the Negro would be the one to suffer for this in the end. Besides, the general political agitation drew the attention of our people away from the more fundamental matters of perfecting themselves in the industries at their doors and in securing property.

The temptations to enter political life were so alluring that I came very near yielding to them at one time, but I was kept from doing so by the feeling that I would be helping in a more substantial way by assisting in the laying of the foundation of the race through a generous education of the hand, head, and heart. I saw colored men who were members of the state legislatures, and county officers, who, in some cases, could not read or write, and whose morals were as weak as their education.

Not long ago, when passing through the streets of a certain city in the South, I heard some brick-masons calling out, from the top of a two-story brick building on which they were working, for the "Governor" to "hurry up and bring up some more bricks." Several times I heard the command, "Hurry up, Governor!" "Hurry up, Governor!" My curiosity was aroused to such an extent that I made inquiry as to who the "Governor" was, and soon found that he was a colored man who at one time had held the position of Lieutenant-Governor of his state.

But not all the colored people who were in office during Reconstruction were unworthy of their positions, by any means. Some of them, like the late Senator B. K. Bruce, Governor Pinchback, and many others, were strong, upright, useful men. Neither were all the class designated as carpetbaggers dishonorable men. Some of them, like ex-Governor Bullock of Georgia, were men of high character and usefulness.

---

[3]Booker T. Washington, *Up from Slavery* (New York: A. L. Burt, 1901), pp. 83–86.

Of course the colored people, so largely without education, and wholly without experience in government, made tremendous mistakes, just as any people similarly situated would have done. Many of the Southern whites have a feeling that, if the Negro is permitted to exercise his political rights now to any degree, the mistakes of the Reconstruction period will repeat themselves. I do not think this would be true, because the Negro is a much stronger and wiser man than he was thirty-five years ago, and he is fast learning the lesson that he cannot afford to act in a manner that will alienate his Southern white neighbors from him. . . .

During the whole of the Reconstruction period our people throughout the South looked to the federal government for everything, very much as a child looks to its mother. This was not unnatural. The central government gave them freedom, and the whole nation had been enriched for more than two centuries by the labor of the Negro. Even as a youth, and later in manhood, I had the feeling that it was cruelly wrong in the central government, at the beginning of our freedom, to fail to make some provision for the general education of our people in addition to what the states might do, so that the people would be the better prepared for the duties of citizenship.

It is easy to find fault, to remark what might have been done, and perhaps, after all, and under all the circumstances, those in charge of the conduct of affairs did the only thing that could be done at the time. Still, as I look back now over the entire period of our freedom, I cannot help feeling that it would have been wiser if some plan could have been put in operation which would have made the possession of a certain amount of education or property, or both, a test for the exercise of the franchise, and a way provided by which this test should be made to apply honestly and squarely to both the white and black races.

Thought Provokers

1. Was the white South ever really defeated in spirit? Would the results have been more satisfactory from its point of view if it had accepted the rule of the conqueror with better grace?
2. What were the major differences between presidential and congressional Reconstruction plans? What accounts for those different approaches? Who had the better constitutional arguments? Who advocated the soundest policies?
3. It has been said that Johnson was his own worst enemy, and that the white Southerners were damaged by his determination to befriend them with a "soft" policy. Comment critically.
4. Present the cases for and against *immediate* and *gradual* black suffrage. Form conclusions. Why have the excesses of the black–white legislatures been overplayed and their achievements downgraded?
5. Why did organizations like the Ku Klux Klan flourish in the Reconstruction South? In what ways did the KKK resemble a modern "terrorist" group?
6. Identify the most serious long-run mistake made during Reconstruction. What have been the effects of that mistake?

Constitution of the United States of America

[Boldface headings and bracketed explanatory matter have been inserted for the reader's convenience. Passages that are no longer operative are printed in italic type.]

Preamble

We the people of the United States, in order to form a more perfect union, establish justice, insure domestic tranquillity, provide for the common defense, promote the general welfare, and secure the blessings of liberty to ourselves and our posterity, do ordain and establish this CONSTITUTION for the United States of America.

Article I. Legislative Department

Section I. Congress

Legislative power vested in a two-house Congress. All legislative powers herein granted shall be vested in a Congress of the United States, which shall consist of a Senate and a House of Representatives.

Section II. House of Representatives

1. **The people to elect representatives biennially.** The House of Representatives shall be composed of members chosen every second year by the people of the several States, and the electors [voters] in each State shall have the qualifications requisite for electors of the most numerous branch of the State Legislature.

2. **Who may be representatives.** No person shall be a Representative who shall not have attained to the age of twenty-five years, and been seven years a citizen of the United States, and who shall not, when elected, be an inhabitant of that State in which he shall be chosen.

3. **Representation in the House based on population; census.** Representatives and direct taxes[1] shall be apportioned among the several States which may be included within this Union, according to their respective numbers, *which shall be determined by adding to the whole number of free persons, including those bound to service for a term of years* [apprentices and indentured servants], *and excluding*

---

[1]Modified in 1913 by the Sixteenth Amendment authorizing income taxes.

Indians not taxed, three-fifths of all other persons [slaves].[1] The actual enumeration [census] shall be made within three years after the first meeting of the Congress of the United States, and within every subsequent term of ten years, in such manner as they shall by law direct. The number of Representatives shall not exceed one for every thirty thousand, but each State shall have at least one Representative; *and until such enumeration shall be made, the State of New Hampshire shall be entitled to choose three, Massachusetts eight, Rhode Island and Providence Plantations one, Connecticut five, New York six, New Jersey four, Pennsylvania eight, Delaware one, Maryland six, Virginia ten, North Carolina five, South Carolina five, and Georgia three.*

4. Vacancies in the House to be filled by election. When vacancies happen in the representation from any State, the Executive authority [governor] thereof shall issue writs of election [call a special election] to fill such vacancies.

5. The House to select its officers; to vote impeachment charges (i.e., indictments). The House of Representatives shall choose their Speaker and other officers; and shall have the sole power of impeachment.

Section III. Senate

1. Senators to represent the states. The Senate of the United States shall be composed of two Senators from each State, *chosen by the legislature thereof,*[2] for six years; and each Senator shall have one vote.

2. One-third of Senators to be chosen every two years; vacancies. *Immediately after they shall be assembled in consequence of the first election, they shall be divided as equally as may be into three classes. The seats of the Senators of the first class shall be vacated at the expiration of the second year, of the second class at the expiration of the fourth year, and of the third class at the expiration of the sixth year,* so that one-third may be chosen every second year; *and if vacancies happen by resignation or otherwise, during the recess of the legislature of any State, the Executive* [governor] *thereof may make temporary appointments until the next meeting of the legislature, which shall then fill such vacancies.*[3]

3. Who may be Senators. No person shall be a Senator who shall not have attained to the age of thirty years, and been nine years a citizen of the United States, and who shall not, when elected, be an inhabitant of that State for which he shall be chosen.

4. The Vice-President to preside over the Senate. The Vice-President of the United States shall be President of the Senate, but shall have no vote, unless they be equally divided [tied].

5. The Senate to choose its other officers. The Senate shall choose their other officers, and also a President pro tempore, in the absence of the Vice-President, or when he shall exercise the office of President of the United States.

6. The Senate to try impeachments. The Senate shall have the sole power

---

[1]The word *slave* appears nowhere in the Constitution; *slavery* appears in the Thirteenth Amendment. The three-fifths rule ceased to be in force when the Thirteenth Amendment was adopted in 1865.

[2]Repealed in favor of popular election in 1913 by the Seventeenth Amendment.

[3]Changed in 1913 by the Seventeenth Amendment.

to try all impeachments. When sitting for that purpose, they shall be on oath or affirmation. When the President of the United States is tried, the Chief Justice shall preside:[1] and no person shall be convicted without the concurrence of two-thirds of the members present.

7. Penalties for impeachment conviction. Judgment in cases of impeachment shall not extend further than to removal from office, and disqualification to hold and enjoy any office of honor, trust or profit under the United States: but the party convicted shall nevertheless be liable and subject to indictment, trial, judgment and punishment, according to law.

Section IV. Election and Meetings of Congress

1. Regulation of elections. The times, places and manner of holding elections for Senators and Representatives shall be prescribed in each State by the legislature thereof; but the Congress may at any time by law make or alter such regulations, except as to the places of choosing Senators.

2. Congress to meet once a year. The Congress shall assemble at least once in every year, and such meeting *shall be on the first Monday in December, unless they shall by law appoint a different day.*[2]

Section V. Organization and Rules of the Houses

1. Each House may reject members; quorums. Each house shall be the judge of the elections, returns and qualifications of its own members, and a majority of each shall constitute a quorum to do business; but a smaller number may adjourn from day to day, and may be authorized to compel the attendance of absent members, in such manner, and under such penalties, as each house may provide.

2. Each House to make its own rules. Each house may determine the rules of its proceedings, punish its members for disorderly behavior, and with the concurrence of two-thirds, expel a member.

3. Each House to publish a record of its proceedings. Each house shall keep a journal of its proceedings, and from time to time publish the same, excepting such parts as may in their judgment require secrecy; and the yeas and nays of the members of either house on any question shall, at the desire of one-fifth of those present, be entered on the journal.

4. Both Houses required to agree on adjournment. Neither house, during the session of Congress, shall, without the consent of the other, adjourn for more than three days, nor to any other place than that in which the two houses shall be sitting.

Section VI. Privileges of and Prohibitions upon Congressmen

1. Congressional salaries; immunities. The Senators and Representatives shall receive a compensation for their services, to be ascertained by law and paid out of the treasury of the United States. They shall in all cases except treason, felony and breach of the peace, be privileged from arrest during their attendance at the

---

[1]The vice-president, as next in line, would be an interested party.
[2]Changed in 1933 to January 3 by the Twentieth Amendment.

session of their respective houses, and in going to and returning from the same; and for any speech or debate in either house, they shall not be questioned in any other place [i.e., they shall be immune from libel suits].[1]

2. Congressmen not to hold incompatible federal civil offices. No Senator or Representative shall, during the time for which he was elected, be appointed to any civil office under the authority of the United States, which shall have been created, or the emoluments whereof shall have been increased, during such time; and no person holding any office under the United States shall be a member of either house during his continuance in office.

Section VII. Method of Making Laws

1. Money bills to originate in the House. All bills for raising revenue shall originate in the House of Representatives; but the Senate may propose or concur with amendments as on other bills.

2. The President's veto power; Congress may override. Every bill which shall have passed the House of Representatives and the Senate, shall, before it become a law, be presented to the President of the United States; if he approve he shall sign it, but if not he shall return it with his objections to that house in which it shall have originated, who shall enter the objections at large on their journal, and proceed to reconsider it. If after such reconsideration two-thirds of that house shall agree to pass the bill, it shall be sent, together with the objections, to the other house, by which it shall likewise be reconsidered, and, if approved by two-thirds of that house, it shall become a law. But in all such cases the votes of both houses shall be determined by yeas and nays, and the names of the persons voting for and against the bill shall be entered on the journal of each house respectively. If any bill shall not be returned by the President within ten days (Sundays excepted) after it shall have been presented to him, the same shall be a law, in like manner as if he had signed it, unless the Congress by their adjournment prevent its return, in which case it shall not be a law [this is the so-called pocket veto].

3. All measures requiring the agreement of both Houses to go to the President for approval. Every order, resolution, or vote to which the concurrence of the Senate and House of Representatives may be necessary (except on a question of adjournment) shall be presented to the President of the United States; and before the same shall take effect, shall be approved by him, or being disapproved by him, shall be repassed by two-thirds of the Senate and House of Representatives, according to the rules and limitations prescribed in the case of a bill.

Section VIII. Powers Granted to Congress

Congress possesses certain enumerated powers:

1. Congress may lay and collect taxes. The Congress shall have power to lay and collect taxes, duties, imposts, and excises, to pay the debts and provide for the common defense and general welfare of the United States; but all duties, imposts and excises shall be uniform throughout the United States;

---

[1] In the 1950s, Senator Joseph R. McCarthy was accused of abusing this privilege.

2. Congress may borrow money. To borrow money on the credit of the United States;

3. Congress may regulate foreign and interstate trade. To regulate commerce with foreign nations, and among the several States, and with the Indian tribes;

4. Congress may pass naturalization and bankruptcy laws. To establish an uniform rule of naturalization, and uniform laws on the subject of bankruptcies throughout the United States;

5. Congress may coin money and regulate weights and measures. To coin money, regulate the value thereof, and of foreign coin, and fix the standard of weights and measures;

6. Congress may punish counterfeiters. To provide for the punishment of counterfeiting the securities and current coin of the United States;

7. Congress may establish a postal service. To establish post offices and post roads;

8. Congress may issue patents and copyrights. To promote the progress of science and useful arts by securing for limited times to authors and inventors the exclusive right to their respective writings and discoveries;

9. Congress may establish inferior courts. To constitute tribunals inferior to the Supreme Court;

10. Congress may punish crimes committed on the high seas. To define and punish piracies and felonies committed on the high seas [i.e., outside the three-mile limit] and offenses against the law of nations [international law];

11. Congress may declare war, may authorize privateering. To declare war,[1] grant letters of marque and reprisal,[2] and make rules concerning captures on land and water;

12. Congress may maintain an army. To raise and support armies, but no appropriation of money to that use shall be for a longer term than two years;[3]

13. Congress may maintain a navy. To provide and maintain a navy;

14. Congress may regulate the army and navy. To make rules for the government and regulation of the land and naval forces;

15. Congress may call out the state militia. To provide for calling forth the militia to execute the laws of the Union, suppress insurrections, and repel invasions;

16. Congress shares with the states control of militia. To provide for organizing, arming, and disciplining the militia, and for governing such part of them as may be employed in the service of the United States, reserving to the States respectively the appointment of the officers, and the authority of training the militia according to the discipline prescribed by Congress;

17. Congress makes laws for the District of Columbia and other federal areas. To exercise exclusive legislation in all cases whatsoever, over such district (not exceeding ten miles square) as may, be cession of particular States, and the acceptance of Congress, become the seat of government of the United States,[4] and to

---

[1]Note that the president, although he can provoke war or wage it after it is declared, cannot declare it.

[2]Papers issued to private citizens in time of war authorizing them to capture enemy ships.

[3]A reflection of fear of standing armies earlier expressed in the Declaration of Independence.

[4]District of Columbia, ten miles square, was established in 1791.

exercise like authority over all places purchased by the consent of the legislature of the State, in which the same shall be, for the erection of forts, magazines, arsenals, dock-yards, and other needful buildings;—and

Congress has certain implied powers:

18. **Congress may enact laws necessary to enforce the Constitution.** To make all laws which shall be necessary and proper for carrying into execution the foregoing powers, and all other powers vested by this Constitution in the government of the United States, or in any department or officer thereof.

Section IX. Powers Denied to the Federal Government

1. **Congressional control of slave trade postponed until 1808.** *The migration or importation of such persons as any of the States now existing shall think proper to admit shall not be prohibited by the Congress prior to the year 1808; but a tax or duty may be imposed on such importation, not exceeding $10 for each person.*

2. **The writ of habeas corpus[1] not to be suspended; exception.** The privilege of the writ of habeas corpus shall not be suspended, unless when in cases of rebellion or invasion the public safety may require it.

3. **Attainders[2] and ex post facto laws[3] forbidden.** No bill of attainder or ex post facto law shall be passed.

4. **Direct taxes to be apportioned according to population.** No capitation [head or poll tax], or other direct, tax shall be laid, unless in proportion to the census or enumeration herein before directed to be taken.[4]

5. **Export taxes forbidden.** No tax or duty shall be laid on articles exported from any State.

6. **Congress not to discriminate among states in regulating commerce; interstate shipping.** No preference shall be given by any regulation of commerce or revenue to the ports of one State over those of another; nor shall vessels bound to, or from, one State, be obliged to enter, clear, or pay duties in another.

7. **Public money not to be spent without Congressional appropriation; accounting.** No money shall be drawn from the treasury, but in consequence of appropriations made by law; and a regular statement and account of the receipts and expenditures of all public money shall be published from time to time.

8. **Titles of nobility prohibited; foreign gifts.** No title of nobility shall be granted by the United States: and no person holding any office of profit or trust under them, shall, without the consent of the Congress, accept of any present, emolument, office, or title, of any kind whatever, from any king, prince, or foreign state.

---

[1]A writ of habeas corpus is a document that enables a person under arrest to obtain an immediate examination in court to ascertain whether he is being legally held.

[2]A bill of attainder is a special legislative act condemning and punishing an individual without a judicial trial.

[3]An ex post facto law is one that fixes punishment for acts committed before the law was passed.

[4]Modified in 1913 by the Sixteenth Amendment.

Section X. Powers Denied to the States

Absolute prohibitions on the states:

1. **The states forbidden certain powers.** No State shall enter into any treaty, alliance, or confederation; grant letters of marque and reprisal [i.e., authorize priva-teers], coin money; emit bills of credit [issue paper money]; make anything but gold and silver coin a [legal] tender in payment of debts; pass any bill of attainder, ex post facto law,[1] or law impairing the obligation of contracts, or grant any title of nobility.

Conditional prohibitions on the states:

2." **The states not to levy duties without the consent of Congress.** No State shall, without the consent of the Congress, lay any imposts or duties on im-ports or exports, except what may be absolutely necessary for executing its inspec-tion laws: and the net produce of all duties and imposts, laid by any State on imports or exports, shall be for the use of the treasury of the United States; and all such laws shall be subject to the revision and control of the Congress.

3. **Other federal powers forbidden the states.** No State shall, without the consent of Congress, lay any duty of tonnage [i.e., duty on ship tonnage], keep [non-militia] troops or ships of war in time of peace, enter into any agreement or compact with another State, or with a foreign power, or engage in war, unless actually in-vaded, or in such imminent danger as will not admit of delay.

Article II. Executive Department

Section I. President and Vice-President

1. **The President the chief executive; his term.** The executive power shall be vested in a President of the United States of America. He shall hold his office dur-ing the term of four years,[2] and, together with the Vice-President, chosen for the same term, be elected as follows:

2. **The President to be chosen by state electors.** Each State shall appoint, in such manner as the legislature thereof may direct, a number of electors, equal to the whole number of Senators and Representatives to which the State may be entitled in the Congress; but no Senator or Representative, or person holding an office of trust or profit under the United States, shall be appointed an elector.

A majority of the electoral votes needed to elect a President. *The electors shall meet in their respective States, and vote by ballot for two persons, of whom one at least shall not be an inhabitant of the same State with themselves. And they shall make a list of all the persons voted for, and of the number of votes for each; which list they shall sign and certify, and transmit sealed to the seat of government of the United States, directed to the President of the Senate. The President of the Senate shall, in the presence of the Senate and House of Representatives, open all the certifi-*

---

[1]For definitions see footnotes 2 and 3 on preceding page.

[2]No reference to reelection; clarified by the anti-third term Twenty-second Amendment.

cates, and the votes shall then be counted. The person having the greatest number of votes shall be the President, if such number be a majority of the whole number of electors appointed; and if there be more than one who have such majority, and have an equal number of votes, then the House of Representatives shall immediately choose by ballot one of them for President; and if no person have a majority, then from the five highest on the list the said house shall in like manner choose the President. But in choosing the President the votes shall be taken by States, the representation from each State having one vote; a quorum for this purpose shall consist of a member or members from two-thirds of the States, and a majority of all the States shall be necessary to a choice. In every case, after the choice of the President, the person having the greatest number of votes of the electors shall be the Vice-President. But if there should remain two or more who have equal votes, the Senate shall choose from them by ballot the Vice-President.[1]

3. Congress to decide time of meeting of Electoral College. The Congress may determine the time of choosing the electors and the day on which they shall give their votes; which day shall be the same throughout the United States.

4. Who may be President. No person except a natural-born citizen, *or a citizen of the United States at the time of the adoption of this Constitution,* shall be eligible to the office of President; neither shall any person be eligible to that office who shall not have attained to the age of thirty-five years, and been fourteen years a resident within the United States [i.e., a legal resident].

5. Replacements for President. In case of the removal of the President from office or of his death, resignation, or inability to discharge the powers and duties of the said office, the same shall devolve on the Vice-President, and the Congress may by law provide for the case of removal, death, resignation, or inability, both of the President and Vice-President, declaring what officer shall then act as President, and such officer shall act accordingly, until the disability be removed, or a President shall be elected.

6. The President's salary. The President shall, at stated times, receive for his services a compensation, which shall neither be increased nor diminished during the period for which he shall have been elected, and he shall not receive within that period any other emolument from the United States, or any of them.

7. The President's oath of office. Before he enter on the execution of his office, he shall take the following oath or affirmation:—"I do solemnly swear (or affirm) that I will faithfully execute the office of President of the United States, and will to the best of my ability preserve, protect and defend the Constitution of the United States."

Section II. Powers of the President

1. The President has important military and civil powers. The President shall be commander in chief of the army and navy of the United States, and of the militia of the several States, when called into the actual service of the United States; he may require the opinion, in writing, of the principal officer in each of the executive departments, upon any subject relating to the duties of their respective offices,

---

[1]Repealed in 1804 by the Twelfth Amendment.

and he shall have power to grant reprieves and pardons for offenses against the United States, except in cases of impeachment.[1]

2. The President may negotiate treaties and nominate federal officials. He shall have power, by and with the advice and consent of the Senate, to make treaties, provided two-thirds of the Senators present concur; and he shall nominate, and by and with the advice and consent of the Senate, shall appoint ambassadors, other public ministers and consuls, judges of the Supreme Court, and all other officers of the United States, whose appointments are not herein otherwise provided for, and which shall be established by law: but the Congress may by law vest the appointment of such inferior officers, as they think proper, in the President alone, in the courts of law, or in the heads of departments.

3. The President may fill vacancies during Senate recess. The President shall have power to fill up all vacancies that may happen during the recess of the Senate, by granting commissions which shall expire at the end of their next session.

Section III. Other Powers and Duties of the President

Submitting messages; calling extra sessions; receiving ambassadors; executing the laws; commissioning officers. He shall from time to time give to the Congress information of the state of the Union, and recommend to their consideration such measures as he shall judge necessary and expedient; he may, on extraordinary occasions, convene both houses, or either of them, and in case of disagreement between them, with respect to the time of adjournment, he may adjourn them to such time as he shall think proper; he shall receive ambassadors and other public ministers; he shall take care that the laws be faithfully executed, and shall commission all the officers of the United States.

Section IV. Impeachment

Civil officers may be removed by impeachment. The President, Vice-President, and all civil officers[2] of the United States shall be removed from office on impeachment for, and on conviction of, treason, bribery, or other high crimes and misdemeanors.

Article III. Judicial Department

Section I. The Federal Courts

The judicial power lodged in the federal courts. The judicial power of the United States shall be vested in one Supreme Court, and in such inferior courts as the Congress may from time to time ordain and establish. The judges, both of the Supreme and inferior courts, shall hold their offices during good behavior, and shall, at stated times, receive for their services a compensation which shall not be diminished during their continuance in office.

---

[1]To prevent the president's pardoning himself or his close associates.

[2]That is, all federal executive and judicial officers, but not members of Congress or military personnel.

Section II. Jurisdiction of Federal Courts

1. **Kinds of cases that may be heard.** The judicial power shall extend to all cases, in law and equity, arising under this Constitution, the laws of the United States, and treaties made, or which shall be made, under their authority;—to all cases affecting ambassadors, other public ministers and consuls;—to all cases of admiralty and maritime jurisdiction;—to controversies to which the United States shall be a party;—to controversies between two or more States;—*between a State and citizens of another State;*[1]—between citizens of different States;—between citizens of the same State claiming lands under grants of different States, and between a State, or the citizens thereof, and foreign states, citizens or subjects.

2. **Jurisdiction of the Supreme Court.** In all cases affecting ambassadors, other public ministers and consuls, and those in which a State shall be party, the Supreme Court shall have original jurisdiction.[2] In all the other cases before mentioned, the Supreme Court shall have appellate jurisdiction,[3] both as to law and fact, with such exceptions, and under such regulations, as the Congress shall make.

3. **Trial for federal crime to be by jury.** The trial of all crimes, except in cases of impeachment, shall be by jury; and such trial shall be held in the State where the said crimes shall have been committed; but when not committed within any State, the trial shall be at such place or places as the Congress may by law have directed.

Section III. Treason

1. **Treason defined; necessary evidence.** Treason against the United States shall consist only in levying war against them, or in adhering to their enemies, giving them aid and comfort. No person shall be convicted of treason unless on the testimony of two witnesses to the same overt act, or on confession in open court.

2. **Congress to fix punishment for treason.** The Congress shall have power to declare the punishment of treason, but no attainder of treason shall work corruption of blood, or forfeiture except during the life of the person attained.[4]

Article IV. Relations of the States to One Another

Section I. Credit to Acts, Records, and Court Proceedings

Each state to respect the public acts of the others. Full faith and credit shall be given in each State to the public acts, records, and judicial proceedings of every other State.[5] And the Congress may by general laws prescribe the manner in which such acts, records, and proceedings shall be proved [attested], and the effect thereof.

---

[1]The Eleventh Amendment restricts this to suits by a state against citizens of another state.

[2]That is, such cases must originate in the Supreme Court.

[3]That is, it hears other cases only when they are appealed to it from a lower federal court or a state court.

[4]That is, punishment only for the offender; none for his heirs.

[5]For example, a marriage valid in one is valid in all.

Section II. Duties of States to States

1. **Citizenship in one state valid in all.** The citizens of each State shall be entitled to all privileges and immunities of citizens in the several States.

2. **Fugitives from justice to be surrendered by the states.** A person charged in any State with treason, felony, or other crime, who shall flee from justice, and be found in another State, shall on demand of the executive authority [governor] of the state from which he fled, be delivered up, to be removed to the State having jurisdiction of the crime.

3. **Slaves and apprentices to be returned.** *No person held to service or labor in one State, under the laws thereof, escaping into another, shall, in consequence of any law or regulation therein, be discharged from such service or labor, but shall be delivered up on claim of the party to whom such service or labor may be due.*[1]

Section III. New States and Territories

1. **Congress to admit new states.** New States may be admitted by the Congress into this Union; but no new State shall be formed or erected within the jurisdiction of any other State, nor any State be formed by the junction of two or more States, or parts of States, without the consent of the legislatures of the States concerned as well as of the Congress.

2. **Congress to regulate federal territory and property.** The Congress shall have power to dispose of and make all needful rules and regulations respecting the territory or other property belonging to the United States; and nothing in this Constitution shall be so construed as to prejudice any claims of the United States, or of any particular State.

Section IV. Protection to the States

Republican form of government guaranteed; also protection against invasion and rebellion. The United States shall guarantee to every State in this Union a republican form of government, and shall protect each of them against invasion; and on application of the legislature, or of the executive [governor] (when the legislature cannot be convened), against domestic violence.

Article V. The Process of Amendment

The Constitution may be amended in one of four ways. The Congress, whenever two-thirds of both houses shall deem it necessary, shall propose amendments to this Constitution, or, on the application of the legislatures of two-thirds of the several States, shall call a convention for proposing amendments, which, in either case, shall be valid to all intents and purposes, as part of this Constitution, when ratified by the legislatures of three-fourths of the several States, or by conventions in three-fourths thereof, as the one or the other mode of ratification may be proposed by the Con-

---

[1]Invalidated in 1865 by the Thirteenth Amendment.

gress; provided *that no amendments which may be made prior to the year one thousand eight hundred and eight shall in any manner affect the first and fourth clauses in the ninth section of the first article,*[1] *and* that no State, without its consent, shall be deprived of its equal suffrage in the Senate.

Article VI. General Provisions

1. The debts of the Confederation secured. All debts contracted and engagements entered into, before the adoption of this Constitution, shall be as valid against the United States under this Constitution, as under the Confederation.

2. The Constitution, federal laws, and treaties the supreme law of the land. This Constitution, and the laws of the United States which shall be made in pursuance thereof; and all treaties made, or which shall be made, under the authority of the United States, shall be the supreme law of the land; and the judges in every State shall be bound thereby, anything in the Constitution or laws of any State to the contrary notwithstanding.

3. Federal and state officers bound by oath to support the Constitution; religious tests forbidden. The Senators and Representatives before mentioned, and the members of the several State legislatures, and all executive and judicial officers, both of the United States and of the several States, shall be bound by oath or affirmation to support this Constitution; but no religious test shall ever be required as a qualification to any office or public trust under the United States.

Article VII. Ratification of the Constitution

The Constitution to become effective when ratified by nine states. The ratification of the conventions of nine States shall be sufficient for the establishment of this Constitution between the States so ratifying the same.

Done in Convention by the unanimous consent of the States present, the seventeenth day of September in the year of our Lord one thousand seven hundred and eighty-seven and of the Independence of the United States of America the twelfth. In witness whereof we have hereunto subscribed our names.

[Signed by]   *G° Washington*
                                                     Presidt and Deputy from Virginia
                                                     [and thirty-eight others]

---

[1] This clause, relating to slave trade and direct taxes, became inoperative in 1808.

AMENDMENTS TO THE CONSTITUTION

Article I. Religious and Political Freedom (1791)

Congress not to interfere with freedom of religion, speech or press, assembly, and petition. Congress shall make no law respecting an establishment of religion, or prohibiting the free exercise thereof; or abridging the freedom of speech, or of the press; or the right of the people peaceably to assemble, and to petition the government for a redress of grievances.

Article II. Right to Bear Arms (1791)

The people secured in their right to bear arms. A well-regulated militia being necessary to the security of a free State, the right of the people to keep and bear arms [i.e., for military purposes] shall not be infringed.

Article III. Quartering of Troops (1791)

Quartering of soldiers on the people restricted. No soldier shall, in time of peace, be quartered in any house without the consent of the owner, nor in time of war, but in a manner to be prescribed by law.

Article IV. Searches and Seizures (1791)

Unreasonable searches forbidden. The right of the people to be secure in their persons, houses, papers, and effects, against unreasonable searches and seizures, shall not be violated, and no [search] warrants shall issue but upon probable cause, supported by oath or affirmation, and particularly describing the place to be searched, and the persons or things to be seized.

Article V. Right to Life, Liberty, and Property (1791)

Individuals guaranteed certain rights when on trial and the right to life, liberty, and property. No person shall be held to answer for a capital, or otherwise infamous, crime, unless on a presentment [formal charge] or indictment of a grand jury, except in cases arising in the land or naval forces, or in the militia, when in actual service in time of war or public danger; nor shall any person be subject for the same offense to be twice put in jeopardy of life or limb; nor shall be compelled in any criminal case to be a witness against himself, nor be deprived of life, liberty, or property, without due process of law; nor shall private property be taken for public use [i.e., by eminent domain] without just compensation.

Article VI. Protection in Criminal Trials (1791)

Accused persons assured of important rights. In all criminal prosecutions, the accused shall enjoy the right to a speedy and public trial, by an impartial jury of the State and district wherein the crime shall have been committed, which district shall have been previously ascertained by law, and to be informed of the nature and cause of the accusation; to be confronted with the witnesses against him; to have compulsory process [subpoena] for obtaining witnesses in his favor, and to have the assistance of counsel for his defense.

Article VII. Suits at Common Law (1791)

The rules of common law recognized. In suits at common law, where the value in controversy shall exceed twenty dollars, the right of trial by jury shall be preserved, and no fact tried by a jury shall be otherwise re-examined in any court of the United States, than according to the rules of the common law.

Article VIII. Bail and Punishments (1791)

Excessive bail, fines, and punishments forbidden. Excessive bail shall not be required, nor excessive fines imposed, nor cruel and unusual punishments inflicted.

Article IX. Concerning Rights Not Enumerated (1791)

The people to retain rights not here enumerated. The enumeration in the Constitution, of certain rights, shall not be construed to deny or disparage others retained by the people.

Article X. Powers Reserved to the States and to the People (1791)

Powers not delegated to the federal government reserved to the states and the people. The powers not delegated to the United States by the Constitution, nor prohibited by it to the States, are reserved to the States respectively, or to the people.

Article XI. Suits Against a State (1798)

The federal courts denied authority in suits by citizens against a state. The judicial power of the United States shall not be construed to extend to any suit in law or equity, commenced or prosecuted against one of the United States by citizens of another State, or by citizens or subjects of any foreign state.

Article XII. Election of President and Vice-President (1804)

1. **Changes in manner of electing President and Vice-President; procedure when no presidential candidate receives electoral majority.** The electors shall meet in their respective States, and vote by ballot for President and Vice-President, one of whom, at least, shall not be an inhabitant of the same State with themselves; they shall name in their ballots the person voted for as President, and in distinct ballots the person voted for as Vice-President, and they shall make distinct lists of all persons voted for as President, and of all persons voted for as Vice-President, and of the number of votes for each, which lists they shall sign and certify, and transmit sealed to the seat of government of the United States, directed to the President of the Senate;—the President of the Senate shall, in the presence of the Senate and House of Representatives, open all the certificates and the votes shall then be counted;—the person having the greatest number of votes for President shall be the President, if such number be a majority of the whole number of electors appointed; and if no person have such majority, then from the persons having the highest numbers not exceeding three on the list of those voted for as President, the House of Representatives shall choose immediately, by ballot, the President. But in choosing the President, the votes shall be taken by States, the representation from each State having one vote; a quorum for this purpose shall consist of a member or members from two-thirds of the States, and a majority of all the States shall be necessary to a choice. And if the House of Representatives shall not choose a President whenever the right of choice shall devolve upon them, before *the fourth day of March*[1] next following, then the Vice-President shall act as President, as in the case of the death or other constitutional disability of the President.

2. **Procedure when no vice-presidential candidate receives electoral majority.** The person having the greatest number of votes as Vice-President shall be the Vice-President, if such number be a majority of the whole number of electors appointed; and if no person have a majority, then from the two highest numbers on the list the Senate shall choose the Vice-President; a quorum for the purpose shall consist of two-thirds of the whole number of Senators, and a majority of the whole number shall be necessary to a choice. But no person constitutionally ineligible to the office of President shall be eligible to that of Vice-President of the United States.

Article XIII. Slavery Prohibited (1865)

1. **Slavery forbidden.** Neither slavery[2] nor involuntary servitude, except as a punishment for crime whereof the party shall have been duly convicted, shall exist within the United States, or any place subject to their jurisdiction.

2. Congress shall have power to enforce this article by appropriate legislation.

---

[1]Changed to January 20 by the Twentieth Amendment.

[2]The only explicit mention of slavery in the Constitution.

Article XIV. Civil Rights for Blacks, etc. (1868)

1. **Citizenship defined; rights of citizens.** All persons born or naturalized in the United States, and subject to the jurisdiction thereof, are citizens of the United States and of the State wherein they reside. No State shall make or enforce any law which shall abridge the privileges or immunities of citizens of the United States; nor shall any State deprive any person of life, liberty, or property, without due process of law; nor deny to any person within its jurisdiction the equal protection of the laws.

2. **When a state denies [Blacks] the vote, its representation shall be reduced.** Representatives shall be apportioned among the several States according to their respective numbers, counting the whole number of persons in each State, excluding Indians not taxed. But when the right to vote at any election for the choice of Electors for President and Vice-President of the United States, Representatives in Congress, the executive and judicial officers of a State, or the members of the legislature thereof, is denied to any of the male inhabitants of such State, being twenty-one years of age and citizens of the United States, or in any way abridged, except for participation in rebellion, or other crime, the basis of representation therein shall be reduced in the proportion which the number of such male citizens shall bear to the whole number of male citizens twenty-one years of age in such State.

3. **Certain ex-Confederates ineligible for federal and state office; removal of disability.** No person shall be a Senator or Representative in Congress, or Elector of President and Vice-President, or hold any office, civil or military, under the United States, or under any State, who, having previously taken an oath, as a member of Congress, or as an officer of the United States, or as a member of any State legislature, or as an executive or judicial officer of any State, to support the Constitution of the United States, shall have engaged in insurrection or rebellion against the same, or given aid or comfort to the enemies thereof. But Congress may, by a vote of two-thirds of each house, remove such disability.

4. **Public debt valid; debt of rebels void.** The validity of the public debt of the United States, authorized by law, including debts incurred for payment of pensions and bounties for services in suppressing insurrection or rebellion, shall not be questioned. But neither the United States nor any State shall assume or pay any debt or obligation incurred in aid of insurrection or rebellion against the United States or any claim for the loss or emancipation of any slave; but all such debts, obligations, and claims shall be held illegal and void.

5. **Enforcement.** The Congress shall have power to enforce, by appropriate legislation, the provisions of this article.

Article XV. Black Suffrage (1870)

Restrictions on denial of vote. *1.* The right of citizens of the United States to vote shall not be denied or abridged by the United States or by any State on account of race, color, or previous condition of servitude.

2. The Congress shall have power to enforce this article by appropriate legislation.

Article XVI. Income Taxes (1913)

Congress empowered to lay and collect income taxes. The Congress shall have power to lay and collect taxes on incomes, from whatever source derived, without apportionment among the several States, and without regard to any census or enumeration.

Article XVII. Direct Election of Senators (1913)

Senators to be elected by popular vote. *1.* The Senate of the United States shall be composed of two Senators from each State, elected by the people thereof, for six years; and each Senator shall have one vote. The electors in each State shall have the qualifications requisite for electors of [voters for] the most numerous branch of the State legislatures.

2. When vacancies happen in the representation of any State in the Senate, the executive authority of such State shall issue writs of election to fill such vacancies: Provided, that the Legislature of any State may empower the executive thereof to make temporary appointments until the people fill the vacancies by election as the Legislature may direct.

3. This amendment shall not be so construed as to affect the election or term of any Senator chosen before it becomes valid as part of the Constitution.

Article XVIII. National Prohibition (1919)

The manufacture, sale, or transportation of intoxicating liquors forbidden. *1. After one year from the ratification of this article the manufacture, sale, or transportation of intoxicating liquors within, the importation thereof into, or the exportation thereof from the United States and all territory subject to the jurisdiction thereof, for beverage purposes, is hereby prohibited.*

2. The Congress and the several States shall have concurrent power to enforce this article by appropriate legislation.

3. This article shall be inoperative unless it shall have been ratified as an amendment to the Constitution by the legislatures of the several States, as provided by the Constitution, within seven years from the date of the submission thereof to the states by the Congress.[1]

Article XIX. Woman Suffrage (1920)

Women permitted to vote. *1.* The right of citizens of the United States to vote shall not be denied or abridged by the United States or by any State on account of sex.

2. Congress shall have power to enforce this article by appropriate legislation.

---

[1]Repealed in 1933 by the Twenty-first Amendment.

Article XX. Presidential and Congressional Terms (1933)

1. **Presidential, vice-presidential, and Congressional terms of office to begin in January.** The terms of the President and Vice-President shall end at noon on the 20th day of January, and the terms of Senators and Representatives at noon on the 3rd day of January, of the years in which such terms would have ended if this article had not been ratified; and the terms of their successors shall then begin.

2. **New meeting date for Congress.** The Congress shall assemble at least once in every year, and such meeting shall begin at noon on the 3rd day of January, unless they shall by law appoint a different day.

3. **Emergency presidential and vice-presidential succession.** If, at the time fixed for the beginning of the term of the President, the President-elect shall have died, the Vice-President-elect shall become President. If a President shall not have been chosen before the time fixed for the beginning of his term, or if the President-elect shall have failed to qualify, then the Vice-President-elect shall act as President until a President shall have qualified; and the Congress may by law provide for the case wherein neither a President-elect nor a Vice-President-elect shall have qualified, declaring who shall then act as President, or the manner in which one who is to act shall be selected, and such persons shall act accordingly until a President or Vice-President shall have qualified.

4. The Congress may by law provide for the case of the death of any of the persons from whom the House of Representatives may choose a President whenever the right of choice shall have devolved upon them, and for the case of the death of any of the persons from whom the Senate may choose a Vice-President whenever the right of choice shall have devolved upon them.

5. Sections 1 and 2 shall take effect on the 15th day of October following the ratification of this article.

6. This article shall be inoperative unless it shall have been ratified as an amendment to the Constitution by the legislatures of three-fourths of the several States within seven years from the date of its submission.

Article XXI. Prohibition Repealed (1933)

1. **Eighteenth Amendment repealed.** The eighteenth article of amendment to the Constitution of the United States is hereby repealed.

2. **Local laws honored.** The transportation or importation into any State, Territory, or Possession of the United States for delivery or use therein of intoxicating liquors, in violation of the laws thereof, is hereby prohibited.

3. This article shall be inoperative unless it shall have been ratified as an amendment to the Constitution by conventions in the several States, as provided in the Constitution, within seven years from the date of the submission thereof to the States by the Congress.

Article XXII. Anti–Third Term Amendment (1951)

The President limited to two terms. *1.* No person shall be elected to the office of President more than twice, and no person who has held the office of President, or acted as President, for more than two years of a term to which some other person was elected President shall be elected to the office of President more than once. But this article shall not apply to any person holding the office of President when this article was proposed by the Congress [i.e., Truman], and shall not prevent any person who may be holding the office of President, or acting as President, during the term within which this article becomes operative [i.e., Truman] from holding the office of President or acting as President during the remainder of such term.

2. This article shall be inoperative unless it shall have been ratified as an amendment to the Constitution by the legislatures of three-fourths of the several States within seven years from the date of its submission to the States by the Congress.

Article XXIII. District of Columbia Vote (1961)

1. Presidential Electors for the District of Columbia. The District constituting the seat of Government of the United States shall appoint in such manner as the Congress may direct:

A number of electors of President and Vice-President equal to the whole number of Senators and Representatives in Congress to which the District would be entitled if it were a State, but in no event more than the least populous State; they shall be in addition to those appointed by the States, but they shall be considered for the purposes of the election of President and Vice-President, to be electors appointed by a State; and they shall meet in the District and perform such duties as provided by the twelfth article of amendment.

2. Enforcement. The Congress shall have the power to enforce this article by appropriate legislation. [Adopted 1961].

Article XXIV. Poll Tax (1964)

1. Payment of poll tax or other taxes not to be prerequisite for voting in federal elections. The right of citizens of the United States to vote in any primary or other election for President or Vice-President, for electors for President or Vice-President, or for Senator or Representative in Congress, shall not be denied or abridged by the United States or any State by reason of failure to pay any poll tax or other tax.

2. Enforcement. The Congress shall have the power to enforce this article by appropriate legislation. [Adopted 1964].

Article XXV. Presidential Succession and Disability[1] (1967)

1. Vice-President to become President. In case of the removal of the President from office or of his death or resignation, the Vice-President shall become President.[2]

---

[1]Passed by a two-thirds vote of both houses of Congress in July 1965; ratified by the requisite three-fourths of the state legislatures, February 1967, or well within the seven-year limit.

[2]The original Constitution (Art. II, Sec. I, para. 5) was vague on this point, stipulating that "the powers and duties" of the president, but not necessarily the title, should "devolve" on the vice-president. President Tyler, the first "accidental president," assumed not only the power and duties but the title as well.

2. Successor to Vice-President provided. Whenever there is a vacancy in the office of the Vice-President, the President shall nominate a Vice-President who shall take office upon confirmation by a majority vote of both Houses of Congress.

3. Vice-President to serve for disabled President. Whenever the President transmits to the President pro tempore of the Senate and the Speaker of the House of Representatives his written declaration that he is unable to discharge the powers and duties of his office, and until he transmits to them a written declaration to the contrary, such powers and duties shall be discharged by the Vice-President as Acting President.

4. Procedure for disqualifying or requalifying President. Whenever the Vice-President and a majority of either the principal officers of the executive departments or of such other body as Congress may by law provide, transmit to the President pro tempore of the Senate and the Speaker of the House of Representatives their written declaration that the President is unable to discharge the powers and duties of his office, the Vice-President shall immediately assume the powers and duties of the office as Acting President.

Thereafter, when the President transmits to the President pro tempore of the Senate and the Speaker of the House of Representatives his written declaration that no inability exists, he shall resume the powers and duties of his office unless the Vice-President and a majority of either the principal officers of the executive department[s] or of such other body as Congress may by law provide, transmit within four days to the President pro tempore of the Senate and the Speaker of the House of Representatives their written declaration that the President is unable to discharge the powers and duties of his office. Thereupon Congress shall decide the issue, assembling within forty-eight hours for that purpose if not in session. If the Congress, within twenty-one days after receipt of the latter written declaration, or, if Congress is not in session, within twenty-one days after Congress is required to assemble, determines by two-thirds vote of both Houses that the President is unable to discharge the powers and duties of his office, the Vice-President shall continue to discharge the same as Acting President; otherwise, the President shall resume the powers and duties of his office.

Article XXVI. Lowering Voting Age (1971)

1. Ballot for eighteen-year-olds. The right of citizens of the United States, who are eighteen years of age or older, to vote shall not be denied or abridged by the United States or by any State on account of age.

2. Enforcement. The Congress shall have power to enforce this article by appropriate legislation.

Article XXVII. Restricting Congressional Pay Raises (1992)

Congress not allowed to increase its current pay. No law varying the compensation for the services of the Senators and Representatives shall take effect, until an election of Representatives shall have intervened.

Index